booksonline

Read this book online today:

With SAP PRESS BooksOnline we offer you online access to knowledge from
the leading SAP experts. Whether you use it as a beneficial supplement or as
an alternative to the printed book, with SAP PRESS BooksOnline you can:

• Access your book anywhere, at any time. All you need is an Internet connection.
• Perform full text searches on your book and on the entire SAP PRESS library.
• Build your own personalized SAP library.

The SAP PRESS customer advantage:

Register this book today at *www.sap-press.com* and obtain exclusive free trial
access to its online version. If you like it (and we think you will), you can choose to
purchase permanent, unrestricted access to the online edition at a very special price!

Here's how to get started:

1. Visit *www.sap-press.com*.
2. Click on the link for SAP PRESS BooksOnline and login (or create an account).
3. Enter your free trial license key, shown below in the corner of the page.
4. Try out your online book with full, unrestricted access for a limited time!

Your personal free trial **license key**
for this online book is: 6kiw-ugam-syn9-j5hr

SAP® Interactive Forms by Adobe®

PRESS

SAP PRESS is a joint initiative of SAP and Galileo Press. The know-how offered by SAP specialists combined with the expertise of the Galileo Press publishing house offers the reader expert books in the field. SAP PRESS features first-hand information and expert advice, and provides useful skills for professional decision-making.

SAP PRESS offers a variety of books on technical and business related topics for the SAP user. For further information, please visit our website: *www.sap-press.com*.

Horst Keller
The Official ABAP Reference (Third Edition)
2012, 1655 pp.
978-1-59229-376-6

Michael Szardenings
Printing in SAP
2011, 286 pp.
978-1-59229-396-4

Martina Kaplan, Christian Oehler
Implementing SAP Enhancement Packages
2011, 220 pp.
978-1-59229-351-3

Stefan Kauf, Viktoria Papadopoulou
Creating Forms in SAP ERP HCM
2009, 229 pp.
978-1-59229-282-0

Jürgen Hauser, Andreas Deutesfield, Stephan Rehmann,
and Thomas Szücs

SAP® Interactive Forms by Adobe®

Galileo Press

Bonn • Boston

Galileo Press is named after the Italian physicist, mathematician and philosopher Galileo Galilei (1564–1642). He is known as one of the founders of modern science and an advocate of our contemporary, heliocentric worldview. His words *Eppur si muove* (And yet it moves) have become legendary. The Galileo Press logo depicts Jupiter orbited by the four Galilean moons, which were discovered by Galileo in 1610.

Editor Patricia Kremer
English Edition Editor Kelly Grace Harris
Translation Lemoine International, Inc., Salt Lake City, UT
Copyeditor Pamela Siska
Cover Design Nadine Kohl, Graham Geary
Photo Credit Getty Images/Thomas Barwick
Layout Design Vera Brauner
Production Kelly O'Callaghan, Graham Geary
Typesetting Publishers' Design and Production Services, Inc.
Printed and bound in Canada

ISBN 978-1-59229-398-8

© 2012 by Galileo Press Inc., Boston (MA)

2nd edition 2012

2nd German edition published 2011 by Galileo Press, Bonn, Germany

Library of Congress Cataloging-in-Publication Data
SAP Interactive forms by Adobe / Jürgen Hauser ... [et al.]. — 2nd ed.
p. cm.
Includes index.
ISBN-13: 978-1-59229-398-8
ISBN-10: 1-59229-398-0
1. SAP Interactive Forms. 2. File conversion (Computer science) 3. Adobe
Acrobat. 4. PDF (Computer file format) I. Hauser, Jürgen. II. SAP AG.
QA76.9.F48S37 2012
005.7'2—dc23
2011026571

Contents at a Glance

Dear Reader,

You hold in your hands your one-stop guide for all questions related to SAP Interactive Forms by Adobe. In this second edition of our best-selling book, you will find updated information on parallelization of print jobs, ABAP Offline Infrastructure, XDC Editor, Secure ADS Connections, and more. This is a reference that may never make it back to your bookshelf—keep it on your desk to help you solve all your SAP Interactive Forms problems, or to learn something you never knew before.

Second editions hold a special challenge for both authors and editors: to match the caliber of the first edition, to seamlessly manage the addition of new content, and—mundane, but crucial!—to keep track of all the new and old screenshots (no small task in a book with 500 figures). I'm happy to say that Jürgen and his co-authors (Andreas, Stephan, and Thomas) handily managed all three of these tasks to deliver, yet again, an outstanding reference on SAP Interactive Forms by Adobe. I'm confident that all readers (whether new to the book, or familiar with the first edition) will greatly benefit from this comprehensive reference produced by stellar authors.

We appreciate your business, and welcome your feedback. Your comments and suggestions are the most useful tools to help us improve our books for you, the reader. We encourage you to visit our website at *www.sap-press.com* and share your feedback about this work.

Thank you for purchasing a book from SAP PRESS!

Kelly Grace Harris
Editor, SAP PRESS

Galileo Press
Boston, MA

kelly.harris@galileo-press.com
www.sap-press.com

Contents

6   Form Output 229

13 Advanced Installation and Configuration 695

This book describes the SAP® Interactive Forms by Adobe® technology. It provides all of the required details for print and interactive scenarios and uses step-by-step examples to explain the usage of the relevant tools.

1 Introduction

In 2002, SAP and Adobe Systems entered a strategic partnership that still continues. The aim was to integrate interactive forms and Adobe's print and design expertise with the SAP NetWeaver technology platform and make them available to customers via SAP's business applications.

▶ At this time, Adobe already had the required technology: the Adobe LiveCycle® product group, whose core area is the conversion of form templates and their corresponding data into various output formats, such as different Printer Definition Languages (PDLs) or Portable Document Format (PDF) documents. In addition to the generation of output formats, Adobe focused on the design of forms. For this reason, Adobe provided the Adobe LiveCycle Designer®, a graphically interactive tool that enables users to create the layout of a form.

▶ For the integration of the tools with SAP NetWeaver, SAP contributed its knowledge gained from the development of SAPscript and SAP Smart Forms. SAP Smart Forms provided the outline for integrating Adobe technology with SAP applications. This facilitated the implementation of the new technologies for most developers.

Today, the development tasks are divided between Adobe and SAP to a large extent: While Adobe develops the core technology, SAP improves the integration and the frameworks that are based on the technology.

In 2005, SAP finally brought SAP Interactive Forms by Adobe to market. For the SAP NetWeaver 2004 release, SAP Interactive Forms by Adobe was available as an SAP NetWeaver solution extension for SAP customers for the first time. Today, it is used in numerous SAP customer projects and even SAP uses the new technology in its own applications. With each Enhancement Package (EHP) for the SAP Business Suite, SAP provides more and more converted print forms and changes to this new technology either from SAPscript or from SAP Smart Forms. With the release of EHP4 for SAP ERP 6.0, SAP now provides more than 2,200 PDF-based print forms that use this technology. With SAP Business Suite 7, approximately 2,400 PDF-based print forms are available for SAP customer. Therefore, now is the right time to become familiar with this technology. Reading this book is the best way to do so.

The benefits of the newest, PDF-based print forms technology are obvious: In addition to the mere print output, the generation of interactive PDF forms (that is, PDF files that provide interactive form fields when you open them with Adobe Reader®) allows for usage options that have not been available in the SAP world. Various SAP solutions use interactive forms. You can find numerous examples for SAP Business Suite 7 in the Financial and HCM areas. For example, as of version 5.0, SAP Customer Relationship Management (CRM) also provides an interactive form for Lead Management via a partner enterprise in the standard.

The revised second edition now also explains the configuration of a secure ADS connection, introduces you to the creation and use of job profiles, and discusses ABAP Offline Infrastructure. In addition to these new topics, the other chapters were completely revised and updated for SAP NetWeaver 7.0 Enhancement Package 2 (EHP2).

Structure of the Book

To give you a better overview of the book's topic, the following sections introduce the structure and content of the individual chapters:

▶ **Chapter 2**, Use of SAP Interactive Forms by Adobe, lays the foundation for understanding the concepts and technologies underlying SAP Interactive Forms by Adobe. This chapter considers different usage scenarios for interactive forms and helps you select the appropriate scenario. One of the basic principles is understanding the integration of the Adobe technology with the SAP NetWeaver technology platform.

▶ **Chapter 3**, Installation and Configuration, describes how you can implement the software to work with SAP Interactive Forms by Adobe. It also details the configuration of the software components. This chapter guides you through the individual steps and indicates possible problems and their solutions.

▶ **Chapter 4**, Interface and Form Context, introduces the print form topic. The procedure is explained using an example, which you can reproduce in your system. You get to know Transaction SFP, important concepts, and the relationship between interfaces, form context, and form design.

▶ In **Chapter 5**, Creating Form Templates, you begin using Adobe LiveCycle Designer to design the layout of print forms. Based on the interface and the context of the previous chapter, this chapter provides step-by-step instructions on how to use Adobe LiveCycle Designer and helps you understand the underlying technology. In this context, it considers critical topics, such as the process of structuring forms by means of subforms and data binding of form fields.

▶ **Chapter 6**, Form Output, introduces you to the development of print programs. Print programs generate the print output using the interfaces and context that were created in Chapter 4 and the form template that was developed in Chapter 5. This chapter requires some ABAP skills.

▶ Now that you are familiar with designing PDF forms, **Chapter 7**, Advanced Form Template Creation, covers more complex topics, such as output formatting, pagination, and script programming. It also explains the usage of tables in forms and discusses the creation of interactive PDF forms in preparation for the following chapters.

▶ **Chapter 8**, Integration with Web Dynpro ABAP, describes the integration of PDF forms with Web Dynpro ABAP. Web Dynpro is the first of two environments that this book considers. It enables you to implement online scenarios. Various examples explain how you can integrate an interactive form with a Web Dynpro application. Furthermore, it illustrates how you can use Web Dynpro ABAP for offline scenarios, for the print scenario, and for combined online and offline scenarios.

▶ **Chapter 9**, Internal Service Requests (ISR), introduces the ISR framework, whose technology is based on Web Dynpro. It describes the usage of this framework within the SAP infrastructure and offers a clear example. In the next step, the customizing and programming of complex scenarios are explained. This chapter concludes with links to additional technical documentation.

▶ **Chapter 10**, ABAP Offline Infrastructure, introduces the implementation of offline scenarios in ABAP. An example describes the configuration of the infrastructure. The infrastructure is based on the interface concepts and the print program. For the processing, an offline handler needs to be programmed. To reproduce the example, you need Business Communication Services.

▶ In **Chapter 11**, ABAP PDF Object, we leave the framework world and introduce you to a deeper level of ABAP programming. This chapter also uses programming examples to show how you can use the functions for PDF forms through the PDF object in ABAP. Among other things, it focuses on the implementation of offline scenarios.

▶ **Chapter 12**, Offline Scenarios via Web Services, demonstrates an alternative method for integrating PDF forms with an SAP system via Web services, which can be used to implement offline scenarios. It discusses the two possible approaches to using Web services: The first approach is directly supported by Adobe Live-Cycle Designer; the second approach uses the Simple Object Access Protocol (SOAP) object in JavaScript.

▶ Finally, **Chapter 13**, Advanced Installation and Configuration, discusses advanced configuration and installation topics. Among other things, you learn how to configure a secure connection for ADS. This chapter also introduces the XDC Editor as well as the creation and management of job profiles.

Depending on your special fields of interest, you can jump to different chapters in this book. The following list provides an overview of which chapters are relevant regarding particular concerns and interests.

▶ **Installed system available**
If you already have a completely installed and configured SAP system and are not interested in the installation, configuration, and administration, you can skip Chapter 3.

▶ **Administration of Adobe Document Services**
Read Chapter 3 and Chapter 13 if you want to specialize in the usage of Adobe Document Services.

▶ **Creating PDF forms**
The procedures for creating print forms and interactive forms are largely identical. Chapter 5 introduces the creation of PDF forms. If you are already familiar with this topic, you can skip this chapter and read only Chapter 7, which addresses the advanced form designer.

▶ **Implementation of print outputs**
If you want to focus on the creation of print outputs, first read Chapter 4 and Chapter 6.

▶ **Implementation of interactive online scenarios**
If you are interested in the implementation of online scenarios, you can proceed with Chapter 8 and Chapter 9.

▶ **Implementation of interactive offline scenarios**
If you are interested in offline scenarios, read Chapter 10, Chapter 11, and Chapter 12.

System Requirements and Sample Files

If nothing is specified, the descriptions in this book are based on SAP NetWeaver 7.0 EHP2, including Version 8.2 of Adobe LiveCycle Designer and Version 9.4 of Adobe Reader®.

If your system is older, you can set up or configure a system as described in Chapter 3 to become familiar with the new developments introduced in this book.

You can find the form templates and listings that were created for this book at *http://www.sap-press.com*. You can also download a transport for the Web Dynpro ABAP examples here, so that you can directly reproduce the exercises in your system.

Acknowledgments

The writing of this book was quite a complex project, and the description of the multilayer integration with the SAP environment was no easy task and could only be mastered with a team of authors. That is why I am particularly glad that I could enlist the appropriate expert for each topic. I would like to thank my coauthors, *Andreas Deutesfeld* (Chapter 3, Chapter 4, Chapter 6, and Chapter 11), *Dr. Stephan Rehmann* (Chapter 9), and *Thomas Szücs* (Chapter 8) for their excellent cooperation. Owing to the collaboration with Andreas Deutesfeld, the second edition could be extended with a completely new chapter, Chapter 10.

Special thanks are due to *Niklas Gussek,* who helped me describe the configuration of a secure connection for ADS in Chapter 13.

A team of authors also depends on experts' counterchecks. We were provided with valuable feedback that contributed to the book's quality. For this, we would like to thank Christina Vogt, Martin Plummer, Ralf Ruth, and Dr. Simon Hoeg.

Additionally, we would also like to say thanks to Sanjay Dhiman, Dave Nikkel, Judy Toombs, Les Woolsey, Matthias Zeller, Blair Powell, Dave Welch, and Inder Narang at Adobe. At SAP, we would like to thank Dr. Wolfgang Weiss, Yasuo Nagao, Markus Meisl, and Dirk Michael Schulze. They contributed considerably to the success of SAP Interactive Forms by Adobe.

A special thank you also goes to Patricia Kremer, Kelly Harris, and Stefan Proksch, our editors at Galileo Press, for their excellent collaboration.

Dr. Jürgen Hauser
Adobe Product Manager SAP Interactive Forms by Adobe

This chapter introduces SAP Interactive Forms by Adobe and discusses various application scenarios. It also specifies the software components used and the architecture for integration with SAP NetWeaver.

2 Use of SAP Interactive Forms by Adobe

This chapter introduces you to the basic terminology associated with the use of SAP Interactive Forms by Adobe, such as Portable Document Format (PDF)-based print forms and interactive forms. A classification of online and offline application scenarios is outlined for interactive forms; additionally, you are provided with support for deciding in which cases you should use interactive forms. Furthermore, this chapter compares Adobe Acrobat® and Adobe Reader and explains why it is sufficient to deploy Adobe Reader for the use of SAP Interactive Forms by Adobe. Finally, this chapter introduces the software components of Adobe, Adobe Live-Cycle Designer, and Adobe Document Services and their integration with the SAP NetWeaver stack.

2.1 PDF, PDF-Based Print Forms, and Interactive PDF Forms

The following sections detail PDFs and the two main concepts of this book—PDF-based print forms and interactive PDF forms.

2.1.1 PDF File Format

In the early 1990s, Adobe Systems launched the first version of PDFs. At that time, Adobe was well known for its PostScript printer language, Adobe Illustrator (a vector-based drawing tool), and Adobe Photoshop (image editing). The idea behind PDF was to develop a platform-independent file format that enabled high-quality exchange and printout of documents. The primary focus was on the exchange of documents and not on an editable document format.

The specification of PDF is published; therefore, everyone can get an overview of this file format. The International Organization for Standardization (ISO) lists the

PDF format under Standard 32000. The PDF/A format for archiving documents is already an ISO standard; however, it has not yet become a part of SAP Interactive Forms by Adobe.

PDFs enable you to flexibly describe the structure of individual pages of a document. PDF is a flat file format and knows only the concept of a page as the structuring element. Compared to PostScript, it is a pure descriptive language and therefore contains no programming language constructs.

The most commonly known use of PDF is high-quality print output: A document is converted into a PDF file and can then be displayed or printed on different platforms and operating systems via Adobe Reader. The presentation of a document as a PDF ensures that the document always has the same layout regardless of the user's operating system or platform. The user requires only a PDF display tool, for example, Adobe Reader.

In addition to the pure display and printout, you can also use PDF documents for data entry. To do this, forms that are based on PDF contain interactive form fields that enable the user to interact with the PDF document. This way, you can enter data and execute calculations that are based on this data directly during entry. For this reason, Adobe Reader supports JavaScript as one of the scripting languages.

2.1.2　PDF-Based Print Forms

Forms are a well-known structuring method for data output (for example, a telephone bill) or data entry (for example, official application forms). One of the essential aspects of forms is a uniform layout that enables and supports the recognition of forms. The structure of each telephone bill is identical and the customer knows where to find certain information on the bill—just like annual tax forms.

This feature requires the form designer to use a clear and comprehensible layout for the form. The layout describes what information is located in which position on the form. It must also specify how to handle a large number of data records, which is usually done by distributing them throughout multiple pages.

The task of a form designer is to create form templates. Based on the form template, a specific form is generated and—in most cases—filled with data during the generation process. Consequently, the form template plays a central role in all form-based processes. Therefore, the form designer must be optimally supported in his task with a user-friendly and intuitive tool.

Forms can be output both on paper and electronically; however, the electronic output has significant advantages (for example, electronic transmission or archiving). For this reason, SAP Interactive Forms by Adobe enables you to output forms in different printer languages or as PDF files.

Supported Printer Languages

The printer languages supported include Adobe PostScript® (PS), Printer Command Language® (PCL) developed by Hewlett-Packard®, and Zebra Programming Language® (ZPL) for printing barcodes on Zebra label printers. Printers must be able to process one of the aforementioned printer languages to ensure that they are supported by SAP Interactive Forms by Adobe.

Supported Printer Languages
SAP Interactive Forms by Adobe supports the following printer languages: ▸ Adobe PostScript Levels 2 and 3, where Level 3 is the default setting. To create Level 2, the corresponding XML Device Configuration (XDC) file must be copied and customized (see Section 3.5.6, XDCs).   ▸ PCL 5 in monochrome and color.   ▸ ZPL-II is supported in different resolutions, for example, 200, 300, and 600 Dots per Inch (DPI).

The print output and the PDF file are created based on Adobe XML Forms Architecture (XFA) technology, which is a specification published by Adobe. This specification describes the XML-based structure of a form template and the behavior of display and conversion programs at runtime. The XFA specification is a very good source of information and can be downloaded from the Adobe website (*http://partners. adobe.com/public/developer/xml/index_arch.html*).

Support of Barcodes

Another important area supported by SAP Interactive Forms by Adobe is barcodes. A barcode encodes information that can be read by a scanner and then processed. You can find barcodes on virtually every product package read at a checkout counter. You can determine the scanned product and its price based on the information encoded in the barcode.

SAP Interactive Forms by Adobe supports most of the common barcodes. Currently, there are 34 different barcodes, including EAN8, EAN13, and Code 128, for example.

There are also barcodes that can be supported only by the printer itself. If this is the case, the output is done as a PDF file, and a gray rectangle will be displayed instead of the barcode. It is also possible to exclusively create a barcode and print it on a barcode printer. Currently, this is supported for Zebra label printers.

There is no way to define barcodes yourself. For barcodes that are not supported, you have to rely on their support in one of the more recent releases.

Simplex and Duplex Printing

The double-sided print output and paper tray selection are supported as of SAP NetWeaver 7.0 Support Package 13. Simplex and duplex printing, that is, single-sided and double-sided printing, are controlled by means of the page sets and master pages. The form designer assigns the individual form pages to master pages to specify whether a page appears on the front side or the back side. Very complex scenarios are possible here (for example, combining simplex and duplex prints in one form) that require skillful use of master pages and conditional page breaks.

Paper Tray Control

The selection for the paper tray control requires multiple configuration steps because the corresponding control codes need to be determined for the printer and assigned to the available paper types. The control codes are contained in the XDC files, and their assignment is carried out by editing the XDC files located on the server.

PDF-Based Print Forms, SAP Smart Forms, and SAPscript

The print output, which is based on PDF-based print forms, provides an alternative to the SAPscript and SAP Smart Forms technologies provided by SAP. There is no full equivalence with regard to functions and properties between the technologies due to technological differences. The option to navigate to a callback of an ABAP function during the layout creation is not possible for PDF-based print forms due to technological reasons.

> **SAP Smart Forms versus SAP Interactive Forms by Adobe**
>
> SAP Note 1009567 describes the functional differences between SAP Smart Forms and SAP Interactive Forms by Adobe.

SAP Interactive Forms by Adobe provides advanced and complex innovations, such as enhanced layout options (for example, rectangles with rounded corners) or support of a scripting language (for instance, implementing calculations and validations in interactive PDF forms). These enhanced options can impact performance and file sizes; for example, shadings affect the output in PCL format.

Another innovation compared to the already-existing technologies is the option to create interactive PDF forms. These are described in greater detail in the following section.

2.1.3 Interactive PDF Forms

PDF documents provide much more than just the known display and print functionality: They can contain interactive form fields. These fields are called "interactive" because the user can make changes by means of the mouse or the keyboard.

Possibilities

Interactive form fields include input fields for text and numbers that are entered via the keyboard. Moreover, you are provided with radio buttons or checkboxes, which are primarily operated using the mouse. In addition, more complex fields, such as the DATE SELECTION field (a calendar appears for simplified selection), list boxes, and dropdown lists are available. List fields or dropdown lists are particularly helpful if the user of the form is supposed to select an input value from a predefined list. The list can display all list entries so that the user does not have to remember all possible input options.

Interactive PDF forms are used for structured data entry by the user. If multiple users enter data, this is called *mass data entry*. In this case, electronic support is especially beneficial because the processing and saving of data can be automated.

Interactive form fields enable the user to interact directly with the document. Data that are stored in the interactive PDF form are changed during the interaction. For integration with electronic processes, you can extract or insert data on the server side. In specific cases, this is also possible at the user's work station, for example, if only the data contained in the PDF form are to be sent by email.

For SAP Interactive Forms by Adobe, the XFA-based technology is used. Here, the form template is stored in XML format and the data contained in the PDF form are stored as an XML data record.

Static and Dynamic PDF Forms

For interactive PDF forms, you can differentiate between static and dynamic PDF forms depending on whether the form layout changes during the interaction or not. An example is dynamic tables in which users can insert new rows or delete old rows. Another example is to hide parts of the form depending on the previous entries. This is possible only for dynamic PDF forms.

For dynamic PDF forms, the form layout is created directly in Adobe Reader. This is done based on the form template and the data contained therein. As of Adobe Reader version 8.1, the display of dynamic forms is considerably faster than in older versions. It is recommended that you use Adobe Reader version 8.1 or higher if you utilize dynamic functions intensively. It is recommended that you use the current Adobe Reader version. Nevertheless, it is possible that the use of frameworks (for example, Web Dynpro frameworks) may result in restrictions or cause delays in the support. If this is the case, the corresponding chapters of this book refer to the relevant SAP note.

2.1.4 Accessibility of PDF Forms

Because you can use interactive PDF forms as a part of user interfaces, the accessibility of PDF forms is of significance. Interactive forms enable you to create accessible PDF forms. Accessible means, for example, that visually handicapped users can also utilize the PDF form. Although Adobe Reader provides a function for reading PDF documents out loud (VIEW • READ OUT LOUD), third-party software, such as JAWS® from Freedom Scientific®, is usually used. Accessibility also means that mobility-impaired users can work with an application or a document (for example, by means of the voice control).

Accessibility impacts the size of the PDF file because additional information needs to be added. This information must be generated on the server during the creation of the PDF document, which also requires extra time. Therefore, you should consider whether a PDF form should always be accessible or not. A user-specific control is one option to avoid additional work. For example, you can use the user settings for the print preview in SAP GUI.

The form layout does not always result in an accessible form. The design tool to form templates supports you in the creation of accessible forms—for example, for the positioning of form fields, which influences the sequence. However, if the layout of the form is so complex that it is difficult to use, it is predictable that accessibility problems will occur. In such cases, it is extremely helpful to reconsider and revise the form layout.

2.1.5   Using Interactive PDF Forms

You have been introduced to several significant properties of PDF forms:

▶ A PDF form may or may not be interactive. If not, it is a PDF-based print form.

▶ In addition, a PDF form can be static or dynamic.

These properties are either determined by the individual frameworks that integrate the PDF forms, for example, in Web Dynpro ABAP it is a preset that creates dynamic PDF forms, or are available as parameters in the programming interfaces.

The benefit of interactive PDF forms in electronic business processes in the SAP environment is that you just need Adobe Reader and a Web browser or email program to use them. The wide distribution of Adobe Reader and the common email programs and Web browsers facilitates their use considerably.

2.2   Adobe Reader and Adobe Acrobat Family

Adobe offers two products for displaying PDF files: the free Adobe Reader and the Adobe Acrobat family that is subject to charge. The Adobe Acrobat 9 family comprises three separate products: Adobe Acrobat Standard, Adobe Acrobat Pro, and Adobe Pro Extended.

> **Note on the Usage of SAP Interactive Forms by Adobe**
>
> Adobe Reader is sufficient for the use of SAP Interactive Forms by Adobe! Most notably, it is not necessary to purchase Adobe Acrobat licenses. Adobe Reader is distributed by Adobe Systems and not by SAP; that is, Adobe Reader can be downloaded only from the Adobe website (*http://www.adobe.com/reader*).

Adobe Reader 9.4.2 is used throughout this book. If you use an older version of Adobe Reader, you should update Adobe Reader to this version or a higher version after you have read this chapter.

The fee-based products of the Adobe Acrobat family provide more functionality than the free Adobe Reader. Section 2.2.1, Comparing Adobe Reader and Acrobat Professional, details why it is still sufficient to use Adobe Reader.

> **Interactive Forms on Mobile Devices**
>
> SAP Note 1002905 describes the supported mobile devices and the existing restrictions from the point of view of SAP Interactive Forms by Adobe. Currently, interactive forms are supported by Adobe Reader for Pocket PC.

2.2.1   Comparing Adobe Reader and Acrobat Professional

Adobe Acrobat products provide more functionality than the free Adobe Reader. This functionality includes, for example, the creation of PDF documents and their manipulation. Adobe Acrobat Pro Extended enables the conversion of different 3D formats into a PDF document.

Parts of this functionality are also included in Adobe Reader; however, they are hidden and must first be activated. For their activation, a PDF document must be provided with a corresponding ID, called usage rights, during their creation.

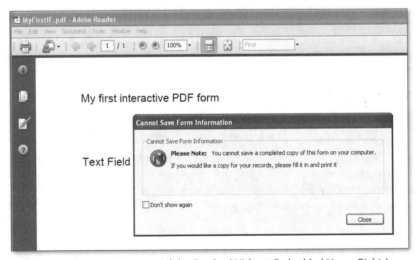

Figure 2.1   Interactive Forms in Adobe Reader (Without Embedded Usage Rights)

Figure 2.1 shows a simple interactive PDF form in Adobe Reader 9.4, which contains interactive form fields. After a change has been made in the first form field, the dialog shown in the figure appears. It notifies the user that the data entered cannot be saved using Adobe Reader. In Adobe Acrobat, this functionality is always activated.

Usage Rights for Adobe Reader

By embedding usage rights into the PDF itself, you can activate the following additional functions in Adobe Reader:

▶ **Saving of interactive PDF forms**
This eliminates the behavior of Adobe Reader described earlier, in which data that were entered in an interactive PDF form cannot be saved.

▶ **Digital signature**
If the PDF form includes a signature field, the user can digitally sign the PDF, provided that this functionality has been activated.

The qualified digital signature required in Germany, for example, is not supported in the standard version of Adobe Reader. This functionality can be added by using a plug-in.

▶ **Add comments and markups**
This functionality enables you to comment on the opened PDF document. To do this, you are provided with sticky notes that allow you to enter free text (see Figure 2.2). In addition, you can use custom stamps.

Commenting on dynamic PDF forms is not possible presently.

▶ **Add PDF file attachments**
You can add file attachments to PDF documents. Two types of file attachments are distinguished here: document-wide file attachments and file attachments on specific pages and in specific positions (also referred to as *file attachment comments*). A setting exists for these file attachments that prevents the file attachment from opening at the click of a mouse. This setting can be found under EDIT • PREFERENCES • TRUST MANAGER.

For dynamic PDF forms, you are provided with only document-wide file attachments.

▶ **Call Web services**
Calling Web services is also a functionality that can only be used with usage rights.

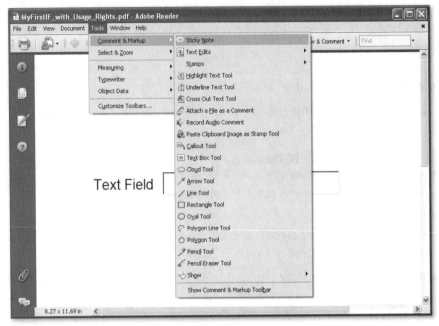

Figure 2.2 Enabled Menu for Comment & Markup

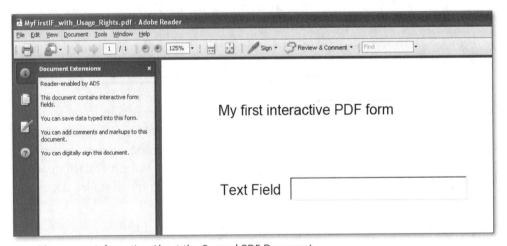

Figure 2.3 Information About the Opened PDF Document

Figure 2.3 shows the same PDF form that was displayed in Figure 2.1. The difference is that usage rights are now embedded. You are provided with additional information about the currently opened document if you click on the blue I symbol in the top left corner. The information for the example shown in this figure indicates that the document contains interactive form fields and lists the embedded usage rights in descriptive form.

The intention behind SAP Interactive Forms by Adobe is to add usage rights to interactive PDF forms. Therefore, Adobe Reader is sufficient for viewing.

For adding usage rights, you must install a *credential* in SAP NetWeaver together with SAP Interactive Forms by Adobe. This credential is not required for PDF-based print forms. Chapter 3, Installation and Configuration, describes how you can obtain this credential and how it is installed in the SAP NetWeaver stack.

2.2.2 Selecting the Appropriate Adobe Reader Version

New releases of SAP Interactive Forms by Adobe usually include new functions. Because of this, there is a recommended minimum version number for every release of SAP Interactive Forms by Adobe to utilize the full functionality.

For a project that uses SAP Interactive Forms by Adobe, you must always determine the Adobe Reader version(s) to be used. If you use different Adobe Reader versions, it is recommended that you test them (for example, a new version of Adobe Reader may correct errors in older versions).

Selecting the Adobe Reader Version

If you use functionality that was introduced together with a specific SAP NetWeaver support package, you must consider the lowest version number. New Adobe Reader versions are downward compatible; that is, you can always use a newer version of Adobe Reader.

▶ If you use Adobe LiveCycle Designer 8.1 and SAP NetWeaver 7.0 Enhancement Package 1 (EHP1), Adobe Reader 8.2 is the minimum version.

▶ As of SAP NetWeaver 7.0 EHP2, and if you use Adobe LiveCycle Designer 8.2, you should use Adobe Reader 9.4 or higher. You must also observe whether an integration environment (such as Web Dynpro) specifies the Adobe Reader version to be used.

It is also useful to visit the Adobe Systems Web site (*http://www.adobe.com/reader*) to obtain information about the latest Adobe Reader version. There you can find new versions if, for example, a security problem occurred that was remedied by a new version.

2.2.3 Useful Settings of Adobe Reader

In Adobe Reader, there are some preferences that enable you to customize the behavior of Adobe Reader for the use of interactive forms. These preferences can be found under the menu path EDIT • PREFERENCES....

▶ Under the Forms category you can find multiple options with regard to the display and behavior for filling out an interactive PDF form. The ALWAYS HIDE FORMS DOCUMENT MESSAGE BAR option is particularly interesting. You can select this option if document messages are sensitive (for example, if the document contains interactive form fields) or if you want to provide more space for the form itself.

▶ In the INTERNET category you can find the DISPLAY PDF IN BROWSER option. This option specifies whether Adobe Reader is started embedded in the browser. Users frequently search for this option when they find out that Adobe Reader always opens externally and want to change this setting.

2.3 Examples of PDF-Based Print Forms and Interactive PDF Forms

If you have an SAP system at hand that is already installed and configured for the use of SAP Interactive Forms by Adobe, you can continue to the following two examples. If you do not have such a system, you can set up a test system as described in Chapter 3 and then follow the examples. The first example demonstrates the print output; the second example creates an interactive PDF form that is prefilled with data.

2.3.1 Example for Print Output

This example is intended to demonstrate the integration of the print output with the SAP NetWeaver ABAP stack via PDF-based print forms. To do this, you call a print program, enter the parameters, and then create a print output. You can display the print output as a print preview instead of sending it to a printer.

The example assumes that the flight database is filled with data. If required, the flight database can be filled by executing the SAPBC_DATA_GENERATOR program in Transaction SE38.

The print output is viewed at runtime when the print program and the form design have already been created. The print program performs the data retrieval and preparation and then initiates the creation of the print output. The print output can be either a printer language (PS, PCL, or ZPL) or a PDF.

1. Log on to the SAP system via the SAP GUI.

2. Start Transaction SE38 to open the ABAP Editor.

3. Enter FP_TEST_03 as the name of the program. Figure 2.4 shows what the screen should look like.

Figure 2.4 Selecting and Starting a Print Program

4. Then, start the program by clicking on the corresponding icon in the toolbar (the clock with the green checkmark) or by pressing the F8 key.

5. The print program is now executed and the screen shown in Figure 2.5 is displayed. You can accept the displayed parameters. After you have run the example, you can change the parameters.

6. You can also select another form by changing the FORM parameter in this screen. However, you cannot select just any form—only forms with the same interface. Chapter 4, Interface and Form Context, provides detailed information on this topic.

Figure 2.5 Entering Parameters for the Print Program Example

For example, select FP_TEST_03 or FP_TEST_03_TABLE. Again, click on the clock icon or press the F8 key to run the program. This opens the PRINT dialog for selecting the output device (see Figure 2.6).

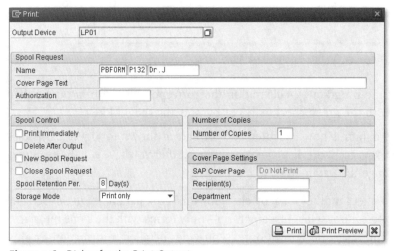

Figure 2.6 Dialog for the Print Output

7. In this dialog, you must select an output device. You can enter "LP01" as text; LP01 is a sample printer present in many SAP systems. If this printer is not available on your SAP system, you must search for an output device via the input help or contact your system administrator.

8. Next, click on the PRINT PREVIEW button (not PRINT) to obtain a preview of the print output.

9. If all steps were performed correctly, Adobe Reader will be displayed in the SAP GUI as shown in Figure 2.7. In this case, Adobe Reader displays the print output as a PDF document. You can see an excerpt from the flight-booking database in accordance with the selected form.

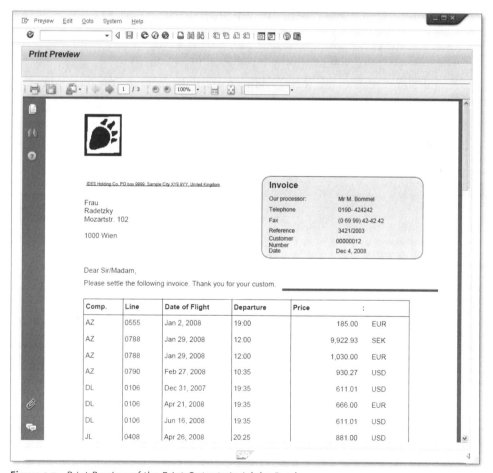

Figure 2.7 Print Preview of the Print Output via Adobe Reader

This example indicates which parts of the print output are identical for all forms. This includes the form layout that describes the appearance of the formatted output and the structure of data. The data quantity per form output is the only variable that is changeable and thus changes at runtime during the various calls. This is based on parameters and therefore different data are selected from the database and processed.

2.3.2 Creating an Interactive PDF Form

The second example considers the creation of an interactive PDF form. SAP provides a test program for this as well. You can test it as described here:

1. Go back to the initial screen of the ABAP Editor (see Figure 2.4).

2. In contrast to the print example, start the FP_TEST_IA_01 program. You can change the parameters for the test in the following screen.

3. Do not make any changes in the FORM area for the initial test.

4. In the DATA area you can set individual parts of the form to EDITABLE or LOCKED (READ-ONLY).

5. You can change the values that are used for filling the individual form fields during creation. You can accept these defaults or change them as shown in Figure 2.8.

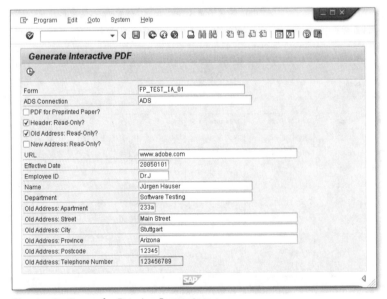

Figure 2.8 Screen for Entering Parameters

6. Start the program.

7. In the subsequent PRINT dialog, select a configured printer—just as in the print example—and click on PRINT PREVIEW to confirm.

An interactive PDF form as shown in Figure 2.9 is displayed in the preview of the print output. This form is used for a change of address for an employee. Accordingly, the form includes an area that provides general information, such as name and department, and an area with the old, currently saved address. The NEW ADDRESS area contains interactive form fields for entering a new address.

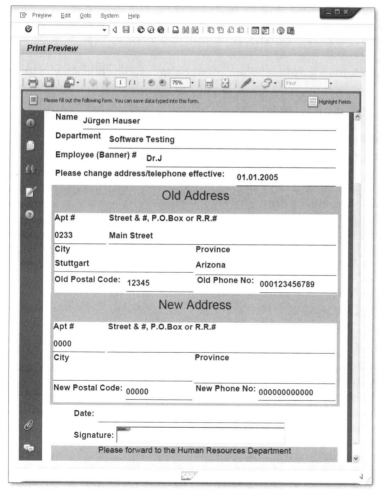

Figure 2.9 Preview of the Interactive PDF Form Example

Below the NEW ADDRESS area, there are two more form fields that you can test (you may have to scroll down the visible area of the PDF form to see them).

▶ The first field is a date field that provides a convenient date selection screen.

▶ The second field is the field for a digital signature.

At this point, you may test the procedure for applying a digital signature. To do this, a certificate must be installed on your PC. Adobe Reader indicates the certificates available. You can also check which usage rights have been added to the form (see Section 2.2.1 for more details).

2.4   Using Interactive Forms in Business Processes

The creation of interactive forms is the second important application area in addition to the print output. Interactive forms can be used to optimize individual steps of a business process. In this case, optimizing processes means the following:

▶ **Increasing the data integrity**
Errors can occur whenever data are transmitted or processed manually. If, for example, the handwriting on a paper form is illegible or cannot be read entirely after transmission by fax, this may result in problems during further processing.

So what are you supposed to do if you want to enter the data into the system? In most cases, you would simply guess. Guessing may result in higher costs, if, for example, electronic bank transfers fail or a second manual revision is necessary. Consistent electronic entry of data can remedy this problem.

▶ **Eliminating manual steps**
Manual entry of data must be carried out by a person. However, before this person can start entering data, the data must be sent to the person in paper form. The transfer of data to the entering person can be done by fax or by mail. Frequently, the documents are scanned in and the data are then provided in electronic form.

Another example is the entry of data during a telephone call (for instance, telephone orders). Usually, you cannot control the data entered on either side.

All of these manual steps result in processing delays. These delays ultimately prolong the overall duration of the business process, which means, for example, that products are delivered with a delay and suppliers receive their payment later.

Consistent electronic processing can considerably accelerate business processes by eliminating manual steps.

For the use of interactive forms in business processes, there are two different types of scenarios: online scenarios and offline scenarios. In this case, the concepts online and offline do not indicate whether the users have network access but whether the users are logged on to an SAP system or not.

2.4.1 Online Scenarios

Online scenarios mainly feature the following two characteristics:

▶ **Direct access to an SAP system is required and possible**
During the use of a PDF form, it is possible to call an SAP system, for example, to perform validations, implement a value help, or carry out complex calculations. This requires that the user is known in the system and that he is logged on to an SAP system.

▶ **Integration with other user-interface technology**
PDF forms are never displayed alone. They are displayed in a Web browser and are surrounded by other Web technology that calls Adobe Reader embedded in an (HTML) page.

A typical online scenario may look like the following: The user is logged on to SAP NetWeaver Portal. In the portal, he can view the pages of a Web Dynpro application in an iView. Web Dynpro enables you to integrate a PDF form with a view as a user-interface element and supports the implementation of value helps, validations, etc., for PDF forms.

2.4.2 Offline Scenarios

Offline scenarios may be characterized as follows:

▶ **Access to an SAP system is not possible or required**
When the user processes a form, he cannot (and does not have to) call an SAP system. Therefore, value helps, validations, and simple calculations must be contained in the PDF form by means of a scripting language. When the processing of the PDF form is completed, it is transferred to an SAP system. This transfer is done either indirectly (for example, via an email that contains the PDF form

as an attachment) or directly by logging on to the SAP system and uploading the PDF form to an application.

For example, if the user is not logged on to the company intranet, it is usually not possible to access an SAP system. If the user is logged on to the intranet, he can send the PDF form, or the data contained therein, to an SAP system via a Web service or HTTP call.

▶ **Independence of other user-interface technologies**
PDF forms are opened and processed with Adobe Reader exclusively. Therefore, integration with another technology for creating user interfaces is not necessary.

These two characteristics require only that the PDF form contain all of the necessary information (such as value helps and data). This may result in larger PDF files, which can impact the transfer time. This is important if the network connection is slow, for example.

The fact that all necessary information is already contained in the PDF form and that no access to an SAP system is required entails very interesting application options. Consider the following implementation example of an offline scenario:

A user receives an email including a request to increase the budget of a cost center. The details of this request (currently approved budget, requested budget, and already-spent budget) are contained in an interactive PDF form that has already been sent to the user as an email attachment. Therefore, this interactive PDF form provides all of the necessary information for making a decision. Additional access to an SAP system is not required to fulfill the task. After the decision has been made (approval, rejection, or approval of a different budget), the form, including all changes, can be transferred as follows:

▶ It is returned to the SAP system via *email* for further processing.

▶ Or the PDF form can be sent to the user as an *attachment to a proposal for an appointment*. At the customer's site, you can then enter all of the relevant data in the form. Subsequently, it is returned to the SAP system for updating.

▶ A *portal* can also provide the option to download an interactive PDF form, fill it out, and start a process when it is returned to the SAP system.

2.4.3 Combining Online and Offline Scenarios

Another approach is to provide the user with an option to go offline midway through the process. This constitutes a mixture of offline and online scenarios. Examples of this include the entry of travel expenses or working time.

When planning a business trip in the enterprise portal, you can prepare the entry of travel expenses. One step of the business process could be the display of a PDF form in which the user can enter the expenses. Depending on the process implementation, the user could download the form or receive it via email. During the business trip, he can fill out the PDF form on his laptop. The user interface for travel expenses enables the business traveler to upload the PDF form via a portal upon his return. It is then displayed for checking, the entries are validated, and possible confirmations are displayed. Corrections to the form can be done online.

2.4.4 When Do You Use Online and Offline Scenarios?

In addition to the question about the functioning and programming of the technology, you must also consider when you want to use interactive forms. To do this, the following lists provide some support. Interactive forms are suitable as a method for implementation if at least one of the following criteria applies:

▶ **Imitating the layout of well-known forms**
A well-known form implies that the user already knows how to handle it. This familiarity enables a fast transfer of the former paper-based process into an electronic process. The (re)use of a well-known form can reduce training costs.

▶ **Simple user interface for occasional SAP users**
Interactive forms allow for the creation of simple interfaces for occasional users of SAP systems. Instead of logging on to an SAP system, the user receives all of

the necessary information for the operation in a compact PDF form. This enables a fast and convenient participation in the business process.

▶ **Creating a document for archiving**
In contrast to other technologies (for example, all HTML-based Web technologies), completed PDF forms are available for further use. This way, they can be archived to fulfill regulatory requirements of traceability.

▶ **Local print output of the form**
PDF forms enable you to quickly create high-quality prints on site. For many user-interface technologies (for example, HTML) this is possible only with some difficulty and extra effort.

▶ **Support of digital signatures**
PDF forms can contain fields for digital signatures. However, country-specific requirements must be taken into account. You can insert multiple digital signatures into a form within workflows (the respective fields must be contained in the form).

▶ **Several persons are required for data entry**
PDF forms support data entry that cannot be implemented by one single person. Frequently, forms cannot be completed by one person only because the required information must be provided by several people (for example, information on products and finances).

You should consider the implementation of an offline scenario if one of the following criteria is met:

▶ **Integration of external users**
A person who is not an employee of the enterprise is supposed to participate in a business process but must not have access to the enterprise's SAP systems.

▶ **Offline use of a form**
The user group of the form is in the service field or on a business trip and therefore has no access to the intranet and hence no access to the SAP system.

An alternative approach is the analysis of existing business processes. If you can identify manual steps or detect intermediate statuses in processing that are similar to the following two examples, you should consider the use of interactive forms for process optimization:

▶ **Conversion of existing paper-based processes**
It is possible that today's paper-based forms can be replaced with electronic

versions. With the introduction of electronic forms, you can digitize parts of or complete processes.

▶ **Approval processes**
In approval processes, you either change or create new system data, for example, master data. However, this modification is supposed to become effective in the system only after it has been approved. In this case, interactive PDF forms are well suited as data containers. The data saved in the PDF form are transferred to the SAP system only after approval.

If you compare the various options available in online and offline scenarios, you will notice that the full efficiency of interactive PDF forms is utilized in offline scenarios. The need to integrate external users with business processes indicates that an implementation using interactive forms makes sense. This ultimately results in a faster execution of the business process and higher data quality—and therefore optimized process costs.

2.4.5   Notes on the Use of Interactive Forms

"The why and the how" play a decisive role in the use of interactive forms in the implementation of business processes.

Note for Offline Scenarios

In offline scenarios, the usability of interactive forms primarily depends on the forms' size. The larger the forms are, the more difficult it is for the user to navigate within the form. For this reason, it is useful to use the concepts of dynamic forms.

Depending on the data (for example, marital status, nationality, or answers to yes/no questions), some parts of the forms can be either hidden or displayed. This way, you can reduce the size and the complexity of the form. In extreme cases, you can implement navigation with tabs that are similar to user interfaces.

A welcome side effect is that the behavior with regard to performance sometimes considerably improves if, for example, large dynamic forms (more than ten pages) do not have to be constantly re-created in Adobe Reader.

Notes for Online Scenarios

Online scenarios entail that you ensure a balance between the user interface parts of the embedded technology (for example, Web Dynpro) and the interactive form. Consider some extreme examples that illustrate this concept:

▶ If an interactive form with multiple pages is embedded in Web Dynpro and if the Web Dynpro screen does not include any interface elements, the user faces a complex navigation in the interactive form.

▶ Another extreme example is multiple dynamic tables—tables in which you can insert or delete rows—which are distributed to multiple pages.

A possible solution for these cases is to reduce the complexity—just as for offline scenarios. In both cases, you should check why interactive forms are used (see Section 2.4.4, When Do You Use Online and Offline Scenarios?) to ensure that interactive forms are not used just because they are easy to implement.

Interactive Forms are not a Replacement for Complex User Interfaces

SAP Interactive Forms by Adobe is a form technology that is oriented toward the creation of forms. There are fewer functions provided, particularly in comparison to user-interface technologies; for example, it is not possible to program a form entirely in JavaScript without creating a form template in Adobe LiveCycle Designer.

Therefore, you should use SAP Interactive Forms by Adobe for form-based scenarios and not as a replacement for a user-interface technology. You will encounter difficulties if you still use forms as a replacement for user interfaces.

Notes for Combined Online/Offline Scenarios

If you combine online and offline scenarios, for example, to map the completing and processing of a form, you should carefully consider whether you should use one and the same form in both scenarios. Consider the notes provided in Section 2.4.4 to check whether an interactive form is required for the online scenario. Keep in mind that the effort saved for the design and the implementation of the application interface usually entails a greater development and maintenance effort.

2.5   Software Components and Architecture

Now that you have learned what PDF-based print forms and interactive forms are and when they can be used, let us look at the required software components and their integration with SAP NetWeaver. SAP Interactive Forms by Adobe mainly consists of three software components, which can be used only after they have been integrated with different SAP environments:

▶ **Adobe LiveCycle Designer**
Adobe LiveCycle Designer is used at design and implementation time.

▶ **Adobe Reader**
Adobe Reader is required on the user's PC at runtime.

▶ **Adobe Document Services (ADS)**
ADS must be installed and configured in the SAP NetWeaver stack at runtime.

Adobe Reader must be downloaded from the Adobe Website. ADS and Adobe LiveCycle Designer are available directly from SAP. They are provided via the SAP Service Marketplace (*http://service.sap.com*) or via SAP Solution Manager.

2.5.1 Adobe LiveCycle Designer

Adobe LiveCycle Designer is a tool that the form designer uses to create the layout of forms. The layouts of PDF-based print forms and interactive forms are created in the same way. The same tool, Adobe LiveCycle Designer, is used for both types of forms. Figure 2.10 shows how you can use Adobe LiveCycle Designer as a desktop application.

Figure 2.10 Adobe LiveCycle Designer

Adobe LiveCycle Designer is a graphical interactive tool; many of the required steps can be implemented using the mouse. The layout of the form is displayed graphically at design time (the window shown in the middle of Figure 2.10). Changes, such as the positioning of form fields, are carried out using drag and drop.

In addition to the layout, Adobe LiveCycle Designer graphically displays the form hierarchy and the data context:

► The form hierarchy indicates the structure of the pages that consist of the form fields used and the subforms. Subforms are structuring elements that enable you to create and maintain more complex forms. Nested subforms therefore constitute a form hierarchy.

► The data context describes the data structure of the form. Technically, a form is based on an XML data structure with a corresponding XML schema. In the SAP environment, Adobe LiveCycle Designer is used almost exclusively in the context of a framework. These frameworks create the XML schema at design time. During runtime, the XML data required for form output are generated automatically.

Adobe LiveCycle Designer provides all of the available form fields in a library. From this library, you can insert new form fields into the form layout using drag and drop. After a new form field has been added to the form, you can define additional properties using the palettes. Some examples are the appearance of buttons or edit and display patterns. The appearance determines whether a button has a border or a 3D effect. The edit and display pattern can be used to format figures, times, or a date.

Very complex behavior of forms can also be implemented using script programming. Forms are based on an event model and you can create a script program for many predefined events (for example, the `initialize` event for the time of initialization of a field).

You can choose between two different scripting languages:

► **JavaScript**
The first option is JavaScript, a scripting language from Web programming. It allows for easy access to script programming for form creation.

▶ **FormCalc**

The second option is Adobe's proprietary scripting language, FormCalc. Form-Calc has a higher performance rate than JavaScript. In particular, calculations that are based on tabular data structures can be implemented more easily with FormCalc than with JavaScript.

Most PDF-based print forms can be used without any script programming. Interactive forms with dynamic behavior, however, often require scripts to implement this dynamic behavior (for example, inserting or deleting table rows).

SAP Version of Adobe LiveCycle Designer

You must use the SAP version of Adobe LiveCycle Designer for the development of PDF-based print forms and interactive forms, and not the version available from Adobe (for example, as part of Adobe Acrobat Professional or other Adobe LiveCycle products). Therefore, you must download Adobe LiveCycle Designer from the SAP Service Marketplace.

Embedding Adobe LiveCycle Designer in SAP Development Environments

Adobe LiveCycle Designer is already embedded in the development environments for the use in the SAP environment. This results in the following benefits:

▶ Adobe LiveCycle Designer is integrated with the development process and can be called at the right point and at the right time.

▶ Adobe LiveCycle Designer is always called in the context of the current development work. Therefore, the form to be processed is already opened and the data view already displays the underlying data structure.

As a result, the form design must be saved in the surrounding development environments. Therefore, the embedded Adobe LiveCycle Designer does not provide any FILE menu. You cannot find the menu item for file properties under FILE • FORM PROPERTIES… as is the case in the independent Adobe LiveCycle Designer; instead, it is available under EDIT • FORM PROPERTIES…

Figure 2.11 shows the embedding of Adobe LiveCycle Designer in the SAP GUI. Here, Adobe LiveCycle Designer is integrated with Form Builder. Form Builder is the environment in the ABAP Workbench that bundles all of the development tools required for the use of SAP Interactive Forms by Adobe.

Figure 2.11 Adobe LiveCycle Designer Embedded in the SAP GUI

To check whether your installation is correct, you must call Form Builder and navigate to the form template shown in Figure 2.11.

1. To do this, start the SAP GUI and call Transaction SFP. The screen shown in Figure 2.12 should appear.

2. Enter the name of the form in the FORM input field—in this case FP_TEST_03_TABLE.

3. Then click on the DISPLAY button.

4. In the following screen, select the LAYOUT tab to go to the screen shown in Figure 2.11.

Figure 2.12 Initial Screen of Transaction SFP

For the sake of completeness, Figure 2.13 shows how Adobe LiveCycle Designer is embedded in the SAP NetWeaver Developer Studio. The SAP NetWeaver Developer Studio is an Eclipse-based development tool that is usually used for development in Java.

Figure 2.13 Adobe Designer Embedded in the SAP NetWeaver Developer Studio

In SAP's Java world, there is only one integration of SAP Interactive Forms by Adobe, that is, the integration with Web Dynpro Java. This book focuses on development using ABAP because multiple integrations exist here. For this reason, the main focus is on integration with Web Dynpro ABAP and not with Web Dynpro Java.

2.5.2 Adobe Document Services

ADS is the server component installed on the SAP NetWeaver stack; strictly speaking, it is installed on the Java stack and comprises Java and C++ coding. It must be configured after the installation and prior to the first usage. A configuration is also necessary on the ABAP side. In a nutshell, the ABAP stack must be notified of which ADS installation is to be used and how it can be reached. Only after these two configurations have been completed can ADS be used by ABAP.

> **ADS and Adobe Document Server**
>
> ADS is a software component of SAP Interactive Forms by Adobe. Do not confuse this component with Adobe Document Server.
>
> Adobe Document Server is an Adobe product that is maintained only within the framework of warranty services and will be taken off the market soon. Adobe LiveCycle provides a similar scope of functions.

First let us consider how you can use ADS within the ABAP and Java world (see Figure 2.14). On both sides, there is a PDF object that represents the lowest usable interface. The PDF object calls ADS.

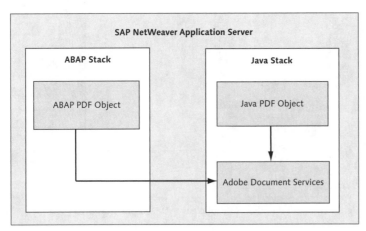

Figure 2.14 Main Components from the Developer's View

The PDF object is used exclusively whereby you can use only the functionality existing in the respective PDF object. Currently, the PDF object in ABAP provides considerably more functionality. The Java PDF object is mainly used in Web Dynpro runtime; the ABAP PDF object, however, calls ADS from the Java stack. The Java stack is still required for ADS for applications that are completely implemented in ABAP.

> **ADS Requires the Java Stack**
>
> ADS constitutes an SAP NetWeaver solution extension that can be installed and operated only on the Java stack of SAP NetWeaver Application Server. Therefore, you need a Java instance in your system landscape, even if the PDF forms are used only in the ABAP world.

Using ADS

Figure 2.15 illustrates which frameworks are based on the two PDF objects or on other frameworks.

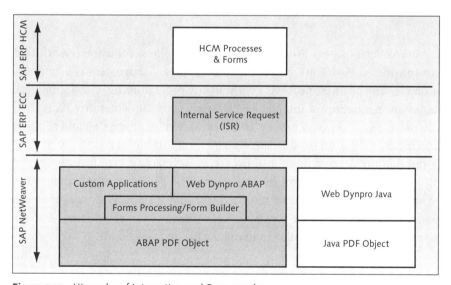

Figure 2.15 Hierarchy of Integration and Frameworks

The PDF object is the lowest layer. Web Dynpro is based on the PDF object in both worlds (ABAP and Java). In the ABAP world, you are also provided with Form Builder and the Forms Processing runtime. You can also develop custom applications that use the PDF object directly. In this case, Form Builder is used to create the PDF forms and save them in the repository. This functionality is available in SAP NetWeaver directly.

SAP Enterprise Core Component (ECC) contains the Internal Service Request (ISR) framework, which is based on Web Dynpro. In more recent releases of SAP NetWeaver, it is based on Web Dynpro ABAP; in the past, it utilized Web Dynpro Java. ISR supports the implementation of online scenarios using a workflow integration.

This book considers all integrations that are displayed in gray in Figure 2.15. It imparts the necessary basics that also apply to the frameworks and application options not considered within the scope of this book. These are briefly explained in the following text for the sake of completeness.

▶ HCM Processes & Forms is a framework that has been developed specifically for personnel administration. It is part of SAP HCM and allows for the implementation of processes in personnel administration using interactive PDF forms. It is a specialization and further development of the ISR framework. For this reason, this book considers only the ISR framework because it provides all necessary basics.

▶ SAP NetWeaver Business Process Management is the second framework that is not considered. SAP NetWeaver Business Process Management is a complex tool for creating business processes without any programming. This framework includes an integration of interactive PDF forms for implementing individual offline steps of a process. A process is either started by processing and sending an interactive PDF form (to the SAP system) or an offline step is required midway through the process flow. In this case, an interactive PDF form is sent to the user, who then participates in the process. The process is stopped until the user has processed the PDF and returned it to the system. With regard to the integration of interactive PDF forms, SAP NetWeaver Business Process Management provides functions similar to the older Guided Procedures.

▶ There is also indirect integration. Indirect integration includes all options in which interactive PDF forms are not directly integrated with a technology or framework; however, they can be integrated with an existing framework using another technology. An example is the integration of a Web Dynpro application with SAP Business Workflow, with SAP NetWeaver Business Process Management, or with Guided Procedures. This way, the mentioned frameworks can be used to support online or offline scenarios. For the implementation of interactive PDF forms in SAP Business Workflow, you need a working knowledge of the frameworks with which you want to integrate and of the integration of interactive PDF forms with Web Dynpro. This book provides details about the latter. However, it would go beyond the scope of this book to describe SAP Business Workflow, SAP NetWeaver Business Process Management, or Guided Procedures.

Communication between PDF Objects and ADS

PDF objects are implemented either in Java or ABAP. The communication structure with ADS is illustrated in Figure 2.16; it is identical for both languages.

Figure 2.16   Interaction of PDF Object and ADS

The communication between the PDF object and ADS is carried out by calling a Web service. The PDF object implements a Web service stub, which is utilized to call ADS.

The PDF object itself does not contain a lot of logic. Its main task is to correctly call ADS via the Web service stub based on the parameters and the required functionality. Both the PDF objects and ADS are located on the SAP NetWeaver Application Server (AS). ADS is always installed on the Java stack.

Structure of ADS

ADS comprises two components: Document Services and Core Adobe Document Services (see the lower part of Figure 2.16):

▶ Core Adobe Document Services provide the main functionality for the server side. This includes, for example, the creation of a PDF or various printer languages, extraction of data from the PDF, insertion of a server-side signature, or adding of usage rights for a PDF. Functions, such as the administration of fonts or certificates stored on the server, are part of Core Adobe Document Services.

▶ Document Services are on the next abstraction level. These utilize the functions made available by Core Adobe Document Services; however, they provide an application programming interface that comprises more than just simple basic functions. This enables you to perform multiple tasks in one Document Services call. Document Services ensure that basic functions are used in the correct sequence and that you require only one Web service call. You can save a lot of administration and communication effort with just one single call. This is particularly significant if you call multiple fast functions individually.

Interface to ADS

Document Services are combined and managed in an Enterprise JavaBean. The interface of these JavaBeans is provided as a Web service and the interface of the Web service via a Web Service Definition Language (WSDL file). The Web service stub for the PDF objects can be created from the WSDL file. This is illustrated in Figure 2.16.

The Web service of ADS is a public Web service that cannot be used directly. You can find it in developer and administration tools within SAP NetWeaver without any problems—the documentation of the Web service and its parameters, however, is not published. Ultimately, it is the interface agreed upon by SAP and Adobe.

The PDF object abstracts from this Web service interface and is the lowest interface to ADS that is released for application development. This abstraction provides SAP and Adobe a wider scope for future developments.

2.5.3   Interaction of Components

Up to now, this chapter has described individual software components and the interaction of PDF objects and ADS. The following sections detail the overall architecture of the integration at both development time and at runtime. You will need this information when reading the following chapters, for example, to understand and solve problems or to comprehend why certain decisions were made in frameworks.

Considering Development Time

First, development time is discussed. Figure 2.17 illustrates how you can use the development environment to create a form template (which is based on a specific context) and make it available for further use.

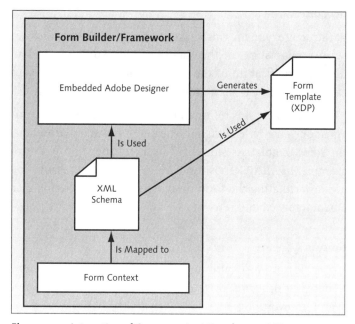

Figure 2.17   Interaction of Components at Development Time

1. At development time, Adobe LiveCycle Designer, which is integrated with the SAP environments, is used to create form templates, which are then converted into PDF documents or print outputs at runtime. This form template corresponds to the description of a data structure.

2. All development environments have a form context (often also referred to as context). In most cases, this context must be set up manually prior to the actual form template creation. The context is the intermediary element between the SAP framework and the Adobe components.

3. The development environment creates an XML schema based on the context. This XML schema includes the description of the data structure, which is based on the form template. This description is transferred to Adobe LiveCycle Designer and is displayed in the data view of the form designer's screen. This is done automatically.

4. Now, the form designer creates the form template. To do this, Adobe LiveCycle Designer, which is embedded in the development environment, is started. The form template includes the form layout; for interactive PDF forms, you must specify the behavior and integrate the form with the data structure. By integrating the form template with the data structure, you always create a form template for a specific data structure.

   If you change the data structure, you may also have to change the form template; this is the case for structural changes of the data hierarchy. Adding new data nodes does not require a modification of the form template; however, if you want to use the data node, you must extend the form template accordingly.

5. When you save the form template, it is returned to the SAP development environment that embeds Adobe LiveCycle Designer. The development environment then ensures that the form template is stored at the correct position with the correct name (for example, in ABAP Repository). There are several reasons for this automation, such as facilitating the form designer's work or ensuring that form templates can be referenced and retrieved.

Considering the Runtime

Every framework has a specific runtime environment in addition to a development environment—for PDF-based print forms, it is the Forms Processing runtime and for Web Dynpro the Web Dynpro runtime.

1. At runtime, form data must be created that corresponds to the data description and therefore to the context and the XML schema. The data can be read from the database or are already available in the framework, for example.

2. Before the data are transferred to the PDF object, they must be prepared and converted into XML format, which must correspond to the XML schema.

3. In the next step, the runtime must locate the form template required for the current task and transfer it to the PDF object.

4. For the actual call of the PDF object, the runtime environment decides on the required output format or whether usage rights should be added in case of an interactive PDF form. It then calls ADS via the PDF object.

Figure 2.18 summarizes the steps at runtime up to the call of the PDF object.

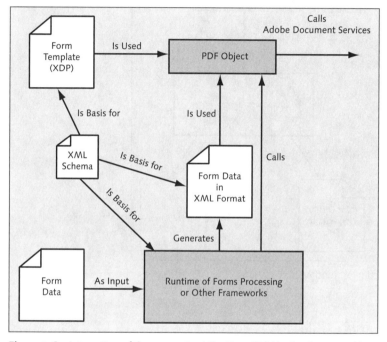

Figure 2.18   Interaction of Components at Runtime (Within the Framework)

Figure 2.19 summarizes how input data (form data and form templates) are transferred to ADS using the PDF object at runtime.

1. The PDF object uses the form data and form template that were provided by the runtime environment.

2. In this process, the PDF object calls ADS. The data, the form template, and the parameters are transferred to ADS in accordance with the interface definition.

3. ADS processes the data and form templates according to the parameters and thus creates the required output format.

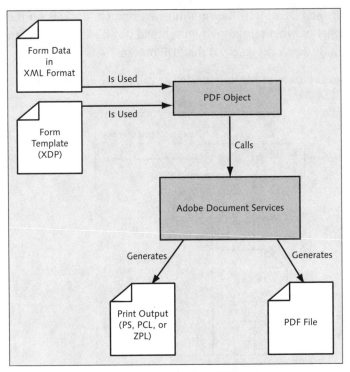

Figure 2.19 Interaction at Runtime (Call of ADS)

2.6 Summary

This chapter briefly introduced you to the terminology used for PDFs. In this context, two central concepts, PDF-based print forms and interactive forms, were detailed.

Knowledge of the classification of application scenarios in offline and online scenarios enables you to select the correct framework for your implementation. Furthermore, you were provided with decision support for assigning business processes to scenarios. This chapter also provided support to answer the question whether you should use interactive forms at all.

Users who participate in business processes comprising interactive forms must install Adobe Reader on their computers. In this context, this chapter compared Adobe Reader and Adobe Acrobat and pointed out the relevance of the various versions. Adobe LiveCycle Designer was presented as a tool that you can use to create form templates during development. The form templates and data from the SAP systems are converted into different output formats (printer languages and PDF) at runtime using ADS.

Finally, you learned about the integration of ADS with SAP NetWeaver. This information is particularly useful for Chapter 3. It can also be beneficial for troubleshooting. If you already have an installed and configured system at your disposal, you can skip Chapter 3.

This chapter details how to configure the SAP system for using SAP Interactive Forms by Adobe. It also gives an overview of the scenario-dependent configuration of the runtime components and of optional setting options.

3 Installation and Configuration

This chapter details how to set up a development environment for SAP Interactive Forms by Adobe. A prerequisite here is that both NetWeaver Application Server ABAP and Java are available. This chapter describes the specifics that must be considered in addition to the ADS operation and the configuration required.

3.1 Prerequisites

To work with SAP Interactive Forms by Adobe, you need ADS and Adobe Live-Cycle Designer. ADS is integrated with the SAP NetWeaver Java application server; however, you also need an ABAP application server to reproduce certain scenarios that are described in this book. Chapter 9, Internal Service Requests, details the requirements for the creation of ISR scenarios.

Note on the Subsequent Presentation

The following description assumes that the ABAP and Java systems have already been installed in Versions 7.0 EHP2 (NetWeaver ABAP) and 7.20 (NetWeaver Composition Environment 7.2) or higher. The configuration of ADS is outlined beginning with Section 3.2, Basic Configuration.

Test Version

If no installed systems are available, you can download and install test versions. A start page on these versions is available via the following link in the SAP Developer Network (SDN): *https://www.sdn.sap.com/irj/sdn/adobe*. Log on or register to the SDN. Download the Java and ABAP trial versions for SAP NetWeaver 7.0 or higher via their respective links.

3.1.1 Credentials and Password for SAP Interactive Forms by Adobe

You can also download a ReaderRights credential, which is valid for a limited period and required for the generation of interactive forms, via the SDN.

1. To do this, go to *http://sdn.sap.com* and log on or register.

2. In the main navigation, select DOWNLOADS and then SOFTWARE DOWNLOADS • SAP NETWEAVER MAIN RELEASES. You can also access this page directly via *http://www.sdn.sap.com/irj/sdn/nw-downloads*.

3. From the software packages available, you need CREDENTIALS AND PASSWORD FOR SAP INTERACTIVE FORMS BY ADOBE. The download includes an archive file (*.zip*) that contains a password-protected private key (credential). The format of the file corresponds to the Public Key Cryptography Standards (PKCS) #12 specification; the file has the extension *.p12* or *.pfx*. In addition to the key, the ZIP archive also contains a text file (*.txt*), which stores the corresponding password.

3.1.2 Adobe LiveCycle Designer 8.2

You can download version 8.2 of Adobe LiveCycle Designer from the SAP Service Marketplace.

1. To do this, go to *http://service.sap.com/installations* and log on.

2. Then select the ENTRY BY APPLICATION GROUP menu entry.

3. Navigate to SAP NETWEAVER • SAP NETWEAVER • SAP NETWEAVER 7.0 • INSTALLATION AND UPGRADE • <OPERATING SYSTEM> • <DATABASE>. Here you can specify any combination of operating system and database, because it is a local PC application.

4. Use the ADOBE LIVECYCLE DESIGNER 8.2 entry in the DOWNLOADS tab to download the software.

3.2 Basic Configuration

This section describes the individual steps required to set up ADS. In this context, distinctions are made between the basic, scenario-dependent, and optional configuration. This section also introduces the tools used and check options for each configuration aspect.

You can call ADS via a Web service interface. The provided function is wrapped in the Portable Document Format (PDF) object that is available in both the ABAP and the Java environment. Therefore, to use ADS, access to the Web service must be configured. For this purpose, the following steps are required.

3.2.1 ADSUSER

First, create a user in the Java system through which you can call ADS.

1. Start NetWeaver Administrator (NWA) via the URL *http://<server>:<port>/nwa*, for instance, *http://localhost:50000/nwa*, if you are on the Java system locally (see Figure 3.1).

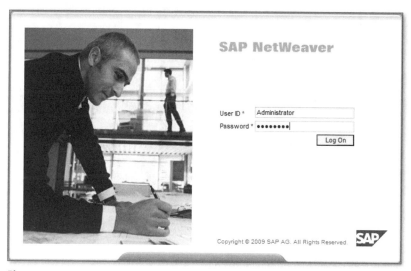

Figure 3.1 SAP NetWeaver Administrator Java Logon Page

2. Enter "Administrator" as the user name and the corresponding password.
3. Select the CONFIGURATION MANAGEMENT tab.
4. Click on the IDENTITY MANAGEMENT link (see Figure 3.2).

Figure 3.2 Configuration Management

5. You are now in the user administration of the Java system (see Figure 3.3).

Figure 3.3 Identity Management (User Administration)

Here you must create the user via which the functions of ADS are addressed. This user is usually called ADSUser. First check whether the user already exists. To do so, enter "ADSUser" in the input field of Figure 3.3, and click on Go to confirm. If the user doesn't exist, continue with this procedure to create it. If the user is already available, you can check the settings accordingly.

6. Define the password and other technical settings in the DETAILS section (see Figure 3.4). First, enter a password under DEFINE PASSWORD and CONFIRM PASSWORD. Memorize this password because you will need it later on in the Web service configuration.

Figure 3.4 Creating the ADSUser

7. Enter any name in the LAST NAME field because this is a required field.

8. Select TECHNICAL USER under SECURITY POLICY.

9. Go to the ASSIGNED ROLES tab. The system now displays Figure 3.5. Enter "SAP_ADSCALLER" as the role on the left-hand side and click on GO.

10. Select this role and click on ADD TO ASSIGN IT TO THE ADSUSER.

11. Remember to save the user settings by clicking on the SAVE button.

Figure 3.5 Role Maintenance in the User Administration

You have now created an ADSUser with the SAP_ADSCALLER role through which you can call ADS.

3.2.2 ADSCaller

The SAP_ADSCALLER role is linked with various applications to access ADS. You can check them in the IDENTITY MANAGEMENT of NetWeaver Administrator.

1. To do so, select the ROLE option as the SEARCH CRITERIA, and enter "SAP_ADSCALLER" in the input field on the right. Click on GO (see Figure 3.6).

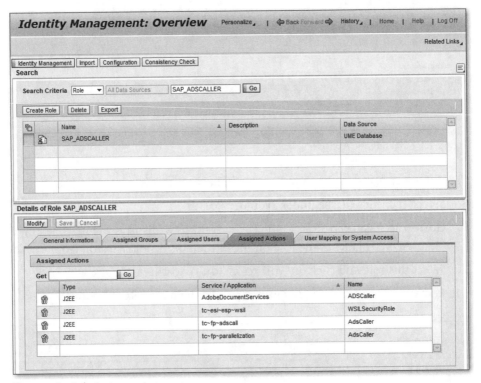

Figure 3.6 Role Assignments

2. Select the result displayed.

3. In the DETAILS section you can view various applications that are linked with the role.

3.2.3 Web Service Test

The previously described configuration steps allow for a password-protected call of ADS. You can test this via the Web services navigator.

1. To do this, go to URL *http://<server>:<port>/wsnavigator*, and log on as the administrator using the corresponding password (see Figure 3.7).

Figure 3.7   Web Services Navigator

2. Click on PROVIDER SYSTEM under SEARCH TYPE, and then choose the SEARCH button (see Figure 3.8).

Figure 3.8   Selecting Web Services

69

3. The system displays a list of available Web services (see Figure 3.8). Choose ADOBEDOCUMENTSERVICESV1 and click on NEXT.

4. You can view the `rpData` method under OPERATIONS. Select it and click on NEXT (see Figure 3.9).

Figure 3.9 Testing Adobe Document Services

5. You could additionally set call parameters (INVOCATION PARAMETERS button) as shown in in Figure 3.10. This is not required for this test, however. Simply click on NEXT again.

Figure 3.10 Call Parameter of the rpData Method

6. The dialog for entering the user parameters opens. Enter "ADSUser" and the password you selected in Figure 3.4 (see Figure 3.11).

Figure 3.11 Logon for the Web Service Test

7. By clicking on OK, you receive the response of the Web service call (see Figure 3.12).

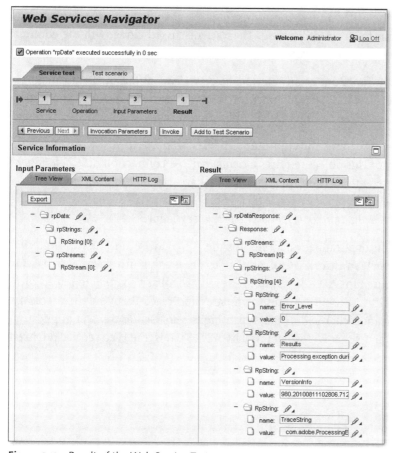

Figure 3.12 Result of the Web Service Test

You do not enter any additional data in this test and thus you cannot simulate any correct processing by ADS. The purpose of this test is to check whether the communication was established successfully. Without any data, you receive, as expected, an error message (COM.ADOBE.PROCESSINGEXCEPTION: REQUIRED STREAM: "PDFDOCUMENT" NOT FOUND IN REQUEST OR ITS LENGTH IS ZERO) under RESULT. However, this message indicates that the Web service call was successful, as it originates from ADS itself.

3.3   Scenario-Dependent Configuration

Section 3.2, Basic Configuration, described the basic configuration of ADS that all scenarios require. The following sections detail the configuration steps that are necessary for the different usage options. Figure 3.14 illustrates the components that are relevant for form processing. They are discussed along with the communication channels that these components use.

The Web service functions as an interface to ADS. Two different client categories access this interface: the Remote Function Call (*RFC) destination* (ABAP application server) and the *Web service proxy* (Java application server).

Both ABAP print programs and applications in Web Dynpro ABAP use the *ABAP PDF object* at runtime. This object requires a *configured RFC* connection (*RFC destination*) to communicate with ADS. Form scenarios that are executed on the Java application server, such as applications in Web Dynpro Java, and ISR scenarios, access the ADS Web service via a proxy (*Web service proxy*, see Figure 3.13).

There is an additional callback channel for the ABAP form runtime—the Internet Communication Framework (ICF) service. To access this interface, a *destination* must be configured for ADS. The system uses this feedback channel to reload form templates because ADS buffers these templates and reads them only if necessary. This communication channel for mass printing is also used to transfer application data and documents that were generated by ADS. That is, the Web service call itself contains only control data in these scenarios.

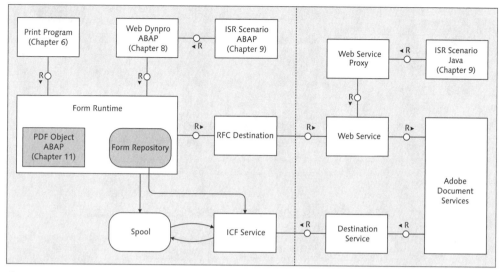

Figure 3.13 Architecture

3.3.1 RFC Destination

To call ADS from an ABAP application server, an RFC connection must be configured, which is done in Transaction SM59 (Configuration of RFC Connections).

1. Click on the CREATE button and enter a name for the connection. The default connection must be called "ADS." You can also configure additional connections. The application program controls the ADS call by transferring a connection name. Select G (HTTP CONNECTION TO EXTERNAL SERVER) as the connection type.

2. In the TECHNICAL SETTINGS tab (see Figure 3.14), enter the computer name into the TARGET HOST field, the HTTP port into SERVICE NO., and the path of the ADS Web service (/ADOBEDOCUMENTSERVICES/CONFIG?STYLE=RPC) into PATH PREFIX. After you have entered the path, the system displays a warning that you can skip by pressing the Enter key.

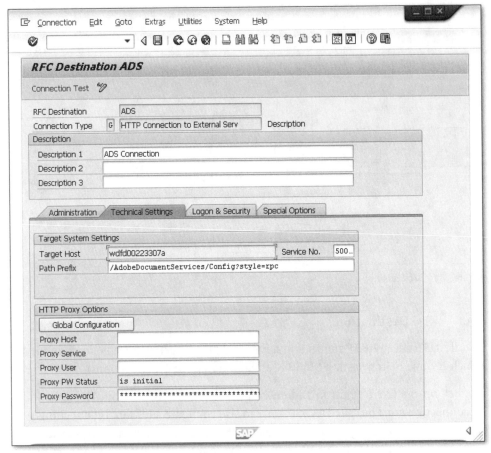

Figure 3.14 Configuration of RFC Connections

3. Navigate to the LOGON & SECURITY tab and select the BASIC AUTHENTICATION option (see Figure 3.15). Enter "ADSUser" and the master password that you previously defined. Click on SAVE to complete the configuration.

4. You can then test the RFC connection using the FP_PDF_TEST_00 program. The connection test that Transaction SM59 provides does not work here because it does not support Simple Object Access Protocol (SOAP). Therefore, call Transaction SE38 (if you do not have the necessary authorization, you can also use Transaction SA38), and run the FP_PDF_TEST_00 program by specifying the RFC connection

that you have configured (ADS in this example). If a connection has been set up successfully, the system returns the internal version number of ADS.

Figure 3.15 Credentials for Accessing ADS

3.3.2 Destination and ICF Service

While ADS is called through a SOAP protocol via the RFC connection that is configured in Transaction SM59, the actual user data, such as form templates and business data (large data volumes in some scenarios), are transported via a separate HTTP connection. This enables ADS to cache form templates because the call contains only a reference to the used template. Moreover, the system thus uses a time stamp to decide whether the local cache needs to be updated or whether the already-cached template can be used. Moreover, the separate connection enables you to bypass SOAP restrictions because this protocol is not designed for the exchange of large data volumes.

ADS_AGENT

First, you must create a service user that is used for the communication between ADS and the ABAP application server. The following two roles are assigned to this user:

- ▶ SAP_BC_FP_ICF
- ▶ SAP_BC_FPADS_ICF

To start, you must generate the roles for these profiles if this has not been done in your system yet.

1. Call Transaction PFCG (Role Maintenance) to display the roles.

2. Then navigate to the AUTHORIZATIONS tab, and click on the DISPLAY AUTHORIZATION DATA button on the MAINTAIN AUTHORIZATION DATA AND GENERATE PROFILES area (see Figure 3.16). The system now displays all authorizations for this role. You can use the GENERATE button to generate a current profile.

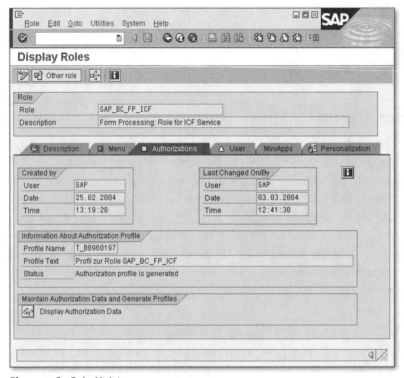

Figure 3.16 Role Maintenance

3. After the system has generated both profiles, call Transaction SU01 (User Maintenance) to create the user. Enter "ADS_AGENT" as the name and click on CREATE.

4. In the ADDRESS tab, you must fill in the LAST NAME field; you should repeat the user name here. Go to the LOGON DATA tab, and select the SERVICE USER CATEGORY. Configure a password.

5. Navigate to the ROLES tab and assign the two previously mentioned roles to the user (see Figure 3.17). Finally, click on the SAVE button.

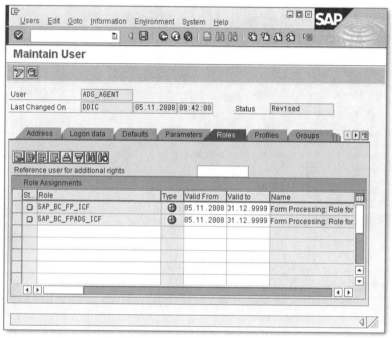

Figure 3.17 Maintaining Users

SICF

Then you must activate the two ICF services that are called by ADS:

1. To do this, call Transaction SICF (Maintain Services) and click on the EXECUTE button.

2. Navigate to the DEFAULT_HOST • SAP • BC • FP node, and select the ACTIVATE SERVICE option from the context menu (see Figure 3.18).

Figure 3.18 Activating ICF Services

3. Repeat this step for the DEFAULT_HOST • SAP • BC • FPADS node.

Testing the ADS_AGENT User and the ICF Services

You can use a Web browser to test the ICF service, which is used to access the ABAP form repository. To do this, you must first determine the computer name and the HTTP port of the ABAP application server.

1. Call Transaction SICF, click on EXECUTE, and then select the PORT INFORMATION entry from the GOTO menu. The system displays a table in a dialog box. In the PROTOCOL column, search for the HTTP entry, and write down or copy the corresponding entries in the HOST NAME and SERVICE columns.

2. Start the Web browser, and enter the following URL: *http://<server>:<port>/sap/ bc/fp/form/layout/FP_TEST_03_TABLE.XDP*. The name of the <server> is identical to the previously determined host name and <port> to the HTTP port.

3. When you call this URL, the system prompts you to enter a user name and password. Enter "ADS_AGENT" and the password that you previously defined. If the authentication has been successful, you can view an XML file. This file is the FP_TEST_03_TABLE template that is stored in the ABAP form repository in its original language (see Figure 3.19).

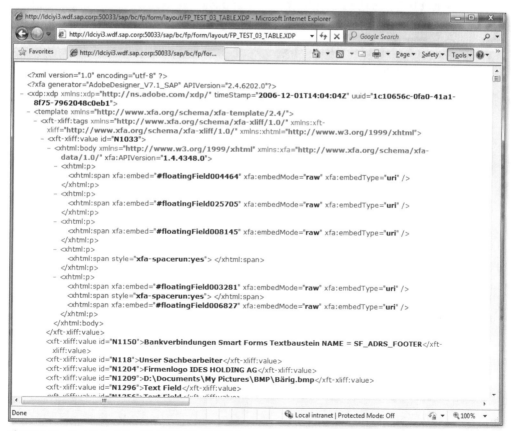

Figure 3.19 Test Call of the FP_TEST_03_TABLE Form

Destination

After you have configured the ABAP application server for access by ADS, you must create a destination on the Java application server that refers to the released services. ADS uses this destination to access the ICF service in the ABAP application server.

1. Start SAP NetWeaver Administrator.

2. Select the DESTINATIONS entry in the CONFIGURATION MANAGEMENT tab (see Figure 3.2).

3. Click on the CREATE button to create a new destination (see Figure 3.20).

4. Select FP_ICF_DATA_<SID> as the DESTINATION NAME. You must replace <SID> with the system ID of the ABAP system.

5. Select HTTP as the DESTINATION TYPE and click on NEXT.

Figure 3.20 Creating the FP_ICF_DATA_<SID> Destination

6. Enter the same server and port as the URL (in the form of *http://<server>:<port>*) as the ones you used in the connection test (see Figure 3.19). This time, however, you do not enter a path, as shown in Figure 3.21.

7. Specify the system ID and the client in which you have configured the ADS_ AGENT user.

8. Choose NEXT.

Figure 3.21 Connection Settings

9. Select the BASIC (USER ID AND PASSWORD) ENTRY AS AUTHENTICATION, as shown in Figure 3.22.

Figure 3.22 Logon Information

10. Enter ADS_AGENT as the USER NAME and the corresponding password.

11. Choose FINISH.

Testing the Destination

The connection test from NetWeaver Administrator generally generates an error message for the connection because the URL stores only the name of the computer and the HTTP port. The path specifications for the respective service are not added until runtime. To perform a test anyway, you can temporarily extend the stored URL.

1. Add the */sap/bc/fp/form/layout/FP_TEST_03_TABLE.XDP* path to the URL, and click on PING DESTINATION without saving the changes. If this test has been successfully executed, the system displays an INFO screen with the following message: ... RESPONSE CODE 200, CONTENT TYPE TEXT/XML.

2. Click on CANCEL because you have added the path only for testing purposes. This test simulated that the FP_TEST_03_TABLE form template from the ABAP form repository was read.

You can also test the configuration from the ABAP application server.

1. To do this, call the FP_CHECK_DESTINATION_SERVICE test program (Transaction SE38 or SA38).

2. Enter the name of the configured RFC connection (ADS) and select the WITH DESTINATION SERVICE option.

3. When you click on EXECUTE, the system calls ADS, which then generates a PDF form. For this process, the callback channel that you previously configured is used, and the system displays a brief INFO message (...BYTES TRANSFERRED) in the case of a successful result.

3.3.3 Web Service Proxy

The Java PDF object accesses ADS via a Web service proxy. To use applications in Web Dynpro Java, the proxy must be configured on the respective client system. This may either be a local call of the same system or a remote Java application server.

Notes on the Subsequent Step Sequence

The following description assumes that you have not configured the Web service proxy in your system yet. It is absolutely essential to know the configuration, for example, if you need to change the connection.

You now configure the Web service proxy to access ADS from Web Dynpro Java.

1. Again, start SAP NetWeaver Administrator as shown in Figure 3.1.

2. Select the SOA MANAGEMENT tab and click on the DESTINATION TEMPLATE MANAGEMENT tab (see Figure 3.23).

3. Click on NEW to create a new entry.

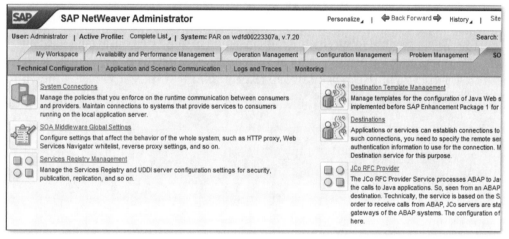

Figure 3.23 SOA Management Tab

4. An input screen opens (see Figure 3.24) where you select WSIL for the DESTINATION TYPE and define CONFIGPORT_DOCUMENT as the DESTINATION NAME.

5. The form of the URL should be *http://<server>:<port>/inspection.wsil.*

6. Choose NEXT.

Figure 3.24 Creating a Web Service Proxy

7. You now need to specify the authentication because every user (also a technical user) must log on to the system to access ADS. Select the HTTP AUTHENTICATION ENTRY WITH USER ID/PASSWORD (BASIC) UNDER AUTHENTICATION, as shown in Figure 3.25.

Figure 3.25 Credentials For the Web Service Proxy

8. Enter "ADSUser" as the USER ID and the password that you have selected.

9. Click on FINISH to complete the configuration and save the changes.

10. Select OPERATION MANAGEMENT • SYSTEMS • START & STOP • JAVA APPLICATIONS.

11. Start the `tc~wd~pdfobject` application.

With this configuration, the Web Dynpro Java runtime can access ADS.

3.3.4 ReaderRights Credential

To generate interactive forms with usage rights, a private key is required—the ReaderRights credential. Based on the usage rights, additional functions are released in Adobe Reader. You can download the corresponding key with a trial period for evaluation and test purposes from the SDN (see Section 3.1, Credentials and Password for SAP Interactive Forms by Adobe). To obtain a ReaderRights credential to use the product, read SAP Note 736902.

You configure the key within SAP NetWeaver Administrator. There you can manage credentials, certificates, and Certificate Revocation Lists (CRLs) for ADS. In the following, you configure the ReaderRights credential.

1. Start SAP NetWeaver Administrator.

2. Select the CONFIGURATION MANAGEMENT tab and the INFRASTRUCTURE link (see Figure 3.26).

3. Click on the ADOBE DOCUMENT SERVICES link.

Figure 3.26 Configuration Management Tab

4. In the subsequent screen (see Figure 3.27), you can manage credentials, certificates, and certificate revocations, or you can monitor the license status. You can also use the application to manage job profiles.

5. Initially, select CREDENTIALS in the SHOW field and click on MANAGE P12 FILES.

Figure 3.27 Initial Screen for Managing Credentials

6. Use the subsequent dialog (see Figure 3.28) to load the credential to your system.

7. Click on the ADD NEW FILE button. A dialog opens where you choose the pfx file via the BROWSE button.

8. Choose the UPLOAD button.

Figure 3.28 Managing Credentials

9. Click on CLOSE to close the dialog from Figure 3.28.

10. You can now configure the credential by selecting the ADD NEW OBJECT button as shown in Figure 3.27.

11. Figure 3.30 opens. Choose ReaderRights and set the type to P12.

12. Open the list of P12 files and select your credential.

13. Enter the password which you received as part of the credentials (text file in the zip file) under Password and Confirm Password.

14. Close the dialog by clicking on SAVE.

Figure 3.29 Selecting the ReaderRights Credential

ADS is now configured and you can use the ReaderRights credential.

Consider the expiry date if it is a test credential from SDN (see Figure 3.30).

Figure 3.30 Fully Configured ReaderRights Credential

To complete the configuration, you must restart the services on the Java server because otherwise the changes made will not be effective.

1. Start the two services, *Document Services Trust Manager* and *PDF Manipulation Module—Low Encryption*.

2. Go to the OPERATION MANAGEMENT tab in SAP NetWeaver Administrator.

3. Choose SYSTEMS and then START & STOP.

4. Select JAVA SERVICES, and enter "adobe" under SERVICE COMPONENT. Press the ⌷Enter⌷ key.

5. You can now select the two services from the list and restart them.

Testing the ReaderRights Credential

You can test whether the ReaderRights credential has been installed correctly with the FP_TEST_03 program. Call this test program in Transaction SA38 and select the X (INTERACTIVE FORM WITH ADDITIONAL USAGE RIGHTS) option for the FORM • INTERACTIVE parameter. If you then display the print preview of the form, Adobe Reader indicates that it is an interactive form.

3.3.5 FPCONNECT

You can make additional settings for the previously configured RFC connection (see Section 3.3.1, RFC Destination) in the FPCONNECT table.

1. Call Transaction SM30 (Maintain Table Views). Enter "FPCONNECT" in the TABLE/VIEW field, and click on the MAINTAIN button. You can skip the warning displayed (CAUTION: THE TABLE IS CROSS-CLIENT).

2. To add settings for an RFC connection, click on NEW ENTRIES. Then enter the respective name (for example, "ADS," see Figure 3.31) in the RFC DESTINATION column.

3. In the DIR_GLOBAL column, you can specify whether the installation is a dual-stack system, in which case the ABAP and Java application server share a global directory. Nevertheless, if it is a dual-stack installation, you must set the value to TRUE. Therefore, the data is directly exchanged via the global directory. This is probably not the case in your system.

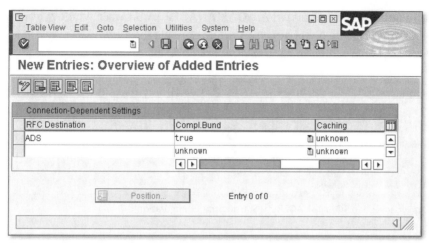

Figure 3.31 Maintaining the FPCONNECT Table

4. The COMPL.BUND column allows for the cross-system control of form bundling. To activate this function, select the TRUE value. This significantly reduces the runtime of print jobs with a lot of small or medium-sized forms as long as the print program outputs these forms in one print job (see Section 6.6.1, Bundling Forms). This is a cross-system setting; alternatively, ABAP print programs can control the form bundling via a parameter.

5. To save the changes of a table entry, click on the SAVE button. For all other table columns, you should use default values.

3.4 Configuration for Parallelization

You must configure two Web services to parallelize print jobs (see Section 6.7). One service (FpPrintRequestService) is responsible for the actual parallelization, while the other service (FpQueueAdminService) is required for administration and monitoring.

The Web services are configured via the SOA management.

1. For this purpose, start Transaction SOAMANAGER. A browser window opens (see Figure 3.32), which you can also start directly via the *http://<server>:<port>/ sap/bc/webdynpro/sap/appl_soap_management?sap-language=EN* link.

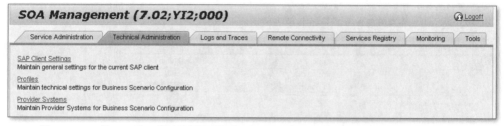

Figure 3.32 Transaction SOAMANAGER for Starting the Configuration

---

Client-Dependency of the Web Service Connection

Note that Web service connections are *client-dependent*. You must implement the connection from every client from which this parallelization is supposed to be used. Remember: The direct connection to ADS via Transaction SM59 was *client-independent*.

---

2. Next, choose the SERVICE ADMINISTRATION tab and then the WEB SERVICE CONFIGURATION link (see Figure 3.33).

Figure 3.33 Service Administration

3. In the subsequent screen (see Figure 3.34), switch the search mode from SERVICE to CONSUMER PROXY and enter "FP*" as the search pattern. Click on the START button to display the search results. Figure 3.34 also shows the search list with the result.

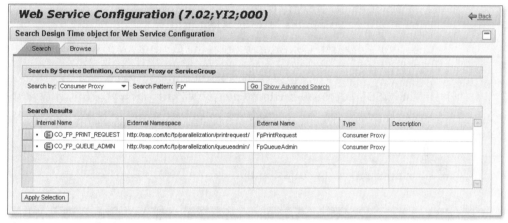

Figure 3.34 List of Relevant Consumer Proxies

The configuration of these two Web services is described in Sections 3.4.1, Web Service for Parallelization, and 3.4.2, Web Service for Monitoring.

3.4.1 Web Service for Parallelization

This section describes the configuration of the Web service for actual parallelization.

1. First, choose the FPPRINTREQUEST entry, and click on APPLY SELECTION. The lower area of the screen now displays the details of the proxy definition. Click on the CONFIGURATIONS tab to navigate to the logical ports (see Figure 3.35).

Figure 3.35 Overview of Logical Ports

2. Choose the CREATE button. A new window opens (see Figure 3.36), in which you make the following settings:

   ▸ You can enter any name under LOGICAL PORT NAME, for example, "ADS."

   ▸ By selecting the LOGICAL PORT IS DEFAULT checkbox, you define that it is the default port.

   ▸ Enter a DESCRIPTION in the correspondent field.

   ▸ Choose WSDL BASED CONFIGURATION as the CONFIGURATION TYPE.

   ▸ Leave the WSDL ACCESS settings at VIA HTTP ACCESS.

   ▸ In the WSDL LOCATION section, enter *http://<server>:<port>/FpPrintRequest-Service/FpPrintRequest?wsdl &mode=ws_policy* as the URL FOR WSDL ACCESS. Here you must replace <server> and <port> with the parameters of your Java stack.

   ▸ Click on the APPLY SETTINGS button.

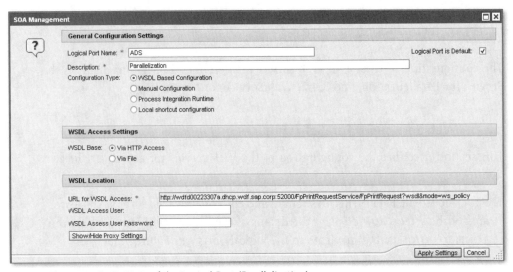

Figure 3.36 Settings of the Logical Port (Parallelization)

3. The system takes you back to the Web service administration, where you must make the security settings (see Figure 3.37). In this case, the `sapsp:HTTPBasic` authentication method is used by default, whereby an authentication with user and password is sufficient.

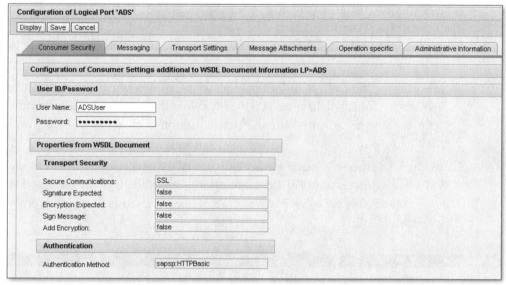

Figure 3.37 Security Settings of the Logical Port

4. Enter the user for ADS (ADSUser) and the previously defined password.

5. Choose SAVE.

6. SOA Manager displays a success message, as shown in in the upper area of Figure 3.38.

Figure 3.38 Success Message of the Web Service Configuration

3.4.2 Web Service for Monitoring

After you have configured the Web service for parallelization, turn your attention to the second Web service from Figure 3.34. The FpQueueAdminService service is required for monitoring and managing jobs.

1. Select the FPQUEUEADMIN entry in SOA Manager (see Figure 3.34), and click on the APPLY SELECTION button. The lower area of the screen now displays the details of the proxy definition. Click on the CONFIGURATIONS tab to navigate to the logical ports.

2. Now perform the same steps for this Web service as described in Section 3.4.1, Web Service for Parallelization. It is essential that the logical port has the same name as the one you used for the parallelization Web service, in this case "ADS."

3. The decisive change is made in the URL FOR WSDL ACCESS INPUT field in the WSDL LOCATION section. For the monitoring service, the URL for the access is *http://<server>:<port>/FpQueueAdminService/FpQueue Admin?wsdl&mode=ws_policy* (see Figure 3.39).

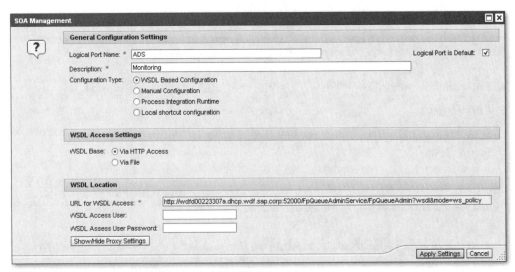

Figure 3.39 Settings of the Logical Port (Monitoring)

Maintain the security settings as shown in Figure 3.37, and save your entries. A success message as shown in Figure 3.38 appears.

3.4.3 Connection Test for the Two Web Services

You can use a simple connection test to check whether the Web services for parallelization can be addressed from the ABAP stack.

1. To do so, select a consumer proxy from Figure 3.34, click on the APPLY SELECTION button, choose the previously created logical port (ADS), and then click on the PING WEB SERVICE button (see Figure 3.40).

Figure 3.40 Connection Test of a Web Service

2. The system is automatically checks whether the technical connection settings are correct, whether the services are available in the Java stack, and whether you entered the security settings correctly (for instance, user and password).

3. A success message as illustrated in Figure 3.41 appears.

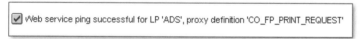

Figure 3.41 Configuration Tested Successfully

3.4.4 Assigning the Logical Port to the ADS Connection

The connection to ADS is made in the ABAP program via an SM59 connection, which usually bears the name "ADS." If you select another name, you must explicitly specify it in every application program. To be able to use parallelization, it is necessary to define a mapping between this SM59 connection and the created logical ports.

You define this mapping in the FPCONNECT table, through which you also specify the settings for bundling (see Section 3.3.5, FPCONNECT).

1. Start Transaction SM30 for table maintenance.

2. Enter "FPCONNECT" as the table, and click on the MAINTAIN button.

3. Confirm the information with regard to client independence by pressing the Enter key.

4. Select the connection entry for ADS and scroll to the right until you can view the Logical Port field.

5. Enter the name of the logical port, which you selected in Section 3.4.1, Web Service for Parallelization, or Section 3.4.2, Web Service for Monitoring (see Figure 3.42).

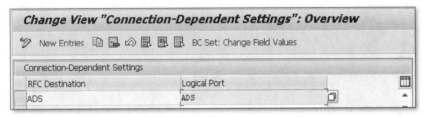

Figure 3.42 Assigning the Logical Port

Parallelization is basically possible with and without bundling of forms. With bundling, however, you also reduce the name of ADS calls, as is the case in sequential processing.

3.5   Optional Configuration

This section discusses additional settings of ADS.

3.5.1   Licensing

To generate customer-specific, interactive forms, you require an additional license. ADS provides a component that monitors usage, subject to licensing, and allows changing of the license status.

1. To view the corresponding usage data and make changes to the status, start SAP NetWeaver Administrator and there the ADOBE DOCUMENT SERVICES application as described for the configuration of the ReaderRights credential (see Section 3.3.4, ReaderRights Credential). The screen shown in Figure 3.27 is displayed.

2. Select the LICENSING tab.

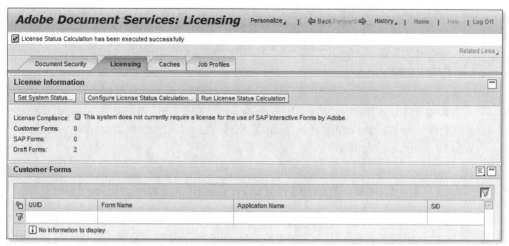

Figure 3.43 Licensing Tab

3. As shown in Figure 3.43, you can view the number of the forms that were processed on this system. These forms are divided into the following three categories:

   ▶ **Number of SAP Forms**
   This number indicates how many forms have been processed that were delivered by SAP and were not or only slightly changed. These forms do not require an additional license.

   ▶ **Number of Customer Forms**
   Customer forms are custom-developed, interactive forms or SAP forms that have been changed to a large extent. Fundamental changes include a customization of the data binding, which is required for adding new data fields, for example.

   ▶ **Number of Draft Forms**
   Forms that are generated from nonproduction systems or clients are not considered in the determination of the license status.

4. Once customer forms that require a license have been processed, the status (LICENSE COMPLIANCE) changes from green to red. When you purchase a license, you can configure this in the system by clicking on the SET SYSTEM STATUS button field and selecting the corresponding field in the subsequent dialog (THIS SERVER

97

IS LICENSED FOR THE USE OF SAP INTERACTIVE FORMS BY ADOBE). Then the status changes from red to green again. In addition to displaying the license status in the administration interface, ADS writes a log entry when a license is required but the status has not been configured.

The CUSTOMER FORMS table in the bottom area of the user interface displays all customer forms that require a license and any additional information, such as the SAP system ID and client from which ADS was called, and the name of the form and calling application.

3.5.2 Credentials, Trusted Anchors, Certificate Revocation Lists

You can use ADS to generate and check digital signatures. In this context, you must distinguish between certification and signature. When a PDF document is certified, it is assigned an invisible signature that ensures the integrity of the form; that is, once the PDF document has been manipulated, the certification is regarded as invalid—both in Adobe Reader and by ADS. You can add any number of signatures to the document, which can be inserted in business processes for approval steps, for example. To use digital signatures, you need credentials, trusted anchors, and certificate revocation lists.

Credentials

The PDF object (ABAP and Java) provides different methods to certify and add signatures. These methods also enable you to specify the key that is supposed to be used via a configured alias. However, if these optional parameters are not provided, ADS uses the following default values:

▶ DocumentCertification as the alias for the certification

▶ ServerSignature as the alias for the digital signature

The approach for the installation and configuration of these and other keys is identical to the one for the ReaderRights credential (see Section 3.3.4, ReaderRights Credential). You only need to spell the alias correctly and enter a valid password. As already mentioned in the description of the ReaderRights credential, you must restart the services *Document Services Trust Manager* and *PDF Manipulation Module— Low Encryption* for additional keys.

The CREDENTIALS tab displays a table of all registered keys. ADS checks the expiration dates and write log entries daily when the current date approaches or exceeds the expiration date. Therefore, the system administrators do not have to regularly check the expiration data of the keys via this user interface. Instead, they only have to monitor the log files.

In the CONFIGURE EXPIRY CHECK area, you can configure the settings for the log entries. For example, you can customize the time of the daily executed check process. You can also define the period for which warnings are supposed to be written to the log file before a key expires.

Trusted Anchors

ADS enables you to check signatures in PDF forms. To do this, you need to configure trusted certificates that are either the public key of a private key that is used for a signature or the public key of the issuing authority—a so-called root certificate. These public keys are managed via the TRUSTED ANCHORS tab. The following shows how to define a list of trusted certificates in your system.

1. As shown in Figure 3.27, choose the TRUSTED ANCHORS entry instead of CREDENTIALS. Via the MANAGE CER FILES key, you can load the CER file for trusted anchors into the system just as you did for the ReaderRights credential.

2. Subsequently, you can select this file via ADD NEW OBJECT (see Figure 3.30).

3. Define the intended use for the certificate via the checkboxes (TRUSTED FOR) (Figure 3.44):

   ▶ **Signatures and as Trusted Root**
   You use this option to define whether the certificate is supposed to be used to validate signatures.

   ▶ **Certified Documents**
   If you want to use the public key to check certified PDF forms, you must select this field.

   ▶ **Embedded High Privilege JavaScript**
   Interactive forms may contain JavaScript statements. You can use this option to define whether such PDF forms can also be considered trustworthy if they are certified. This option is available for selection only when you select CERTIFIED DOCUMENTS.

Figure 3.44 Managing Trusted Anchors

4. Complete the registration of the public key by clicking on SAVE. This key is then listed in the `Trusted Anchors` table.

5. Restart the two services *Document Services Trust Manager* and *PDF Manipulation Module—Low Encryption*.

Now the list of trusted certificates is active in your system.

Certificate Revocation Lists

Certificate revocation lists enable you to retroactively select keys as invalid that you have initially categorized as trustworthy. These lists are also managed in the DOCUMENT SECURITY tab, but you must select CERTIFICATE REVOCATION LIST to specify the revoked certificates.

1. Similar to the ReaderRights credential and the trusted anchors, you must load the Certificate Revocation List (CRL) into the system via MANAGE CRL FILES.

2. By selecting the ADD NEW OBJECT button, you navigate to the selection of available CRLs (see Figure 3.45). Additionally fill out the URL field. This is a unique identifier, which is contained in the keys (`crldp` field) that can be revoked via this list. Usually, the certificate revocation list can also be called via this URL.

3. Click on SAVE to complete the registration. The list is now displayed in the CRLs TABLE.

Figure 3.45 Certificate Revocation List

After having configured the certificate revocation lists, you must restart the two services *Document Services Trust Manager* and *PDF Manipulation Module—Low Encryption*.

Secure Sockets Layer (SSL)

To use certifications and signatures, the ADS Web service must be called via a secure SSL connection. Chapter 13, Advanced Installation and Configuration, describes the SSL configuration; you can find a detailed description of how to perform the necessary configuration steps in the SAP Help Portal (*http://help.sap.com*). There, navigate via SAP SOLUTIONS • SAP NETWEAVER • SAP NETWEAVER 7.x to the ADOBE DOCUMENT SERVICES CONFIGURATION GUIDE. The CONFIGURATION OF THE WEB SERVICE SSL CONNECTION chapter describes the SSL configuration.

3.5.3 Service Properties

There are additional properties whose settings are important: the size of the destination cache for buffering forms, the number of processes that can process documents in parallel, and the number of parallel jobs that can be used for parallelization of print jobs.

Destination Cache

As mentioned in Section 3.3.2, Destination and ICF Service, ADS has a local cache, which is used to store form templates. To modify the size of the cache, again call

ADOBE DOCUMENT SERVICES in NetWeaver Administrator under CONFIGURATION MANAGEMENT • INFRASTRUCTURE.

1. Select the CACHES tab.

2. The current size of the cache is displayed in MB. The default value is 4MB.

3. You can change the value via the CONFIGURE DESTINATION CACHE button. If you use large form templates or forms in different languages, you should increase this value so that the cache can be optimally utilized.

4. The two other buttons, CLEAR DESTINATION CACHE and CLEAR PDF CACHE, could be useful if you need to reset the cache again. This usually should not be required. In case of an error, for instance, if a form change does not appear in the completed document, you can manually delete the buffer here.

PoolMax

For the *XML Form Module* and *PDF Manipulation Module—Low Encryption* services, there is the respective PoolMax property that indicates how many documents can be processed simultaneously. The *XML Form Module* service generates PDF documents and print forms. Its default value is four processes.

The *PDF Manipulation Module* service is required for adding usage rights and digital signatures. Its default value is two. If you send parallel requests to ADS and if you have a machine with several processors, you can increase these values to optimally utilize the resources.

1. You cannot make this setting via NetWeaver Administrator. Instead, start the Config Tool. You can find it at operating system level under */usr/sap/<SID>/ J<instance>/j2ee/configtool/configtool.bat* (or sh).

2. Open the tree structure under SERVICES. There you can find COM.ADOBE~ XMLFORMSERVICE and COM.ADOBE~PDFMANIPULATION (see Figure 3.46).

3. The POOLMAX setting is available for both entries. Here you can specify the number of processes.

4. Choose FILE • APPLY CHANGES in the menu.

5. You must then restart the cluster, for instance, via the SAP Management Console.

Figure 3.46 Config Tool—Setting PoolMax

3.5.4 Number of Parallel Print Jobs

The individual requests are distributed to parallel processes in the parallelization of print jobs. You can configure the number of requests to be started in parallel.

1. Start NetWeaver Administrator, and choose the APPLICATION MODULES link under CONFIGURATION MANAGEMENT • INFRASTRUCTURE.

2. Select SAP.COM~TC~FP~PARALLELIZATION~EJB.JAR as the name (see Figure 3.47).

3. Choose FPXFAREQUESTPROCESSORBEAN in the EJB MODULE DETAILS.

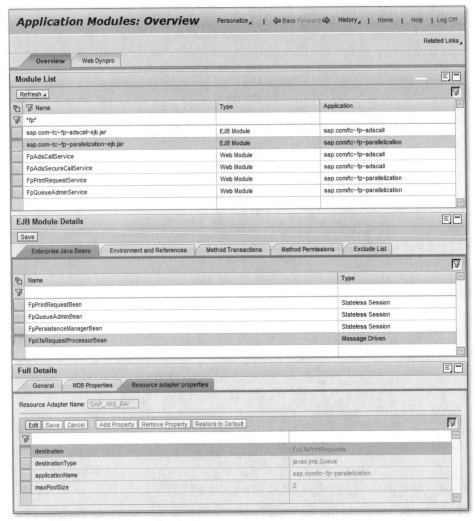

Figure 3.47 Number of Parallel Print Jobs

4. Select the EDIT button.

5. Change the value MAXPOOLSIZE to the number that is supposed to be processed in parallel in the parallelization framework.

6. Save your settings.

3.5.5   Fonts

The installation of ADS comprises numerous fonts, which are stored in the following directory: */usr/sap/<SID>/ J2E/J<instance>/j2ee/os_libs/adssap/FontManagerService/ fonts/adobe*. To use additional fonts for the form output, you must make the respective fonts available to the Document Services Font Manager.

1. For this purpose, copy the fonts to the directory, */usr/sap/<SID>/SYS/global/ AdobeDocumentServices/FontManagerService/fonts/customer*.

2. The following types are supported:

    ▶ OpenType® (*.otf*)

    ▶ TrueType® (*.ttf*)

    ▶ PostScript® Type 1 (*.pfb*, *.pfm*)

3. Before you can use the newly installed fonts, you must restart two ADS components. Call SAP NetWeaver Administrator.

4. Select OPERATION MANAGEMENT • SYSTEMS • START & STOP • JAVA SERVICES. Restart the DOCUMENT SERVICES FONT MANAGER service.

5. Select the JAVA APPLICATIONS tab. Restart the ADOBEDOCUMENTSERVICES application.

3.5.6   XDCs

To generate form outputs, you need the ADS XFA Device Configuration (XFA) files. They are XML files that describe the printer or output to the printer. You can find the XDC files in the */usr/sap/<SID>/SYS/global/AdobeDocumentServices/lib* directory.

You can add modified or additional XDC files by copying the files to the *XDC/ Customer* subdirectory. The provided XDC files should remain unchanged in principle. Section 6.3, Device Types for the Output, provides more information on XDC files and the necessary assignment to device types on the ABAP application server.

3.6   Error Analysis

This section discusses typical error messages and possible causes for these problems. The overview in Table 3.1 enables you to easily find common (configuration) errors and eliminate them.

Errors when Calling ADS from the ABAP Application Server	
The ENTER LOGON DATA dialog box opens.	Possible causes: Either the ADSUSER user is locked (see Section 3.2.1) or you have entered a wrong password for the RFC connection data (see Section 3.3.1).
The "HTTP receive failed with exception communication_failure" message is displayed (possibly as a part of a more detailed error message).	Possible causes: You have entered a wrong computer name or HTTP port for the RFC connection data (see Section 3.3.1).
The "HTTP send returned with status code" message is displayed (possibly as a part of a more detailed error message).	Possible cause: You have entered a wrong path for the RFC connection data (see Section 3.3.1).
The error message contains "com.adobe. ProcessingException: Problem accessing data from destination..."	Possible causes: The ADS_AGENT user is either locked or does not have the necessary authorizations. The ICF services are not activated. You have entered a wrong computer name or HTTP port for the destination or the password is not correct (see Section 3.3.2).
Errors when Calling ADS from the Java Application Server	
The "com.sap.tc.Web Dynpro.pdfobject.core. PDFObjectRuntimeException: Service call exception" message is displayed (possibly as a part of a more detailed error message).	Possible causes: Either the ADSUSER user is locked (see Section 3.2.1) or you have entered the wrong details in the Web service proxy (password, computer name, HTTP port, or path). The Java PDF object was not restarted after changes had been made to the configuration (see Section 3.3.3, Web Service Proxy). Usually, the stack trace, which includes the previously mentioned exception, contains further information that indicates the cause of the error.

Table 3.1 Typical Error Messages when Calling ADS and Possible Causes Using ADS

General Errors when Calling ADS	
The "User ADSUSER does not have access to method rpData" message is displayed (possibly as a part of a more detailed error message).	Possible cause: The ADSUSER user is not linked to the ADSCaller role (see Figure 3.7).
The "com.adobe.ProcessingException: Could not retrieve a password for credential: ReaderRights" message is displayed (possibly, as a part of a more detailed error message).	Possible causes: The ReaderRights credential has not been configured or has been configured with a wrong alias (see Section 3.3.4).
The "com.adobe.ProcessingException: Not allowed by credential error while applying usage rights to PDF" message is displayed (possibly as a part of a more detailed error message).	Possible cause: The ReaderRights credential has expired (see Section 3.3.4).
The error message contains "com.adobe.ProcessingException: Credential login error while applying usage rights to PDF."	Possible cause: The two services *Document Services Trust Manager* and *PDF Manipulation Module—Low Encryption* were not restarted after changes had been made to the configuration (see Section 3.3.4).

Table 3.1 Typical Error Messages when Calling ADS and Possible Causes Using ADS (Cont.)

3.7 Using ADS

This section covers critical aspects of the usage of ADS. These include monitoring the individual components and settings, and logging or tracing errors.

3.7.1 Monitoring and Performance Tracing

You can find information on the Java system's performance behavior in NetWeaver Administrator. The following steps show how to obtain details on ADS.

1. Start NetWeaver Administrator and select the AVAILABILITY AND PERFORMANCE MANAGEMENT tab.

2. Then select RESOURCE MONITORING and AS JAVA STATISTICS.

3. You can filter the ADS calls, for instance, by entering "ADSUser" as the user (see Figure 3.48).

Figure 3.48 Performance Tracing

4. You can view the response times in the RESPONSE TIME column. You can also find information on the memory consumption (ALLOCATED MEMORY column).

3.7.2 Log Configurator

You can use the Log Configurator service, which is available in NetWeaver Administrator, to configure which components are supposed to write how many logs or traces. To obtain detailed processing information from ADS, proceed as follows:

1. Select the PROBLEM MANAGEMENT tab and then LOGS AND TRACES.

2. Click on the LOG CONFIGURATION link.

3. Select TRACING CATEGORIES, and navigate to the ROOT LOCATION • COM • ADOBE node (see Figure 3.49).

4. Select the ALL value for SEVERITY, and click on the COPY SEVERITY TO SUBTREE and SAVE CONFIGURATION buttons. This means that all subcomponents of ADS

write the maximum number of traces, which can be helpful for troubleshooting and are frequently required by the support team.

5. To return to the default setting, click on the DEFAULT CONFIGURATION button.

Figure 3.49 Tracing ADS

Log Viewer

You can use the LOG VIEWER to view log and trace files in NetWeaver Administrator.

1. Select the PROBLEM MANAGEMENT tab and then LOGS AND TRACES.

2. Click on the LOG VIEWER link.

3. Choose SHOW VIEW • GENERAL • DEFAULT TRACE (JAVA).

4. Filter the results by entering "com.adobe" in the LOCATION column.

3.8   Installation of Adobe LiveCycle Designer

To install Adobe LiveCycle Designer, you must first unpack the downloaded archive (see Section 3.1.2, Adobe LiveCycle Designer 8.2) to a temporary directory. Then open the setup program contained therein.

Once you have confirmed the installation directory, the program components are installed. You can now use Adobe LiveCycle Designer together with the SAP GUI.

3.9   Automatic Configuration via CTC

This chapter has comprehensively described the configuration required for using ADS in an ABAP environment. It is essential to know the basic concepts in order to find errors quickly. But you are now also able to adapt the required settings if changes are made to the system landscape.

The configuration can be run automatically. For this purpose, SAP provides a CTC template to set up an ABAP system and a Java system in such a way that ADS can be used directly. This template can be called multiple times, for example, if you want to run a second ABAP system with the same ADS. The ADS is operated as a hub (see Section 3.10). Some configuration steps may be omitted because the configuration is based on a wizard.

You start the automatic configuration in NetWeaver Administrator.

1. Select the CONFIGURATION MANAGEMENT tab (see Figure 3.2).

2. Click on the SCENARIOS link.

3. Start the CONFIGURATION WIZARD.

4. Select the CONFIGURATION OF THE ADOBE DOCUMENT SERVICES AS A HUB entry, and click on the START button (see Figure 3.50).

5. The system guides you through 14 configuration steps.

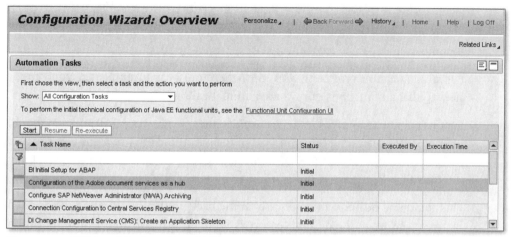

Figure 3.50 CTC-Based Configuration of ADS

3.10 ADS Hub

ADS provides central services for PDF-based scenarios. Because they are implemented in a JEE-based environment, you must install a NetWeaver Java stack.

The application systems required by ADS can be set up in ABAP and in Java. Most applications (and all applications that are discussed in this book) are developed in ABAP. For this reason, the installation of the Java stack is always an additional application server.

This additional effort enables you to link various ABAP systems with ADS. Besides sizing, which must be considered separately, you must also answer the basic question of release dependency between the two stacks here.

SAP positions ADS as a hub. This means that the independent ADS system is interoperable with other systems (as part of NetWeaver AS Java). ADS also has its own patch cycle, for instance, compared with an SAP ERP system that calls ADS. The minimum requirement on both sides is NetWeaver 7.0 SP13 respectively. As of this support package, you can combine various versions with one another. For instance, it is possible to use Version 7.0 in ABAP while the Java stack is used in Version 7.20. This combination (lower ABAP release) is ensured thanks to the backwards compatibility of ADS and the stable Web service interface.

It is interesting to combine a more recent ABAP release with an older Java release. This is also possible as of Release 7.0 SP13. However, new functions of ADS, which become available in subsequent releases, cannot be supported.

For all application programs, you must therefore bear in mind that you cannot assume that all functions of ADS are automatically available.

For this purpose, SAP provides an availability query that every ABAP program should call before it uses a new function via the form runtime environment (see Chapter 6, Form Output) or the ABAP PDF object (see Chapter 11, ABAP PDF Object). Only if this availability query is successful may a function be used.

This could also be done automatically in the background, but it cannot be decided in general whether the desired feature is required or optional for the application scenario. In the former case, you would either output an error message or have to program a workaround. In the latter case, you simply omit this function. Therefore, the decision must be made in the respective application program.

If the release of your ADS should always be higher or identical to the ABAP release, you can go without this query.

The availability query is implemented via an ABAP class CL_FP_FEATURE_TEST, which offers a static method, IS_AVAILABLE. A Boolean value is returned that provides information as to whether the desired feature can be used.

The feature itself is transferred to the IS_AVAILABLE method. The possible values depend on the ABAP stack release and are listed as attributes of the CP_FP_FEATURE_TEST class.

Table 3.2 shows the values from Release 7.0 EHP2.

Feature	Description
GC_JOB_PROFILES	Job profiles
GC_CLEAR_TEMPLATE_CACHE	Delete the form buffer
GC_SELF_TEST	Self-test
GC_ZCI_SCRIPT_INJECTION	ZCI Script Injection
GC_HIGHLIGHT_FIELDS_ON_ERROR	Highlight fields in case of error

Table 3.2 Features That Can be Used For the Query

Feature	Description
GC_ASSEMBLE_STITCH	Merge in one PDF document, also for very large PDFs
GC_NO_DROP_DOWN_TO_ZCI	Do not send dropdown lists to ZCI
GC_XDC_API	XDC-API

Table 3.2 Features That Can be Used For the Query (Cont.)

You probably will not use any of these features directly in your programs. Rather, these are functions that are queried internally, for instance, in Web Dynpro ABAP.

Job profiles (GC_JOB_PROFILES) may be of interest to you and are described in Chapters 6 and 13. But because they are available as of the first version, which supports the ADS hub concept (Release 7.0 SP13), you can omit the query.

Listing 3.1 shows the basic call of the feature test.

```
DATA lv_flag TYPE ABAP_BOOL.
DATA lx_exception TYPE REF TO cx_fp_runtime.
TRY.
  lv_flag =
     cl_fp_feature_test=>is_available(
        lv_feature = cl_fp_feature_test=>gc_job_profiles )
CATCH cx_fp_runtime INTO lx_exception.
* Error during ADS communication.
ENDTRY.
IF lv_flag = ABAP_TRUE.
* OK
...
```

Listing 3.1 Availability Query of an ADS Feature

The feature test itself utilizes a cached version number of ADS and executes a remote call only in exceptional cases. For this reason, the query is not critical for performance.

The ADS hub concept is also described in the ADS Hub—Central Installation of Adobe Document Services blog of the SAP Developer Network (SDN), which is available at: *http://www.sdn.sap.com/irj/scn/weblogs?blog=/pub/wlg/14106*.

3.11　Summary

In this chapter, you have learned how you can configure the ABAP and Java systems for the use of ADS. This is necessary to understand and test the examples in the subsequent chapters. The chapter also provided an overview of the individual components of the solution and their interactions. Moreover, it provided information on critical aspects of using ADS and enabled you to trace and eliminate typical (configuration) errors yourself.

To create forms or extend existing forms, you need to understand the structure of a form and its components. This chapter provides you with basic information on interfaces and context.

4 Interface and Form Context

The following sections detail and describe the structure of a form and the maintenance of individual components. The main focus is data definition and form logic.

4.1 Structure of a Form

A form describes the appearance of a document, that is, the structure of the pages and the positioning of objects, such as texts, graphics, fields, or even tables. Most forms use fields that must be filled with application data at runtime. The number of rows in a table depends on the data available for a specific document. Therefore, a form constitutes a dynamic object that can create the finished document only in conjunction with the application.

The form designer defines an *interface* so that you can assign the application data between an ABAP program and a form. This interface is an independent form object; the form itself consists of a context and a layout. Within the context you can access data of the interface where you determine the hierarchy of the data. Through the context you define a schema, which is available later on for layout creation. This means that there are two form objects: the interface and the form. Form objects are maintained either using the Object Navigator of the ABAP Workbench (Transaction SE80) or directly via Form Builder (Transaction SFP). As Workbench objects they can be transported, have a package assignment, and can be translated. Interface and form are independent objects that are maintained separately.

The interface defines what data are maintained by a print program and can be used in multiple forms. An interface is referenced from a form whereby the form uses this interface for the print program. The form itself comprises the context and the layout—they form a unit.

Figure 4.1 shows the interaction of interface and form where multiple forms can exist for one interface. The form contains the context and the layout.

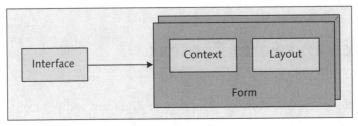

Figure 4.1 Interface and Form Context/Layout

It does not make any difference whether you process a form in the ABAP Workbench or directly in Form Builder. Form Builder provides direct access and the screen offers more space for processing.

In the ABAP Workbench, you can navigate within the packages and have an overview of multiple form objects from which you can select one by double-clicking on it. Additionally, the ABAP Workbench provides you with a where-used list that is very important if you want to know which forms use a specific interface. This way, you can determine which forms should be adapted if you want to extend an interface.

If you know the name of a form, you can work in Form Builder directly. The ABAP Workbench provides a good overview of the contained form objects in case you assign packages to your forms. This book uses direct access to Form Builder.

4.2   Interface of a Form

The interface of a form has a unique name and is defined in Form Builder. All application data that are supposed to be transferred to a form are listed here and typed accordingly.

There are three different types of interfaces:

► **ABAP Dictionary-based interface**
The ABAP Dictionary-based interface is the most commonly used interface and is therefore described in great detail within this chapter.

► **XML schema-based interface**
The XML schema-based interface is relevant for applications that work with an XML schema without any ABAP Dictionary reference.

► **Smart Forms-compatible interface**
The Smart Forms-compatible interface is generated during the migration of a Smart Form into a Portable Document Format (PDF)-based form.

For a better understanding, we will show you how to create an interface.

1. Start Transaction SFP, click on the Interface radio button, and enter the name Z_IFBA_BOOK_DDIC_01 (see Figure 4.2). Then click on Create.

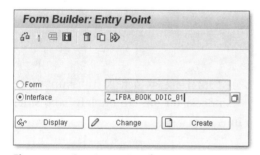

Figure 4.2 Creating an Interface

2. In the resulting dialog box, enter a description and keep all other values unchanged (see Figure 4.3). Choose Save.

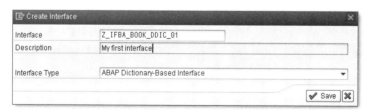

Figure 4.3 Specifying Interface Properties

3. An interface is a transportable object with a package assignment, so you are asked for a package. If you enter a package, you must assign a transport request.

For these examples, however, it is sufficient to use local objects because they cannot be transported and are only used locally on the system on which they were created.

4. Click on Local Object or enter $TMP as the package. Save your entries (see Figure 4.4).

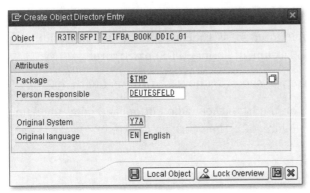

Figure 4.4 Package Assignment

Form Builder now shows the newly created interface, which is still empty (see Figure 4.5) and saved locally. It will be extended later on. On the left-hand side, you can see the different elements of an interface:

Figure 4.5 Interface

- Form interface
- Global definitions
- Initialization
- Currency/quantity fields

The following sections describe the purpose of the individual categories and the properties that can be specified.

4.2.1 ABAP Dictionary-Based Interface

The name of the ABAP Dictionary-based interface derives from the fact that all parameters have an ABAP Dictionary reference and are based on tables, structures, or data elements that are defined in the ABAP Dictionary. When you created an interface in Section 4.2, Interface of a Form, and accepted the default values in the dialog box shown in Figure 4.3, the ABAP Dictionary-based interface had already been selected as the interface category by default. This interface category is the most important one for most applications. For this reason, it is described in great detail within the scope of this book.

You can make comprehensive definitions within an interface, where the definition of the import parameters is the most significant one. Here, you specify the application data to be maintained. These data are relevant both for the design of the form and at runtime when a print program wants to transfer data to the form.

The present interface must be extended by other parameters, which is detailed based on an example. In addition, you are provided with various processing options. The interface will use structures and tables from the flight-booking model (SCUSTOM, SBOOK, and SPFLI), which are employed in numerous SAP examples. In Section 4.3, Context of a Form, you will use this data model to establish the context of a form to enable a tabular output. The layout of the form is developed in Chapter 5, Creating Form Templates, while Chapter 6, Form Output, discusses the output of the form.

Form Interface

Import and export parameters and exceptions are identified within the form interface. More notably, you can define new import parameters here. The export parameters and exceptions are predefined and can neither be changed nor extended.

Import Parameter

When you double-click on the IMPORT entry in Form Builder (see Figure 4.5), the system displays a parameter on the right that is predefined in every interface: /1BCDWB/DOCPARAMS TYPE SFPDOCPARAMS. By double-clicking on the SFPDOCPARAMS type name, you can navigate to the definition of this Dictionary structure; the system now displays the components of the structure (see Figure 4.6).

Figure 4.6 Defining the Default Parameter of an Interface

Table 4.1 describes the meaning of the individual fields in the default parameter.

Component	Meaning
LANGU	Output language of the form
COUNTRY	The country and the language is relevant for the formatting of dates and figures
FILLABLE	Indicator for whether the form is to be created as an interactive form
DYNAMIC	Property of interactive forms
DARATAB	Archive information if optical archiving is requested for the output
REPLANGU1	Replacement language if the form is not available in the requested language
REPLANGU2	Another replacement language
REPLANGU3	Another replacement language

Table 4.1 Components of the Default Parameter

You will come across these fields again if you want to write a print program and output a form. For now, you do not have to consider these fields.

Now that you know how to navigate to the definition of a parameter using a double-click, we will define some parameters for setting up a form context in the following examples.

1. In Form Builder, you are provided with various buttons that you can use to process an interface (see Figure 4.5). They enable you to append, insert, delete, or duplicate rows.

2. To add a new parameter, click on APPEND ROW. The system creates an empty row below the default parameter.

3. Enter CUSTOMER as the parameter name, TYPE as the type assignment, and SCUSTOM as the type name. The result is shown in Figure 4.7.

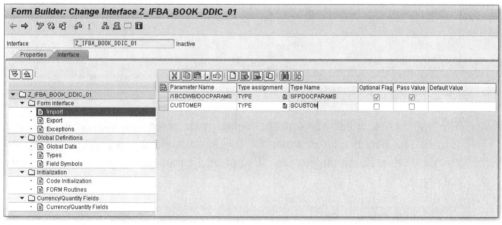

Figure 4.7 Newly Created Parameter

▶ The structure of the import parameter is similar to a function module interface; you can reference different Dictionary categories, for example, data elements, structures, or table types. In fact, you will generate a function module interface from the form interface later on.

▶ You can use the two checkboxes, OPTIONAL FLAG and PASS VALUE, to specify whether a parameter is required at runtime and whether it is transferred as a value or as a reference. If you set the parameter to OPTIONAL FLAG, it does not have to be transferred by the application when a form is called. You will require most parameters; however, you can provide an additional optional parameter that can be transferred by the print program at runtime. A pass by value is usually not considered for structures and tables because, in most cases, it is more efficient to refer just to the data.

> ▶ TYPE is the only type assignment permitted for ABAP Dictionary-based interfaces.

4. Now create two more parameters: BOOKINGS with the data type TY_BOOKINGS and CONNECTIONS with the data type TY_CONNECTIONS.

5. You are required to transfer an elementary field of the DATE type as another optional parameter. To do this, create a DATE parameter with the SYDATUM data type, and select the OPTIONAL FLAG checkbox for this parameter (see Figure 4.8).

Parameter Name	Type assignment	Type Name	Optional Flag	Pass Value	Default Value
/1BCDWB/DOCPARAMS	TYPE	SFPDOCPARAMS	☑	☑	
CUSTOMER	TYPE	SCUSTOM	☐	☐	
BOOKINGS	TYPE	TY_BOOKINGS	☐	☐	
CONNECTIONS	TYPE	TY_CONNECTIONS	☐	☐	
DATE	TYPE	SYDATUM	☑	☐	

Figure 4.8 Completed Interface

The interface now has one optional default parameter, /1BCDWB/DOCPARAMS, and four custom parameters, of which CUSTOMER is a flat structure, and BOOKINGS and CONNECTIONS are both table types. The optional parameter, DATE, is an elementary data type.

Navigating to ABAP Dictionary

The definition of the data types can be displayed at any time by double-clicking on the corresponding type name. The system displays a message if you have not saved the interface yet. You can now go to the ABAP Dictionary to navigate to the next step or back to Form Builder.

Export Parameter

The system displays the export parameters if you double-click on EXPORT on the left-hand side. For the ABAP Dictionary-based interface, only one parameter (/1BCDWB/FORMOUTPUT) exists that you cannot change—neither is it possible to add custom export parameters. The predefined parameter is used in some application programs, for example, to process a generated PDF.

Exceptions

You can view the exceptions by double-clicking on EXCEPTIONS. There are three predefined exceptions for each interface:

▸ **USAGE_ERROR**
The USAGE_ERROR exception is triggered at runtime if the transferred call parameters do not enable form creation, for example, an unknown form or an invalid output device.

▸ **SYSTEM_ERROR**
The SYSTEM_ERROR exception indicates a runtime error, for example, if errors occur for the connection definition for Adobe Document Services (ADS).

▸ **INTERNAL_ERROR**
The INTERNAL_ERROR exception is reserved for unforeseen errors.

Meaning of the Interface at Runtime
As mentioned previously, the interface definition forms the basis for a function module interface in which you can find the import parameters, export parameters, and exceptions.
For this reason, a form interface must always be in line with the application program (except for the optional parameters). A program terminates if parameters that are expected by the interface are not transferred.

Activating the Interface

You should activate the interface prior to defining the other components, because only then can you use it in a form.

1. To do so, select the ACTIVATE button, as shown in Figure 4.9.

Figure 4.9 Activating the Interface

2. If you made an error in the definition of the interface, for example, if you used an unknown data type, the system notifies you accordingly during activation.

3. You can check the interface at any time. To do so, select the CHECK button, which is positioned on the left side of the activation icon. The system checks whether all data types used exist and displays error messages, if necessary.

Global Definitions

The global definitions include global data, types, and field symbols. Here, you can define custom fields that you can use in the entire form, for example, to implement calculations that are not provided by the application program.

Global Data

Global data usually provides data that are required for the creation of sums.

In the present example, you define a SUM_BOOKINGS table and specify it as the TY_BOOKINGS data type.

1. To do so, double-click on GLOBAL DATA on the left-hand side, and insert a row on the right, similar to the procedure used for the import parameters.

2. Now enter "SUM_BOOKINGS" as the variable name and "TY_BOOKINGS" as the type name (see Figure 4.10).

Figure 4.10 Global Data of an Interface

Types

For the TYPES, you can define custom data types if no corresponding ABAP Dictionary type exists and you want to address multiple fields at the same time. The data types are recorded in the source code, just as in the ABAP program.

Field Symbols

FIELD SYMBOLS are an efficient option for using pointers in nested tables or for large data quantities. By using field symbols you do not copy any data that improve the memory requirement and the runtime. This is illustrated in Listing 4.1.

Initialization

The initialization enables you to process data from the interface and initialize global data. An interesting option is that you can select data from a database depending on the interface parameters. You can therefore output more data on a form than are intended by the SAP application without having to modify the application program. SELECT statements can read data from the SAP database in initialization coding, whose result is stored in global data. You can then use and output this data in a form even though the actual application program would not. The interface between the application and the form remains unchanged. You fill in only global data, which you can then use in the context and the layout of the form.

> **Extending Data Retrieval**
>
> If you need more data than provided in the standard, it is more efficient to extend the data retrieval in the application program, for example, by adding or enhancing an existing SELECT statement in ABAP. If you read data during initialization, this basically constitutes another database access; therefore, you must decide which procedure is best suited for the concrete case.

Code Initialization

Under CODE INITIALIZATION of the interface, you can enter the initialization code in an ABAP Editor. Here, you specify the input parameters that you want to access in read-only mode and determine which output parameters to fill. The output parameters are the global data that you created for the global definitions.

In this example, you fill the internal table, SUM_BOOKINGS, with sums from the import parameter BOOKINGS. To do this, you perform a currency-dependent summation to sum different currencies individually.

1. Click on APPEND ROW and define the input parameter BOOKINGS.

2. Again, select APPEND ROW for the output parameters and enter the name SUM_BOOKINGS.

3. A type assignment of the parameters is not required because the system automatically determines the assignment to the interface parameters or the global data.

4. For the summation, use the LOOP statement in ABAP and the COLLECT command (see Listing 4.1).

```
FIELD-SYMBOLS <lfs_bookings> TYPE sbook.
DATA lv_sums LIKE LINE OF sum_bookings.
LOOP AT bookings ASSIGNING <lfs_bookings>.
  lv_sums-forcuram = <lfs_bookings>-forcuram.
  lv_sums-forcurkey = <lfs_bookings>-forcurkey.
  COLLECT lv_sums INTO sum_bookings.
        ENDLOOP.
```

Listing 4.1 Initialization Code

As a result, a row is created for each FORCURKEY currency (EUR, USD, etc.) in the SUM_BOOKINGS table, and the FORCURAM values are summed separately for each of these currencies.

5. In the Editor, you can use the PRETTY PRINTER, whose button is positioned on the left-hand side of the Editor. There, you can also find the button for PATTERNS, which you can use to insert various statement patterns into your coding.

6. The results should appear as illustrated in Figure 4.11. Save the interface.

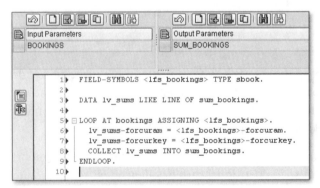

Figure 4.11 Initialization Code

Form Routines

If your initialization codes contain recurring program sections, you can outsource and call them in FORM ROUTINES, as it is common in ABAP. The Editor is the same as the one you already know from the initialization code. For this example, there is no need for form routines because it is rather simple.

Currency/Quantity Fields

The CURRENCY/QUANTITY FIELDS are a special case with regard to data: They are particularly important in business documents and require additional information for the output, which you as the form developer must pay special attention to.

Currency fields have the Dictionary data type CURR and the quantity fields the data type QUAN. These fields each contain the amount; for the correct output, however, you also require the unit. For this reason, the currency is stored in a field of the CUKY data type and the quantity unit in a field of the UNIT data type.

1. Let's take a look at the SBOOK database table in the ABAP Dictionary. To do so, start Transaction SE11 and enter "SBOOK" in the database table field. Select DISPLAY to view all fields of the table.

2. The FORCURAM field comprises the S_F_CUR_PR data element and CURR as the data type (length 15, decimal places 2). Now you can process any currency in this field.

   The definition specifies two decimal places; however, this is only the internal display and this value is not relevant for the output. For example, the Euro (EUR) has two decimal places, whereas Japanese currency (JPY) does not require any. The definition of decimal places for each currency is specified in the TCURX table.

3. If you now output the FORCURAM field, the currency is taken from the assigned reference field, which is defined in the SBOOK table.

4. By clicking on CURRENCY/QUANTITY FIELDS (see Figure 4.12), you can see that the FORCURKEY reference field is also contained in the SBOOK table. This field provides the currency (EUR, JPY, USD, etc.), and the runtime environment can implement the formatting correctly.

   The same applies to quantity fields. The LUGGWEIGHT field has the WUNIT reference field in the same SBOOK table.

Automatic Assignment of Amount and Unit

The special feature of both cases is that the amount and unit are stored in the same table. Therefore, the system automatically implements correct formatting.

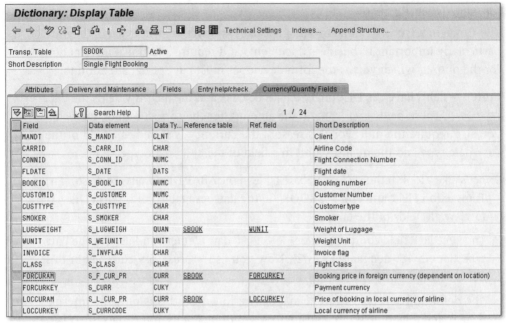

Figure 4.12 Definition of Currency and Quantity Fields

However, if the unit (CUKY or UNIT) is stored in a separate table, the system cannot establish the reference automatically. In this case, you must reassign the reference fields for the interface definition.

1. To do this, select CURRENCY/QUANTITY FIELDS in the interface.

2. Enter a field name, such as TAB1-FELD, and specify an assigned reference field, TAB2-REFFELD.

3. Select CURR or QUAN as the data type, depending on whether a currency or quantity is involved (see Figure 4.13).

Field Name	Reference Field	Data Type
BOOKINGS-FORCURAM	BOOKINGS-FORCURKEY	CURR
T_SUMS-FORCURAM	T_SUMS-FORCURKEY	CURR

Figure 4.13 Defining Reference Fields

4. Remember to activate the interface!

Amount and Unit from Different Tables

If you do not make this specification and the fields are not contained in the same table, the system will not implement correct formatting. In this case, no error message is output.

If these values are not output correctly in your forms, it is advisable to check the definition of the currency and quantity fields in the ABAP Dictionary and in the form interface and to make the assignments in the interface, if required.

4.2.2 XML Schema-Based Interface

The XML schema-based interface is used when an application does not process ABAP Dictionary data, but XML data directly. This interface category is used for Web Dynpro ABAP that defines its own data context. During definition, the interface is provided with only a local file including the XML schema, which must correspond to the W3C standard.

1. Now create a new interface, Z_IFBA_BOOK_XML_01, and select XML schema-based interface as the interface category (see Figure 4.14).

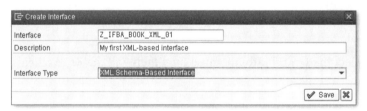

Figure 4.14 XML Schema-Based Interface

2. Save the interface as a local object.

3. Now go to the properties of the interface, which look completely different compared to the ABAP Dictionary-based interface (see Figures 4.5 and 4.15).

4. There are two different settings for the source: FILE and GENERATED. You cannot make any manual selections here because the GENERATED setting is intended for applications that generate an interface via Application Programming Interface (API), such as Web Dynpro ABAP.

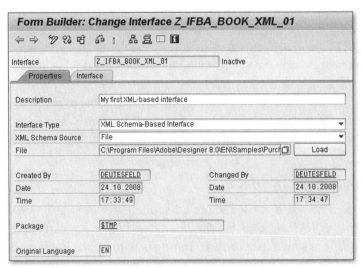

Figure 4.15 Properties of an XML Schema-Based Interface

5. Enter the complete path to the XML schema file in the FILE input field using the input help. Select an XML schema file via a dialog.

   Relative to the installation directory of Adobe LiveCycle Designer, you can find a sample file you can use under *\EN\Samples\Purchase Order\Schema\Schema\ Purchase Order.xsd*.

6. Remember to select the LOAD button because only then will the XML schema be loaded into the interface.

7. You can then save and activate the interface.

8. The system displays the XML schema if you select the INTERFACE tab. However, you cannot make any changes here.

9. As usual, you can display the import and export parameters and the exceptions on the left-hand side. However, adding further parameters or exceptions to an XML schema-based interface is not possible.

10. The XML schema-based interface has two import parameters:

    ▶ /1BCDWB/DOCPARAMS

    ▶ /1BCDWB/DOCXML

    You already know the first parameter from the ABAP Dictionary-based interface. The second parameter is of the XSTRING type and exports the XML data in binary format at runtime. The calling application must transfer the XML data with a formatting that corresponds to the XML schema and can be processed by ADS.

The XML schema is the final format of the form design and you do not have to define a context for this interface category.

The XML schema-based interface is particularly interesting if the application can provide the data in XML format already and no further data modeling is required via a form context. Therefore, this interface category is suitable for Web Dynpro ABAP, for example, because it already provides data modeling.

4.2.3 Smart Forms-Compatible Interface

Finally, you are provided with information on the last interface category, the Smart Forms-compatible interface. Its name suggests that forms with this interface can be called by applications that have used Smart Forms previously.

Normally, such interfaces are created by migrating a Smart Form into a PDF-based print form; however, you can also create an interface of this category yourself. The Smart Forms-compatible interface contains the same parameters and exceptions as the interface of a Smart Form.

1. Therefore, create a Z_IFBA_BOOK_SF_01 interface as usual and select the category as illustrated in Figure 4.16. You cannot change the predefined import parameters.

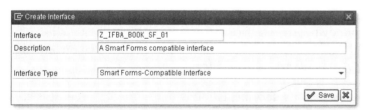

Figure 4.16 Smart Forms-Compatible Interface

2. The parameters are different from those of the ABAP Dictionary-based interface. Another difference is that you are now provided with tables (see Figure 4.17), which are transferred to a function module as table parameters at runtime. In ABAP Dictionary-based forms, this is done by directly transferring the table types using the import parameters.

Figure 4.17 Parameters of the Smart Forms–Compatible Interface

3. You can define custom export parameters for the Smart Forms-compatible interface. You already know the global definitions, the initialization, and the currency/quantity fields from the ABAP Dictionary-based interface.

The benefit of this interface category is that you can address it from existing Smart Forms print programs (for example, by migrating a Smart Form); however, this interface does not provide all of the options available in the SAP Interactive Forms by Adobe solution. Therefore, this interface category is used only in rare cases.

4.2.4 Documentation of a Form Interface

You can document your own form interface to store information about their significance. The documentation is integrated with the normal documentation environment that you can access using Transaction SE61.

If an interface is transported, its documentation is transported as well. It is also taken into account for other activities, such as copying, deleting, or renaming. You can consult the documentation of predefined interfaces to see whether it provides valuable notes for the form development (provided that the interfaces are documented).

1. To record the documentation, enter the Z_IFBA_BOOK_DDIC_01 interface in the initial screen of Form Builder and follow the menu path GOTO • DOCUMENTATION • CHANGE.

2. You can now document the interface. To do this, you are provided with the following categories (see Figure 4.18):

- ▸ Use (&USE&)
- ▸ Structure (&STRUCTURE&)
- ▸ Enhancements (&ENHANCEMENTS&)
- ▸ Further hints (&FURTHER_HINTS&)

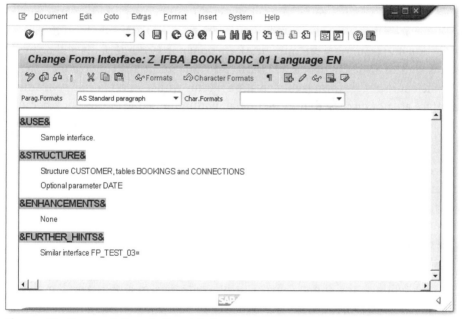

Figure 4.18 Documentation of a Form Interface

3. To complete the documentation, you must set the status to ACTIVE.

4. You can access an existing interface documentation from the Form Builder menu via the path GOTO • DOCUMENTATION • DISPLAY.

5. You can also access the documentation from within Form Builder. Simply select the menu path GOTO • DOCUMENTATION. The system displays the documentation or you can edit it, depending on whether you are in display or edit mode.

4.3 Context of a Form

The context of a form constitutes the form object only in conjunction with the layout and it is thus not an independent object (like the form interface). The following sections focus on the context, while Chapter 5 describes the creation of the layout.

Forms are maintained in Form Builder or in the ABAP Workbench—just like the interfaces. They can also be transported, have a package assignment, and be translated. To create a new form, you need an existing and active interface. The different interface categories, along with their properties, have already been discussed in Section 4.2; from now on, only ABAP Dictionary-based interfaces will be used. Forms with an XML schema-based interface do not require any context: the schema is sufficient to enable form layout creation. Forms with a Smart Forms-compatible interface are not discussed in further detail within the scope of this book because the descriptions focus on the SAP Interactive Forms by Adobe solution and its new options.

The context defines what data from the layout is available for the layout; the main task of the context is the data modeling. The ABAP Dictionary data of the interface is mapped in a hierarchy and constitutes the logical data model of the form. You can consider the context as a modeling tool that transforms a lot of input data (structures, tables, and elementary fields from the interface) into a data schema. In this process, you create an XML schema that is available for Adobe LiveCycle Designer.

However, you use the context not just to include data in a hierarchy but also to add additional objects, such as texts (SAPscript include texts and Smart Forms text modules), graphics, or addresses. The selection of these objects may depend on the interface data. An address is typically generated from an address number that is transferred to the form by the application print program via the interface. You can also add texts dynamically depending on the transfer values. Additionally, you can reference graphics or transfer their content in binary form. These objects will be specified in detail later on. For now, it is important only that the form context constitutes the link between application data and the form layout.

4.3.1 Creating a Form

You can now create a form to establish the context. To do so, you use Form Builder again.

1. Start Transaction SFP and click on FORM. Enter Z_IFBA_BOOK_FORM_01 as the name.

2. Then click on CREATE (see Figure 4.19).

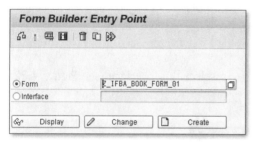

Figure 4.19 Creating a Form

3. Enter a description in the dialog box that opens (see Figure 4.20). Additionally, you must select the form interface for the form. You can use the Z_IFBA_BOOK_DDIC_01 interface that you created in Section 4.2. If you know the name of an interface, you can always enter it directly.

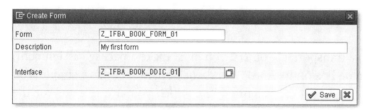

Figure 4.20 Assigning an Interface

Alternatively, you can also utilize the input help. To do so, simply press the F4 key when the cursor is in the input field of the interface, or click on the icon on the right of the input field. A dialog box opens in which you can search for interfaces of a specific author or enter the creation or change date, for example.

4. If you know only a specific part of the interface name, you can enter it in the dialog box (see Figure 4.20). For example, the existing interfaces start with the letter Z and contain the term BOOK. So enter Z*BOOK* as the name of the interface and press the F4 key (see Figure 4.21).

Figure 4.21 Searching for an Interface

5. Double-click on Z_IFBA_BOOK_DDIC_01 to select the interface (see Figure 4.22) and click on SAVE.

Figure 4.22 Selecting the Interface Using the Input Help

6. Because a form is a transportable object, you must make a package assignment. To do this, the dialog box of the ABAP Workbench opens. For this example, you can select the package $TMP (see Figure 4.23), which you also selected for the interfaces. In doing so, the form is created as a local object. You can also click on the LOCAL OBJECT button.

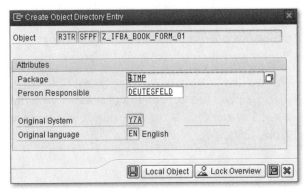

Figure 4.23 Package Assignment

7. Form Builder now displays the empty context of the created form (see Figure 4.24); the form itself was stored locally. The following sections detail how to define the context of the form.

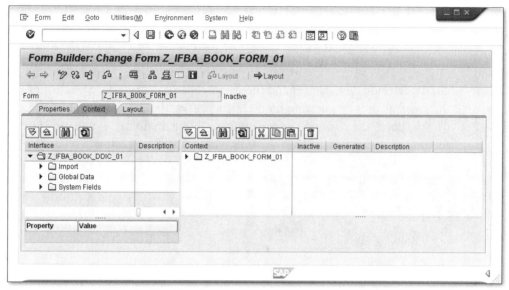

Figure 4.24 Empty Context of the New Form

4.3.2 Structure of a Form

You can see three tabs for the elements of a form:

▸ **Properties**
In the PROPERTIES tab, you can view general information, such as the assigned interface, the creator, the last processor and the corresponding time stamps. In addition, you can find information on the package assignment and the original language of the form. The original language is always the language you logged on to the SAP system with during creation. The form should only be changed in this language later on.

▸ **Context**
The CONTEXT tab is selected by default. On the left side, you can see the form interface (in this case Z_IFBA_BOOK_DDIC_01); the context itself is displayed

on the right. It is still empty, which is why you can only see the root node, Z_IFBA_BOOK_FORM_01.

▶ **Layout**
The LAYOUT tab is not considered at this point. Feel free to click on this tab—Adobe LiveCycle Designer is started within the Form Designer.

The following steps describe how you can obtain information about the interface and the field definitions within the form.

1. On the left side, you can expand the parameters of the interface by clicking on the small arrows or selecting the EXPAND SUBTREE button (see Figure 4.25). To do this, you must position the cursor on a subtree; in doing so, you can expand the import parameters only or the entire interface, for example.

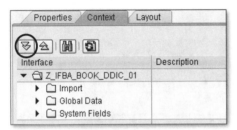

Figure 4.25 Expanding the Interface

For this interface, expanding it still makes sense to some extent; for complex and comprehensive interfaces, you should expand only the part that is relevant for your work to keep a better overview. You can compress individual subtrees again at any time. Figure 4.26 show the fully expanded interface.

2. You can see the import parameters and the global data as you have defined them in the interface, Z_IFBA_BOOK_DDIC_01. A CUSTOMER structure exists whose fields are all shown; additionally, there are two tables, BOOKINGS and CONNECTIONS, and an elementary field, DATE. The different object types, such as structures, tables, or fields, are marked by a corresponding icon. The global data shows a SUM_BOOKINGS table that you created as well.

3. Double-click on a field to view the properties in the field list in the lower left. Figure 4.27 shows the full name of the CUSTOMER-CITY field, its description, and its type information.

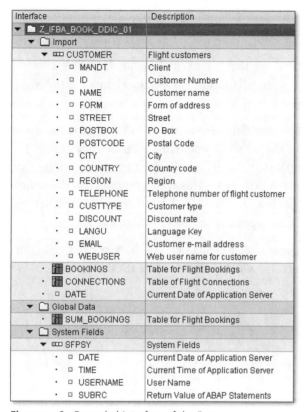

Figure 4.26 Expanded Interface of the Form

Property	Value
General	
Name	CUSTOMER-CITY
Description	City
Type Information	
Type Category	Dictionary Type
Type Name	CITY

Figure 4.27 Properties of an Interface Field

The TYPE INFORMATION includes the TYPE CATEGORY and TYPE NAME. The following type categories exist:

▶ Built-in type (for example, `STRING`)

▶ Dictionary type (reference to a data element)

▶ Flat structure (a structure without a hierarchy)

▶ Deep structure (a structure with subelements, for example, tables)

▶ Internal table

The CITY type name is underlined for the CUSTOMER-CITY field. Double-click on the underlined name to navigate to the definition of this data element in the ABAP Dictionary.

By double-clicking on CUSTOMER, you can view in the field list that it has a flat structure; by double-clicking on the SCUSTOM type name, you can navigate to the definition. A double-click on BOOKINGS displays its properties; they indicate that it is an internal table of the TY_BOOKINGS type. This way, you can view the definition of tables, structures, and fields at any time without displaying the interface separately or searching for the data types in the ABAP Dictionary.

Below the interface, there are some system fields that you have not defined yourself; they involve the SFPSY structure, which provides some useful fields (see Table 4.2).

Field Name	Meaning
DATE	Current date
TIME	Current time
USERNAME	Name of the logged-on user
SUBRC	Result of a single record node

Table 4.2 System Fields

The SFPSY-SUBRC field can be evaluated only according to a single record node. This node type is discussed in detail in Section 4.3.10, Single Record Nodes.

The following sections describe the individual node types on which the form context is based. All nodes are created below the root node, which is a folder that may contain any number of nodes. Node types are listed in Table 4.3.

Node Type	Meaning
Structure	Data structure
Data	Field

Table 4.3 Different Node Types

Node Type	Meaning
Text	Smart Forms text module, SAPscript includes text or dynamic text
Graphic	Graphic (reference or content)
Address	Address from the central address management
Alternative	Alternative subtrees, depending on the condition
Loop	Table with recurring elements
Single record	Direct access to an individual table row
Folder	Grouping option for multiple nodes

Table 4.3 Different Node Types (Cont.)

In addition, there are conditions that can be defined for almost every node type (except for the alternative node type). If a condition is defined for a node, that node is processed only when the condition is met.

The different processing options of the context are indicated based on the structure node type.

4.3.3 Structures

The simplest way to add a node to the context from the interface is to drag and drop.

1. For example, drag the CUSTOMER structure from the import parameter list to the root node of the context; as a result, the CUSTOMER structure is added to the context and displayed as expanded (see Figure 4.28).

2. Alternatively, you can right-click on the root node and select CREATE • STRUCTURE from the context menu.

3. A dialog box opens in which you can use the input help to display all available structures. In this case, CUSTOMER and SFPSY are provided.

4. Double-click on CUSTOMER to select it and choose NEXT. The result is identical: The CUSTOMER structure has been added to the context, as illustrated in Figure 4.28.

141

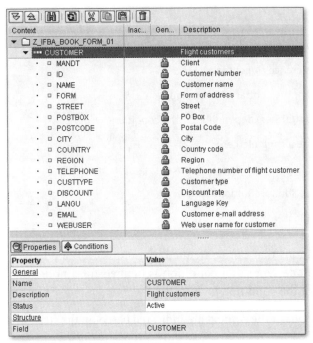

Figure 4.28 Adding the CUSTOMER Structure

In the context, you are provided with a number of different processing options. You can delete, cut, copy, or paste nodes or subtrees. This is done either using the context menu or via the toolbar above the context. You can search for nodes and expand or collapse subtrees for more convenient processing.

The node properties are displayed at the bottom right if you double-click on a node in the context. Each node has two important properties:

▶ **Generated**
A generated node cannot be deleted because it is an elementary part of a superordinate node. After you have added the CUSTOMER structure, a lock icon is displayed for every field of the structure. Because these fields are part of the structure, they cannot be removed from the context. You can delete only the entire structure; therefore, no lock icon is displayed for the CUSTOMER structure.

▶ **Active/Inactive**

Initially, all nodes you insert are ACTIVE. An active node can be used for creating a layout and is provided with data at runtime.

You can set a node or subtree to INACTIVE by right-clicking on it and selecting DEACTIVATE. This can also be done via the node properties. Here, the status is displayed. You can set it to ACTIVE or INACTIVE via the selection list. You can also select multiple nodes simultaneously. Hold down the `Ctrl` key to select additional nodes. Use the `SHIFT` key to select whole areas. When you have made all your selections, you can set the status for all selected nodes via the context menu.

Note that you can set generated nodes to INACTIVE but not delete or move them.

Why Is It Important to Deactivate One or More Nodes?

Structures often contain numerous fields, of which only a few are necessary for the form output. You should always set the status of unnecessary fields to INACTIVE so that the data schema becomes clearer for Adobe LiveCycle Designer, that is, so that the fields are not displayed at all later on and the creation of the layout becomes more comprehensible.

The status of the fields is also relevant at runtime. Only the fields with an ACTIVE status are provided with values and transferred to ADS. So if you deactivate fields that are not required, then this results in fewer data being created and transferred. Therefore, you can reduce the memory requirement and improve the performance. This is particularly important for complex structures or tables.

---

1. In this example, you need only the following fields: ID, NAME, FORM, STREET, POSTBOX, POSTCODE, CITY, COUNTRY, and EMAIL.

2. For all other fields, set their status to INACTIVE.
   You do not have to set all fields to INACTIVE if they are not used. But you should do so if large data quantities or entire substructures can thus be hidden. If you are not sure whether you will require a field in the future, you can keep its status set to ACTIVE.

3. The context should now look as illustrated in Figure 4.29.

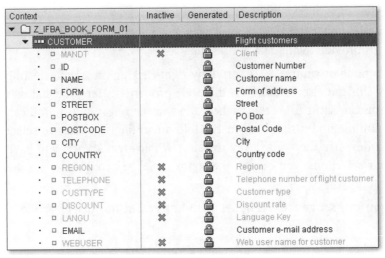

Figure 4.29 Setting Nodes that Are not Required to Inactive

4.3.4 Data Nodes

You can also include individual fields into the context. These can already be contained as such in the interface or originate from the structures. The difference is, however, that the field is dragged separately into the context. This is particularly useful if you need only one field from a structure. To include the entire structure and deactivate all of the fields not required would be too cumbersome and would decrease the clarity of the context. Therefore, you can add individual fields to the context.

1. You can add the DATE field from the SFPSY structure of the system fields. (You can also include the complete SFPSY structure and set the status of the fields not required to INACTIVE; however, this example is intended to show you how to work with individual fields in the context.)

2. To do this, expand the system fields and the SFPSY structure. Drag and drop the DATE field to the root node of the context, Z_IFBA_BOOK_FORM_01. The system displays an individual field, DATE, below the CUSTOMER structure.

3. If you collapse the CUSTOMER structure, you obtain a better overview of the context. Below the root node, it contains two objects: the CUSTOMER structure and the DATE field.

4. Double-clicking on the DATE field displays its properties below the context. Under DATA, the system shows that the field is provided with data from the SFPSY structure. However, its name is DATE and it is addressed with this name in the context and in the layout.

5. Because there is a DATE interface parameter that you want to use in the context, rename the parameter you just added by overwriting the DATE name with "SYSTEM_DATE" in the properties and by pressing the ENTER key. The name is updated in the context (see Figure 4.30).

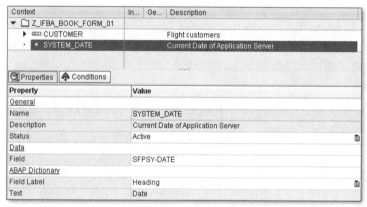

Figure 4.30 Added Field "SFPSY-DATE"

Uniqueness of Field Names

If you insert a field multiple times, it is automatically renamed by the system (for example, DATE1) to ensure uniqueness. The data binding, which you can check in the properties, remains the same.

You can also create a field via the context menu.

1. To do so, right-click on the Z_IFBA_BOOK_FORM_01 root node of the context.

2. Select CREATE • DATA. A dialog opens, where you use the input help. All fields you can directly add to the context are displayed. In this example, these are all fields of the two structures: CUSTOMER and SFPSY.

3. Double-clicking on SFPSY-DATE displays the same result as previously.

Fields that you add to the context are not generated. No lock icon is displayed in contrast to the structure fields; therefore, you can delete these fields directly.

4.3.5 Text Nodes

A form does not just output data—rather, texts including additional information are important for the form. On one hand, these texts can be defined in the layout directly, which is discussed later on. On the other hand, they can also be provided via the context. To do this, three different text sources are supported:

▸ SAP Smart Forms text modules

▸ SAPscript include texts

▸ Dynamic texts

SAP Smart Forms and SAPscript are existing form solutions from SAP and include texts that can be integrated with both solutions. SAP Smart Forms also enable the maintenance of text modules. Both text types can be used within SAP Interactive Forms by Adobe.

The Smart Forms text modules and SAPscript include texts that are stored in the database and can be used in forms.

Smart Forms Text Modules

Smart Forms text modules (in the following referred to only as text modules) are maintained using Transaction SMARTFORMS. They have a unique name, can exist in multiple languages, have a transport connection, and are client-independent.

A text module contains frequently recurring texts, such as the footers of a form, to output the business connection. For the present form, you use the SF_ADRS_FOOTER text module. You can also display this text directly.

1. Start Transaction SMARTFORMS and click on Text Module.

2. Enter SF_ADRS_FOOTER in the input field and click on Display. An address and bank details are now displayed. This text is supposed to be included in the form, which is why you add it to the context.

3. Right-click on the root node of the Z_IFBA_BOOK_FORM_01 context and select Create • Text. In doing so, you append the text to the end of the form.

4. You should select a meaningful name and a description for the properties of the text so that you can identify the text in the context. To do this, overwrite the value TEXT with FOOTER and enter a proper description, for example, "business connection."

5. The status is displayed as another property, so you can set text modules to INAC-TIVE as well.

You now must specify the text module to be used so that the text can be added to the output at runtime.

1. Open the input help for the TEXT NAME field to display all text modules available on the system.

2. If you double-click on the SF_ADRS_FOOTER entry, the system adds the name to the properties. You can also enter the name directly. Note, however, that you enclose the name in single quotation marks (see Figure 4.31).

Text	
Text Type	Text Module
Text Module	
Text Name	'SF_ADRS_FOOTER'

Figure 4.31 Text Name Enclosed in Single Quotation Marks

If you enter SF_ADRS_FOOTER directly without the single quotation marks, the system will notify you that the SF_ADRS_FOOTER field does not exist. The system also checks whether a text module that you specified exists and will display an error message if the text cannot be found.

Specifying the Text via a Field

A name without single quotation marks indicates a field; the name of the text module would be determined only at runtime. This way, it is possible to drag texts depending on fields that are transferred via the interface by the application.

3. In this example, you do not have to determine the language because the text is requested in the language of the form.

4. If you want to specify a text using a field, you can simply drag and drop the field to the text name from the interface. It is then entered in the properties. However, the system cannot check whether the text already exists because the value of the field is not known until runtime.

Therefore, you can specify, for the properties of a text module, whether a runtime error should be triggered if a text module cannot be found during output. In this case, select the NO ERROR IF TEXT NOT AVAILABLE checkbox.

5. The system also provides the Copy Style From Text Module checkbox and an input field for the style as further properties. Each text module is assigned with a style that defines the paragraph and character formats that can be used in a text. The style enables you, for example, to specify the fonts and different paragraph properties, such as the alignment.

In this case, select the Copy Style From Text Module checkbox and leave the Style field empty. As a result, the system uses the style that was statically assigned to the text; for the SF_ADRS_FOOTER text, it is the SAPADRS style.

Limitations to the Use of Text Modules

Within SAP Interactive Forms by Adobe, not all components are supported in text modules and style properties; this applies to the following properties and elements:

- ▶ Page protection
- ▶ Outline paragraphs
- ▶ Superscript and subscript
- ▶ Barcodes
- ▶ Special characters
- ▶ Hyperlinks
- ▶ Smart Forms system fields
- ▶ There are limitations for the tabulators and the SAP characters.

Note

Details about the limitations can be found in the SAP online documentation for Transaction SFP under PDF-Based Print Forms • Designing Forms With Form Builder • Context In Form Builder • Inserting A Text •Entering Text Module Properties.

---

6. If you want to assign another style later on, you can simply use the input help for the Style field and select a style by double-clicking on it.

7. The context now appears as shown in Figure 4.32.

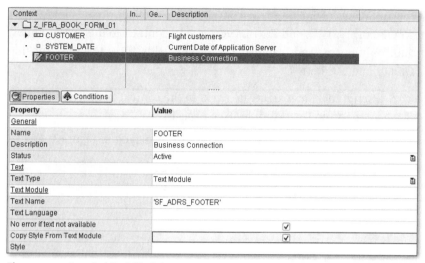

Context	In...	Ge...	Description
▼ ☐ Z_IFBA_BOOK_FORM_01			
▶ 📇 CUSTOMER			Flight customers
• ☐ SYSTEM_DATE			Current Date of Application Server
• 📝 FOOTER			Business Connection

| 🔍 Properties | 🔷 Conditions |

Property	Value
General	
Name	FOOTER
Description	Business Connection
Status	Active
Text	
Text Type	Text Module
Text Module	
Text Name	'SF_ADRS_FOOTER'
Text Language	
No error if text not available	☑
Copy Style From Text Module	☑
Style	

Figure 4.32 Inserted Text Module

SAPscript Include Texts

SAPscript include texts can be used in SAPscript forms and in Smart Forms. These are texts that are maintained in application transactions or in Customizing, for example, request texts, document texts, or vendor texts. They are classified by various text objects. In addition, you are provided with standard texts comprising the TEXT text object; these texts are maintained using Transaction SO10.

SAPscript include texts are client-dependent and can exist in multiple languages; they are not transported automatically. The key of SAPscript texts comprises four fields:

▶ Text name

▶ Text object

▶ Text ID

▶ Text language

The text object classifies the application, whereas the text ID enables sub-grouping within a text object. Each text has a name and can exist in multiple languages. The client is another key field that you may not define in the form. The text is always read in the client in which the application program is executed.

The key for an SAPscript include text contains the aforementioned fields: TEXT NAME, TEXT OBJECT, TEXT ID, and TEXT LANGUAGE. In contrast to the text modules, which include only a name and a language as the key fields, these texts also include the TEXT OBJECT and the TEXT ID.

1. To use an SAPscript include text, create a text in the context as described in Section 4.3.5, Smart Forms Text Modules (see page 146).

2. Select INCLUDE TEXT as the text type. The result is displayed in Figure 4.33.

Property	Value
General	
Name	TEXT
Description	Text Node TEXT
Status	Active
Text	
Text Type	Include Text
Include Text	
Text Name	
Text Object	
Text ID	
Text Language	
No error if text not available	☐
Standard Paragraph	
First Paragraph	
Style	

Figure 4.33 Properties of an SAPscript Include Text

3. You can display the definition of the text objects using Transaction SE75. You can view the corresponding text ID by double-clicking on a text object.

   If you want to create your own SAPscript include text for testing, simply use an SAPscript standard text, which you can create by means of Transaction SO10. TEXT is predefined as the text object; you can use the ST standard value as the text ID. A general standard text will be created.

4. For this example, you do not require any SAPscript include text. You can also insert a text via the input help.

5. The NO ERROR IF TEXT NOT AVAILABLE checkbox (see Figure 4.34) has the same meaning as for the text modules. If you select this checkbox, no runtime error occurs if the desired text is not available. You can specify the text key statically (with single quotation marks) or dynamically using fields. In this process, a specific part of the key (for example, the text object and the text ID) can be static and only the name specified in a field.

Property	Value
General	
Name	TEXT
Description	Text Node TEXT
Status	Active 📄
Text	
Text Type	Include Text 📄
Include Text	
Text Name	'ADRS_FOOTER'
Text Object	'TEXT'
Text ID	'ST'
Text Language	'EN'
No error if text not available	☑
Standard Paragraph	
First Paragraph	
Style	

Figure 4.34 Inserting an SAPscript Include Text

6. Again, you can define a style that describes the formatting properties of the text. Note that you can use only a Smart Forms style, not an SAPscript style. This style must provide the required paragraph and character formats.

7. You can select a paragraph format in the STANDARD PARAGRAPH field and therefore override the standard paragraphs in the SAPscript include text.

The FIRST PARAGRAPH field enables you to format the first paragraph of an include text using this paragraph format. If you have not specified a standard paragraph, all standard paragraphs of the text are also formatted with this format.

Limitations to the Use of SAPscript Include Texts

Not all elements can be supported for the use of SAPscript include texts. The properties not supported include the following:

- SAPscript styles (A Smart Forms style must be used.)
- Control commands
- Page protection
- Outline paragraphs
- Superscript and subscript
- Barcodes
- Special characters
- Hyperlinks
- SAPscript system icons and standard icons

> **Note**
>
> There are limitations for the tabulators and the SAP characters.
>
> Note that no control commands are evaluated, they are simply ignored. As a result, both branches are output in the case of an IF/ELSE statement, for example. INCLUDE statements are not executed.

Dynamic Texts

It is sometimes possible that an application has already read the text from the database and transferred it to the parameters. In some cases, the text can also originate from a source that the text-reading functions of SAPscript and Smart Forms texts cannot access. If your applications make use of such texts and you want to transfer the text content into the interface, you need a dynamic text.

1. To use dynamic text, create a text in the context as it has been described previously.

2. Select DYNAMIC TEXT as the TEXT TYPE. The result is displayed in Figure 4.35.

Property	Value	
General		
Name	TEXT	
Description	Text Node TEXT	
Status	Active	🗎
Text		
Text Type	Dynamic Text	🗎
Dynamic Text		
Field		
Text Language		
Style		

Figure 4.35 Dynamic Text

3. In the STYLE field, define the style to describe the paragraph and character formats.

4. You should specify the text language because it may be relevant for the text display.

5. Enter the text under FIELD; an internal table of the TSFTEXT type is expected here. The structure of this table type is TLINE, which includes the fields TDFORMAT and TDLINE (see Figure 4.36).

The components TDFORMAT and TDLINE describe the text in Interchange Text Format (ITF) format. For more information on the structure of this format, refer to the SAP online documentation about the SAPscript topic via the help of Transaction SO10.

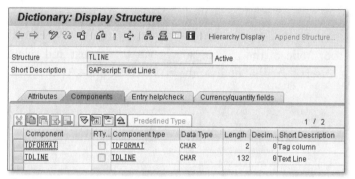

Figure 4.36 Structure of a Dynamic Text

4.3.6 Graphic Nodes

Graphics are frequently used in forms, for example, to output a company logo. You can use scanned drawings, scanned signatures at the end of a document, or small images in item lists showing a material.

You are provided with various options for inserting graphics into a document. For example, you can provide a graphic via the data or specify it in the layout of the form. In the former case, the context provides the option both to transfer the content of a graphic, that is, its binary format, and to reference the graphic via a URL.

Because this chapter is limited to the context of the form, it describes the two alternatives of how a graphic can be specified within the context. The graphic node is available for this reason.

Note on the Sample Form

Because the sample form does not use any graphics in the context, you can skip the following descriptions. The graphic nodes created here will be deleted again.

If required, you can come back to this section if you want to transfer graphics into your custom forms using a program, for example, because you read them from a repository. In this case, the graphic node in the context is the only option.

However, a general example cannot be provided because it depends on your system environment. You can still provide such a graphic in your form context and insert it in the layout.

---

1. Right-click on the root node of the Z_IFBA_BOOK_FORM_01 context and select CREATE • GRAPHIC to insert a graphic node at the end (see Figure 4.37).

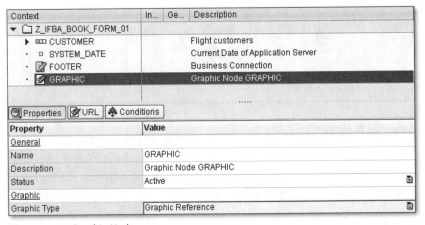

Figure 4.37 Graphic Node

2. You already know the properties of a graphic node from the other node types. Like all the other node types, it has a name, a textual description, and a status (ACTIVE or INACTIVE).

3. You can specify the graphic type as another property. It is set to GRAPHIC REFERENCE by default. You can switch between GRAPHIC REFERENCE and GRAPHIC CONTENT using the input help.

4. Press the [Enter] key after you have made your selection in the input help. An additional dialog box opens in which you must confirm your selection because the additional attributes detailed next will get lost.

Graphic Reference

In Figure 4.37, you can see the URL button on the right-hand side of the PROPERTIES button.

1. Let's assume your company logo is available at *http://www.addressofyourcompany. com/images/companylogo.jpg*.

2. Select the URL button, insert a new row using the APPEND ROW button, and enter the URL in single quotation marks, as illustrated in Figure 4.38. Remove the DELIMITER.

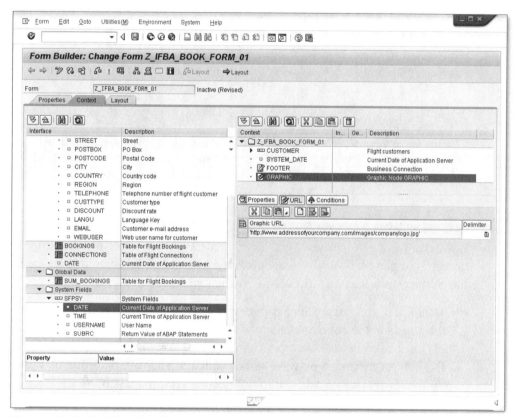

Figure 4.38 Static URL with Reference to the Graphic

3. If you want to specify the graphic reference dynamically, you can also use fields that refer to the graphic at runtime. A part of the URL can even be static, whereas only the name of the graphic is dynamic.

▶ Therefore, it is possible that all graphics are available at *http://www.address ofyourcompany.com/images/* and that you can transfer the value (*company_logo. jpg*) at runtime in a GRAPHIC field, which must exist in your interface. Then, you would only have to enter the static part 'HTTP://WWW.ADDRESSOFY-OURCOMPANY.COM/IMAGES' in the first row (see Figure 4.39), select the slash / as the delimiter, and insert a second row, which contains only the GRAPHIC field.

Figure 4.39 Compound URL for a Graphic

Access to a Graphic Reference

For the use of a graphic reference, ADS must be able to access the graphic. For an HTTP-URL, it is therefore important that no logon is required. A file reference (FILE-URL) is also possible, in which case the file must also be accessible at runtime.

Graphic Content

If you changed the properties to graphic content (see Figure 4.40), the URL button is no longer displayed. Instead, you are provided with additional fields for the properties of the graphic content. These involve the two fields FIELD and MIME TYPE.

▶ Under FIELD, you can specify a parameter from your interface or the global data, which include the content of the graphic in binary form. The data type of the field must be of the XSTRING type. The STRING data type is also supported; in this case, however, the data must be Base64-coded. If your interface provides such a field, you can drag and drop it to this position. It is the task of the application program to read the graphic from the corresponding source, for example, from the database or the MIME Repository, and to make it available via the form interface.

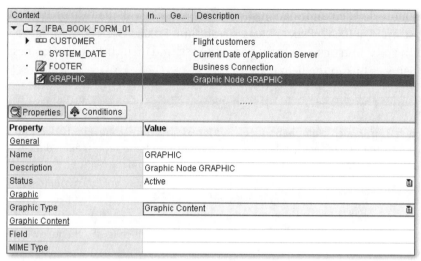

Figure 4.40 Specifying the Graphic via the Content

▶ The MIME type indicates the graphic format and has the "image/gif" form here. The list of supported formats is available in the Adobe LiveCycle documentation. You can also define the MIME Type dynamically via a field, which has to be provided by the interface.

4.3.7 Address Nodes

Addresses are used in various forms, for example, invoices or delivery notes. Usually, not all fields, such as name, ZIP code, and city, are transferred; instead, the system uses addresses that are managed and formatted via Business Address Services (BAS).

An address in a form depends not only on the correct values but also on the correct formatting. Whether you must position the ZIP code on the left or right side of the city, whether you must add a country key in front of the ZIP code, or whether you must print a country name in a specific language below the address depends on the regulations of the respective country and whether a document is sent within a country or from one country to another.

This complex logic cannot be reproduced in every form. Instead, you are provided with BAS whose task it is to retrieve the relevant information and to visually format the address. The application obtains only an address number and can specify some additional information.

To obtain more detailed information about these services, call the help of Transaction SFP, select PDF-BASED PRINT FORMS • DESIGNING FORMS WITH FORM BUILDER • CONTEXT IN FORM BUILDER • INSERTING AN ADDRESS, and then click on the Business Address Services link in the help text.

Note
This section describes the information required for address formatting and the existing configuration options. For the sample form, you only position some address fields directly in the layout. Therefore, you can skip the rest of the section initially.
The following sections, however, describe how you can search for an address number in your system via an input help. If you have found an address, you can extend your form context by one address and position the address in the layout.
You can find address nodes in many forms provided by SAP, which is why the following is particularly important and should be kept in mind.

There are three different types of addresses (see Table 4.4).

Address Type	Internal	Description
Company addresses	1	A typical business address that is specified by an address number.
Personal addresses	2	A personal address that is specified by a person number. Because a person can have multiple addresses, you must also define an address number additionally.
Workplace addresses	3	The address of a contact partner within an enterprise. Again, you must specify a person number and an address number.

Table 4.4 Address Types

To insert an address in a form, right-click on the root node of the Z_IFBA_BOOK_FORM_01 context and select CREATE • ADDRESS. An address node is added at the end and can be moved to another position in the context using the mouse. Figure 4.41 illustrates the properties of an address node.

▶ Under ADDRESS TYPE, the company address is specified by default, which you can change using the input help. You can also select this property dynamically; however, you must provide a field that contains the address type at runtime. To do this, select DEFINE DYNAMICALLY as the address type in the address node — the DYNAMIC ADDRESS TYPE field is now ready for input. The values must correspond to the values provided in Table 4.4.

▸ The PERSON NUMBER is ready for input only if the address type is PRIVATE ADDRESS or CONTACT PARTNER ADDRESS.

Addresses Must be Available at Runtime

The address number and, if applicable, the person number are mandatory values. An address cannot be formatted without these values because the corresponding data cannot be read. Because addresses are usually specified dynamically, this cannot be checked in Form Builder.

If the values are not available at runtime during the creation of the form, runtime errors occur and the print job is canceled.

Property	Value
General	
Name	ADDRESS
Description	Address Node ADDRESS
Status	Active
Address	
Address Type	Organization, Company
Dynamic Address Type	
Address Number	
Person Number	
Handle for Address Number	
Handle for Person Number	
Additional Specifications	
Number of Lines to be Used	'10'
Sending Country	
If PO box and street exist	PO box has priority over street
Dynamic Priority	
Fixed Language for Country Indicator	
Different Recipient Language	
Country Indicator in Recipient Language	
Uppercase/Lowercase Spelling	
Priority of Lines	
Person Above Organization	
SAP Business Partner Details	
Time-Dependent Business Partner Name	No
Dynamic Time Dependency	
Time Stamp	
Business Partner Number for Organization, Company	
Business Partner Number for Person	

Figure 4.41 Properties of an Address Node

▸ The fields HANDLE FOR ADDRESS NUMBER and HANDLE FOR PERSON NUMBER are intended for temporary addresses. Refer to SAP Note 1059819 if these fields are not displayed on your system.

▸ You can use the address number's input help to search for addresses on your system. To do so, extend the form interface by a field for the address number (AD_ADDRNUM data type) and use this field in the address node of the context.

▸ During your initial tests you can leave the ADDITIONAL SPECIFICATIONS of the address node unchanged. However, you must enter a SENDING COUNTRY in any case. If this value is missing you cannot activate the form, and an error message is displayed.

▸ The NUMBER OF LINES TO BE USED is set to 10 by default. You can enter a smaller value. During formatting via BAS, the program attempts to suppress lines.

▸ Under ADDITIONAL SPECIFICATIONS, you can detail how the address is to be formatted if both a PO box and a street are available. Here, you can also determine language settings for the country names. The UPPERCASE/LOWERCASE SPELLING checkbox is also interesting. If it is not set, then the city and country are output in uppercase letters.

▸ In the last section, you can define properties of a business partner. For detailed information, refer to the BAS documentation.

4.3.8   Alternatives

Forms include a lot of dynamic content, for example, some objects are supposed to be output only under certain conditions. For this reason, alternatives are available. An alternative is a node that comprises a condition and two subnodes. Under CONDITION, you can check and logically link different fields. The names of the two subnodes are TRUE and FALSE and are carried out if the condition is met (TRUE) or not (FALSE). The TRUE/FALSE branches can contain any number of subnodes, which are processed accordingly.

There is an optional parameter, DATE, in the interface, as has been described in Section 4.2.1, ABAP Dictionary-Based Interface. This value can be transferred by the application program at runtime; however, the form may not rely on it because the parameter is optional.

A simply structured example illustrates the use of the alternative node. If the optional parameter, DATE, does not contain any value, use the system date that you already added to the context as the SYSTEM_DATE field (see Figure 4.30).

1. To add an alternative to your form, right-click on the root node of the Z_IFBA_BOOK_FORM_01 context and select CREATE • ALTERNATIVE. An alternative node is added at the end and can be moved to another position in the context using the mouse.

2. Move the alternative further upward by dragging it to the SYSTEM_DATE field.

3. Rename the node ALT_DATE and enter an appropriate description. The result is displayed in Figure 4.42. Before expanding the two branches of the alternative, you should first set the condition for the alternative.

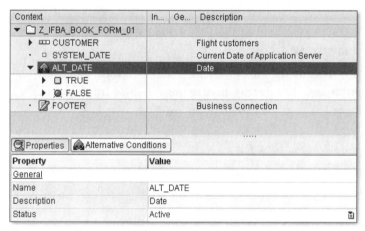

Figure 4.42 Alternative Node

4. Select the ALTERNATIVE CONDITIONS button and then APPEND ROW in the new screen.

5. You want to check whether the optional parameter, DATE, has a value or not. To do this, drag the DATE field from the interface and drop it in the first field, Operand; the equals sign (=) is already proposed as the relational operator.

6. In the second OPERAND field, you can check against another field or a concrete value. Because you want to test whether the value is initial, you can enter INITIAL directly into the field. You probably already know this concept from ABAP programming. The result should look like the one illustrated in Figure 4.43.

Figure 4.43 Alternative Condition

7. Different relational operators are available and you can interlink various conditions. For example, insert multiple rows and specify the operator, AND or OR, for each row. In the first row, the operator field remains empty.

This completes the condition for the alternative and you can now expand the two subnodes, TRUE and FALSE. If the condition is met at runtime, this means that the optional parameter, DATE, contains no value. For this reason, you use the system date that you already inserted in the context as the SYSTEM_DATE field.

1. Simply drag the SYSTEM_DATE field to the TRUE node, where it is inserted as a subnode by using the mouse.

2. The FALSE branch now contains the DATE field, because in this case it provides the value you want to use. For this reason, drag the DATE field from the interface to the FALSE branch. The result is shown in Figure 4.44.

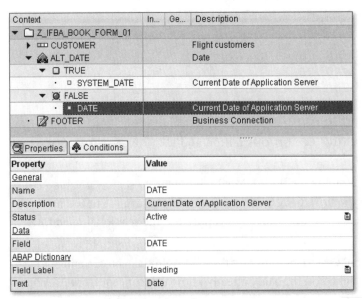

Figure 4.44 Expanded Alternative Node

3. You can insert the fields below the TRUE or FALSE node via the context menu as usual. Through the alternative, either the value of the DATE field or the value of the current system date is used.

4.3.9   Tables or Loops

You come across tabular output of data in many forms, for example, in invoices, order confirmations, and delivery notes. In this regard, tables in forms means internal ABAP tables that are provided in the import parameters or global data of the interface. The number of table rows has not yet been specified at design time because the corresponding rows are not provided until form output, depending on the application data. The column structure determines which fields can be output within a row.

Tables can also be nested, where multiple subitems can exist for an item row. However, it is also possible that the interface contains two (internal) tables. Here, a foreign key dependency exists between the data: In the second table, a data record exists for each item of the first table. Both data records form a common table row in the output table of the form.

This is exactly the case in the sample interface, where there are two internal tables, BOOKINGS and CONNECTIONS:

- The CONNECTIONS table contains the CARRID and CONNID key fields and defines a quantity of flight schedules, which are described by the two fields, CARRID (airline carrier) and CONNID (connection ID). A connection between two airports is uniquely defined by the pair; according to this, it is an access key.

- The BOOKINGS table has the key fields CARRID, CONNID, FLDATE, and BOOKID, and is the table of the actual flight bookings. To describe a booked flight, you require the flight connection. Therefore, the table contains the two key fields, CARRID and CONNID. However, this is not sufficient to uniquely describe the flight booking. An actual booking is done on a specific day and multiple persons can book the same flight. Therefore, the booking table also provides the two key fields FLDATE (flight date) and BOOKID (booking ID). These four key fields uniquely identify a booking.

Because both tables include the client in the key, the entries are client-dependent. In this example, this is not significant because you obtain different values at runtime depending only on the client used for running the print program.

If you want to output the booking table, you may need information from the connection table. This section details how you can read information from a table during the output of another table, for example, the flight time.

1. To add the booking table to your form, drag and drop the BOOKINGS table from the interface to the context. The table is inserted at the end of the context.

2. You can move the table upward, for example, by dragging the FOOTER text node to the BOOKINGS table. Text node and table swap the sequence and the BOOKINGS table is fully expanded automatically.

   The icon on the left side of the node name indicates that it is a table. A DATA node is automatically generated below the table node, which you can identify as a structure based on the icon. The table node encapsulates a lot of similar data records, which are described by a structure.

3. Disable the fields you do not need for the output. Particularly for tables, you should disable all fields that will not be relevant later on. Set all fields to INACTIVE except for CARRID, CONNID, FLDATE, FORCURAM, and FORCURKEY. The result of your work is displayed in Figure 4.45.

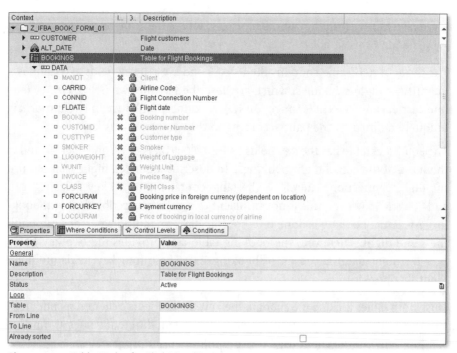

Figure 4.45 Table Nodes for Flight Bookings

You can also create a table via the context menu.

1. Right-click on the root node of the Z_IFBA_BOOK_FORM_01 context and select CREATE • LOOP.

2. A dialog opens in which you enter the table name directly or use the input help to select from the available tables.

3. For the properties of the table node in the lower part of Figure 4.45, you can see two fields, FROM LINE and TO LINE. Here, you can limit the value range to be output. The ALREADY SORTED checkbox is discussed later on, together with the control level.

4. The WHERE CONDITIONS button enables you to specify limitations for the output. This basically corresponds to the WHERE conditions, which you already know from the LOOP statement in ABAP. You can define conditions to limit the data quantity.

   Because you want to output all data records of the BOOKINGS flight booking table that are passed by the application at runtime, you do not specify any Where conditions.

5. However, you can add such a condition to your form. If, for example, you want to suppress all data records that are in the past, you can set the FLDATE fields of the BOOKINGS table in relation to the DATE field of the SFPSY system structure. The comparison could appear as illustrated in Figure 4.46.

Figure 4.46 Limitation via a Where Condition

Avoiding Input Errors

The best way to avoid errors during input is to drag and drop the fields to the corresponding positions.

You now create a control level for groups according to one or more data fields. For example, a grouping according to airline carrier would make sense.

1. Select the CONTROL LEVELS button and insert a row. Drag the CARRID field to the field and check the SORT IN ASCENDING ORDER checkbox (see Figure 4.47).

Figure 4.47 Control Level with Ascending Sorting

2. This changes the structure of the context. The CARRID field is positioned at the very top, whereas all other fields grouped via the control level are below the GROUP node.

Figure 4.48 shows the context after the control level has been created.

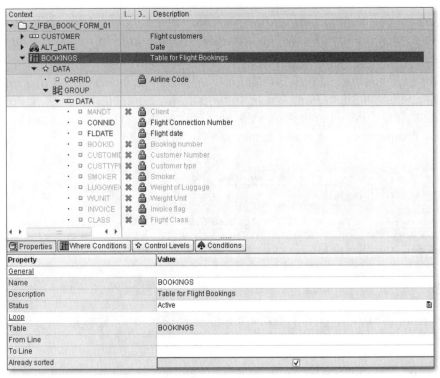

Figure 4.48 Context with Control Level

3. Now select the ALREADY SORTED checkbox (in the PROPERTIES area of Figure 4.48). You leave it up to the application program to transfer the data already sorted by the airline carrier. As a result, the runtime environment will not carry out a new sorting again.

4. In the interface, you are provided with an additional table, SUM_BOOKINGS, for the global data whose values have been calculated in the initialization code (see Listing 4.1). Add this table to the context and position it directly after the BOOKINGS table. Drag and drop the SUM_BOOKINGS table to the context and move it within the hierarchy, if required.

4.3.10 Single Record Nodes

Section 4.3.9, Tables or Loops, stated that the CONNECTIONS table contains information about a flight connection. The table including the flight bookings requires information from the connections table, so you can nest the CONNECTIONS table in the BOOKINGS table.

In this case, this is not required because one data record exists for each connection. Therefore, you can read this data record from the connections table specifically and add the data via the single record node that is provided for this purpose. In ABAP, a single record node corresponds to a READ TABLE <tab> WITH KEY <key> statement.

You now read the flight time for each booking from this table. To do so, you add a single record node to the table output.

1. Expand the BOOKINGS table in the context, if you have not done that yet.

2. Right-click on the DATA node and select CREATE • SINGLE RECORD.

3. In the resulting dialog box, enter the CONNECTIONS table directly or use the input help to select the table from the value list.

4. Figure 4.49 illustrates that the single record node has been positioned below the DATA node. This means that for each data record from the BOOKINGS table, one data record is read from the CONNECTIONS table.

5. You must specify a read condition so that the system knows how the CONNECTIONS table is to be accessed. If you double-click on the single record node, you can select the WITH KEY CONDITIONS button in the lower part of the screen.

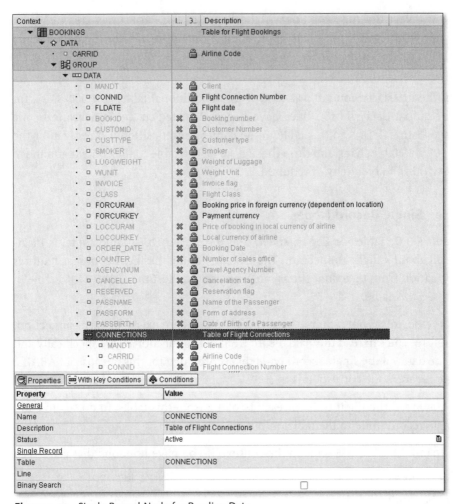

Figure 4.49 Single Record Node for Reading Data

6. The two fields, CARRID and CONNID, link the two tables. Initially, drag the CARRID field from the context of the CONNECTIONS table and drop it in the left OPERAND field.

7. Create a second row and add the CONNID field.

8. On the right side, specify the comparison fields, BOOKINGS-CARRID and BOOKINGS-CONNID, which you can drag and drop from the BOOKINGS table of the context. You can also enter the field names directly.

9. Set the status of the fields not required to Inactive. Because you want to read only the flight time, set all fields to inactive except for FLTIME.

Figure 4.50 shows the result.

Figure 4.50 With Key Conditions of the Single Record Node

Act with Caution for Fields with Conversion Routines

If you implement a form check (Check button), a warning is displayed that informs you that the CONNECTIONS-FLTIME field has a conversion routine. See SAP Note 796755 for more information.

A conversion routine can perform a formatting at runtime and create a value that does not correspond to the schema definition. The FLTIME field is defined as 4-byte integer in the ABAP Dictionary; however, the SDURA conversion routine is defined in the assigned domain, S_DURA. Therefore, the CONVERSION_EXIT_SDURA_OUTPUT function module is called at runtime to implement the data formatting. The result is transferred to Adobe Document Services in the data stream.

If you call this function module in the single test and, for example, enter the value 250 (the value is expected in minutes), the result is 4:10, that is, four hours and ten minutes. The display of 4:10, however, is not a valid number value because it contains a colon. Therefore, you must pay special attention to fields with conversion routines with regard to the definition of the layout and set the data type to a character type in Adobe LiveCycle Designer.

4.3.11 Conditions

You have already come across different forms of conditions in the previous node types, for example, the conditions for a table, the single record node, and alternatives. By means of a condition, you influence the behavior of the form at runtime depending on specific values.

For each node type (except for alternatives) you can also define a condition in the properties. You can do this via the CONDITIONS button as shown in Figure 4.50.

If you define a condition for a node, a decision is made at runtime whether this node is processed or not. Therefore, a text node can be output only under certain prerequisites. The output of a graphic can depend on different conditions, or you can suppress a complete table.

> **Processing Conditions**
>
> Note that if a condition is not met, both the node itself and its subnodes are not processed and are thus not displayed in the layout.
>
> In the creation of the layout, you learn more about the options to efficiently and effectively hide and display parts of the form by means of the form design and the conditions.

You can now add a condition to the form. To do this, look at the definition of the BOOKINGS table (SBOOK structure): You can see the CANCELLED field, which identifies all flights cancelled. Now you need to suppress all data records for which this indicator is set.

1. Because you need to suppress the complete table row, you define the condition for the DATA node below the control level in the BOOKINGS table.

2. Double-click on the DATA node and select the CONDITIONS button in the node properties.

3. Select the APPEND ROW button. Drag and drop the `CANCELLED` field to the first operand field and enter an X enclosed in single quotation marks (`'X'`) in the second operand field.

4. Set the relational operator to NOT EQUAL TO (≠). The result is displayed in Figure 4.51.

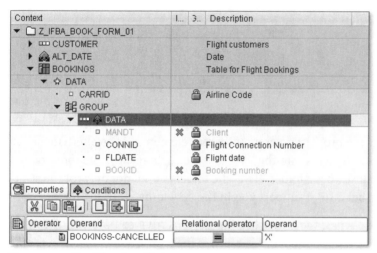

Figure 4.51 Condition for a Node

5. Different relational operators are available, and you can interlink any number of conditions using `AND` or `OR`.

6. A corresponding icon in the context tree, which is displayed between the actual node icon and the node name, indicates whether a condition is defined for a node. If data are missing in the output of your forms, you should check the corresponding conditions in the context.

4.3.12 Folders

The folder is described as the last node type (see Figure 4.52). Folders are required to structure the context and you can combine various node types in one folder. You can also group multiple folders into one folder.

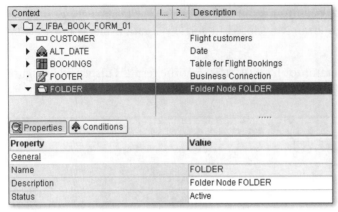

Figure 4.52 Folder

You already know the property to group different elements: As an alternative, you can group multiple elements into the TRUE and FALSE branches. The root node of the context also constitutes a folder. Here, the folder is used not only for the structuring and clarity but also to support you in the development of the form.

Like all other node types, the folder has the status ACTIVE or INACTIVE. If you set the status to INACTIVE, no subnodes are output so that you can temporarily set some parts to INACTIVE during the test phase. If you create a folder retroactively, you can drag and drop already-existing node types to the folder.

4.4   Documentation of a Form

You can document your own forms to store information about their significance. The documentation is identical to the procedure described in Section 4.2.4, Documentation of a Form Interface. For existing forms, you can refer to the documentation to find notes about possible extensions if you use a form provided by SAP as a template.

1. The documentation is available via the initial screen of Form Builder. Select the FORM radio button and enter Z_IFBA_BOOK_FORM_01 as the name. Use the following menu path: GOTO • DOCUMENTATION • CHANGE.

2. You can now document the form. To do this, you are provided with the following categories:

- Use (&USE&)
- Constraints (&CONSTRAINTS&)
- Call (&CALLUP&)
- Context (&CONTEXT&)
- Layout (&LAYOUT&)
- Further hints (&FURTHER_HINTS&)

3. To complete the documentation, you must set the status to ACTIVE.

4. You can also access the documentation from within Form Builder. Follow the menu path GOTO • DOCUMENTATION.

4.5 Summary

This chapter introduced you to the interface and form context. For the interface, the focus was on the ABAP Dictionary-based interface. In addition, you learned how you can add parameters to an interface to use them in a form later on.

This was followed by a presentation of the form context as a modeling tool of the interface data. You mapped data from the interface in a hierarchy and learned how to enrich the context with various objects, such as texts, graphics, addresses, and conditions. Particular attention was paid to tables because they are used in many forms and provide interesting functions, for example, control levels.

Chapter 5 describes how you create the layout based on a form context using Adobe LiveCycle Designer.

This chapter introduces you to the design of form templates. The techniques explained here can be used for print forms and interactive forms. This chapter describes step-by-step how you can use Adobe LiveCycle Designer to create form templates.

5   Creating Form Templates

In Chapter 4, Interface and Form Context, you created an ABAP Dictionary-based interface and used it as the basis for the form context. This chapter describes step-by-step how you can create a form template that is based on this context.

During the course of this chapter you will learn how to use Adobe LiveCycle Designer and design a form template so you become familiar with the basic principles of creating one. However, let's begin with an introduction to Adobe LiveCycle Designer and its integration with the SAP GUI.

5.1   Adobe LiveCycle Designer

So that it can be used in SAP environments, Adobe LiveCycle Designer is integrated with the SAP GUI and SAP NetWeaver Developer Studio. This section describes how Adobe LiveCycle Designer is integrated and used with the SAP GUI to help you create a form template for print output. The first feature of Adobe LiveCycle Designer is that it does not have a FILE menu; you save the form template using the SAP GUI or SAP NetWeaver Developer Studio.

Figure 5.1 illustrates how Adobe LiveCycle Designer is embedded in Form Builder (which can be accessed with Transaction SFP) and thus in the SAP GUI. Adobe LiveCycle Designer provides its own menu bar and toolbar.

Figure 5.1 Adobe Designer Embedded in Form Builder

Adobe LiveCycle Designer and the SAP Version of Adobe LiveCycle Designer

Adobe LiveCycle Designer, which is embedded in the SAP GUI and SAP NetWeaver Developer Studio, has a slightly different menu structure compared to the standalone version. The WINDOW menu is called PALETTES, there is no FILE menu, and required menu items were moved to the EDIT menu. Therefore, the toolbar has fewer icons.

In addition to the obvious visual changes, the SAP version of Adobe LiveCycle Designer provides additional libraries for Web Dynpro and the Internal Service Request (ISR) framework. This version is also synchronized with the Adobe Document Services (ADS) version; that is, you need a particular version of ADS to use all of the functions for generating (print) outputs. This also applies to Adobe Reader; however, if you do not use any new features, Adobe Designer is backwards compatible.

For example, you can use Adobe Designer 8.0 to create PDF forms for Adobe Reader 7.0, but you cannot customize the appearance of checkboxes, because this is not supported by Adobe Reader 7.0.

If you develop forms in the SAP environment, you must use the SAP version of Adobe Designer.

The following sections provide an overview of the relevant areas of the Adobe LiveCycle Designer user interface.

5.1.1 Menu Bar and Toolbar

Adobe LiveCycle Designer provides its own menu bar and toolbar (see Figure 5.2). Thus, as shown in Figure 5.1, there are two menu bars and several toolbars available.

Figure 5.2 Menu Bar and Toolbar

As already mentioned, Adobe LiveCycle Designer does not have a FILE menu. The NEW DATA CONNECTION…, FORM OBJECT COLLECTIONS…, and FORM PROPERTIES… menu items were moved from the FILE menu to the EDIT menu. The environment that embeds Adobe Designer loads the form templates.

For the SAP GUI this means that form templates are saved via the menu bar or toolbar of the SAP GUI itself. In Figure 5.1, for example, you can see the disk icon for saving in the top toolbar.

There is a toolbar directly below the menu bar. This toolbar enables you to quickly and easily call frequently required functions. Like most programs, Adobe Designer also allows hiding and displaying individual toolbars. Section 5.8.1, Customizing the Toolbars, provides you with tips for the configuration of the toolbar.

5.1.2 Script Editor

As you can see in Figure 5.3, Adobe LiveCycle Designer offers a script editor in which you can enter scripts for the two supported script languages, JavaScript and

FormCalc. The LANGUAGE screen element provides a dropdown list for selecting the corresponding language.

Figure 5.3 Script Editor

Various events occur while forms are generated and edited. You can create specific script programs for the respective events at the level of the individual form elements. The SHOW screen element enables you to select the scripts you want to display. In addition, you can create and edit so-called script objects, which you can use to combine and reuse individual script programs.

Script programming is further discussed in Chapter 7, Advanced Form Template Creation.

5.1.3 Hierarchy and Data View

The HIERARCHY and DATA VIEW represent two different aspects of the form template in a tree structure. You will often switch between these two views during the creation of the form.

The form hierarchy shown in Figure 5.4 illustrates the structure of a form template. Because the information on the structure of a form template is required in various areas (for example, for binding form fields to data or for script programming), it is very helpful to display the information accordingly. As in most tree structures, you can expand or collapse individual branches.

Figure 5.4 Form Hierarchy

The DATA VIEW (see Figure 5.5) is a critical source of information for the creation of the form template because it displays the structure of the data that is supposed to be output via the form template. The information on the data structure is also required for data binding and script programming.

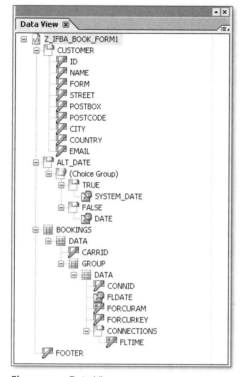

Figure 5.5   Data View

In addition to the structure of the data, DATA VIEW can also display the structure of request and response parameters for Web services.

Data Structure for Forms/Data Connections

Every form is based on exactly one XML-based data structure. This is generally defined by an XML schema-based data connection. You can also set up data connections based on sample data. However, in these cases—compared to XML schemas—structure information is missing.

The two remaining types of data connections, OLEDB-based and Web Service Definition Language (WSDL)-based, are not designed to describe the data structure on which a form is based. OLEDB-based data connections are not discussed in this book, but Chapter 12, Offline Scenarios via Web Services, provides more information on WSDL-based data connections.

In addition to the structure, the system displays further information, such as the identified field type, in the form of icons to the left of the name of the data node. For XML schema-based data connections, for example, Adobe LiveCycle Designer can determine this information automatically.

Section 5.3.1, Defining the Data Binding, describes how data view uses an icon to indicate which data nodes are bound to form fields. Thus, in the data view, you can easily determine to what extent you actually use the data that is transferred via the interface.

5.1.4 Library and Object Palette

The right side of the Adobe LiveCycle Designer interface contains two other important palettes, for example, the LIBRARY palette (see Figure 5.6). The STANDARD library displays all available form field types:

▶ So-called static form fields (image, text, line, or rectangle)

▶ Form fields for the input and output of data (text field, decimal field, or checkbox)

▶ Interactive form fields (buttons or dropdown lists)

This chapter and Chapter 7 explain the usage of nearly all form fields by means of examples. At this point, you should take your time and look at the form fields illustrated in Figure 5.6. This figure gives a first overview of the functions that you can implement in forms.

The BARCODES library contains all supported barcodes. A look at this library shows which barcodes are supported by SAP Interactive Forms by Adobe; however, you cannot define your own barcode types.

Figure 5.6 Form Field Library

One of the most important palettes is the OBJECT palette. This palette, illustrated in Figure 5.7, provides different tabs depending on the form object selected. In these tabs you can define the properties of the form fields.

Figure 5.7 "Object" Palette

To speed up the work with Adobe LiveCycle Designer, you should know on which tabs you can find the corresponding properties. At the beginning of this chapter, you are guided to each tab; however, later on, the chapter will not describe in detail how you can navigate to the respective tab.

5.1.5 Form Design Area

The form design area (see Figure 5.8) is the most important area. For this reason, it should also occupy the largest part of the screen. The DESIGN VIEW and MASTER PAGES tabs provide an exact view of the form template's layout.

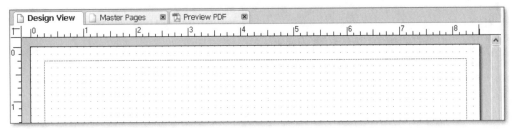

Figure 5.8 Form Design Area

Figure 5.8 shows the DESIGN VIEW, in which you define the layout of the individual pages. In the MASTER PAGES tab, you can create the background of the pages that can be used for multiple form pages. Both views enable you to add form fields in a graphical interactive way via drag and drop and changing the layout.

The PREVIEW PDF tab is extremely helpful to quickly view the output as a PDF in Adobe Designer. For this reason, Adobe LiveCycle Designer creates a PDF from the form template and displays it in its user interface. Bear in mind that this is only a preview. Sections 5.2.2, Using Text Fields, and 5.3.2, Using Preview Data, discuss this aspect in more detail.

5.2 The Basic Principles of the Form Template Design

You already created the interface and context for the first form template in Chapter 4. In the next step, you prepared a form template that corresponds to the context. You are also already familiar with Form Builder from Chapter 4. This section now describes the options that the LAYOUT tab provides in more detail.

If you are not in Form Builder yet, execute Transaction SFP to start Form Builder. To begin creating the form template, perform the following steps:

1. Select FORM, and enter Z_IFBA_BOOK_FORM_01 to select the form object that you created in Section 4.3, Context of a Form.

2. Start to edit it by clicking on the CHANGE button.

3. Then select the LAYOUT tab. The screen should now appear as illustrated in Figure 5.1.

4. Ensure that DESIGN VIEW is selected for the form design area. If it is not selected, click on the DESIGN VIEW tab. This design view displays an empty form template. Within the blue frame, you can add form fields.

   The alternative, MASTER PAGES, is discussed in Section 5.5, Using Master Pages and Rich Text Fields.

5. Now, close all libraries but the STANDARD library. The library should now appear as illustrated in Figure 5.6.

6. Select the hierarchy, and take a closer look at it. The form template has a master page—PAGE1—and an unnamed form page (UNTITLED SUBFORM) (PAGE 1).

In Section 5.2.1, Getting Started, you begin creating your first form template. Figure 5.9 illustrates what the form template is supposed to look like at the end of this chapter.

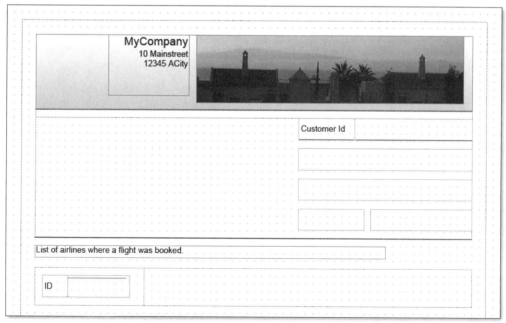

Figure 5.9 Form Template that is Supposed to be Created

5.2.1 Getting Started

Begin creating the form template as follows:

1. First, drag and drop an IMAGE form field from the Library palette to the first page of the form. You can position the image wherever you like. The correct positioning is discussed in Section 5.2.2, Using Text Fields.

2. Then select the OBJECT PALETTE. It contains the DRAW tab (see Figure 5.10) that displays the input field for the URL of the image data. Next to the input field, there is a button to select the corresponding file. Select any image from your hard drive. For the example in Figure 5.9, we chose an image of a landscape.

Figure 5.10 "Draw" Tab for an Image

3. Then select the EMBED IMAGE DATA option. Because the image is the same for each form output, embed the data for the image into the form template. The reason for doing so is that the system is not supposed to access the image data to import or transfer it via the form context for each generation process.

4. Define that the size is supposed to be copied from the image file. To do this, select the USE ORIGINAL SIZE option for the size.

The letterhead is supposed to contain the name and address of the company. For this, a static text object is used, as follows:

1. As the next object, you drag and drop a TEXT form field from the Standard library to the form template.

2. You can change the size of the form fields directly in the design view using the mouse. To do this, select the previously added text if it is not selected yet. As you can see in Figure 5.11, the system now displays an object frame for the form field. You can use this frame to adjust the size of the form field.

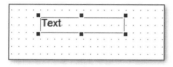

Figure 5.11 Object Frame for a Text Field

3. Enlarge the TEXT form field until it has about the same height as the image. Confirm the next dialog with OK. It is not relevant in this context.

4. You can change the position of a form field in a page in a similar way via drag and drop. To do this, click on the form field, and keep the left mouse button pressed. Now, move the mouse and change the position of the form field in the page.

5. In the next step, add a line to visually separate the areas of the form.

6. In the DRAW tab of the OBJECT palette, set the width of the line to "0.015in" (see Figure 5.12).

Figure 5.12 "Draw" Tab for a Line

7. Move the line to the left border of the blue rectangle and extend the line over the entire page.

8. Now, add a rectangle to the page.

9. In the DRAW tab of the OBJECT palette, select the LINEAR—TO BOTTOM fill. Then select any shade of white as the first color and any shade of gray as the second color. Set the LINE STYLE to NONE (see Figure 5.13).

Figure 5.13 "Draw" Tab for a Rectangle

Gradients and PostScript Level 2

When a form is output in the PostScript Level 2 printer language, gradients are emulated because they are not directly supported by PostScript Level 2. Therefore, you should avoid using gradients for performance reasons.

10. Select and right-click on the rectangle. Select the SEND TO BACK menu item in the context menu that opens. This way, you define that the rectangle is positioned behind all other form fields.

To check the first steps, compare your form template with the example shown in Figure 5.14. Note that you have not yet arranged the form fields; arrange them now as illustrated in Figure 5.15. If necessary, change the size of the fields. Now, the layout of the letterhead is defined.

Figure 5.14 First Preliminary Result

Figure 5.15 Form Template After Having Arranged the Fields

5.2.2 Using Text Fields

Text fields are the easiest option for outputting data in a form. To output information on the customer, such as customer ID and address, you must enhance the form template in the example as follows:

1. Add a text field to the form template. To do this, drag and drop a text field from the STANDARD library to the page of the form template and arrange the text field below the line.

2. Next, change the caption of the text field. To do this, double-click on the TEXT FIELD caption of the previously added text field and enter "Customer Id" as the new caption.

3. Take a closer look at the text field. You can see a vertical orange line between the caption and the input field (see Figure 5.16). It can be used to split the available space between the caption and the input field.

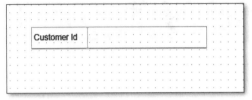

Figure 5.16   Text Field

Use the mouse to move this line to the right to increase the distance between the caption and the input field.

4. Navigate to the Field tab of the OBJECT palette for the text field and make sure that the text field is selected (see Figure 5.17). Here, select the NONE option for appearance to remove the frame for the input field of the customer ID.

Figure 5.17   "Field" Tab for a Text Field

The frame is quite helpful for interactive forms because it is easier for the user to recognize the fields that require input. For the mere print output, this does not look very nice in most cases.

To further edit the form template, you require additional palettes.

1. Display the two palettes LAYOUT and BORDER by selecting the two corresponding menu items in the PALETTES menu.

2. Select the previously added text field. Navigate to the BORDER palette and select the EDIT INDIVIDUALLY option for Edges. Then select SOLID for the bottom border.

3. Add another four text fields to the form design.

4. After having configured the properties for these four fields, you must align them as required. To do this, perform the following steps for each of the four fields.

   ▶ Select the corresponding text field and navigate to the Object palette. In the Field tab, set the Appearance to NONE.

   ▶ Then navigate to the LAYOUT palette and also set the POSITION in CAPTION to NONE (see Figure 5.18).

Selecting and Editing Multiple Text Fields

If you left-click on and hold down the Ctrl key simultaneously, you can select several form fields consecutively, which enables you to edit the form fields simultaneously. You can perform the previous steps faster by editing the four text fields at once.

Figure 5.18 "Layout" Palette for a Text Field

Aligning Form Fields

This section shows you how to arrange the text fields for the customer information in the form in an appealing way. To make it easier to align the form fields, you can decrease the mesh size of the grid according to where the form fields are aligned.

1. To do this, open the drawing aids by calling the DRAWING AIDS menu item via the PALETTES menu. This menu enables you to activate and deactivate the grid and define the distance of its grid lines (see Figure 5.19).

Figure 5.19   Drawing Aids

2. In INTERVAL, set the distance for both X and Y to "8/in."

3. Close the DRAWING AIDS palette.

The grid is also required for the tabbing order and for accessible forms because the order of the form fields is also defined by their position in these two cases. In this context, the position is evaluated from the top left to the bottom right. Therefore, you must position the form fields exactly.

Drawing Aids

In addition to the grid options, the drawing aid also provides the option to specify the units of measurement. Available units of measurement are inches, centimeters, millimeters, and points.

In the next step, we will align the text fields. Proceed as follows:

1. Arrange and size the fields in accordance with the example shown in Figure 5.20.

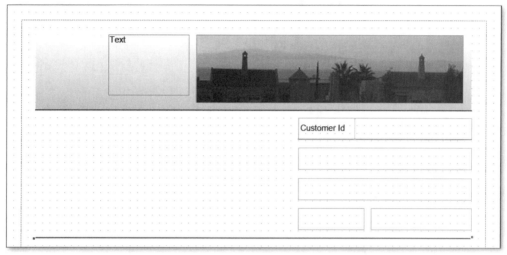

Figure 5.20 Alignment of the Text Fields

2. Insert the line that you can see in the figure below the fields.

3. Set the width of the line to "0.015in."

Naming Form Fields

Finally, you assign names to all form fields; however, do not confuse names and captions of form fields. The captions are visible in the form, while the names of the form fields are part of the structure of the form template.

1. To do this, select all of the added form fields consecutively in the hierarchy and either press ⬚F2⬚ or open the context menu with the right mouse button and select the RENAME OBJECT menu item.

2. Rename the form fields sequentially: "CustomerID," "Name," "Street," "ZIP," and "City." During this process, check which text field you have selected in the design view to generate a correct address at a later stage, that is, to ensure that the street is displayed in the correct position.

3. Compare your hierarchy with the one shown in Figure 5.21. This enables you to determine whether you have added and named all form fields correctly.

Figure 5.21 "Hierarchy" After Having Renamed the Fields

Naming form fields is particularly critical for advanced form development. Theoretically, you can also create form templates without naming the form fields.

Naming Form Fields

Assigning names to form fields has the following benefits: A form template becomes much clearer when you use meaningful names for form fields (for example, Street instead of TEXTFIELD3). Meaningful names also enable third parties to easily understand the structure of the form.

In addition, writing scripts is much easier because you can use the logically meaningful names of the form fields in the script programs.

Therefore, clear names considerably facilitate the maintenance of your form.

Using the Preview PDF Option

In the next step, the form template is displayed as a PDF document.

1. To do this, select the PREVIEW PDF tab in the form design area.

2. Above the PDF, there is a note highlighted in purple that indicates that you cannot save data that are embedded in the form. In the top right of the screen, a

button for selecting fields is displayed. Click on this button and wait. The fields for the address are highlighted. See Figure 5.22.

The system has generated a preview of an interactive PDF. Adobe LiveCycle Designer cannot assign usage rights to this PDF form, which means that you cannot store the embedded data.

3. Because this chapter does not discuss interactive PDF forms, you will change the PDF preview to a print form in the next step. Call the FORM PROPERTIES... menu item in EDIT.

4. Navigate to the PREVIEW tab. Set the PREVIEW TYPE to PRINT FORM (ONE-SIDED).

5. Switch to PREVIEW PDF again. As you can see, the note and the button are no longer displayed.

Figure 5.22 Form Template as a PDF Document

PDF Preview in Adobe LiveCycle Designer

The Preview PDF option in Adobe LiveCycle Designer is used to test form templates. As you have already seen, no usage rights are assigned to PDF forms.

However, the forms need to be generated via ADS to be used in applications. This is done by the frameworks that are also responsible for assigning usage rights.

5.2.3   Formatting Texts

You must now again edit the Text form field that you inserted at the beginning. To do this, you must display two additional palettes if they are not visible yet: the

Font palette and the Paragraph palette. You can display them by selecting the corresponding menu items in the Palette menu.

To edit the text, proceed as follows:

1. Enlarge the field using the object frame and position it in such a way that it attaches to the image with only a small distance on the left.

2. Select the field by double-clicking on it. This way, you select the entire existing text so that you can easily delete it by pressing the ⟨Del⟩ key.

3. Enter each of the following three texts into a new line (you can go to the next line by pressing the ⟨ENTER⟩ key): "MyCompany," "10 Mainstreet," and "12345 ACity" (see Figure 5.23).

4. Select the first line by double-clicking on it, and navigate to the Font palette (see Figure 5.23).

Figure 5.23 "Font" Palette

5. Here, set the font size to 14 and the style to Bold. Then select the third line in the text and set the font size to 14 here, too.

6. Finally, edit the paragraph because the text is supposed to be right-aligned. To do this, select the text (the form field) and navigate to the Paragraph palette.

7. Here, select the icon for the right-aligned text and the icon for Align Vertical Center.

The text should now look as illustrated in Figure 5.24.

Figure 5.24 Completely Formatted Text for the Company Address

Further Options with Adobe LiveCycle Designer 8.2

To enable you to enhance the appearance of texts, new functions were added to the Font palette in Adobe LiveCycle Designer (see Figure 5.23). Besides baseline shift, character spacing, and vertical and horizontal scaling, the most important new function is automatic kerning. Automatic *kerning* adjusts the spacing between specific pairs of letters, such as "WA" or "Te" in order to create the appearance of even spacing.

5.3   Data Binding for Form Fields

To define exactly where the form data is supposed to be output from the SAP system, you can link form fields to the data structure by means of data binding. In the next step, we will bind the address fields of the customer to the data structure.

5.3.1   Defining the Data Binding

To define the data binding, proceed as follows:

1. First, select the text field for the customer ID.

2. Navigate to the OBJECT palette and select the BINDING tab.

3. The BINDING tab contains an input field for the default binding. On the right of this field there is a button. Click on this button, and follow the menu path Z_IFBA_BOOK_FORM_01 • CUSTOMER • ID. Figure 5.25 shows this selection.

Figure 5.25   Selecting the "Default Binding"

4. The field of the default binding now contains a binding expression ($.CUSTOMER.ID) that indicates where the data for the customer ID can be found in the data structure.

   Z_IFBA_BOOK_FORM_01 is the name of the data binding that is also displayed in the data view. For the binding expressions, it is replaced by $. This is followed by the path in the data hierarchy separated by a period (.). You could have also entered this binding expression directly with the keyboard.

5. If the message box for the binding properties is displayed, select the DON'T UPDATE ANY RELATED PROPERTIES and DON'T SHOW AGAIN options because you are supposed to perform all of the steps in this example manually.

6. The DATA VIEW displays an icon for bound data nodes after the ID data node. Navigate to the data view and compare it with Figure 5.26.

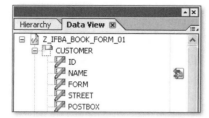

Figure 5.26 Icon for Bound Data Nodes

You can also define the default binding directly from the data view via drag and drop. To do this, you must first select the data view and expand it until the fields below the CUSTOMER node are visible. For the remaining four fields, you should use this alternative and proceed as follows:

1. You can find the data nodes that are supposed to be bound under the CUSTOMER node. This includes child nodes, such as NAME, STREET, POSTCODE, and CITY.

2. Now, select a first node (for example, NAME) and keep the left mouse button pressed. Move the mouse pointer to the text field below the customer ID in the design view, and release the left mouse button.

3. You have now defined the data binding for the second text field. You can check this by selecting the BINDING tab in the OBJECT palette and viewing the binding expression. Here, you should find an expression that starts with $ (older Adobe LiveCycle versions use $record).

4. Proceed in the same way for the remaining three text fields.

> **Using "$" and "$record" in Binding Expressions**
>
> The $ and $record binding expressions have the same meaning and can replace each other. With the release of Adobe LiveCycle Designer 8.2, $ has been used in the user interface because it is shorter. However, this has not been implemented in all areas yet.

As you can see, the second method for defining the data binding is quicker and easier than the method that was described first. However, there are various steps involved in the creation of form templates for which you must use the first method, for example, the usage of floating fields or the manual creation of tables or subform structures, if required.

Section 5.5, Using Master Pages and Rich Text Fields, introduces a method that further simplifies this process: generating a form field with the correct binding directly from the data view.

5.3.2 Using Preview Data

To create the PDF preview, Adobe LiveCycle Designer generates a PDF from the form template. During this process, it may also process data; however, this must be explicitly defined for the preview. To do this, Adobe Designer allows you to refer to a data file.

1. Define the name and the path to the file in the FORM PROPERTIES dialog, which you call via the menu path EDIT • FORM PROPERTIES....

2. Then navigate to the PREVIEW tab. Here, you can find an input field for the name and for the path of the data file (see Figure 5.27).

Figure 5.27 "Preview" Tab of the "Form Properties"

3. Next to the input field, there is a button to open a file search dialog. You can select a data file from the file system directly; this should be an XML file that corresponds to the XML schema used in the form template. If this is not the case, the system displays an error message when you switch to the PDF preview. You can also use a local file. However, if others want to open your form and view it in the preview, this file may be missing.

> **Note**
>
> Section 6.5.1, Trace and PDF with Additional Information, shows you how you can retrieve sample data that were used to generate the output via a print program. You can then store these data locally and use them for your preview.

4. As of Adobe LiveCycle Designer 8.0, you are provided with the option to have the system generate a data file. To do this, the DEFAULTS tab of the form properties contains the GENERATE PREVIEW DATA...; click on this button (see Figure 5.27). The dialog that opens again displays the structure of the data. Click on the GENERATE button to generate a data file.

5. After already having bound the address fields to the data and being provided with the data for the preview, call the PREVIEW PDF option again. As you can see, all fields are now filled with data, and the form is no longer an interactive PDF form (see Figure 5.28).

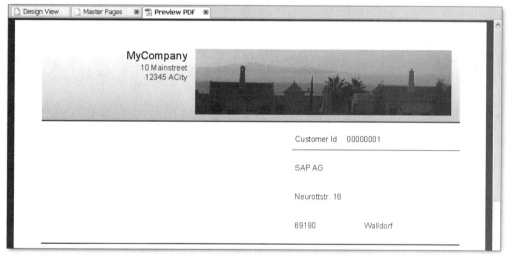

Figure 5.28   "PDF Preview" Tab with Bound Address Data

5.4 Structuring Form Templates with Subforms

Take a closer look at the form hierarchy in Figure 5.21: All form fields are now below the node for page 1 of the form template; it is a flat hierarchy.

Subforms are an option to combine several form fields and structure the form hierarchy. It makes sense to combine logically associated form fields in a subform because this helps the form designer keep the overview of the form template.

Because the individual data nodes are usually also logically grouped in the data structure, it is often helpful to assign a similar structure to the form hierarchy.

5.4.1   Adding a Hierarchy

In the next step, we will add all of the address fields to a subform.

1. Use the mouse to select the text fields by clicking in the upper-left part of the text field for the customer ID, keeping the left mouse button pressed, and selecting all fields via the "rubber band." Move the mouse until you are to the right, below the text field for the city. Release the left mouse button. Now, all of the fields should be selected.

2. To add all of the fields to a subform, press the right mouse button and select the WRAP IN SUBFORM menu item from the displayed context menu (see Figure 5.29).

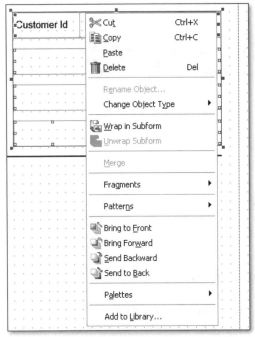

Figure 5.29   Adding Fields to a Subform

3. To include the form fields of the letterhead in a subform, you must perform the same steps for the respective form fields.

4. Drag and drop the hierarchy to add Line 2 to the UNTITLED SUBFORM. To do this, select Line 2 and keep the left mouse button pressed. Then move the mouse

upward. Move the mouse upward until the UNTITLED SUBFORM is highlighted (see Figure 5.30). Now, release the left mouse button. You can see that the subform has been increased in the form design area.

Figure 5.30 Adding the Line to the Subform

5. Now, assign a name to the two subforms. Depending on their content, name them "Letterhead" and "Address."

6. You should then take a closer look at the form hierarchy. The plus (+) and minus (–) signs to the left of the subforms enable you to display or hide the content of subforms. Hide the content of the Letterhead and Address subforms.

7. Now, select the two new subforms consecutively in the hierarchy by pressing the ⌈Ctrl⌉ key.

8. If you then right-click on them, the context menu opens (see Figure 5.31). Select the WRAP IN SUBFORM menu item to add the two subforms to a new subform.

It is also possible to create subforms in the hierarchy. The most complex way would have been to add the subforms to the form template from the Standard library and then add the fields to the subforms.

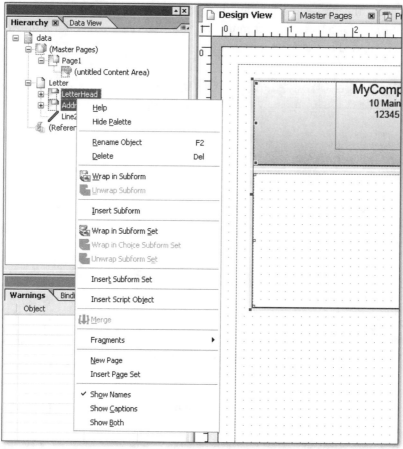

Figure 5.31 Wrapping Subforms in Subforms

1. Next, assign the name "Introduction" to the new template.

2. Now, assign the name "Letter" to page 1.

3. Accordingly, change the default binding of page 1 in the BINDING tab of the OBJECT palette from NORMAL to NONE.

If you have performed these steps correctly, your hierarchy will look like the one illustrated in Figure 5.32.

Figure 5.32 "Hierarchy" Tab After Having Implemented the Subforms

You have changed only the structure of the form template and not the layout. At this point, you can call the PDF preview and check this. The result is identical to the output in Figure 5.28.

5.4.2 Extending the Form Template

Subforms can be used for much more than structuring the form hierarchy. The following sections discuss the usage of subforms in more detail.

1. Add another Text form field to the form template.

2. Position the form field with a small distance below Line 2 and on the right-hand side of the left border of the design area of the form template. Increase the width of the form field and enter the following text: "List of airlines where a flight was booked."

3. Then drag and drop a subform from the STANDARD library to the form template. Position the subform directly below the previously added form field. Increase the width of the subform until it covers the entire page. Finally, name it "AirlinesList."

4. In the next step, drag and drop a second subform from the STANDARD library into the first subform.

5. Name the second subform "Airline."

Creating Form Fields with Correct Data Binding from the Data View

Next, we will add a text field to the second subform for specifying the flight line ID. Proceed as follows:

1. Navigate to the Data View tab.

2. Search for the CARRID data node, which you can find under Z_IFBA_BOOK_FORM_01 •
   BOOKINGS • DATA. Figure 5.5 showed the entire data hierarchy.

3. Select CARRID and drag and drop it to the second subform (see Figure 5.33).

Figure 5.33 "Hierarchy" Tab with Unnamed Subforms

4. The newly created area of the form template should now look as illustrated in Figure 5.34.

Figure 5.34 Extending the Form by Subforms

In addition to defining data connections from the data view via drag and drop, you can also use the drag-and-drop method to directly generate fields. To do this, the information from the XML schema is evaluated to determine which form field type is supposed to be used. The data view directly displays the result of the evaluation in the form of an icon to the left of the node name.

In this context, take a closer look at the data view. You can see icons for text fields, date fields, subforms, tables, and table rows. In addition to the type of the form field, its data binding is also known and set. In the case of the CARRID data node, the system automatically creates a text field with the correct data binding.

In addition to the two procedures mentioned in Section 5.3, Data Bindings for Form Fields, this is the third procedure for defining data bindings of form fields. It is also the easiest method because you can create the form field and the data binding in one step.

For form templates that are based on ABAP Dictionary-based interfaces, this procedure provides even more benefits. The generated XML schema contains the caption that is already defined in the ABAP Dictionary. You can easily test this by adding the Z_IFBA_BOOK_FORM_01 • CUSTOMER • FORM data node to the form. The system automatically assigns the FORM OF caption to the text field.

After having tested this, delete the field from the form template again.

Completing the Layout of the Airline List

Next, we will edit the AIRLINE subform and the CARRID text field.

1. Reduce the size of the CARRID text field and the caption area.

2. Then move the text field to the upper-left corner of the subform for the airline.

3. Finally, reduce the size of the subform for the airline. However, the subform still needs to be larger than the text field.

4. If you used Adobe LiveCycle Designer to generate preview data, you should now refresh the data. To do this, call the FORM PROPERTIES dialog via the menu path EDIT • FORM PROPERTIES..., and navigate to the DEFAULT tab. Generate the data as described at the beginning.

5. Now, call PREVIEW PDF. The result should be similar to the one shown in Figure 5.35, which displays the airline ID of the first airline.

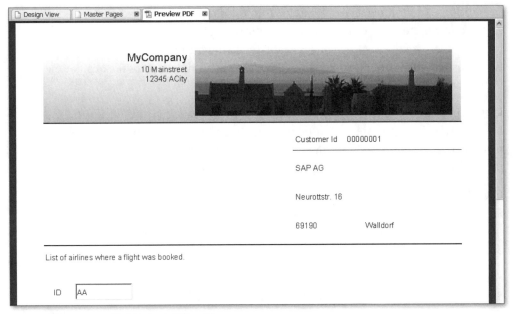

Figure 5.35 First Output Airline ID

Defining the Data Binding of the New Subforms

In this step, we will output the complete list of the airline IDs. To do this, edit the default binding for the AIRLINE subform as follows:

1. Select the subform and navigate to the BINDING tab of the OBJECT palette.

2. Click on the icon to the right of the input field for the default binding.

3. Follow the menu path Z_IFBA_BOOK_FORM_01 • BOOKINGS • DATA. Ensure that you select the first option for which no submenu is displayed (see Figure 5.36).

Figure 5.36 Data Binding for the "Airline" Subform

4. Look at the binding expression of the subform, which is $.BOOKINGS.DATA[*]. The expression contains an asterisk in square brackets ([*]), because Adobe LiveCycle Designer has determined from the data structure that the DATA data node under BOOKINGS is a node that can be repeated any number of times. This was defined in Chapter 4, Interface and Form Context.

The Airline subform was bound to the DATA node under BOOKINGS. The DATA node itself does not represent any data values: it is used only to structure the data.

5. Select the AirlinesList subform and navigate to the SUBFORM tab of the OBJECT palette (see Figure 5.37).

Regarding the content, the tab provides two options (POSITIONED and FLOWED) to define how the form fields that the subform contains are arranged in the form area. The first option, POSITIONED, defines that the form fields have an absolute position based on the X and Y coordinates. The positioning takes place at the design time of the form template.

6. Select the second option, FLOWED, for the form template. The FLOWED option defines that the form fields that are contained in the subform during the creation of the form output are positioned. However, you must still specify how the form fields are supposed to be positioned. To do this, the FLOW DIRECTION input field has been activated (see Figure 5.37). This field provides two options for defining the order (TOP TO BOTTOM and WESTERN TEXT). For this form template, select WESTERN TEXT.

Figure 5.37 "Subform" Tab

7. Then take another look at the data binding of the Airline subform (in the BINDING tab of the OBJECT palette). Because the default binding contains an asterisk in

square brackets ([*]) and because the FLOWED option is selected for the content of the wrapping subform, the REPEAT SUBFORM FOR EACH DATA ITEM option is now available. Select this option for the form template. This defines that the number of subform outputs depends on the number of data nodes in the data stream.

8. Next, look at the default binding of the CARRID text field. The binding expression is CARRID, that is, without $..., and is often called the relative binding of the form fields. The CARRID text field has a relative binding to the wrapping subform whose binding expression is $.BOOKINGS.DATA[*]. Thus, the CARRID text field has a unique binding.

9. Note that the first subform now occupies less space in the template. Its actual size during the form output is now determined by the content. Navigate to the PDF preview. The system now displays a list of all airline IDs similar to the one shown in Figure 5.38.

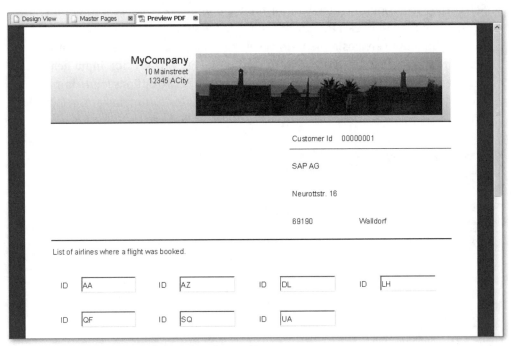

Figure 5.38 Output of the Airline IDs as a List

Repeating Subforms

You can have the system repeat subforms when they have a data binding to repeating data itself and when you have selected the FLOWED option for the content of the wrapping subform.

You can use the minimum, maximum, and initial counter to control the minimum or maximum number of instances of the subform. The initial counter defines how many instances are initially instanced. Therefore, a subform can be displayed five times, for example, although the data includes the corresponding node only three times.

Subforms are discussed further in Chapter 7.

Data Binding to Repeating Data

You can implement a data binding to repeating data only once. Such binding expressions are indicated by [*]. For the example in this chapter, this means that you cannot output the list of the airline IDs another time. The data are used up, so to speak, and is no longer available for further data bindings.

You can easily check this by copying the AirlinesList subform (select it, open the context menu by right-clicking on it, and select the Copy entry) and inserting it again further below into the form template (open the context menu by right-clicking on it, select the PASTE entry, and correct the position if required). In the preview, you can see that the second list displays only one empty text field.

5.5   Using Master Pages and Rich Text Fields

In the following section, we will add a footer to the form template. The content of the footer is supposed to be a formatted text that is maintained outside the form template. The FOOTER data node has already been provided for this in the interface and context of the form (see Section 4.3.3, Structures, and Figure 5.5).

5.5.1   Customizing the Master Page

Master pages enable you to define a page background that is displayed on multiple form pages. To display the footer on all form pages, you must customize the master page as follows:

1. Navigate to the MASTER PAGES tab to go to the form design area for master pages. Check whether PAGE1 is selected. If it is not selected, select it.

2. PAGE1 has a content area, which has a pink border in the MASTER PAGES view. It defines the area of the design area in which form fields can be added to the form template. This area is shown on the right in Figure 5.39.

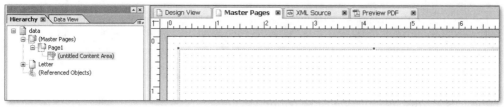

Figure 5.39 Master Pages

3. In the next step, we will increase the space available in the bottom area of the master page. To do this, select the content area with the mouse. If required, you must move the master page upward using the scroll bars.

4. To have more space available on the page, you must decrease the content area. The content area provides the same object frame as any other form field. Move the bottom edge of the content area upward (see Figure 5.40).

Figure 5.40 Bottom Area of the Master Page

5.5.2 Rich Text Fields

Now, add a text field and edit its properties.

1. Drag and drop a text field from the STANDARD library to the area that you have previously created by decreasing the content area.

2. To edit the properties, first navigate to the LAYOUT palette and set the position in CAPTIONS to NONE to hide the caption of the text field.

3. Then select the Object palette and navigate to the Field tab. Here, set Appearance to None to deactivate the border of the text field and set the checkmark in Allow Multiple Lines (see Figure 5.41).

Figure 5.41 "Field" Tab for a Rich Text Field

4. Because the text in the footer is later transferred as it has been formatted, set the Field Format to Rich Text.

Text Fields and Formatted Text

Formatted text can be displayed by rich text fields. The text is transferred by the data and must be formatted according to an XHTML subset. Among other things, paragraphs and changes of the font style are supported.

You can find a list of the supported elements of the XML Forms Architecture Specification in Section 7.7.3.

5. Move the text field to the left of the content area and enlarge the text field with the mouse until it is more or less as wide as the content area.

Figure 5.42 "Binding" Tab for a Rich Text Field

6. Also, enlarge it in such a way that a text with multiple lines easily fits into it. The system displays a message box, which you confirm by clicking OK.

7. Drag and drop the FOOTER node from the data view to the text field to create the default binding. The default binding should now appear as illustrated in Figure 5.42. Remember: The FOOTER node is a Smart Forms text module; the text of a text module is transferred in XHTML format.

8. If you used Adobe LiveCycle Designer to generate preview data, you should now refresh the data. To do this, you need a trick to retrieve the data for the footer:

   Add the FOOTER to the design view. Generate the preview data and then delete the previously generated FOOTER text field from your form template again. The system does not generate preview data for the fields on the master pages. For this reason, a field for the generation of the preview data has been temporarily added to the design view.

9. Navigate to PREVIEW PDF to view the result, which should look like the one illustrated in Figure 5.43. You may have to scroll down to see this.

16, Sample Street · Sample City XY9 0YY, PO box 9999 GB Sample City XY9 0YY, Phone +1/2 12/99 10 99 Fax +1/2 12/99 12 99 Telex 4 99 009 sam gb
Payment by RFT1 Credit Transfer: To Paymaster for the credit of IDES Holding A/c 33456 quoting our invoice number
Payment by BACS: Account name: IDES Holding Account number: 033456000 Sort code: 01-01-01 Bank: Bank of England Branch: Head Office London ABC 23D Swift code: BKENGB2LA
Payment by check: Checks should be made payable to IDES Holding and sent to IDES Holding Finance Branch at the address stated above.
UK VAT Registration No: YX099 European VAT registration no: 888 8D18
Executive Board: Thomas Schmidt · Sharon Bishop · Chantal Willemin · Sigeruh Takahashi

Figure 5.43 PDF Preview of the Footer

5.5.3   Alternative Method for Adding the Footer

This section discusses in detail how you can create form fields directly from the data view.

1. Delete the text field for the footer.

2. Now, drag and drop the footers from the data view to the master page. In this case, the system evaluates information from the schema and automatically configures the properties for the form fields.

3. Select the FOOTER node in the data view and keep the left mouse button pressed. Drag and drop the FOOTER node to the area below the content area and release the mouse button. Check the data format in the BINDING tab of the OBJECT palette for the text field. It has already been set to XHTML, just as the field format has already been set to RICH TEXT (FIELD tab, see Figures 5.41 and 5.42).

4. Customize the appearance and captions as described and the position and size of the text field.

5.5.4   Activating Forms

Like all objects in the ABAP development, the form must be activated before you can use it. To do this, click on the ACTIVATION icon. The procedure is identical to the activation of an interface as described in Section 4.2.1, ABAP Dictionary-Based Interface. In Chapter 6, Form Output, you will use the created form template to create a print output.

5.6   Reusing Form Objects

Form objects enable you to reuse segments of a form template. If some of the segments are identical in multiple forms, or if you want to reuse script programs, you can use form objects.

For the method described in this section, the form objects are stored locally on the computer of the user. If other users need to have access to these form objects, you must manually copy them.

Form objects can be grouped; this enables you to logically combine the form objects that are thematically linked. You can name these groups and display or hide them in the user interface of Adobe LiveCycle Designer as required.

The version of Adobe LiveCycle Designer delivered by SAP provides three additional libraries with form objects: two libraries for Web Dynpro and one library for the ISR framework. The form objects of these libraries contain scripts for the integration with Web Dynpro or the ISR framework. When you use these two integrations, you must use the form objects from the respective library instead of the form fields from the STANDARD library to ensure correct processing.

Form Fragments in Adobe LiveCycle Designer

The form fragments in Adobe LiveCycle Designer are not yet available in this SAP environment. Form fragments externally manage parts of forms and integrate them with a form template through references.

Next, we will create a library and store the address part of the form template in this library.

5.6.1 Creating Your Own Libraries

Begin creating a new group in the library.

1. To do this, click on the icon marked in Figure 5.44, and select the ADD GROUP… item in the menu that opens.

Figure 5.44 Menu for Managing Libraries

2. A dialog box appears in which you must specify the name of the group. Enter the name "My Form Objects." Click the icon on the right-hand side of the "My Form Objects" library (it is identical to the icon that is selected in Figure 5.44), and select the group properties.

3. The system displays the dialog shown in Figure 5.45. Here, you can change the name of the group; LOCATION indicates the storage location for your form objects. You can also define what needs to be done with the form objects (add, remove, or modify).

Figure 5.45 Library Group Properties

5.6.2 Adding Form Objects

Form objects can consist of single form fields or subforms. Let's add the subform that contains the text fields for displaying the address as a form object to the previously created library.

1. There are two options for adding the subform to the library:

   ▶ For the first option, you must select the subform in the design area and open the context menu by right-clicking on it. At the very bottom, this menu includes the ADD TO LIBRARY... menu item.

   ▶ For the second option, you must select the subform and keep the left mouse button pressed. Then drag and drop the subform into the newly created library and release the mouse button.

2. In both cases, the system displays the same dialog, where you must enter the name, a description of the form object, and its usage. Finally, you must define to which library the form object is supposed to be added. Figure 5.46 shows an example of a possible input.

> **Note**
>
> In the hierarchy, there is no context menu to add an object to a library. Also, you cannot drag and drop an object from the hierarchy directly to a library.

Figure 5.46   Add Library Object Dialog

3. The library should now appear as illustrated in Figure 5.47.

Figure 5.47   Library with Your Own Group and Form Object

5.6.3   Using Form Objects

The following section uses an example to demonstrate using form objects.

1. Move the mouse to the newly added form object and wait a moment. The system then displays a note. This note is the description that you entered when adding the object to the library.

Like form fields, you can also drag and drop add form objects from the STAN-DARD library to a form template.

2. Try this: Select the ADDRESS SUBFORM form object, and drag and drop it to the form template. Now the system adds a new subform to the form template. This subform contains the same text fields with all previously set properties.

3. You can use the PREVIEW PDF option to see that the address data is now output twice.

5.7 Implicit Data Binding

So far, you have been introduced to so-called explicit binding. Here, the binding expressions for binding the data are explicitly specified (for example, $.CUSTOMER.ID). An explicit binding also enables you to use relative binding expressions, for example, a relative data binding to the wrapping subform. You already used relative binding expressions in Section 5.3 for form fields. The CARRID field has a relative binding to the AIRLINE subform.

The following sections introduce an additional option for binding form fields to data structures. For implicit data bindings, the binding to the data is derived from the form hierarchy and the name of the form fields (and from the subforms). This requires that the form hierarchy has a structure that is similar to the data structure.

This can be best explained using an example: To do this, create a copy of the form template and change the data binding from an explicit data binding to an implicit data binding. You can either use the PDF preview or refer to Section 6.1, Print Program, to find out that the output for these two options is identical.

5.7.1 Creating Copies of Forms

To keep the original form template, create a copy of the already-created form template first. Proceed as follows:

1. Save the form layout if you have not done so yet.

2. Navigate to the Form Builder start page (Transaction SFP).

3. In the start page, select FORM and enter Z_IFBA_BOOK_FORM_01 as the name. Then click on the button that is used to copy objects in the toolbar.

4. This opens the dialog shown in Figure 5.48. Enter Z_IFBA_BOOK_FORM_01_IMPL into the COPY TO field and click on the button with the green checkmark.

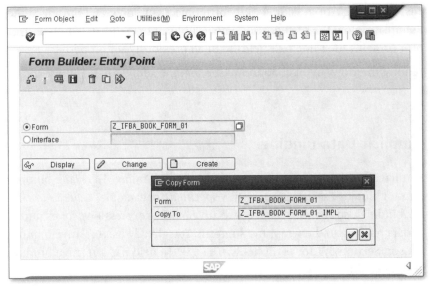

Figure 5.48 Copying a Form Object

5. In the next dialog, Create Object Dictionary Entry, create the copy of the form as a local object. At this point, you should look at Figure 5.21.

6. After having created the new form, return to the Form Builder start page. The name of the previously created form is already entered in the input field. Thus, you can start by clicking on the CHANGE button.

5.7.2 Implementing the Implicit Data Binding

Now let's change the data binding for the sample form from explicit to implicit.

1. First, compare the CUSTOMER data node and its child nodes (ID, NAME, etc.) with the Address subform and the form fields contained therein. Both have the same structure.

2. Then rename the ADDRESS subform. To do this, select it in the form hierarchy, and press the F2 key. Name it "CUSTOMER." Ensure that you spell it exactly as it is displayed in the data view.

3. Select the BINDING tab of the OBJECT palette for the subform, and change the default binding from NONE to NORMAL to activate implicit binding (see Figure 5.49).

Figure 5.49 "Binding" Tab for the "CUSTOMER" Subform

The next step considers the text fields that are contained in the CUSTOMER subform.

1. First, rename the "CustomerId," "Name," "Street," "ZIP," and "City" fields to "ID," "NAME," "STREET," "POSTCODE," and "CITY." The data view defines how you must name the fields. Please note that case sensitivity is important here.

2. Then set the DEFAULT BINDING for each text field to NORMAL.

3. For the list of the airlines, view the structure under the BOOKINGS data node (up to the CARRID node) in the data view (see Figure 5.5).

4. Return to the hierarchy, and rename the AirlinesList subform to BOOKINGS and the Airline subform to DATA.

   The text field already has the correct name, because you have added it to the form template via drag and drop.

5. For the BOOKINGS and DATA subforms and for the CARRID text field, sequentially set the default binding to NORMAL. Ignore the previous specifications of the default binding.

6. Finally, go to the master page, and set the default binding to NORMAL for the footer field (FOOTER).

7. In the BINDINGS of the REPORT palette, you can display the form fields grouped by their type of default binding. Select Fields with Normal Data Binding and the system displays all form fields (see Figure 5.50). To check whether you have

changed the setting for all form fields, you can select FIELDS WITH DATA BINDING BY REFERENCE. If you have considered all form fields, the system no longer displays any fields.

Figure 5.50 Checking the Bindings

8. Your form hierarchy should now look as illustrated in Figure 5.51.

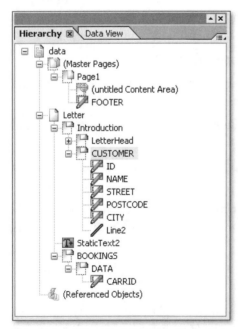

Figure 5.51 "Hierarchy" Tab After Having Renamed the Fields

9. You can use the PDF preview to check whether the form is output in the same way as before the changes were made. If everything is correct, you will not see any difference.

10. Finally, activate this form template.

Implicit Binding to Data

For implicit binding (indicated by the Normal value for the default binding) the same applies as for explicit bindings to repeating data. Data that have been bound once are no longer available for the binding of additional fields.

You can easily check this by copying the CUSTOMER subform and adding it to the form template for a second time. If you now navigate to the PDF preview, you can see that the second CUSTOMER subform is empty.

Implicit and Explicit Binding

Now that you are familiar with the two main binding types, we can provide the following recommendation: Do not use implicit and explicit binding in one form! We advise against it because you must know exactly how these two interconnect. Among other things, the order in the hierarchy is relevant. It also significantly reduces the maintainability of the form template.

However, with regard to comparing the performance of explicit and implicit data binding, note the following: During the generation of a print output or a PDF, the system must evaluate the data bindings.

▸ For explicit binding, the system always needs to process the complete binding expression for each binding, which requires additional time. You should therefore use relative binding expressions, because the system can evaluate them more easily.

▸ The same applies to implicit binding. Here too, it is often not necessary to evaluate complete binding expressions. However, note that for the implicit data binding the form fields have to be clearly assigned to the data, otherwise you may obtain unwanted results for the data binding and thus for the output.

Therefore, the form hierarchy and the data structure should be as similar as possible to efficiently use implicit binding and obtain a clear result. If so, you should use implicit data binding. Alternatively, use explicit binding and relative binding expressions.

5.8 Useful Functions in Adobe LiveCycle Designer

This section discusses some useful functions of Adobe LiveCycle Designer.

5.8.1 Customizing the Toolbars

To have more space available for the design area, you should carefully consider how many toolbars you require and actually use. Simply hide the toolbars that you do not need; the use of palettes is preferable. If you want to follow this recommendation, deactivate all toolbars but the STANDARD toolbar.

You can also reduce the size of the buttons for the remaining STANDARD toolbars. To do this, right-click on the toolbar and select the CUSTOMIZE... menu item in the menu that opens. In the next dialog (see Figure 5.52), remove the selection (green checkmark) for the LARGE BUTTONS option.

Figure 5.52 "Customize" Dialog in Adobe LiveCycle Designer

5.8.2 Object Editor

To simplify and accelerate the development of forms, Version 8.0 of Adobe Live-Cycle Designer introduced the so-called object editor that you can activate via the VIEW • OBJECT EDITOR menu path.

Figure 5.53 displays the object editor. It provides two details adjacent to the field: the name of the field and the type of field. You can change these two details here directly and do not have to navigate to the hierarchy to rename the fields. In addition, you can also use the object editor to call the context menu.

Figure 5.53   Object Editor

5.8.3   Spelling

Version 8.0 of Adobe LiveCycle Designer also introduced a spell check so that the system automatically checks the text for spelling mistakes when you enter text. If the system finds a spelling mistake, it underlines it with a red wave. This line is visible only if the respective text is ready for input.

You can trigger the check for the complete form template via the TOOLS • CHECK SPELLING... menu path anytime.

5.8.4   Hyphenation

As of Version 8.2 of Adobe LiveCycle Designer, hyphenation is supported for a more uniform body image. For this purpose, a hyphenation dictionary is used. Hyphenation is supported for form fields that enable text input and output and it is supported for the captions of all form fields

You can activate hyphenation via TOOLS • OPTIONS for new form templates or via EDIT • FORM PROPERTIES... for existing form templates. Figure 5.54 shows the possible options in the HYPHENATION area of the FORMATTING tab.

The FORMATTING tab of the FORM PROPERTIES dialog additionally contains two buttons for activating and deactivating hyphenation for all form fields (see Figure 5.54).

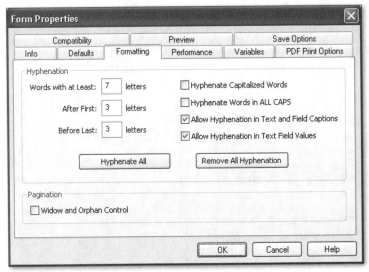

Figure 5.54 "Formatting" Tab of the Form Properties

The PARAGRAPH palette provides an option for individually setting hyphenation for each form field. For this purpose, select the HYPHENATE option if required or deselect it in order to deactivate hyphenation (see Figure 5.55).

Figure 5.55 "Paragraph" Palette

5.8.5 Managing Multiple Form Fields

Adobe LiveCycle Designer provides various functions to facilitate the processing of form templates with numerous form fields. You can navigate to the following functions via the EDIT menu:

▶ **Lock Text**
The LOCK TEXT option enables you to define that you must double-click on the text to begin editing the text. By default, it is sufficient to single-click on the text. You should select this option to avoid that you do not start the text editor by mistake.

▶ **Lock Static Objects**
With the LOCK STATIC OBJECTS option, you can avoid selecting static objects. In the created form template, for example, the letterhead only consists of static objects. After having completed the creation, you can lock these objects to prevent objects from being moved by mistake.

▶ **Lock Fields**
Like the option for locking static objects, you can use this option to lock the nonstatic objects. You should use this and the previous option depending on the requirements and task.

5.8.6 Managing Data Bindings

For data bindings, Adobe LiveCycle Designer provides setting options to facilitate their management. You can access these options via the TOOLS • OPTIONS menu in the DATA BINDINGS tab.

Depending on your preferred data connection, you can select the NORMAL default value for implicit data bindings or the NONE default value for explicit data bindings in the SUBFORM BINDING AREA. This way, you do not have to check or set the binding of a subform each time you add a new subform.

You can also activate a warning. This is very useful if you work with preview data. In this case, when you open a form, Adobe LiveCycle Designer informs you that the file with the preview data cannot be accessed (for example, if the form has been copied but not the preview data file).

5.8.7 Adobe Reader Target Version for a Form Template

If you have to create forms for different Adobe Reader versions (for example, in offline scenarios with an integration of external users), Adobe LiveCycle Designer provides a useful function for defining the target version. The target version is the minimum Adobe Reader version that can be used to display and edit a form. Figure 5.56 shows the DEFAULTS tab of the FORM PROPERTIES dialog. You can call this dialog via EDIT •FORM PROPERTIES.... In the TARGET VERSION area, you can define the minimum Adobe Reader version.

Figure 5.56 "Defaults" Tab of the Form Properties

If you use a function during the creation of a form template that is not supported in the defined target version (for example, hyphenation for text fields), the WARNINGS palette outputs the respective warning (see Figure 5.57). The SUPPORTED IN column indicates which function is supported in which Adobe Reader version.

	Object	Description	Type	Supported in	Code
⚠	FOOTER	Target version does not support vertical paragraph alignment for field values.	Target Version	Reader 7.0.5	1205
⚠	data	Target version does not support the Preserve Scripting Changes To Form When Saved option.	Target Version	Reader 8.0	1305
⚠		Target version does not support this use of text hyphenation for the current file type.	Target Version	Reader 9.0	1603

Figure 5.57   Target Versions Warnings in the "Warnings" Palette

This book considers solely the case where Acrobat and Adobe Reader 9.0 or a higher version is selected, that is, that the Adobe Reader version for Adobe Live-Cycle Designer 8.2 is used.

5.8.8   Defining the Tab Order

Usually, the tab order is automatically determined by the layout and structure of the form template. If you want to change this, you can use the function that is provided in the TAB ORDER tab. You can display or hide this tab using the PALETTE • TAB ORDER menu item. Figure 5.58 illustrates the tab and the numbering of the form fields according to the order in the design view.

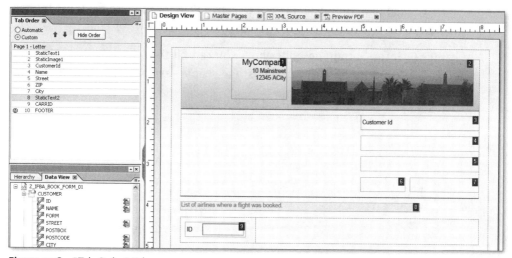

Figure 5.58   "Tab Order" Tab

The TAB ORDER tab is not required in the other chapters of this book. Therefore, hide the tab by clicking on the CLOSE icon or selecting the PALETTES • TAB ORDER menu item.

5.8.9 PDF Structure

The PDF structure issue is mentioned solely for the sake of completeness. This function is not available in the SAP environment, so you should hide the corresponding tab.

If the PDF STRUCTURE tab is displayed, hide it by clicking on the CLOSE icon or selecting the PALETTES • PDF STRUCTURE menu item.

5.9 Summary

This chapter introduced the tool for creating form templates, Adobe LiveCycle Designer, and described its usage. You created a form template based on the context of Chapter 4, Interface and Form Context, (and therefore based on the interface prepared there) with an example.

You also created a template for a print form. The explained method applies to the creation of both print forms and interactive PDF forms. In a print form, the text fields are used to output data. In an interactive PDF form, these fields are interactive and allow you to change their content.

Chapter 6, Form Output, describes how you can fill the form template with data and generate a print output. To do this, the chapter explains the creation of a so-called print program in detail.

This chapter describes how you can output a form and quickly analyze the cause of an error. It also details the translation of forms and a connection option to external form software via a certified interface.

6 Form Output

So far, you have learned how to create a form interface and a form. The form interface constitutes the connection between the print program and the form. It defines what parameters are expected at runtime and provides them for the form. The form context models the data of the interface and, if necessary, enriches the data structure with texts, addresses, or graphics. Here, the data of the interface are arranged as is logically required in the form. The context, particularly its option to define conditions for different node types, makes it an efficient tool for defining form logic.

The form layout refers to the schema that is generated from the context; the fields of this schema are arranged in the layout and formatted in accordance with their requirements. Here, the appearance of the form is specified through fonts and other design characteristics.

This chapter details how you can create a completed document on the basis of a form and enrich it with data. Because problems may occur during the form output, you are provided with the most important alternatives for analyzing errors and resolving them. The translation of forms is another important topic because many enterprises use different languages for corresponding with business partners. You will learn how to manage language-dependent layouts and how to translate forms.

The various options for performance optimization (bundling and parallelization of print jobs) also constitute an essential part of this chapter.

If you already use other form software within your systems and want to integrate them with the print programs of your SAP system, you are provided with a certified interface. This chapter presents the options for this interface and details about how it can be used.

6.1 Print Program

The print program is an ABAP program and is responsible for data retrieval, the type of output, and the selection of forms. The complexity of data retrieval may vary and strongly depends on the application.

In this example, you only have to read data for a customer from the CUSTOMER table and flight connections with the respective information from the two tables SBOOK and SPFLI. Because this chapter focuses on the interaction of print program and form, you do not require any complicated data logic; the principle is always identical. The sample program therefore includes a simple selection screen and some SELECT statements for database access.

6.1.1 Data Selection

Now, first create an ABAP program and implement the following steps (Transaction SE38).

1. Enter Z_IFBA_BOOK_PRINT as the program name and save it as a local object.

2. Listing 6.1 shows the first part of the program that defines the selection screen and reads the data from the database for the specified customer:
   - The P_CUSTOM parameter expects the customer ID. Enter the Z_IFBA_BOOK_FORM_01 form for the P_FORM parameter; the default value corresponds to the form that you have already created.
   - P_LANGU specifies the form language and defines—together with the country from P_CTRY—the formatting of the number and date fields.
   - P_DATE expects a date.
   - The first SELECT statement reads the customer information from the SCUSTOM table. Here, the customer ID of the selection screen is the access key.
   - The second SELECT statement imports all bookings of the customer in a sorted manner.
   - The third SELECT statement reads the flight connections for all bookings.

```
PROGRAM z_ifba_book_print.
TYPE-POOLS: abap.

PARAMETER: p_custom TYPE s_customer   DEFAULT 1,
           p_form   TYPE fpwbformname
                    DEFAULT 'Z_IFBA_BOOK_FORM_01',
           p_langu  TYPE spras        DEFAULT 'D',
           p_ctry   TYPE land1        DEFAULT 'DE',
           p_date   TYPE sydatum.

DATA: gs_customer    TYPE         scustom,
      gt_bookings    TYPE         ty_bookings,
      gt_connections TYPE         ty_connections,
      gs_outputpar   TYPE         sfpoutputparams,
      gv_fmname      TYPE         rs38l_fnam,
      gx_exc_api     TYPE REF TO  cx_fp_api,
      gv_err_string  TYPE         string,
      gs_docparams   TYPE         sfpdocparams.

* Select data.
SELECT SINGLE * FROM scustom INTO gs_customer
               WHERE id = p_custom.
IF sy-subrc <> 0.
*    Error handling. No data for customer found.
  EXIT.
ENDIF.
SELECT * FROM sbook INTO TABLE gt_bookings
        WHERE customid = p_custom
        ORDER BY PRIMARY KEY.
IF sy-subrc <> 0.
*    Error handling. No data for booking found.
  EXIT.
ENDIF.
SELECT * FROM spfli INTO TABLE gt_connections
        FOR ALL ENTRIES IN gt_bookings
        WHERE carrid = gt_bookings-carrid
          AND connid = gt_bookings-connid
        ORDER BY PRIMARY KEY.
IF sy-subrc <> 0.
*    Error handling. No flight connection information found.
  EXIT.
ENDIF.
```

Listing 6.1 Selecting Data

> **Note on Error Handling**
>
> Note that at this point not much effort has been invested in error handling. For example, if no data exist for the customer, the program terminates without any notification. This should never occur in live programs.
>
> Good error handling often requires a lot of space compared to the actual coding. Because this book focuses only on the essential elements and the call of a form, minimum error handling is sufficient for demonstration purposes.

3. If you navigate to the texts in the program via the menu path GOTO • TEXT ELEMENTS • SELECTION TEXTS, you can activate the DICTIONARY REFERENCE checkbox. As a result, the texts are displayed in the selection screen at runtime.

4. To check this, activate and start the program. The result should then appear as shown in Figure 6.1.

Figure 6.1 Completed Selection Screen of the Print Program

The application data required for the present form is now available in the global field, GS_CUSTOMER, or in the global tables, GT_BOOKINGS and GT_CONNECTIONS.

6.1.2 Determining the Generated Function Module

You cannot directly address the form that you created as a form object. Instead, an ABAP function module is created from the form. This function module inherits the parameters of the form interface, which were defined there, including all properties (name, data type, optional, pass by value). In addition, it also includes the coding to communicate with the form runtime environment. You do not have to consider this because the form is simply a function module at runtime to which you transfer all required data of the form interface. The formatting of data and call to Adobe Document Services (ADS) runs automatically.

Because you cannot simply use the name of the function module as the name of the form, a mapping exists between the two objects. The assigned name must be provided to you via the FP_FUNCTION_MODULE_NAME function module and the function module is generated upon the first call. If you change the form, this is determined upon calling the FP_FUNCTION_MODULE_NAME function module and regeneration takes place.

Never Use the Name of the Generated Function Module Directly!

The name of the generated function module is different in every system because it is not transported. If you transport your form from the development system to the test or live system, it has a different name in each system. Therefore, you should never address the form via a generated name directly, even if you know it in a system.

In another system, this name almost always stands for another form. If the interface does not match, a runtime error is triggered. Note, however, that no error occurs for a compatible interface, and a wrong form would be output.

In addition, it is very likely that the function module does not exist in the target system at all. The generation is done by calling the FP_FUNCTION_MODULE_NAME function module.

Let's expand the program to determine the name of the generated function module.

1. Add the coding provided in Listing 6.2 directly to the coding provided in Listing 6.1.

```
* Retrieve name of generated function module.
DATA gx_exc_api TYPE REF TO cp_fp_api.
TRY.
    CALL FUNCTION 'FP_FUNCTION_MODULE_NAME'
      EXPORTING
        i_name      = p_form
      IMPORTING
        e_funcname = gv_fmname.
  CATCH cx_fp_api INTO gx_exc_api.
    gv_err_string = gx_exc_api->get_text( ).
    MESSAGE gv_err_string type 'E'.
ENDTRY.
```

Listing 6.2 Determining the Generated Function Module

2. Transfer the name of the form to the `FP_FUNCTION_MODULE_NAME` function module. The return is the name of the generated function module that you will call later on.

3. Note that class-based exceptions are used here, which you must catch. Certainly, the most critical error is that the desired form does not exist.

The error-handling simple catches all errors in the same manner, outputs the error text, and terminates the program.

6.1.3 Opening a Print Job

Before you can call a form, you must consider the general output options. This includes, for example, whether you want to print a form or send a completed PDF document.

The ABAP function module `FP_JOB_OPEN` must be called at the beginning of the form output and determines these settings.

1. Insert the call to the `FP_JOB_OPEN` function module at the end of the program. To do so, simply select the PATTERN button in ABAP Editor.

2. Removing the comments of the inserted coding results in a pregenerated error handling. The function module includes a `CHANGING` parameter with the name `IE_OUTPUTPARAMS`. In this program, a `GS_OUTPUTPAR` variable has already been defined, which you can transfer.

3. Listing 6.3 shows the finished coding, which directly follows Listing 6.2.

```
* Start print job.
gs_outputpar-reqnew = abap_true.
CALL FUNCTION 'FP_JOB_OPEN'
  CHANGING
    ie_outputparams = gs_outputpar
  EXCEPTIONS
    cancel          = 1
    usage_error     = 2
    system_error    = 3
    internal_error  = 4
    OTHERS          = 5.
IF sy-subrc <> 0.
  MESSAGE ID sy-msgid TYPE sy-msgty NUMBER sy-msgno
```

```
            WITH sy-msgv1 sy-msgv2 sy-msgv3 sy-msgv4.
  ENDIF.
```

Listing 6.3 Initializing the Form Output

The `CHANGING` parameter of the `FP_JOB_OPEN` function module is typed as the `SFPOUTPUTPARAMS` structure. From the ABAP Editor, you can navigate to the structure's definition in the Dictionary by double-clicking on the structure name. Table 6.1 lists the most critical parameters of the `SFPOUTPUTPARAMS` structure.

Field Name	Meaning
NODIALOG	Suppresses the dialog box for the output
PREVIEW	Initially selects a print preview
GETPDF	Requests the return of a PDF document
GETPDL	Requests the return of a print data stream
GETXML	Requests the return of application data
CONNECTION	Connection to ADS
ADSTRLEVEL	Trace level of ADS
JOB_PROFILE	Name of a job profile
BUMODE	Bundling mode
ASSEMBLE	Assembles in one PDF document.
PARALLEL	Activates the parallelization of print jobs
DEST	Defines the output device (printer)
REQNEW	Creates a new spool request
REQIMM	Immediate output of the spool request
REQDEL	Deletes the spool request after the output has been implemented
REQFINAL	Completes the spool request
SPOOLID	Adds the output to this spool ID
COPIES	Number of copies
PDLTYPE	Printer language for the return of the print data stream

Table 6.1 Important Parameters of the SFPOUTPUTPARAMS Structure

Field Name	Meaning
XDCNAME	XDC file for the return of the print data stream
ARCMODE	Archiving mode
NOARMCH	No modification of the archiving mode
NOPREVIEW	No preview possible from the print dialog
NOPRINT	No print possible from the print dialog
NOARCHIVE	No archiving possible from the print dialog
XFP	Activates the XFP output
XFPTYPE	Type of the XFP output
XFPOUTDEV	Device of the XFP output

Table 6.1 Important Parameters of the SFPOUTPUTPARAMS Structure (Cont.)

You do not need these parameters for the initial tests. If you call the FP_JOB_OPEN function module with the initial parameter IE_OUTPUTPARAMS, a print dialog appears in which you can make all of the settings for a print output or preview.

Numerous fields are prepopulated with meaningful values. For example, if you do not specify any values, the connection with the name ADS is always used for the connection to ADS. You can override this connection using the CONNECTION parameter, for example, if you connect different systems and test them against different versions. If you do not specify a printer in the DEST parameter, the system tries to read the value from your user defaults.

REQNEW is an important parameter. If you do not set this parameter, the system tries to attach the new documents to an existing spool request during print output. You must decide for each application whether this behavior is desired. For this test program, the creation of a new spool request is supposed to be enforced. Therefore, the parameter was set to ABAP_TRUE.

Using the JOB_PROFILE parameter, you can add a job profile to Adobe Document Services to influence processing.

6.1.4 Calling the Generated Function Module

To add a form to the print job, proceed as follows:

1. Call the generated function module whose name has already been determined in Listing 6.2.

2. For the ABAP statement CALL FUNCTION, you must remember to enter the GV_FMNAME variable as the function module and not enclose it in single quotation marks; otherwise the system will try to call a function module with the name GV_FMNAME, which presumably does not exist.

   If you enter the GV_FMNAME variable directly, this is equivalent to a dynamic call. The decision about which function module is called is not made until runtime and depends on the value of GV_FMNAME. Due to this dynamic call, it cannot be checked whether all parameters are transferred correctly at development time.

3. But you can use a trick to program the correct call: Call the FP_FUNCTION_MODULE_NAME function module in the single test from Function Builder (Transaction SE37), enter Z_IFBA_BOOK_FORM_01 as the name of the form for the I_NAME parameter, and select EXECUTE (see Figure 6.2). If the function module has not been generated yet, this may take a few seconds. But the following call will be considerably faster.

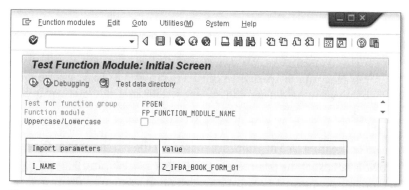

Figure 6.2 Determining the Generated Function Module

4. In the result screen (see Figure 6.3), you can see the assigned generated function module for the E_FUNCNAME parameter. In the present system, this is /1BCDWB/SM00000185; a different value might be displayed by your system, however.

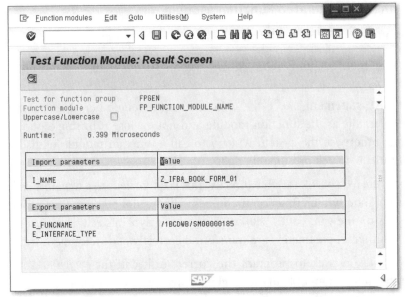

Figure 6.3 Name of the Generated Function Module

5. By entering the pattern for your function module, you can have your print program generate the call pattern. Thus, the available parameters of the interface are automatically inserted into the program call.

Calling the Function Module Dynamically

Always call the generated function module dynamically. However, you must remember to remove the name again and to specify the call via the GV_FMNAME field because the function module obtains another name in the target system after the form has been transported.

---

6. You can recognize the interface of your form based on the parameters of the call. You must provide values for the parameters CUSTOMER, BOOKINGS, and CONNECTIONS. The DATE parameter is optional because it was defined as such in the interface; the /1BCDWB/DOCPARAMS parameter requires the known structure, SFPDOCPARAMS, via which you can determine the form language, for example.

7. Listing 6.4 shows the completed call of the generated function module. Add the coding directly to the coding provided in Listing 6.3. You do not need the /1BCDWB/FORMOUTPUT return parameter with the FPFORMOUTPUT structure in this

program because it provides information about the number of generated pages. Keep the error handling as simple as possible.

```
* Set language and country.
gs_docparams-langu   = p_langu.
gs_docparams-country = p_ctry.
* Call generated function module (form).
CALL FUNCTION gv_fmname
  EXPORTING
    /1bcdwb/docparams        = gs_docparams
    customer                 = gs_customer
    bookings                 = gt_bookings
    connections              = gt_connections
    date                     = p_date
* IMPORTING
*   /1BCDWB/FORMOUTPUT       =
  EXCEPTIONS
    usage_error              = 1
    system_error             = 2
    internal_error           = 3
    OTHERS                   = 4.

IF sy-subrc <> 0.
  MESSAGE ID sy-msgid TYPE sy-msgty NUMBER sy-msgno
          WITH sy-msgv1 sy-msgv2 sy-msgv3 sy-msgv4.
ENDIF.
```

Listing 6.4 Calling the Generated Function Module

6.1.5 Closing the Print Job

The form output must be closed by all means—to do this, you are provided with the FP_JOB_CLOSE function module. Depending on the type of form output you select, this function module displays a print preview or, if applicable, concludes the spool request.

1. Add the call of the FP_JOB_CLOSE function module to your program and use the statement pattern again.

2. Listing 6.5 shows the finished coding, which you add directly to the coding from Listing 6.4.

```
* Close print job.
CALL FUNCTION 'FP_JOB_CLOSE'
```

```
*  IMPORTING
*     E_RESULT              =
   EXCEPTIONS
      usage_error        = 1
      system_error       = 2
      internal_error     = 3
      OTHERS             = 4.
IF sy-subrc <> 0.
   MESSAGE ID sy-msgid TYPE sy-msgty NUMBER sy-msgno
           WITH sy-msgv1 sy-msgv2 sy-msgv3 sy-msgv4.
ENDIF.
```

Listing 6.5 Closing the Print Job

3. The E_RESULT return parameter with the SFPJOBOUTPUT structure is not required in this program. However, you can use information from this structure, for example, the number of forms or the number of the generated spool request.

6.1.6 Form Output

The program is now complete and contains all of the necessary elements for the form output. You could invest more effort in error handling, but you already have all of the elements required to print a form.

Structure of a Print Program

A print program has the following basic structure:
- Data selection (see Listing 6.1)
- Determining the generated function module (see Listing 6.2)
- Opening the print jobs (see Listing 6.3)
- Calling the generated function module (see Listing 6.4)
- Closing the print job (see Listing 6.5)

Note that you can output multiple forms or the same form several times within a print job. To do so, simply call multiple generated function modules between the function modules, FP_JOB_OPEN and FP_JOB_CLOSE, for example, in a LOOP statement in ABAP. You can also call the FP_FUNCTION_MODULE_NAME function module several times for different forms. For performance reasons, you should generally implement the determination of a function module prior to opening the print job and not repeatedly within a loop.

1. After you have activated the program, you can start it. The selection screen (see Figure 6.1) appears, and the default values have already been preselected for the first call. The customer number is 1, the language of the form output is English, the country for formatting the date and number fields is United States, and the name defined for the form is Z_IFBA_BOOK_FORM_01. The date is optional and you can therefore call the form with or without the date.

2. If you select EXECUTE in the selection screen, a print dialog appears as illustrated in Figure 6.4.

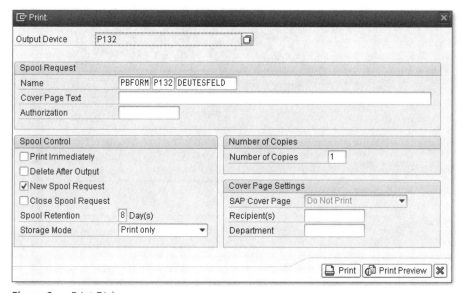

Figure 6.4 Print Dialog

3. If no output device is displayed, you can select it via the input help, if required. When calling the FP_JOB_OPEN function module, you can also provide GS_OUTPAR-DEST with the name of the printer or alternatively define an output device in your user defaults.

4. In the lower left-hand part of the dialog, you can see that the NEW SPOOL REQUEST checkbox is activated in the SPOOL CONTROL area. This was set in Listing 6.3.

5. Select the PRINT PREVIEW button in the dialog. Now all forms are processed internally; in this case, it is only one form. The ABAP Dictionary data, which you transferred in the interface, is converted into an XML data stream based on

the context definition, and ADS is called on the Java stack for creating a PDF document. Figure 6.5 shows the PDF document for your form.

Figure 6.5 Print Preview of a Form

6. If you receive an error message, you should proceed as described in Section 6.5, Error Analysis. If your system does not contain the data records for the flight-booking model, you can regenerate them via the ABAP program, SAPBC_DATA_GENERATOR (start using Transaction SE38). The program automatically creates the entries in the required database tables.

7. Adobe Reader is required for displaying the PDF document. Different display options are available; for example, you can save the document or print it locally.

However, the SERVER-BASED PRINT OUTPUT option is more important. You can find this button in the application toolbar. If you select this button, the document is sent via the SAP spool system to the printer that you defined in your program or in the print dialog.

8. Printing via the SAP spool system creates a spool request. However, you can also print without the print preview by clicking on the PRINT button in the print dialog (see Figure 6.4). Section 6.2, Spool System, provides detailed information on spool requests.

You can customize the behavior in many ways using the parameters listed in Table 6.1, which you transfer when calling the FP_JOB_OPEN function module. For example, if you set NODIALOG to 'X', then no print dialog is displayed. You can then use the PREVIEW parameter to define whether the preview is to be displayed ('X' means show preview). If you do not want to display a print dialog, you should implicitly define an output device in the DEST field; otherwise, the value is taken from your user defaults.

Output Device must be Known at Runtime

If you have not specified an output device in your user defaults and do not transfer an output device in the DEST parameter, the system asks for it. In this case, the print dialog opens, even though you suppressed it via the NODIALOG parameter. Provided that no connection exists to the front end, for example, because your program runs in background mode, a runtime error occurs because not enough information is available for further processing.

You can also use your print program for other forms, provided that they have the same interface. You can output the forms that you created in Chapter 4, Interface and Form Context, and Chapter 5, Creating Form Templates, without any changes to the print program.

Caution: Error in Generation After a Transport

In some cases it may be possible that data are formatted incorrectly in the form after it was transported to the target system. This particularly affects number fields where the reference field is not evaluated correctly. This error only occurs if the form needs to be generated anew (which is always the case after a transport), and the print program runs in update. In this case, the FP_FUNCTION_MODULE_NAME function module is called by another function module, which was started with the IN UPDATE TASK addition.

Not all data types are determined correctly due to this program error. This error occurs only in the ABAP Dictionary-based interface.

There are two ways to solve this problem:

▶ You have the option to manually regenerate the function module using the `FP_GENERATE_FUNCTION_MODULE` program (see SAP Note 1076159).

▶ You can integrate the correction of SAP Note 1518283 or import the relevant support package. As a result, the problem is avoided in future transports. Note that manual regeneration is required additionally for function modules that have already been generated.

6.2 Spool System

A spool request is necessary to print a completed form via the SAP system. A spool request can be sent to the printer either automatically or manually, and you can view the completed document once again on the system—before and after the output.

For a better understanding, create a spool request by calling the `Z_IFBA_BOOK_PRINT` program and clicking on the PRINT button in the print dialog (see Figure 6.4). Make sure that you specify a valid printer; the requirements that must be met to use an output device for SAP Interactive Forms by Adobe are detailed later on. The checkboxes, in particular PRINT IMMEDIATELY and NEW SPOOL REQUEST, should be selected as illustrated in Figure 6.4. As a result, a new spool request is created that is not printed immediately.

To display the spool requests, you are provided with different options for accessing the output controller. You can start Transaction SP01 and limit the selection by various criteria, for example, by the creator or the creation date of the spool request. You can also use Transaction SP02 as a direct access to your requests. You can access the list of your own spool request via the menu path SYSTEM • OWN SPOOL REQUESTS. As a result, a new mode is opened and a list of your requests is displayed in a new window. Figure 6.6 shows how this list may look.

There are different types of spool requests, which are identified by different icons. The requests that you created using SAP Interactive Forms by Adobe are identified by the Adobe Reader icon and PDF DOCUMENT is displayed as the tooltip.

Figure 6.6 List of Spool Requests

To create an output request from the spool request, activate the checkbox of the corresponding spool number on the left side of the column, and select the PRINT DIRECTLY button. The document is then sent to the output device.

You can display the spool requests from this transaction both before and after the output. To do so, click on the PDF DOCUMENT icon or select the spool request and choose the DISPLAY CONTENTS button. Since Release 7.01, the system then directly displays the first document of the spool request (in older versions, this was possible only via the interim step of a part list).

Activating the Part List As in Previous Versions

The part list shows the individual parts of a spool request. A new entry is made for each call of Adobe Document Services. The list of all entries is referred to as part list. If required, you can activate it across the system if you prefer this type of display—for instance, for error analysis in the test system. Refer to the description in SAP Note 1134660.

1. Start the RSPO0021 program.

2. Enter SHOW_PART_LIST as the spool option.

3. Select ACTIVATE or DEACTIVATE.

4. Press the [F8] key (Execute).

You can print multiple documents in one spool request either by calling multiple generated function modules between the two function modules, FP_JOB_OPEN and FP_JOB_CLOSE, or by not setting the REQNEW parameter when calling FP_JOB_OPEN; the system then tries to attach the document to an existing spool request.

Use the arrow buttons to navigate between the individual documents (see Figure 6.7).

Figure 6.7   Navigation Buttons in a Larger Spool Request

For more information on spool requests and output requests, call the application help via Transaction SP01. To do so, follow the menu path HELP • APPLICATION HELP.

6.3   Device Types for the Output

All printers that are provided for the output via the SAP system are managed through the spool administration, which is available via Transaction SPAD. An output device has different settings. The spool administration is not an integral part of this book; however, it is provides some specifics for the output via the SAP Interactive Forms by Adobe solution concerning output devices.

Basically, each output device is assigned to a device type. These device types, however, are required for other form solutions, such as SAPscript or SAP Smart Forms. For printing via ADS, they are not used directly because the formatting is done on the Java stack. For more information on device types, refer to the online documentation of Transaction SPAD, which you can reach by starting Transaction SPAD and following the HELP • APPLICATION HELP menu path.

However, ADS requires information about the printer for which formatting is requested. For this reason, the spool administration was extended by a mapping between the SAP device types and the printer information for ADS. The benefit here is that the information does not have to be defined for each output device—only for the corresponding device types.

Device Types for Printing Using ADS

You can assign the following device types to output devices:

- PostScript
- PCL
- ZPL (for Zebra label printers)
- IPL (Intermec Printer Language)
- TPCL (Toshiba)
- DPL (DATAMAX)
- PDF (for printers that understand PDF directly)

You need a reference to this information for each device type you assigned to your output devices so that you can use the devices for print output via ADS. SAP provides an assignment for some device types, which you can display and enhance using the RSPO0022 program.

1. Start the RSPO0022 program using Transaction SE38 and click on the DISPLAY XDC ENTRIES button in the initial screen. The result should appear as in Figure 6.8.

Figure 6.8 Assigning Device Types

2. You can see, for example, that the POST2 device type was mapped to the Post-Script printer language (*.ps*). However, this information is not always sufficient for formatting because many different PostScript printers exist, each providing different options. These differences are of particular concern regarding paper trays or additional fonts, which are provided via enhancements.

For this reason, you must specify an assignment to an XML Device Configuration (XDC) file. These files comprise device descriptions, some of which have already been delivered.

3. The processing of the XDC files is done using the XDC Editor. You can find information on the installation of the XDC Editor in Section 3.6.5, Installing and Using the XDC Editor.

If you created new XDC files, you must assign them to an SAP device type, which is done using the RSPO0022 program.

1. In the initial screen, select CREATE/CHANGE XDC ENTRY and specify a device type and print settings.

2. A dialog box opens in which you select your XDC file. After confirming your selection, the system assigns the SAP device type and the XDC file (see Figure 6.9).

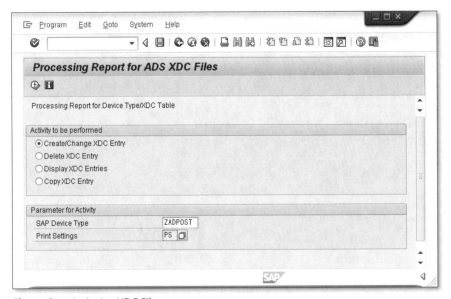

Figure 6.9 Assigning XDC Files

If you receive an error message stating "Cannot find PDL type for output device XYZ" (FPRUNX 113), this may be because no XDC file has been assigned to the corresponding device type. For more information, see SAP Note 685571.

6.4 Special Output Scenarios

Additional options for output processing exist. So far, you have learned that a document can be displayed as a PDF in a preview or that a spool request can be created directly. In addition, you have many more options to influence document creation and process completed documents yourself. The following descriptions provide you with some valuable information.

6.4.1 Archiving

Frequently, statutory requirements necessitate the optical archiving of business documents. You can do this with SAP ArchiveLink interface, which enables integration with the archiving solutions.

To archive a completed PDF document, you only have to set the archiving mode accordingly using the `ARCMODE` parameter when calling the `FP_JOB_OPEN` function module. The following values exist (see Table 6.2):

ARCMODE Value	Meaning
1 or SPACE	Print only
2	Archive only
3	Print and archive

Table 6.2 Archiving Options

If you set this value to 1 or enter no value at all in the program, only a print output is generated; if you set it to 2, the document is transferred to the archive and no print output is created. The value 3 means both—creating a print output and archiving the PDF document.

A PDF document requires an index so that it can be stored in the archive. This index cannot be transferred when the `FP_JOB_OPEN` function module is called because a print job can contain multiple forms. Therefore, you must transfer such an index for each call of the generated function module.

The index is part of the /1BCDWB/DOCPARAMS parameter. The assigned structure, SFPDOCPARAMS, contains a DARATAB table of the TFPDARA type and is a table that includes archive indexes. According to this, multiple archive indexes can be transferred with each document, but usually only one entry is used. The row type of the table is TOA_DARA. At runtime, the completed PDF document is transferred to SAP ArchiveLink together with the archiving information. For more information on SAP ArchiveLink, refer to the online documentation (*http://help.sap.com/saphelp_nw70/helpdata/EN/5e/566039b85f9443e10000000a114084/frameset.htm*).

If you set the STORAGE MODE in the print dialog (see Figure 6.4), archiving is possible only when the application program transfers the indexes for the documents. If you want to prevent the user from changing the storage mode, you must set the NOARMCH parameter to 'X' when calling the FP_JOB_OPEN function module. This disables the selection list in the print dialog.

6.4.2 Returning Documents

Another interesting option is to return the created document to the application. Thus, the calling program assumes full control of further distribution—for example, no print preview is displayed or no print output is triggered. The application program receives the document in formatted form and can, for example, send it via email, store it in a repository, or provide it via a Web service.

The following sections briefly describe how you can request a PDF document and save it locally. To do this, you will copy and change the Z_IFBA_BOOK_PRINT program.

1. Copy the Z_IFBA_BOOK_PRINT program and rename the copy as Z_IFBA_BOOK_DOWNLOAD. Listing 6.6 shows the completed program for requesting the PDF and saving it locally.

```
PROGRAM z_ifba_book_download.
TYPE-POOLS: abap.
INCLUDE fp_utilities.
PARAMETER: p_custom TYPE s_customer    DEFAULT 1,
           p_form    TYPE fpwbformname
                     DEFAULT 'Z_IFBA_BOOK_FORM_01',
           p_langu   TYPE spras         DEFAULT 'D',
           p_ctry    TYPE land1         DEFAULT 'DE',
           p_date    TYPE sydatum,
           p_pdf     TYPE localfile OBLIGATORY.
DATA: gs_customer    TYPE          scustom,
```

```
      gt_bookings      TYPE          ty_bookings,
      gt_connections   TYPE          ty_connections,
      gs_outputpar     TYPE          sfpoutputparams,
      gv_fmname        TYPE          rs38l_fnam,
      gx_exc_api       TYPE REF TO   cx_fp_api,
      gv_err_string    TYPE          string,
      gs_docparams     TYPE          sfpdocparams,
      gs_formoutput    TYPE          fpformoutput.
AT SELECTION-SCREEN ON VALUE-REQUEST FOR p_pdf.
  PERFORM value_help_for_output_file USING 'PDF'
                                     CHANGING p_pdf.
START-OF-SELECTION.
* Select data.
  SELECT SINGLE * FROM scustom INTO gs_customer
               WHERE id = p_custom.
  IF sy-subrc <> 0.
*    Error handling. No data for customer found.
    EXIT.
  ENDIF.
  SELECT * FROM sbook INTO TABLE gt_bookings
          WHERE customid = p_custom
          ORDER BY PRIMARY KEY.
  IF sy-subrc <> 0.
*    Error handling. No data for booking found.
    EXIT.
  ENDIF.
  SELECT * FROM spfli INTO TABLE gt_connections
          FOR ALL ENTRIES IN gt_bookings
          WHERE carrid = gt_bookings-carrid
            AND connid = gt_bookings-connid
          ORDER BY PRIMARY KEY.
  IF sy-subrc <> 0.
*    Error handling. No flight connection information found.
    EXIT.
  ENDIF.
* Retrieve name of generated function module.
  TRY.
      CALL FUNCTION 'FP_FUNCTION_MODULE_NAME'
        EXPORTING
          i_name    = p_form
        IMPORTING
          e_funcname = gv_fmname.
    CATCH cx_fp_api_repository
```

```
            cx_fp_api_usage
            cx_fp_api_internal INTO gx_exc_api.
        gv_err_string = gx_exc_api->get_text( ).
        MESSAGE  gv_err_string TYPE 'E'.
    ENDTRY.
* Request PDF document.
  gs_outputpar-nodialog = abap_true.
  gs_outputpar-getpdf   = abap_true.
  CALL FUNCTION 'FP_JOB_OPEN'
    CHANGING
      ie_outputparams = gs_outputpar
    EXCEPTIONS
      cancel          = 1
      usage_error     = 2
      system_error    = 3
      internal_error  = 4
      OTHERS          = 5.
  IF sy-subrc <> 0.
    MESSAGE ID sy-msgid TYPE sy-msgty NUMBER sy-msgno
            WITH sy-msgv1 sy-msgv2 sy-msgv3 sy-msgv4.
  ENDIF.
* Set language and country.
  gs_docparams-langu   = p_langu.
  gs_docparams-country = p_ctry.
* Call generated function module (form).
  CALL FUNCTION gv_fmname
    EXPORTING
      /1bcdwb/docparams  = gs_docparams
      customer           = gs_customer
      bookings           = gt_bookings
      connections        = gt_connections
      date               = p_date
    IMPORTING
      /1bcdwb/formoutput = gs_formoutput "Returns PDF!
    EXCEPTIONS
      usage_error        = 1
      system_error       = 2
      internal_error     = 3
      OTHERS             = 4.
  IF sy-subrc <> 0.
    MESSAGE ID sy-msgid TYPE sy-msgty NUMBER sy-msgno
            WITH sy-msgv1 sy-msgv2 sy-msgv3 sy-msgv4.
  ENDIF.
```

```
* Close print job.
  CALL FUNCTION 'FP_JOB_CLOSE'
* IMPORTING
*   E_RESULT              =
    EXCEPTIONS
      usage_error         = 1
      system_error        = 2
      internal_error      = 3
      OTHERS              = 4.
  IF sy-subrc <> 0.
    MESSAGE ID sy-msgid TYPE sy-msgty NUMBER sy-msgno
            WITH sy-msgv1 sy-msgv2 sy-msgv3 sy-msgv4.
  ENDIF.
* Save PDF document.
  PERFORM download_file USING gs_formoutput-pdf p_pdf.
```

Listing 6.6 Requesting a PDF Document

2. The basic difference is the call to the FP_JOB_OPEN function module; by setting the NODIALOG parameter, you suppress the print dialog. To notify the system that you want to receive a PDF, you must set the GETPDF parameter to 'X'. Now, when the generated function module is called, the document in the PDF field of the /1BCDWB/FORMOUTPUT import parameter is returned. At the end of the program, save this document into the local file system.

3. For the input help and for saving, access the FP_UTILITIES include, which is used in many test programs for the form processing topic and provides useful routines, such as, uploading and downloading files.

4. When you start the program and enter a local file under FILE NAME in the selection screen, a PDF document is created and saved on your PC.

5. To create an interactive PDF document, you must set the FILLABLE field in the GS_DOCPARAMS parameter when calling the generated function module. Once you have done this, the fields of the PDF document become ready for input.

6. You can also request the document in another printer language by setting the GETPDL parameter. To do this, you must specify which printer language is to be created and which XDC files are to be used.

   You specify the printer language in the PDLTYPE field and the XDC file in the XDCNAME field, for example, "ps_plain.xdc." The completed print data stream is returned in the /1BCDWB/FORMOUTPUT-PDL field after the generated function module has been called. You can also request both formats in one call.

6.5 Error Analysis

Errors can occur in the development phase of a form. Basically, there are two types of errors: cancellations that prevent a form output or a generated document that is not structured as desired.

Because you work in a complex system landscape, it is important to have good error-analysis tools at hand. The following sections present a few simple examples of the importance of error-handling tools.

6.5.1 Trace and PDF with Additional Information

To gather additional information during document generation, ADS provides options to generate a trace or to enrich a PDF document with additional information. The trace contains detailed information about the process that is rather technical, but also enables you to draw conclusions about the error cause. The trace can be returned to the calling application or saved locally on your PC.

A PDF document can include file attachments that you can display and save in Adobe Reader. The PDF becomes a data container that contains all documents important for the output and analysis. Transaction SFP provides you with some setting options to create a PDF with additional information. For more information on this topic, refer to SAP Note 944221.

1. Start Transaction SFP and follow the UTILITIES • SETTINGS menu path. A dialog box as illustrated in Figure 6.10 appears.

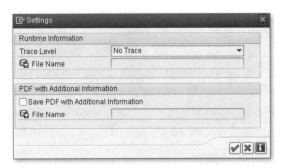

Figure 6.10 Settings for Error Analysis

2. In the upper half of the screen, you can request a trace, which you can store on your local PC. Different trace levels with increasing levels of detail are available.

Select a level other than No Trace and the input field of the file name becomes ready for input. Enter a name for a text file to save the trace.

3. The most interesting option for error analysis is the aforementioned PDF with additional information. This PDF is created by ADS if you set the trace level to the highest value, Very detailed trace, in the selection list.

Note on the Settings Made

The settings are maintained until you change them again or log off from the system. They also apply to any other session of your logon.

4. Now start the Z_IFBA_BOOK_PRINT print program and create a print preview. The PDF looks as usual but now contains different file attachments (see Figure 6.11). You can display them by clicking on the Paper Clip icon on the left.

Figure 6.11 PDF with Additional Information

Meaning of the File Attachments

Some file attachments listed are useful for further error analysis. A lot of the information is relevant only for the support team, so you do not have to know it in detail. Nevertheless, you should know the meaning of the individual files and which conclusions you can draw.

► **.xdc**
Files with the extension *.xdc* are files for printer configuration, which were discussed in Section 6.3, Device Types for the Output. Because a print preview has been requested in this example, a file for both the PDF (*adobepdf.xdc*) and for the print output (*hppcl5e.xdc*) are attached. Your system may also contain another XDC file depending on the printer selection.

Here, you can see whether the desired XDC file has been used at all. If, for example, you created your own XDC file, the list indicates whether ADS has used it for form creation. Basically, you can open all files using Adobe Reader or save them locally to check whether the content of the XDC file meets your expectations.

If problems occur for the print output, you should assign the original XDC file to the device type. As a result, however, your additionally defined fonts or paper trays are not available.

► **xfa.xci**
The *xfa.xci* file contains some configurations. If you have not changed the file or have not created a *custom_xfa.xci* file with your own configuration, you do not have to consider it.

► **trace.txt**
The *trace.txt* file contains the trace with the maximum level of detail. Here, you can find information about the operating system and the version of ADS that is particularly important for the support team. Warning or possible errors that occur during document creation and information about the runtime duration can be found in this file.

► **error.pdf**
Another file existing here is called *error.pdf* and includes warnings and errors in readable form.

► **XFD.xml**
The file attachment with the name *XFD.xml* contains application data that are transferred to ADS in XML format. If values are not displayed or displayed

incorrectly in your form, you can check this file to determine whether the values are still correct here. The schema of the XML data stream corresponds to the context definition of your form. You can also use this file to create a preview of the form in Adobe LiveCycle Designer.

▶ **Z_IFBA_BOOK_FORM_01.XDP — form template**
The list of file attachments also contains the form template, which was used for document creation — in this example, *Z_IFBA_BOOK_FORM_01.XDP*. Here, you can see whether the correct form has been used.

▶ **pdfDocument.xml**
The *pdfDocument.xml* file contains the work instructions for ADS. You do not have to know the structure; nevertheless, the file comprises some information that can be useful for quick error analysis. Here, for example, is transferred the locale for which the document is to be formatted. It consists of the language and the country; for the present example, it is en_US.

If problems occur with the number formats or the date display in the completed document, you should check here to see whether the correct locale has been used and examine the call in the print program. Language and country are transferred when calling the generated function module.

Saving the PDF Document with Additional Information

If a problem occurs, you should always first try to generate a PDF with additional information. This allows for initial conclusions with regard to the error cause.

Such a PDF can be displayed only if you implement a print preview. In case of a print output without a PDF, it is useful to save the PDF after generation:

1. To do this, you should activate the SAVE PDF WITH ADDITIONAL INFORMATION checkbox in the lower part of the dialog box illustrated in Figure 6.10 and enter a file name for the PDF, for example, *C:\TEMP\INFO.PDF*. Make sure that the directory exists and use the input help, if required.

2. Press the ENTER key to close the window.

3. If you now create a print request without preview, you can find the PDF with additional information in the specified location.

Perhaps you noticed in the dialog box shown in Figure 6.10 that the input field for the file name of the PDF document is always ready for input. The PDF with additional information is also created if a serious error occurs in the processing done by ADS.

6.5.2 Activating and Retrieving the Trace in the Print Program

You can activate and save or display the trace in the print program. To activate the trace, you must call the FP_JOB_OPEN function module, where you can find the ADSTRLEVEL field in the IE_OUTPUTPARAMS parameter. The values ranging from 00 to 04 correspond to the values of the dialog illustrated in Figure 6.10, where 00 is no trace and 04 means maximum level of detail.

The trace is provided in the calling application program and you can retrieve it after the call of the generated function module by calling the FP_GET_LAST_ADS_TRACE function module. This function module contains only E_ADSTRACE as a parameter and includes the trace of the last call of ADS.

6.5.3 More Detailed Error Messages

A T100 error message is created if a runtime error occurs. This error message is output dynamically in the programs in ABAP via the MESSAGE statement. For example, the errors can be triggered by the form processing, the spool interface, or ADS.

If the error message is triggered by ADS, its text is usually longer than can be output in the message, and some information may not be displayed. This error text is available in the trace or in the PDF with additional information; you can also query the error text in the program. To do this, call the FP_GET_LAST_ADS_ERRSTR function module. If it provides a result, you can write the error text to the application log or display it to the user.

6.5.4 ICF Recorder

You can analyze errors relatively easily using the procedure described in Section 6.5.1, Trace and PDF with Additional Information. However, if an error occurs during background processing, you need other options to root out the problem. Even if the error occurs only sporadically, for example, within a billing run, you should log the calls to ADS.

To do this, use the Internet Communication Framework (ICF) Recorder. The ICF Recorder can log both inbound and outbound requests. In this case, the ABAP stack of SAP NetWeaver calls ADS on a Java stack. Hence, the ABAP system acts as a client. Refer to SAP Note 724804 to obtain a detailed description on the usage options of the ICF Recorder.

The following sections describe how you can record outbound requests using the ICF Recorder.

1. To start the ICF Recorder, use Transaction SICF and select the F8 key or the EXECUTE button in the initial screen, MAINTAIN SERVICES.

2. In the next screen, follow the menu path CLIENT • RECORDER • ACTIVATE RECORD-ING. Now, you can log outbound requests.

   You can find a similar path under EDIT • RECORDER • ACTIVATE RECORDING, which is intended for inbound requests, however. So, you must make sure to activate the correct recorder.

3. Enter "/adobedocumentservices/config" in the CLIENT URL PATH field as illustrated in Figure 6.12.

Figure 6.12 Settings for the ICF Recorder

4. Select the REQUEST + RESPONSE radio button to ensure that both the outbound request and the ADS response are logged.

5. Click on the ACTIVATE button. The status bar should then display a message stating that the recording has been activated.

6. You can now start the Z_IFBA_BOOK_PRINT print program and create a print output as described in Section 6.1.6, Form Output.

7. You can find the recordings of the ICF Recorder via the menu path CLIENT • RECORDER • DISPLAY RECORDING. In the following dialog box (see Figure 6.13), enter "/adobedocumentservices/config" as the REQUEST PATH. Click on the EXECUTE button.

Figure 6.13   Display Options for the Recordings

8. You can see a list of recordings for the outbound requests (see Figure 6.14), including the date, time, and the user who called ADS.

ICF Recordings

⇐ HTTP Service Hierarchy   ⇒ External aliases

Client Requests	Request Path	Stat	Date	Time	User Name	Status	Message ID	Session (Se
▸ ☑ /adobedocumentservices/config	/adobedocumentservices/config	200 C	22.11.2008	14:28:41	DEUTESFELD		0A421591697949280909049900000000	1
	/adobedocumentservices/config	200 C	22.11.2008	14:28:48	DEUTESFELD		0A42159169794928091004 9B00000000	1
	/adobedocumentservices/config	200 C	22.11.2008	14:28:57	DEUTESFELD		0A421591697949280919049D00000000	1
	/adobedocumentservices/config		22.11.2008	14:29:05	DEUTESFELD		0A421591697949280921049F00000000	1
	/adobedocumentservices/config	200 C	22.11.2008	14:28:09	DEUTESFELD		0A4215916B91492808E91D8300000000	2
	/adobedocumentservices/config	200 C	22.11.2008	14:28:06	DEUTESFELD		0A4215916B91492808E61D8000000000	3
	/adobedocumentservices/config	200 C	22.11.2008	14:28:04	DEUTESFELD		0A4215916B91492808E41D7D0000000C	4
	/adobedocumentservices/config	200 C	22.11.2008	14:28:01	DEUTESFELD		0A4215916B91492808E11D7A00000000	5
	/adobedocumentservices/config	200 C	22.11.2008	14:27:58	DEUTESFELD		0A4215916B91492808DE1D770000000C	6
	/adobedocumentservices/config	200 C	22.11.2008	14:27:54	DEUTESFELD		0A4215916B91492808DA1D740000000C	7

Figure 6.14   List of ICF Recordings

9. The STATUS of the recording is an important field. In Figure 6.14, the status is OK (HTTP Code 200). An error code is displayed here if a problem occurs with the connection to ADS.

However, the OK status does not indicate whether a request was processed successfully for a document processing. It states only that the communication between the ABAP and the Java stack worked properly from a technical point of view. This is a necessary prerequisite for a successful processing. Whether an individual document has been formatted correctly can be determined only in the response of the respective request.

The following sections detail how you can display recorded data and which information can be obtained.

1. To display a request, highlight it and select the DISPLAY option.

2. Select REQUEST in the menu that opens. The request that was used to call ADS is then displayed in the lower part of the screen.

"PDF Document"

In this context, PDFDOCUMENT is of some importance. This is a file attachment from a PDF with additional information; that is, it includes work instructions for ADS.

Due to transfer reasons, the XML is Base64-coded, which you can reconvert to the original XML using a Base64 decoder. These steps are all very technical, but in extreme cases this procedure can be useful or may even be the only option for analyzing the error.

---

3. Whether additional sections such as XFD exist depends on the respective call. The form runtime environment decides whether the data is transferred as part of the Web service communication or is provided using a reference.

4. Now you can display the response. To do this, select the DISPLAY button and then RESPONSE for the highlighted request.

   Depending on the scenario, one or more larger Base64-coded sections, such as PDLOut or PDFOut, may be displayed in the response, which contains the print output or the PDF in Base64-coded form. You can copy the sections and reconvert them to their original format to display the files.

5. If you scroll farther down, you can see multiple sections that are marked with RpString (see Figure 6.15). The most important entry is RpString with the name Results. It provides information about whether ADS was able to correctly process the request. In this case, the value is OK.

   If an error occurs, however, an error text is displayed here instead. Incidentally, this is the same error text that you determined using the FP_GET_LAST_ADS_ERRSTR function module (see Section 6.5.3, More Detailed Error Messages) or contained in the error message of the ABAP message.

6. The RenderPageCount entry specifies the number of created pages, while VersionInfo indicates the version of ADS. TraceString includes more or less detailed information depending on the trace level, which is particularly important in case of an error.

Figure 6.15 Response of ADS

Deactivating the ICF Recorder

After the analysis, remember to switch off the ICF Recorder again; otherwise, the requests continue to be recorded, and the system's performance decreases.

---

7. Exit the screen, including the list of recordings, and switch off the ICF Recorder via the menu path CLIENT • RECORDER • DEACTIVATE RECORDER. Again, enter "/adobedocumentservices/config" as the client URL path and select DEACTIVATE.

8. A dialog box opens in which usually only one entry is displayed. You can see multiple entries here if other users have activated the ICF Recorder as well.

9. Select your entry and choose DEACTIVATE. You can still display the recordings later on.

6.6   Performance Optimization Through Bundling

Performance is frequently a critical topic for the output of documents. The processing speed is particularly important for a high volume of documents, such as for mass printing.

Most of the performance-critical SAP print programs run in the ABAP stack; therefore, in mass printing, a high volume of data must be transferred to the Java stack, where the documents are formatted by ADS. The finished documents (PDF or print formats) must then be sent to the ABAP stack again because the SAP spool system implements the output here.

Therefore, performance is always a combination of the times for rendering the form and the times for the communication between the systems. The time required for the data transfer becomes particularly noticeable if you process multiple small documents. This is the case in many mass printing scenarios—many documents are generated that only comprise one or two pages. Depending on the complexity of the documents, the system conditions, and the network speed, it may be possible that the communication itself takes longer than the actual formatting of the documents.

6.6.1   Bundling Forms

This section describes the bundling of form calls. As of Release 7.0 EHP2 (ABAP) and 7.2 (Java), you have the additional option of print job parallelization, which is described in Section 6.7, Parallelization of Print Jobs.

You have the option to bundle multiple calls to ADS and transfer them collectively. This reduces the initial communication overhead and the initialization time. Bundling means that you collect the data of multiple forms in the form runtime environment and call ADS when a specific data volume has been reached. The data are collected in such a way that the system can assign it to the individual forms. A combination of different forms is also supported.

Therefore, if you alternately output order confirmation, delivery note, and invoice in any sequence, the system ensures the correct assignment. The number of forms that are bundled in one call is dynamic and depends on the number of pages of the individual forms. The system tries to obtain an optimal bundle volume with regard to performance. Therefore, at the beginning of a print job, there is a learning phase during which statistics are gathered about the forms. The optimal volume can be determined after some calls have been made.

The benefit of bundling is that you need to make hardly any settings in your print programs:

► The most critical aspect is that the system requirements are met for bundling. Section 3.3.2, Destination and ICF Service, discussed this topic.

► Another important aspect is the method of how the print program calls forms. Remember that a print job is enclosed within the function modules FP_JOB_OPEN and FP_JOB_CLOSE. You can bundle only forms that are called within *one* such enclosure. However, bundling is not possible if a program only outputs one form per job, concludes the job, and reopens for the next form.

Therefore, you must ensure that the loop is within the function modules, FP_JOB_OPEN and FP_JOB_CLOSE, and that you do not reopen the spool job for each form.

The system provides bundling support for the following scenarios:

► Print output

► Archiving

► Print output and archiving

► PDF return

For returning the PDF, you must make some changes to the program, which are discussed later on. If you request the PDF using the GETPDF parameter, bundling is not implemented initially. Bundling switches off automatically when the print data stream is requested using the GETPDL parameter.

The print output and archiving scenarios and their combination are the most important ones for a mass output of documents. When you implement a print preview, the system automatically deactivates bundling. Bundling does not take place if you request an interactive PDF document.

6.6.2 Activating Bundling

If you activate the bundling in the FPCONNECT table as described in Chapter 3, you do not have to attend to the bundling any longer. Only in some cases do you have to consider certain aspects.

You can also explicitly activate and deactivate bundling in every print program. For this reason, the BUMODE field is available in the IE_OUTPUTPARAMS parameter when the FP_JOB_OPEN function module is called.

Table 6.3 shows the possible values for the BUMODE parameter.

Value	Meaning
space	Setting is taken from the FPCONNECT table
M	Bundling
–	No bundling
X	Obsolete, do not use

Table 6.3 Possible Values of the BUMODE Parameter

If you do not specify a value, the setting in the FPCONNECT table (MBATCHING field) decides whether bundling is implemented or not. If you enter 'M' in the BUMODE field, this enables the bundling for the print program to be independent of the setting in the FPCONNECT table. However, you can also deactivate the bundling for individual print programs by entering '–' in the BUMODE field during the call.

6.6.3 Deactivating Bundling

Bundling is automatically deactivated for those scenarios for which bundling is not supported, for example, the print preview. But it may still be necessary to deactivate bundling. This may be due to the delayed processing of documents.

Normally, a call of the generated function module also entails the synchronous call to ADS. As a result, the document is created and the application receives some information. For example, the application learns whether the form could be created successfully and how many pages it contains. This would not be possible with bundling because a call of the generated function module saves the data only internally, and the call to ADS is carried out only when another generated function module is called later on. This generated function module can even stand for another form type.

If the call of the generated function module was successful for the bundling, this means only that the call was marked for implementation. However, if an exception occurs, the entire processing of the last bundle was unsuccessful.

The number of return pages is a good orientation point.

- If the number of pages is zero, the form was marked for bundling.
- If the number of pages is returned after the call of a generated function module, then the entire bundle was created successfully and the number of pages indicates the total of all documents in the bundle.

It is not possible to determine the number of pages of individual documents contained in the bundle. However, the overall number of pages of all documents is available and is provided in the spool system later on.

The fact that you don't get a feedback for each document sets some criteria for when you should deactivate the bundling in a print program:

- If the print program requires the number of pages of every document, you must not bundle the forms.
- If the processing status of the document must be recorded in real time, for example, for updates, bundling should be deactivated.
- If you have to assign occurring errors to exactly one document, it is recommended that you use individual processing.

Bundling is particularly effective in improving performance for the generation of multiple small documents. For large documents, the benefits of bundling can hardly be noticed, as fewer forms are bundled in a call. Beyond a specific size, the forms are automatically processed in single calls. This is automatically controlled by the form runtime environment.

6.6.4 Bundling Example

SAP provides the `FP_CHECK_BATCH_SPOOL_OUTPUT` sample program as an example for bundling and for testing purposes. The structure of the program is very similar to the `Z_IFBA_BOOK_PRINT` program and is also based on the flight data model.

When you look at the program in Transaction SE38, you can determine that two different forms are used for output: Initially, you specify the generated function modules for the forms: `FP_TEST_03_TABLE` and `FP_TEST_02` (see Listing 6.7).

```
CALL FUNCTION 'FP_FUNCTION_MODULE_NAME'
  EXPORTING
    i_name      = 'FP_TEST_03_TABLE'
  IMPORTING
```

```
   e_funcname = fm_name_1.
CALL FUNCTION 'FP_FUNCTION_MODULE_NAME'
  EXPORTING
    i_name      = 'FP_TEST_02'
  IMPORTING
    e_funcname = fm_name_2.
```
Listing 6.7 Using Two Forms in the Print Job

The lines provided in Listing 6.8 open a new spool job, deactivate the immediate output (you do not want to send several thousands of pages directly to the printer), disable the print preview, and activate the bundling. If you set the MBATCHING field of the FPCONNECT table to 'X' you do not require this line.

```
* Set output parameters and open spool job
  fp_outputparams-reqnew     = 'X'.
  fp_outputparams-reqimm     = ' '.
  fp_outputparams-nopreview  = 'X'.
  fp_outputparams-connection = p_conn.
  fp_outputparams-bumode     = 'M'.
```
Listing 6.8 Setting the Parameters for Bundling

Prior to calling the first generated function module, you can see that the program switches between two different form languages (see Listing 6.9). Section 6.8, Translating Forms, describes how you can provide forms in multiple languages.

```
* change language and country
  help = index MOD 2.
  IF help = 0.
    fp_docparams-langu   = 'D'.
    fp_docparams-country = 'DE'.
  ELSE.
    fp_docparams-langu   = 'E'.
    fp_docparams-country = 'US'.
  ENDIF.
```
Listing 6.9 Switching between Two Form Languages

The FP_TEST_00 form is inserted at regular intervals at the end of the loop (see Listing 6.10).

```
help = index MOD 7.
IF help = 0.
  CALL FUNCTION fm_name_2
    EXPORTING
      /1bcdwb/docparams  = fp_docparams
      mychar             = sy-uname
      mydate             = sy-datum
      mytime             = sy-uzeit
      mynum              = '042'
      myint              = index.
ENDIF.
```
Listing 6.10 Adding a Second Form to the Job

1. Now start the program. In the selection screen, you can specify a range of customer numbers. If you select a larger interval here, for example, 1 to 100 or 1,000, a spool request with many documents is created.

2. If an error occurs during output, you can assume that your system is not configured for bundling. The necessary configuration steps are detailed in Chapter 3, Installation in Configuration.

3. Display your spool requests when the program is complete. To do so, call Transaction SP02 or select SYSTEM • OWN SPOOL REQUESTS from the menu as described in Section 6.2.

4. If you have activated the display of the part list in your system, the system shows a list and not the PDF documents directly (Figure 6.16 shows an example). Each part can contain multiple documents. The page count starts with a low value and gradually increases with every part number. This is the aforementioned learning phase of the system, in which it tries to specify the optimal bundle volume for the forms involved. In this case, the optimum of approximately 200 pages per bundle was reached after some 20 calls (one call corresponds to one part).

5. You can display the individual documents by selecting a part and choosing the DISPLAY CONTENTS button. This may take some time if you carry out this process for a part for the first time because the PDF is created for display upon request. If your system does not display any part list and the PDF documents are displayed directly, you can conveniently navigate through the PDF documents (see Figure 6.7).

Part List of PDF Spool Request   26.229

Part No.	Date	Time	Pages	From Page	To Page
1	22.11.2008	14:33:18	2	1	2
2	22.11.2008	14:33:22	5	3	7
3	22.11.2008	14:33:26	7	8	14
4	22.11.2008	14:33:26	2	15	16
5	22.11.2008	14:33:27	1	17	17
6	22.11.2008	14:33:27	2	18	19
7	22.11.2008	14:33:31	11	20	30
8	22.11.2008	14:33:36	15	31	45
9	22.11.2008	14:33:41	19	46	64
10	22.11.2008	14:33:45	17	65	81
11	22.11.2008	14:33:50	23	82	104
12	22.11.2008	14:33:56	31	105	135
13	22.11.2008	14:34:02	42	136	177
14	22.11.2008	14:34:08	40	178	217
15	22.11.2008	14:34:15	47	218	264
16	22.11.2008	14:34:23	60	265	324
17	22.11.2008	14:34:30	53	325	377
18	22.11.2008	14:34:38	80	378	457
19	22.11.2008	14:34:46	65	458	522
20	22.11.2008	14:34:55	98	523	620
21	22.11.2008	14:35:07	100	621	720
22	22.11.2008	14:35:18	125	721	845
23	22.11.2008	14:35:30	139	846	984
24	22.11.2008	14:35:44	161	985	1.145
25	22.11.2008	14:35:59	195	1.146	1.340
26	22.11.2008	14:36:15	177	1.341	1.517
27	22.11.2008	14:36:31	196	1.518	1.713
28	22.11.2008	14:36:47	199	1.714	1.912
29	22.11.2008	14:37:03	201	1.913	2.113
30	22.11.2008	14:37:13	92	2.114	2.205

Figure 6.16 Part List with Activated Bundling

6. If you want to experiment with the bundling, you can enhance your program with a DO loop and output the same form repeatedly. Alternatively, you can enhance the selection conditions and output data for multiple customers. You can also provide the bundling mode as a selection parameter and thus run the program with and without bundling. Here, you should consider the runtimes for both execution variants.

6.6.5   Bundling the PDF Return

The option to obtain a completed PDF document after the call of the generated function module has already been detailed in Section 6.4.2, Returning Documents. Here, the GETPDF parameter was simply set to 'X' during the call of the FP_JOB_OPEN function module. Then the PDF was available after the call of the generated function module.

This is not possible for activated bundling because not every call of the generated function module results in a call to ADS. When a bundle is completed, it contains the output of multiple forms. Because such a bundle cannot be returned by the generated function module, a program that wants to activate the bundling for the PDF return must look different.

SAP delivers the FP_CHECK_BATCH_PDF_RETURN sample program for bundling the PDF return. You must explicitly activate this special bundling variant in the program by setting the GETPDF parameter to 'M'. You then must receive a table of PDF documents after each call of the generated function module. In most calls, this table is empty, but as soon as a bundle is completed, the table contains all PDF documents of the bundle. The name of the function module you must use to receive the table of PDF documents is FP_GET_PDF_TABLE.

> **The Last Bundle Is Available Only at a Later Stage**
>
> Because a bundle can be completed only when the FP_JOB_CLOSE function module is called, you must also query the table of PDF documents after the call of this function module. Otherwise, the last bundle might be missing.

Set the bundling mode to 'M' when you start the program if, in your system, the FPCONNECT table contains no entry where MBATCHING equals 'X'. Double-click on the individual PDF documents in the results list to select them.

6.7 Parallelization of Print Jobs

The processing of documents by Adobe Document Services—as it has been described so far in this chapter—has always been sequential. A print program is responsible for retrieving data of various documents and communicates with the form runtime environment in the ABAP stack. In doing so, the application data are first transformed into a suitable XML presentation, and the parameters are determined for Adobe Document Services. The Web service call communicates with Adobe Document Services, which is installed on the Java stack and is responsible for formatting the finished documents.

Because Web service calls are synchronous, the process waits in the ABAP stack until the formatting has been processed successfully. Conversely, there is no activity on the Java stack as long as the ABAP process is engaged in data retrieval.

Section 6.6, Performance Optimization Through Bundling, presented a bundling of Web service calls, which reduced the overhead required for communication and initialization. Even in this case, the processing is always synchronous. Put simply, either the ABAP process or the Java process is engaged in the processing of documents of an application program.

Typically, the formatting of forms by ADS requires more effort and time, which is why the Java stack works most of the time and the ABAP process waits. A typical ratio is 80% for the Java stack and 20% for the ABAP stack (single-sided and double-sided documents, CPU speed of the stack similar). In absolute terms, you can utilize several Java processes for one ABAP process.

If you want to reduce the total time consumed for formatting, it is not sufficient to provide multiple CPUs. These would simply not be used due to the synchronous and sequential processing.

You can utilize various CPUs only if an application program already plans a splitting of print jobs into various smaller jobs that are then scheduled in parallel. However, this is included in only a few print programs. A general disadvantage of such a parallelization in the ABAP stack is that no information about the Java stack's resources is available. So if you have various print programs that format documents completely independently of each other, there is no resource distribution. If too many processes are started in parallel in ABAP, the requests accumulate in the queue in the Web Dispatcher or at EJB level in the Java stack.

The situation gets even worse if several ABAP systems use a central Java system with ADS. A cross-system resource management is not possible here.

The solution is to have a central location for parallelization. SAP supports such a parallelization of print jobs since ABAP 7.0 EHP2 and Java 7.2, which occurs in the Java stack. You can thus avoid the problems mentioned above. The form processing in the ABAP stack has been adapted accordingly so that no or few changes need to be done to the application programs. The form runtime processing ensures the correct control of parallelization, the correct sequence of documents, and the final status confirmation to the application program.

The following sections present parallelization, possibly required adaptations, monitoring, and error analysis.

6.7.1 Activating Parallelization in the Print Program

To utilize parallelization, you must activate it in the print program. For this purpose, you only need to set a parameter before you call the FP_JOB_OPEN function module:

```
fp_outputparams-parallel = 'X'.
```
Listing 6.11 Activating Parallelization

Moreover, you also need to configure the system for parallelization (Section 3.4, Configuration for Parallelization). If the configuration has not yet been done, the system recognizes this automatically and ignores the PARALLEL parameter—the system then processes all requests sequentially as usual.

You should deploy parallelization only in cases where many documents are output with the FP_JOB_OPEN and FP_JOB_CLOSE function modules. In principle, it is recommended that you use bundling at the same time to reduce the runtime costs for management.

> **When Should You Use Parallelization?**
>
> Activate parallelization if you need to output many forms (more than 1,000). The output must be made within FP_JOB_OPEN and FP_JOB_CLOSE because otherwise parallelization is not possible. You should activate bundling simultaneously. The best effect can be achieved if you output many small documents.

Additional changes are not required in the programs. The form runtime environment automatically ensures that the documents are in the correct sequence in the spool request despite the parallel processing of documents. The sequence results as usual from the call sequence of forms in the print program.

1. The output's status is not available after the call of a generated function module due to the asynchronous processing. An exception can be triggered for such a call, but the assignment to the call is no longer easily possible. The final status is not available until the FP_JOB_CLOSE function module is called. The form runtime environment waits until all requests have been processed on the Java stack. The status is required periodically via an internal API.

2. If an error occurs at a given point in time, the processing is terminated as soon as possible. The system waits for the end of the ADS processes currently working in parallel, deletes the queue with the requests, and notifies the application program about the error via an exception.

3. After the processing has been implemented completely and successfully, the `FP_JOB_CLOSE` function module is exited, and the control is returned to the application program. Now you can evaluate the number of generated pages from the output parameters, for example.

In case of an error, the spool request is closed, and the system deletes all documents which have possibly been generated and are logically located after the error in the sequence. This avoid gaps in the output.

If your program needs to determine the status for each form or the page count immediately after the call of the generated function module, you cannot use parallelization. The bundling should then be deactivated.

You can use the `FP_CHECK_BATCH_SPOOL_OUTPUT` program provided by SAP to generate larger print jobs also using parallelization. If your system is configured for parallelization, the program displays a PARALLEL PROCESSING checkbox in the selection screen. Activate this checkbox and increase the value for the REPETITIONS field to generate a large data volume. Start the output. After the program has been terminated, a spool request is available as usual.

This is all you will notice about parallelization in the ABAP system, where only an ABAP process runs for the print program as usual. The parallel Java processes are controlled internally.

The processes running during processing are very interesting. This is described in the Section 6.7.2, Monitoring Requests.

6.7.2 Monitoring Requests

You can monitor the status of the currently running and the already completed parallelization jobs in the ABAP system using the `FP_MONITOR_PARALLEL_PROCESSING` program. Moreover, you have the option to cancel jobs if required (which triggers an error in the running application program).

The initial screen of the program provides two buttons: DELETE ALL SUCCESSFUL JOBS and DELETE ALL COMPLETED JOBS.

Press F8 as shown in Figure 6.17 to obtain an overview of the current jobs. If print jobs have already been processed in parallel in your system, you receive a list, which can be similar to the one shown in Figure 6.18. If no list is displayed, start a print program as described in Section 6.7.1, Activating Parallelization in the Print Program.

Figure 6.17 Monitor for Parallel Processing

Depending on your spool authorizations, the system displays only your own jobs or all jobs of the system.

Monitor for Parallel Processing

Job ID	SAP System	Cl.	Spool no.	User Name	Created on	Time	Changed On	Time	Not processed	Successful	With errors	Status	Status Te...	Action
20110120145603.2397130	Y12	000	2.388	DEUTESFELD	20.01.2011	15:56:01	20.01.2011	15:58:03	0	34	0	✔		🗑
20110119090627.4070000	Y13	000	2.105	DEUTESFELD	19.01.2011	10:06:29	19.01.2011	10:08:56	0	0	1			🗑
20110119141726.1720000	Y13	000	2.114	DEUTESFELD	19.01.2011	15:17:28	19.01.2011	15:20:07	0	2	1			🗑
20110120093127.9993850	Y13	000	3.695	PRATAPISSACE	20.01.2011	10:31:29	20.01.2011	10:34:38	0	30	0	✔		🗑
20110120124653.2243220	Y13	000	1.760	DEUTESFELD	20.01.2011	13:46:52	20.01.2011	13:50:03	0	30	0	✔		🗑
20110124111813.5901760	Y13	000	4.211	DEUTESFELD	24.01.2011	12:18:14	24.01.2011	12:18:49	0	14	0	✔		🗑
20110507110024.7886880	Y13	000	17.581	DEUTESFELD	07.05.2011	13:00:24	07.05.2011	13:00:56	1	13	0	🚂		⊖

Figure 6.18 Status of the Individual Requests of Parallelization

The overview (see Figure 6.18) shows the status of each job and the system from which it was started, as well as the user, date, and time. The status is indicated by symbols. A green checkmark means that the job was completed successfully. A yellow warning sign is shown in case of an error. Running jobs are indicated with a train icon. You can remove completed jobs, whether successful or with errors, from the list using the action icons. You can cancel running jobs via the STOP icon.

The columns NOT PROCESSED, SUCCESSFUL, and WITH ERRORS provide detailed information, particularly about running jobs.

Unprocessed jobs have already been transferred by the ABAP system from the parallelization framework to the Java system but have not been processed by ADS yet.

If you click on the JOB ID of a running job in Figure 6.18, the program takes you to the details, where you can view the individual ADS jobs (see Figure 6.19). This figure shows an example of what these details typically look like. Some requests have already been processed, two are currently being processed, and the requests with the clock icon are still in the queue.

Jobs in the queue have already been transferred by the ABAP system for processing, but have not been assigned to a free process of ADS.

Request ID	Created on	Time	Changed On	Time	Status	Status Te...	Number of Pag...
SPOOL0000017582_00006	07.05.2011	13:03:52	07.05.2011	13:03:53	✔		8
SPOOL0000017582_00007	07.05.2011	13:03:53	07.05.2011	13:03:54	✔		15
SPOOL0000017582_00008	07.05.2011	13:03:54	07.05.2011	13:03:56	✔		18
SPOOL0000017582_00009	07.05.2011	13:03:56	07.05.2011	13:03:58	✔		22
SPOOL0000017582_00010	07.05.2011	13:03:58	07.05.2011	13:04:00	✔		23
SPOOL0000017582_00011	07.05.2011	13:04:00	07.05.2011	13:04:03	✔		34
SPOOL0000017582_00012	07.05.2011	13:04:04	07.05.2011	13:04:07	✔		39
SPOOL0000017582_00013	07.05.2011	13:04:07	07.05.2011	13:04:12	✔		41
SPOOL0000017582_00014	07.05.2011	13:04:12	07.05.2011	13:04:16	✔		51
SPOOL0000017582_00015	07.05.2011	13:04:17	07.05.2011	13:04:21	✔		51
SPOOL0000017582_00016	07.05.2011	13:04:22	07.05.2011	13:04:28	✔		68
SPOOL0000017582_00017	07.05.2011	13:04:28	07.05.2011	13:04:36	✔		89
SPOOL0000017582_00018	07.05.2011	13:04:36	07.05.2011	13:04:44	✔		90
SPOOL0000017582_00019	07.05.2011	13:04:44	07.05.2011	13:04:54	✔		113
SPOOL0000017582_00020	07.05.2011	13:04:55	07.05.2011	13:05:06	✔		126
SPOOL0000017582_00021	07.05.2011	13:05:06	07.05.2011	13:05:19	✔		148
SPOOL0000017582_00022	07.05.2011	13:05:20	07.05.2011	13:05:35	✔		173
SPOOL0000017582_00023	07.05.2011	13:05:36	07.05.2011	13:05:54	✔		182
SPOOL0000017582_00024	07.05.2011	13:05:55	07.05.2011	13:06:16	✔		215
SPOOL0000017582_00025	07.05.2011	13:06:17	07.05.2011	13:06:39	✔		225
SPOOL0000017582_00026	07.05.2011	13:06:41	07.05.2011	13:07:13	✔		280
SPOOL0000017582_00027	07.05.2011	13:07:14		00:00:00	🖨		0
SPOOL0000017582_00028	07.05.2011	13:07:15		00:00:00	🖨		0
SPOOL0000017582_00029		00:00:00		00:00:00	🕐		0
SPOOL0000017582_00030		00:00:00		00:00:00	🕐		0
SPOOL0000017582_00031		00:00:00		00:00:00	🕐		0
SPOOL0000017582_00032		00:00:00		00:00:00	🕐		0
SPOOL0000017582_00033		00:00:00		00:00:00	🕐		0

Figure 6.19 Detailed Overview of a Request

The number of pages per call usually increases initially because the bundling of forms is still in the self-learning phase. The program tries to reach a bundle size of approximately 200 pages. Until then, the calls are still run synchronously so that the ABAP system obtains direct information on the number of pages generated. Only when the bundling works optimally after a few calls does the system automatically switch to asynchronous processing and run several ADS processes.

It is therefore important that you use parallelization only for large print jobs. If you only have a few pages, the system does not have the opportunity to determine the optimal bundle size and switch to the asynchronous parallel processing. The forms are therefore still processed sequentially, which does not result in any performance gains. On the contrary, the processing could even be slowed down due to the low management overhead.

There are still some requests in the queue, as you can see in the example of Figure 6.19. This means that the print job utilizes ADS well. If required, in such a case you could release more processes for parallelization to reduce the overall processing time (see Section 3.5.4, Number of Parallel Print Jobs).

If you click on an entry in the REQUEST ID column in Figure 6.19, you obtain a detailed overview of a single ADS request, including the number of pages and a trace, for example (see Figure 6.20). You can find useful information here in case of an error.

Figure 6.20 Status of an ADS Call During Parallelization

6.7.3   Tracing Using the SOA Manager

You can trace the communication for parallelization jobs using the SOA Manager. Here you can record the communication between the ABAP stack and the Java stack, and you have valuable information at hand in case of an error.

First, you need to activate the trace for communication.

1. Start Transaction SOAMANAGER in your ABAP system, and select the LOGS AND TRACES tab in the SOA management (see Figure 6.21).

| Service Administration | Technical Administration | **Logs and Traces** | Remote Connectivity | Services Registry | Monitoring | Tools |

Web Service Configuration Log
Web Service Configuration Log Viewer

SOA Runtime Log/Trace Viewer
Display log and trace records of SOA runtime

SOA Runtime Logs Configuration
Configure SOA runtime logs

SOA Runtime Trace Configuration
Configure SOA runtime traces

SOA Runtime Trace Patterns
SOA runtime trace patterns

SOA Configuration Trace: Administration and Viewer
Analyze and administer the SOA configuration trace

Figure 6.21 Logs and Traces Tab

2. Select SOA RUNTIME TRACE CONFIGURATION.

3. The manager takes you to the trace configuration (see Figure 6.22).

Trace Configuration   Back

Tracing

Expiration Time	User Name	Interface	Trace Level	Accept Trace	Export Trace	Trace Pattern
2999-12-31 13:00:00			Errors	✓	✓	

Reset to default tracing | Switch tracing off | Refresh table
Add new | Edit | Delete

Figure 6.22 Trace Configuration

4. Click on the ADD NEW button to add a new configuration.

5. Define some attributes in the settings (see Figure 6.23) to log the information you require. This is important because the recording can create large data volumes and also impacts the runtime.

6. Select a recording duration (EXPIRATION TIME (SECONDS) field). You can also deactivate the recording manually later. But because users easily forget this option, you should limit the recording time right from the start.

7. Enter the USER NAME of the user who starts the ABAP print program. If you leave this field blank, the system logs all calls.

8. Specify "CO_FP_PRINT_REQUEST" as the Interface because you want to log only calls for parallelization.

9. Choose the Full Trace entry as the Trace Level.

10. Click on the Add new button to activate the setting.

Figure 6.23 Settings for the Trace

By making these settings, you have added a new entry to the trace configuration in Figure 6.22.

Now all calls of parallelization are logged. Start a print program for parallelization, for instance, FP_CHECK_BATCH_SPOOL_OUTPUT, and wait until it is completed. The recorded trace is now available.

1. To display the recorded trace, select SOA Runtime Log/Trace Viewer in the SOA Manager (see Figure 6.21).

Figure 6.24 Settings for the Trace Display

2. Accept the suggested values from Figure 6.24, and click on Start.

3. You can view several entries sorted by time stamp. Various call types are shown in the Communication Pattern column. Method:startJob indicates the start of parallelization job (see Figure 6.25).

4. The individual calls are either Method:processRequest or Method:queueRequest. A processRequest identifies a synchronous call, while a queueRequest places a

request for asynchronous processing in the queue. When processing starts, the list contains entries of the `processRequest` type almost exclusively because the system is still in the synchronous learning phase and determines the optimal size for the form bundle. Both types will be included in the list after several calls, and after a while only entries of the `queueRequest` type will occur. Parallelization now works optimally because all requests are placed in the queue and can be processed in parallel.

Figure 6.25 Logged Data Records

5. Now select an entry with the communication pattern `processRequest` or `queueRequest`.

6. In the details area under HEADER, you are provided with information, for instance, SUCCESSFULLY PROCESSED (WS).

7. Choose the PAYLOAD TRACE tab to view the details of the REQUEST (call) and the RESPONSE. This information may be useful for the support team and presents a

single call of ADS. In Figure 6.26, you can also see the Status of the communication itself (HTTP 200 OK). Note that this is only the status of the communication. An error message of ADS is also transferred with this status. This status indicates only whether a communication problem has occurred.

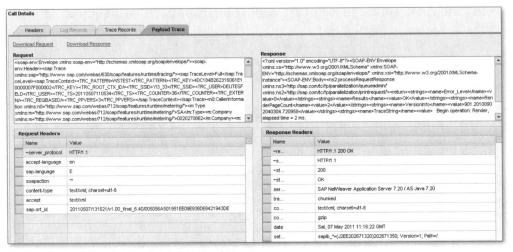

Figure 6.26 Details of a Call (Payload Trace)

Tracing with the SOA manager is indeed very technical. The goal of this description is to provide you with the option to obtain information at the right points in case of an error so that you can narrow down the cause as quickly as possible.

Parallelization is a powerful framework that reduces the runtime of large print jobs and takes place in the background. In the print program, you only need to activate parallelization and observe a very few specifics (many forms within the `FP_JOB_OPEN` and `FP_JOB_CLOSE` function modules, no individual processing). If you "parallelize" an individual form, this has no effect and the system processes as usual. The parallelization framework is used unnecessarily.

Despite asynchronous processing, the system automatically takes care of the sequence. The application program assumes control again when all forms have been processed completely. Its benefits fully unfold only in case of a large number of forms (more than 1,000). If sufficient processes are available for parallelization, the total runtime can be reduced by a factor of 3 to 5.

This improvement can be very important if longer print jobs must be completed over night or in a specific timeframe.

6.8   Translating Forms

Because business documents usually have to be output in different languages, an option must be available to translate a created form. When you create a new form, it automatically obtains an original language. This is the language with which you are logged on to the SAP system at that point in time. Future extensions of the form should always be implemented in the original language. In Form Builder, the original language of the form is indicated under properties. If you try to change a form in another language the system notifies you accordingly.

Forms include a language-independent part and texts that are relevant for translation. The language-independent components comprise, for example, the interface used, the structure of the context, and the arrangement of the layout elements you created using Adobe LiveCycle Designer. Texts, however, are language-dependent—therefore, you are provided with an option to translate them into multiple languages.

The following sections describe how you can translate forms yourself.

1. Start Transaction SFP in the display mode for your form, for example, Z_IFBA_BOOK_FORM_01.

2. Follow the menu path GOTO • TRANSLATION. A dialog box opens where you enter the target language of the translation. For example, select DE for German.

3. Do not change the default for the source language (English). For further translations, it may be useful to select another source language (if the form has already been translated into other languages) depending on the language skills of the respective translator. Choose the TRANSLATE button.

4. In the following screen (see Figure 6.27), you are provided with three text categories:

   ▶ **<AD> PDF-Based Forms**
     AD stands for the form documentation. This entry is displayed only if documentation exists for the form.

▶ **<PDFB> PDF-Based Forms**
PDFB identifies texts that you entered directly in the layout of the form using Adobe LiveCycle Designer.

▶ **<TLGS> Lockable Logical Objects (Short Texts)**
TLGS identifies the short texts that you entered in the context.

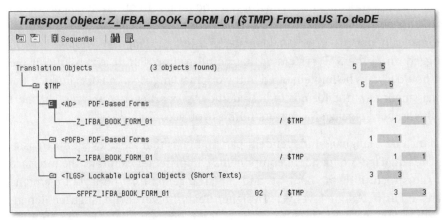

Figure 6.27 Starting Up the Translation of a Form

6.8.1 Translating Short Texts

The following sections describe the translation of short texts in a form.

1. Initially, double-click on the entry for the short text, SFPFZ_IFBA_BOOK_FORM_01. In the following screen (see Figure 6.28) you can see three texts available for translation. If you return to this screen after the translation, the already-translated texts will be displayed here.

2. The text "My first form" is the short text you entered during creation of the form. Translate it to "Mein erstes Formular." Translate the texts "Date" or "Business Connection" into "Datum" and "Geschäftsverbindung."

3. Save the text prior to returning to the previous screen (see Figure 6.27).

4. You can check the translated texts by logging on to the system in German and displaying the context of the form. There, you can see the two texts, "Datum"

and "Geschäftsverbindung," which you just entered. Under PROPERTIES (EIGEN-SCHAFTEN), you can find the text "Mein erstes Formular."

Figure 6.28 Translating Short Texts

6.8.2 Translating Long Texts

This section describes how to handle long texts. Because all texts from the layout are saved in XML format, the translation is a bit more complex.

1. Double-click on the Z_IFBA_BOOK_FORM_01 entry (see Figure 6.27).

2. The following screen (see Figure 6.29) displays an XML document in the upper area containing the texts of the original language. The target language is displayed in the lower area.

   If you call the translation of long texts for a form for the first time, the target language is still the primary. Therefore, select the COPY SOURCE TEXT button.

3. In the lower area, you can change the texts highlighted in blue. Because you copied the source language as a suggestion, the texts to be translated are located in the correct position and you can overwrite them with German texts. You cannot and must not change the surrounding XML sections because the texts cannot be assigned in the translated form any longer.

4. Save your entries when you have translated all texts. To check the translation, log on to the system in the target language and start Adobe LiveCycle Designer in Form Builder. The texts you just translated are now displayed.

Figure 6.29 Translating Long Texts

6.8.3 Output of a Translated Form

After you have translated a form, you can call it at runtime. To do so, start the print program and enter the required language in the LANGU parameter when calling the generated function module. If the form is not available in the language selected, the system tries to find a replacement language. You can influence this process by filling the values REPLANGU1, …, REPLANGU3, with replacement languages.

Provided that no replacement languages are set or that the form is not available in the requested languages, the system tries to output the form in the logon language.

> **Propagating Layout Changes**
>
> Provided that you extend the form in the original language after the translation has already been carried out, these changes are copied to the existing translations upon activation. The new texts are simply copied here. So when you call a form in the foreign language, the texts are displayed in the original language until you update the translation.
>
> When you transport a form, this synchronization is done in the target system if other translations already exist there.
>
> If you start the translation transaction after the layout has been changed, the system displays a mixture of languages. Texts that have already been translated exist in the target language. New texts, however, are copied from the original language and must still be replaced by their translations.

For the translation of forms, you must note that longer texts may change the layout. So you should always provide sufficient space for fields and labels in the layout.

If the form is output in a language with a text flow from right to left (for example, Hebrew or Arabic), the layout is not mirrored. But because the layout is uniform for all languages, in this case you must create a copy of the form in which the layout can be arranged as required.

6.9 XFP Output

If you need to connect another form solution to the SAP system, you can use the XFP interface. It may be necessary to use an external solution, for example, because another form solution is already in use or advanced printer control requirements exist.

Interfaces for external form providers are also available for the other two form solutions provided by SAP—SAPscript and SAP Smart Forms—which both have been on the market for quite a while. These interfaces include the Raw Data Interface (RDI) for SAPscript and the Smart Forms XSF interface, which works on an XML basis. The XFP interface for SAP Interactive Forms by Adobe is very similar to the XSF interface.

The primary aim of the XFP interface is to continue to use the existing application programs and to forward only the application data to the external software. The layout formatting is not implemented here directly—instead, this task is assumed by the form software. The external form software is responsible for the creation of documents based on the application data. Furthermore, it is also responsible for distributing the documents to the correct output devices.

The XFP interface involves an interface certified by SAP. You can obtain information on the certified partners of this interface in the Partner Information Center at *http://www.sap.com/ecosystem/customers/directories/SearchSolution.epx.*

There are two variants of the XFP data stream: The application data can be transferred with or without context evaluation.

▶ For the XFP variant with context evaluation, the application data of the interface is processed in the same way as if it was transferred to ADS. Here, only minor adaptations are made to the XML namespaces. The system is also provided with additional information so that the external software knows which output will be created.

▶ For the XFP variant without context evaluation, the application data of the interface is directly transferred into an XML format without considering the context. Graphics, addresses, or texts from the context are not consider here either.

Facts like the complexity of the application data and whether the external software can support the variant without context evaluation determine which XFP variant is more suitable for the respective scenario. The variant without context evaluation may be appropriate for plain forms that contain hardly any logic in the context, because the XFP data stream can be created faster.

Further information on the XFP interface is available in the SAP online documentation for Transaction SFP. Follow the menu path HELP • APPLICATION HELP in the menu. On the help page, select SAP INTERACTIVE FORMS BY ADOBE • PDF-BASED PRINT FORMS • FORM OUTPUT • OUTPUT IN XFP FORMAT.

You can activate and control the XFP interface using parameters when calling the `FP_JOB_OPEN` function module:

▶ **XFP**
Use the `XFP` parameter, and enter `'X'` to activate the XFP output.

▶ **XFPTYPE**
You can control this variant of the XFP output (with or without context evaluation) using the `XFPTYPE` parameter. The initial value means with context evaluation; if you enter `'R'`, the application data is directly transferred in XML format.

▸ **XFPOUTDEV**

XFPOUTDEV is an optional parameter that controls the connection to the external system. This parameter is described in the following text.

The SAP spool system is used for the connection of the external system and the transfer of data. The form runtime environment utilizes the virtual output device, XFP, which must have the XFP device type. To use the XFP interface, you must create such an output device. If you select another name, you must transfer it via the XFPOUTDEV parameter. You must assign the XFP device type to the output device in any case; otherwise, the data stream is not formatted correctly.

For an XFP output, the data is not transferred via the output device that is used by the application (DEST parameter). A spool request is created not for this printer but for the XFP device that is used for each transfer to the external form software. You can create multiple virtual output devices and then distribute the data to the respective print programs depending on the scenario. The actual printer is provided in the XFP data stream together with other metainformation and is available to the external system.

SAP Printing Guide

You can obtain detailed information on the definition of output devices in the SAP Printing Guide. A link to this document can be found in XFP documentation.

The way data is received by the external system and which settings must be made depends on the respective form software.

6.10 Summary

This chapter outlined the meaning and the tasks of the print program and its interaction with the form interface. The print program is responsible for data retrieval as well as for the output and print job control. Besides data selection, the specification of the correct form is also important.

This chapter discussed different output scenarios, such as print preview, print output, archiving, or return of PDF documents. In this context, you gained an insight into the SAP spool system and the necessary device definitions for the use of printers using the SAP Interactive Forms by Adobe solution. Error analysis constituted another important topic. You learned how you can create a PDF with additional information or operate the ICF Recorder to log the communication between the SAP system and ADS. Then you learned about bundling for form output and its effects on performance.

Parallelization of print requests was presented as an essential innovation in Release 7.0 EHP2. You learned about the basic principle of parallelization and how you can use parallelization to improve the performance of your print scenarios. This chapter also included information about monitoring and error analysis.

Another section dealt with the translation of forms. You learned how to translate your own forms to provide them in different languages.

The final section introduced you to the XFP output. You learned how to use this certified interface to connect third-party form software to the SAP system.

This second chapter on the creation of forms addresses advanced form designs. Here, the example regarding the creation of form templates from Chapter 5, Creating Form Templates, is further developed, and you are introduced to the basic principles of creating interactive forms.

7 Advanced Form Template Design

In Chapter 5, you created a first form template for the print output. In this context, you were introduced to the first form fields and used them to create a form template that outputs one page. The output itself was generated by a print program, which you developed in Chapter 6, Form Output. You can continue to use this print program for the first part of this chapter.

The form template from Chapter 5 will be extended in this chapter, for example, by implementing tables and page breaks. Furthermore, you will move from the creation of form templates for print forms to the creation of form templates for interactive PDF forms. This chapter then lays the foundation for the creation of interactive PDF forms, as they are required in the following chapters, by introducing you to the implementation of script programs, providing notes on how to increase performance, and describing the creation of accessible PDF forms.

7.1 Advanced Techniques for Print Forms

In this section, we will extend the form templates created in Chapter 5 using advanced techniques to output a list of flight bookings by means of tables, for example. This list has several pages; that is, you need to define page breaks. Another critical aspect of the output is the formatting of the individual data values. At the end of this chapter, we will prepare a form template for duplex printing.

7.1.1 Preparations

First, prepare the form template from Chapter 5 for further usage. To keep the old form template, copy it, and then customize it. Proceed as follows:

1. Start Transaction SFP in the SAP GUI and create a new form template with the name "Z_IFBA_BOOK_FORM_02" by copying the form from Chapter 5 (`Z_IFBA_BOOK_FORM_01`).

2. Start editing the newly created form and navigate to the LAYOUT view.

3. For the AIRLINESLIST subform, set the content from FLOWED to POSITIONED to facilitate the editing process for the next steps.

4. Then delete the AIRLINE subform by selecting it in the hierarchy and pressing the DEL key.

5. Finally, increase the height of the subform to approximately 2 inches. You can check the size using the LAYOUT palette.

The preparations are now complete, and you can begin extending the form template.

> **Tip for Editing Subform Structures**
>
> To create more complex structures, such as nested subforms, or tables, it is often much easier to handle subforms with positioned content than subforms with flow content. By carefully switching the content type, you can facilitate the management of the form templates in Adobe LiveCycle Designer. Start with the subforms with positioned content and then proceed with switching to flowed content.

7.1.2 Floating Fields

Floating fields enable you to embed data (for example, a name, a date, or an amount of money) in a static text. This process can be best explained using an example. To do this, extend the form template as follows:

1. First, select the static text above the subform for `Airlineslist` in the hierarchy and rename it "LetterText."

2. Then navigate to the design view and increase the static text until it more or less reaches the right border; leave some space in the vertical direction, too.

3. Move the `Airlineslist` subform down until it no longer overlaps the static text.

4. Replace the text of the static text, LETTERTEXT, with the following: "List of airlines where a flight was booked. This list was also sent to the email address." The text

field enlarges if the text exceeds the right border; you can use the [ENTER] key to jump to a new line.

5. Set the size of the font to 12 POINTS.

6. Now, wrap the LETTERTEXT text in a subform and name it LetterTF.

7. Select the static text and place the mouse pointer directly after the word "address." Now, insert a so-called "floating" field into the static text by selecting the menu path INSERT • FLOATING FIELD.

8. Then insert a space between the word "address" and the just inserted floating field.

Figure 7.1 shows a part of the form template and what it should look like. The system automatically inserted a text field into the form hierarchy. This represents the floating field in the form hierarchy and is thus invisible in the form template. In the text of the form template, the floating field is enclosed in curly brackets. The text reads: {EMAILFLOATINGFIELD}.

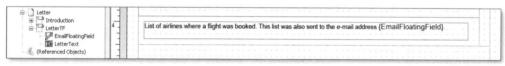

Figure 7.1 Floating Field

In the next step, you format the floating field as follows:

1. Select the floating field in the form hierarchy (it is the text field in the LetterTF subform), and rename it "EmailFloatingField."

2. You can also format the text. To do this, navigate to the FONT palette, and set the font size to 14 POINTS and the style to BOLD.

3. Finally, define the data binding for the field. To do this, navigate to the BINDING tab of the OBJECT palette. Bind the field to the EMAIL node under the CUSTOMER structure.

4. Look at the output using the PDF preview (see Section 5.3.2, Using Preview Data) or use the print program from Section 6.5.1, Trace and PDF with Additional Information.

Figure 7.2 shows the result of the text output. The text format enables you to determine how the content of the EMAIL data node was inserted in the text.

List of airlines where a flight was booked. This list was also sent to the e-mail address **info@sap.de**.

Figure 7.2 Floating Field for Output

7.1.3 Using Tables

Next, you need to output the flight connections with the form. To do this, tables are available as structure elements for the creation of form templates.

View the structure under the BOOKINGS node in the data view. The data structure is a nested table that groups the data according to the IDs of the airlines. The data for the output are already provided in groups by the Z_IFBA_BOOK_PRINT print program, which was created in Section 6.1, Print Program. The reason for this is that the sorting of data is not supported for the output as a PDF or in print languages.

Adding a Table to a Form

To insert a table, you can drag and drop form fields, or even complete structures, directly from the data view to the form template. Proceed as follows:

1. Check whether the AIRLINESLIST subform is visible in the DESIGN VIEW and whether the DESIGN VIEW is displayed.

2. Then drag and drop the BOOKINGS node via from the data view to the AIRLINESLIST subform.

3. Confirm the dialog that indicates that there is not enough space available in the form to add the table. You will solve this problem in the next step.

Working with Tables in Adobe LiveCycle Designer

To better handle the creation and processing of tables, you should search for the key word "using tables" in the Adobe LiveCycle Designer Help or navigate the menu path USING LIVECYCLE DESIGNER • WORKING WITH FORM DESIGNS • USING TABLES • SELECTING, COPYING, MOVING, AND NAVIGATING and read the SELECTING, COPYING, MOVING, AND NAVIGATING section. This section explains how you can select the entire table, rows, or columns using the mouse pointer.

By performing the previous steps, you added the table to the form template. The following description involves several steps to initially format the table.

1. Click in the cell for the ID column heading. Open the context menu, and select the EDIT TEXT... menu item.

2. Then change the column heading from ID to AIRLINE ID and set the style of the font to BOLD. Click in the cell below the AIRLINE ID column heading, and reduce the size of the cell (and therefore of the column) so that the column heading only just fits into the cell. To enlarge the first row for the table heading, click on the upper edge of the still selected cell using the mouse and drag it downward. This does not reduce the size of the cell but increases the size of the preceding row.

3. Select the cell for the GROUP column heading, specify CONNECTIONS as the new column heading, and set the style of the heading's font to BOLD.

4. Select the cell below the No. column heading, and reduce the cell to approximately two-thirds of the original width. Also, decrease the width of the DATE column.

5. Next, edit the FLTIME form field that displays the duration of the flight in the form. To do this, select it, and change the form field type to DATE/TIME FIELD. The reason for this is that—as described in Section 4.3.8, Alternatives—the duration is stored as a decimal value and is mapped through a conversion routine in the hours/minutes format.

6. Set the appearance to NONE. Then deactivate the caption (in the LAYOUT palette). Finally, decrease the size of the field until it no longer exceeds the cell of the table.

7. Change the column heading of the CONNECTIONS column to DURATION.

8. Select all column headings of the inner table while pressing the Ctrl key, and set the style of the font to BOLD.

9. Display the BORDER palette via the PALETTE • BORDER menu path. Again, select all column headings of the internal table, and navigate to the BORDER palette. Here, set the style from NONE to SOLID in the BACKGROUND FILL area and select a light shade of gray as the color.

10. Perform the previous two steps for the two column headings of the external table, too.

The table in the form template should now appear as illustrated in Figure 7.3. The column headings have a gray background. The rows and cells in which data is included for the output have a white background.

Airline ID	Connections					
	No.	Date	Amount (for.currncy)	Curr.	Duration	

Figure 7.3 Structure of the Table in the Form Template

Structure of Tables

The structure and the data binding of tables are described using the previously inserted table as an example. First, this section discusses the structure of the table in the hierarchy of the form template. This hierarchy is also shown in Figure 7.4.

Figure 7.4 Hierarchy of the Form Template After Having Inserted the Table

In general, a table is displayed with one node for the table itself and two child nodes that map the header and a data row, respectively. This is displayed by the corresponding icons in the hierarchy. In the example, the table is mapped by the BOOKINGS node. Below it, the header of the first table is mapped by the overflowLeader node. This table has two columns and therefore two static texts for the column headings. The name of the data row (also called the body row) is DATA. In the first column, there is a text field with the name CARRID that outputs the airline ID. The second column contains a new table. This table is thus a nested table. The second table is mapped by the GROUP node and, in turn, has an untitled header and a data row, DATA. The second table has five columns for the data output.

The structure of the table contains only one data row to describe the structure. The number of data rows that the table actually contains during the output depends on the data volume that was provided for the output.

Data Binding for Tables

This section uses the table for the flight bookings to explain the procedure of binding the data of a table.

▶ First, look at the BOOKINGS table node and its default binding (BINDING tab in the OBJECT palette). Due to the $.BOOKINGS binding expression, the table has an explicit data binding to a data node. In most cases, the data structure has one node to which the table can be bound. In particular, this is the case if forms are created with Transaction SFP and if an ABAP Dictionary-based interface is used. However, you may also use tables where only the data row has a binding.

▶ Now look at the default binding of the DATA data row in the first table. This data row has a relative binding due to the DATA[*] expression. These expressions for subforms were detailed in Chapter 5. This is a binding expression that binds data nodes that can repeat any number of times in the data stream. Accordingly, the REPEAT ROW FOR EACH DATA ITEM option is selected. In the form, this data row is therefore displayed as many times as the data node exists in the data stream.

▶ A relative binding expression for the individual fields of the data cells defines how the individual cells of the tables are filled. You can check this by viewing the default binding for the CARRID field. The expression is CARRID. Therefore, the value is defined in relation to the data node that is bound to the table row.

> **Tip for Problems with the Output of Tables**
>
> Problems with the output of tables, for example, if the data are not displayed at all or in the wrong position, are often caused by an incorrect data binding of the individual table rows. For problems with tables, you should always check the data binding of the table first.
>
> To do this, first check the table element in the hierarchy and then the rows. Finally, check whether the cells have a relative binding to the row. Note that headers usually do not require a data binding. Thus, you can set the default binding for headers to NONE.

> **Note for Tables with Empty Cells**
>
> For tables where the data stream does not include the data nodes for empty fields, you must follow the instructions described in this section. Otherwise, table cells may be moved. You can easily recognize this because the binding expression for the cell contains the [*] string in this case.

7.1.4   Page Breaks

Before you extend the form template, you should have a look at the output. You can use the `Z_IFBA_BOOK_PRINT` print program from Section 6.1, or call the PDF preview as described in Section 5.3.2. If everything functions correctly, your output should appear as shown in Figure 7.5.

Note that the output still consists of only a single page. The table no longer fits on one page because it has too many data rows. You can correct this by implementing page breaks.

Extending the Form Template for the Usage of Page Breaks

If you look at the SUBFORM tab in the OBJECT palette for the LETTER page and AIRLINESLIST subform, you see that both have an absolute position (with X and Y coordinates) on the page or in the subform defined for the contained form fields. Because you cannot define the size of the table until the output is generated, you must change the setting for the form template from POSITIONED to FLOWED. Proceed as follows:

1. First, select the LETTER page in the hierarchy. In the SUBFORM tab of the OBJECT palette, change the content type from POSITIONED to FLOWED.

List of airlines where a flight was booked. This list was also sent to the e-mail address info@sap.de.

Airline ID	Connections					
AA	No.	Date	Amount (for.currncy)	Curr.	Duration	
	0017	Jul 18, 2007	686.59	SGD	6:01	
AZ	No.	Date	Amount (for.currncy)	Curr.	Duration	
	0555	Mar 28, 2007	166.50	EUR	2:05	
	0790	May 23, 2007	1,312.90	CAD	13:35	
	0790	May 23, 2007	1,357.03	CHF	13:35	
DL	No.	Date	Amount (for.currncy)	Curr.	Duration	
	1984	Apr 23, 2007	380.65	USD	5:25	
LH	No.	Date	Amount (for.currncy)	Curr.	Duration	
	0400	May 26, 2007	371.84	GBP	7:24	
	0401	Aug 28, 2007	549.91	USD	7:15	
	0402	Apr 23, 2007	549.91	USD	7:35	
	0402	Aug 13, 2007	549.91	USD	7:35	
	2402	Jun 23, 2007	217.80	EUR	1:05	
	2402	Aug 18, 2007	435.60	EUR	1:05	
	2407	Apr 28, 2007	217.80	EUR	1:05	
QF	No.	Date	Amount (for.currncy)	Curr.	Duration	
	0005	Jun 22, 2007		USD	13:45	
	0005	Aug 17, 2007	866.97	USD	13:45	

Figure 7.5 Print Output After Having Inserted the Table

2. Set the flow direction to TOP to BOTTOM.

3. Check whether the ALLOW PAGE BREAKS WITHIN CONTENT option is enabled.

4. Select the AIRLINESLIST subform, and perform the same steps as for the LETTER subform.

Due to this modification, the subforms are now aligned along the left border of the page and may have slightly moved to the left. The subforms directly adjoin each other at the top or bottom border. This is not relevant for this example.

In those cases where this is not wanted and you want the form fields to have an absolute position, wrap them in a subform, and retain the POSITIONED option for the content. A flowed subform can contain the newly inserted subform without any problems.

Due to the previous modifications, the subforms can grow along with their content and, if required, span multiple pages after page breaks. The next step deals with the table:

1. Navigate to the TABLE tab in the OBJECT palette for the BOOKINGS table.

2. Check whether the ALLOW PAGE BREAKS WITHIN CONTENT option is already enabled.

3. Next, go to the Row tab for the data row of the BOOKINGS table. Here, the ALLOW PAGE BREAKS WITHIN CONTENT option is not selected.

This means that page breaks are allowed within the table but only between the rows and not within the content of a row, that is, the internal table in our example. As a result, all connections of an airline must always be output as a block. If this block does not fit on the page as a whole, it is moved to the next page. You can check this by having a look at the output. The system outputs multiple pages so that all connections are visible.

For this definition of page breaks, it is assumed that all connections of an airline fit on one page. You can modify the form template in such a way that the system also allows page breaks for the internal table.

1. Select the DATA data row of the BOOKINGS table.

2. Select the ALLOW PAGE BREAKS WITHIN CONTENT option in the Row tab of the OBJECT palette.

3. Select the inner table, GROUP, and check whether the ALLOW PAGE BREAKS WITHIN CONTENT option is enabled in the CELL-TABLE tab.

Take another look at the output. For this book, we used the customer with the customer ID 1 so that the page break for the internal table occurs on the first page. Thus, the form template can manage lists of flight connections of any length. A disadvantage is that the airline ID is not repeated on the next page for page breaks within the internal table.

Finally, view the DATA data row of the GROUP table. For this row, the ALLOW PAGE BREAKS WITHIN CONTENT option is not selected. This option would be relevant only if the size of one of the form fields in the cells of the row would change, which would require a page break in the data row itself. A typical example for this case is a multiple line text field for which you do not know the number of lines in advance.

> **Tip for Form Templates with Layout Problems**
>
> If you have problems with the page breaks of your form, you should check whether all relevant subforms have flow content.
>
> To do this, you must trace back the hierarchy from the form element that has the problem to the subform that displays the page. In this context, check whether the FLOWED option is selected in the respective SUBFORM tab of the OBJECT palette.
>
> For tables, check whether the ALLOW PAGE BREAKS WITHIN CONTENT option is set correctly (that is, as described in this section) for the table and the data row(s).

Outputting the Page Numbering in the Form

The output of the sample form now spans several pages. In the next step, we will extend the form template in such a way that the current page number and the total page count are output on each page. To do this, customize the master page as follows:

1. Navigate to the master page view, and move the visible part of the master page so that you can view the lower part.

2. Below the text field for the footer, add a new static text, and replace the text with ""Page /". Set the paragraph to CENTER. You can do this via the PARAGRAPH palette. Then navigate to the FONT palette, and set the font size to 12 POINTS.

3. Next, center the text on the page. To do this, select the text and follow the LAYOUT • CENTER IN PAGE • HORIZONTALLY menu path.

4. Navigate to the edit mode for the text, and move the mouse pointer to the left of the slash. Use the INSERT • CURRENT PAGE NUMBER menu path to insert a placeholder for the current page number in the text.

5. Then move the mouse pointer to the right of the slash, and follow the INSERT • NUMBER OF PAGES menu path to insert a placeholder for the total page count in the text.

6. Finally, rename the static text from "StaticText2" to "NumberofPages."

The bottom area of the master page should now appear as illustrated in Figure 7.6. Look at the form template output to view the result of the changes made to the master page.

Figure 7.6 Bottom Area of the Master Page After Adding the Output of the Page Numbering

7.1.5 Subform Set

You can use a subform set to group subforms and define the order in which the subforms are output. There are two types of subform sets that distinguish themselves as follows:

▶ **Normal subform sets**
This type defines the output order for the creation of the form. This order is derived from the order of the subforms in the hierarchy.

▶ **Choice subform sets**
For this type, you can define an expression to specify whether the subform is supposed to be output or not. The most common method is to define a data binding for the subforms and display or hide the subforms when the data is generated by adding or omitting a data node.

For the form interface used in this form template, DATE was set as an optional parameter. In Section 4.3.8, an alternative was inserted in the form context to use the system date if the DATE parameter is not transferred. To implement this for the form template creation, use a choice subform set.

In the following steps, we will customize the form template in such a way that if a date was transferred, the respective date is output, and if no date was transferred, the system date is output.

1. Drag and drop the ALT_DATE node via from the data view to the ADDRESS subform and navigate to the hierarchy to view how the subform set is displayed.

The subform set is mapped by a specific node in the hierarchy. This node has subforms and child nodes (see Figure 7.7).

Figure 7.7 Representation of the Subform Set in the Hierarchy

2. Enlarge the ALT_DATE subform and the SYSTEM_DATE and DATE date fields. Then, provide more space for the caption of these two date fields.

3. Select the SYSTEM_DATE field, and change its caption to "Date of (SYS)." (SYS) enables you to later recognize what date was used for the output.

4. Select the DATE field, change its caption to "Date of," select the subform set in the ALT_DATE subform, and rename it "DateAlternative."

5. Navigate to the SUBFORM SET tab of the OBJECT palette. As you can see, the SELECT ONE SUBFORM FROM ALTERNATIVES option is selected for the type. The tab contains another button, EDIT ALTERNATIVES.... Click on it.

6. This opens the dialog shown in Figure 7.8. In this dialog, you can see that the CHOOSE SUBFORM USING EXPRESSION option is selected and the data binding is defined. A relative binding to the wrapping subform was used.

For both subforms, there is one area in which you can define the binding of the subform. In this example, the names for the data node and the subform are the same. In addition, you can specify an expression to further limit the choice for the two subforms. However, this is not required in the example shown here.

Figure 7.8 Dialog for Defining the Selection Criteria of the Subforms

7. Select CANCEL to close the dialog. Then navigate to the BINDING tab of the sub-form set. This tab contains the REPEAT SUBFORM SET FOR EACH DATA ITEM option that defines whether the system is supposed to evaluate the subform as many times as data nodes exist in the data stream. For our example, this option is not selected because there is only one alternative in the data stream.

8. Now you can output the form and check which subform is used for the date output. You can use the Z_IFBA_BOOK_PRINT program to try both variants. The two variants are distinguished by whether the data is transferred as an optional parameter or not.

> **Sections and Choice Sections in Tables**
>
> The subform set concept also exists for tables. For tables, the subform set is called SEC-TION and the choice subform set is the CHOICE SECTION. The usage is identical.

7.1.6 Using Patterns for Display Formatting

If you look at the current appearance of the form output, you will probably notice that the status date, the costs for a flight, and the flight duration are not output in the correct format in the form. By means of the developed sample form, you format one date, one number, and one time in the following sections, respectively. The corresponding pattern that is used is explained, too, and the general documentation describes the structure of the patterns in detail. The documentation is part of the XML Forms Architecture (XFA) specification (see Section 7.7.3, XML Forms Architecture).

Formatting Date Fields

First look at the SYSTEM_DATE and DATE date fields. The goal of the following formatting process for the output is to display the day of the week (spelled out) in front of the date.

1. Increase the size of the ALT_DATE subform so that there is more space available to the right of both date fields. This is necessary to have sufficient space for the formatted output of the date.

2. Next, enlarge the TRUE subform and then the SYSTEM_DATE date field until the space created in the previous step is also used.

3. Select the SYSTEM_DATE date field and navigate to the FIELD tab of the OBJECT palette. Here, set the appearance to NONE.

4. This tab also includes the PATTERNS... button (see Figure 7.9). You can use this button to enter the display pattern.

Figure 7.9   Field Tab with Patterns... Button

5. Click the PATTERNS... button. The system opens the dialog shown in Figure 7.10, where you can enter the display pattern.

6. Enter "date{EEEE, MMMM D, YYYY}" in the PATTERN: field.

7. Perform the last four steps the same way for the DATE date field.

Figure 7.10   The Patterns Dialog

The pattern has the following structure: It starts with the DATE CATEGORY, which you use to determine a date pattern. The pattern itself is enclosed within curly brackets. To output the spelled-out day of the week (for example, Monday), by definition the E must be used four times for the day-of-the-week pattern. The four Ms define that the month is also spelled out (for example, July). This is followed by the day of the month, which is mapped by a single D. The single D indicates that the day is output in one or two digits. The four Ys define that the year is output in four digits. Therefore, this pattern is supposed to output a date in the following format: "Wednesday, December 24, 2020."

Formatting Numeric Values

In the next step, we will modify the FORCURAM field. This fields outputs the costs for a flight. It is a field that formats amounts according to the corresponding currency and outputs them with the correct alignment. Note that in this context, Japanese currency, for example, has no decimal places and that there are Arabic currencies that have three decimal places. For all formats of amounts, the decimal points need to be positioned below each other to have a uniform appearance in the form. This can be achieved as follows.

1. Select the FORCURAM field and navigate to the CELL tab in the OBJECT palette.

2. You must use display patterns for the formatting described at the beginning of this section. To do this, deselect the LIMIT LEADING DIGITS and LIMIT TRAILING DIGITS options.

3. Click the PATTERNS... button.

4. Then enter the following pattern as the display pattern in the PATTERN: field: "num{zzz,zzz,zz9.888}".

5. Navigate to the PARAGRAPH palette and select RADIX ALIGNMENT (see Figure 7.11). In the now-active input field to the right of the radix icon, enter "0.3in" to set the decimal point's distance to the right border to 0.3 inches. This defines that all decimal points of the table rows are positioned below each other.

Figure 7.11 Paragraph Palette

The num category followed by curly brackets indicates that a pattern is provided for a numeric value. The output pattern uses the small z to specify that the system is only supposed to display a digit here if the digit does not equal zero. No leading zeros should be output. The 9 in the output pattern defines that the system is supposed to output a zero for the digits here. This enables you to map amounts that have a "0.xx" format. The 8 indicates that these digits are output only if the original data have a digit here, too. This is used for Japanese currency, for example, because this currency does not have decimal places and thus does not provide decimal places in the data. The comma is the thousands separator and the point the decimal point. Both are to be output for the used pattern. Later, they are replaced by the correct signs according to the locale. For example, in Germany the decimal point is mapped by a comma and in the U.S. by a point.

Formatting Time Outputs

The third and last formatting type is the formatting of the flight duration.

1. Select the FLTIME field and navigate to the BINDING tab in the OBJECT palette.

2. Set the date format to TIME.

3. Navigate to the FIELD tab and click on the PATTERNS... button.

4. Enter the display pattern "time{HH:MM}" directly in the PATTERN: field.

5. Navigate to the PARAGRAPH palette and select the right-aligned paragraph.

In this context, note that a time format was selected to map the flight duration, which means that the flight time is supported only up to 23:59 hours. A rather simple pattern can be used in this case. The two Hs indicate that the time is to be output in a 24-hour format. The "MM" stands for the two-digit output of the minutes. The time category is used if you want to specify a pattern for a time.

Display Formatting

Now it is time to look at the output. The form looks much more harmonious now (see Figure 7.12). You should always use display patterns to format the output, if possible.

Airline ID	Connections					
	No.	Date	Amount (for.currncy)	Curr.	Duration
AA	0017	Jul 18, 2007	686.59	SGD	6:01
	No.	Date	Amount (for.currncy)	Curr.	Duration
AZ	0555	Mar 28, 2007	166.50	EUR	2:05
	0790	May 23, 2007	1,312.90	CAD	13:35

Figure 7.12 Excerpt for the Formatted Output of Date, Amounts, and Times

This section introduced formatting using patterns by means of output formatting. However, there are two other cases where patterns are critical and allow for a generalization of the usage of patterns—displays and data patterns.

Display and Data Patterns

In the earlier example, you used only display patterns, which is sufficient for understanding the structure and usage of patterns. However, in more complex form scenarios, you can also use patterns to process data from the XML data stream underlying the form. So-called data patterns define how the system is supposed to interpret strings in the XML data stream. You specify the data patterns in the BINDING tab of the OBJECT palette.

For the example in this chapter, it was not necessary to define the data patterns because the system automatically identified the data during the generation of the XML data stream thanks to the form field types and the corresponding mapping to a default pattern.

However, for interactive PDF forms, there are two other cases where patterns are critical. In this context, patterns are used to input data and to validate the input. This is described in Section 7.2.2, From PDF-Based Print Forms to Interactive PDF Forms.

7.1.7 Conditional Page Breaks

The example is now extended so that only the flight connections of an individual airline are output on one page. A condition is specified for this purpose. If this condition occurs when the output is generated, a page break needs to be made.

If requested, you can create a copy of the form template at this point and perform the page break example with this copy.

Proceed as follows to define a conditional page break:

1. Select the DATA node under the BOOKINGS node (this is the data row of the external table).

2. Go to the PAGINATION tab of the OBJECT palette. There you can find the EDIT... button next to the CONDITIONAL BREAKS: 0 output. Click on this button to open the EDIT CONDITIONAL BREAKS dialog, where you must create a new condition.

3. To add a new condition, click on the green ✚ icon. Set the language to JAVASCRIPT to define that the condition is entered in JavaScript.

4. Check whether the Before option is selected. If it is not, select it. With this option you define that the page break is to occur before you continue with processing.

5. For the to field, select the Top of Next Page option via the button located on the right-hand side of the field.

6. Finally, you must define the condition itself. To do so, enter the following in the when field: `(this.resolveNode("DATA[-1] .CARRID").rawValue !=` `this.resolveNode("DATA.CARRID").rawValue).`

The condition compares the value of the `CARRID` field of the preceding table row with the value of the current row. If the values differ, a page break needs to be made.

You can add the following statement to intercept the case of processing the first table row because there is no preceding row: `if` `(this.resolveNode("BOOKINGS. DATA[-1].CARRID") != null).` The previous condition must then be added to the curly brackets of the `If` statement. Section 7.3.8, Access to Data Nodes and Form Fields, discusses the `resolveNode` function. The dialog should now look as illustrated in Figure 7.13.

Figure 7.13 Dialog for Processing Conditional Page Breaks

Now look at the output. It now includes seven instead of the original two pages. Every airline ID is output on a new page as desired and defined in the condition for a page break.

Notes on Conditional Page Breaks

You can define various conditions for page breaks. Because every condition can have different effects (defined by the BEFORE, AFTER, and To options), the sequence is of relevance. For this reason, you can change the sequence using the two arrow icons in the dialog for editing conditional page breaks.

You can use the ▣ icon to the left of the condition's field to automatically create a proposal for a condition. If you click on this button, the system offers various form fields for which it can generate a condition.

Note on Pagination

In addition to the conditional page breaks, you can also define the placement of subforms and the use of overflow footer areas and overflow header areas in the PAGINATION tab of the OBJECT palette. You can find more notes on this topic in the Adobe LiveCycle Designer Help, where you can enter the search term "pagination subforms" and select the first help topic.

7.1.8 Form Output with Duplex Printing

The last modification of the form template is configuring for the support of duplex printing when the form is output on a duplex printer. To achieve this, you must use one page set and two master pages (one for the front and one for the back). To do so, you must extend the example of this chapter as follows:

1. Select the node (MASTER PAGES) that is located directly under the Data node in the hierarchy and rename it PageSet.

2. Click on the right mouse button on the Pageset node to display the context menu for the page set and select the NEW MASTER PAGE menu item.

3. Copy the static text, "NumberofPages," of PAGE1 by selecting it and following the EDIT • COPY menu path.

4. Paste the previously copied text to PAGE2. To do so, move PAGE2 until you can view the bottom area, then open the context menu below the content area with a right click to select the PASTE menu item.

5. Rename PAGE2 to "back" and PAGE1 to "front."

6. Move the static text, NUMBEROFPAGES, to the right on the front and to the left on the back. You can also set the paragraph for the NUMBEROFPAGES text on the front to right-aligned and on the back to left-aligned.

7. In addition, you can copy the `Footer` form field from the front to the back so that the footer is displayed on both the front and the back.

Up to now, you have carried out only preparations. In the next step, you actually configure the duplex printing.

1. Select the `Pageset` node.

2. The PAGE SET tab of the OBJECT palette includes the PRINTING dropdown list. Here, select the PRINT ON BOTH SIDES option. Confirm the dialog that indicates that this is supported only for PDFs with Adobe Reader/Adobe Acrobat 8.0 and later.

3. Select the front, and navigate to the PAGINATION tab in the OBJECT palette. Select the ODD (FRONT) PAGES option for the ODD/EVEN field. For the back, select the EVEN (BACK) PAGES option for the ODD/EVEN field (same procedure).

To test whether the last actions were successful, you must output the form on a printer that allows for duplex printing. However, the PDF preview or print view also enables you to recognize whether the pages were correctly assigned.

Note on the Placement of Master Pages

The previously mentioned PAGINATION tab of the OBJECT palette allows for a more accurate specification of the master pages' position in the output. The default setting "No Placement Restriction" was selected in this example.

To specify that an even number of pages is output, you can extend the previous example by adding another master page and selecting the EVEN (BACK) PAGES option in the ODD/EVEN field and setting the PLACEMENT to LAST PAGE (IN PAGE SET). Then this master page is used only if it is the last page and on a back page.

Complex Simplex and Duplex Printing Scenarios

This example considered a very simple duplex printing scenario. You can also use several page sets and combine them via the tray control. To select the page sets, you need conditional page breaks.

The Adobe LiveCycle Designer Help provides more information on this if you search for the key word "page set." You can also refer to SAP Note 1122142.

7.1.9 Output of the Completed Form Template

By outputting the form with duplex printing, you have completed the creation of a PDF-based print form. Figure 7.14 displays the form template for comparison.

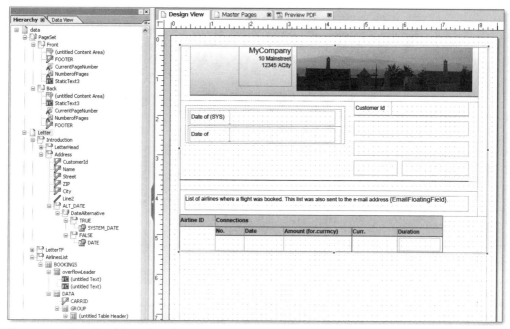

Figure 7.14 Completed Form Template

You can compare it with your form template and use it as a reference for the positioning of the form fields and the structure of the hierarchy. For a better overview of the output, Figure 7.15 shows the first page of a sample output (without conditional page breaks).

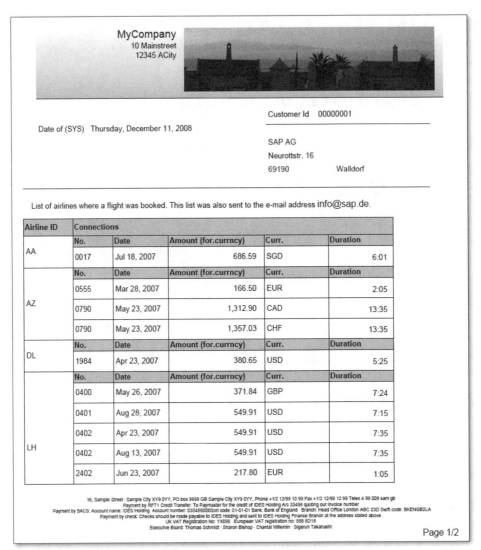

MyCompany
10 Mainstreet
12345 ACity

Customer Id   00000001

Date of (SYS)   Thursday, December 11, 2008

SAP AG
Neurottstr. 16
69190   Walldorf

List of airlines where a flight was booked. This list was also sent to the e-mail address info@sap.de.

Airline ID	Connections					
AA	No.	Date	Amount (for.currncy)	Curr.	Duration	
	0017	Jul 18, 2007	686.59	SGD	6:01	
AZ	No.	Date	Amount (for.currncy)	Curr.	Duration	
	0555	Mar 28, 2007	166.50	EUR	2:05	
	0790	May 23, 2007	1,312.90	CAD	13:35	
	0790	May 23, 2007	1,357.03	CHF	13:35	
DL	No.	Date	Amount (for.currncy)	Curr.	Duration	
	1984	Apr 23, 2007	380.65	USD	5:25	
LH	No.	Date	Amount (for.currncy)	Curr.	Duration	
	0400	May 26, 2007	371.84	GBP	7:24	
	0401	Aug 28, 2007	549.91	USD	7:15	
	0402	Apr 23, 2007	549.91	USD	7:35	
	0402	Aug 13, 2007	549.91	USD	7:35	
	2402	Jun 23, 2007	217.80	EUR	1:05	

16, Sample Street · Sample City XY9 0YY, PO box 9999 GB Sample City XY9 0YY, Phone +1/2 12/99 10 99 Fax +1/2 12/99 12 99 Telex 4 99 009 sam gb
Payment by RFT1 Credit Transfer: To Paymaster for the credit of IDES Holding A/c 33456 quoting our invoice number
Payment by BACS: Account name: IDES Holding Account number: 03345600 Sort code: 01-01-01 Bank: Bank of England Branch: Head Office London ABC 23D Swift code: BKENGB2LA
Payment by check: Checks should be made payable to IDES Holding and sent to IDES Holding Finance Branch at the address stated above.
UK VAT Registration No: YXD99 European VAT registration no: 888 8D18
Executive Board: Thomas Schmidt · Sharon Bishop · Chantal Willemin · Sigerun Takahashi

Page 1/2

Figure 7.15   First Page of the Final Output

7.2   Interactive PDF Forms

Whereas the creation of print outputs was the primary focus of the previous sections, the following sections concentrate on the creation of interactive PDF forms. These are required for Chapter 8, Integration with Web Dynpro ABAP; Chapter 9,

Internal Service Requests; Chapter 10, ABAP PDF Object; Chapter 11, ABAP PDF Object; and Chapter 12, Offline Scenarios via Web Services.

The behavior of the already-known form fields in interactive PDF forms is described first. Then the following sections introduce additional form fields and so-called dynamic properties.

7.2.1 Preparations

You must first prepare a new form object to reproduce the individual sections. To quickly check it, use the PDF preview. To do this, create a print program, and then specify the preview data for the form.

Creating a New Form

For the first steps for the interactive PDF forms, you need a simple interface that consists of only one table. You need to use the customer table from the flight-booking application here. Proceed as follows to create the interface (Section 4.2.1, ABAP Dictionary-Based Interface, provides a detailed description of the procedure):

1. Start Transaction SFP and create a new interface with the name Z_IFBA_ BOOK_DDIC_02.

2. Add a parameter to the interface. Enter CUSTOMERS as the name, TYPE as the type, and TY_CUSTOMERS as the type name. The parameter is not optional and the values are not passed.

3. Finally, save and activate the interface.

Next, create a new form. Proceed as follows (Section 4.3, Context of a Form, provides a detailed description of the procedure):

1. Create a new form with the name Z_IFBA_BOOK_FORM_03 in the start screen of Transaction SFP.

2. Add the CUSTOMERS interface parameter to the context.

3. Deactivate all of the fields but ID and NAME.

4. Save the form.

At a later stage, you must not forget to activate it after saving. However, this is not required at this point because you are just creating the form.

Print Program to Generate Preview Data

Now you need a print program to test the form in the print view or to generate test data. Section 6.1 describes how to create a print program in detail. Create the print program for this chapter as follows:

1. Start Transaction SE38 and create a new program with the name `Z_IFBA_BOOK_INTERACTIVE`.

2. Use the ABAP programming code in Listing 7.1.

3. Save and activate the program.

4. Now, create the preview data as described in Section 6.5.1. The usage of preview data is described in Section 5.3.2.

Note that in this context the print program in Listing 7.1 creates a dynamic, interactive PDF form for the preview. To do this, the two fields, `fillable` and `dynamic`, are set in `docparams`. These two code lines are bold in Listing 7.1.

```
PROGRAM z_ifba_book_interactive.
PARAMETERS: p_form   TYPE fpwbformname
                     DEFAULT 'Z_IFBA_BOOK_FORM_03',
            p_langu TYPE spras       DEFAULT 'D',
            p_ctry  TYPE land1       DEFAULT 'DE'.
DATA: gt_customers  TYPE        ty_customers,
      gs_outputpar  TYPE        sfpoutputparams,
      gv_fmname     TYPE        rs38l_fnam,
      gx_exc_api    TYPE REF TO cx_fp_api,
      gv_err_string TYPE        string,
      gs_docparams  TYPE        sfpdocparams.

SELECT * FROM scustom INTO TABLE gt_customers
   UP TO 10 ROWS
        ORDER BY PRIMARY KEY.
* Retrieve name of generated function module.
TRY.
    CALL FUNCTION 'FP_FUNCTION_MODULE_NAME'
      EXPORTING
        i_name     = p_form
      IMPORTING
        e_funcname = gv_fmname.
  CATCH cx_fp_api_repository
        cx_fp_api_usage
        cx_fp_api_internal INTO gx_exc_api.
```

```
      gv_err_string = gx_exc_api->get_text( ).
      MESSAGE  gv_err_string TYPE 'E'.
ENDTRY.
* Start print job.
gs_outputpar-reqnew = abap_true.
CALL FUNCTION 'FP_JOB_OPEN'
  CHANGING
    ie_outputparams = gs_outputpar
  EXCEPTIONS
    cancel          = 1
    usage_error     = 2
    system_error    = 3
    internal_error  = 4
    OTHERS          = 5.
IF sy-subrc <> 0.
  MESSAGE ID sy-msgid TYPE sy-msgty NUMBER sy-msgno
          WITH sy-msgv1 sy-msgv2 sy-msgv3 sy-msgv4.
ENDIF.
* Set language and country.
gs_docparams-langu    = p_langu.
gs_docparams-country  = p_ctry.
gs_docparams-fillable = abap_true.
gs_docparams-dynamic  = abap_true.
* Call generated function module (form).
CALL FUNCTION gv_fmname
  EXPORTING
    /1bcdwb/docparams       = gs_docparams
    customers               = gt_customers
* IMPORTING
*   /1BCDWB/FORMOUTPUT      =
  EXCEPTIONS
    usage_error             = 1
    system_error            = 2
    internal_error          = 3
    OTHERS                  = 4.
IF sy-subrc <> 0.
  MESSAGE ID sy-msgid TYPE sy-msgty NUMBER sy-msgno
          WITH sy-msgv1 sy-msgv2 sy-msgv3 sy-msgv4.
ENDIF.
* Close print job.
CALL FUNCTION 'FP_JOB_CLOSE'
* IMPORTING
*   E_RESULT                =
```

```
EXCEPTIONS
    usage_error         = 1
    system_error        = 2
    internal_error      = 3
    OTHERS              = 4.
IF sy-subrc <> 0.
  MESSAGE ID sy-msgid TYPE sy-msgty NUMBER sy-msgno
          WITH sy-msgv1 sy-msgv2 sy-msgv3 sy-msgv4.
ENDIF.
```

Listing 7.1 Print Program for the Interactive PDF Form

Preparing the PDF Preview

To use the PDF preview, define the properties of the PDF preview. Proceed as follows:

1. Start Transaction SFP, select the previously created form, Z_IFBA_BOOK_FORM_03, and then navigate to the form editing functions (in CHANGE MODE).

2. Here, go to the LAYOUT tab to display the form in Adobe LiveCycle Designer.

3. Follow the EDIT • FORM PROPERTIES… menu path, and navigate to the PREVIEW tab of the dialog that opens.

The following three steps define the properties of the PDF form for the preview. Like the print program, the PDF preview is supposed to display a dynamic, interactive PDF form. In addition, you can specify the preview data. Figure 7.16 shows the FORM PROPERTIES dialog and the corresponding tab.

Figure 7.16 Preview Tab of the Form Properties Dialog

1. Set the PREVIEW TYPE to INTERACTIVE FORM.

2. Select the DYNAMIC XML FORM entry in the PREVIEW ADOBE XML FORM AS field.

3. For the DATA FILE, select the file that you created in the previous section when generating the preview data.

PDF Preview of Interactive PDF Forms

No usage rights are added for the generation of a PDF document in Adobe LiveCycle Designer. If you use the PDF preview to test interactive PDF forms, the system displays a warning that the input cannot be stored (see Section 2.2.1, Comparing Adobe Reader and Acrobat Professional). You can select the DON'T SHOW AGAIN option to not to have to confirm this dialog for each test.

Note that some functions may be restricted due to missing usage rights. In this case, you must generate the PDF form using the print program created in this chapter and then use it for testing.

Copying the Form Template for Reuse in Multiple Examples

At this point, you can copy the previously created form; the procedure was described in Section 5.7.1, Creating Copies of Forms. This enables you to distribute the following examples across several forms for test purposes; for example, you can create a new form after each section according to your requirements by copying the empty form.

Now, create a copy of the `Z_IFBA_BOOK_FORM_03` form and assign the following name to it: `Z_IFBA_BOOK_FORM_03_EMPTY`. The preparations are now complete. The following sections introduce the different aspects of interactive PDF forms in detail.

7.2.2   From PDF-Based Print Forms to Interactive PDF Forms

In Chapter 5 and during the course of this chapter, you created a print form. Everything that you have learned about form creation so far also applies to the creation of interactive PDF forms. This section discusses those fields that also have an interactive behavior. These include text fields, decimal fields, and date/time fields. These form fields are used to describe the editable status of form fields and to extend the usage of patterns to input and validation.

Text Fields

In interactive PDF forms, text fields enable you to enter a text. The text can have one or more lines. The fact that you do not know the text length in advance is the most important aspect when handling text fields. Look at the first example, which shows how this is handled when no preparations were made during the form template creation.

1. Start Transaction SFP, open the Z_IFBA_BOOK_FORM_03 form in change mode, and navigate to the LAYOUT tab.
2. Drag and drop a text field from the STANDARD library to the upper left of the form template.
3. Then call the PDF preview, and enter a text that exceeds the text field.
4. Exit the text fields either by clicking next to the field or pressing the TAB key.

Examine the result (see Figure 7.17). Because the text does not fit into the text field, the system displays a plus sign in the lower right-hand corner of the text field. The following sections detail four different options for handling this case.

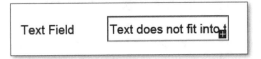

Text Field   Text does not fit into

Figure 7.17 Display of Text Fields with Exceeding Text

1. Return to the DESIGN VIEW, and select the text field.
2. Increase the width of the text field so that you can enter more text.
3. Navigate to the FIELD tab of the OBJECT palette.
4. Here, select the LIMIT LENGTH TO VISIBLE AREA option (see Figure 7.18).
5. Check the behavior of the text field in the PDF preview.

Now you can only enter as much text as fits into the text field. This procedure limits the length of the text to the visible area but has the disadvantage that you do not know the number of characters.

It is therefore better to define the number of characters that can be entered because the data are to be processed and thus are usually subject to length restrictions. Proceed as follows:

Figure 7.18 Field Tab for a Text Field

1. Return to the DESIGN VIEW and select the text field.

2. Deselect the LIMIT LENGTH TO VISIBLE AREA option and select the LIMIT LENGTH option instead. Enter "30" into the MAX. CHARS input field, for example.

3. Check the behavior in the PDF preview. The number of possible characters is limited to a maximum of 30. The text field does not accept further input.

So far, we have discussed only how to limit the input. Alternatively, the system can automatically adapt the font size or enlarge the text field. Let's first look at how to adapt the font size in the following example:

1. Navigate to the DESIGN VIEW and add another text field to the form template.

2. Select the new text field, and enable the ALLOW MULTIPLE LINES option.

3. Increase the width and the height of the text field so that you can enter more text. If the EXPAND TO FIT message is displayed, confirm it. You already selected the option in the previous step.

4. Navigate to the PARAGRAPH palette and select ALIGN LEFT and ALIGN TOP for the caption and the value (see Figure 7.19).

Figure 7.19   Paragraph Palette

5. Then navigate to the FONT palette. Here, select that you only want to edit the value properties.

6. Enter "0" into the size input field to activate the automatic determination of the font size. This value is not provided in the dropdown list (see Figure 7.20).

Figure 7.20   Font Palette with Font Size 0

7. Go to the PDF preview to check the behavior.

If you enter more text than fits into the text field, the system automatically decreases the font size. The advantage of this is that the complete text is always visible. However, it makes sense to select this option only for large, multiple-line text fields; otherwise, the font quickly becomes too small and illegible.

The options detailed so far do not affect the layout of the form. The following procedure, however, uses so-called *resizable text fields* and thus affects the layout.

The following description shows how you can add such text fields to the form template.

1. Add a third text field to the form template.

2. Select it and activate the ALLOW MULTIPLE LINES option in the FIELD tab of the OBJECT palette.

3. In the DESIGN VIEW, increase the width and the height so that you can enter more text.

4. Navigate to the PARAGRAPH palette and select ALIGN TOP for the caption and the value.

5. Go to the PDF preview to check the behavior.

If you now enter a multiple-line text that does not fit into the text field, a scrollbar appears on the right of the text field when you enter the text (see Figure 7.21). When you exit the field, the scrollbar disappears, and the system no longer displays the entire text. The plus sign (+) is displayed again to indicate that the entire text is not visible.

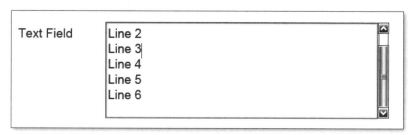

Figure 7.21 Scrollbar in a Text Field During the Input

To have the system display the entire text, you must define that the height of the text field is allowed to change. The text field then becomes a resizable text field.

1. To do this, select the third text field and navigate to the PARAGRAPH palette.

2. Here, select the EXPAND TO FIT option below the input field for the height to define that the system may adapt the height of the field after text has been entered (see Figure 7.22).

3. Check the behavior in the PDF preview.

Figure 7.22 Layout Palette with the EXPAND TO FIT Option Selected

Let's look at a case where more text is entered than fits into the field. During the input, the scrollbar is displayed, but the size of the text field is adapted accordingly after you have exited it. If you delete lines at a later stage, the system decreases the size of the text field again. However, the size of the text field never falls below the values that you specified during the creation of the form template because this defines the minimum height of the text field.

Using Resizable Text Fields

You must use resizable text fields in a subform hierarchy that has flow content. Otherwise, the form may become illegible due to overlapping form fields. For the sake of simplicity, the example did not discuss these aspects. This concept is described in Section 7.1.4, Page Breaks.

Editable State of Form Fields

All text fields that you previously added to the interactive PDF form were automatically ready for input. However, this is not wanted in all cases. The form may contain areas that have been filled in with data in advance that are not supposed to be modified by the user because it is for information only. An example of this may be a customer ID that has been assigned by the system and is not supposed to be changed by the customer.

This section discusses the following three editable states that assume a critical role:

▶ **User Entered — Optional**
For this option, the input for the form field is optional; that is, it is not relevant for the further processing of the form whether data has been entered or not.

▶ **User Entered — Required**
This option defines that the user must enter data into this form field for further processing. The form processor receives a message in three cases. If the user exits the form field without entering data or making a selection, the system outputs a message in the form of a dialog. The form can be submitted only if all required fields are populated. In Adobe Reader, you can highlight form fields; that is, form fields that require input are indicated by a red frame.

▶ **Read Only**
This option defines that this is just an output field. The user of the form cannot change the value or selection.

The following example illustrates a case where input is required. To do this, define the ready-for-input status for a text field as follows:

1. Select the initially added text field.

2. Navigate to the VALUE tab of the OBJECT palette.

3. For TYPE, select the USER ENTERED–REQUIRED entry.

4. In the EMPTY MESSAGE input field that is displayed after having selected the option in the previous step, enter the text "Please fill in field." (See Figure 7.23).

5. For fields that require input, you must specify a data binding. Therefore, define the data binding for the text field by dragging and dropping the NAME node under DATA from the data view to the text field.

   You can ignore that the data binding contains [*] in the binding expression (due to the repeating data in the table structure). Only the first data value is output.

Figure 7.23 Value Tab of the Object Palette for the Text Field

6. Now, call the PDF PREVIEW.

7. Select HIGHLIGHT FIELDS in the upper-right corner of Adobe Reader (see Figure 7.24). This highlights all form fields that are ready for input in gray-blue; the text field that requires an input is indicated by a red frame.

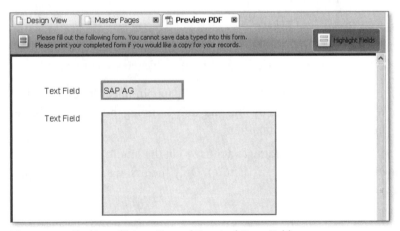

Figure 7.24 Marking of Interactive and Required Form Fields

8. In the last step, delete the content of the first text field and exit the text field by clicking next to it or pressing the TAB key. A dialog box opens that displays the previously specified error message.

Defining the Editable State of Form Fields

For interactive PDF forms, you need to define the editable status for all form fields so that the user can only modify the content of those fields for which this is intended. This aspect is not relevant for the print output because all form fields are always inactive here.

Decimal Field

For the print output, a decimal field was used to output the costs for the flights. For interactive PDF forms, the decimal fields are used to enter numeric values. Because decimal fields always require the input of a numeric value, you cannot use all characters. For example, the letter A does not make sense for numbers and thus cannot be entered. In addition, the decimal fields provide an easy option for limiting the number of leading and trailing digits. This is illustrated in the following example.

1. Drag and drop a decimal field from the STANDARD library to the form template.

2. Select the decimal field and navigate to the FIELD tab of the OBJECT palette.

3. Select LIMIT LEADING DIGITS, and enter "3" into the input field.

4. Select LIMIT TRAILING DIGITS and enter "2" into the input field.

5. Check the behavior by navigating to the PDF preview and entering various values.

You can check that you can only enter digits and, for example, a minus sign at the beginning, or a comma, but no characters. If decimal places are not allowed (due to limiting the number of trailing digits to zero), it is because the system does not accept decimal points.

Using Decimal Fields and Numeric Fields

In addition to decimal fields, numeric fields are also available. You should use decimal fields because the integrated support for leading and trailing digits facilitates the creation of form templates.

Date/Time Field

The date/time field that is used for the print output can be used for a formatted output and for the input of a date or time. There are two options for entering a date: either directly with the keyboard or with the mouse using a so-called datepicker (see Figure 7.25).

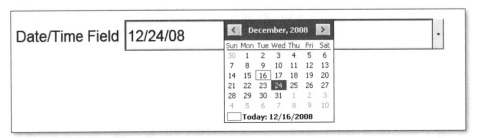

Figure 7.25 Datepicker to Input a Date

The following example illustrates this:

1. Drag and drop a date/time field from the STANDARD library to the form template.

2. Check whether the data format in the BINDING tab of the OBJECT palette is set to DATE.

3. Go to the FIELD tab of the OBJECT palette, and click on the PATTERNS... button. Enter "date{EEEE, D. MMMM YYYY}" in the PATTERN: field of the DISPLAY tab in the pattern dialog.

4. Enlarge the date field until the complete date can be displayed.

5. Navigate to PREVIEW PDF.

You should first try to enter the date directly into the field using the keyboard. If you correctly enter the date, it is displayed in the long form. You probably noticed that it was quite difficult to enter the date directly. The reason for this is that no explicit input pattern has been specified—the default pattern is MM/DD/YY. Try again to enter a date.

It is considerably easier to use the datepicker. When you click into the date field, the system displays a button on the right (see Figure 7.25). By clicking on this button, the calendar window opens, and you can select a day by clicking on it or go from month to month in the upper half of the calendar window.

In the context of the direct entry of data, you were introduced to the edit patterns. Using the previously added date field as an example, the following sections discuss these patterns in detail.

Patterns

So far, you know of two types of patterns: display and data patterns. For interactive PDF forms, however, there are two additional patterns: the edit and the validation pattern.

Edit and Validation Patterns

Edit and validation patterns are used to increase the quality of the input data. They enable you to validate the input directly when the user processes the form and to have the user correct the input, if required. Therefore, you should use them whenever possible (for example, for email addresses, telephone numbers, customer names, etc.).

The use of edit and validation patterns is explained in the following sections using the previously added date field as an example. The procedure is the same for all form field types.

Using Edit Patterns

To test the usage of edit patterns, navigate to the PDF preview, and enter "01/01/2008" into the date field. Because the date is not spelled out after you enter it, you know that the entry was not accepted. No message is output here. This is further discussed in Section 7.2.2. First, you need to facilitate the entry using another edit pattern. Proceed as follows:

1. Return to the DESIGN VIEW and select the date field.

2. Click on PATTERNS... in the FIELD tab of the OBJECT palette to open the PATTERNS dialog. Go to the EDIT tab and enter "date{M/D/YYYY}" as the pattern.

   To facilitate the input, the system is accepts the one-digit input of the day and month. In the M/D/YYYY edit pattern, the single M or D represents the one- or two-digit input of the month or day. If you use MM (or DD), the user always has to enter the month or day with two digits, for example, 12/24/2020.

3. Check the PDF preview to see whether the previously defined edit pattern is accepted.

For example, enter "12/24/20." This input is not accepted by the edit pattern because it expects you to enter a four-digit year. Because the short version for years is often used in dates, you must modify the edit pattern so that it accepts both alternatives — the two-digit and the four-digit input for the year. Proceed as follows:

1. Return to the DESIGN VIEW.

2. Select the date field, and navigate to the EDIT tab of the pattern dialog.

3. Enter "date{M/D/YYYY}|date{M/D/YY}" in the Pattern field.

   By using the vertical slash in edit patterns, you can define two or more alternative patterns. The order is important here. The complete pattern is read from left to right, and the first pattern that can be successfully implemented cancels the processing.

   In this example, the difference between these two alternatives is the two- or four-digit year, mapped accordingly by YY or YYYY in the edit pattern.

4. Return to the PDF preview and enter dates with different formats to see what happens.

Using Validation Patterns

The next problem that you must solve is the missing message that should be displayed when the date has been entered with the wrong format. To do this, you use a validation pattern. Validation patterns are a comfortable way to check whether the correct input format was used for the input. A correct format also implies that no nonexistent days or months are used for the date. You can check this by simply entering "13" for the month: The system will not display a message.

To solve this problem, customize the form template as follows:

1. Return to the DESIGN VIEW, and select the date field if it is no longer selected.

2. Then go to the VALUE tab and click on the VALIDATION PATTERN... button to open the PATTERN dialog. The VALIDATION tab is selected automatically.

3. Enter "date{M/D/YYYY}|date{M/D/YY}" in the PATTERN field. It is the same pattern as the edit pattern and also uses the alternative of two- or four-digit years.

4. Click OK to close the PATTERN dialog.

5. Enter the following text into the VALIDATION PATTERN MESSAGE input field (see Figure 7.26): "Please enter a valid date using one of the following patterns M/D/YY or M/D/YYYY."

Figure 7.26 Defining the Validation Pattern in the Value Tab

6. Finally, select the ERROR option (located directly above the input field for the message) to define that it is an error if the validation of the input fails. This affects further processing.

7. Navigate to the PDF preview, and enter a date with an invalid month or day (for example, "12/32/20""). You receive a dialog (see Figure 7.27) that displays the text that you defined in the example. The problem of the missing message is now solved.

Figure 7.27 Message for Failed Validation

Complex Display Patterns

To complement the example, take a closer look at the display patterns again. You are already familiar with the definition of alternatives. Now you can use this knowledge in the following sections to output a text if no values exists for the date field. Proceed as follows:

1. Return to the DESIGN VIEW, and select the date field.

2. Go to the FIELD tab of the OBJECT palette and click on PATTERNS....

3. Here, enter the following new pattern: "null{'M/D/YYYY or M/D/YY'}|date{EEEE, MMMM D, YYYY}."

4. Return to the PDF preview.

The new display pattern uses so-called *pattern categories*:

▶ On one hand, the date category is used for the date pattern.

▶ On the other hand, the special category null is used to process null values (nonexisting values).

In the curly brackets, the pattern for the category is specified. In the example, the string itself is used as the display pattern for null values. The string does not contain formatting symbols. Therefore, the text is displayed in the date field (see Figure 7.28). If a value exists, it is formatted according to the date pattern. The previously defined display pattern is used.

Figure 7.28 Display of the Date Field in the Case of Missing Values

The XFA describes patterns in more detail. For more information on this specification, refer to Section 7.7.3.

7.2.3 Form Fields of Interactive PDF Forms

In addition to the already-described form fields that can be used for the print output and for interactive PDF forms, there are several form fields that are specific for use in interactive PDF forms. They can also be used for the print output but are not functional there. Instead, they display the current status.

Example: Specific Fields from Interactive Forms for Print Output

For example, they display the selected list item for dropdown lists or display whether a checkbox is selected or not.

The following sections discuss password fields, buttons, image fields, checkboxes, radio buttons, dropdown lists, and list boxes successively. They are added to the template to enable you to test their behavior. Figure 7.29 illustrates what the form fields mentioned earlier look like in an interactive PDF form.

Figure 7.29 Overview of the Interactive Form Fields

Password Field

Password fields enable you to enter a text without displaying the characters and numbers on the screen.

1. Drag and drop a password field from the STANDARD library to the form template.

2. Navigate to the FIELD tab of the OBJECT palette.

3. Here, you can define which character or sign is supposed to be displayed for the entered characters or numbers. To do this, you must specify the character in the PASSWORD DISPLAY CHARACTER input field.

In the PDF preview, you can enter a text into the password field. The system displays only the previously defined display character instead of the characters and numbers entered. The entered password cannot be read on the screen, but it is provided as clear text in the data. If a password is supposed to be encrypted, the encryption must be implemented by a script program.

Buttons

Buttons are a common part of user interfaces. If you click on them, an action is triggered. For this example, the action is the submission of an interactive PDF form as an email attachment. This can be achieved as follows:

1. Add a button to the form template.

2. Then select the button and navigate to the FIELD tab.

3. Set the CONTROL TYPE to SUBMIT. An additional tab is displayed in the OBJECT palette.

By default, the control type is set to NORMAL. In this case, the action must be implemented via script programming (see Section 7.3.1, First Script Program). These two special cases—the call of a Web service and the submission to a URL—are supported by a specific control type; the process of calling a Web service (EXECUTE control type) is described in detail in Chapter 12. This section deals only with the submission.

To define the exact activities for the submission, proceed as follows:

1. Navigate to the SUBMIT tab.

2. Enter the following text into the SUBMIT TO URL input field: "mailto:<email address>." Replace <email address> with your actual email address (see Figure 7.30).

Figure 7.30 Submit Tab for the Button

3. Select PDF for Submit As. This defines that the system is supposed to submit the PDF itself. All other options are not discussed in this section.

4. To test the submission of the PDF, you must use the print program to generate the PDF because this process requires usage rights. By clicking on the button, your email program is started and a window opens where you can edit a new email. The PDF is already attached to this new email. Thus, the email program is responsible for the actual submission.

5. At this point, have another look at the required input and the validation patterns. Delete the content of the first text field for which the input is required and click on the button to submit the PDF. The system displays the message that indicates that at least one form field that requires input is not filled. In addition, this field is highlighted with a red frame. The email cannot be submitted until all required form fields are filled.

6. Enter text into the form field so that you can test the validation pattern for the date field at a later stage.

7. Enter an incorrect date (for example, 1/2/3) into the date field. A message is displayed that reads that the date is not correct.

8. Then click on the button to submit the PDF. The dialog is displayed again to inform you prior to the submission that the date field is filled incorrectly. After having confirmed the dialog, the system displays another dialog that indicates

that the submission has been cancelled. The reason is that you defined that it is regarded as an error if the validation with the pattern fails for the validation pattern.

Image Field

Image fields are different from static images in that they are interactive and thus enable you to upload an image to the PDF form. You can also define a data binding here. A data binding enables you to provide image data via the XML data stream. If you want to contain the image data in the XML data stream, you must set the image field to READ-ONLY, as described in Section 7.3.5, Editable State of Form Fields.

You can add an image field to the form template for testing purposes. The following file formats are supported: Windows Bitmap (BMP), Joint Picture Experts Group (JPG), Graphic Interchange Format (GIF), Portable Network Graphics (PNG), and some variants of the Tagged Image File (TIF) format. You can find those in the Adobe LiveCycle Designer Help using the key words "image fields overview."

Checkboxes

You can use checkboxes to provide options in interactive PDF forms, for example, a checkbox in a form for renting a car. The user can then select or deselect these options. In addition to the car itself, the requester can use checkboxes to select an insurance category and a GPS device.

Three definitions must be examined for using checkboxes:

▶ **States**
In the FIELD tab of the OBJECT palette, you can define whether the checkbox should have two (ON/OFF) or three (ON/OFF/NEUTRAL) states.

▶ **Value for the states**
In the BINDING tab, you can specify the data value for the states.

▶ **Appearance and check style**
The appearance and check style of the checkbox are again defined in the FIELD tab. For appearance, you are provided with the following options: SUNKEN CIRCLE, SUNKEN SQUARE, SOLID CIRCLE, and SOLID SQUARE. For the check style, you can choose from DEFAULT, CHECK, CIRCLE, CROSS, DIAMOND, SQUARE, and STAR.

At this point, test the behavior of the checkboxes by adding three checkboxes to the form template, for example, and selecting different combinations of the appearance and check style. You should also use a checkbox with three states and check in the PDF preview how the neutral state is mapped. In contrast to the ON state, the icon (for example, CHECK) is mapped in gray instead of black.

Radio Button

Generally, radio buttons behave the same way as checkboxes. However, there is one difference: Radio buttons are combined in so-called *radio button groups*. Exactly one radio button can be selected for one radio button group. For this reason, radio button groups are also often referred to as *exclusion groups*. However, multiple radio button groups can be used in one form.

Example for Using a Radio Button Group

In a form for renting a car, you can use a radio button group to select either partial or comprehensive coverage, because these two options exclude each other.

The use of radio button groups is illustrated using the following example:

1. Navigate to the DESIGN VIEW and add four radio buttons to the form template.

2. In the HIERARCHY palette, you can see that all four radio buttons of a radio button list (this is the name of the exclusion group) were added.

3. Right-click on the third radio button in the hierarchy (or design view) to display its context menu for the page set, and select the WRAP IN NEW RADIO BUTTON GROUP menu item to create a new exclusion group.

4. Drag and drop the last added (fourth) radio button in the hierarchy to the second exclusion group. The black bar indicates where you would add the radio button if you released the mouse button (see Figure 7.31).

In the PDF preview, you can make sure that the user can only select a single option in both exclusion groups. To use radio buttons, you must specify the data values for the individual options in the BINDING OF THE OBJECT palette.

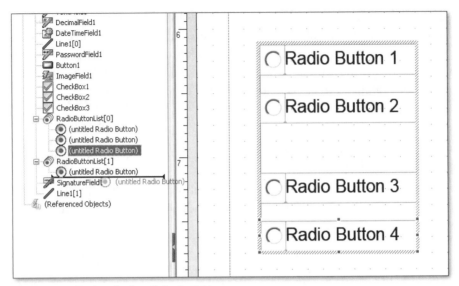

Figure 7.31 Moving the Fourth Radio Button

Document Signature Field

Document signature fields enable you to prevent further entries to the form fields and identify the user that signed the PDF form by means of their certificate. When processing a signed document, you can check whether the document has been modified since the last signature and which certificate was used for the signature. The certificates must be assigned to the users by the application itself.

If you have a certificate, you can reproduce the following example. Here, you need to use the print program again, because the corresponding usage right is required for the digital signature.

1. Add a signature field to the form template.

2. Navigate to the SIGNATURE tab of the OBJECT palette and select the LOCK FIELDS AFTER SIGNING option.

3. In the dropdown list, select ALL FIELDS IN DOCUMENT.

You can test the document signature field in the PDF preview.

▶ Once you have signed the document, the system locks all input fields.

▶ After having deleted the signature via the CLEAR SIGNATURE menu item in the context menu of the signature field, the form fields are ready for input again.

▶ You can define the list of the form fields that are to be locked by using collections. This is illustrated in the Adobe LiveCycle Designer Help under the key word "collections."

Section 11.4.3, Validation of a Digital Signature, analyzes the usage of signature fields and the validation of the signature in more detail.

Note on the Usage of Document Signatures

SAP Note 834573 states that you need at least Adobe Reader 8.1 to use document signatures. Another point is the size of the PDF files when you use document signatures. With each document signature, the size of the PDF file increases because additional information on the state of the PDF at the time of the signature must be added. This cannot be avoided for the document signature function and thus needs to be considered in its usage.

Dropdown List and List Box

Finally we look at the dropdown list and the list box. Both provide a list of entries the user can select from. For dropdown lists, the user can view the list only during the selection and can only select one entry. In contrast, for list boxes, part of the list or the entire list is visible and you can define whether multiple entries can be selected or not. However, the direct input of a value is only enabled by dropdown lists. To test this, supplement the form template as follows:

1. Navigate to the DESIGN VIEW.

2. Add a dropdown list to the form template.

3. Add a list box to the right of the dropdown list.

4. Select the dropdown list and navigate to the FIELD tab of the OBJECT palette.

5. Here, select the ALLOW CUSTOM ENTRY option.

For the test, the most important element is missing: the list of the entries. Both the dropdown list and the list box enable you to compile these list entries in the FIELD and BINDING tabs (both belong to the OBJECT palette). An entry in the list consists of the text of the list entry that is displayed in the PDF form and the input value that is used in the data model.

The definition of the list entries in the form template has the disadvantage that the lists must be maintained twice if the entries are not known in advance or if the entries frequently change; that is, they must be maintained in Customizing and in the form template. For these cases, a better approach is to transfer list entries through data when generating the PDF form. This is enabled by so-called *dynamic properties*.

7.2.4 Dynamic Properties

Dynamic properties enable you to dynamically define a form template at runtime instead of during creation. These properties include list entries of dropdown lists and list boxes, captions of form fields, validation messages and tool tips, and user-defined screen reader text for the input/output help (see Section 7.6, Introduction to Accessible PDF Forms). The properties are defined via bindings to data nodes. How this works is described next.

Activation of the Dynamic Properties

To use dynamic properties, you must first activate them.

1. To do this, follow the TOOLS • OPTIONS... menu path and navigate to the DATA BINDING area.

2. The DYNAMIC PROPERTIES area contains the SHOW DYNAMIC PROPERTIES option (see Figure 7.32). Select this option.

3. If you want to, you can define a color for the label of the input fields of Adobe LiveCycle Designer (the default setting is green).

Figure 7.32 Data Binding Options

Dynamic Population of Dropdown Lists

Similar to hyperlinks, the system underlines properties of form fields that can be defined by dynamic properties and maps them in green. Figure 7.33 illustrates this for the CAPTION and the LIST ITEMS of the dropdown list. In addition, the figure displays a little chain icon after the LIST ITEMS field. This is visible after a dynamic property has been defined, for example, the list entries in this case.

Figure 7.33 Caption and List Items as Dynamic Properties

To define the list entries for the dropdown list, proceed as follows:

1. Select the dropdown list and navigate to the FIELD tab of the OBJECT palette.

2. Click on LIST ITEMS to open the DYNAMIC PROPERTIES dialog.

3. Similar to the procedure for defining the data binding manually (see Section 5.3.1, Defining the Data Binding), define the binding for the items to the repeating node, DATA, under CUSTOMERS.

4. Then you implement a binding of the item text and the item value as NAME and ID. This is relative to the binding of the items. Figure 7.34 illustrates what the dialog for the definition of the dynamic properties should look like after you have performed the preceding steps.

Figure 7.34 Dynamic Properties for the List Items Dialog

5. In the data view, nodes that are bound by a dynamic property are indicated by a specific icon. This icon is shown in Figure 7.35.

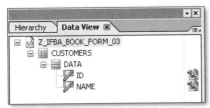

Figure 7.35 Indicator in the Data View for Nodes That Are Bound by Dynamic Properties

6. The procedure for defining list entries for list boxes is identical to the procedure for dropdown lists. Therefore, perform the same steps for the list box.

7. You can check in the PDF preview which entries were used to populate the list and how the selected entry is displayed (see Figure 7.36). For the DROP-DOWN LIST, the selected entry is mapped in an input field. For the LIST BOX, the selected entries are highlighted by a blue background.

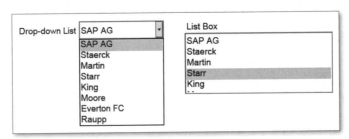

Figure 7.36 Open Dropdown List and List Box

Dynamic Captions and Texts

In addition to the dynamic population of the list entries of dropdown lists and list boxes, the dynamic properties also enable you to provide captions, texts, and messages. The following section describes this procedure using the caption as an example:

1. Select a form field and navigate to the FIELD tab of the OBJECT palette.
2. Click on CAPTION to open the dialog that is shown in Figure 7.37.

Figure 7.37 Dynamic Properties for the List Items Dialog

3. In this dialog, you can define the Binding for the caption text the same way as for normal data bindings.

For the transfer of fields, no fields are provided in the context that is based on the example for the interactive forms. To check the functionality for this example, you can bind the caption to the CUSTOMERS • DATA • NAME node. This works without problems in the example. However, in real-life scenarios, you should not bind captions to a repeating data node because every caption should be uniquely bound to one data node.

7.3 Using Script Programs

In some cases, the desired functionality cannot be defined in a graphical interactive way due to its complexity. Some examples include validations that go beyond the mere use of patterns, complex calculations based on data and user entries, and the dynamic behavior of interactive PDF forms, such as displaying and hiding form fields or adding or deleting table rows. Therefore, form creation also supports the programming of script programs.

The following sections use examples to introduce you to using script programs in interactive PDF forms. Figure 7.39 illustrates the form template that you will develop in this section. You can also use script programs for print forms. Chapter 12 provides additional examples that make extended use of script programs.

This topic is described in more detail in Section 7.7.2, Adobe Designer Scripting Reference and in the documentation mentioned in Section 7.7.3, XML Forms Architecture. It contains more examples and the names of the properties that are used in the following script programs.

7.3.1   First Script Program

The basic principles and the usage of script programs can be illustrated with a simple example, which we will look at in the following sections.

Script Languages and Events

You can create script programs in two script languages. The first language is JavaScript, which is commonly known. The second language is called FormCalc, which is a script language developed by Adobe. The use of FormCalc is somewhat easier if you want to carry out calculations, particularly on the basis of table structures. The advantage of JavaScript is its popularity.

The execution of script programs is always triggered by an event. For example, by clicking on a button, the `click` event is triggered. Another example is the `docReady` event. It occurs after all preparations and required processes have been completed. The difference between these two examples is that the `click` event requires a user interaction, whereas the `docReady` event requires no interaction at all. Therefore, events can be divided into two groups: *interaction events* and *system events*.

This book uses JavaScript as the script language, again, due to its popularity. It is expected that you are familiar with its basic principles. Forms provided by SAP mostly use FormCalc. Section 7.7.3 contains more information on FormCalc.

Preparations

To reproduce the description, you need a new form template. Proceed as follows:

1. Start Transaction SFP.

2. Create a new form template, Z_IFBA_BOOK_FORM_04, by copying the backup copy (Z_IFBA_BOOK_FORM_03_EMPTY) that you created in Section 7.2.1, Preparations.

3. Start editing the new form template by navigating to the LAYOUT tab in Form Builder. Then, call the dialog for defining the form properties via the EDIT • FORM PROPERTIES... menu path.

   In this dialog (see Figure 7.38), you set two default values to simplify the procedure of creating new script programs for the following examples.

Figure 7.38 Form Properties for Scripting

4. Click on the DEFAULTS tab in the dialog.

5. In the SCRIPTING area, set the DEFAULT LANGUAGE to JAVASCRIPT.

6. Then check whether DEFAULT RUN AT is set to CLIENT.

This way, you have defined that all new script programs are, by default, created in JavaScript and that the script programs are displayed in Adobe Reader (client) so that you can easily test them. The alternatives are to have the system run the script programs at the server (SERVER option) or to combine both types (CLIENT AND SERVER option).

Script Editor

First, create a script program that is called when you click a particular button.

1. Add a new button to the form template.

2. If the script editor is hidden, display it via the PALETTES • SCRIPT EDITOR menu path (see Figure 7.39).

Figure 7.39 Script Editor with Script Program for the Example

3. Enlarge the area for the script editor by keeping the mouse button pressed and moving the border at the bottom of the script editor downward to have more space available for entering script programs.

4. Open the SHOW dropdown list and select the click event from the list of all available events.

5. Go to the input field and enter the following programming code:

```
xfa.host.messageBox("SAP Interactive Forms by Adobe");
```

The messageBox function opens a message box that outputs a text (the parameter). The xfa.host expression identifies an object that provides the basic functions and properties. The currentPage property indicates the currently displayed page. When entering the program code, you probably noticed that a selection area was displayed after the point (.) for supporting completion of the code. This box provides all available functions and properties, including a short description (see Figure 7.40).

344

Figure 7.40 Completion of Script Code

6. Test the form in the PDF preview. After you have clicked on the button on the form, the system opens a message box that displays the text "SAP Interactive Forms by Adobe."

7. To proceed, you must confirm the dialog by clicking OK.

Syntax Check for Script Programs

As of Adobe LiveCycle Designer 8.1, you can check script programs for syntax errors. You can run this check via the CHECK SCRIPT SYNTAX button (🗩) or via the TOOLS • CHECK SCRIPT SYNTAX menu path. This check always considers all script programs up to the first syntax error, not only the script programs for the selected form field. Use the following example to reproduce the syntax check:

1. Select the button for the message box from the first example and go to the script editor.

2. Delete parts of the statement to generate a syntax error (see the example of Figure 7.41).

3. Click on the CHECK SCRIPT SYNTAX button or select the menu item to trigger the check.

4. The program should now display the message shown in Figure 7.41. The script editor highlights in red the row with the syntax error.

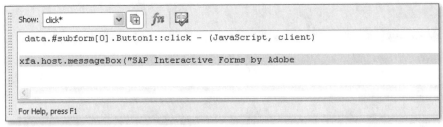

Figure 7.41 Highlighted Syntax Error in the Script Editor

The syntax errors are also displayed in the WARNINGS tab of the REPORT palette. If they are hidden, select the PALETTES • REPORT menu to show them. Because the program always checks all script programs, the form field is displayed with a description of the error (see Figure 7.42). By double-clicking on the error message, you can select the form field and call the script program directly in the script editor to remedy the syntax error.

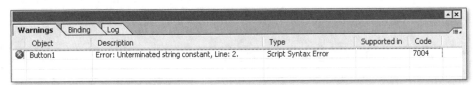

Figure 7.42 Warnings Palette with Syntax Error Message

7.3.2 Tips for Debugging Script Programs

When testing script programs, it is often difficult to determine at which point the execution of the script program was aborted. For example, the execution of the script program may be aborted due to expressions invalid at runtime, nonexistent objects, or a syntax error not remedied. Before describing further examples, the following sections therefore provide some useful tips for debugging script programs.

Using the Message Box

Using the message box enables you to easily define whether a script was executed up to a specific line of the script program or not. Simply add the program code of the previous example to your script program. If the system displays the dialog during the execution, you know that the script program has been executed up to that point.

In addition, you can also output the values of variables. If you replace the script program from the previous example with Listing 7.2, the message box outputs the value of a variable.

```
var i = 10;
xfa.host.messageBox(
  "SAP Interactive Forms by Adobe : i = " + i);
```

Listing 7.2 Message Box for the Output of a Variable Value

Displaying the Console for Errors and Messages

As of Adobe Reader 8, a very useful function is available that can be used to debug scripts: the console of the JavaScript debugger. For the development of interactive PDF forms, only the console is relevant. It outputs messages when errors occur during the execution of the script.

1. First, you must activate the console. You can do this in the basic settings of Adobe Reader via the EDIT • PREFERENCES... menu path.

2. The JavaScript category contains the JAVASCRIPT DEBUGGER area. Here, select the SHOW CONSOLE ON ERRORS AND MESSAGES option.

3. To test this function, add a third program line to the script program of the `click` event for the button. This line only contains the word `test`.

4. Then, navigate to the PDF preview, and click on the button. The console opens and the system displays a message that the `test` symbol is not defined (see Figure 7.43). In the bottom right corner of the dialog is the "trash can" icon. You can use it to delete the content of the console between the individual test runs.

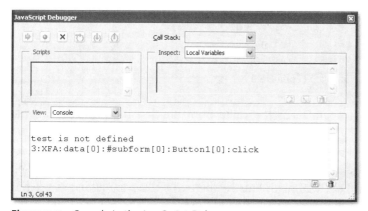

Figure 7.43 Console in the JavaScript Debugger

> **Using the Console as of Adobe Reader 8**
>
> As of Adobe Reader Version 8, you can also use coding to show the console. To do this, use the `console.show()` statement. You can then output a text in the console using the `console.println("<text>")` statement.

7.3.3 Calculations via Script Programs

To facilitate the input, you can have interactive PDF forms carry out calculations automatically. For example, for travel expenses, the form can automatically add the costs for individual items, such as flight tickets, hotels, and so on, and display the total for the user. Therefore, you do not have to add the costs manually, and the result is immediately available.

Let's reproduce this case with the following example. To do this, extend the form template as follows:

1. Add three decimal fields to the form template. Arrange the fields below each other.

2. Modify the caption of the form fields as follows (from top to bottom): VALUE1, VALUE2, and SUM. Then select the third decimal field.

3. Navigate to the VALUE tab of the OBJECT palette, and set the TYPE TO CALCULATED – READ ONLY.

4. Go to the script editor and select the `calculate` event for SHOW to enter a script program for calculations.

5. Enter Listing 7.3.

```
var value1 = parseInt(DecimalField1.rawValue);
var value2 = parseInt(DecimalField2.rawValue);
this.rawValue = value1 + value2;
```

Listing 7.3 Sum for a Calculated Form Field

First, the script program reads the value from the first input field (`rawValue` property). The field itself is referenced in the hierarchy through its name (`DecimalField1`). For decimal fields, a string is returned for the input value. Thus, the string is additionally converted into an integer. The same is carried out for the second decimal field. Finally, the two entries are added and set as the new value for the third decimal field. This is also the field for which the `calculate` event was called. It can be referenced with `this`.

6. Navigate to the PDF preview, and check to see whether the entered values are added.

Naming Variables in JavaScript

When naming variables, do not use names of properties (for example, `value`), because the property will be used instead of the variable from the script program. You should always add a prefix or postfix to the variable, for example, `aValue` instead of `value`, to avoid this problem.

7.3.4 Input Validation via Script Programs

In those cases where validation patterns are no longer sufficient, you can use script programs to implement validations. The validation for whether an input value is within a specific interval—for example, greater than 10 and less than 20—cannot be mapped by patterns. Thus, the validation for this example must be carried out by a script program. The example can be implemented as follows:

1. Add another decimal field to the form template.

2. Navigate to the VALUE tab of the OBJECT palette.

3. Enter the following text for the VALIDATION SCRIPT MESSAGE: "The entered value must be greater than 10 and less than 20."

4. Select ERROR to define that it is regarded as an error if the validation fails. The VALUE tab should now look as illustrated in Figure 7.44.

Figure 7.44 Settings for the Validation

5. Navigate to the script editor and select the `validate` event.

6. Enter Listing 7.4 as the script program.

```
aValue = parseInt(this.rawValue);
(aValue > 10 && aValue < 20);
```

Listing 7.4 Input Validation via Script Program

In Listing 7.4, the input value of the current field (`this`) is read first, and the returned string is converted into an integer as described in the last example. The last line contains a logical expression that implements the interval limits. The system evaluates this expression either as true or false.

If the condition is false, the system displays the previously defined error message. You can check this in the PDF preview by entering the value 5 and then exiting the field, for example. The program should now display the error message shown in Figure 7.45.

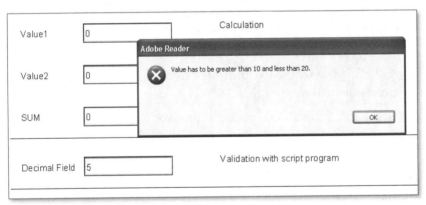

Figure 7.45 Error Message of Input Validation

7.3.5 Controlling the Ready-for-Input Status and Visibility of Form Fields

Another very critical function that can be implemented via script programs is the dynamic modification of the editable status of form fields. In the same context, you also frequently need the option to display or hide form fields or complete subforms. Some examples include forms that are supposed to dynamically adapt after a payment method or marital status has been selected to reduce the input options for the user to a minimum. An additional example where the editable status is often modified via script programs is the image field. The implementation of this example is illustrated next:

1. Add four buttons to the form template. Arrange the buttons in a 2×2 matrix.

2. Add a text field to the right of the buttons.

3. Enter "Read-only" and "Editable" as captions for the two buttons at the top. Enter "Invisible" and "Visible" as captions for the two buttons at the bottom.

4. Select the two upper buttons and add one line from the program code of Listing 7.5 to the `click` event. The comments in Listing 7.5 facilitate the selection of the correct program line. Carry out the same process for the two buttons at the bottom as well.

```
// Set form field to read only
TextField1.access ="readOnly";
// Set form field to editable
TextField1.access ="open";
// Exclude form field from layout ("hidden") and
// hence make it invisible, "invisible" also makes
// form fields invisible but it still occupies
// space in the layout
TextField1.presence ="hidden";
// Make form field visible
TextField1.presence ="visible";
```

Listing 7.5 Program Lines for Controlling the Ready-for-input Status and Visibility

The programming code in Listing 7.5 assumes that the text field in your example also has the name `TextField1`. You can check this in the hierarchy. If this is not the case, you must change either the name of the text field or the reference in the program code.

5. You can modify the status of the text field in the PDF preview by clicking on the respective buttons. This example requires that the PDF is a dynamic PDF form.

7.3.6 Determining the Recipient Address for an Email Message at Runtime

In Section 7.2.2, From PDF-Based Print Forms to Interactive PDF Forms, you created a button for sending a PDF form. In this process, you entered the email address directly in the Submit tab. This is not desirable in all cases because the address is included in the form template then and you do not always know beforehand to which (return) address the PDF form is to be sent. Moreover, you must continuously update the form in case the address should change. A much better approach is to transfer the email address as part of the data and use it dynamically at runtime.

To illustrate this, modify the form template at runtime in the following example. Proceed as follows:

1. Add a new button to the form template.

2. Navigate to the Field tab of the Object palette. Enter "Submit PDF" as the caption, and set the Control Type to Submit. A new Submit tab is display subsequently.

3. Go to the Submit tab.

4. Enter the following text under Submit To Url: "mailto:a@b.com." In the form template, the program thus creates all required nodes which are to be changed later on using the script program.

5. Select PDF in the dropdown list under Submit As.

6. Next, select the button and go to the script editor. Then select the `initialize` event from the Show dropdown list.

7. Enter the script program from Listing 7.6. You can define the parameter for the `resolveNode` method using the documentation for XFA. You must look this up in the "Part 2: XFA Grammar Specification" documentation under "The field element." Section 7.7.3, XML Forms Architecture, details how to obtain this documentation.

```
if (this.resolveNode("#event.#submit") != null)
{
    this.resolveNode("#event.#submit").target =
                           "<an email address>";
}
```

Listing 7.6 Script Program for Defining an Email Address

Notes on Email Addresses in this Example

You should always use your personal email address for this example. Therefore, replace *<an email address>* in the listings with your personal email address.

As you can see, this example uses the email address as part of the script itself. It is therefore still part of the form template.

In Section 7.3.8, Access to Data Nodes and Form Fields, you learn how you can read values from the data underlying the form. Section 10.3, Configuring the Email Inbound, presents an example in which the email address is actually provided via the data.

8. Test the form template by navigating to the PDF PREVIEW.

9. Click the SUBMIT PDF BUTTON. A window opens where you can select the email client. Select an appropriate program.

10. Then a new email message is displayed that already includes the PDF form as an attachment. The last step is to actually send the email message.

You can also customize the email message. This is useful because it is usually sent to a person. Listing 7.7 shows how you can define the subject and the message text. However, you cannot change the name of the PDF file in the attachment. This name is taken from the PDF to be sent.

```
xfa.resolveNode(
    "data.#subform.Button6.#event.#submit").target =
        "mailto:"+"<an email address>"
    + "?subject="+"Form Attached"
    + "&body="+"Please find attached the form.";
```

Listing 7.7 Defining the Subject and Message Text

It is not necessary that the event and the script program, in which you make the adaptations, belong to the form field that is to be changed. You can also use the `xfa.resolveNode` method instead of the `this.resolveNode` method. Listing 7.7 is an example for this. Note that in this case, `Button6` is the name of the form field; `#subform` stands for an unnamed subform. Section 7.3.8, Access to Data Nodes and Form Fields, discusses the use of `resolveNode` in more detail.

7.3.7 Querying Reader Version Information

In some cases, it is useful to check whether the users of a PDF form use an Adobe Reader version that can handle a specific or very new function. Even though

Adobe Reader checks this and notifies the user about updates, the program does not update automatically (this may also be prohibited by the respective system administrators).

The following example shows how you can use script programming in form templates to access script objects and methods of Acrobat JavaScript programming via the app object. You can find more information on the available objects and methods in Section 7.7.4, Acrobat JavaScript Reference. To reproduce the example, proceed as follows:

1. Add another button to the form template.

2. Change the caption of the button to "Get version."

3. Select the button and go to the script editor.

4. Choose the click event under SHOW, and enter the program code of Listing 7.8.

```
// app is a defined object in Adobe Acrobat and Adobe Reader
// (see AcroJS documentation)
var aType = app.viewerType;
var aVariation = app.viewerVariation;
var aVersion = app.viewerVersion;
var aText = "This PDF is rendered in: Type=" + aType
            + ", Variant=" + aVariation
            + ", Version=" + aVersion;
if (aVersion >= 9 )
{
   aText = aText + "\nIt is  Version 9 or newer.";
}
xfa.host.messageBox(aText);
```

Listing 7.8 Version Query Script Program

5. Test the form in the PDF PREVIEW.

6. Click GET VERSION. The system shows a message box like the one shown in Figure 7.46. The version number may vary depending on the Adobe Reader version used.

You can find additional information (for instance, the values for using Adobe Acrobat instead of Adobe Reader) in the Acrobat JavaScript reference (see Section 7.7.4) under the app object as well as the viewerType and viewerVariation attributes.

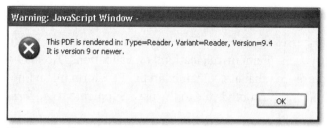

Figure 7.46 Output For The Version Information Query

Figure 7.47 displays the form template for the previous examples as a reference for the arrangement and captions of the individual form fields.

Button	xfa.host.messageBox

Value1		Calculation
Value2	
SUM	

| Decimal Field | | Validation with script program |

| Read-only | Editable | Control visibility and edit mode |
| Invisible | Visible | Text Field |

Submit PDF

Get version

Figure 7.47 Form Template for the Script Programs as a Reference

355

7.3.8 Access to Data Nodes and Form Fields

The next script example discusses the access to data nodes and form fields, which are often accessed when you implement calculations or validations. Accessing data nodes enables you to use data that are contained in the PDF form but are not bound to any form field and are thus not visible to the user. Supplement the form template as follows:

1. Create a new form template, Z_IFBA_BOOK_FORM_05, by copying the backup copy (Z_IFBA_BOOK_FORM03_Empty). Figure 7.47 shows the complete form template as a reference.

2. Add a button to the new form template. Change the CAPTION of the button to "Access D + F."

3. Navigate to the script editor while the button is selected and have the system display the click event.

4. Enter the script program from Listing 7.9.

   The script program first uses the resolveNodes method to reference all data nodes that have been identified by the parameter in a list. Then, a for loop reads the value (value) for each data node and compiles a string from those values. The second part repeats these steps. The only difference is that the references to form fields are defined in a table and that rawValue accesses the values of the form fields.

```
//accessing data nodes
var theFields = xfa.resolveNodes(
        "xfa.datasets.data.data.CUSTOMERS.DATA[*].NAME");
var aString = "";
for (var i = 0; i < theFields.length; i++) {
  aString = aString + theFields.item(i).value;
  if (i<theFields.length-1) { aString = aString + ", ";}
}
// Accessing form fields
var theFields = xfa.resolveNodes(
                "xfa.form.data.CUSTOMERS.DATA[*].NAME");
aString = aString + "\n";
for (var i = 0; i < theFields.length; i++) {
  aString = aString + theFields.item(i).rawValue;
  if (i<theFields.length-1) { aString = aString + ", ";}
```

```
      }
xfa.host.messageBox(aString);
```

Listing 7.9 Script Program for Accessing Data Nodes and Form Fields

> **Using resolveNode and resolveNodes**
>
> The two methods, `resolveNode` and `resolveNodes`, enable you to define references to one or more data nodes or form fields. You can use them if unknown subforms or form fields are supposed to be referenced for repeating data.
>
> To do this, you need so-called Scripting Object Model (SOM) expressions. These expressions begin with `xfa.datasets.data.` for the access to data and with `xfa.form` for access to form fields. In both cases, this is followed by the name of the data structure's root node, and a path in the data hierarchy is specified for the data nodes and a path in the form hierarchy for the form fields. You can use the data view or hierarchy if you want to specify a path because they graphically map the hierarchy. Listing 7.9 contains an example of these two cases.

5. Then navigate to the PDF preview, and click on the ACCESS D + F button to test the script program. A dialog box (see Figure 7.48) opens that outputs a text with two lines. Both lines should be identical.

   ▶ The text of the first line was determined from the underlying data of the form.

   ▶ The second text line shows the same result; however, in this case the text was determined from the values of the form fields.

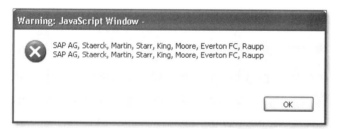

Figure 7.48 Output for the Data Node and Form Field Access

7.3.9 Dynamic Tables

The final example discusses dynamic tables. Dynamic tables enable you to add new table rows, delete existing rows, or change the order of rows at runtime. Some examples of using this function include order forms that display the details of an order as a table and work reports that contain information on individual tasks and required material. In both examples, the content of the table varies from case to case and is not specified until the form is used.

> **Using Dynamic Tables**
>
> If you want to use dynamic tables via integration or a framework, you must check to see whether the framework also supports dynamic tables.

For subforms, the so-called *instance manager* is used for the implementation of dynamic tables. Tables are technically based on subforms. Therefore, this description not only applies to tables but also to subforms. The instance manager provides three functions:

- Creating a new instance (`addInstance`)
- Deleting an instance (`removeInstance`)
- Changing the order of the instances (`moveInstance`)

To use these functions, the table rows or subforms must be bound to repeating data and dynamic PDF forms must be generated. The following section describes the creation of an example to test these functions.

1. Add a table to the form template by dragging and dropping the CUSTOMERS data table from the data view to the design view.

2. Decrease the width of the two table columns and add an additional column by selecting the right column and following the TABLE • INSERT • COLUMNS TO THE RIGHT menu path.

3. Increase the width of the previously added column by selecting its right border using the mouse and moving it to the right while keeping the mouse button pressed.

4. In the cell of the data row of the third column, insert a subform to the far right by dragging and dropping a subform from the STANDARD library to the table cell. During this process, the static text is replaced by the subform.

5. Check whether the content of the subform is set to FLOWED and whether the flow direction is set to WESTERN TEXT.

6. The subform is required to insert two buttons in the subform in this step. Enter "Add" as the caption for the left button and "Remove" as the caption for the right button.

7. You can avoid the yellow warning messages by setting the value of the CONTENT field to FLOWED for the pages and enable page breaks for the page itself, the table, and the data row of the table.

8. Supplement the `click` event of the left button with the script program from Listing 7.10 to enable the user to add rows. To do this, click on the ADD button, navigate to the script editor, display the script for the `click` event, and add the program code.

```
var anInstanceManager =
   this.parent.parent.instanceManager;
var newInstance = anInstanceManager.addInstance(1);
var aToIndex = this.parent.parent.index + 1;
var aFromIndex = newInstance.index;
   anInstanceManager.moveInstance(aFromIndex, aToIndex);
```

Listing 7.10 Adding a Table Row

The script program first specifies the instance manager (`instanceManager`) for the individual table rows. To do this, the system navigates twice from the button (`this`) to the parent node in the form hierarchy (`parent`). The first parent node is the subform, whose parent node is the table row. Then, the system calls the `addInstance` method with the parameter value 1 to generate a new instance and merge it with the data (parameter value 1). The system always adds new instances to the end of a table. The `index` property therefore defines in which row the button was clicked and which index the newly added row has. The `moveInstance` method can then move the instance from the old to the new position.

Dynamic Tables and Calculations

If the table contains calculations, the following function call must be used to trigger the new calculation: `xfa.form.recalculate(1)`.

9. Analogous to the previous step, add Listing 7.11 to the `click` event of the REMOVE button to enable the user to delete rows.

```
this.parent.parent.instanceManager.removeInstance(
                              this.parent.parent.index);
```

Listing 7.11 Removing a Table Row

As in Listing 7.10, the instance manager for the table row is determined and the `removeInstance` method is called in Listing 7.11. This method includes a parameter that maps the index of the instances (rows) that are supposed to be removed. this.parent.parent.index identifies the index of the row that contained the button that was clicked.

Navigate to the PDF preview. The table has been filled with some rows in advance; two buttons exist for each row (see Figure 7.49):

▶ The ADD button adds a new table row directly after the row that contained the button that was clicked.

▶ The REMOVE button deletes the row that contains the button that was clicked.

Cust. No.	Customer name		
Dynamic Table			
00000001	SAP AG	Add	Remove
00000004	Staerck	Add	Remove
00000005	Martin	Add	Remove
00000006	Starr	Add	Remove
00000007	King	Add	Remove
00000008	Moore	Add	Remove
00000009	Everton FC	Add	Remove
00000010	Raupp	Add	Remove

Figure 7.49 Dynamic Table with Buttons to Add or Remove Table Rows

The example does not include error handling, for example, querying the minimum and maximum number of rows. The instance manager provides two properties, `occur.min` and `occur.max`, to determine the allowed minimum and maximum number of rows, respectively. The `count` property of the instance manager returns the current number of instances. Finally, Figure 7.50 displays the form template for the last two examples as a reference for the arrangement and captions of the individual form fields.

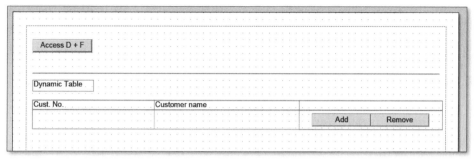

Figure 7.50 Form Template for the Script Programs as a Reference

7.4   Using Barcodes

Using barcodes is rather easy because barcodes behave like normal form fields and can be dragged and dropped into a form template. You can define the value to be encoded to the barcode using data bindings. The supported barcodes are provided separately in the BARCODES library (see Figure 7.51).

▼ Barcodes				☰
Aztec	AUS Post Custor	AUS Post Custor	AUS Post Reply	AUS Post Standard
Codabar	Code 11	Code 128	Code 128A	Code 128B
Code 128C	Code 128SSCC	Code 2 of 5 Indu	Code 2 of 5 Inte	Code 2 of 5 Matrix
Code 2 of 5 Star	Code 3 of 9	Code 49	Code 93	Data Matrix
EAN13	EAN8	Logmars	MSI	PDF 417
Paper Forms Bar	Planet Code	Plessey	QR Code	RFID
RSS 14	RSS 14 Stacked	RSS 14 Stacked	RSS 14 Truncate	RSS Expanded
RSS Limited	UK Post RM4SC	UPC EAN2	UPC EAN5	UPC-A
UPC-E	UPS Maxicode	US Postal DPBC	US Postal Stand	US Postal Zip-5

Figure 7.51 Supported Barcodes in the Barcodes Library

Availability of Barcodes

There is no way to define new barcodes yourself: you depend on the availability of barcodes. New versions of Adobe LiveCycle Designer usually add new barcodes to the barcodes library.

Note here that you must use at least the ADS version that was introduced with the Adobe LiveCycle Designer version. In case of Adobe LiveCycle Designer 8.2, this involves the version that is provided with SAP NetWeaver 7.0, Enhancement Package 2.

7.4.1 Properties of Barcodes

These are two barcode categories:

- ▸ **1D barcode**
  For one-dimensional barcodes, the encoded value is output in one dimension (usually, horizontally). These barcodes generally have a checksum because no redundancy is integrated into the barcode pattern itself.

- ▸ **2D barcode**
  For this barcode category, the encoded value is output in two dimensions, that is, horizontally and vertically. Due to the two-dimensional output, you can use the redundancy to correct errors. The data matrix, QR, and PDF 417 barcodes are 2D barcodes.

The differences are illustrated in Figure 7.52.

Also of importance is whether a barcode is directly supported only by Zebra label printers or whether the barcode can also be output in PDF forms and to other printers. This is indicated in the BARCODES library by the printer icon (▦, see Figure 7.51). For PDFs or outputs to other printers, only a gray rectangle is provided. An example of a barcode that can only be output to a Zebra label printer is the CODE 11 barcode. CODE 128 is a barcode that can also be output in PDF forms and to other printers.

Figure 7.52 1D Barcode (Code 128) and 2D Barcode (PDF 417)

Using the Paper Form Barcode

The paper form barcode is a specific barcode that enables you to encode the underlying data of a form. During the interaction with the PDF form, the system continuously updates the paper form barcode to display the current state. If the paper form barcode is printed and scanned, it contains the data that had been entered in the form prior to printing.

You can use this barcode, for example, to print a form after having completed it and then sign the printed form manually. For further processing, the paper form barcode can be scanned so that the system can decode the data. In this scenario, you do not have to manually enter the data again.

To be able to use paper form barcodes, you must add the barcode usage right. This is not done by default and must be implemented manually or by using a job profile. You require a ReaderRights credential for this purpose. Credentials that have been delivered since early 2009 enable this. Contact SAP to obtain a new credential if you want to use the paper form barcodes and still have an older credential version.

7.4.2 Notes on the Output of Barcodes with Zebra Label Printers

You must consider the following three points when you create forms that can be output to Zebra label printers:

▶ You must define a specific paper type for the page. This paper type must match the label format. To do this, you must select the master page, and then select the CUSTOM value for the PAPER TYPE in the MASTER PAGES tab of the OBJECT palette. You can enter the size of the labels into the HEIGHT and WIDTH input fields.

▶ Zebra label printers support 200 and 300 Dots per Inch (DPI). For output to a printer, you must configure the correct device type (see Section 6.3, Device Types for the Output).

7.5 Tips for Increasing Performance

The creation of form templates is a complex process where the way in which the template is created may considerably affect performance. This section provides tips that you should consider when creating form templates, or that can support you in analyzing the performance of existing form templates.

7.5.1 Merging Static Texts

If you use multiple adjacent static texts in one form template, you should merge these static texts. This is especially the case if a normal PDF is imported for the creation of a form template. In this case, numerous texts from the original are mapped as single static texts.

To solve this problem, the context menu of the hierarchy or the design view contains the Merge Selected Text Objects menu item if multiple static texts are selected simultaneously. By using this function several times, you can reduce the number of static texts and thus increase output performance.

7.5.2 Resolution of Used Images

If you use images (company logos, for example), you should use an external application to reduce them to the proper size. It is also possible to use the original images in Adobe LiveCycle Designer for the output; however, this has the following disadvantages:

▶ The image is added to the form template in its original size. This increases the size of the form template and thus the PDF file.

▶ It involves additional effort to correct the scaling.

These two aspects can be prevented by adapting the image.

7.5.3 Ensuring Correct Data Bindings

When a form output is generated, the system must evaluate all data bindings. It is therefore important to define only required data bindings. Some examples of unnecessary data bindings include headings in tables, which only use static texts but have the Normal default binding. The same applies to subforms. Here, you must ensure that you do not combine the implicit and explicit binding for nested subforms and that no subform with the Normal default binding is accidently included.

In addition to avoiding unnecessary data bindings, using relative data bindings also increases performance. Relative binding expressions were introduced in Section 5.3, Data Bindings for Form Fields.

7.5.4 Nesting Depth of Subforms

The number of the subforms used in one form template affects processing time because each subform must be processed separately. Therefore, you should not use unnecessary subforms in form templates.

The content and the data binding of the subform indicate whether or not this is required. A subform is not required if it contains only one subform and if the data binding is set to NONE. However, you must check every case.

7.5.5 Gradient Fills for PostScript Level 2

Gradient fills (gradients) are not supported by PostScript Level 2 and must be simulated for the output. This affects the size of the generated PostScript output and the required processing time. Therefore, if you need to use PostScript Level 2, you should not use gradient fills.

7.5.6 Using Script Programs

It is quite easy to use complex calculations and loops in the supported script languages. However, because they affect the output time, you should consider whether the calculations need to be carried out in the form or whether you can increase performance by carrying them out during the data formatting in the print program.

Long running script programs can cause delays for interactive PDF forms, for example, when you open script programs that are located in the `initialize`, `form:ready`, `layout:ready` or `doc:ready`, event, or when you interact with PDF forms. In the latter case, the script programs are usually located in the `click`, `enter`, `exit`, or `change` event.

If there are considerable delays, check the events mentioned previously. A tip for selecting the script language: Compared with JavaScript, FormCalc usually has a higher performance when it comes to calculations on the basis of table-like structures.

7.5.7 Enforcing Strict Scoping Rules in JavaScript

As of Adobe Reader 8.1, you can define stricter scoping rules for object references in Java Script and thus clean up and release the storage more frequently. This has a positive effect on the memory consumption and the performance of JavaScript programs. If object references are released more frequently, this often has the result that objects or variables no longer exist. In script programming, you must therefore ensure that the programs do not automatically assume that a variable, which was used in preceding program runs, still exists.

Because the retroactive activation of strict scoping rules can result in compatibility problems, you must enable this behavior explicitly. This is done in the DEFAULT tab of the form properties by activating the ENFORCE STRICT SCOPING RULES IN JAVASCRIPT. It is recommended that you activate this option and adapt it accordingly in script programming.

7.5.8 Limiting the Volume of Transferred Data for the Form Output

The data volume that is used for the generation of the output affects the overall duration of the generation process for the output. It is therefore important to transfer only the data required via a context.

To do this, let's look at the data view. If there are multiple data nodes that are not bound to a form field, you should view the context, for example, with Transaction SFP if you used Form Builder to create the form template (see Section 4.3.3, Structures).

If you used an implicit data binding, this information cannot be taken from the data view that easily. In this case, you must compare the structure in the hierarchy with the data view. Remember: The implicit data binding requires a structure that is as similar as possible in terms of structure and names (see Section 5.7, Implicit Data Binding).

7.5.9 Using Fonts

The number of fonts used affects the size of PDF files or print language outputs — if the font is not supported by the printer hardware itself. You should use as few fonts as possible in a form.

7.6 Introduction to Accessible PDF Forms

Accessible PDF documents must have a so-called *tag structure* to enable access to the content of a document together with tools that are often referred to as screen readers. The tag structure includes details on the contained elements; it also provides information on the structural relationship between these elements. The system needs to generate the tag structure during the creation of the PDF document.

You can easily check whether a PDF document has a tag structure by following the File • Properties menu path. The dialog that opens, Document Properties, contains a note, *Tagged PDF: Yes*, in the Advanced area of the Description tab if the PDF has a tag structure. For dynamic PDF forms, Adobe Reader can "decide" to create the tag structure only if a screen reader is available to improve performance.

Adobe Reader and Adobe Acrobat already provide a tool that reads the document content out loud. You can select it via the View • Read Out Loud • Activate Read Out Loud menu path. The same menu can also be used to have the system read only the current page or to the end of the document. You can also pause or stop this option via this menu.

To externally access the tag structure using additional screen readers, Adobe Reader supports the Microsoft® Active Accessibility® (MSAA) interface. You can use the JAWS® screen reader by Freedom Scientific®, for example.

> **Generation of Accessible PDF Forms for Print Outputs**
>
> To display a PDF form in the print view, the system reads the corresponding setting of the SAP GUI to define whether a tag structure should be generated or not. When a PDF form is archived or returned, the system always generates the tag structure.

7.6.1 Creating Accessible PDF Forms

Adobe LiveCycle Designer provides a palette solely for the text definition that is to be output by the screen reader. This is the Accessibility palette (see Figure 7.53). If this palette is hidden in Adobe LiveCycle Designer, you can use the Palettes • Accessibility menu path to display it.

You can use the Screen Reader Precedence dropdown list to define which text is output for a form field by the screen reader. In addition to the None option for no output, the following four options are available:

▶ **Custom Text**
Using the Custom Text option, you can enter a specific text, which is not displayed in the form.

▶ **Tool Tip**
This is a specific text that is also displayed in the form when the mouse pointer is positioned on a particular field for a few seconds.

▶ **Caption**

If you use this option, the caption of a form field is output.

▶ **Name**

If this option is selected, the system outputs the (technical) name from the form hierarchy.

Figure 7.53 Accessibility Palette

For the last two options, the screen reader determines the text from the form template. For the first two options, you must enter the text in the ACCESSIBILITY palette. To do this, you are provided with the two input fields, TOOL TIP and CUSTOM SCREEN READER TEXT. Both texts can also be made available via the underlying data of the form. To do this, you can define the data binding and a binding expression via the dynamic properties.

7.6.2 Tips for Creating Accessible PDF Forms

When creating form templates, you must take into account the following aspects:

▶ All form fields should be provided with a caption.

▶ For the captions, you should use the caption option available for form fields.

▶ You should not use abbreviations, such as "pcs." for "pieces," in texts, because the screen reader tries to read out loud "pcs."

▶ The form fields arrangement is important. You should therefore use the grid or the subforms with the FLOWED option for the content.

▶ You can view the order of form fields via the VIEW • TAB ORDER menu path.

▶ You should not use colors and effects to provide additional information.

▶ You should provide descriptive text for all images.

> **The Structure of the Forms Must Support the Accessibility**
>
> In addition to practical tips, it is also important to consider the structure of the form. The structure of the PDF forms needs to be designed for accessibility. That means that the structure must be rather simple. If the structure of a form is too complex to be understood by the user, even the best technology is no longer helpful.

7.7 Additional Information

This book cannot describe all of the topics relevant for the creation of form templates in detail.

7.7.1 Additional Information on the Internet

A wide range of additional information sources are available on the Internet:

▶ The SAP Community Network should be mentioned first. There is a complete area for SAP Interactive Forms by Adobe (at *https://www.sdn.sap.com/irj/sdn/adobe*). In addition, there are numerous blogs on specific topics regarding the creation of forms. A separate forum publishes questions about the creation of forms and frameworks, which are answered by the community. You can find this forum at *https://www.sdn.sap.com/irj/sdn/forum?forumID=155*.

▶ You can also access further information on the Adobe Web site. The pages on Adobe Developer Connection contain a separate area for Adobe LiveCycle Designer. The URL is *http://www.adobe.com/devnet/livecycle/*.

▶ Adobe also provides general information on the partnership between SAP and Adobe Systems (*http://www.adobe.com/enterprise/partners/sap.html*).

The following sections list information sources and describe the information provided on these Internet pages. Various chapters in this book also refer to these URLs.

7.7.2 Adobe Designer Scripting Reference

You can find a more detailed introduction to the usage of script programs for the creation of forms at *://www.adobe.com/go/learn_lc_scriptingBasics_82*.

7.7.3 XFA

XFA describes the underlying technology of the PDF-based and interactive PDF forms. It includes references for the following four areas:

▶ *Part 2: XFA Grammar Specifications* contains the template reference. For the properties of the form fields, you can find the names that are relevant to the creation of scripts here (such as the `presence` property that controls the visibility of the form fields).

▶ *Part 3: Other XFA-Related References* contains the FormCalc specification and a lot of additional information on the FormCalc script language.

▶ *Part 3: Other XFA-Related References* also includes the picture clause specification. It describes in detail how you create, display, and edit data and validation patterns.

▶ The last part that should be mentioned is the Rich Text Reference. It provides detailed information on how you must format the XHTML text for rich text fields.

You can find the XFA at *http://partners.adobe.com/public/developer/xml/index_arch.html*. The release of SAP Interactive Forms by Adobe described in this book is based on Version 2.8.

> **Notes on XFA**
>
> The document on the XFA is a specification of the underlying technology, which is mainly implemented by Adobe LiveCycle Designer and ADS. If you use elements that cannot be accessed via the user interface of Adobe LiveCycle Designer, you should carefully check whether your specific requirements can be implemented at all. For Version 2.8, you must also consider that you need at least Adobe Reader 9 and ADS for SAP NetWeaver 7.0 Enhancement Package 2.

7.7.4 Acrobat JavaScript Reference

When creating interactive PDF forms, you can also use objects and functions that are defined in Acrobat JavaScript. Regardless of the name, they also function in Adobe Reader. You can find the following two documents at *http://www.adobe.com/devnet/acrobat/javascript.html*:

- *JavaScript for Acrobat API Reference*

- *Developing Acrobat Applications Using JavaScript*

The reference details the available options; the second document describes their usage by means of examples.

Functions Only Available for Interactive Forms

The functions that are described in the two Acrobat JavaScript references are available only for interactive PDF forms and not for PDF-based print forms!

7.8   Summary

This chapter first introduced you to the advanced topics of the creation of print outputs by extending the form template from Chapter 5. It then moved toward interactive PDF forms by transferring the knowledge about print forms to interactive forms. The chapter also introduced the form fields that are specifically used for interactive PDF forms. The creation of script programs, tips for increasing performance, and the introduction to the creation of accessible PDF forms finally complemented the advanced topics.

This chapter has laid the foundation for the next chapters, which introduce interactive PDF forms in even more detail.

This chapter details the integration of SAP Interactive Forms by Adobe with Web Dynpro ABAP. Many of the scenarios described here can also be used in Web Dynpro Java without a lot of adaptations, because Web Dynpro ABAP and Web Dynpro Java have the same programming model (except for platform-specific modifications).

8   Integration with Web Dynpro ABAP

This chapter provides you with an overview of the options for integrating Adobe with Web Dynpro ABAP. The first part of this chapter details the structure of a component in Web Dynpro ABAP based on a plain Hello World example (see Section 8.1, Web Dynpro ABAP). This is followed by a presentation of the individual scenarios of SAP Interactive Forms by Adobe in Web Dynpro ABAP (see Section 8.2, Scenarios for the Integration of Interactive Forms), with a particular focus on the InteractiveForm User Interface (UI) element (see Section 8.3, The Interactive-Form UI Element).

Chapter 4, Interface and Form Context, introduced form templates, which you can also use in Web Dynpro ABAP. Section 8.4, Interaction with Form Builder, outlines the creation and integration of form templates with your Web Dynpro application. The information and techniques provided in the first sections of this chapter form the basis for Section 8.5, Implementing the Scenarios Using Web Dynpro ABAP, where you will learn step-by-step instructions on how to implement individual scenarios of the Adobe integration using Web Dynpro ABAP.

In real project life, many SAP customers use various SAP releases in parallel. In this context, architects must answer the questions as to which functions are available as of which release or whether changes are necessary after an upgrade. For this reason, this chapter contains information that is not limited to the functions that are available in NetWeaver 7.0 EHP2. It also describes in detail as of which SAP release—and, if necessary, as of which support package—a specific function can be used. The same applies to Adobe LiveCycle Designer and Adobe Reader. Furthermore, this chapter offers a checklist to optimally support you in your project. The examples are structured in such a way that they work with the lowest possible release. Basic information on compatibility of SAP release, Adobe LiveCycle Designer, Adobe Reader, and various browser versions is available in the Product Availability Matrix (PAM), which you can find in the SAP Service Marketplace.

8.1   Web Dynpro ABAP

Web Dynpro is SAP's latest user interface technology. It is a technology that is independent of the client and the platform:

▶ Client independence means that an application that was developed with Web Dynpro can be run via different clients (web browsers, SAP NetWeaver Business Client).

▶ Platform independence, however, relates to the programming model and the architecture of Web Dynpro on the server. At present, Web Dynpro has been implemented on two platforms by SAP—SAP NetWeaver ABAP and Java stack. Applications that have been created for one of the platforms can be ported to the other.

Web Dynpro for the Java platform was first delivered with SAP NetWeaver 6.40. Web Dynpro ABAP followed with release 7.0.

8.1.1   Initial Overview

The Web Dynpro component is the core object of every Web Dynpro application. It is a new Workbench object and can be created and manipulated using Transaction SE80 (just like reports or classes, for example). A separate transaction for Web Dynpro—similar to Transaction SE38 for reports or Transaction SE24 for classes—does not exist. The environment, integrated with Transaction SE80 for developing Web Dynpro components, is called Web Dynpro Explorer.

A Web Dynpro component is a normal Workbench object and has a development class assigned to it. Hence, it can be transported to other systems.

The architecture of Web Dynpro is based on the established Model View Controller (MVC) approach; that is, data, layout, and program logic can be separated from each other. The data storage (in the model) is carried out via the context.

The context is a hierarchical structure that can be freely defined by the application developer. This structure consists of nodes, which, in turn, can have attributes. A node may comprise zero, one, or more elements at runtime—similar to the rows of an internal table. You can establish a simple recursion between nodes, for example, to map trees with an indefinite depth. The area in which you can define the context is called the Context Editor.

The program logic is defined in controllers. Basic object-oriented programming for a controller includes attributes, methods, and events. Depending on the controller type, specific attributes and methods are predefined by Web Dynpro. Therefore, the constructor of a controller is called `wdDoInit`, whereas `wd_this` is the name of the attribute that indicates its attributes and methods.

A Web Dynpro component consists of various subobjects, which, in turn, are used for different tasks. According to the MVC approach, these subobjects each contain a controller and a context. The most important subobjects with their respective controllers are listed in the following:

▶ **View** (includes ViewController)
You can use the view to design the layout of a screen, that is, to add UI elements and specify their properties. Properties have additional settings; the most important ones are listed below:

  ▶ The data type (Boolean, string, enumeration type, and so on).

  ▶ Whether the property can (or even must) be bound to a context attribute or a context node. This way, a connection is established between the view and the model. By modifying the data in the model, you can change the content and the appearance of the UI elements dynamically at runtime.

  ▶ Whether the property contains text or data. If it contains text, the text is automatically stored in the Online Text Repository (OTR).

The layout of a view consists of UI elements that can be arranged in a hierarchical structure. However, specific (simple) rules apply here. For example, the grouping of UI elements is implemented using containers. This is a UI element that, in turn, can contain other UI elements. The area in which you can define the layout of a view is called the ViewDesigner.

A component can have any number of views; however, it is not recommended that you use more than 15 views due to performance reasons.

▶ **Window** (includes WindowController)
In addition, you can define a hierarchical structure of views by embedding one view of a window inside another. You can also define which views you can navigate by connecting them using outbound and inbound plugs. In a way, a window represents the views of a component to the user. A view cannot be displayed in the screen directly. This is always done via a window. A component can have several windows. However, this usually makes sense only if you want to define additional pop-up windows. The area in which you can define the structure of a window is called the WindowEditor.

A Web Dynpro component can comprise several controllers. These include:

▶ **ComponentController** (part of each component)
The ComponentController is a central controller that exists in every Web Dynpro component. Data that you would like to share with all other controllers can be stored here centrally. The first option concerns the storage of the data in the context. You can access the data from another controller via context mapping. The second option concerns the storage of data directly in the attributes of the controller. As soon as you select an attribute as `public`, you can access it from every other controller.

▶ **CustomController**
This is a controller to which you can outsource data (similar to the Component-Controller) that are supposed to be shared by other controllers. This structure has been created to enable the application developer to group shared data logically. This means that you do not have to store all shared data in the ComponentController. Your Web Dynpro component then includes a CustomController with the address data of a business partner and a second Custom Controller including the marketing attributes. The ComponentController is a specially configured CustomController.

▶ **InterfaceController**
In the InterfaceController, you can view all context nodes, methods, and events of the ComponentController that can be used by other Web Dynpro components. You can define them in the ComponentController using the properties `interface` or `public`.

▶ **ConfigController**
This is a special controller that can be used for the configuration of a Web Dyn-

pro component. For further information on the configuration topic, refer to the online help for Web Dynpro. In this chapter, no configuration is carried out.

A Web Dynpro application package consists of a Web Dynpro application and a Web Dynpro component. It is the executable unit for a Web Dynpro component. A Web Dynpro application is a Workbench object, too. A user never sees a window of a component directly, but always indirectly via a Web Dynpro application. As a result, a Web Dynpro application package refers to the window of a component. In addition, you can also specify other properties, for example, parameters or the help linking.

It is also useful to subdivide larger Web Dynpro application packages into multiple Web Dynpro components. This is done either through direct embedding of the other component or using a ComponentInterface.

Each Web Dynpro component implements a ComponentInterface, which is also a Workbench object. When you create a component using the Web Dynpro Explorer, you automatically generate a ComponentInterface of the same name, which is implemented by the Web Dynpro component.

In addition, you can also create a ComponentInterface as a single object using the Web Dynpro Explorer and implement it in any number of Web Dynpro components. A ComponentInterface contains an InterfaceController and a window. The definitions made here are also available in all external implementing components. This enables you to use a simple form of polymorphism between different Web Dynpro components.

If a component uses a ComponentInterface (not implemented, but referenced), you must specify at runtime which component is actually supposed to be used. The component then must implement this ComponentInterface.

Each component can also have an assistance class. This is an ordinary ABAP objects class to which you can outsource source code for better tool support. In this context, the assistance class acts as the interaction layer; that is, UI-based services are implemented there. In smaller applications it can also assume the role of the business logic. The assistance class must inherit from `CL_WD_COMPONENT_ASSISTANCE` class. It is recommended that you use an assistance class for the following reasons:

▶ An assistance class is a regular ABAP OO class and thus offers all ABAP OO language features as well as full tool support. In contrast to the editors in the Web

Dynpro environment, you can use exceptions, a ClassConstructor, or ABAP units. Moreover, you have comprehensive refactoring options.

▶ In a real-life project, various developers work on the same topic, or change requests must be implemented in parallel after a go-live. In the Web Dynpro environment, the lock is set on the controller (for instance, the view, the window, and so on). In the ABAP OO environment, however, the lock is set on the individual methods of a class. The use of an assistance class thus allows for a greater parallelism in the development phase and accelerated simultaneous processing of change requests in the maintenance phase.

> **Note on the Examples of this Chapter**
>
> Internet Explorer 6 and 8 were used as the browser and Windows XP Professional as the operating system for all examples provided in this chapter. Throughout this chapter, Adobe Reader Version 9.3.2 was used and Adobe Reader 8.0 was used for testing purposes. The use of older and other browser and reader versions is also possible as per PAM.
>
> The examples, which are available for download, were tested in various SAP releases. They can be used not only in the current release NetWeaver 7.0 EHP2, but also up to NetWeaver 7.0 SP 16. They readily work in an SAP ERP system with version SAP ECC 6.0, whereas none of the examples requires the additional functions provided by SAP ERP. Before testing the examples, you should load the flight data model first.
>
> The examples also work with the products combined under Business Suite 7 Innovations 2010 as well as every SAP product that has NetWeaver 7.0 as the basis. The examples were also tested under SAP CRM 5.0 (based on NetWeaver 7.0) and SAP CRM 7.0 (based on NetWeaver 7.0 EHP1) and partly used in actual customer projects (in extended form).

8.1.2 Step by Step: Hello World

Prior to getting started on the Adobe integration examples, let's look at the concepts detailed in Section 8.1.1, Initial Overview, based on a simple example. The aim here is to use a practical example so that you can understand the other examples in this chapter without having any previous knowledge of Web Dynpro ABAP.

As shown in Figure 8.1, a Web Dynpro component is created in the Web Dynpro Explorer using Transaction SE80.

1. Therefore, start Transaction SE80 and select the WEB-DYNPRO COMP./INTF. entry.

Figure 8.1 Selecting the Category in Transaction SE80

2. Enter the name of the Web Dynpro component to be created and press the
   [ENTER] key. In this example, the name of the Web Dynpro component is
   ZADB_HELLO_WORLD.

3. If the component does not exist yet, the system automatically asks whether a component is to be created. To confirm, click on the YES button (see Figure 8.2).

Figure 8.2 Newly Created Component After Entering the Name of the Web Dynpro Component and Pressing Enter

4. Another dialog opens in which you can enter a descriptive text for the component. Here, the text is "Example: "Hello World"" (see Figure 8.3). The system automatically creates a window. You can specify the name in the WINDOW NAME field. Depending on the release of your system, you can also specify the name of a

view in this dialog. This view is also automatically created by the system and embedded in the window.

Figure 8.3 Creating a Web Dynpro Component

5. To confirm the dialog, click on the button with the green checkmark. The system then creates the Web Dynpro component. Because it is a Workbench object, you are prompted to select a package to assign the Web Dynpro component to.

6. Each Web Dynpro component contains a ComponentInterface through which other components can use released functions of this component. For this reason, a second dialog opens in which you must select the ComponentInterface package. Select the same package as for the component. This is not mandatory, but useful, because you usually want to transport both objects together later on. If you select a package whose objects are transported, you must select a transport request for the component and the ComponentInterface, respectively.

7. Then the component and its subobjects—the window and, if applicable, the view—are displayed in the tree of the Web Dynpro Explorer.

If the automatic creation of a view was not provided in the dialog for creating the component due to a lower release, then you must create a new view. To do so, right-click on the name of the component and select the corresponding entry from the context menu that appears (see Figure 8.4).

8. A dialog opens in which you enter the name of the view and a description, if required. Confirm the dialog. The new view is displayed together with the ViewDesigner to show its layout in the correct area of the Web Dynpro Explorer. The ViewDesigner is divided into three different areas:

▶ The upper-right area of the ViewDesigner provides the hierarchical structure of the layout. Currently, it includes only an empty container called ROOTUIELEMENTCONTAINER.

Figure 8.4 Creating a New View via the Context Menu

▸ The lower right area shows the properties of this container.

▸ The left-hand side shows a layout preview displaying the still-empty container. The layout preview can be hidden and shown using the respective buttons in the toolbar.

9. Now is a good time to save your work. To do so, click on the button with the SAVE icon in the SAP GUI toolbar.

To output the text "Hello World," you must add a suitable UI element to the view because the container only defines an area where other UI elements can be placed inside.

1. As shown in Figure 8.5, right-click on the ROOTUIELEMENTCONTAINER entry in the upper-right area of the ViewDesigner. In the context menu, select the INSERT ELEMENT entry.

Figure 8.5 Inserting a New UI Element

2. Another dialog opens in which you can further specify the new UI element. For the text output, you need a TextView UI element. Select this UI element

from the lower dropdown list (see Figure 8.6). In the view, the UI element also requires a unique name as the identifier. Specify such a name, for example, "SOME_TEXT."

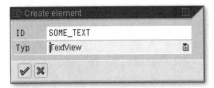

Figure 8.6 Creating a UI Element

3. Confirm the dialog. The new UI element now appears as a subelement of ROO-TUIELEMENTCONTAINER in the ViewDesigner (see Figure 8.7).

Property	Value	Bindi...
Properties (TextView)		
ID	SOME_TEXT	
design	standard	
enabled	☑	
hAlign	auto	
layout	native	
semanticColor	standard	
text		
textDirection	inherit	
tooltip		
visible	Visible	
wrapping	☐	
Layout Data (FlowData)		
cellDesign	padless	
vGutter	none	

☐ CONTEXT_MENUS
▽ ☐ ROOTUIELEMENTCONTAINER
    ☐ SOME_TEXT

Figure 8.7 TextView as a Subelement of RootUIElementContainer

4. Enter the string "Hello World" in the Text property of the SOME_TEXT TextView. After you have pressed the [ENTER] key, the text appears in the layout preview in the middle of the screen (see Figure 8.8).

5. If, depending on the release of the system, you were not provided with the option that the view is automatically generated during the creation of the component, you must embed it manually in the window. To do so, navigate to the window

by double-clicking on its name in the tree of the Web Dynpro Explorer. The right-hand side switches from ViewDesigner to WindowEditor.

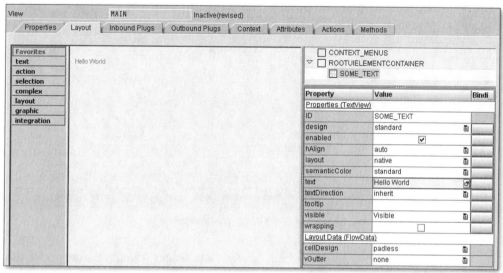

Figure 8.8 Layout Preview

6. Drag and drop the view from the tree of the Web Dynpro Explorer to the root node of the window structure displayed on the right-hand side. You can also select the view by choosing the EMBED VIEW entry from the context menu of the WND_MAIN window in the window structure. The result should then appear as shown in Figure 8.9.

7. Activate the component by right-clicking on its name in the tree of the Web Dynpro Explorer and selecting the appropriate menu entry. You may have to switch to the display mode for the window to prevent locking yourself out.

8. Now, create a new Web Dynpro application with the name of the component using the context menu path, CREATE • WEB DYNPRO APPLICATION.

9. The name of the component is suggested as the name of the application in the dialog that now appears. This is acceptable because both are different Workbench objects and may have the same name due to their different types. Retain the default value of the name and enter an optional description. Confirm the dialog.

Figure 8.9 MAIN View Embedded in the WND_MAIN Window

10. The system prompts you again to select a package. Select the same package as for the component. If the package can be transported, you must specify a transport request. Then the application is displayed in the Web Dynpro Explorer as illustrated in Figure 8.10.

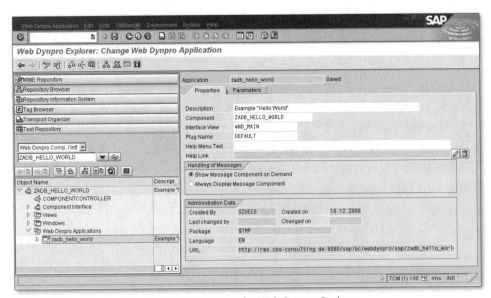

Figure 8.10 Application After the Creation in the Web Dynpro Explorer

11. To start the application, press the ⌈F8⌉ key or select the Test entry from the context menu of the application in the tree of the Web Dynpro Explorer. The browser is started automatically and the Web Dynpro application is executed therein. Depending on the setting of your system, you may have to log on again.

12. You then see the "Hello World" text in your default browser (see Figure 8.11).

Figure 8.11 Hello World Example in the Web Browser

8.2 Scenarios for the Integration of Interactive Forms

SAP provides three basic scenarios for the integration of interactive forms. They are created in such a way that they can be combined freely and therefore cover virtually all kinds of application cases. This section provides you with an overview of how you can use these scenarios by means of Web Dynpro. For more information on the individual scenarios, refer to Chapter 2, Use of SAP Interactive Forms by Adobe.

8.2.1 Print Scenario

In the print scenario, the system either displays a Portable Document Format (PDF) file or automatically creates a noninteractive PDF form based on a form template. Because every PDF form is also a PDF file, it is displayed within the Web Dynpro application package using Adobe Reader. You can find the example shown in Figure 8.12 in the Web Dynpro component, ZADB_DISPLAY_PDF, for testing purposes. You can start it using the application of the same name.

Figure 8.12 Displaying a PDF File Using Web Dynpro ABAP

Caution: Differences in Terminology!

In Chapter 4, Interface and Form Context, Chapter 5, Creating Form Templates, and Chapter 6, Form Output, you learned how to create a PDF form based on a PDF form template and input data. The same mechanisms are used internally by the Web Dynpro runtime environment to automatically create a PDF form at runtime according to your specifications.

In this chapter, the following linguistic simplifications are therefore used to prevent confusions: If the terms form and form template are used, they always stand for PDF form and PDF form template. Furthermore, the term PDF form is used instead of PDF file if the focus is on the display or modification of data.

Particularly in Chapter 4, which is about Form Builder, the term form is used instead of form template. This abbreviated term is alright from the Form Builder viewpoint because it exclusively deals with form templates. The term form is used consistently within this transaction.

In Web Dynpro, however, you must differentiate between design-time object and run-time object. For this reason, within Web Dynpro, the forms created in Form Builder are called form templates. Therefore, the corresponding property in the `InteractiveForm` UI element is called `templateSource`. The runtime object, that is, the object the users can view in Adobe Reader and in which they can enter their data, is called the form. The data contained in the form are called form data.

A form in which a user enters data or can trigger actions on the server is an interactive form. Here, it is insignificant whether the application suppresses the input depending on the situation—for example, in the display mode. Every PDF form is also a PDF file, which is displayed in Adobe Reader. If the focus is on the file character of a form, for example, for the download or upload, the term PDF file is used.

8.2.2 Online Scenario

In the online scenario, the user is provided with a PDF form that is ready for input. Therefore, the user can directly fill out the fields in the form and have the inputs checked by the server. This is basically an alternative UI in which the user works with a PDF-based view that is equivalent to the paper form.

Similar to the print scenario, the PDF form is directly embedded in the application in Web Dynpro ABAP using Adobe Reader. This way, the Web Dynpro application package can navigate between different PDF forms, for example.

As an application developer, you are provided with some very convenient options for implementing the online scenario. For example, it is usually sufficient to specify the name of a form template and to supply the data in the Web Dynpro context according to their structure in the form interface. The creation of the PDF form and the return transport of the user's inputs are automatically carried out by the Web Dynpro runtime.

You can find an example of a simple Web Dynpro application package that shows the online scenario in `ZADB_ONLINE_EXAMPLE` (see Figure 8.13). The input field in Adobe Reader and the `readOnly` input field in the browser below Adobe Reader both bind to the same context attribute. After a value is entered in Adobe Reader, this value is also displayed in the `readOnly` input field. The source code in your application can access the entered data or prepopulate the fields via the connection to the Web Dynpro context. You can obtain more detailed information on this scenario in Section 8.5.2, Online Scenario.

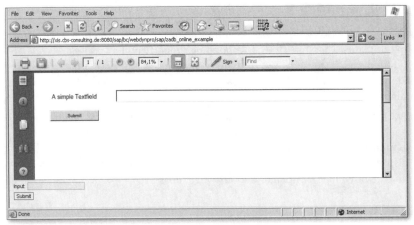

Figure 8.13 Interactive Form in a Web Dynpro Application

8.2.3 Offline Scenario

In the offline scenario, similar to the online scenario, the PDF form is ready for input. However, Adobe Reader is not embedded in a Web Dynpro application in the browser, but runs in a standalone mode. As a result, you do not need a permanent connection to the server. In a typical offline scenario, the user downloads the PDF form from a server to his computer, fills it out offline, and sends the filled-out copy back to the server as soon as he is online again. The following lists some real-life examples implementing Web Dynpro:

► A request form for a government agency that can be filled out by a citizen. The offline nature of this scenario involves the citizen receiving a (printable) copy; the government agency does not have to set up a user account on the system for every single citizen. With Web Dynpro, you create an application for downloading, uploading, and (optionally) for reviewing the form. After the upload, the Web Dynpro application package triggers follow-up processes for processing the request.

► In a key account scenario, the key account manager has stored some blank PDF forms on his notebook so he can open them when he visits a customer. At the customer's site, he can then fill out the forms as required and save them as a copy. When the key account manager returns to the office, he can upload the filled-out copies to the server, for example, using a Web Dynpro application. From the Web Dynpro application package, follow-up processes are triggered for processing the data further.

In contrast to a pure offline scenario, you can use Web Dynpro to create a mixed offline/online scenario. The key account manager would then work with the online scenario while he is in the office and with the offline scenario when he is with a customer or at home. The online scenario could also be implemented using a pure Web Dynpro UI.

Furthermore, an offline/print scenario is possible. The user receives (for instance, by mail) a printed form (possibly an invitation to an event). The user fills out this form and returns it to the organizer by email, fax, or regular mail. The form includes a barcode to easily identify both the participant and the data concerning the event. Additionally, the I ATTEND checkbox can be evaluated via a simple OCR identification. If the user receives the form via email, he can fill out the form electronically offline, print it, and return the signed form. The filled-out data can then be read easily using a paper form barcode. Web Dynpro can be used as an application for manual postprocessing of such replies (for example, integrated with a workflow).

You can find an example for a simple Web Dynpro application package that shows the offline scenario in `ZADB_OFFLINE_EXAMPLE`. For more details on the implementation of the different offline scenario variants using Web Dynpro ABAP, refer to Section 8.5.3, Offline Scenario.

8.3   The InteractiveForm UI Element

The use of the `InteractiveForm` UI element is the core of the Adobe integration with Web Dynpro ABAP. This UI element enables you to map all of the scenarios presented in Section 8.2. For this reason, the UI element comprises several properties (see Figure 8.14). The most important of these are:

▶ **enabled**
Indicates that a PDF form is ready for input. The capacity to enter data is already set on the server. Using this property, you can toggle between the print scenario and the online scenario.

▶ **readOnly**
Indicates that the PDF form is ready for input in the online scenario. To ensure that this property functions, switch on the online scenario by means of the `enabled` property. The capacity to enter data is set in the client. In contrast to switching the `enabled` property, this has the following benefits:

▶ It provides a higher performance because the server does not have to create a new PDF form.

▶ Adobe Reader does not lose its current scroll status by loading a new PDF form.

▶ **dataSource**
Specifies the context node that the displayed form data is stored on, provided that a form template has been specified. Therefore, this special context node is also called the dataSource node.

▶ **templateSource**
If you use a form template, you can enter its name here. dataSource and templateSource are always paired. It does not make any sense to only specify one of them because the system automatically creates the PDF form based on the form data and the form template.

▶ **pdfSource**
Binds to the context attribute on which the PDF file is stored. This property is particularly significant for the print and the offline scenario. In the online scenario, it enables you to store the form as a PDF file on the server.

Property	Value	Bindi
□ CONTEXT_MENUS		
▽ □ ROOTUIELEMENTCONTAINER		
◇ INTERACTIVE_FORM		
Property	**Value**	**Bindi**
Properties (InteractiveForm)		
ID	INTERACTIVE_FORM	
additionalArchives		
dataSource		
displayType	native	
enabled	□	
height	300px	
pdfSource		
readOnly	□	
templateSource		
tooltip		
visible	Visible	
width	300px	
Events		
onSubmit		
Layout Data (FlowData)		
cellDesign	padless	
vGutter	none	

Figure 8.14 UI Element/InteractiveForm

It primarily depends on the scenario whether and how these properties must be set. Section 8.4 and Section 8.5 each include examples that provide more detailed information.

8.4   Interaction with Form Builder

The ViewDesigner in Web Dynpro provides direct access to Form Builder (Transaction SFP). Therefore, you can conveniently navigate from the `InteractiveForm` UI element to the used form template and adjust changes to both objects, if necessary. For more detailed information on form templates and the use of Transaction SFP, refer to Chapter 4, Interface and Form Context, and Chapter 5, Creating Form Templates.

8.4.1   Using Form Templates

A form template can be used simply by entering its name in the `templateSource` property of the `InteractiveForm` UI element or by selecting the connected input help.

Provided that the entered form template exists and that the `dataSource` property has not been bound yet, the system immediately provides you with the option to create a tree of nodes and attributes in the context that is equivalent to the form interface and to bind the `dataSource` property to the root of this tree. The system attempts to give the generated node the same name as the form template. It is possible that the name will be shortened to comply with the name-length restrictions in the context. If a node of the same name already exists, an appropriate sequential number is appended to the name of the new node.

Using a Form Interface in ViewDesigner

You can find an example of an existing form template in the Web Dynpro component, `ZADB_DISPLAY_EXIST_TEMPL`. It is a quasi Web Dynpro equivalent of the SAP example report `FP_EXAMPLE_01`. The report creates—based on the form template of the same name—a form that includes flight-booking data.

The following list provides a step-by-step guide to how the existing form template, `FP_EXAMPLE_01`, was integrated with the Web Dynpro component:

1. Create a new Web Dynpro component, including a view.

2. Navigate to the view and create an `InteractiveForm` UI element there.

3. At first, neither `templateSource` nor `dataSource` of the `InteractiveForm` UI element is filled or bound.

4. You can select the already-existing form template `FP_EXAMPLE_01` via the input help of the `templateSource` property (see Figure 8.15).

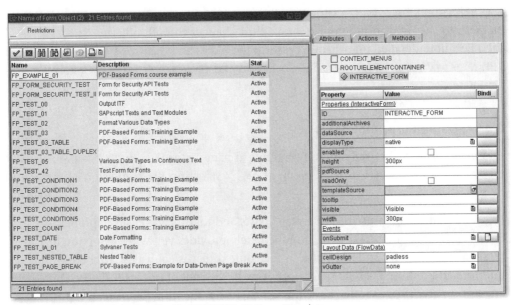

Figure 8.15 Selecting the FP_EXAMPLE_01 Form Template

5. A dialog opens in which the system offers to automatically create the context nodes. Select YES to confirm.

6. Then the system fills the TEMPLATESOURCE and binds the DATASOURCE to the newly-created context node (see Figure 8.16).

7. DATASOURCE binds to the `FP_EXAMPLE_01` node generated by the system, which received the name of the form template (see Figure 8.17) by the system.

8. You can find the source code for populating the context nodes generated from the form template in the `wdDoInit` method (see Listing 8.1). It is implemented similar to the SAP example report, `FP_EXAMPLE_01`. This allows you to compare the two implementations.

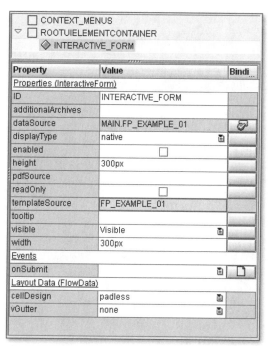

Figure 8.16 Automatically Bound Properties, dataSource and templateSource

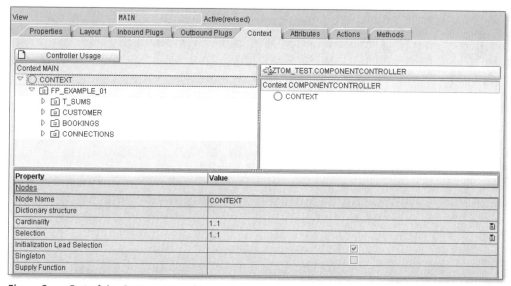

Figure 8.17 Part of the Context Created by the System

```
METHOD wddoinit.
  DATA:
    ls_customer          TYPE scustom,
    lt_bookings          TYPE ty_bookings,
    lt_connections       TYPE ty_connections,
    lt_sums              TYPE TABLE OF sbook,
    lr_form_node         TYPE REF TO if_wd_context_node,
    lr_customer_node     TYPE REF TO if_wd_context_node,
    lr_connections_node  TYPE REF TO if_wd_context_node,
    lr_bookings_node     TYPE REF TO if_wd_context_node,
    lr_t_sums_node       TYPE REF TO if_wd_context_node,
    ls_sums              LIKE LINE OF lt_sums.

  FIELD-SYMBOLS:
    <booking> LIKE LINE OF lt_bookings.

* get the data of the invoice from the database
  SELECT SINGLE * FROM SCUSTOM INTO ls_customer
              WHERE ID = '38'.
  CHECK sy-subrc = 0.
  SELECT * FROM sbook INTO TABLE lt_bookings
          WHERE customid = ls_customer-id
            AND carrid   = 'LH'
          ORDER BY PRIMARY KEY.
  IF lt_bookings[] IS NOT INITIAL.
    SELECT * FROM spfli INTO TABLE lt_connections
            FOR ALL ENTRIES IN lt_bookings
            WHERE carrid = lt_bookings-carrid
              AND connid = lt_bookings-connid
            ORDER BY PRIMARY KEY.
  ENDIF.

* currency key dependent summary
  LOOP AT lt_bookings ASSIGNING <booking>.
    ls_sums-forcuram  = <booking>-forcuram.
    ls_sums-forcurkey = <booking>-forcurkey.
    COLLECT ls_sums INTO lt_sums.
  ENDLOOP.

* bind the selected values their respective context nodes
  lr_form_node       = wd_context->get_child_node(
                          wd_this->wdctx_fp_example_01 ).
  lr_customer_node   = lr_form_node->get_child_node(
```

```
                          wd_this->wdctx_customer ).
lr_connections_node = lr_form_node->get_child_node(
                          wd_this->wdctx_connections ).
lr_bookings_node    = lr_form_node->get_child_node(
                          wd_this->wdctx_bookings ).
lr_t_sums_node      = lr_form_node->get_child_node(
                          wd_this->wdctx_t_sums ).

  lr_customer_node->bind_structure( ls_customer ).
  lr_connections_node->bind_table( lt_connections ).
  lr_bookings_node->bind_table( lt_bookings ).
  lr_t_sums_node->bind_table( lt_sums ).
ENDMETHOD.
```

Listing 8.1 wdDoInit Method

You can also create a completely new form template using ViewDesigner.

1. Define the structure of the new form interface in the context—in this example, this is the DATA_SOURCE node with a 1:1 cardinality and with a VALUE attribute of the STRING type (see Figure 8.18).

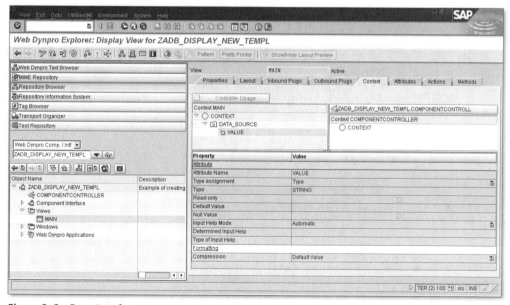

Figure 8.18 Form Interface

2. Enter the name of the new form template in the `templateSource` property of the `InteractiveForm` UI element and confirm your entry by pressing the ⌈ENTER⌋ key.

3. A dialog opens in which you can either use an already-existing form interface or have the system generate a new one via a subtree of the context. Because a new interface is to be created, enter its name, `ZADB_DISPLAY_NEW_TEMPL`, and click on the CONTEXT button (see Figure 8.19).

Figure 8.19 Specify New Form Interface

4. Then click on the `DATA_SOURCE` node in the ContextViewer that opens. Its structure will be used for the new form interface (see Figure 8.20). Confirm your selection by clicking on the button with the green checkmark.

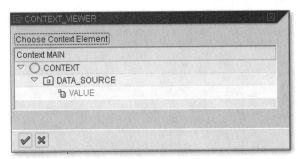

Figure 8.20 Selecting the Root Node of the New Form Interface in the CONTEXTVIEWER

5. The system then automatically creates a new form interface and subsequently a form template (see Figure 8.21).

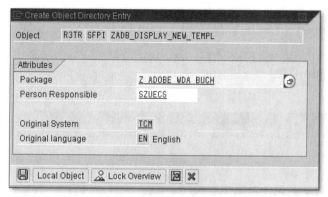

Figure 8.21 Create Object Directory Entry

6. Form Builder opens, and you can process the newly created form template. For print forms, you should first change the LAYOUT TYPE to STANDARD LAYOUT. You can find this setting in the PROPERTIES tab of Form Builder (see Figure 8.22).

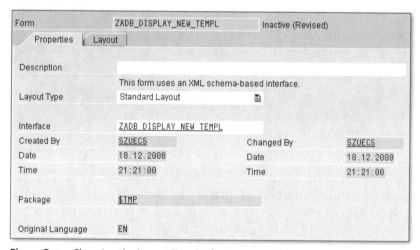

Figure 8.22 Changing the Layout Type in the Properties Tab

7. Switch to the LAYOUT tab. Drag and drop the VALUE attribute from the DATA VIEW palette to the work area of Form Builder—the system creates the binding automatically and correctly (see Figure 8.23).

> **Caution: Do Not Forget Activation!**
>
> Remember to select ACTIVATE before you return to the ViewDesigner, otherwise the ViewDesigner does not recognize the new form template.

Figure 8.23 Form with VALUE Attribute

8. After returning to the ViewDesigner, the system automatically binds the DATA-SOURCE property to the previously selected context node (see Figure 8.24).

9. It is recommended that you set the width of the INTERACTIVEFORM UI element to 100% and the height to 500 pixels (provided that the screen size is big enough) after you have created the form template. The corresponding properties are called WIDTH and HEIGHT.

10. Before testing the application, you must fill in the VALUE context attribute. The source code in Listing 8.2 implements this in the supply function, S_DATA_SOURCE, of the DATA_SOURCE node.

```
METHOD s_data_source.
  DATA:
    ls_data_source TYPE wd_this->element_data_source.
```

```
ls_data_source-value = '42'.
  node->bind_structure( new_item = ls_data_source ).
ENDMETHOD.
```

Listing 8.2 S_DATA_SOURCE Supply Function

Figure 8.24 Automatically Bound dataSource Property

Web Dynpro ABAP supports DDIC and XML-based form interfaces for form templates. Form templates that are based on an SAP Smart Forms interface cannot be used.

The additional features of DDIC interfaces, which were covered in Chapter 4, Interface and Form Context, are supported only in the print scenario. In the online and offline scenarios, the 1:1 conversion between form data and context data is mandatory. As a result, you cannot use any calculating or data-limiting functions. This is because user entries must be reconverted from the form into the Web Dynpro context. SAP recommends using DDIC interfaces in the print scenario only. For more information, see SAP Note 1252350.

The relationship among the Web Dynpro context, the interface of a form, and the form itself is illustrated in Figure 8.25. As you can see, Web Dynpro uses the context to access the form template or the PDF form that was automatically created by the Web Dynpro runtime via the form interface. In the print scenario, the arrows go in only one direction: from the Web Dynpro context to the PDF form.

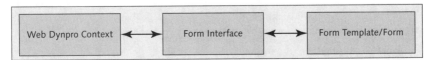

Figure 8.25 Relationships among the Web Dynpro Context, Form Interface, and Form Template/Form

Adjusting Changes to the Form Interface

If the form interface was changed, you should also change the context of the Web Dynpro views that use the forms involved. Therefore, Web Dynpro ABAP provides the option to update the context from the definition of the interface. A prerequisite is that the form template has been specified via the `templateSource` property in the `InteractiveForm` UI element. If the `dataSource` property is bound, the context node behind it is updated; otherwise, a new context node is created.

The adjustment is implemented by calling the context menu in the `InteractiveForm` UI element of the ViewDesigner. Figure 8.26 shows the menu entry GENERATE CONTEXT.

At present, you do not necessarily have to adjust the context to the changed form interface if the change was additive. In this case, the new interface fields or nodes are not provided with data by Web Dynpro and are thus empty in the form. For interactive forms, these new fields must not be ready for input.

But then, the extension of a form template serves a specific purpose. Usually, the additional fields are supposed to be filled from all applications involved. To avoid the cumbersome regeneration of the context, you should define the design from the outset. To do so, proceed as follows:

▶ Use a data structuring that is as useful as possible. Even if your table currently has only one entry, you should not make it "flatter" than it actually is. Treat yourself with a real table node with a 0:N cardinality and have Web Dynpro set the `leadSelection` automatically. Then it is always positioned as the first entry. Thus, your table node acts like a structure, while ensuring extensibility without any structure adjustment.

Figure 8.26 Regenerating the Context from the Form Interface

▶ Benefit from the option to define a DDIC structure for a context node. This way, you do not have to adjust the node any longer if a new field is added. Simply add the field to your DDIC structure. It is then automatically available as an attribute in the context node.

▶ In ABAP, and therefore in Web Dynpro ABAP, you must use uppercase spelling. In an XML-based form interface, you must also use uppercase letters for the name of the data nodes.

Adjusting Changes to the Web Dynpro Context

Changes to the Web Dynpro context must be transferred to the form template in the following cases:

▶ Changing the data type of an attribute, for example, from STRING to MATNR

▶ Adding or deleting an attribute

► Changing the properties of a node (for example, converting a structure into a table)

► Adding or deleting a node

In these cases, you must also adjust the form interface.

If it is an interface generated by the ViewDesigner, and if you navigate to the form template from the ViewDesigner, the system notifies you that the two definitions no longer match (see Figure 8.27). You then have the option of having the system update the form interface.

Figure 8.27 Automatic Interface Adjustment

You can also update the interface manually anytime. To do so, right-click on the InteractiveForm UI element in the ViewDesigner and select the GENERATE XML SCHEMA entry (see Figure 8.28). The adjustment of an interface may also affect other forms. The system provides a corresponding warning (see Figure 8.29).

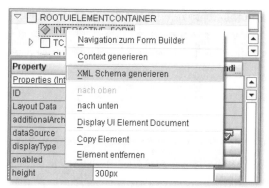

Figure 8.28 Starting the Schema Generation

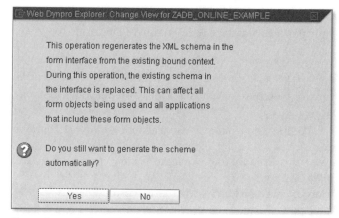

Figure 8.29 System Warning

The regeneration of an XML-based interface is possible only if the interface has been created using the ViewDesigner. The logic for the adjustment was implemented at that time in SAP NetWeaver 7.0 SP 12 and completed with SP 14. Refer to the corresponding SAP notes if you have a system with a lower support package level.

You will come across the previously presented type of adjustment when you implement a field extension in a project and want to display the value of this field in the PDF form, for example. Here, you should note that you can append the additional field to the context node without any modifications (via an enhancement of the node or possibly via an append structure for the node's DDIC structure). However, the necessary form interface/form template change is possible only with modifications.

The best approach is to copy the form template provided by SAP (including its interface) to the customer namespace. Then overwrite the value of the `templateSource` property using an implicit enhancement at the end of the `wdDoModifyView` method.

8.4.2   The pdfOnly Case

The pdfOnly case is a special case in which it is your responsibility to generate a PDF form on the basis of a form template and data. If it is an interactive form, you are also responsible for the data extraction. For this reason, only the `pdfSource` property is bound to the context in this case. `templateSource` and `dataSource` are not used. In the online scenario, this approach only functions in combination with the outdated Active Component Framework (ACF) integration (see Section 8.5.2). Therefore, the `pdfSource` property contains an ACF-enabled PDF form.

Note on the Usage of the Procedure

In principle, you should use this procedure only if you want to use functions that are already contained in Adobe Reader, but are not yet supported by SAP.

▶ In the online scenario, it is not recommended to use this option of direct control. Doing this not only takes a lot of effort, but the internal specifications of the SAP Adobe integration, which are then used without any encapsulation, could be changed by SAP anytime. In addition, the pdfOnly case only functions with the outdated ACF integration, which is no longer developed by SAP. This also indicates that SAP is not interested in continuing the pdfOnly case for the online scenario.

▶ In the print scenario, however, the pdfOnly variant enables you to use functions of Adobe Document Services (ADS) by means of the `PDF Object` programming interface, which is not yet supported by Web Dynpro.

▶ You should only use the pdfOnly option in offline scenarios if you do not intend to use a mixed offline/online scenario.

8.5   Implementing Scenarios Using Web Dynpro ABAP

In this section, we will implement different scenarios of the Adobe integration by means of Web Dynpro ABAP with the help of examples. First, we will discuss two rather comprehensive variants of the print scenario. Then we will look at the implementation of online and offline scenarios.

8.5.1 Print Scenario

The print scenario can be implemented in two different ways: you can display an already-existing PDF file or the Web Dynpro runtime can automatically create a PDF form based on a form template and data via ADS. In both cases, the file is presented to a user via the `InteractiveForm` UI element.

Displaying a PDF File

To implement this scenario, transfer a PDF file that is located in the MIME Repository or in a database table to a context attribute of type `XSTRING`. Then, bind the `pdfSource` property of the `InteractiveForm` UI element to this context attribute.

You can use the code shown in Listing 8.3 to access a file in the MIME Repository:

```
DATA:
  lr_mime_repository TYPE REF TO if_mr_api,
  content            TYPE XSTRING.

CONSTANTS:
  url TYPE STRING VALUE '/SAP/BC/WebDynpro/SAP/ZADB_DISPLAY_PDF/
acrobatpro_datasheet.pdf'.

lr_mime_repository =
  cl_mime_repository_api=>get_api( ).
lr_mime_repository->get(
  EXPORTING
    i_url = url
  IMPORTING
    e_content = content ).
wd_context->set_attribute(
  NAME  = 'PDF'
  VALUE = content ).
```

Listing 8.3 Loading a PDF File from the MIME Repository

The `wdDoInit` method of the view is a good location to load the already-existing PDF file in this example. If the file is used by multiple views, you should use the same method of the ComponentController or a CustomController. You can also use a load-on-demand by moving the source code to an action handler.

With regard to Listing 8.3, the path provided in the URL constant points to the file in the MIME Repository. The file itself is located within the ZADB_DISPLAY_PDF component. You can recognize this by the components of the path, which are described as follows:

▶ **/SAP/BC/WebDynpro**
Path to the Web Dynpro component

▶ **/SAP/ZADB_DISPLAY_PDF/**
Name of the Web Dynpro component

Components without a namespace always receive the name prefix, /SAP/. If you use a custom namespace, it changes from /SAP/ to /CBSGMBH/, for example, for component /CBSGMBH/MY_WDA_COMPONENT (see Figure 8.30).

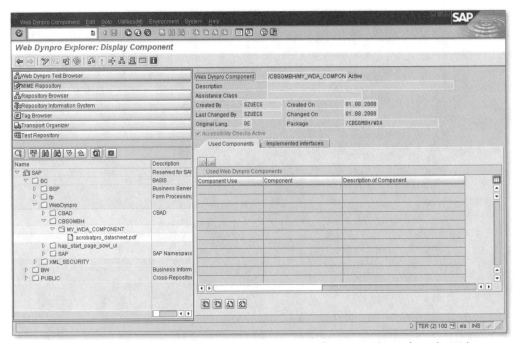

Figure 8.30 Folder Structure Is Available per Namespace for MIME Objects from the Web Dynpro Components

These are all of the steps required. The PDF file is displayed after executing the application. You can find the example in the Web Dynpro component, ZADB_DISPLAY_PDF.

> ### Caution: Pitfall!
>
> In early support packages of SAP NetWeaver 7.0, the default value of the `enabled` property of the `InteractiveForm` UI element is set to `true`. Later on, this was changed in the ViewDesigner to better support the print scenario. Therefore, in SAP NetWeaver 7.0 you should always check to see whether the `enabled` property is switched off. Only then is the print scenario active. In EHP2, the new default value is enabled from the outset.
>
> The Application Program Interface (API) of the `InteractiveForm` UI element by means of the `CL_WD_INTERACTIVE_FORM` class has not been changed by SAP so as to not jeopardize the functionality of existing Web Dynpro applications. There, the default value is still set to `true`. If you make use of dynamic programming with the `InteractiveForm` UI element, you must consider this.

Because the `pdfSource` property is bound to a context attribute in this scenario, its value can be changed—even at runtime. This way, you can create an application that enables the user to navigate between different PDF files. You can find an example of this in the Web Dynpro component, `ZADB_DISPLAY_PDF_NAV`. The corresponding application has the same name. Multiple PDF files are provided in a context node of the 0:N cardinality and made available in the `DropdownByIndex` UI element for selection by the user using the `LeadSelection` of the connected context node (see Figure 8.31).

Figure 8.31 Switching between Different PDF Files Using a Dropdown List

Displaying a PDF Form According to a Form Template

This variant of the print scenario is based on a form template. A PDF form is generated based on it containing data stored in the context. The resulting PDF form is then displayed by the system. All of this is done automatically by the Web Dynpro runtime.

Section 8.4, Interaction with Form Builder, already detailed how you can define a form template in the `InteractiveForm` UI element or generate a new form template from the ViewDesigner. This information is sufficient to allow you to display a PDF form. For this reason, you have to load only the corresponding data into the context structure to which the `dataSource` property binds. This functions in the same way as if you were working with Web Dynpro—for example, by means of a supply function or direct population from other methods of the View Controller.

This is where you can benefit from the use of a form template: Layout and data are separated. This way, you can use different form templates while reusing the same data structures and program logic. A classic example is the rollout of a solution in different regions, for example, from the United States to Japan. Here, the pure translation of texts in the form template is usually not sufficient.

Using DDIC Interfaces versus XML-based Form Interfaces

Up to this point, form templates and their use in Web Dynpro ABAP have been considered only from the integration point of view. The following sections take a look at the technical background. You already know from the previous chapters of this book that each form template has an interface. This interface can either be an SAP Smart Forms, DDIC, or XML-based interface. Web Dynpro ABAP supports both DDIC and XML-based interfaces. SAP recommends using the XML-based interface for new form templates. Legacy SAP Smart Forms–based interfaces are not supported.

Despite the many benefits of the XML-based interface, which will be detailed in the course of this chapter, users often select the "outdated" DDIC interface—particularly for the print scenario. Compared to the XML-based interface, it enables the use of additional functions, for example, the display of addresses that you would otherwise have to implement yourself. In addition, old forms often use the DDIC interface.

With regard to the integration with Web Dynpro, you will not see any difference between the two interface types at first glance. An equivalent context is generated for equivalent interfaces. Among other aspects, this enables you to change a form interface from DDIC to XML later on without having to change the Web Dynpro components involved.

> **Note on Form Templates from the ViewDesigner**
>
> Form templates that you create using the ViewDesigner always have an XML-based interface. In addition, they are protected against external changes, for example, by means of Transaction SFP.
>
> Such forms are intended as ad hoc forms that are mostly used in a single Web Dynpro component. This can be very useful.
>
> If you do not want this dependency, create the form template externally using Transaction SFP. However, an automatic adjustment from the Web Dynpro context is no longer possible then.

Using the jobProfile Property

You can enter the name of a job profile in this property. The `JobProfile` property enables you to use special additional functions for a form in ADS, for instance, duplex prints for older forms that were created using Adobe LiveCycle Designer 7.1. Section 13.2, Managing and Creating Job Profiles, provides more information on the `JobProfile` property and the job profile editor. This function is available in Web Dynpro ABAP as of NetWeaver 7.0 EHP2.

With regard to Web Dynpro ABAP, there are several restrictions concerning the usage of job profiles:

- You require NetWeaver 7.0 EHP2 of the SAP system as well as the correct minimum version of ADS. Customers do not always upgrade ADS, which may be available at a central location, when they upgrade their SAP system. ADS Version 800.20070401.012023 is the required minimum version.

- Job profiles are supported only for ZCI-based forms in the online scenario. More information on ZCI-based forms is available in the next section in which the online scenario is discussed.

- You can use job profiles from Web Dynpro ABAP only for forms that have an XML-based interface.

It is important for you to know that ADS uses a job profile in the form. The content of the job profile is not evaluated within the Web Dynpro ABAP runtime environment. Therefore, you enter only the name of the job profile in the `InteractiveForm` UI element.

Using a job profile, you can also enable features in the form that you must not implement in the Web Dynpro environment; for instance, to convert a print form into an interactive form. You can interfere with the correct functioning of a Web Dynpro runtime environment using such a job profile. If you notice unexpected effects after having used a `Job Profile`, simply delete the content of the `jobProfile` property. If, after doing this, the problem no longer exists, it was caused by an operation not supported within the job profile.

SAP provides a sample application on the job profile topic. The Web Dynpro application is called DEMO_IFBA_JOB_PROFILES.

pdfSource Property in the Print Scenario with Form Templates

One property of the `InteractiveForm` UI element, which has not been considered in detail so far, is important for the print scenario with form templates. It is the `pdfSource` property, which was mentioned in the section on displaying a PDF file. If you bind this property to a context attribute of the type `XSTRING`, you are provided with the currently displayed PDF form in the next roundtrip. Note that the transfer of the PDF form to the context requires some time per roundtrip. Therefore, you should not bind the property to the context if you do not need the PDF form. The same applies to the online scenario that is described in more detail in the following section.

8.5.2 Online Scenario

In the online scenario, a PDF form is ready for input in the browser. Furthermore, you are provided with several additional functions, for example, the value help from Web Dynpro ABAP as an input support. But before you can start to use interactive forms in Web Dynpro ABAP, let's look at the basic technologies for interactive forms.

Basic Technologies for Interactive Forms in the Online Scenario

In the online scenario, interactive forms are based on one of two completely different technologies: outdated ACF (Active Component Framework) and ZCI (Zero Client Installation). They indicate the type of embedding and the control of Adobe Reader in the browser. As a developer, but particularly as an architect, you should know both variants because you will find the corresponding setting options in the `InteractiveForm` UI element and in Form Designer. Today, only the use of ZCI makes sense. As of NetWeaver 7.0 EHP2, SAP has labeled the use of ACF for interactive forms as *deprecated*. For more detailed information, refer to SAP Note 1249189.

▶ **ACF**

ACF is a technology that is used to integrate ActiveX controls or Java applets selected by SAP with Web Dynpro. It is a wrapper around the actual ActiveX control or Java applet. It provides a defined interface to the calling framework (Web Dynpro). ACF is not only used for Adobe integration, but also for other UI elements such as `Network`, `Gantt`, and `OfficeControl`.

An ActiveX wrapper is used in the case of Adobe Reader. This reveals a disadvantage of this solution: Its use is limited to Internet Explorer. An ACF-based Adobe integration cannot function in Firefox, for example. Another disadvantage of the ActiveX solution is that such a control must be installed on the client PC and maintained by an administrator. This, in turn, incurs a higher total cost of ownership (TCO).

However, the ACF integration has one advantage: You can use almost any PDF form template here because it does not require any special adjustments compared to the ZCI integration.

This benefit no longer exists within SAP NetWeaver 7.0 EHP1 after the ZCI integration has been improved. SAP therefore recommends that you no longer use the ACF integration for interactive forms. For more information, refer to SAP Note 1249189. SAP does not further develop the ACF integration but still provides support within the scope of normal maintenance. If you use ACF integration in your project, you will not benefit from the new Adobe integration features.

▶ **ZCI**

The ZCI integration is the successor technology of the ACF integration and has been available to customers since SAP NetWeaver 7.0 SP 10. In contrast to the ACF approach, there is no wrapper around Adobe Reader; Adobe Reader is controlled per JavaScript via a special API provided by Adobe. As a result, this solution functions in all browsers supported by SAP. Therefore, as of SAP NetWeaver 7.0 SP 15, not only Internet Explorer, but Firefox is also supported for Adobe integration (see SAP Note 1098009).

Up to SAP NetWeaver 7.0 EHP1 not every form template is suitable for the ZCI integration. To use ZCI, you first had to insert the ZCI script into the form template. This can be done either via the menu path UTILITIES • INSERT WEB DYNPRO SCRIPT (see Figure 8.32) or via the `FP_ZCI_UPDATE` report for several form templates in one go. As of SAP NetWeaver 7.0 EHP1, ADS automatically inserts the ZCI script in the form. For this purpose, ADS must have a ZCI script that corresponds to the linked ABAP stack.

Figure 8.32 Inserting the ZCI Script via the Menu

The ZCI script is constantly developed further by Adobe, which is why there are different versions of this script. Each version is bound to a specific release and therefore to a specific support package of SAP NetWeaver. So—prior to NetWeaver 7.0 EHP1—if you import a support package, you may have to adapt the ZCI script for all form templates you use. From a technical point of view, this constitutes a modification of the form templates provided by SAP.

For your developer PC the basic rule applies that different versions of Adobe LiveCycle Designer also entail different versions of the ZCI script. Newly created form templates receive the ZCI script that is currently installed on your computer. Ensure that it matches the support package level of the SAP system if the SAP system does not yet include NetWeaver EHP1.

Also note that before using NetWeaver 7.0 EHP1 you must update the ZCI script on ADS and also adapt the ZCI script on the PCs of all project members.

Otherwise, an obsolete ZCI script is inserted into new forms; then you have to replace it using the ZCI conversion report, `FP_ZCI_UPDATE`.

In addition to the ZCI script, there are different versions of the respective controls that must correspond to the version of the ZCI script. The ZCI conversion report is used to update them.

Important Note: Automatically Updating the ZCI Script

Up to SAP NetWeaver 7.0 SP 15, there are some serious errors and deficiencies within the ZCI integration. Therefore, you should install SP 16 or higher for this release if you want to use the online scenario. Otherwise, you must expect several errors (for example, when locking the form against input and when using pop-up windows) and deficiencies (such as the lack of input/output conversion).

With Enhancement Package 1 of SAP NetWeaver 7.0, there is an automatic update of the ZCI script. Here, the form template no longer has to contain a ZCI script. It is automatically added and updated by ADS at runtime. Therefore, version problems due to obsolete form templates are a thing of the past. Make use of this option to avoid problems right from the outset.

If you use SAP NetWeaver 7.0 EHP1, for example, within the framework of an EHP of SAP ERP or CRM 7.0, you should note that ADS runs on the Java platform. The automatic update of the ZCI script is not included in SAP's allowed combination of SAP NetWeaver ABAP 7.0 EHP1 and SAP NetWeaver Java 7.0. For this reason, you would have to install SAP NetWeaver Java 7.0 EHP1 or higher.

With SAP NetWeaver 7.0 EHP2, all of these problems are solved because SAP also offers an appropriate ADS version. It is also important to ensure that you use ADS that corresponds to the version. If not, you cannot use specific features from EHP2, for instance, the new value helps.

Problematic Aspects of the Interactive Online Scenario

There are several problematic aspects that you should consider if you want to use the online scenario:

- Adobe Reader is a separate UI environment. This is required for the offline scenario—in the online scenario; however, it constrains the full integration with Web Dynpro. For example, within Adobe Reader some Web Dynpro features do not function, such as personalization. Developers are not provided with the wide range of UI elements to create highly interactive applications to the degree provided by Web Dynpro. The structuring of data by means of a `Tree` UI element is not possible either.

▸ Forms that have been created for the offline scenario are usually not suitable for the online scenario. This is because forms in offline scenarios usually contain additional data (for example, summarized in dropdown lists), which may result in large forms. This in turn is not suitable for an online scenario in which all form data are continuously exchanged with the server. Here, you would only create fields with small value sets as dropdown lists and include a value help for cases with many entries. Overall, this would result in better performance. However, this is not suitable for filling out a form offline due to the missing server connection.

▸ Adobe Reader fully occupies the intended area in the browser. Combining it with Web Dynpro UI elements is not possible. Prior to SAP NetWeaver 7.0 SP 11, it was possible to specify the height and width of this area in fixed sizes only (for example, pixel); that is, until then it was impossible to automatically adjust the size of the form to the size of the browser.

▸ Web Dynpro only supports some features of the PDF standard and Adobe Reader. It will always be a technology that must implement support for new functions of ADS, the PDF standard, and Adobe Reader before you as the application developer can use them from Web Dynpro. SAP strives to do so; however, the PDF standard alone is too extensive to implement completely.

For example, digital signatures are currently not supported in Web Dynpro ABAP. In addition, only a subset of the controls available in Adobe LiveCycle Designer has been released for use in Web Dynpro. SAP has not even implemented a series of controls in the xACF and ZCI libraries that have been developed by Adobe specifically for Web Dynpro.

▸ You cannot display multiple interactive forms in the browser at the same time, for example, to compare the content of two forms. However, this is enabled for noninteractive forms, that is, for forms that have been created according to the print scenario. The same applies to the user of the InteractiveForm UI element in a dialog.

▸ Whereas you can apply a consistent corporate design to Web Dynpro without changing the application, this is not possible for a form template. It can have only a single design. If the corporate design is changed, you must readjust every form template concerned.

▸ Problem effects observed in the browser (for example, no data transfer after a roundtrip) cannot always be traced back to a problem with the Adobe integration because Adobe Reader has a high error tolerance. For this reason, Adobe Reader does not always display an error message for problems.

▶ Forms of the online scenario created by the Web Dynpro runtime always constitute a dynamic PDF. Adobe specifies a maximum of twelve pages, which should not be exceeded due to performance reasons. More information is available on the Adobe Web site at *http://www.adobe.com/devnet/livecycle/articles/DynamicInteractiveFormPerformance.pdf*.

▶ Up to Release SAP NetWeaver 7.0, ZCI-based forms must already contain the source code for communication with the Web Dynpro framework—the ZCI script. As of Release 7.0 EHP1, the script for creating the PDF form is automatically added by ADS. So, if you use SAP NetWeaver 7.0, you must pay special attention to the use of the correct ZCI script and always keep it up to date. This can be very tedious or even impossible.

▶ It is a technical challenge to integrate an ActiveX control with a browser that interacts with its environment via a JavaScript framework, which must not lose its contents between roundtrips, and is supposed to be performant. The alternative is to use the two technologies and their strengths directly, for example, Web Dynpro for online scenarios and SAP Interactive Forms by Adobe for offline scenarios.

▶ Client certificates are not supported by the ZCI integration at present. If you must use client certificates, you can only revert to the ACF integration (which has not been and will not be further developed by SAP) or exchange the interactive form embedded in Web Dynpro with a pure Web Dynpro application package.

▶ HTTPS is supported by the ZCI integration as of Adobe Reader 8.1. If you use an older version of Adobe Reader, you must revert to the unsecure HTTP variant or to the ACF integration. For this reason, it is always advisable to schedule the rollout of the latest Adobe Reader version recommended by SAP at the start of a project. Note that you receive Adobe support only if your enterprise uses Adobe Reader 8.4 or higher (status at the time this book went to press).

Due to the numerous problems and the unsteady integration of the two technologies (browser and Adobe Reader) you should use the online scenario with special care. However, there are also some good usage options, which are presented below.

Reasonable Usage of the Online Scenario

Typically, the scenario is used in two areas:

- For entering data in simple forms, for example, paper. The permanent connection to the server for the online scenario enables the immediate check of entries, the support of value helps, and the possible start of follow-up processes.

- For the online review of small forms from the offline scenario.

The implementation of the two online scenarios is discussed in the course of this chapter, whereas the review of offline forms is included in Section 8.5.3.

It is useful to answer some questions and clarify issues prior to the use of the online scenario. Some of these questions result from the list of problematic aspects of the use of the online scenario. The following checklist should help you with your projects:

- Check whether an implementation using Web Dynpro (or another technology) without interactive forms would be more reasonable. In a pure online scenario, it usually makes no sense to embed an Adobe form in a Web Dynpro environment because the maintenance and development effort resulting from the combination of the two technologies is usually greater than if you focused on only one technology.

- Decide whether the entries in the browser are supposed to be made via Adobe Reader or Web Dynpro. This means that there should be virtually no dependencies between the UI logic outside and inside Adobe Reader. Such dependencies can arise if you position the same input field both within Adobe Reader and outside Adobe Reader in a Web Dynpro application package, for example, to provide users with the option to enter data either in the form or in the Web Dynpro environment. This usually results in problems because the sequence for transferring changes between Adobe Reader and Web Dynpro is undefined.

  This design principle also applies to interconnected input fields. For example, you should never provide the `City` field in the form and the `Country` field in the Web Dynpro environment with ready-for-input status. This would be hard for the user to understand. The best solution is to establish groups of logically related fields and to implement them completely in one of the two technologies.

- ZCI is used as the integration technology right from the start of the project because the ACF integration is no longer developed by SAP.

- Ensure that all project members use the same version of Adobe LiveCycle Designer.

- If you use SAP NetWeaver 7.0 EHP1 or higher, check whether ADS has this or a higher version. Otherwise, the ZCI script will not be used automatically. If you upgrade ADS or import a support package, you must allow for test effort that is required for regression tests of the form processes in connected systems.

- Prior to NetWeaver 7.0 EHP1, the rule applies that the same version of ZCI is stored on ADS as on the project members' PCs. The latest and, in particular, the same ZCI script is used in all form templates right from the outset. No new support package is imported during the project or else the ZCI script must be updated in the form templates already created. After an update of the ZCI script (in all used form templates, on all PCs and ADS) the business scenarios concerned are retested.

- The used form templates only have a manageable number of fields. The resulting PDF form has a maximum of twelve pages because Adobe has set this limit for dynamic PDFs due to performance issues.

- The form is primarily developed for the online scenario and not for the offline scenario. This is a typical (unconscious) error when converting an existing paper form into a form template for the online scenario. This includes, for example, that dropdown lists are used sparingly and may contain only a small, manageable number of entries (less than or equal to seven). Otherwise, you should add a value help to the `Text Field` control. Dropdown lists of any size can cause performance problems.

- The page size remains Letter or DIN A4 only in exceptional cases, such as displaying an existing paper form. In all other cases, the size of the form is adapted so that its content is just enclosed. This way, you can avoid unnecessary scrollbars within Adobe Reader and increase the initial magnification of the form. This improves the readability and usability of the form considerably. The worst that can happen is that the user must select a suitable form magnification by means of Adobe Reader's zoom function after the form has been loaded.

For converted paper forms, you should also check whether Letter or DIN A4 is a useful format. Because the user works online, you can split a large form into many small forms and interlink them using a wizard created by means of Web Dynpro UI elements. For example, consider a program for filling out an annual tax declaration: Here, you are guided through the individual sections of the form step by step.

- At the beginning of the project you must check whether the support of client certificates is necessary because they are not currently supported by the ZCI integration.

- If you do not use the latest Adobe Reader version, there are restrictions with regard to using the VPN connection. Up to Version 8, Adobe Reader sets up a separate communication channel to the server without using the communication object of the browser. This is possible as of Version 9.

- Always use the latest version of Adobe Reader recommended by SAP. This way, you can prevent some of the problems mentioned here. Schedule the rollout of a possible Adobe Reader update.

- Do not use the DECFLOAT data type. This new data type was introduced in ABAP in NetWeaver 7.0 EHP2. It is not supported yet in the Adobe integration.

- Ensure that in an XML-based form interface the names of all elements and attributes only consist of uppercase letters; otherwise, you cannot set the focus on a field or navigate from a message to a field.

- In SAP NetWeaver 7.0 EHP2, new XFOs for value helps were implemented at the same time. For this purpose, you require Adobe LiveCycle Designer Version 8.2 as well as Adobe Document Services Version 820.20080812.034112.

If you consider these rules, there is nothing to prevent a successful use of the online scenario.

Updating the ZCI Script Prior to SAP NetWeaver 7.0 EHP1

Because version problems of the script occur in every project in which a version lower than SAP NetWeaver 7.0 EHP1 is used, the following sections describe how you can detect and resolve them. The first question to ask is how to determine the version of the ZCI script.

1. To do so, start Form Builder (Transaction SFP) and open the form template concerned.

2. Go to the LAYOUT view and select the HIERARCHY palette there.

3. You can find the included ZCI script under (VARIABLES). It has the name, CONTAINERFOUNDATION_JS. Click on it.

4. The beginning of the file should now appear in the Script area. There you will find the version information. In Figure 8.33, the version number is 802.20070 810081039.413428.411870. The area directly after the first dot is important: It includes the date and enables you to determine the up-to-dateness of the script. The structure of the date is year/month/day—in this case August 10, 2007. If the script area is not displayed, you can expand it using the blue slider.

Figure 8.33 Determining the Version of the ZCI Script in the Layout View

The next question is whether the determined version is obsolete, just right, or too new. Here, the rule applies that up to SP 16 the version mentioned is the correct version. You need a more recent version of the ZCI scripts for higher support package versions or after downloading SAP Notes 1229392, 1227102, and 1180004.

If the ZCI script is obsolete, you have two options for updating it:

▸ Via Transaction SFP_ZCI_UPDATE for several forms
▸ Using Form Builder (Transaction SFP) for exactly one form

In the former case, the new ZCI script must be available on ADS. For more information, refer to SAP Note 956074. In the latter case, the ZCI script must be available in different directories on your computer. Let's look at this case more closely.

1. The ZCI script is located in subdirectories of the Adobe LiveCycle Designer directory together with the controls and sorted by language. For version 8.2, for example, the path is *C:\Programs\Adobe\Designer 8.2*. The subdirectories are called *DE*, *EN*, etc.

   Each of these subdirectories includes a *Templates* subdirectory. The ZCI script should at least be found in the subdirectories, *Web Dynpro* and *Custom*. The corresponding file is called *Web DynproInteractiveForm.tds* and can be opened with a text editor. You can find the version entry within the file.

2. For an update, this file must be replaced consistently in all subdirectories for all languages used. For later versions of the file, refer to the respective SAP notes (for example, SAP Note 956074).

3. Once you have restarted Adobe LiveCycle Designer, the new version of the file is used. If this does not work, delete the cache directory of Adobe LiveCycle Designer under *C:\Documents and Settings\<developer>\Application data\Adobe\ Designer*. You must replace the *<developer>* path component with the name of the current Windows user.

If you use SAP NetWeaver 7.0 EHP1 or higher, you are no longer displayed a ZCI script within the form template. The ADS version is decisive then. The rule of thumb is that ADS should at least have the version of the SAP NetWeaver ABAP stack to be able use all features.

The following sections present different techniques that will be used in a real online example later on.

Processing Input Fields

In the first and simplest example, you are to create an interactive PDF form that "only" contains one single input field and a button for sending the input to the server. The text entered in the form is displayed in a Web Dynpro input field for verification outside the form after the SEND button has been activated. You can find an example in the Web Dynpro component, ZADB_ONLINE_INPUT_FIELD.

Carry out the following steps to create such a component:

1. Create a new Web Dynpro component using Transaction SE80. The component should contain a view (MAIN) and a window (WND_MAIN).

2. In the context of the view, create a DATA_SOURCE node with the cardinality 1:1 and with a VALUE context attribute of the type STRING (see Figure 8.34).

3. Use the following UI elements in the layout of the view:

   ▶ an Inputfield with Label

   ▶ an optional Button

   ▶ an InteractiveForm UI element

4. Bind the value property of the Inputfield to the VALUE context attribute.

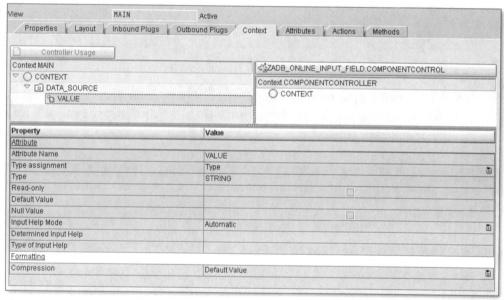

Figure 8.34 Context of the View

5. Activate the enabled property for the InteractiveForm UI element so that the PDF form becomes interactive.

6. Next, create a new form template from the ViewDesigner as described in Section 8.4.1, Using Form Templates. In this form template, a text field binds to the VALUE attribute from the data view of Form Builder.

7. Because you want to create a ZCI-based interactive PDF form, you first have to set the layout type in the PROPERTIES tab to ZCI LAYOUT (see Figure 8.35).

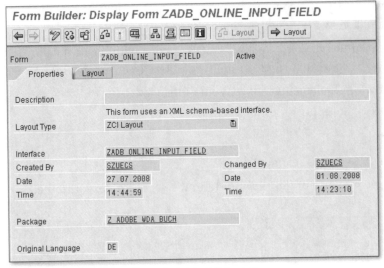

Figure 8.35 Layout Type Manually Set to ZCI Layout

8. Add a SEND button from the WEB DYNPRO NATIVE library (see Figure 8.36). If the ZCI script is not yet displayed in the HIERARCHY palette, you can add it to the form template later on.

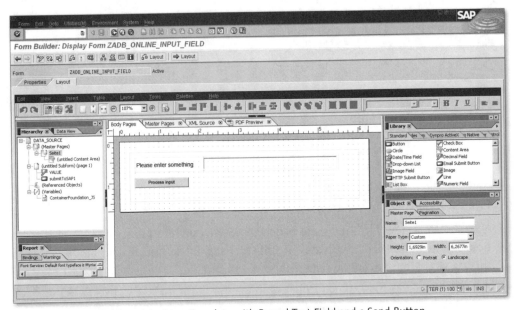

Figure 8.36 Complete Form Template with Bound Text Field and a Send Button

Two Web Dynpro Tabs in Form Builder

There are two Web Dynpro libraries in Form Builder: WEB DYNPRO ACTIVEX and WEB DYN-PRO NATIVE. The ActiveX library contains controls for the use in ACF-based form templates. The Native library contains the controls intended for ZCI-based form templates.

A form template must use the controls of the corresponding library depending on the layout type; otherwise, the interactive form will not function properly. Unfortunately, the system does not display an error message if an incorrect control is used. For example, if you use the wrong SEND button, you can still activate the form template without any problems. No error message is provided at runtime either. Clicking on the button triggers absolutely nothing—a frequent source of error whose cause is not obvious. So it is your responsibility to ensure that the right controls are used.

9. Return to the ViewDesigner in Web Dynpro after the new form template and form interface have been activated. The `dataSource` property of the `InteractiveForm` UI element was automatically bound by the system (see Figure 8.37).

Property	Value		Binding
Properties (InteractiveForm)			
ID	INTERACTIVE_FORM		
Layout Data	MatrixHeadData	🗏	
additionalArchives			
dataSource	MAIN.DATA_SOURCE		🖑
displayType	native	🗏	
enabled	☑		
height	400px		
pdfSource			
readOnly	☐		
templateSource	ZADB_ONLINE_INPUT_FIELD		
tooltip			
visible	Visible	🗏	
width	100%		
Events			
onSubmit		🗏	
Layout Data (MatrixHeadData)			
cellBackgroundDesign	transparent	🗏	
cellDesign	rPad	🗏	
colSpan	1		

Figure 8.37 Automatically Bound dataSource Property

10. If you created a `Button` UI element above the `InteractiveForm` UI element, it is only active in the Web browser if you assigned an action to its `onSubmit` event. Because the action is to do nothing but trigger a roundtrip to the server, it is sufficient to create an action without source code. The transfer of the entries

from the PDF form to the input field is done automatically because they both bind to the same context attribute.

For the example created just now, `Inputfield`, the `readOnly` property should only be set to prevent accidental inputs. The user is supposed to make the entries only in the PDF form. You can also use a `TextView` UI element. However, in this case the user would not recognize that a specific area contains information or is supposed to receive information.

11. Create a Web Dynpro application package as the last step for the Web Dynpro component and start it. After you have entered a text and clicked on one of the two buttons, the browser should then appear as illustrated in Figure 8.38. After you have entered "to appear above" in the PDF form and clicked one of the two buttons, the input appears in `Inputfield` above the PDF form.

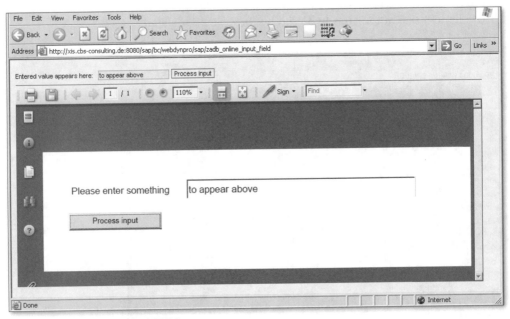

Figure 8.38 Finished PDF Form

In this example, it is not important whether you click on the SEND button in the PDF form or the Web Dynpro button outside the form. In both cases, you trigger a roundtrip to the server and your entries are transferred from the form into the Web Dynpro context. This, in turn, means that you could omit the SEND button in the form. It would then be closer to a real paper form.

One decisive "what-if?" question has not been considered yet. This involves the option of using already-existing form templates with a DDIC interface. In principle, these form templates can also be used for interactive forms in Web Dynpro ABAP — even if this is not recommended by SAP. However, the DDIC interface may not carry out any operations for the inbound data (conversions, limiting or extending user input, and so on).

Experiment!

Due to its simplicity, this example is perfectly suited to consider some what-if situations:

▶ For example, change the capacity to enter data for the two input fields via the properties `readOnly` and `enabled`. What happens if both input fields are ready for input at the same time? (This is undefined.)

▶ Can you use existing form templates that were created using Form Builder? (Yes.)

▶ What happens if you use the SEND button from the wrong library in Form Builder? (The text field is ready for input, but clicking on the SEND button has no effect.)

▶ Can you retroactively change the layout type from ZCI to another value? (That is not possible retroactively. A conversion in the other direction is possible using the ZCI update report that was presented earlier.)

You can also experiment with this example in other browsers or Adobe Reader versions if you have the chance. If a complex example does not function in a project, this simple example may help you to exclude these and similar infrastructure problems.

Because no option exists for application developers to define the re-transformation of an input from the form into the Web Dynpro context, the input of a user would probably not be processed. As long as you stick to this rule, you can also use the form template with DDIC interface as interactive forms.

This feature was not intended originally. Form templates with DDIC interface were supposed to be used only as pure print forms. Upon request of users, this option has been retroactively provided. For this reason, it is not sufficient to switch on the `enabled` property for a form template with DDIC interface to make the resulting form interactive.

Existing Web Dynpro applications with print forms that have a DDIC interface could become interactive. For those, the value of the `enabled` property was irrelevant prior to the implementation of this feature; they have never been ready for input. Therefore, a method handler was assigned to the `InteractiveForm` UI element. You may know the method handler from other Web Dynpro UI elements, such as

OfficeControl, BIApplicationFrame, or Table. A method handler enables the Web Dynpro developer to call additional functions on a UI element, which cannot be mapped via a property or for which SAP did not want to introduce a new property due to the special role of the feature.

In this case, the latter applies. The additional property that can be addressed using the method handler is called legacyEditingEnabled. It is a Boolean value that is switched off by default. The method handler includes a set and a get method to change or read the current value. You can access the method handler only via the UI element. For this reason, you should position the respective code in the wdDoModifyView method of the view on which the InteractiveForm UI element can be found.

You can use the code shown in Listing 8.4 to access the method handler and set legacyEditingEnabled to true.

```
METHOD wddomodifyview.
  DATA:
    lr_interactive_form TYPE REF TO
      cl_wd_interactive_form,
    lr_method_handler   TYPE REF TO
      if_wd_iactive_form_method_hndl.

* make sure that it's only done once
  CHECK first_time = abap_true.

* get the InteractiveForm ui element
  lr_interactive_form ?= view->get_element( 'INTERACTIVE_FORM' ).

* get the method handler of the InteractiveForm
* ui element
  lr_method_handler ?= lr_interactive_form->_method_handler.

* set legacyEditingEnabled to true
  lr_method_handler->set_legacy_editing_enabled( abap_true ).
ENDMETHOD.
```

Listing 8.4 Setting legacyEditingEnabled in wdDoModifyView

Now, the interactive form with the DDIC interface is ready for input. You can find the corresponding example in the Web Dynpro component, ZADB_ONLINE_INPFLD_DDIC.

Background Information: Integrating ACF-Based Forms

Now that the ZCI integration has been described in great detail, only one aspect remains to be discussed—the integration of ACF-based form templates. Because SAP does not develop new features for such form templates and because ACF form templates have the disadvantages previously discussed, you should always use the ZCI integration for new form templates.

Before ZCI was developed, customers used ACF and went live with their projects. Because a retroactive changeover to ZCI is not required as long as the conditions remain unchanged (e.g., system, user requirements) or a changeover is not yet worthwhile, you will still come across ACF-based form templates. Therefore, the following briefly discusses ACF integration.

You must implement the following when using ACF form templates:

▸ Set the layout type of the form template to XACF LAYOUT

▸ Use the controls from the ACTIVEX palette of Form Builder

▸ Do not add any ZCI script to the form

▸ Change the `displayType` from NATIVE (ZCI) to ACTIVEX (ACF) in the `InteractiveForm` UI element

In more recent support packages, the `displayType` property is automatically set to NATIVE after inserting an `InteractiveForm` UI element so that a useful default value is specified for the ZCI form templates. Note that the default value in the `CL_WD_INTERACTIVE_FORM` class is still set to ACTIVEX due to the necessary downward compatibility.

> **Caution: Pitfall!**
>
> There are numerous pitfalls in the creation of interactive PDF forms. The following is a checklist. The ZCI-based form becomes interactive only if all of these points are met.
>
> ▸ The `enabled` property is activated.
>
> ▸ The `readOnly` property is not activated.
>
> ▸ The `displayType` property has the `Native` value. (Note: In older support packages, the default value is `activeX`.)
>
> ▸ For a DDIC form template, `legacyEditingEnabled`, was activated using the method handler.
>
> ▸ The layout type of the form template is ZCI.

> ▶ The controls from the correct Web Dynpro palette in Form Builder were used.
>
> ▶ Prior to NetWeaver 7.0 EHP1: The ZCI script is available and up to date.

Connecting Value Help

This section discusses a convenient function that is indispensable when running an average business application in the SAP environment—value help. The design of the value help connection ensures that the user can use the same scope of input help types for an interactive form as is available in Web Dynpro. You can set the type of value help in the corresponding context attribute as usual. The connection of the Object Value Selector (OVS) or a freely programmed value help is also fully identical.

Refer to the Web Dynpro online help for more information on the integration of value helps with Web Dynpro ABAP. There you will find a comprehensive description of the options available. In addition, you will find an implementation of all these options in an interactive PDF form in the Web Dynpro component, ZADB_ONLINE_VALUE_HELP.

What is new is the connection of the value help to the Web Dynpro context by means of Form Builder. Here you must note that the availability of a value help must already be specified in Form Builder via a corresponding control at design time. For a Web Dynpro Inputfield this is done only at runtime. This means that the VALUE HELP button is always visible in interactive forms—even if no value help is defined in the context attribute at runtime.

The other effect is that the VALUE HELP button occupies space in the form. If a table field is supposed to receive a VALUE HELP button, this button is always visible for all rows of this column. In Web Dynpro it is visible only if you click on or put the focus on Inputfield, for example, through tabbing. Therefore, an interactive form with a value help does not correspond to a paper form. Here, you must make a compromise between the detailed mapping of a paper form and user-friendliness.

But how do you actually integrate a value help with an interactive form?

1. Create a Web Dynpro component with a simple interactive form according to the description under "Processing Input Fields" in Section 8.5.2.

2. Use a data element that already contains a value help, for example, S_CARR_ID (the airline), as the type of the context attribute that is assigned to the Textfield

in the PDF form. This way, the Web Dynpro runtime environment knows which value help to display. The value selected by the user is automatically populated to the context attribute.

3. A trigger is required in the PDF form to display the value help. For this reason, the WEB DYNPRO NATIVE library contains the `Value Help` control (see Figure 8.39). Drag and drop this control next to the `Text Field`.

> **Caution: Pitfall!**
>
> The `Value Help Drop-Down List` control is available in addition to the `Value Help` control. This value help is displayed as a dropdown list. Unfortunately, only the OVS can be displayed this way. All other value sets resulting from value helps cannot be provided as a dropdown list by the user (more than one result field, too large data quantity, filter options available via the value help, and so on).
>
> If this was the case, you could also use a dropdown list directly. The alternative of opening an empty dropdown list with a subsequent value help dialog for the other value help types does not make sense from a usability standpoint. For these reasons, Web Dynpro ABAP does not support this control.

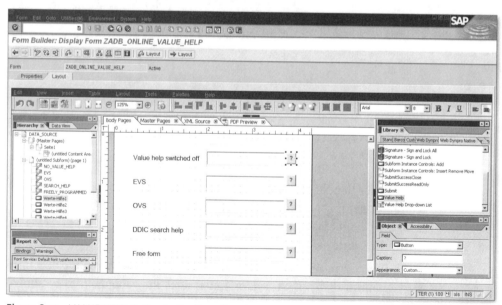

Figure 8.39 VALUE HELP Button in the Form Template

4. If you execute your application now, you will see that nothing happens. The reason is that the VALUE HELP button does not know which Text Field it belongs to. Because the layout and the data are separated also in a form template, the VALUE HELP button contains a data binding instead of a reference to another control.

   This data binding cannot be set via the object properties; it must be entered manually in the button's script. To do so, click on the VALUE HELP button and open the script area in Form Builder.

5. Then enter the value of the binding in the row below the comment. The result for the binding to the NO_VALUE_HELP attribute is: var fieldName = "NO_VALUE_HELP"; Figure 8.40 illustrates this.

Figure 8.40 Data Path Sent to the Server via the Value Help Button

You may notice that this is not a classic binding, but rather some kind of pointer or reference that is sent to the server when the button is activated. The VALUE HELP button uses the script of the click event to send the data path to the server for which the value help is to be called.

The Web Dynpro runtime on the server maps this data path from the PDF form back to a path in the context. It then determines the value help to be shown and displays it as a pop-up window. If no value help is available, a message is displayed.

Web Dynpro ABAP supports the connection of a value help to ZCI form templates as of SAP NetWeaver 7.0 SP 12. SAP Note 1029721 describes the necessary adaptations.

Caution: Pitfall!

If you forget to set the data path in the script, no error message is displayed either in Form Builder or at runtime. Clicking the VALUE HELP button does not trigger any reaction of the system.

If the path cannot be mapped in the Web Dynpro context, a short dump is triggered at runtime. In the ViewDesigner, no error message is sent at design time.

If you change a form interface, you should check to see whether the script of the VALUE HELP buttons must be adapted.

New Value Helps in Adobe LiveCycle Designer 8.2

As of Adobe LiveCycle Designer Version 8.2, SAP supports the following three new types of value helps:

▸ Numeric field value help

▸ Decimal field value help

▸ Text field value help

These new value helps each combine an input field and a value help button in one control. The benefit is that the VALUE HELP button in tables is only visible if the associated input field is in the focus. This significantly increases the clarity in tables. You should therefore always use these new input helps (see Figure 8.41). Note that—in contrast to Web Dynpro—the space for the invisible value help is not released dynamically. This means that you will have a small empty stripe in the table column on the right of the input field.

You can find a demo example for the new values helps in the DEMO_IFBA_VALUEHELP_XFO Web Dynpro application. Note that ADS must have Version 820.20080812.034112 or higher so that you can use this feature.

Figure 8.41 New Input Help

Using Dropdown Lists

As of SAP NetWeaver 7.0 SP 10 or with SAP Note 983699, application developers have the option to integrate dropdown lists with their ZCI form template whose entries are automatically set by the system. Up to that point, values in dropdown lists had to be included in the form template at design time.

As with the Web Dynpro UI element, DropdownByKey, the entries of a dropdown list in a ZCI form template are taken from the ValueSet of the context attribute to which the dropdown list binds. If the type of the context attribute includes a domain with fixed values, these are automatically used. The NodeInfo of a context node provides the option to set a ValueSet dynamically at runtime via the SET_ATTRIBUTE_VALUE_SET method.

The following example illustrates the use of a dropdown list in an interactive PDF form. You can find the example in the Web Dynpro component, ZADB_ONLINE_DROPDOWN.

1. Create a Web Dynpro component with a view and a window.

2. In the view, create a DATA_SOURCE node with the cardinality 1:1 and with a CLASS attribute of type S_CLASS (see Figure 8.42). This data element already contains a domain with three fixed values for the cabin classes on an airplane (first, business, economy). These values are to be displayed as a dropdown list in an interactive form later on.

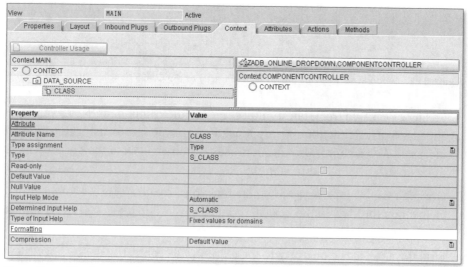

Figure 8.42 The Context Editor Automatically Recognizes that the Context Attribute CLASS has Fixed Values

3. Set the layout of RootUIElementContainer to RowLayout. In the view, create a DropdownByKey with Label and a Button with a dummy Action for triggering a roundtrip. The selectedKey property of DropdownByKey should bind to the CLASS context attribute (see Figure 8.43).

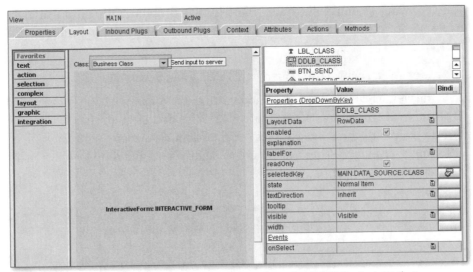

Figure 8.43 DropdownByKey UI Element Binds Directly to the CLASS Context Attribute

4. Create a Web Dynpro application package for the component. Now, you have already created a functioning dropdown list in an application using the onboard means of Web Dynpro. Use this option as a countercheck to the dropdown list in the interactive PDF form later on.

5. Once the Web Dynpro dropdown list functions, create an `InteractiveForm` UI element on the view in the next step. Set its `LayoutData` to `RowHeadData` so that it appears in a new row.

6. Bind the `dataSource` property to the `DATA_SOURCE` context node.

7. Create a new ZCI-based form template by entering the name of a new form template in the `templateSource` property and using the context node. Form Builder displays the CLASS attribute as a dropdown list in the BODY PAGES palette (see Figure 8.44).

Caution: Pitfall!

Even if a dropdown list is already displayed for the CLASS attribute in the DATA VIEW, you must not drag and drop the attribute to the form template.

Although Adobe LiveCycle Designer automatically creates a dropdown list in the empty form template, this dropdown list is still an ordinary dropdown list and not a ZCI-based dropdown list from the WEB DYNPRO NATIVE library. It does not provide the option to automatically assign a value set from the Web Dynpro context.

Figure 8.44 Form Builder Visualizes the CLASS Attributes as a Dropdown List

8. In the WEB DYNPRO NATIVE library, you are provided with three different drop-down lists:

 ▸ NUMBERED DROP-DOWN LIST

 ▸ NUMBERED DROP-DOWN LIST (NO SELECTION)

 ▸ VALUE HELP DROP-DOWN LIST

 Only the two types of numbered dropdown lists are real dropdown lists; that is, they represent the ValueSet of a context attribute. For more information on the VALUE HELP DROP-DOWN LIST see "Connecting the Value Help" in Section 8.5.2.

9. The difference between the two actual dropdown lists is that you do not have to select an entry for NUMBERED DROP-DOWN LIST (NO SELECTION). This is mapped in the context with the initial value of the context attribute.

 Because the user has to select first class, business class, or economy for a flight booking in the present example, choose the NUMBERED DROP-DOWN LIST and drag and drop it to the form template. The data binding is also done by drag and drop. To do this, drag the CLASS attribute from the data view to the previously created dropdown list.

10. Change the text of the dropdown list to "Class," adjust the size of the form template, and add a SEND button. The intermediate result should appear as illustrated in Figure 8.45.

Figure 8.45 Finished Form Template

A Historical Excursion

In Adobe LiveCycle Designer 7.1, you must also specify a binding path for the items of the dropdowns. This can be done via a special dialog in the BINDING tab that is called via the SPECIFY ITEM VALUE link. In the displayed path, `$record.sap-vhlist.REPLACE_THIS.item[*]`, you must replace REPLACE_THIS with the name of the attribute (see Figure 8.46). As of Adobe LiveCycle Designer 8, this is no longer required (see Figure 8.47).

---

11. Activate the form template and the form interface. But first, check to see whether you have removed all of the pitfalls for interactive forms (ZCI script available, ZCI layout type) and return to the ViewDesigner in Web Dynpro.

12. Activate the `enabled` property for the `InteractiveForm` UI element.

13. Activate the view and test the application. The interactive form should now be displayed in the browser. If the dropdown list is changed within the form, and if a roundtrip is triggered, the change should be displayed in the `DropdownByKey` UI element.

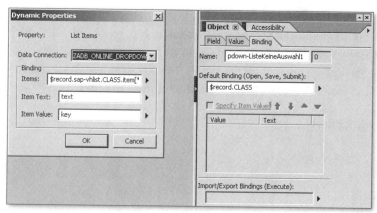

Figure 8.46 Dynamic Properties—Adobe LiveCycle Designer 7.1

Figure 8.47 Dynamic Properties—Adobe LiveCycle Designer 8

In the next section, we look at the form data. You can export the data from the PDF form using a function from the Adobe Reader menu. Unfortunately, the Adobe Reader menu is not visible if it is displayed within Web Dynpro in the browser. The corresponding function is not available via the Adobe Reader toolbar either.

1. Therefore, start the Web Dynpro application package and save the form as a PDF file on your computer using Adobe Reader.

2. Open the PDF file in a separate window. In Adobe Reader, follow the menu path DOCUMENT • FORMS • EXPORT DATA…

3. Save the XML file on your computer, and double-click on the file to open it.

4. Below the XML Node, `<sap-vhlist>`, you will find the items existing in the drop-down list (see Figure 8.48). If a second context node, `FOO`, was available, which would also include a ValueSet, an XML node, `FOO`, with an equivalent substructure would appear parallel to the XML node, `CLASS`. The XML node, `CLASS`, directly below the XML node, `DATA_SOURCE`, contains the input of the user.

```
<?xml version="1.0" encoding="UTF-8" ?>
- <DATA_SOURCE>
    <CLASS />
  - <sap-vhlist>
    - <CLASS>
      - <item>
          <key>C</key>
          <text>Business Class</text>
        </item>
      - <item>
          <key>Y</key>
          <text>Economy Class</text>
        </item>
      - <item>
          <key>F</key>
          <text>First Class</text>
        </item>
      </CLASS>
    </sap-vhlist>
  </DATA_SOURCE>
```

Figure 8.48 Form Data Exported from the PDF Form

This XML is exchanged between Adobe Reader and the server in each roundtrip. Therefore, you can draw the following two conclusions:

▶ Because the value quantities are constantly transported back and forth, drop-down lists can have a decisive influence on the performance of an interactive form. Make sure that you use as few entries as possible in a dropdown list and utilize an input help for larger value quantities.

▶ There is no dynamic reload of the items of the dropdown list. All values of all dropdown lists are always available in the data XML.

Regarding performance in terms of generating an interactive PDF form via ADS, this process is considerably decelerated on the server as of a specific number of entries per dropdown list. Depending on the ADS version used and the hardware, an upper limit of 50 entries should not be exceeded (see SAP Note 1013227 for Web Dynpro Java. With regard to the upper limit, this also applies to Web Dynpro ABAP, although the `sap.valuesetlimit.maxondemand` parameter does not exist on the ABAP stack).

Integrating Tables

Not all forms consist of only individual fields. Frequently, users must enter similar data whose number is not specified in advance—just consider the items of a sales order, for example. The representation of such data is usually done row by row in a table.

This option is also available in SAP Interactive Forms by Adobe. In combination with Web Dynpro, the data of the table originates from the context of the view in which the InteractiveForm UI element is located. In the next section, we will create a corresponding example. You can find the result in the Web Dynpro component, ZADB_ONLINE_TABLE.

1. Create a new Web Dynpro component with a view, a window, and an appropriate application. In the context of the view, create a DATA_SOURCE node with the cardinality 1:1 and with a SCARR subnode of type SCARR (the database table; see Figure 8.49).

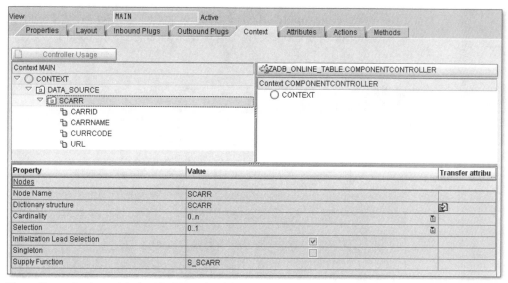

Figure 8.49 Context with the SCARR Node of the SCARR Type (List of Airlines)

2. This node is populated with the content of the database table later on. To do this, create a supply function, S_SCARR, and populate the node as shown in Listing 8.5:

```
METHOD s_scarr.
  DATA:
    lt_scarr TYPE wd_this->elements_scarr.

* get the list of carriers from database
  SELECT * FROM scarr INTO TABLE lt_scarr UP TO 13 ROWS.

* bind all the elements
  node->bind_table( new_items = lt_scarr ).
ENDMETHOD.
```

Listing 8.5 S_SCARR Supply Function

3. As in the previous example, you should first check to see whether the implementation can be done using pure Web Dynpro means. To do this, create a `Table` UI element in the view and bind the `dataSource` property to the `SCARR` node.

4. Then use the table wizard to generate the columns of each table containing an `Inputfield` as the `CellEditor`.

5. Activate the `readOnly` property for the table because the user is supposed to enter his data in the InteractiveForm UI element later on. The table is used to check the inputs in the PDF form only (see Figure 8.50).

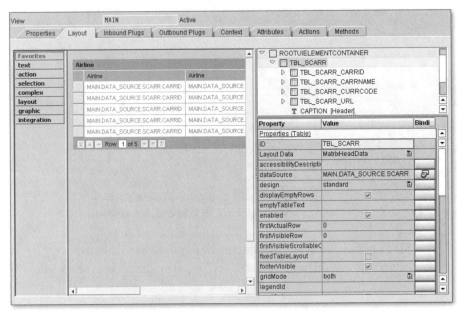

Figure 8.50 Using a Web Dynpro Table for Displaying the List of Airlines

6. Now, activate all items and start the application you previously created. The table should be populated with the list of airlines in the browser (see Figure 8.51).

Figure 8.51 Table Containing the List of Airlines

If the application works and the table is displayed in the browser, your next task is to create a form template with an equivalent table.

1. To do so, create an `InteractiveForm` UI element in the view.

2. Generate a new ZCI-based form template from the ViewDesigner, just as in the previous examples.

3. Again, use the `DATA_SOURCE` node as the root node for the interface of your form template. If you switch to Form Builder, you should see the table and its fields in the DATA VIEW palette.

   You should notice immediately that a `DATA` node was added between `SCARR` and the table fields (see Figure 8.52). This extra node is necessary whenever a 0:N or 1:N context node is used by Web Dynpro. It symbolizes the table row; in Web Dynpro, this is a context element.

Figure 8.52 Converted Structure of the SCARR Context Node in the Data View Palette

4. The easiest way to generate the table is to drag and drop the table node from the data view to the form template. Here, a column, including a column header, is automatically created for each attribute (see Figure 8.53). For each respective table column, the system automatically selects an editor suitable for the attribute type and establishes the corresponding binding.

Figure 8.53 Table Generated via Dragging and Dropping the SCARR Node from the Data View

Provided that a dropdown list is generated automatically, you must replace it with a corresponding dropdown list from the WEB DYNPRO NATIVE library. For more information on this topic, please refer to "Using Dropdown Lists" in Section 8.5.2.

5. Add a SEND button above the table so that the data entries can be sent to the server (see Figure 8.54).

6. Make all other necessary ZCI settings. Activate the form template and return to the ViewDesigner in Web Dynpro. Activate the view and start the Web Dynpro application package associated with the component. The system displays the ready-for-input table in the form.

Change a field of the table displayed in the form, for example, change the URL of Air Berlin from ".de" to ".com" (see Figure 8.55).

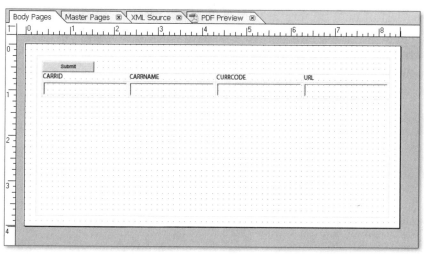

Figure 8.54 Added Send Button above the Table

Figure 8.55 Ready-for-Input Table

7. If you click on the SEND button, the change is sent to the server. It then appears in the superordinate Web Dynpro table.

The form data of the PDF form that is available as XML are also interesting in this example. Extract the data analog to the dropdown list example (see "Using Dropdown Lists" in Section 8.5.2). As shown in Figure 8.56, the data XML always contains all of the table rows. Because the data XML is always sent back and forth between the server and Adobe Reader, you should do the following:

▶ Avoid tables with a high number of rows due to performance reasons

▶ Limit the number of columns to the required minimum

```xml
<?xml version="1.0" encoding="UTF-8" ?>
<DATA_SOURCE>
 <SCARR>
  <DATA>
    <CARRID>AA</CARRID>
    <CARRNAME>American Airlines</CARRNAME>
    <CURRCODE>USD</CURRCODE>
    <URL>http://www.aa.com</URL>
    <MANDT>100</MANDT>
  </DATA>
  <DATA>
    <CARRID>AB</CARRID>
    <CARRNAME>Air Berlin</CARRNAME>
    <CURRCODE>EUR</CURRCODE>
    <URL>http://www.airberlin.com</URL>
    <MANDT>100</MANDT>
  </DATA>
```

Figure 8.56 Excerpt of the Data XML of the Table Example

With regard to the table rows, different aspects exist for interactive forms (in contrast to static print forms), which are discussed in more detail in the following sections.

Adding or Deleting Table Rows from the Form

Adding or deleting table rows from the form was not easy prior to SAP NetWeaver 7.0 EHP2. Although you had the option to add new table rows to a table or delete existing ones via a script in the form at runtime, you still had to consistently transfer this change to the server.

The Web Dynpro runtime receives the data from Adobe Reader and examines it to see if one or more context attributes should be updated. For table-like data, this examination is done row by row. If a row is missing in the received data, the attribute values of the subsequent rows overwrite their former preceding rows. The last row (corresponding to the last Web Dynpro context element) was not deleted or changed prior to SAP NetWeaver 7.0 EHP2. Its content is available twice. This was enhanced in SAP NetWeaver 7.0 EHP2. The context menu is now deleted automatically.

If, however, the received data contains an additional row, prior to SAP NetWeaver 7.0 EHP2 the update of the attribute values of the last table row in the appropriate context node failed because no corresponding context element had been created. This resulted in a RABAX (short dump). As of SAP NetWeaver 7.0 EHP2, a new context element is created automatically.

A solution for the deletion problem was to use a hidden column with a deletion indicator. If it is set, you can delete the unnecessary row from the context node through coding, for example, in the wdDoBeforeAction method.

There were two possible solutions to the problem of adding rows:

▶ You could always provide a specific number of empty context elements in the context node of the table, which the user could fill. Once all of these context elements were filled, you could generate new ones on the server.

▶ You could completely omit the script in the form and generate new rows via the server. To do this, you created a Group UI element around the InteractiveForm UI element. There, you inserted a Toolbar in the Group, and placed an "Add row" ToolbarButton there (see Figure 8.57). You can find an example in the Web Dynpro component, ZADB_ONLINE_TABLE_DYN.

The same procedure was also an alternative for solving the deletion problem. You had to note that a user was not permitted to decide which row to delete using the button outside the form. Here, you required a separate selection column in your table that you had to evaluate on the server.

All of these settings are no longer required as of NetWeaver 7.0 EHP2 because the Web Dynpro runtime automatically manages the context elements. You only need to ensure the following:

▶ Activate this new functionality via the SET_DYNAMIC_TABLES_ENABLED method of the method handler of the InteractiveForm UI element

▶ Create or delete the subform of the relevant row using scripting in the form via instanceManager.addInstances or instanceManager.removeInstance

You can find an example in the DEMO_IFBA_DYNAMIC_TABLE Web Dynpro application.

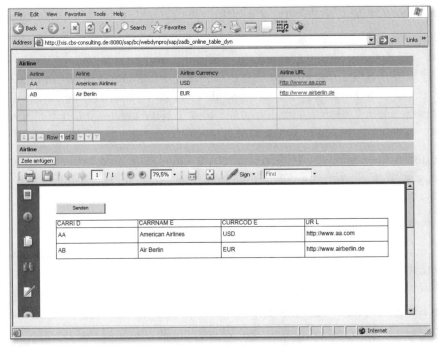

Figure 8.57 Adding New Rows Using GROUP with TOOLBAR

Caution: Performance Pitfall!

According to the SAP support team, performance and memory problems can occur when table rows are dynamically added to or deleted from a PDF form.

Also, refer to the information and recommendations provided by Adobe regarding the performance of dynamic interactive forms. It is available on the Adobe Web site at *http://www.adobe.com/devnet/livecycle/articles/DynamicInteractiveFormPerformance.pdf*.

In this context, you should also consider omitting the PDF form in your online scenario and creating the form directly in Web Dynpro using only the Table UI element. Another case in which such a step makes sense is discussed in "Can You Use LeadSelection and Selection in a PDF Form?" in Section 8.5.2.

The Table Content is Larger Than the Page

If a table is larger than the page height specified in Form Builder, the table is cut off at the end of the page. You can avoid this by activating the FLOWED property for the page. The disadvantage of this procedure is that the elements cannot be positioned on the page any longer. Remember that you can also specify whether a table row is moved completely to the next page (see Chapter 7, Advanced Form Template Creation). This setting is useful for interactive forms.

To prevent this problem, you can use the numerous binding options in Form Builder to distribute the table to multiple pages. In the table example presented, you could insert a 0:N context node between DATA_SOURCE and SCARR for the current page.

To keep this example as simple as possible, in the ZADB_ONLINE_TABLE sample table, the number of selected airlines was restricted to 13 so that the page size is not exceeded.

Can You Use LeadSelection and Selection in a PDF Form?

The short answer is: The two Web Dynpro concepts are not directly supported for interactive PDF forms that are embedded in Web Dynpro.

The long answer is that you can reproduce this functionality in a form using two hidden Boolean attributes and scripts. However, it would go beyond the scope of this chapter to implement and document an example. But the techniques presented here should enable you to create such an application.

> **Caution: Complexity Pitfall!**
>
> When defining the implementation of such complex requirements, you should think twice about the technology to be used. It is recommended avoiding the implementation of such complicated and complex requirements within an interactive PDF form. Instead, consider fulfilling your requirements via onboard means of Web Dynpro. There, you can create a plain master/detailed navigation via LeadSelection (for example, to display the list of available flight connections of a selected airline) with just a few clicks and without having to write any source code.
>
> For complex master/detailed scenarios you also need to write source code in Web Dynpro, for example, to recover entered detail data if LeadSelection of the master node is changed at the same time. Implementing such a requirement by means of an interactive PDF form is questionable due to the incurring development costs and the resulting TCO. Here, the use of Web Dynpro is the more cost-efficient alternative.

onSubmit Event

In all of the previous examples, a SEND button was positioned on the PDF form. It was used to send the entered data to the server. The InteractiveForm UI element contains an onSubmit event that is triggered as soon as you click on the SEND button on the PDF form.

The following example discusses the behavior of the button, the sending of data to the server, and triggering of the event in detail. The example is kept simple intentionally: A counter is increased by one each time the event is triggered.

1. Create a new Web Dynpro component with a view, a window, and an appropriate application.

2. In the view, place an Inputfield UI element along with a Label (displays the current counter reading) and a Button to trigger roundtrips to the server. Bind the value property of the Inputfield to a COUNTER context attribute of type I and set the Inputfield to readOnly.

3. Create an InteractiveForm UI element. Bind the dataSource property to a new context node with the VALUE attribute of the STRING type.

4. Create a new ZCI-based form template from the ViewDesigner. On the form template, place a Text Field that binds to the VALUE attribute from the DATA VIEW palette.

5. Add a SEND button to the form template.

6. The WEB DYNPRO NATIVE library contains other buttons in addition to the SEND button. However, they are not supported by Web Dynpro ABAP (SAP Note 1098009). To illustrate the side effects of using the wrong button, add the CHECK BOX button to the form. Form Builder automatically labels the button with CHECK (see Figure 8.58).

7. Activate the form template and return to the ViewDesigner in Web Dynpro.

8. Create a new ON_SUBMIT action and bind it to the onSubmit event of the InteractiveForm UI element. The counter should increase by one within the action. This is done using Listing 8.6.

```
METHOD onactionon_submit.
  DATA:
    counter TYPE I.

* increase the counter by 1
  wd_context->get_attribute(
    EXPORTING
      name = 'COUNTER'
    IMPORTING
```

```
      value = counter ).
  ADD 1 TO counter.
  wd_context->set_attribute(
    name  = 'COUNTER'
    value = counter ).
ENDMETHOD.
```

Listing 8.6 Action Handler of the ON_SUBMIT Action

Figure 8.58 Completed Form

9. Activate the Web Dynpro component and start the application you created previously (see Figure 8.59).

By means of this application, you can examine the behavior of the onSubmit event of the InteractiveForm UI element. The behavior is as follows:

▶ Clicking the Web Dynpro button does not trigger the onSubmit event. This is because in Web Dynpro only one event can be triggered within a roundtrip, so only the action of this event can be processed. Therefore, the onAction event of the button is used. As described in the previous sections, the data change to the form is transferred to the server and is available in the action handler of the button event.

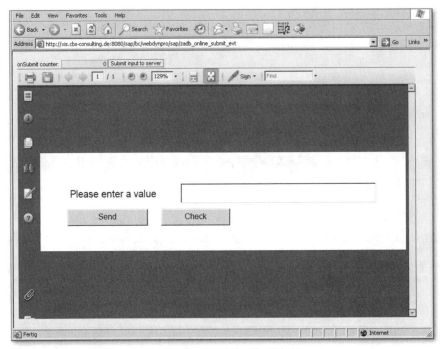

Figure 8.59 Completed Application for Examining the Behavior of the onSubmit Event

▶ Only if the request is submitted from within the PDF form to the server is the onSubmit event of InteractiveForm UI element triggered. This can be done by clicking on SEND or CHECK.

▶ There is no difference between SEND and CHECK because the CHECK BOX control behind CHECK is not supported by Web Dynpro ABAP. The SEND button is the only control supported by Web Dynpro ABAP that you can use to send data to the server.

▶ Triggering the onSubmit event is independent of a data change in the form. The onSubmit event is triggered for each click of the SEND button.

Hiding the Toolbar of Adobe Reader

In the online scenario, the Adobe Reader toolbars may be irrelevant if the user does not use the functions provided there in the context of the particular application. However, they occupy a certain space in Adobe Reader.

Due to this requirement, SAP has developed an option so you can hide these toolbars. The method handler of the `InteractiveForm` UI element provides two corresponding methods — `SET_HIDE_TOOLBARS` for setting the visibility and `GET_HIDE_TOOLBARS` for reading a previously made setting.

> **Caution: Pitfall!**
>
> A user can display (and hide) the toolbars anytime using the F8 key. So do not assume that the toolbars are inaccessible. The result is that the `GET_HIDE_TOOLBARS` method only returns the last value set by you or the default value, but not the current visibility state of the toolbars in Adobe Reader.

The following example details how you can hide toolbars in Adobe Reader. You can find this example in the Web Dynpro component, `ZADB_ONLINE_HIDE_TOOLBAR`.

1. Create a new Web Dynpro component. Here, you can use and copy the input field example for implementing the online scenario. It is the simplest example to add this new feature.

2. In the `wdDoModifyView` method of the view, add the source code shown in Listing 8.7:

```
METHOD wddomodifyview.
  DATA:
    lr_interactive_form TYPE REF TO
      cl_wd_interactive_form.

* make sure that it's only done once
  CHECK first_time = abap_true.

* get the InteractiveForm ui element
  lr_interactive_form ?= view->get_element(
                          'INTERACTIVE_FORM' ).

* get the method handler of the InteractiveForm
* ui element
  wd_this->m_method_handler ?=
    lr_interactive_form->_method_handler.

* set hideToolbars to true
  wd_this->m_method_handler->set_hide_toolbars
```

```
  ( abap_true ).
ENDMETHOD.
```
Listing 8.7 wdDoModifyView Method

3. To activate the source code, you must create a new M_METHOD_HANDLER attribute of the IF_WD_IACTIVE_FORM_METHOD_HNDL type in the ATTRIBUTES tab of the view. This is the interface of the method handler.

   In contrast to the DDIC variant for the input field example, the method handler is now stored in the view for testing purposes to toggle the visibility of the toolbars according to the display of Adobe Reader. Provided that you do not want to implement this test, you can also define the method handler as a local variable in the source code of wdDoModifyView.

4. To test the toolbar toggle functionality, create a new Button UI element, TOGGLE_TOOLBAR, in the view and define a new action in the onAction event. Within the action handler, the system first reads the status of the toolbar visibility that is available on the server; then it changes the status and defines the changed value by calling the method handler.

   The source code of the ON_TOGGLE_TOOLBAR action handler shows the individual steps (see Listing 8.8).

```
METHOD onactionon_toggle_toolbar.
  DATA:
    hide_toolbars TYPE abap_bool.

* get the current value of the hideToolbars
  hide_toolbars =
    wd_this->m_method_handler->get_hide_toolbars( ).

* toggle the boolean
  IF hide_toolbars = abap_true.
    hide_toolbars = abap_false.
  ELSE.
    hide_toolbars = abap_true.
  ENDIF.

* save the new value
  wd_this->m_method_handler->set_hide_toolbars(
```

```
        hide_toolbars ).
ENDMETHOD.
```

Listing 8.8 Action Handler of the ON_TOGGLE_TOOLBAR Action

5. Activate the Web Dynpro component, create a new Web Dynpro application for the component, and start it. You can observe the following effects:

   ▸ Initially, the toolbar is deactivated properly.

   ▸ You can show the toolbar again by pressing the [F8] key.

   ▸ A click on the Web Dynpro button for toggling the toolbar neither shows the toolbar nor hides the toolbar that was displayed using the [F8] key. Nothing happens at all.

The toolbar is only visible in the roundtrip when the InteractiveForm UI element becomes visible.

> **Caution: Pitfall!**
>
> Linking the effect of SET_HIDE_TOOLBARS with a regeneration of the PDF form in the Web Dynpro runtime is more accurate than linking a change to the visibility of the Interactive-Form UI element. At present, the visibility of the toolbars in Adobe Reader is influenced only by the generation of a PDF file.
>
> However, the PDF generation is still implemented under more circumstances than the change of the visibility of the InteractiveForm UI element, to which the setting of SET_HIDE_TOOLBARS also applies:
>
> ▸ You also bind the pdfSource property.
>
> ▸ You toggle between print and online scenario by changing the enabled property.
>
> Therefore, it is recommended to call SET_HIDE_TOOLBARS once and then make no more changes. This way, you can avoid troubleshooting for side effects.

Try the following to check the two aspects mentioned in the previous box:

▸ Bind the pdfSource property to a new context attribute of type XSTRING. Display its content by means of a second InteractiveForm UI element, in which you only bind the pdfSource property to the same context attribute. Nothing happens after the first switch. This indicates that the population of the XSTRING type context attribute always lags one roundtrip behind the pdfSource property with the PDF file. The effect becomes even clearer if you use a ToggleButton instead of a Button for toggling the visibility of the toolbars.

▶ Create a `ToggleButton` in the view, and bind its `checked` property to a new `ENABLED` context attribute of type `WDY_BOOLEAN` with 'X' as the default value. Also, bind the `enabled` property of the `InteractiveForm` UI element to this context attribute.

The sample component, `ZADB_ONLINE_HIDE_TOOLBARS`, also contains these two cases to illustrate the side effects of the downstream change of the visibility of toolbars in Adobe Reader.

Disabling the Print Button in the Toolbar of Adobe Reader

Similar to hiding the toolbar, you can also dynamically hide the print button in the Adobe Reader toolbar. For this purpose, Web Dynpro ABAP offers the two methods, `SET_DISABLE_PRINT_BUTTON` and `GET_DISABLE_PRINT_BUTTON`, in the method handler of the `InteractiveForm` UI element as of SAP NetWeaver 7.0 EHP2.

Hiding the Navigation Panel in Adobe Reader

Additionally, you can dynamically show and hide the navigation panel in Adobe Reader. For this purpose, Web Dynpro ABAP offers the two methods, `SET_HIDE_NAVIGATION_PANEL` and `GET_HIDE_NAVIGATION_PANEL`, in the method handler of the `InteractiveForm` UI element as of SAP NetWeaver 7.0 EHP2.

Message Display, Message Navigation, and Focus Change

The validation errors are also displayed in the form as of SAP NetWeaver 7.0 EHP2. The field relating to an error message receives a different color. Moreover, the message text is directly displayed in the field as a tooltip. Clicking a message in the Web Dynpro MESSAGEAREA sets the focus on the associated input field in the form. A side product of this new feature is that you can now also directly set the focus on a field as usual in the Web Dynpro runtime.

Using Attachments in the Online Scenario

Contrary to the information provided in SAP Note 1080205, attachments are not supported for the online scenario in Web Dynpro ABAP up to SAP NetWeaver 7.0 EHP2—not even as of SAP NetWeaver 7.0 SP 14 or 7.10 SP 4. SAP Note 1080203 clarifies this. The reason is the (natural) poor performance of this feature, because in the online scenario data in Adobe Reader is continuously exchanged with the server. This also applies to attachments that are directly defined in the PDF form.

Attachments may lead to performance problems due to the data volume to be processed. Frequently, you do not just attach a small text file of only a few kilobytes to the PDF form, but also design drawings or other documents, for example.

If you want to support attachments, you should send them to the server in Web Dynpro via the `FileUpload` UI element and outside Adobe Reader. For example, you can use a table to indicate which files are already available on the server. If users want to take the form with them (i.e., for use in an offline scenario), you can generate a new PDF file for them on the server using the PDF object API and attach the previously uploaded files.

In Section 8.5.3, Offline Scenario, you can find detailed information of how you can provide a PDF file to users.

As of SAP NetWeaver 7.0 EHP2, SAP provides two new methods in the method handler of the `InteractiveForm` UI element. Their names are SET_ATTACHMENTS and GET_ATTACHMENTS. With these two methods, you can add attachments to a form or read existing attachments. The previously described notes on performance and user-friendliness still apply despite this attachment support which is convenient for the developer.

Example: Contact Management Using an Interactive Form

In this section, we will put into practice the information obtained in the previous sections about the implementation of the online scenario. Naturally, the example is more complex and longer than the previous examples. However, it provides the opportunity to experience the different aspects of Web Dynpro ABAP in combination with the online scenario of the Adobe integration. This example could also be implemented in a real-life customer project (with some minor cosmetic enhancements).

You can find the example in the Web Dynpro component, ZADB_ONLINE_CONTACT_MGMT. The corresponding PDF form template and its form interface have the same name.

Scenario Description

The fictitious enterprise Dual Use Goods Inc. is present at many trade shows to canvass customers. By the end of each day, the employees have gathered a lot of business cards. In addition, the enterprise provides paper contact forms that are filled out by potential customers. These data must then be entered into the enterprise's SAP Customer Relationship Management (CRM) system. This data entry occupies employees who would otherwise be available for consulting tasks.

To accelerate the input of the numerous business cards and contact forms, the enterprise created an Adobe form that looks like an average business card. It replaces the Web application in the enterprise's CRM system that has been used by the employees up to now.

The computer is freely accessible at the booth, and potential customers can enter their data themselves. The benefit of this approach is that the completion of a paper form and the associated manual or Optical Character Recognition (OCR)-supported input of data into the CRM system are omitted.

A business card always contains the following basic data:

▶ Name of the company

▶ Name of the contact partner

▶ Function of the contact partner within the company

▶ Address of the contact partner in the company

For the sake of simplicity, the following restrictions apply:

▶ Only the first two of the four possible lines are to be used for the company name.

▶ For the name of the contact partner, only the first and the last name are used. In addition, you can specify the title (e.g., Mr., Mrs.). German is specified as the correspondence language.

▶ For the address of the company, you consider only the fields, street, house number, ZIP code, and city. Germany is specified as the country.

▶ In addition to the address, you can enter the telephone number, fax number, and email address as communication data.

After the form has been submitted, the system implements the following:

▶ The entered company is created as a business partner in the prospect role provided that no company of the same name already exists in the system.

▶ The address of the company is created if it does not exist yet.

▶ The contact partner is created as a business partner in the "contact" role provided that no business partner of the same name already exists in the system.

▶ The "Has Contact Person" relationship is created between the contact and the prospect. The previously created address is assigned to the relationship as the standard address. All additional communication data are assigned to the relationship.

This example can be continued by populating additional fields. In addition, you could automatically assign an employee responsible for the new company. Or you could trigger a workflow process to integrate the company with the processes.

1. In the first step, create the interface to the form. It must contain all fields that can be entered by the user. Ideally, you do this within the Web Dynpro component in the context of the view because you can easily structure the data there (see Figure 8.60). The completed context contains the structured composition fields of the business card, typed with Business Application Programming Interface (BAPI) structures.

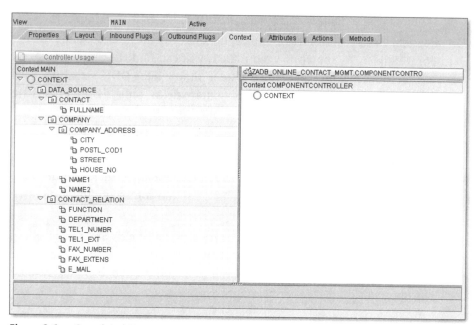

Figure 8.60 Completed Context

2. In SAP CRM, business partners are saved in the BUT000 tables and addresses of organizations in the ADRC table. There are also several dependent tables with detail data. The BAPI_BUPA_CREATE_FROM_DATA function module is available for the creation of a business partner (including the address). This function module has its own structures for data transfer whose field names are partly different from the database tables. For this reason, instead of the database tables, the structures from the call of the function module are specified in the context nodes as follows:

   ▸ CONTACT with BAPIBUS1006_CENTRAL_PERSON

   ▸ COMPANY with BAPIBUS1006_CENTRAL_ORGAN

   ▸ COMPANY_ADDRESS with BAPIBUS1006_ADDRESS

   ▸ CONTACT_RELATION with BAPIBUS1006002_CENTRAL

3. Now, add the InteractiveForm UI element to the view. After you have bound the dataSource property to the top-level node of the previously created node hierarchy in the context and set the enabled property, enter the name of the interface to be created in the templateSource property.

4. Press the [ENTER] key. Then create a new form interface as described in Section 8.4.1 and select the same node from the context that you already bound to the dataSource property. In this example, it is the DATA_SOURCE node.

5. The system creates a new form template together with the interface and switches to Form Builder. As shown in Figure 8.61, you can find the fields previously created in the context on the left-hand side. Although the DDIC structures used by the context node contain considerably more fields, only the used fields are transferred.

6. Now, drag and drop the individual attributes from the DATA VIEW palette to the form template area. Remember the structure of a real business card when you arrange the text fields. Bear in mind that you must display the fields for the function and the department as dropdown lists. Use the corresponding dropdown list from the WEB DYNPRO NATIVE library.

7. Specify the height and width of the form so that all fields are enclosed and no unnecessary space is wasted on the right-hand side and at the bottom. The aim is that the user does not have to scroll in the interactive form. Figure 8.62 shows the result.

Figure 8.61 Form Builder with Used Fields of the BAPI Structures

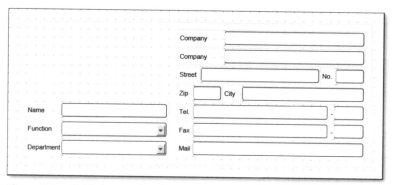

Figure 8.62 Fields Arranged in the Form

8. To improve user acceptance, you could specify a color for the controls. You can change the appearance of a control by selecting the control and choosing the USER-DEFINED… entry from the APPEARANCE DROPDOWN list in the Field subarea of the OBJECT tab. A dialog opens in which you can, for example, round off the corners or specify a background color.

9. Activate the form template and the corresponding interface and return to the ViewDesigner. Remember to remove the ZCI pitfalls.

10. Because the form has no SEND button, create a `Button` UI element above the `InteractiveForm` UI element to send the entries to the server and to trigger further processing of the contact data. To do this, create a new `ON_SEND` action for the `onAction` event of the `Button`.

11. You must also create a `ValueSet` for the dropdown lists because the individual characteristic values of the function and department are not available as fixed values on the domain. They are each stored in a separate database table. The source code in Listing 8.9 from the `wdDoInit` method of the view adds the entries to the respective context attributes.

```
METHOD wddoinit.
  DATA:
    lr_node_info TYPE REF TO if_wd_context_node_info,
    lt_value_set TYPE wdr_context_attr_value_list.

* get the contact relation node info in order to fill
* fixed values
    lr_node_info = wd_context->get_node_info( ).
    lr_node_info = lr_node_info->get_child_node(
                      wd_this->wdctx_data_source ).
    lr_node_info = lr_node_info->get_child_node(
                      wd_this->wdctx_contact_relation ).

* fill the values of possible functions
    SELECT pafkt AS value bez30 AS text FROM tb913
          INTO TABLE lt_value_set
          WHERE spras = sy-langu.
    lr_node_info->set_attribute_value_set(
      EXPORTING
        name      = 'FUNCTION'
        value_set = lt_value_set ).

* fill the values of possible departments
    CLEAR lt_value_set[].
    SELECT abtnr AS value bez20 AS text FROM tb911
          INTO TABLE lt_value_set
          WHERE spras = sy-langu.
    lr_node_info->set_attribute_value_set(
      EXPORTING
        name      = 'DEPARTMENT'
```

```
        value_set = lt_value_set ).
  ENDMETHOD.
```

Listing 8.9 wdDoInit Method

12. Activate the Web Dynpro component and create a new Web Dynpro application for the component.

13. You now have an interactive form whose input is sent to the server. Execute the Web Dynpro application to test the form. For example, you can set a breakpoint in the action handler of the ON_SEND action to see for yourself whether your inputs are sent to the server and transferred to the corresponding context attribute. Have the system display the context of your view in the new ABAP Debugger.

14. If everything functions correctly, you can implement the BAPI call in the action handler of the ON_SEND action. Read the input of the user from the respective context node. The types have already been selected at the beginning in accordance with the BAPI calls so that it is simple to implement this step. The source code in Listing 8.10 shows the necessary calls.

```
METHOD onactionon_send.
  DATA:
    lr_data_source        TYPE REF TO if_wd_context_node,
    lr_contact            TYPE REF TO if_wd_context_node,
    lr_company            TYPE REF TO if_wd_context_node,
    lr_company_address    TYPE REF TO if_wd_context_node,
    lr_contact_relation   TYPE REF TO if_wd_context_node,
    lv_company            TYPE bu_partner,
    lv_contact            TYPE bu_partner,
    lt_return             TYPE bapiret2_tab,
    ls_centraldata        TYPE bapibus1006_central,
    ls_company_org_data   TYPE bapibus1006_central_organ,
    ls_company_address    TYPE bapibus1006_address,
    ls_contact_data       TYPE bapibus1006_central_person,
    ls_contact_relation_data
                          TYPE bapibus1006002_central,
    lv_company_address_guid
                          TYPE guid,
    lv_company_address_guid2
                          TYPE bu_address_guid_bapi.

  DATA:
```

461

```
        lr_api_controller    TYPE REF TO if_wd_controller,
        lr_message_manager   TYPE REF TO
                               if_wd_message_manager.

    FIELD-SYMBOLS:
      <return> LIKE LINE OF lt_return.

* get all the context data that contain the data
    lr_data_source      = wd_context->get_child_node(
      wd_this->wdctx_data_source ).
    lr_contact          = lr_data_source->get_child_node(
      wd_this->wdctx_contact ).
    lr_company          = lr_data_source->get_child_node(
      wd_this->wdctx_company ).
    lr_company_address  = lr_company->get_child_node(
      wd_this->wdctx_company_address ).
    lr_contact_relation = lr_data_source->get_child_node(
      wd_this->wdctx_contact_relation ).

* get all the structures with their values out of the
* nodes
    lr_company->get_static_attributes(
      IMPORTING
        static_attributes = ls_company_org_data ).
    lr_company_address->get_static_attributes(
      IMPORTING
        static_attributes = ls_company_address ).
    lr_contact->get_static_attributes(
      IMPORTING
        static_attributes = ls_contact_data ).
    lr_contact_relation->get_static_attributes(
      IMPORTING
        static_attributes = ls_contact_relation_data ).

* add the country to the address, which always DE here
    ls_company_address-country = 'DE'.

* create the company
    CALL FUNCTION 'BAPI_BUPA_CREATE_FROM_DATA'
      EXPORTING
        partnercategory        = '2' "organisation
        centraldata            = ls_centraldata
        centraldataorganization = ls_company_org_data
```

```
    addressdata                = ls_company_address
    duplicate_message_type  = 'W'
    accept_error               = 'X'
  IMPORTING
    businesspartner            = lv_company
  TABLES
    return                     = lt_return.
LOOP AT lt_return ASSIGNING <return>
    WHERE type CA 'AXE'.
  CALL FUNCTION 'BAPI_TRANSACTION_ROLLBACK'.
  display_messages( lt_return ).
  RETURN.
ENDLOOP.

* add role prospect to it
  CLEAR lt_return[].
  CALL FUNCTION 'BAPI_BUPA_ROLE_ADD_2'
    EXPORTING
      businesspartner             = lv_company
      businesspartnerrolecategory = 'BUP002'
      businesspartnerrole         = 'BUP002'
    TABLES
      return                      = lt_return.
  LOOP AT lt_return ASSIGNING <return>
      WHERE type CA 'AXE'.
    CALL FUNCTION 'BAPI_TRANSACTION_ROLLBACK'.
    display_messages( lt_return ).
    RETURN.
  ENDLOOP.

* create the contact
  SPLIT ls_contact_data-fullname AT ' '
      INTO ls_contact_data-firstname
           ls_contact_data-lastname.
  CALL FUNCTION 'BAPI_BUPA_CREATE_FROM_DATA'
    EXPORTING
      partnercategory      = '1' "person
      centraldata          = ls_centraldata
      centraldataperson    = ls_contact_data
      duplicate_message_type = 'W'
      accept_error         = 'X'
    IMPORTING
      businesspartner      = lv_contact
```

463

```
    TABLES
      return                  = lt_return.
  LOOP AT lt_return ASSIGNING <return>
      WHERE type CA 'AXE'.
    CALL FUNCTION 'BAPI_TRANSACTION_ROLLBACK'.
    display_messages( lt_return ).
    RETURN.
  ENDLOOP.

* add role contact to the contact
  CLEAR lt_return[].
  CALL FUNCTION 'BAPI_BUPA_ROLE_ADD_2'
    EXPORTING
      businesspartner           = lv_contact
      businesspartnerrolecategory = 'BUP001'
      businesspartnerrole       = 'BUP001'
    TABLES
      return                    = lt_return.
  LOOP AT lt_return ASSIGNING <return>
      WHERE type CA 'AXE'.
    CALL FUNCTION 'BAPI_TRANSACTION_ROLLBACK'.
    display_messages( lt_return ).
    RETURN.
  ENDLOOP.

* get the previously created address of the company
  CALL FUNCTION 'BAPI_BUPA_ADDRESSES_GET'
    EXPORTING
      businesspartner    = lv_company
    IMPORTING
      standardaddressguid = lv_company_address_guid
    TABLES
      return             = lt_return.
  LOOP AT lt_return ASSIGNING <return>
      WHERE type CA 'AXE'.
    CALL FUNCTION 'BAPI_TRANSACTION_ROLLBACK'.
    display_messages( lt_return ).
    RETURN.
  ENDLOOP.

* create the contact relation between the company and the
* contact
  lv_company_address_guid2 = lv_company_address_guid.
```

```
CALL FUNCTION 'BAPI_BUPR_CONTP_CREATE'
  EXPORTING
    businesspartner = lv_company
    contactperson   = lv_contact
    addressguid     = lv_company_address_guid2
    centraldata     = ls_contact_relation_data
  TABLES
    return          = lt_return.
LOOP AT lt_return ASSIGNING <return>
    WHERE type CA 'AXE'.
  CALL FUNCTION 'BAPI_TRANSACTION_ROLLBACK'.
  display_messages( lt_return ).
  RETURN.
ENDLOOP.

* commit the changes
  CALL FUNCTION 'BAPI_TRANSACTION_COMMIT'.

* display a success message
  lr_api_controller ?= wd_this->wd_get_api( ).
  lr_message_manager =
    lr_api_controller->get_message_manager( ).
  CALL METHOD lr_message_manager->report_success
    EXPORTING
      message_text =
  'Ihre Kontaktdaten wurden erfolgreich gespeichert.'.

* clear all fields so that the next person can continue
  lr_data_source->invalidate( ).
ENDMETHOD.
```

Listing 8.10 Action Handler of the ON_SEND Action

15. Create the DISPLAY_MESSAGES method on the view to display messages from the BAPI function module. The method receives the IT_RETURN importing parameter of the BAPIRET2_TAB type. Listing 8.11 shows the source code for displaying the messages.

```
METHOD display_messages.
  DATA:
    lo_api_controller     TYPE REF TO if_wd_controller,
    lo_message_manager    TYPE REF TO
                          if_wd_message_manager.
```

```
FIELD-SYMBOLS:
  <return> LIKE LINE OF it_return.

* get message manager
  lo_api_controller ?= wd_this->wd_get_api( ).
  lo_message_manager =
    lo_api_controller->get_message_manager( ).

* report the messages
  LOOP AT it_return ASSIGNING <return>.
    CALL METHOD lo_message_manager->report_t100_message
      EXPORTING
        msgid = <return>-id
        msgno = <return>-number
        msgty = <return>-type
        p1    = <return>-message_v1
        p2    = <return>-message_v2
        p3    = <return>-message_v3
        p4    = <return>-message_v4.
  ENDLOOP.
ENDMETHOD.
```

Listing 8.11 DISPLAY_MESSAGES Method

This message is called if a message of the E, X, or A type occurs after a BAPI call, that is, if an error occurs. Any further processing is cancelled and a rollback using the BAPI_TRANSACTION_ROLLBACK function module is implemented.

A success message is displayed at the end of processing. Then all input fields of the form are reset. This way, the next future contact partner of an interested company can enter his data at the booth terminal.

This example can also be enhanced with additional features. For example, you can add a second Button UI element to the view that checks the entries of the user without posting them directly in the system.

The following figures show the inputs of a PDF form that is embedded in the Web Dynpro application package and data created in the system later on.

1. The user enters his contact data in the business card (see Figure 8.63).

2. A success message is displayed in the top-left corner after clicking on the WEB DYNPRO button to send the data. The fields are cleared for the entries of the next user (see Figure 8.64).

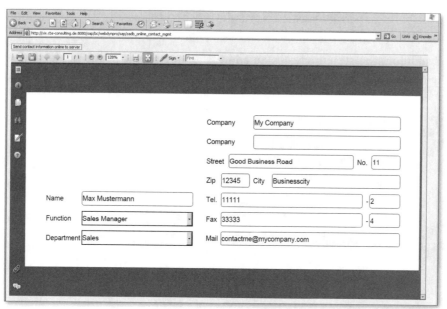

Figure 8.63 Entered Contact Data of the Contact Partner

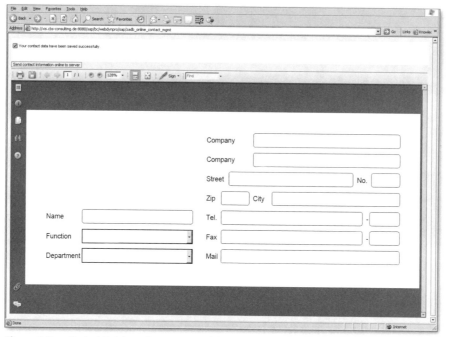

Figure 8.64 Posted Entries—Data Inputs of the Next Contact Person Possible

3. In the business partner master record, the prospect is created as an organization using the data from the business card (see Figure 8.65).

4. In addition, the system creates an address and assigns it to the prospect (see Figure 8.66).

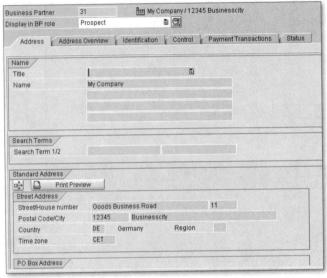

Figure 8.65 Prospect in the Business Partner Master Record

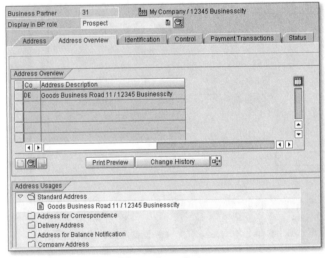

Figure 8.66 Address of the Business Partner

5. The system also creates a contact partner and generates a contact relation between the prospect and the contact (see Figure 8.67).

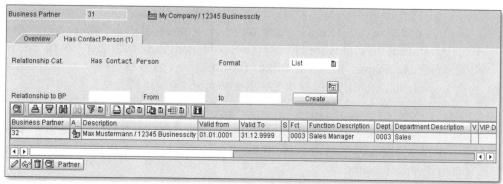

Figure 8.67 Generated Contact Relation and Assigned Address

This example illustrates how simple it is to implement a functioning online scenario using the Adobe integration with Web Dynpro ABAP for a real-life situation. Indeed, the application is not restricted to pure online processing. For example, users can save the (empty or partially completed) form on a memory stick, fill it out offline, and submit it via email or web upload. These and similar offline scenarios are discussed in the following section.

8.5.3 Offline Scenario

In contrast to the online scenario, the offline scenario provides the option to fill out an Adobe form outside the browser and without a network connection to the server.

The lower license costs can be an advantage of the offline scenario compared to the online scenario. Usually, users can download forms from the intranet (or the Internet in external scenarios). Here, the system does not require any named user—unless the respective user is supposed to receive a form that is already partially filled out specifically for him. This can be achieved by means of integrating with Web Dynpro ABAP although it is not required very often. (We will look at the corresponding techniques in the course of this section.) For this reason, the offline scenario is very popular for any type of request, for instance, vacation, transfer, insurance, agricultural subsidies, participation in an event. Customers or business partners can enter their data themselves without having direct access to your SAP system.

Once the user has downloaded and filled out the form, he can return it to the server via various channels. The most common options are uploading via a Web application (for example, on the Web site on which the form was downloaded) or submission via email. This section details the implementation of the download and upload of a form in different application cases by means of Web Dynpro ABAP. The integration of the offline scenario in the email-based ABAP Offline Infrastructure is discussed in Chapter 10, ABAP Offline Infrastructure. Web Dynpro ABAP supports this scenario automatically as of SAP NetWeaver 7.0 EHP2.

At this point, it is important to note that an offline form can be filled out and sent any number of times. Consider this fact when you receive the form via the Web Dynpro application package (avoid duplicate entry) or update the original form (avoid version conflicts).

Providing a Form to the Users

This section describes the options available in Web Dynpro ABAP to provide files to the users for download.

In the first phase of the offline scenario, you provide the PDF form to the user. The options range from a plain download up to sophisticated variants in which the server partially prepopulates the PDF form with data that has been entered by a user in previously implemented business steps.

LinkToURL

The LinkToURL UI element is one of the most convenient ways to provide a file to a user. The file is stored on a web server. The URL that indicates the storage location is entered in the reference property. This value can be dynamized through the context binding. A textual description in the text property is presented as a web link to the user. This link is executed by the browser.

SAP NetWeaver can also be used as the web server. In this case, you are provided with a number of options (from the simple Internet Communication framework (ICF) server to access to the Knowledge Warehouse).

You can find an example of the LinkToURL UI element in the Web Dynpro component, ZADB_LINK_TO_URL. It was implemented in the simplest possible way. The PDF file that contains the form was embedded in the component. The LinkToURL UI element points to the file (see Figure 8.68). Source code is not required.

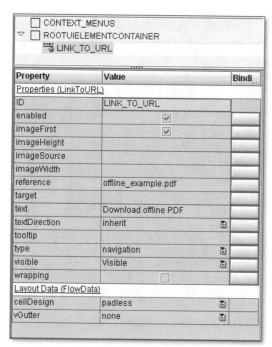

Figure 8.68 LinkToURL UI Element

FileDownload

For the `FileDownload` UI element, you must provide the data in the roundtrip in which the `FileDownload` UI element is displayed (before the user clicks on it). This way, a PDF form can be generated based on parameters of a previous step, for example. The name of the file is entered in the `fileName` property. You must select the `Application/PDF` value for a PDF file as the MIME type in the `mimeType` property. The file itself is kept in the context and connected via the `data` property. Here, the context attribute should be of the `XSTRING` type. The `FileDownload` UI element is presented as a link to the user. The corresponding text is defined in the `text` property.

The first example that you can find in the Web Dynpro component, `ZADB_FILE_DOWNLOAD`, illustrates how you must activate a `FileDownload` UI element so that the user can download a file. Its functionality is identical to the `LinkToURL` example and enables you to compare the two approaches. In contrast to the `LinkToURL` UI element, for the `FileDownload` UI element you must first load the file into the context attribute that the `data` property binds to. In the example, the context has a `PDF` attribute of the `XSTRING` type (see Figure 8.69).

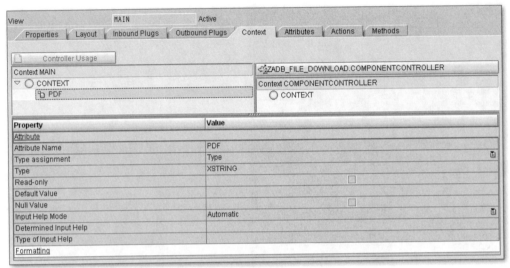

Figure 8.69 PDF File is Loaded into the PDF Context Attribute Later On

The context attribute is populated in the `wdDoInit` method of the view according to the procedure described in Section 8.5.1, Print Scenario (see Listing 8.12).

```
METHOD wddoinit.
  DATA:
    lr_mime_repository TYPE REF TO if_mr_api,
    content            TYPE XSTRING.

  CONSTANTS:
    url TYPE STRING VALUE
'/SAP/BC/WebDynpro/SAP/ZADB_FILE_DOWNLOAD/offline_example.pdf'.

  lr_mime_repository = cl_mime_repository_api=>get_api( ).
  lr_mime_repository->get(
    EXPORTING
      i_url = url
    IMPORTING
      e_content = content ).
  wd_context->set_attribute(
    name = 'PDF'
```

```
    value = content ).
ENDMETHOD.
```

Listing 8.12 wdDoInit Method

Compared to the `LinkToURL` UI element, this example does not provide any additional benefit. Instead, it requires more effort to implement it. A `LinkToURL` UI element would have been sufficient here.

For this reason, the PDF form is prepopulated with a value in the next example. To do this, extend the application with an `Inputfield` and a `Button` labeled with CHECK INPUT. If a user wants to continue his work offline, he can have the system generate a PDF form that includes his current entries and can be filled out offline using the CONVERT TO PDF button. The completely generated PDF file can then be provided to the user via the `FileDownload` UI element.

You can find an example in the Web Dynpro component, `ZADB_FILE_DOWNLOAD_GENPDF`. Figure 8.70 shows the layout of the `MAIN` view of the component.

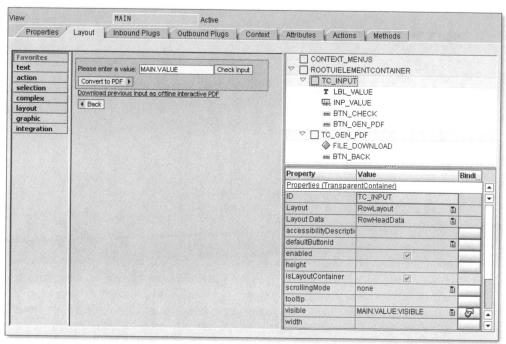

Figure 8.70 Layout of the MAIN View of the Sample Component

The view includes two `TransparentContainer` elements that are visible alternately. The user can activate the buttons, CONVERT TO PDF and BACK, to toggle between the content of the two containers. The `Inputfield` and the `FileDownload` UI element must not be visible at the same time because the current input must be converted into a PDF form prior to the download. Otherwise, the PDF form would only contain the input previously sent to the server.

The use of a supply function for generating a PDF is not a solution either. Although the file would be generated by the supply function in the roundtrip in which the PDF form would be retrieved for the first time, another change to the value in the Inputfield and a subsequent click on the FileDownload UI element would not result in another PDF generation.

The context of the view contains a `VALUE` attribute of the `STRING` type for the entered value and a `PDF` attribute of the `XSTRING` type for the generated PDF form. The VISIBLE property of the `TC_INPUT` TransparentContainer binds to the `visible` property of the `VALUE` context attribute (see Figure 8.71). For `TC_GEN_PDF`, it is the same property in the `PDF` context attribute.

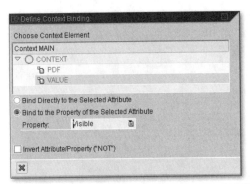

Figure 8.71 TC_INPUT.visible Binds to VALUE:Visible

Note

If you want to follow this example in an old SAP NetWeaver 7.0 system whose support package level is lower than SP 13, you are not provided with the additional properties of context attributes used here. In this case, you must create additional context attributes of the `WDY_BOOLEAN` type to control the visibility of the two TRANSPARENTCONTAINER elements. Alternatively, you can also use two views instead of only one and toggle between them. Then, you would have to move the `VALUE` attribute to a new context node that would be mapped in the two views using the ComponentController.

Because the visible property is enabled by default, you must ensure that the area for the PDF form download is not visible initially. This is done in the wdDoInit method of the view using the coding shown in Listing 8.13.

```
METHOD wddoinit.
* make the download area invisible initially
  wd_context->set_attribute_property(
    EXPORTING
      attribute_name = 'PDF'
      property = if_wd_context_element=>e_property-visible
      value = abap_false ).
ENDMETHOD.
```

Listing 8.13 wdDoInit Method

A separate action is assigned to each of the onAction events of the two Web Dynpro buttons. Because the BTN_CHECK button is only used to send data to the server, its action handler does not have any source code. The action is also assigned to the onEnter event of the Inputfield UI elements so that a user can also trigger a roundtrip by pressing the [ENTER] key.

In the ONACTIOON_GEN_PDF action handler for the BTN_GEN_PDF button, the source code shown in Listing 8.14 converts the user's input into a PDF file for the FileDownload UI element.

```
METHOD onactionon_gen_pdf.
  DATA:
    value              TYPE STRING,
    fm_name            TYPE rs38l_fnam,
    lt_params          TYPE abap_func_parmbind_tab,
    param              LIKE LINE OF lt_params,
    lt_exceptions      TYPE abap_func_excpbind_tab,
    exception          LIKE LINE OF lt_exceptions,
    pdf_ref            TYPE REF TO fpformoutput,
    fp_docparams       TYPE sfpdocparams,
    fp_formoutput      TYPE fpformoutput,
    fp_outputparams    TYPE sfpoutputparams,
    adserrstr          TYPE STRING,
    pdf                TYPE XSTRING,
    lr_api_controller  TYPE REF TO if_wd_controller,
    lr_message_manager TYPE REF TO if_wd_message_manager.
```

```
* get the current value of the user's input
  wd_context->get_attribute(
    EXPORTING
      name = 'VALUE'
    IMPORTING
      value = value ).

* generate the PDF
* => get the name of the generated function module
  CALL FUNCTION 'FP_FUNCTION_MODULE_NAME'
    EXPORTING
      i_name     = 'ZADB_OFFLINE_EXAMPLE'
    IMPORTING
      e_funcname = fm_name.

* set doc params so that the pdf will be interactive
  fp_docparams-fillable = abap_true.
  param-name = '/1BCDWB/DOCPARAMS'.
  param-kind = abap_func_exporting.
  GET REFERENCE OF fp_docparams INTO param-value.
  INSERT param INTO TABLE lt_params.

* add the value parameter
  param-name = 'VALUE'.
  param-kind = abap_func_exporting.
  GET REFERENCE OF value INTO param-value.
  INSERT param INTO TABLE lt_params.

* add the formoutput exporting parameter
  param-name = '/1BCDWB/FORMOUTPUT'.
  param-kind = abap_func_importing.
  GET REFERENCE OF fp_formoutput INTO param-value.
  INSERT param INTO TABLE lt_params.

* add the exception
  exception-name = 'OTHERS'.
  exception-value = 10.
  INSERT exception INTO TABLE lt_exceptions.

* set output parameters and open spool job
  fp_outputparams-nodialog   = 'X'.
  fp_outputparams-getpdf     = 'X'.
  CALL FUNCTION 'FP_JOB_OPEN'
```

```
          CHANGING
            ie_outputparams = fp_outputparams.

* dynamic call of the generated function module
   CALL FUNCTION fm_name
     PARAMETER-TABLE
       lt_params
     EXCEPTION-TABLE
       lt_exceptions.
   IF sy-subrc <> 0.
*    there was an error; check, if it was an ADS related
*    problem
     CALL FUNCTION 'FP_GET_LAST_ADS_ERRSTR'
       IMPORTING
         e_adserrstr = adserrstr.

*    get message manager
     lr_api_controller ?= wd_this->wd_get_api( ).
     CALL METHOD lr_api_controller->get_message_manager
       RECEIVING
         message_manager = lr_message_manager.

*    report error message returned by ADS
     CALL METHOD lr_message_manager->report_error_message
       EXPORTING
         message_text = adserrstr.

*    abort PDF creation
     RETURN.
   ENDIF.

* close spool job
   CALL FUNCTION 'FP_JOB_CLOSE'.

* get the pdf
   READ TABLE lt_params
       WITH KEY name = '/1BCDWB/FORMOUTPUT'
       INTO param.
   pdf_ref ?= param-value.
   pdf = pdf_ref->pdf.

* save the pdf to context
   wd_context->set_attribute(
```

```
      EXPORTING
        name = 'PDF'
        value = pdf ).

* hide the input area
  wd_context->set_attribute_property(
      EXPORTING
        attribute_name = 'VALUE'
        property = if_wd_context_element=>e_property-visible
        value = abap_false ).

* display the download area
  wd_context->set_attribute_property(
      EXPORTING
        attribute_name = 'PDF'
        property = if_wd_context_element=>e_property-visible
        value = abap_true ).
ENDMETHOD.
```

Listing 8.14 Action Handler of the ON_GEN_PDF Action

Listing 8.14 is comprised of three areas:

1. Reading the current value of the user input

2. Generating the PDF form from the form template with the user's entry as input

3. Changing the visibility of the two areas so that the download areas become visible and the input area invisible

The function module generated by the system is used to generate the PDF form because the form contains a DDIC interface. The completed PDF form is made interactive in the DocParams by setting the `fillable = abap_true` field. The Output-Params (`FP_OUTPUTPARAMS` variable) are set in such a way that no dialog is displayed and a PDF form is returned.

Instead of the fully dynamic call using `parameter-` and `exception-table`, you can also enter the parameters and exceptions directly and only keep the name of the function module variable. However, if you need to supply different form interfaces generically, feel free use this source code for implementing such a requirement.

All that remains now is the source code of the action handler of the `ON_BACK` action of the `BTN_BACK` button. It toggles between the two areas (see Listing 8.15).

```
METHOD onactionon_back.
* display the input area
  wd_context->set_attribute_property(
    EXPORTING
      attribute_name = 'VALUE'
      property = if_wd_context_element=>e_property-visible
      value = abap_true ).

* hide the download area
  wd_context->set_attribute_property(
    EXPORTING
      attribute_name = 'PDF'
      property = if_wd_context_element=>e_property-visible
      value = abap_false ).
ENDMETHOD.
```

Listing 8.15 Action Handler of the ON_BACK Action

This example created two minor weak spots from a usability standpoint:

▶ The user must first click on a button and then on a link to receive the file. It would be better to have the link visible permanently. As soon as the user clicks on it the PDF form would have to be generated immediately.

▶ To avoid having the FileDownload link visible all of the time and the user receiving a possibly outdated PDF form, he must toggle between the mode for input and the mode for form download.

For these reasons, the next example utilizes the option of load-on-demand via a supply function to generate a PDF file for each row of a table and provide the PDF file to the user. The example uses the SPFLI table. You can find the example in the Web Dynpro component, ZADB_FILE_DOWNLOAD_MULTI.

1. The component contains a MAIN view that includes the flight connection table. The table was generated from the context using the table wizard. The context contains a 0:N node of the SPFLI type for receiving data from the database table of the same name. In addition, it contains a PDF subnode with the PDF attribute of the XSTRING type in which the PDF form of the current table row is then generated on demand. This task is assumed by the S_PDF supply function that is assigned to the node (see Figure 8.72).

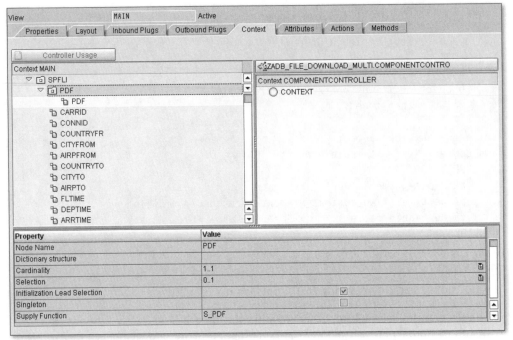

Figure 8.72 Structure of the Context of the Load-on-Demand Example

2. After you have generated the table in the ViewDesigner using the table wizard, you need to manually add another column, TBLCOL_PDF. The `FileDownload` UI element is the `CellEditor` of this column, which binds to the previously mentioned `PDF` context attribute. In addition, select a PDF icon as ImageSource using the property's value help and define the file name in FileName (here, *flugbuchung.pdf*, see Figure 8.73).

3. The example contains a total of two supply functions—one for determining the flight connections and another one for generating the PDF form. The supply function for populating the SPFLI node includes the content shown in Listing 8.16. It is called automatically by the Web Dynpro runtime as soon as the table is displayed for the first time.

```
METHOD s_spfli.
  DATA:
    lt_spfli TYPE wd_this->Elements_spfli.

  SELECT * FROM spfli INTI TABLE lt_spfli.
```

```
* bind all the elements
  node->bind_table( new_items = lt_spfli ).
ENDMETHOD.
```

Listing 8.16 S_SPFLI Supply Function

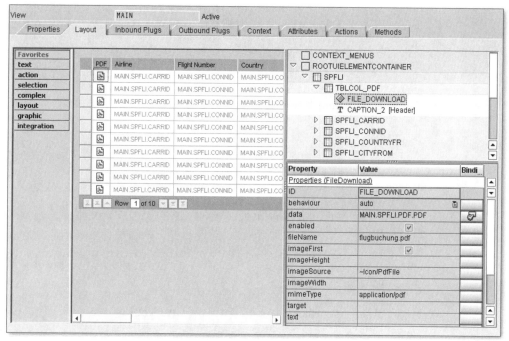

Figure 8.73 First Table Column with FileDownload UI Element

4. As soon as the user clicks on the PDF icon of the `FileDownload` UI element, the Web Dynpro runtime accesses the `PDF` attribute of the `PDF` subnode in this table row. The result is that the `S_PDF` supply function of the context node is called (see Listing 8.17).

```
METHOD s_pdf.
  DATA:
    value                TYPE STRING,
    fm_name              TYPE rs38l_fnam,
    lt_params            TYPE abap_func_parmbind_tab,
    param                LIKE LINE OF lt_params,
    lt_exceptions        TYPE abap_func_excpbind_tab,
    exception            LIKE LINE OF lt_exceptions,
```

```
    pdf_ref              TYPE REF TO fpformoutput,
    fp_docparams         TYPE sfpdocparams,
    fp_formoutput        TYPE fpformoutput,
    fp_outputparams      TYPE sfpoutputparams,
    adserrstr            TYPE STRING,
    pdf                  TYPE XSTRING,
    lr_api_controller    TYPE REF TO if_wd_controller,
    lr_message_manager   TYPE REF TO if_wd_message_manager,
    spfli                TYPE spfli,
    ls_pdf               TYPE wd_this->element_pdf.

* get the data of the parent spfli entry for which we
* were asked to supply the pdf
  parent_element->get_static_attributes(
     IMPORTING
       static_attributes = spfli ).

* generate the PDF
* => get the name of the generated function module
  CALL FUNCTION 'FP_FUNCTION_MODULE_NAME'
     EXPORTING
       i_name      = 'ZADB_FILE_DOWNLOAD_MULTI'
     IMPORTING
       e_funcname = fm_name.

* set doc params so that the pdf will be interactive
  fp_docparams-fillable = abap_true.
  param-name = '/1BCDWB/DOCPARAMS'.
  param-kind = abap_func_exporting.
  GET REFERENCE OF fp_docparams INTO param-value.
  INSERT param INTO TABLE lt_params.

* add the SPFLI parameter
  param-name = 'SPFLI'.
  param-kind = abap_func_exporting.
  GET REFERENCE OF spfli INTO param-value.
  INSERT param INTO TABLE lt_params.

* add the formoutput exporting parameter
  param-name = '/1BCDWB/FORMOUTPUT'.
  param-kind = abap_func_importing.
  GET REFERENCE OF fp_formoutput INTO param-value.
  INSERT param INTO TABLE lt_params.
```

```
* add the exception
  exception-name = 'OTHERS'.
  exception-value = 10.
  INSERT exception INTO TABLE lt_exceptions.

* set output parameters and open spool job
  fp_outputparams-nodialog  = 'X'.
  fp_outputparams-getpdf     = 'X'.
  CALL FUNCTION 'FP_JOB_OPEN'
    CHANGING
      ie_outputparams = fp_outputparams.

* dynamic call of the generated function module
  CALL FUNCTION fm_name
    PARAMETER-TABLE
      lt_params
    EXCEPTION-TABLE
      lt_exceptions.
  IF sy-subrc <> 0.
*     messages don't work inside of supply functions!
*     there was an error; check if it was an ADS related
*     problem
*     CALL FUNCTION 'FP_GET_LAST_ADS_ERRSTR'
*       IMPORTING
*         e_adserrstr = adserrstr.
*
**    get message manager
*     lr_api_controller ?= wd_this->wd_get_api( ).
*     CALL METHOD lr_api_controller->get_message_manager
*       RECEIVING
*         message_manager = lr_message_manager.
*
**    report error message returned by ADS
*     CALL METHOD lr_message_manager->report_error_message
*       EXPORTING
*         message_text = adserrstr.

*    abort PDF creation Ð Web Dynpro runtime will trigger
*    a RABAX due to the missing file
     RETURN.
  ENDIF.
```

```
* close spool job
  CALL FUNCTION 'FP_JOB_CLOSE'.

* get the pdf
  READ TABLE lt_params
       WITH KEY name = '/1BCDWB/FORMOUTPUT'
       INTO param.
  pdf_ref ?= param-value.
  ls_pdf-pdf = pdf_ref->pdf.



* bind a single element
  node->bind_structure( new_item = ls_pdf ).
ENDMETHOD.
```

Listing 8.17 S_PDF Supply Function

Similar to the previous example, this generation of a PDF form is structured as follows:

1. **Reading the data displayed in the PDF form.**
   Here, it is the current SPFLI row.

2. **Generating the PDF form from the form template with the previously read data as input.**
   Note that in a supply function you cannot react to errors by, for example, displaying a message. Therefore, the corresponding source code is commented out.

3. **Processing the generated PDF form.**
   Here, it is written in the PDF attribute of the newly created context element.

The form template was created using Transaction SFP in a previous step. It contains not only the data of the flight connection, but fields from the SCUSTOM database table so that a user could book a flight by filling out the form (see Figure 8.74).

During the generation of the PDF form, the system could fill out some of the fields, for example, name, title, or even address, based on the data of the user (see Figure 8.75). The flight book form also contains a signature field for the electronic signature.

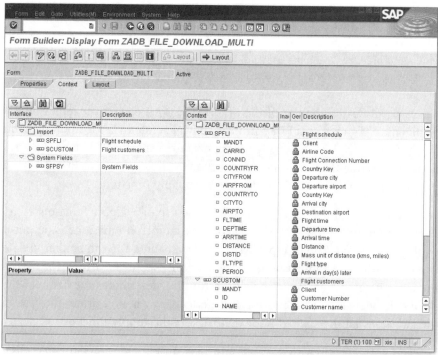

Figure 8.74 DDIC-based Form Template with Fields from the SCUSTOM Database Table

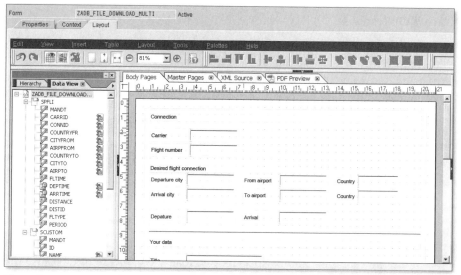

Figure 8.75 Structure of a Complete Form with a Mix of Fields Filled by the System and by the User

> **Note on Using the Electronic Signature**
>
> Observe any legal requirements for using electronic signatures before you put this example into practice. You must use additional hardware and software particularly for implementing the requirement of a qualified electronic signature.

This example discussed the use of the FileDownload UI element together with a supply function. As a result, a PDF form was only generated via a load-on-demand approach if requested by the user. The input data for a specific PDF form is always constant because the data of a flight connection is already known. In contrast to the previous example, this enabled the use of a supply function.

However, the disadvantage of this example is the use of a supply function. Here, a whole range of operations is not allowed, for example, no message is output if something goes wrong (for example, ADS is not available). You can neither update the context attribute of another node nor dynamically set the file name. The reason for the latter is that when the Web Dynpro runtime determines the name of the file during the view rendering process, it is undefined, whether or not the system has already accessed the context node that triggers the supply function.

Therefore, you are provided with another download mechanism called AttachFileToResponse, which is discussed in the following section.

AttachFileToResponse

AttachFileToResponse is not a UI element, but a static method of the class, CL_WD_RUNTIME_SERVICES. It can be called by every action handler (and other methods) and enables the developer to display a "file download dialog box" for one or more files.

In contrast to the FileDownload UI element, the file content does not have to be specified prior to the triggering action. The file can be generated or selected in a targeted manner depending on the current inputs of the user. This is the most flexible way to provide users with a file. You can find an example that provides a good overview of the available options in this method in SAP's Web Dynpro component, WDR_TEST_EVENTS, in the BUTTON section.

Regarding Adobe integration, the ZADB_FILE_DOWNLOAD_GENPDF example is improved in the following example. Here, a special download view was set up because the form could not be generated on the fly by clicking on the FileDownload UI element.

This problem needs to be resolved. You can find this example in the Web Dynpro component, ZADB_ATTACH_FILE_TO_RESP. The layout consists of an Inputfield with Label and a Button. When you click on the GET_PDF button, the system is supposed to generate a PDF form with the current input and provide it to the user for processing or saving.

In the action handler, the PDF form is generated in the same way as detailed in the FileDownload UI element example. The following call at the end of the source code is new (see Listing 8.18). It causes the system to display a FILE DOWNLOAD dialog in the browser that provides the generated PDF form as *myOfflinePdf.pdf* (see Figure 8.76).

```
* transfer the pdf to the user
  cl_wd_runtime_services=>attach_file_to_response(
    i_filename    = 'myOfflinePdf.pdf'
    i_content     = pdf
    i_mime_type   = 'application/pdf' ).
```

Listing 8.18 Calling AttachFileToResponse

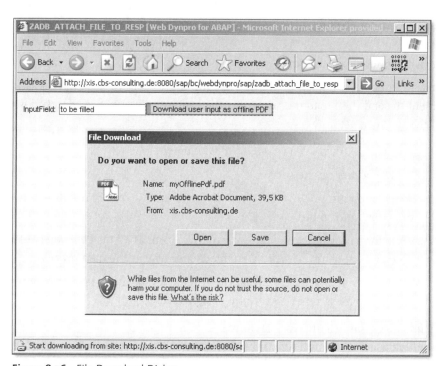

Figure 8.76 File Download Dialog

Furthermore, this method contains the optional parameters, I_IN_NEW_WINDOW and I_INPLACE. If I_INPLACE is set to ABAP_TRUE, then the file is immediately displayed in the browser window. The I_IN_NEW_WINDOW parameter controls whether the current or a new browser window is used.

The benefits of AttachFileToResponse are obvious: The application runs smoother, it enables direct storage of the file, and it is easier to implement from a developer's standpoint.

For this example of generating a PDF form from the input of the user, AttachFileToResponse is the best choice.

Enabling Users to Send the Form to the Server

In the subject area of form upload, you are provided with many options ranging from email dispatch to a web application for checking in the PDF file. This section describes how to upload a PDF form that was filled out offline using a web application implemented with Web Dynpro ABAP. Basically, there are two different cases: a pure upload with input confirmation and an upload with subsequent online review of the PDF form.

Upload with Input Confirmation

This first option of PDF upload uses—just like the subsequent case—a FileUpload UI element to send the file to the server via the browser. The upload process consists of the following steps:

1. Upload of the PDF form via a FileUpload UI element
2. The following occurs on the server:
   - Check the incoming PDF form (for duplicate entry, version of the form, authorization, and so on)
   - If the PDF form is okay: extract the data from the form using the PDF object API to ADS (see Chapter 11, ABAP PDF Object) and trigger the data processing
   - Inform the user about the confirmation or rejection of the file by displaying an appropriate message or a specially designed screen

You can find an example in the Web Dynpro component, ZADB_OFFLINE_BASIC. The component consists of the following three views:

▶ DOWNLOAD_PDF

For downloading the PDF form to fill out. In a real-life application this step is omitted because the user either obtains the file via a separate application or receives it by other means.

▶ UPLOAD_PDF

For uploading the filled-out PDF form

▶ REVIEW_VALUE

For confirming the inputs of the user that the system extracted from the PDF form

All three views are interlinked via outbound and inbound plugs so that the user can carry out all of the steps sequentially; in the WND_MAIN window, the views are interlinked via navigation links (see Figure 8.77).

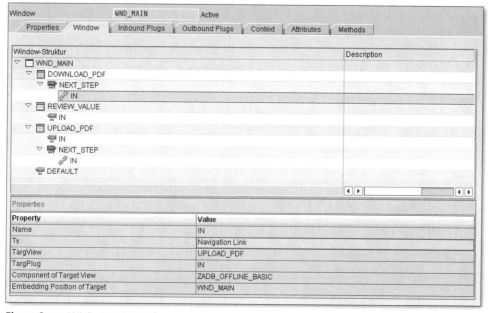

Figure 8.77 WND_MAIN Window

▶ The DOWNLOAD_PDF view contains a download option for the PDF form according to the example of the LinkToURL UI element. An additional button enables you to navigate to the UPLOAD_PDF view.

▶ The `FileUpload` UI element is located on the `UPLOAD_PDF` view. Because the file is required in the next `REVIEW_VALUE` view, the `data` property of this UI element binds to a `CONTENT` attribute of the `PDF_FILE` node that is mapped to the node of the same name at ComponentController. The PDF file specified in `FileUpload` is sent to the server via a `Button` UI element with the Upload label , put in the `CONTENT` context attribute, and navigated to the `REVIEW_VALUE` view.

▶ The user's input is extracted from the PDF form in the inbound plug of the `REVIEW_VALUE` view. The user confirms the correct upload in the view and triggers data processing. For this reason, ADS is accessed via the PDF object. Chapter 11 provides detailed information on the use of this interface.

The system then parses the returned XML data (you surely remember the form data from Section 8.5.2, Online Scenario) using the iXML functionality available in SAP NetWeaver and determines the input of the user from the XML (see Listing 8.19).

```
METHOD handlein.
  TYPE-POOLS:
    ixml.

  DATA:
    lr_fp                    TYPE REF TO if_fp,
    lr_pdf_object            TYPE REF TO if_fp_pdf_object,
    lr_pdf_file_node         TYPE REF TO
                               if_wd_context_node,
    pdf                      TYPE XSTRING,
    form_data                TYPE XSTRING,
    lr_ixml                  TYPE REF TO if_ixml,
    lr_ixml_stream_factory   TYPE REF TO
                               if_ixml_stream_factory,
    lr_ixml_istream          TYPE REF TO if_ixml_istream,
    lr_ixml_document         TYPE REF TO if_ixml_document,
    lr_ixml_parser           TYPE REF TO if_ixml_parser,
    lr_ixml_element          TYPE REF TO if_ixml_element,
    value                    TYPE STRING,
    lr_api_controller        TYPE REF TO if_wd_controller,
    lr_message_manager       TYPE REF TO
                               if_wd_message_manager,
    lr_fp_exc                TYPE REF TO cx_fp_runtime,
    message_text             TYPE STRING.
```

```
* extract the data from the pdf
  TRY.
*   get a reference to form processing interface
    lr_fp = cl_fp=>get_reference( ).

*   create a pdf object Ð it will be used to extract the
*   data
    lr_pdf_object = lr_fp->create_pdf_object( ).

*   get the pdf from the context and put it into the pdf
*   object
    lr_pdf_file_node = wd_context->get_child_node(
      wd_this->wdctx_pdf_file ).
    lr_pdf_file_node->get_attribute(
      EXPORTING
        name = 'CONTENT'
      IMPORTING
        value = pdf ).
    lr_pdf_object->set_document( pdfdata = pdf ).

*   set the task to be extracting the data of the pdf
    lr_pdf_object->set_task_extractdata( ).

*   execute the data extraction task
    lr_pdf_object->execute( ).

*   get the data from pdf as xml
    lr_pdf_object->get_data(
      IMPORTING
        formdata = form_data ).

*   extract the value from the xml
    lr_ixml                = cl_ixml=>create( ).
    lr_ixml_stream_factory =
      lr_ixml->create_stream_factory( ).
    lr_ixml_istream =
      lr_ixml_stream_factory->create_istream_xstring(
        form_data ).
    lr_ixml_document = lr_ixml->create_document( ).
    lr_ixml_parser   = lr_ixml->create_parser(
                       stream_factory = lr_ixml_stream_factory
                       istream  = lr_ixml_istream
                       document = lr_ixml_document ).
```

```
     lr_ixml_parser->parse( ).

     lr_ixml_element = lr_ixml_document->find_from_name(
                         'VALUE' ).
     IF lr_ixml_element IS BOUND.
       value = lr_ixml_element->get_value( ).
       wd_context->set_attribute(
         name  = 'VALUE'
         value = value ).
     ENDIF.
     CATCH cx_fp_runtime INTO lr_fp_exc.
*      get message manager
       lr_api_controller ?= wd_this->wd_get_api( ).
       lr_message_manager =
         lr_api_controller->get_message_manager( ).

*      report message
       message_text = lr_fp_exc->get_text( ).
       lr_message_manager->report_error_message(
         message_text = message_text ).
   ENDTRY.
ENDMETHOD.
```

Listing 8.19 Extraction of the User's Input in the Inbound Plug

In this example, the PDF form contains a VALUE Textfield. The current value of this Textfield is copied to a context attribute called VALUE of the STRING type. An Inputfield UI element set to readOnly displays this value later on.

Figure 8.78 Input Confirmed, Further Processing of Data Triggered

Below the `Inputfield`, you can find a `Button` that the user can use to confirm that his input has been extracted correctly. In a real-life application, the input would then be processed further. Clicking on the button deactivates it so that further processing cannot be triggered more than once (see Figure 8.78).

Upload with Online Review of the PDF Form

Interactive PDF forms in the online scenario that do not utilize pure online features, for example, a value help, can also be used as interactive PDF forms in the offline scenario. This is a very convenient option for users because they can save the intermediate result of their work. For example, information that is temporarily not available can be entered offline at a later point in time. Due to its simplicity, the business card example falls into this category as well.

However, the integration of such an offline step requires downloading from and uploading to the server. After the upload, the user can further process the PDF form in the online scenario. You can either confirm that all inputs have been made or carry out a new offline step. In case of a confirmation, the system triggers the further processing of data.

You can find an example in the Web Dynpro component, `ZADB_OFFLINE_ADVANCED`. It is a further development of the `ZADB_OFFLINE_BASIC` component of the previous example for which the `REVIEW_VALUE` view was renamed to `REVIEW_PDF` and extended. The best way to follow this example is to copy and use the example of the previous section.

You do not have to rename the `REVIEW_VALUE` view—if you must rename it, embed the view in the `WND_MAIN` window. Also, modify the navigation links. In the following example, the `REVIEW_PDF` view is used according to the existing example.

Create an `InteractiveForm` UI element on the `REVIEW_PDF` view. Bind the existing form template of your offline form from the previous example. The ViewDesigner gives you the option to generate the context node for the form data—this is the `ZADB_OFFLINE_EXAMPLE` node—and automatically bind the `dataSource` property to it (see Figure 8.79). Make use of this option.

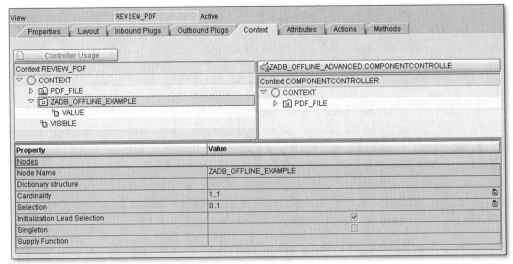

Figure 8.79 Generated Node from the Form Interface

Bear in mind that you are using an interface form from the online scenario. For this reason, you must convert the form template into a ZCI-based form template if you have not done so yet. Then bind the pdfSource property to the CONTENT attribute of the PDF node. This attribute contains the PDF form uploaded by the user.

Within the Web Dynpro runtime, the following happens during the first-time display:

- ▶ The system recognizes that a PDF form is located in the CONTENT context attribute. This form is displayed. If the node that the dataSource property binds to already contains data, this data is ignored. The user can view his uploaded PDF form *only*.

- ▶ Now the user can process the PDF form in the online scenario as usual. Changes are sent to the dataSource node on the server. The PDF form is updated in the CONTENT attribute so that it always contains the current input of the user.

In the subsequent rendering process of the application, the Web Dynpro runtime no longer uses the pdfSource property. This means that you can change the content of the dataSource node later on. You do not have to update the PDF form behind the pdfSource property because this is done automatically by the Web Dynpro runtime from now on.

The benefit of this procedure is that you as the developer do not have to program the extraction of the data from the PDF form yourself. This is all done automatically by the Adobe integration with Web Dynpro ABAP.

Caution: Pitfall!

For this procedure, the `InteractiveForm` UI element must appear for the first time. If the `InteractiveForm` UI element is already visible before the PDF form is put in the context attribute behind the `pdfSource` property, the PDF form is ignored. Instead, the system displays the form data from the `dataSource` node and generates a new PDF form based on this data via ADS. Your PDF form in `pdfSource` is then overwritten.

The extraction of data is not carried out immediately but is implemented by Adobe Reader in the browser. Adobe Reader receives the PDF form and only sends the form data to the server later on. This means that the data from the PDF form is not available until the subsequent roundtrip in the context.

This service functionality for the offline scenario is only enabled when both `pdfSource` and `dataSource` are bound and defined in the `templateSource` of a form template.

Caution: Another Pitfall!

Whenever you use the properties, `dataSource`, `templateSource`, and `pdfSource`, at the same time in an `InteractiveForm` UI element, you must keep this offline case in mind. Because if you switch the `visible` property off and on again, the `InteractiveForm` UI element becomes visible and `pdfSource` has priority over `dataSource`.

Activate the component and create a Web Dynpro application. The example is now complete.

Comparing the Two Upload Procedures

The aim of this section is to differentiate the two procedures and point out their advantages and disadvantages.

The major advantage of the first example is that it is a pure offline procedure. For example, it does not require any ZCI script in the form template, which could become obsolete over time. You can also use all controls in Adobe LiveCycle Designer as required—not only those from the native library. After the upload of the PDF form, the user views his input in an input screen that was created in Web Dynpro. Just as in the second example, he could continue his work here and use the advanced features of Web Dynpro, such as personalization, master/detailed navigation, and high level of interaction and productivity thanks to more than 50 different UI elements.

The disadvantage of the first example is the change of the UI technology which is the advantage of the second scenario. The user always works with the same interactive form that he is already familiar with. He does not have to deal with the two different UI technologies.

This advantage has its price: The PDF form must be an interactive PDF form that can still be filled out offline. To bridge this divide is difficult because an online user wants to have value helps directly from the server and a high performance for the roundtrips, while an offline user selects his data from long dropdown lists and has no performance problems due to the lack of server roundtrips despite the large dropdown lists.

An optional solution for this tradeoff is the creation of separate online and offline forms with nearly identical appearances. In this case, however, you cannot use the service function of Web Dynpro for displaying the PDF form after its upload. The data would have to be extracted separately and provided in the `dataSource` node.

If the processing of data is not supported; that is, if a completely filled-out PDF form is expected on the server, the system can display this form as a print form. To do so, simply deactivate the `enabled` property for the `InteractiveForm` UI element.

The following recommendations are based on practical experience:

▶ If it is an online application in which the users are supposed to have the option to work offline, most SAP applications are too complex to fully implement this by means of a PDF form. Focus on a specific aspect of the application and think about what data you want to include in the offline form. This can be an activity report that is filled out by the employee in-between customer visits in the course of the day, for example.

▶ Provided that it is a pure offline application (for example, a request form), you should use the first scenario and consider that you can omit the review step in a user interface that was created using Web Dynpro if the user receives a confirmation in the follow-up process. If the PDF form contained an incorrect input and the system determined this during the upload, the user can be notified accordingly via a corresponding message. In addition, it is beneficial for the user if he corrects incorrect entries in his PDF form directly: He can access it any time and compare the confirmation, which is then received, with the content of his PDF form.

The second scenario is suitable only for simple forms because performance problems may occur. Consider the restrictions of the online scenario with regard to the maximum number of pages, dropdown lists, and tables with too many entries.

ABAP Offline Infrastructure Support

As of SAP NetWeaver 7.0 EHP2, Web Dynpro ABAP supports ABAP Offline Infrastructure for integrating forms sent by email. As soon as an inbound handler was defined in the form template, Web Dynpro ABAP automatically generates the necessary additional data in the PDF form. SAP provides the DEMO_IFBA_EMAIL demo application to demonstrate the integration with Web Dynpro ABAP. Refer to Chapter 10 to obtain more information on ABAP Offline Infrastructure.

8.5.4   Migrating ACF to ZCI

In SAP Note 1249189, SAP recommends to omit the ACF integration and use the ZCI integration instead. As of SAP NetWeaver 7.0 SP10, you can implement the changeover as follows:

1. Define which form templates are used by the ACF integration and which of these form templates are actually used productively.

2. Decide whether you want to implement a complete or gradual changeover. Consider the complexity of the form templates and the effort required for regression tests.

3. Check whether you can run an upgrade for ADS to NetWeaver 7.0 EHP1 on this occasion. This way, you can use the up-to-dateness of the ZCI script to avoid additional costs caused by the version problems described in Section 8.5.2, Online Scenario.

4. Run the `SFP_ZCI_UPDATE` report for the form templates to be changed. You thus add the ZCI script and change the type of the form template to ZCI. If you use SAP NetWeaver 7.0 EHP1 or higher, it is sufficient to change the type of the form template using the report on ZCI. The ZCI script is then automatically added by ADS at runtime.

5. In the layout of the form template, exchange the controls from the WEB DYNPRO ACTIVEX library with those of the WEB DYNPRO NATIVE library.

6. Change the `displayType` property from ACTIVEX to NATIVE in the ViewDesigner for the `InteractiveForm` UI elements.

7. Create a where-used list for the `CL_WD_INTERACTIVE_FORM` class. Change all locations for dynamically setting the `displayType` property so that they are set to `Native`. This also concerns the dynamic generation of the UI element because the default values is `ActiveX` there.

8. Go through the checklist from Section 8.5.2 (for sensible usage of the online scenario). You must particularly consider the points on setting up the PCs of project members and the required version of ADS for specific features.

9. If you do not use any forms with ACF integration, you can omit the installation and updates for the ACF wrapper for the staff PCs in your enterprise. Remove the ACF wrapper also from preconfigured images. Schedule this activity so that it is performed together with the go-live of the form change or subsequently. Bear in mind that other Web Dynpro UI elements still require an ACF wrapper. If you use these UI elements, you must not schedule uninstallation.

8.5.5 Specialized Topics

This section provides information on the use of digital signatures in the Adobe integration with Web Dynpro ABAP, the controls supported in Form Builder, a list of other interesting information sources, and important SAP Notes.

▶ **Digital signature**
This procedure for signing PDF files or form content is not directly supported by Web Dynpro ABAP. This means that you can only use it in the offline and print scenario, whereas in the print scenario you must generate the PDF file yourself and place it in the `pdfSource` of the `InteractiveForm` UI element.

▶ **Supported ACF and ZCI controls**
At present, Web Dynpro ABAP does not support all controls provided by Adobe LiveCycle Designer under ZCI or ACF. You can find a list of supported controls in SAP Note 1098009.

▶ **Where can you obtain further information?**
On one hand, the SAP Developer Network (SDN) includes an excellent forum for Web Dynpro ABAP with a link to the Wiki area. On the other hand, the continuously updated and comprehensive online help for Web Dynpro ABAP provides detailed information for Adobe integration and for programming Web Dynpro ABAP.

▶ **Important SAP Notes**

The notes listed in Table 8.1 have either been referred to in this chapter or are significant for Adobe integration in the context of Web Dynpro ABAP. They are sorted by their number in descending order so that the latest notes (for the latest support packages) are listed first. Some notes are independent of a specific support package because they contain general information and recommendations. You can recognize them by their title.

SAP Note	Title
1260750	SAP Interactive Forms by Adobe in Web Dynpro ABAP
1252350	Forms with ABAP Dictionary-Based Interface
1249189	Deprecation: ACF No Longer Supported for Adobe
1229392	Adobe: Errors in Adobe Integration
1227102	Adobe: Rabax if Only the pdfSource is Bound
1180004	Adobe: Handling Incorrect Inputs and Conversion Exits
1151340	Error during the XML Schema Generation in Web Dynpro ABAP
1113704	Adobe: User Parameter for Alternative ADS Destination
1098009	Restrictions for Web Dynpro ABAP
1090486	Adobe: Additional Features in DDIC-based Print Forms
1084367	Corrections/Improvements in the Adobe Integration DT for SP 14
1055738	Adobe: Update dataSource from pdfSource According to Template
1029721	Adobe: Support of Input Helps
1013227	Dropdown List Boxes in ZCI-enabled Interactive Forms
983699	Additional Features for Adobe Integration
980437	Toolbar Cannot be Hidden for InteractiveForm
978037	Switching ACF-Based UI Elements to ZCI
962956	Adobe: Interactive DDIC Forms
956074	Using the Update Function for Forms
856882	Adobe: Making the DDIC Mode Partially Ready for Input

Table 8.1 Important SAP Notes for Web Dynpro ABAP and SAP Interactive Forms by Adobe

8.6 Summary

This chapter described how you can integrate SAP Interactive Forms by Adobe with Web Dynpro ABAP. Based on the three basic scenarios, real-life examples, and numerous step-by-step instructions you can implement these scenarios in your own projects.

The Internal Service Request (ISR) enables you to map request scenarios for internal processes that are used to process service requests. In this context, the interactive Adobe form serves as a flexible, modifiable request form.

9 Internal Service Request

This chapter describes the Internal Service Request (ISR), which integrates the interactive Adobe form as a flexible request form. After introducing you to the technical principles of the ISR and the basic conditions for some business request scenarios (see Section 9.1), this chapter analyzes a scenario provided within SAP ERP (see Section 9.2, Scenarios in SAP NetWeaver Portal). Section 9.3, Getting Started—Creating a Plain Scenario, explains what you must consider when creating and setting up a scenario. Sections 9.4, 9.6, and 9.7 introduce and discuss the necessary Customizing settings and program-related enhancement options to refine the request scenario. Section 9.5, Request Forms as Adobe Forms, explains how you can define the Adobe form in the ISR context. Section 9.8 describes the new variant of ISR in the Application Basis (ABA), which was developed for Release SAP NetWeaver 7.0 EHP2.

In addition to Customizing and the program-related ISR details, this chapter focuses on the options provided by the ISR using examples and practical tips. After reading this chapter, you should have a better understanding of the options provided by the ISR framework and be able to implement specific form-based request scenarios according to your requirements.

The ISR and ISR Scenario Concepts

An ISR scenario comprises all settings in an SAP ERP system (for example, SAP ERP 6.0) that are required to map a service request for an internal process.

9.1 Introduction

This section describes the business background and the technical framework for using ISR scenarios within SAP ERP and the required system conditions. It also provides an overview of the ISR framework and names the critical basic concepts.

9.1.1 Concepts in the ISR Framework

The ISR serves to initialize an internal process in which a service defined by the user is processed. The service request enables occasional users to request any service in SAP NetWeaver Portal via an online request form and have the system process the related internal process.

The applicant can implement this without having specific knowledge of the SAP ERP system. The main task here is to provide an input screen as a user-friendly form. This can be ensured via interactive Adobe forms. Due to the free and flexible design options provided by Form Designer, you can design the form for any ISR scenario.

> **Online Form**
>
> ISR supports only online forms. That means that the user must populate and submit the form in the portal; the offline mode is generally not supported.

The following sections describe the ISR framework and the related essential concepts in detail.

Internal Process

An internal process that is appropriate for service requests is usually used and re-used by multiple users. Such processes often require the execution of sometimes complex transactions by specialists or changes to protected data. For example, it makes sense to use a service request to request a system user with a password and the required authorizations for a particular system.

Due to the complexity of such transactions (and the data security-critical or business-critical relevance of the data), or for efficiency reasons, such transactions are usually processed in small, central administrative units that provide the required specialized knowledge. However, a complex internal process may also require the involvement of several departments and may include one or more approval steps.

The main components of the structure of the roles involved in such processes usually remain the same, regardless of the requester.

The applicant is not supposed or allowed to carry out these transactions himself because the occasional user usually does not have the specialized knowledge and the required access permissions to process his service request in the system. However, the user necessarily has the authorization to make the request. It is often left to the occasional user to ensure the success of his service request (via email, telephone, or in written form), using more or less detailed directions in internal process instructions.

Short Description of Service Requests

By completing and submitting the request form in SAP NetWeaver Portal, the SAP ERP system generates a notification for which a processor can be found via the SAP Business Workflow module. The processor can perform activities (for example, sending emails or carrying out transactions) directly from the notification. The request forms and the resulting workflow can be individually adapted to the service request to be implemented and the situation in the respective enterprise.

You can quickly and easily set up your own ISR scenarios. By integrating the Controlling component, you can immediately bill the business costs of the request to the cost object. You can also influence the process and form anytime by means of Business Add-Ins (BAdIs).

Technical Roles

In the context of ISR, various technical roles are involved in the service request process:

- **Applicant**
  If required, the applicant completes and submits the interactive Adobe form to request a service. He tracks the service request status.

- **Approver**
  The approver approves or rejects the service request.

- **Processor**
  The processor ensures that one or more business transactions are carried out in SAP ERP that are necessary for the implementation of the service request.

▶ **Administrator**

The administrator is responsible for the business scenario. He manages the scenario-specific Customizing and the related ABAP programming.

Flexible Framework

The ISR links several applications from SAP NetWeaver 7.0 and SAP ERP 6.0 and provides flexible configuration options via Customizing and the appropriate program interface, which enables you to design customer-specific scenarios. This includes not only mapping the requested process but also integrating SAP Interactive Forms by Adobe as the input screen for the applicant.

In addition to the obligatory input fields, the Adobe form delivers process-specific information and assistance to simplify the request creation. Scenario-specific pre-definitions for input fields, default values, input helps, online data checks, and various events make it easier to complete the form and ensure — when the request is made — a high data quality for the transactions carried out during the process. You can also design the functions and form layout specifically and dynamically for each user.

Plain scenarios require fewer Customizing settings and less programming effort than complex scenarios. However, it is critical that the request form can be easily understood and deployed by occasional users. This can be ensured with an ISR, regardless of the level of complexity.

9.1.2 Prerequisites

To use ISRs with interactive Adobe forms, you must use at least SAP ERP 5.0. The ISR Adobe forms in SAP ERP 5.0 are still based on ACF technology. As of SAP ERP 5.0, you are provided with the ISR interface in Web Dynpro Java. To use interactive Adobe forms, you also need version 6.0.2 or higher of Adobe Reader and at least SAP NetWeaver 6.40. In addition, you need SAP NetWeaver Portal to use all ISR functions. The recommended layout types for Adobe forms is the ZCI Layout (see Section 9.5.1, Specific Properties, and Section 8.5.2, Online Scenario).

As of SAP ERP 6.0 SP 8, the ISR's user interface is also in Web Dynpro ABAP. Besides the functions of the Web Dynpro Java interface, this interface provides some additional functions. Here, the technical prerequisites are SAP NetWeaver 7.0 SP 10 and Adobe Reader 7.08 or higher. You should always use the most recent version of Adobe Reader.

You can find some sample scenarios of the ISR in SAP NetWeaver Portal in various business packages, such as Manager Self-Services (MSS), Business Unit Analyst (BUA), and Employee Self-Services (ESS).

To carry out a service request, the applicant requires various authorizations in the SAP ERP system. Typical error messages due to missing authorizations when starting or submitting a form include:

- **You are not authorized to display users** (01 495)
  This error message is displayed when the authorization for the `S_USER_GRP` authorization object is missing.

- **You have no authorization for the notification type...** (Q0 151)
  This error message is displayed when the authorization for the `B_NOTIF` authorization object is missing.

- **An error occurred while processing the notification...** (IM 277)
  This error message is displayed when the authorization for the `I_QMEL` authorization object is missing.

- **No authorization for this action** (SBDS 106)
  This error message is displayed when the authorization for the `S_BDS_DS` authorization object is missing.

All descriptions in this chapter are based on the functions provided by SAP ERP 6.0; therefore, releases older than SAP ERP 5.0 are not covered in the following sections. The technical solution of the ISR using Web Dynpro ABAP is discussed, but the structurally nearly identical user interface in Web Dynpro Java is not.

9.1.3 What Can Be Configured and Where Can It Be Programmed?

As you will see in the following sections of this chapter, the comprehensive design flexibility of service requests assumes a critical role for the ISR. Numerous settings are configured via Customizing, and numerous BAdI interfaces are provided for further adaptations if you want to use your own ABAP programming. Their implementations are called by the ISR framework when the service request is made and processed.

Figure 9.1 provides an overview of the Customizing settings and the interfaces and illustrates the corresponding relationships.

▶ The diagram focuses on the process from the request creation to its implementation by the processor.

▶ The ISR Customizing settings are indicated in dark gray, notification settings in medium gray, BAdIs are indicated in light gray, and functions modules or ABAP classes in black.

The scenario Customizing is the frame around the entire service request. The following sections describe the different components in greater detail.

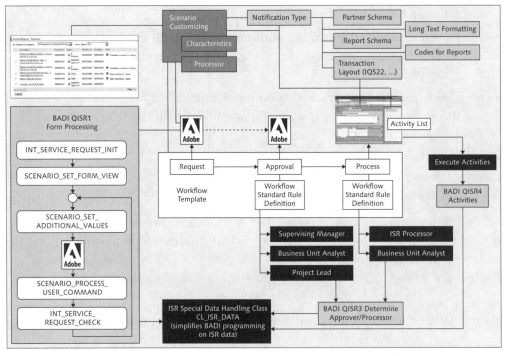

Figure 9.1 Schematic Diagram of the Interdependencies or Assignments of Customizing and BAdI Interfaces

9.2 SAP NetWeaver Portal Scenarios

This section provides an overview of the already-delivered scenarios with interactive Adobe forms and uses a sample implementation of an ISR scenario to illustrate the purpose and use of the framework. In the context of the sample scenario, this section describes the main ISR functions and demonstrates the integration options with the portal.

This chapter provides only an overview of the topic, not a comprehensive description of the functions of the ISR. You can find detailed information on more specific functions in Section 9.4, Section 9.5, and Section 9.6.

9.2.1 Grouping of the Provided Scenarios

SAP ERP provides a lot of scenarios that are usually designed as application examples and thus as a template for customer-specific scenarios. The corresponding Adobe form, in particular, is often customized due to the requirements of customer-specific designs of the layout. Nevertheless, the provided scenarios are fully functional.

The scenarios can be grouped into the following business subject areas:

- Requests for creating or changing master data from SAP ERP, for example, equipment, cost center, internal order, profit center, WBS element, statistical key figures, etc.
- Requests for changing postings in financial accounting
- Requests for changing the budget
- Requests for new cost reports
- Planned value entry in the context of express planning
- Requests for changing HR master data of employees
- HCM processes and forms
- Forms for information or confirmations of specific regulations
- Forms for tax declarations (public sector)
- Notifications

9.2.2 Calling the Request Form in the Portal

The ISR scenario groups mentioned in Section 9.2.1, Grouping of the Provided Scenarios, differ with respect to their business background and the way they can be started. In general, there are three ways the forms of the ISR can be made available to the user in SAP NetWeaver Portal:

▸ **Direct call of the request form as a service link (via URL)**
The request form is started in an iView via a service link (see the *Create Cost Center* example in Section 9.2.3, Applicant Role). You can find generic iViews of the ISR in the portal via the menu path PORTAL CONTENT • ERP COMMON PARTS.

▸ **Indirect call via the ISR Launchpad**
The request form is started in the context of another application via a generated button using the ISR Launchpad. The request includes the business context of the application from which it is called (see the *Create Cost Center* example in Section 9.2.3). This enables the surrounding application to fill out some of the form in advance. Similar to the service link, you can start the request form in a new browser window by clicking on the selection button. Direct communication between the ISR application and the surrounding application is not possible.

▸ **Integrated with a specific application**
Technically, the request form is integrated with another Web Dynpro component. In this case, the Web Dynpro components can exchange data anytime. The request form is started in the same browser mode as the entire application. This applies, for example, to the request scenarios where HR master data are changed (Personnel Change Requests, HCM Processes and Forms).

Section 9.7.3, Usage Options in SAP NetWeaver Portal, describes the technical details of the application options in the portal.

9.2.3   Applicant Role

This section uses the scenario *Create Cost Center* (technical name: SMC1) as an example to illustrate the functionality of the ISR, from making an order to creating the cost center in the system.

In the BUSINESS UNIT ANALYSIS role of the BUA business package, you can call the request form for the CREATE COST CENTER scenario directly as a service link (see Figure 9.2, left column, below the SERVICES folder) and context-dependently from the cost center monitor of the BUA (see Figure 9.2; MASTER DATA iView). In both cases, the QISR_UI_FORM Web Dynpro application is started in the iView (see Section 9.7.3). You can reproduce the complete scenario in your system.

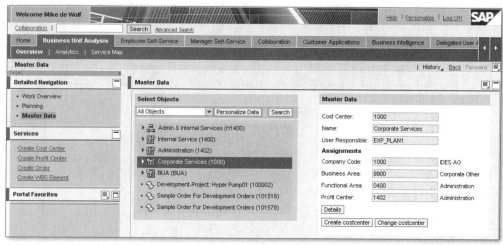

Figure 9.2 Calling "Create Cost Center" as a Service Link and in the Master Data Monitor

The service request consists of three steps. The Roadmap Web Dynpro screen element above the form displays the current step of the three request steps.

1. In the first step, the form is filled out.

2. In the second step, the completed form can be checked and then printed before it is submitted.

3. In the third step, you are informed that your request was sent successfully.

However, this roadmap has nothing to do with the downstream process of the service request implementation.

Three Steps

If you use the `QISR_UI_FORM` Web Dynpro application, these three steps are mandatory. However, if you integrate the ISR request form with your own Web Dynpro application (see Sections 9.2.2, Calling the Request Form in the Portal, and 9.7.3, Usage Options in SAP NetWeaver Portal), you do not have to use this roadmap.

Step 1: Process Form

Figure 9.3 shows a request form that consists of some input fields that are required for requesting a new cost center and some display fields. The personal data of the applicant (name, user data, etc.) are determined and displayed automatically.

Figure 9.3 Request Form after Start

The applicant can copy an existing cost center as the template for the new cost center using the COPY TEMPLATE button. The cost center number 1000 and the controlling area 1000 were copied into the form as templates from the currently selected cost center of the master data monitor.

By clicking on the COPY TEMPLATE button, the master data of cost center 1000 is copied into the corresponding input field for the new cost center in the form. This makes it easier for the applicant to complete the form, because—at least in this business context of the business unit analyst—he can refer to an existing cost center.

In contrast, the context of the template cost center is missing if the request form is started via a service link. In this case, the applicant must enter the template cost center manually, which seems to be no problem in this simple example. However, the applicant can also implement a complex data initialization from the context of a surrounding application. Therefore, how you call the scenario depends on the requirements for the request scenario. You could also use a (programmable) input help here.

> **Programmable Form Process Logic with the QISR1 BAdI**
>
> A function carried out by a button is programmed in the QISR1 BAdI. Besides buttons and data initializations, additional functions in a form include programmable input helps, events in input fields, and form data checks (see Section 9.6, Form Flow Logic).

At the end of the form, you can enter additional specifications or comments into a long text field without having to stick to a format (see Figure 9.4).

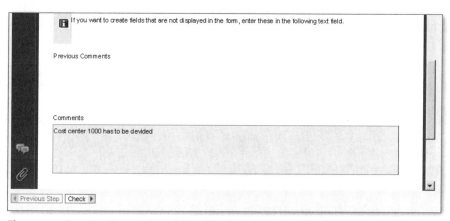

Figure 9.4 Entering Comments and Checking the Form in the First Step

After having completed the form, click on the CHECK (or NEXT STEP) button below the form. At this point, you can have the system check to see whether the form data are correct. These checks are programmed in the QISR1 BAdI (see Section 9.6.3, Programming Examples). If one or more entries in the form contain errors, the processing of the request may be put on hold; for this reason, you can have the system output error messages, which are displayed above the form. In this case, the request remains at step 1 (see Figure 9.5). After the incorrect field values have been corrected, the request changes to step 2 of the form, CHECK AND SEND.

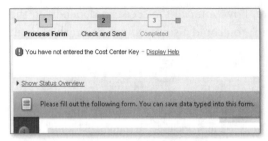

Figure 9.5 Error Message in the First Step

Step 2: Check and Send

In step 2, the form is displayed again but can no longer be changed. You can print the form for documentation purposes using the Adobe Reader function. If the applicant wants to change entries, you can return to step 1 via the PREVIOUS STEP button (see Figure 9.6).

Figure 9.6 Second Step to Check the Entries

If the data are correct, according to the system check and the applicant, you can submit the request by clicking the SEND (or SUBMIT) button.

Step 3: Completed—Output of the Request Number

After the system has generated the request, the request number that corresponds to the notification number in the SAP ERP system (see Figure 9.7) is confirmed in step 3. You can also call the request via a link (QISR_UI_DISPLAY_ONLY Web Dynpro application).

Figure 9.7 Third Step with Notification Number of the Request

Additional Steps after the Creation of the Request

The applicant can now track the status of his service request using the ISR status overview (QISR_UI_STATUSOVERVIEW Web Dynpro application), which is mapped as a separate iView (see Figure 9.8). However, the applicant can also open the status overview via the SHOW STATUS OVERVIEW link within the request form (see Figure 9.3). From here, you can call the form in the display mode and print it anytime.

Service Request: Status Overview

Internal Service Requests Status Overview

Description	Notification	Status	Created on	Changed on	Req. start	Required End	Additional Column 1	Additional Column 2	Warning	Reverse
Cost center 1000 has to be devided	1005410	Open / For Approval	22.12.2008		22.12.2008	20.02.2009	4545	Corporate Services		Reverse
Die Kostenstelle 1000 wird aufgeteilt	1005201	Open / For Approval	26.08.2008		26.08.2008	25.10.2008	1050	Corporate Services	End of processing exceeded since: 58 Day(s)	Reverse
Die Kostenstelle 1000 wird aufgeteilt	1005183	In Process / Approved	22.08.2008	22.08.2008	22.08.2008	21.10.2008	9896	Corporate Services 2	End of processing exceeded since: 62 Day(s)	Reverse
Bitte bis Ende des Monats liefern.	1005181	Open	21.08.2008		21.08.2008	20.10.2008			End of processing exceeded since: 63 Day(s)	Reverse
Report 123456	1005180	Open	21.08.2008		21.08.2008	20.10.2008			End of processing exceeded since: 63 Day(s)	Reverse

Row: 1 of 6

Data from: 22.12.2008 Time: 13:41:44 Refresh

Figure 9.8 Status Overview of all Requests of the Applicant

Depending on the settings, it is at least technically possible that the applicant can modify the request retroactively. This is not possible in this example, however. But the applicant can always view the current status of his request form when starting the form in the status overview. That means, for example, that he can also view the corresponding comment of the approver. The status of the request is OPEN until a processor or approver has processed the request. You can reverse requests with this status anytime via the appropriate function in the ISR status overview. When the status changes to IN PROCESS, the request can no longer be reversed. In additionally configurable columns, you can display up to five selected values of a form (see Section 9.4.5, Characteristics). For request 1005183 in Figure 9.8, the new cost center number and its description are displayed.

9.2.4 Approver Role

After the successful creation of the request, the system generates a notification with the OPEN status. Because the usage of SAP Business Workflow is defined in the Customizing of the corresponding notification type and the ISR, the request creation involved the creation of the corresponding workflow item. The *Create Cost Center* example requires an approval procedure. The system displays this workflow item in the Customizing of the defined approver both in the Universal Worklist (UWL) in SAP NetWeaver Portal and in the inbox of SAP BUSINESS WORKPLACE (Transaction SBWP) in SAP ERP.

The approver can process the request via one of these two inboxes. However, when you open the workflow item, you are provided with various user interfaces. Which request processing type the approver can use depends on the workflow template used (see Section 9.4.8, Processor Determination (BAdI QISR3) and Workflow).

▶ **UWL: starting the form in the portal with approval functions**
   If the approver receives the request in the UWL, the original request form is started in a new browser window (see Figure 9.9). The approver can now make a decision about the request using the APPROVE, REJECT, or BACK TO AUTHOR functions — mapped as buttons below the form (see Figure 9.10).

Figure 9.9 Workflow Item in the UWL of the Approver

Figure 9.10 Comment Entry and Functions for the Approver in the Form

In this scenario, the approver can comment on his decision; however, he cannot change the request data. If the approver selects the REJECT option, the system automatically closes the notification. In contrast, selecting the BACK TO AUTHOR option leads to a new workflow item in the applicant's inbox. The applicant can now modify and resend the request.

The ISR framework also enables the approver to change the request data (see Section 9.7.4, ISR_PROCESS_EVENT Remote Function Call). Whether this makes sense depends on the request scenario. The applicant can view the status change due to the decision of the approver and the comments in the ISR status overview.

▶ **Workplace: starting Transaction IQS22 from the workflow item**
If the approver receives the request in the workplace inbox, Transaction IQS22 (see Figure 9.11) is called. Here, the approver can also approve or reject the request. However, the BACK TO AUTHOR function is not supported.

Figure 9.11 IQS22 Notification Transaction

If the approver approves the request, a new workflow item is generated for the processor who then only uses Transaction IQS22 to process the request.

9.2.5 Processor Role

The processor can call and check the form with the original data through an activity in Transaction IQS22 and view the form data as a table (see Figure 9.12).

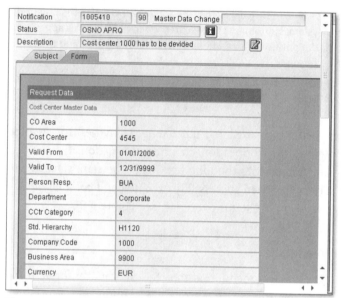

Notification	1005410 90 Master Data Change
Status	OSNO APRQ
Description	Cost center 1000 has to be devided

Subject   Form

Request Data

Cost Center Master Data

CO Area	1000
Cost Center	4545
Valid From	01/01/2006
Valid To	12/31/9999
Person Resp.	BUA
Department	Corporate
CCtr Category	4
Std. Hierarchy	H1120
Company Code	1000
Business Area	9900
Currency	EUR

Figure 9.12 Table View of the Form Data in the Notification

Unlike the approver, the processor is now provided with the means to implement the request service in the system. In this scenario, these include:

▶ **Display Adobe Form**
This activity calls the `QISR_UI_DISPLAY_ONLY` Web Dynpro component in a browser window. In this context, consider the Customizing in Section 9.4.6, Activities and Automatic Updates in Notifications.

▶ **Create Cost Center Master Data**
This activity executes a Business Application Programming Interface (BAPI) to create a cost center; the data for the BAPI are copied from the form data.

▶ **Change Cost Center Master Data**
This activity leads to the change transaction of the cost center.

These activities were defined in the scenario Customizing and programmed in the `QISR4` BAdI (see Section 9.4.6). To display the activity, a text for the link has been defined in the scenario Customizing. An essential setting for the activity is the entry of a function module that executes the activity.

Automatic Execution of an Activity

You can configure the ISR scenario in such a way that the activity for creating the required cost center in the backend system is automatically executed when the request is approved in the form. In doing this, the notification would be closed automatically, and the role of the processor would be obsolete.

Tip: Program the submission of an email as an automatic notification of the applicant in the QISR4 BAdI implementation of the activity (see Section 9.4.6).

After the processor has successfully executed the activity (activities) for creating the cost center, he completes the notification via a menu function. He also has the option of entering a comment into the long text field. The status changes to COMPLETED; thus, the service has been successfully executed and completed. The applicant can check this status in the status overview (see Figure 9.8).

9.2.6 Workflow or Worklist?

By using the notification as the data medium of the request, you can forward the request to the responsible departments or persons via SAP Business Workflow; however, you do not have to use the SAP Business Workflow module. Together with Transaction IQS8 and IQS9, the notification provides so-called worklists, which processors or approvers can use to determine the requests that are relevant to them. From here, the processors or approvers can access the corresponding transaction (IQS22 or IQS23) to process the request. Figure 9.11 displays the user interface of processor Transaction IQS22.

9.3 Getting Started—Creating a Plain Scenario

Now that you know what you can achieve with ISR scenarios, the following section explains the necessary preliminary considerations and procedures for creating your own scenario. Afterward, it describes the ISR wizard for generating a plain scenario. After reading this section, you will know how to design and implement your own scenarios.

9.3.1 Preliminary Considerations for a New ISR Scenario

Prior to creating an ISR scenario, you must answer some questions on the business background of the service request. Table 9.1 can help you describe your preliminary considerations in detail. You should first consider what the overall process should look like. Do not make any detailed considerations until you have a better idea of the process.

Subject Area	Preliminary Considerations
Request form	▸ What input fields (characteristics) should be displayed in the request form? What fields are necessary for completing the service request? ▸ What checks, data initializations, input helps, or specific functions are required by applicants or other roles in the form? ▸ What does the layout for the form look like? ▸ Does a form already exist?
Roles, worklist, and workflow	▸ What roles are provided for the execution of the service? ▸ Do you want to use SAP Business Workflow to process the notification, or do you want to have the processor select his notifications from a worklist? ▸ Are approval steps necessary, and, if so, how many? ▸ Do multiple processors have to be involved simultaneously, or can the processors become active one after the other? ▸ What criteria should be used for the determination of the processor (fixed processor or depending on request fields, organizational structures, costs, last name of the applicant, and so on)?
Request in the backend (notification)	▸ What activities (transaction calls, response email, and so on) should be provided to the processors in the activity list of the notification transaction? ▸ Should individual activities be executed automatically (for example, by the applicant or approver)?
Evaluation	▸ Do you want to create detailed reporting of your request scenario?

Table 9.1 Checklist for the Creation of a Scenario

Subject Area	Preliminary Considerations
Service costs	▸ Do you want to record and evaluate the service costs of your request scenario? ▸ Are plain blanket costs sufficient, or do you want to calculate differentiated service costs?

Table 9.1 Checklist for the Creation of a Scenario (Cont.)

After having answered all of these questions, you can start creating your own ISR scenario. However, before you begin implementing the ISR Customizing directly, you can use the ISR wizard instead. It is particularly helpful if you are working with the ISR framework for the first time.

9.3.2 ISR Wizard

The ISR wizard enables you to create a scenario step by step. You can find the ISR wizard in the Implementation Guide (IMG) (Transaction SPRO • EXECUTE PROJECT or the SAP menu path TOOLS • CUSTOMIZING • IMG) of the SAP ERP system menu path CROSS-APPLICATION COMPONENTS • INTERNET/INTRANET SERVICES • INTERNAL SERVICE REQUEST • SCENARIO DEFINITION • ISR WIZARD.

▸ The Define Scenario with ISR Wizard IMG activity (Transaction QISRCONF) serves to define a scenario.

▸ The Overview of the Scenarios Created in the ISR Wizard IMG activity (Transaction QISRLIST) displays all current scenarios created with the ISR wizard.

Within the wizard, you come across basically the same questions as listed in Table 9.1. In this context, the wizard tries to draft the questions from a business perspective and avoid questions on technical details as much as possible. That means that detailed technical knowledge about the ISR components (notification, workflow, Adobe form, and so on) is not required. The ISR wizard "translates" the answers from the subwizards into technical settings that are later used to generate the Customizing settings for the actual ISR scenario.

Subwizards

The ISR wizard consists of seven individual subwizards for different subject areas; all steps of the subwizards are displayed with a status. Figure 9.13, for example, illustrates the current status of the ISR wizard with all subwizards and their statuses for a scenario that has only been partly processed.

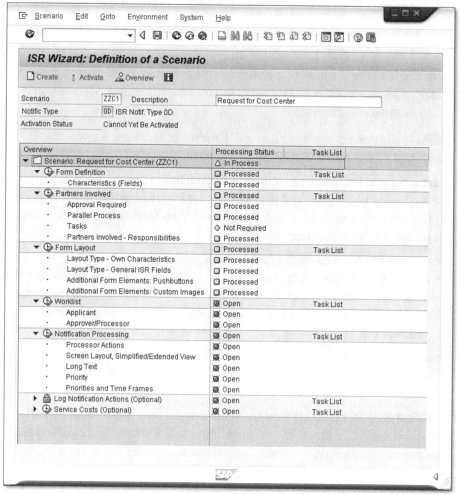

Figure 9.13 ISR Wizard with Status Information

The individual subwizards are partly based on each other and therefore depend on each other. A dependent subwizard cannot be called until the required previous subwizards have been completed. This is indicated accordingly. The interdependencies are explained within every subwizard. Apart from that, you can execute the wizards in any order you like.

Postprocessing a Subwizard

If you postprocess a subwizard—which can be done anytime—you must also carry out the steps in the subsequent, dependent subwizards again to make the necessary adaptations.

The following subwizards are available. One wizard always covers a specific subject area of the ISR. The Customizing or form settings that each subwizard generates are explained in Section 9.4, Customizing and Programming a Scenario, or 9.5, Request Forms as Adobe Forms.

- **Form Definition** (can be executed independent of the other subwizards)
  Here, you define the characteristics of the form.

- **Partners Involved** (can be executed independent of the other subwizards)
  Here, you define the roles and partners that are involved in the business process of the service request and assign user or workflow rules for the determination of the processors at runtime.

- **Form Layout** (depends on the first wizard)
  Here, you specify the rough layout of the form. For example, you define the positioning of characteristics. In addition, you can select fields from the General ISR Fields pool (see Section 9.4.5) and define for which role the characteristic is ready for input.

- **Worklist** (depends on the second wizard)
  Here, you define how the processors can find their service requests. You can also configure the ISR status overview here.

- **Notification Processing** (can be executed independent of the other subwizards)
  Here, you specify the functions of the notification transactions (for example, IQS22) for processing the service request, for example, activities for the processor.

- **Log Notification Actions** (depends on the second and fifth wizard; optional)
  Here, you configure whether and how activities of the notification processing are documented in the notification. These settings are critical for evaluations in notification reporting.

▶ **Service Costs** (can be executed independent of the other subwizards; optional)
Here, you define how the costs of a service request are recorded.

The last two subwizards are optional; that is, you do not have to execute them to activate the scenario. If a subwizard has not been processed yet, its status is OPEN. If a subwizard has been partly processed but is not completed yet, its status is IN PROCESS. If a wizard is completed, its status is PROCESSED. After having completed all subwizards that are not optional, you can activate the scenario.

Activation

The current settings of the subwizards are initially only buffered in the ISR wizard, even though all of the subwizards are not completed yet. You can modify and postprocess any subwizard as long as the scenario is not activated. Not until you activate the entire scenario in the ISR wizard are the settings transferred to the corresponding Customizing tables as a scenario that can be actually used.

However, you cannot generate the Customizing settings for the scenario until all mandatory subwizards have been completed. To do this, you must execute the ACTIVATE function. Only then will the actual ISR scenario be created with the name of the scenario defined in the ISR wizard and the Customizing transferred to the respective Customizing tables. In addition, the system generates a notification type with the corresponding Customizing settings. The ACTIVATION STATUS (CANNOT YET BE ACTIVATED or CAN BE ACTIVATED) indicates whether the scenario is active.

This activation also involves generating a functional interactive Adobe form with all of the required input fields and technical properties—interface, context, data view, script, field binding, and so on (see Figure 9.14). The generated form can then be edited by designing the layout or retroactively extending it with additional fields (see Section 9.5, Request Forms as Adobe Forms), for example.

The name of the form or interface is composed as follows (xxxx refers to the name of the scenario):

▶ Form: Z_ISR_FORM_xxxx
▶ Interface: Z_ISR_IF_xxxx

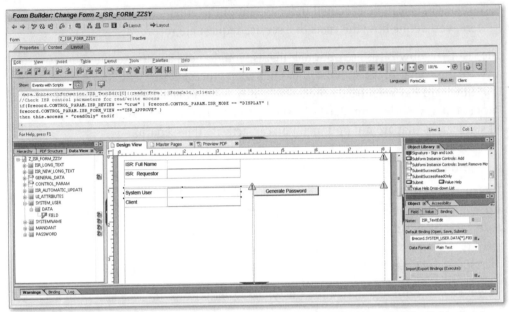

Figure 9.14 Generated Adobe Form with Data View, Data Binding Layout of the Fields, Script

The Customizing settings and the generated Adobe form are collected in the requests that you provided and can therefore be transferred to other systems. For the activation, you need one Customizing and one workbench request each (for SAP Interactive Forms by Adobe). In addition, you are prompted to specify the package assignment for the Adobe form and its interface. You must also activate the corresponding workbench objects in the respective dialog box.

Worklist

After activation, additional changes may have to be made to the Customizing when implementing the new ISR scenario. For this reason, the WORKLIST provides an overview of all generated Customizing settings in an Adobe Portable Document Format (PDF) print form (see Figure 9.15, the example refers to the settings of the ZZSY sample scenario). Among other things, it describes which control functions the respective generated Customizing entry is responsible for and where in the IMG you can find it.

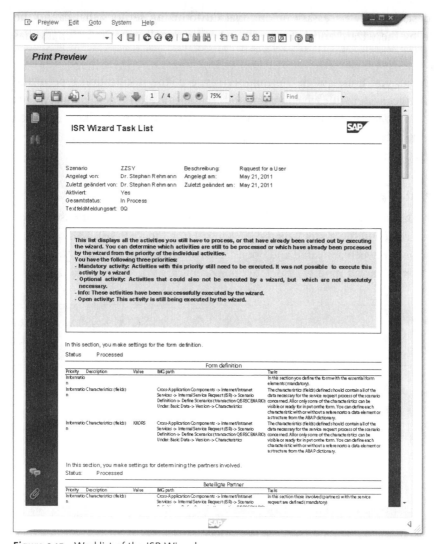

Figure 9.15 Worklist of the ISR Wizard

This list is also used for documentation purposes for the subwizards to track all entries in the wizards, because you can no longer process the scenario in the wizard after it has been activated. You can only process it in the actual IMG activities of the ISR. The worklist displays the current processing status of a partly completed and not activated scenario.

It also describes any necessary or optional Customizing settings that cannot be executed by the wizard and must be carried out manually after the scenario has been activated.

For example, you must assign the number range of the notification type in the required target system in each client and for each notification type separately. This setting cannot be transferred. The components of the ISR scenario that have to be programmed, for example, the implementation of the QISR1 BAdI, are also not generated by the ISR wizard.

ISR Wizard Overview

The SCENARIO LIST of the ISR wizard provides an overview of all of the scenarios that were created in the system via the ISR wizard (see Figure 9.16). This overview distinguishes between activated and open scenarios. In this overview, you can create new scenarios and modify or delete open scenarios.

ISR Wizard: Scenario List

☐ Create   ☞ Open   ⌷ Activate

List of Scenarios	Sc...	Status	Created By	Created ...	Task List	ISR Basic Customizing
▼ ☐ Open Scenarios						
· ⊕ Change of Address	A100	△ In Process	Dr. Stephan R...	22.12.2008	Task List ▦	
· ⊕ Vacation Request	ZH12	◙ Open	Dr. Stephan R...	22.12.2008	Task List ▦	
· ⊕ Request for Cost Center	ZZC1	☐ Processed	Dr. Stephan R...	22.12.2008	Task List ▦	
▼ ☐ Activated Scenarios						
· ▤ Request for System User	ZZSY	☐ Activated	Dr. Stephan R...	22.12.2008	Task List ▦	ISR Basic Customizing

☑ Scenario ZZSY activated successfully   SAP

Figure 9.16   List with Open and Activated Scenarios of the ISR Wizard

Because you cannot modify activated scenarios in the wizard, the ISR wizard cannot be called for activated scenarios. However, the WORKLIST is still available for activated scenarios. In addition, you can navigate directly to the BAdI Builder module for the QISR1 BAdI (see Section 9.6, Form Flow Logic) and basic ISR Customizing, DEFINE SCENARIOS IMG activity (see Section 9.4, Customizing and Programming a Scenario). Here, you can view which settings the system has transferred to the Customizing tables during the activation of the scenario and modify them, if necessary.

Activated Scenario

Only activated scenarios are in the basic ISR Customizing (Transaction QISRSCENARIO). These can no longer be modified or deleted with the ISR wizard but are still listed in the ISR wizard overview (Transaction QISRLIST).

Defining a Scenario

To define a scenario with the ISR wizard, use the following work steps as a guide. The *Request for System User* sample scenario (ZZSY) illustrates this process.

1. Create the ZZSY scenario with Transaction QISRCONF. Subwizards with the CLOCK icon can be executed, subwizards with the LOCK icon cannot. The system automatically determines the NOTIFIC TYPE number (see Figure 9.17).

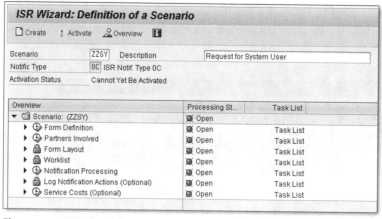

Figure 9.17 ISR Wizard for a New Scenario

2. Process all of the required subwizards until the entire scenario's status is PRO-CESSED. All subwizards have the same structure and usually provide a default value for plain scenarios. That means that you can create a scenario very quickly by accepting the default values in the subwizards.

The first step includes preliminary explanations on the subject area. The definition of the form is shown in Figure 9.18.

Figure 9.18 Step 1 of the Subwizard—Form Definition

3. Next, configure the settings. In the CHARACTERISTICS (FIELDS) step, you can specify the characteristics of the scenario (see Figure 9.19). If you know the reference of a characteristic in the Data Dictionary, enter it here. In Figure 9.19, SYSTEM USER, SYSTEM NAME, CLIENT, and PASSWORD are defined as characteristics.

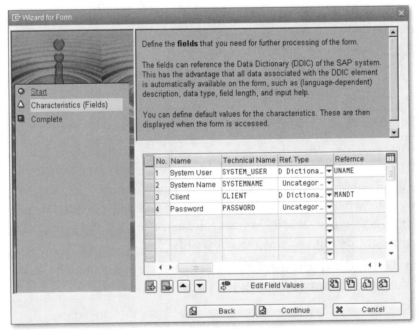

Figure 9.19 Step 2 of the Subwizard—Form Definition

4. The final step is to COMPLETE the subwizard. No specific settings are made in this step.

5. Perform the same steps for the other subwizards with an identical structure. After executing all relevant subwizards (see Figure 9.20), click on the ACTIVATE button.

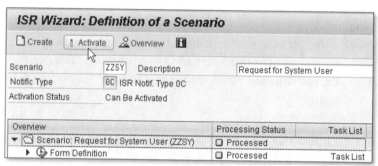

Figure 9.20 Activation of the ISR Scenario

6. Carry out the two additional tasks that are described in the worklist.

9.4 Customizing and Programming a Scenario

You have now created the framework of your ISR scenario using the ISR wizard. You can use the following IMG activities to postprocess and refine the scenario Customizing and scenario-specific programming of available BAdIs.

You can also create ISR scenarios without the wizard. If you are familiar with the ISR, or if you want to use your own or an already-existing ISR scenario as a template, use the following IMG activities.

9.4.1 General Details

The DEFINE SCENARIO IMG activity (Transaction QISRSCENARIO) provides central access to the Customizing of ISR scenarios. The Customizing of these scenarios is often referred to as basic ISR Customizing. It can be found via the menu path CROSS-APPLICATION COMPONENTS • INTERNET/INTRANET SERVICES • INTERNAL SERVICE REQUEST • SCENARIO DEFINITION.

Here, you can view a list of scenarios. Select a scenario, and go to BASIC DATA and VERSION. This brings you to the basic ISR Customizing. From here you can configure the settings for the following subject areas (see Figure 9.21):

▶ **General details**
The general details include the scenario description, the version, and the application (see Section 9.4.2, Application and Version).

▶ **Notification type**
The notification type includes the Customizing for the notification transactions of the (optional) approver and the processor and their functions. The notification type enables you to define the structure process steps of the service (see Section 9.4.3, Notification Type).

▶ **Entry type**
Here, you define the interactive Adobe form as the entry interface for the applicant (see Section 9.4.4, Entry Type).

▶ **Characteristics**
Characteristics enable you to define the input and display fields of the form and any additional fields for processing the service request (see Section 9.4.5, Characteristics).

▶ **Activities**
You define the activities for the roles involved in the process (such as processor and approver) that can be executed manually or automatically (see Section 9.4.6, Activities and Automatic Updates in Notifications, and Section 9.4.7, The Processor's Activities from the Form).

▶ **Processor determination**
If you want to use SAP Business Workflow, you can specify the responsible processor(s) or rules for a system-based determination of one or more processors (see Section 9.4.8, Processor Determination (BAdI QISR3) and Workflow).

▶ **Costs**
You can configure whether or not the internal costs of the service request should be determined in Controlling of the SAP ERP system (see Section 9.4.9, Service Costs and BAdI QISR2).

▶ **Form flow logic**
Here, you specify how the QISR1 BAdI affects the form flow logic. Programmable form flow logic is one of the central functions for ISR and is therefore described separately in Section 9.6, Form Flow Logic.

The central concept, *scenario*, comprises all Customizing settings and programming for a request service.

> **ISR Scenario**
>
> The technical identifier of the ISR scenario is a four-digit, alphanumeric code, ZZSY in this example. The customer namespace is defined by the first character and comprises all characters except for S and all digits from 0 to 9. The scenarios provided by SAP all start with S. The technical key field, SCENARIO, serves to identify the ISR scenario in the entire ISR framework.

Figure 9.21 Basic ISR Customizing

9.4.2 Application and Version

The scenario may consist of multiple versions, only one of which is active. The system automatically determines the version number (starting with 0), and you can define a validity period for every scenario version. This validity period of the version must be unique and must not overlap with the validity period of another version (see Figure 9.22). Provided scenarios are always version 0.

Figure 9.22 Two Versions of a Scenario

When the applicant starts the form, a validity date is provided through the VALIDITY_DATE parameter. This is then used to determine the valid version. You can also select the version via the VERSION parameter. However, this only works if the version is valid (local time). Section 9.7.2, Web Dynpro ABAP Component and Its Usage, provides more details on the transfer of parameters.

The application tends to group multiple scenarios and is only used by specific SAP ERP applications to control their defined properties with respect to the ISR. An application cannot be redefined.

The following SAP applications are currently available:

▶ **Standard Application** (no value in the APPLICATION field)
This is the application for standard scenarios of the ISR.

▶ **HCM Processes and Forms** (H in the APPLICATION field)
You can link a scenario of this application with a form scenario of HCM Administrative Services. For more information, navigate to the Customizing via the menu path PERSONNEL MANAGEMENT • HR ADMINISTRATIVE SERVICES • FORM/PROCESS CONFIGURATION • FORM CONFIGURATION.

▶ **Simplified Interactive Forms** (S in the APPLICATION field)
This is the application for simple forms, which you can integrate with the Express Planning application. You can find more details in the SAP Library via the menu path CROSS-APPLICATION COMPONENTS • EXPRESS PLANNING • PLANNING SERVICES • PLANNING SERVICES WITH CLOSE LINKAGE • ADOBE FORM SERVICE.

▶ **Manual Correspondence** (MC in the APPLICATION field)
This is the application for the public sector.

▶ **Tax and Revenue Management (TRM)** (T in the APPLICATION field)
This is the application for the public sector to process tax forms.

You need to enter an application only if the scenario should be integrated with a special SAP ERP application. Note that such scenarios can only function smoothly within these applications because certain functions are lost or added when specific applications are selected.

If you want to use an application, first get information on the specific documentation of the respective SAP ERP application. If you want to use a request scenario without a connection to an application, you can ignore this setting (see Figure 9.23). The application is usually not needed for customer-specific scenarios. Furthermore, the scenario description is entered here.

Figure 9.23 Access to the Basic ISR Customizing

9.4.3 Notification Type

The notification type is assigned to the scenario (see Figure 9.22). The notification type itself includes the Customizing for the different components of the notification. The Customizing for the notification type can be found via the menu path CROSS-APPLICATION COMPONENTS • INTERNET/INTRANET SERVICES • INTERNAL SERVICE REQUEST • SCENARIO DEFINITION • PREPARE GENERAL NOTIFICATION.

SAP provides a notification type for each subject area mentioned in Section 9.2.1, and comprises several scenarios. If the settings of one of these notification types are not sufficient, you should define your own notification type.

The following settings are linked to the notification type:

▶ Whether or not the scenario requires an approval

▶ The definition of the layout for the notification transaction that is used by the processor to process the service request

▶ The available activities

For simple scenarios, you can use the 01 ("ISR: Incurs Costs"; subject to approval) or 02 ("General"; not subject to approval) notification type. If you need to use your own notification type, you should copy the 01 or 02 notification type and set up your scenarios with your own notification type. The IMG activity can be found via the menu path CROSS-APPLICATION COMPONENTS • INTERNET/INTRANET SERVICES • INTERNAL SERVICE REQUEST • SCENARIO DEFINITION • PREPARE GENERAL NOTIFICATION • NOTIFICATION CREATION • NOTIFICATION TYPE • DEFINE NOTIFICATION TYPES. If your client does not include the 01 or 02 notification type, you can copy these settings from the 000 client using Transaction QISR_SM29.

You should use a provided notification type as a template for defining your own notification type. If you used the ISR wizard to generate an ISR scenario, the system has already generated a new notification type.

Number Range Assignment for the Notification Type

You must assign the notification type in every system to a number range. This Customizing cannot be transferred. Navigate to Transaction IW20 or the IMG via the menu path CROSS-APPLICATION COMPONENTS • INTERNET/INTRANET SERVICES • INTERNAL SERVICE REQUEST • SCENARIO DEFINITION • PREPARE GENERAL NOTIFICATION • NOTIFICATION CREATION • NOTIFICATION TYPE • DEFINE NUMBER RANGES.

If no number range has been assigned, the system outputs one of the following error messages when you send the form: "An error occurred whilst processing the notification" or "An unexpected error occurred during the processing...."

9.4.4 Entry Type

The entry type enables you to define which input screen the applicant should use to enter the service request (see Figure 9.21). Because SAP R/3 4.6C already provided the ISR the first time, there are many entry types available. As of SAP ERP 5.0, the actual recommended entry type is "Entry Using Adobe PDF." Therefore, additional entry types are listed but are not detailed further:

▶ Text Entry Only

▶ Entry Using Internet Transaction Server (ITS) Service

- ▸ Entry Using Notification Transaction
- ▸ Entry Using JavaServer Page (JSP) iView
- ▸ Entry Using Business Server Pages (BSP)
- ▸ Entry Using Adobe PDF

After selecting the ENTRY USING ADOBE PDF option, specify the name of the interactive form. The system then displays the corresponding interface of the form for information purposes. You can regenerate, modify, display, or test the Adobe form from this interface (see Section 9.5, Request Forms as Adobe Forms). These functions are made available in the form via buttons next to the field; you can navigate to Form Builder by clicking on the respective buttons. It is absolutely necessary that the form has some ISR-specific properties so that it can be used in the ISR framework. This is ensured when you process the form using the functions of the basic ISR Customizing.

For each scenario, use a specific form with its own interface. Otherwise, the form or interface may become unusable for other scenarios if you implement changes retroactively. Section 9.5, Request Forms as Adobe Forms, describes the form definition in more detail.

9.4.5   Characteristics

A main aspect of the definition of a service request is the definition of the characteristics (fields) that the service request requires. The necessary input or display fields in the request form should be mentioned first. They are defined as characteristics in the scenario Customizing. Basically, you must define every field as a characteristic that contains data, for example, fields that need to be populated by the applicant.

However, this also includes fields that are only required to display data from the backend or that are populated during the processing of the service. Fields that should not be available to all roles involved, but are required to further process the service request, must also be defined. For example, the form of a request for a system user does not require the technical field for the initial password. The value of this field is generated by the processor.

The characteristics of the ISR Customizing can also have a reference to the Data Dictionary or be freely defined as follows (see Figure 9.24):

▶ Characteristics with reference to a data element of the ABAP Dictionary

▶ Characteristics with reference to a structure of the ABAP Dictionary

▶ Uncategorized characteristics; they have an implicit type, `CHAR250`, without input or output conversion and can thus have a maximum length of 250 characters.

Figure 9.24 Scenario Customizing with the Characteristics List

The following basic conditions apply to the definition of characteristics:

▶ The names of the characteristic or structure fields must be unique within the scenario.

▶ The length of the characteristic or structure field names should not exceed 28 characters.

▶ The data length of the characteristic or structure field names should not exceed 250 characters.

▶ The names of the characteristic or structure fields must not start with "ISR_."

▶ The description of the characteristics can contain up to 40 characters.

In addition to these scenario-specific characteristics, you are provided with numerous default characteristics that can be automatically initialized and displayed in the request form. These include the general ISR fields (see Section 9.5.2, Structure of the Interface and Form Context).

General ISR Fields

For each scenario and form, the ISR framework provides a pool of so-called *general fields* that the system determines automatically at runtime. The list mainly contains address characteristics of the involved processors and technical values, such as scenario, the time of entry of the notification, and so on. You can find the complete list in the `QISRSGENERAL_PARAM` DDIC structure.

You can also use the characteristics definition to define additional functions:

- ▶ **Programmed input help**
  The characteristic should be provided with a programmed input help. To do this, you must define, for the characteristic, which technical name you use for the key value and description for the programming of the `SCENARIO_SET_ADDITIONAL_VALUES` BAdI method of the `QISR1` BAdI (see Section 9.6).

- ▶ **Long text formatting**
  The characteristic should be mapped as a long text field where plain text can be entered. In this case, select the LONG TEXT checkbox (see Figure 9.25). You can also use the `ISR_NEW_LONG_TEXT` standard ISR field (see Section 9.6.2, Default Values for the MODE, USER_COMMAND, and FORM_VIEW Parameters).

Figure 9.25 Customizing for Programmed Input Help and Long Text Formatting

Define the characteristics for the additional columns in the ISR status overview (see Figure 9.8) via THE ADDITIONAL DATA FOR SCENARIO, to which you can navigate via the Customizing of the button with the same description in the basic ISR Customizing. All of the characteristics are available for the definition of up to five columns (see Figure 9.26).

Figure 9.26 Characteristics for the Additional Columns of the Status Overview

9.4.6 Activities and Automatic Updates in Notifications

This section describes the activities that approvers or processors can perform within the scope of the notification transactions. Section 9.4.7, The Processor's Activities from the Form, introduces the activities that processors can carry out from the form. These two activity types involve different technical requirements and require different Customizing.

The Processor's or Approver's Activities in the Notification Transaction

You can distinguish between manual activities for the processor of the service request using notification transactions and activities for automatic updates without using notification transactions. The automatic activity is not performed or triggered by the processor but automatically executed by the system at a specific time.

To define the two activity types, click the ACTION BOX button in the basic ISR Customizing (see Figure 9.21). Activities are defined for each notification type and can be used within all scenarios assigned to this notification type. In the detail screen of the Customizing for the activities, you are provided with the following options:

▶ The CONTROL data settings are critical for the visibility and usability of the activity within the notification transaction.

   ▶ SCENARIO controls the visibility of the activity in the respective scenarios that belong to the notification type.

   ▶ SORT NUMBER controls the order in which the activities are provided in the activity bar of the notification transactions.

   ▶ USAGE controls the visibility of the activities in the notification; default value: ANY VIEW (CREATE, CHANGE, DISPLAY).

   ▶ AND controls the visibility in notifications and/or tasks; default value: NOTIFICATION AND TASK.

   ▶ DOCUMENTATION defines the execution of an activity to see if the notification should document this. (Tip: For the sake of simplicity, select NONE initially.)

▶ In the FUNCTION area, you can define the name of the function module that is processed when the activity is called. The provided scenarios contain some examples of such function modules.

   ▶ In the USER INTERFACE area, you specify the icon and the text that is displayed in the activity bar.

   ▶ In the RULES area, you define the order and dependencies for the execution of the activities.

Define one of the following generic function modules as a FUNCTION if the activity is programmed with the "ISR: Execution of a Function in the Action Box" BAdI. The FUNCTION key word of the activity is required for the implementation of the QISR4 BAdI.

- ISR_ACTIVITY_EXECUTE_TASKDOC

- ISR_ACTIVITY_EXECUTE_ACTIONDOC

- ISR_ACTIVITY_EXECUTE

All three modules can be used the same way and call the same method, EXECUTE_FUNCTION, of the QISR4 BAdI. It depends solely on the specification in the DOCUMENTATION field which function module you use. You can use ISR_ACTIVITY_EXECUTE if DOCUMENTATION = NONE is selected.

Programming an Activity

The function module of an activity must have a defined interface. Because the interface is designed for the requirements of the notification, it makes sense to enter the ISR_ACTIVITY_EXECUTE function module and perform the actual programming in the QISR4 BAdI. The benefit of this approach is that the necessary data for executing the activity are provided in the ISR-typical form for transfer structures. Thus, you can program the activity in the same way as the form flow logic in the QISR1 BAdI.

Activities for Automatic Updates

If you want to use automatic updates, click on the AUTOMATIC UPDATE button. Basically, all activities of the scenario are available for automatic updates. Only activities that are follow-up activities or dependent activities, that is, that require a previous activity, are not provided. You define whether the applicant or the approver performs individual activities for automatic updates, that is, either by submitting or approving the request.

Programming an Activity in the QISR4 BAdI

The automatic activity must be executed without interaction in the backend, that is, without being output or displayed on dynpros. The call should be implemented via the QISR4 BAdI through BAPIs or SELECT commands, for example, and no error message should be output via the RETURN parameter.

The interface of the EXECUTE_FUNCTION method in the QISR4 BAdI provides the corresponding parameters, which are listed in Table 9.2.

Parameter	Type	Description
FLT_VAL	Importing	Scenario name
QMART	Importing	Notification type
FUNCTION	Importing	Key of a function of the activity bar (action box) from the ISR Customizing
RETURN	Exporting	Error message
GENERAL_DATA	Changing	General data
SPECIAL_DATA	Changing	Data of the scenario-dependent fields

Table 9.2 Interface of the QISR4 BAdI

Depending on the selected function (FUNCTION), the required activity is usually executed after the evaluation of the scenario. Let's look at a programming example: The MC1 function creates a cost center via a BAPI. In addition, this function should be executable as an automatic function. The MC3 function executes a transaction and therefore cannot be used as the automatic activity; nevertheless, both functions can be programmed in one implementation (see Listing 9.1). The correct application of the functions must be ensured in the ISR Customizing.

```
METHOD if_ex_qisr4~execute_function.
  DATA: ls_change_data    TYPE fcom_isr_cc,
        lt_return         TYPE TABLE OF bapiret2,
        lt_costcenter     TYPE TABLE OF
                          bapi0012_ccinputlist.

* move form data to local structure
  CALL FUNCTION 'ISR_SPECIAL_DATA_TO_STRUC'
      EXPORTING
          it_special_data = special_data
      CHANGING
          cs_data       = ls_change_data.

  CASE function.
* Create cost center automatically
    WHEN 'MC1'.
* move special data to BAPI structure
*    ...
* Call BAPI to create Cost Center
      CALL FUNCTION 'BAPI_COSTCENTER_CREATEMULTIPLE'
```

```
      EXPORTING

        controllingarea = ls_change_data-co_area
        testrun         = space
      TABLES
        costcenterlist  = lt_costcenter
        return          = lt_return.
    IF lt_return[] IS INITIAL.
      COMMIT WORK.
  ENDIF.

*  Call transaction to change cost center
    WHEN 'MC2'.
      SET PARAMETER ID:
        'CAC' FIELD ls_change_data-co_area,
        'KOS' FIELD ls_change_data-costcenter.
      CALL TRANSACTION 'KS02' AND SKIP FIRST SCREEN.
        WHEN OTHERS.
  ENDCASE.
ENDMETHOD.
```

Listing 9.1 Programming the QISR4 BAdI for Activities

9.4.7 The Processor's Activities from the Form

The processor of a request can carry out multiple activities from the form using the corresponding buttons. The activities are provided as buttons (see Figure 9.27) in the service request (above the form) and can be hidden and displayed via the HIDE ACTIVITY LIST link.

Figure 9.27 The Processor's Activity List above the Form

Define the activities in the Customizing of the Report Launchpad. These activities can be useful when the processor processes the service request only in SAP NetWeaver Portal and does not use notification transactions.

Technical requirements for using the activities are SAP ERP 6.0 SP 12 and SAP NetWeaver Portal. For more information on these requirements, refer to SAP Note 1103969. In addition, you also need one of the following Web Dynpro applications: QISR_FORM or QISR_UI_FORM_DISPLAY_ONLY.

The form is called via the URL parameter, IFV=P. You can also set the FORM_VIEW = ISR_PROCESS container parameter in the workflow. The parameterized URL for a request with the notification number, 000600000110, of the SRCR scenario that is started by the processor in the CHANGE mode, may look as follows:

http://<server>:<port>/sap/bc/webdynpro/sap/qisr_ui_form?sap-language=DE&SCENARIO=SRCR&MODE=CHANGE&NOTIF_NO=000600000110&IFV=P.

You can configure the activities in the Customizing of the Report Launchpad using Transaction LPD_CUST.

1. To use the Report Launchpad correctly, the LPD_EXPERT parameter of your system user must be set to 'X'.

2. Call Transaction LPD_CUST and create a new launchpad.

3. The role must always be QISR. The instance corresponds to your scenario.

4. Select the ACTION LAUNCHPAD flag (see Figure 9.28). In the launchpad itself, you can define activities with various application categories.

Figure 9.28 Customizing of a New Launchpad for Activities

5. Figure 9.29 shows simple examples for application categories. For a detailed explanation of the Report Launchpad, refer to the corresponding documentation.

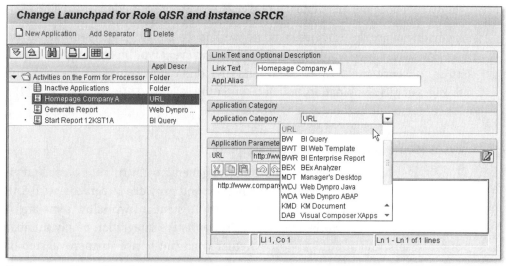

Figure 9.29 Customizing for the Activities of the Form

Analogous to the activities of the notification transaction from Section 9.2.5, Processor Role, or Section 9.4.6, you can also use the QISR4 BAdI.

1. To do this, define an activity with the TRANSACTION application category.

2. Include a variant of the QISRACTIVITY report in the launchpad with a customer-specific transaction.

3. The ISR framework automatically transfers the QMNUM and SCENARIO parameters for the notification number and the scenario.

4. Use the report variant to control the FUNCTION key value of the selected activity. Use Transaction QISRACTIVITY as an orientation point.

9.4.8 Processor Determination (BAdI QISR3) and Workflow

There are several ways to determine the responsible processor or approver of the service request. The use of SAP Business Workflow enables you to have the system automatically determine the processor.

If you do not use SAP Business Workflow, the processor can find the service request he is responsible for via the worklist. To do this, the processor can use Transaction IQS8, which is the variant with the lowest implementation effort. However, the disadvantage is that the processor must actively search for his requests. In this case, the system does not ensure that all service requests are provided.

If you do not use the provided standard workflow templates and if you want to use your own workflow template, you must create an event type linkage for the BUS7051 object category, the CREATED event, and its workflow pattern. For all event type linkages of this combination, you must enter the QGN01_EVENT_NOTIF_CREATED_ISR function module as the CHECK FUNCTION.

WS03100019 Standard Workflow Template

The BUS7051 business object is responsible for generating the runtime object (previously referred to as *notification*) of the request and provides integration with SAP Business Workflow. You can use the WS03100019 standard workflow template of the notification. This workflow template supports the integration of any number of processors, and you can choose whether you want to use an approval step or not.

In the Customizing of the workflow, you must activate the event type linkage for the BUS7051 object category. You can define the responsible processors either directly in the Customizing of the workflow or use the rules of the workflow (Transaction PFAC) to have the system determine them automatically. For approvals, the workflow template only supports the variant with Backend Transaction IQS22.

WS31000009 ISR Workflow Template

If you want to perform *more* than one approval step, the standard workflow template of the notification is not sufficient. As an alternative, you can use the WS31000009 workflow template provided with the ISR framework, which also supports the two request processing options of the approver, that is, in the SAP ERP backend system and in the portal (see Section 9.2.4, Approver Role). This template must be defined in the basic Customizing of the ISR in ADDITIONAL DATA FOR SCENARIO (see Figure 9.30).

Scenario-Specific Workflow Pattern	
Create Notification	WS31000009
Notific. in Process	
Assignment of Processors	
Activation of Event Linkage	

Figure 9.30 Advanced ISR Customizing for the Workflow

You can call the event type linkage in the same screen via the ACTIVATION OF EVENT LINKAGE button. The names of the processors or workflow rules for the automatic determination of processors or approvers must be defined in the ISR Customizing (see Figure 9.31). To do this, click on the ASSIGNMENT OF PROCESSORS button. You should use the WS31000009 ISR workflow template because it is more flexible and can be configured more easily.

In addition to the central Customizing, if you use the WS31000009 workflow template, the current workflow container can be changed for every processor determination by means of a rule for a scenario-specific implementation of the QISR3 BAdI. The rule enables you to determine the responsibilities based on the form data, and the QISR3 BAdI also enables you to control the processor determination. This BAdI has only one method.

Figure 9.31 Processor Assignment to ISR Roles

Table 9.3 describes the interface of the single method, CONTAINER_FOR_ACTOR_DET_FILL. The IS_VIQMEL, IS_TQ80 and IS_VIQMSM parameters provide information on the current notification at runtime, IT_SPECIAL_DATA contains the form data. You can now use these data to adapt the CT_ACT_CONTAINER workflow container. IT_CONT_DEF contains the list of the container elements from the workflow template. Thus, you can evaluate the container content using a workflow rule for the processor determination.

Parameter	Type	Description
IT_CONT_DEF	Importing	Workflow container elements
IS_VIQMEL	Importing	Notification
IS_TQ80	Importing	Notification type
IS_VIQMSM	Importing	Task
IT_SPECIAL_DATA	Importing	Form data
CT_ACT_CONTAINER	Tables	Workflow container

Table 9.3 Interface of the "CONTAINER_FOR_ACTOR_DET_FILL" Method

In this context, let's look at a simple example that describes the processor determination with a workflow rule using the QISR3 BAdI. The processor of the request is determined via the 95000140 rule (see Figure 9.32). According to this rule, all requests of the SMC1 scenario with the characteristic value A* to L* of the persons responsible for a cost center should be assigned to processor Smith.

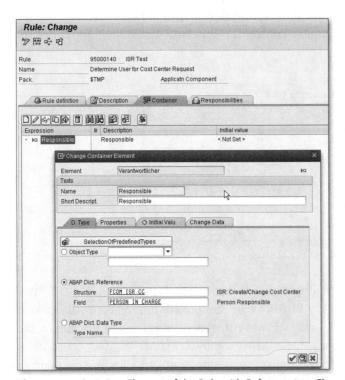

Figure 9.32 Container Element of the Rule with Reference to a Characteristic

If the characteristic value is within the interval M* to Z*, the processor MSS1 is determined (see Figure 9.33). This already works without the QISR3 BAdI. In the BAdI, for example, you can still change the person responsible for a cost center for specific criteria. In this context, you should query the current ISR scenario because this BAdI implementation is used for all scenarios that deploy the so-called work-flow templates (see Listing 9.2).

Name	Priority	Status	Code	Assigned a...	Assigned u...
▼ 🏠 M bis Z		☐ Res...	M bis Z		
· 📄 🗐 Peter Smith			Smith	11/13/2006	12/31/2030
▼ 🏠 A bis L		☐ Res...	A bis L		
· 📄 🗐 MSS1			MSS1	08/26/2008	12/31/2030

Figure 9.33 Definition of the Responsibilities of the Rule

```
METHOD if_ex_qisr3~container_for_actor_det_fill.
DATA: ls_change_data    TYPE fcom_isr_cc,
      ls_act_container TYPE swcont.

* Only Scenario SMC1
  CHECK is_viqmel-auswirk = 'SMC1'.

* Form data in local structure
  CALL FUNCTION 'ISR_SPECIAL_DATA_TO_STRUC'
    EXPORTING
      it_special_data = it_special_data
    CHANGING
      cs_data         = ls_change_data.

* Adaptation of the WF container
  IF ls_change_data-department = 'A123'.
    READ TABLE ct_act_container INTO ls_act_container
        WITH KEY element = 'PERSON_INCHARGE'.
    ls_act_container-value = 'STANDARD_RESPONSIBLE'.
    MODIFY ct_act_container FROM ls_act_container.
  ENDIF.
ENDMETHOD.
```

Listing 9.2 Programming of the QISR3 BAdI

9.4.9 Service Costs and BAdI QISR2

The ISR integrates with the Overhead Cost Controlling function of SAP ERP 6.0. This function allows for a cost-related control of the available service requests in the enterprise. If a department in your enterprise provides one or more services to employees, you can internally allocate the overhead costs that were incurred in this department.

The ISR provides three options for cost determination:

▶ **Template allocation of Easy Cost Planning**
Easy Cost Planning enables you to link a complex cost determination process with the service request. The options and functions of this tool are not explained in detail here because this would go beyond the scope of this chapter.

▶ **Estimated costs**
Estimated costs result in an entry of the costs into the notification. However, these costs are not transferred to Overhead Cost Controlling.

▶ **Price list**
The price list determines the cost of a request. This section describes the price list procedure.

Costs are automatically posted to a cost object, such as an internal order or cost center of the applicant, when the notification that was created with the ISR is completed. The cost center of this service department accepts these costs as an activity based on a price that you can define.

You can implement the automatic cost determination by configuring only a few settings (see Figure 9.34):

1. In the basic ISR Customizing, select the THE SCENARIO INCURS COSTS flag.

2. Then, enter the CONTROLLING AREA.

3. Use the PRICE LIST to determine the cost sender. To do this, select the PRICE LIST flag and click on EDIT PRICE LIST.

4. In the price list, define the combination of the cost center and the activity type of the service provider (for example, cost center of the service department). Enter the "costs" of a service request into the ISR Price field.

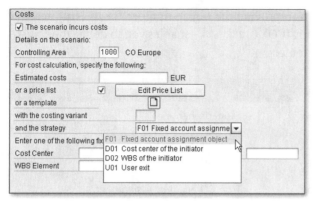

Figure 9.34 Basic ISR Customizing for Service Costs

5. You can also create multiple prices. The DEFAULT flag controls which price is used (see Figure 9.35).

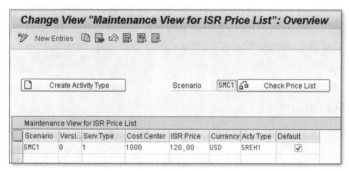

Figure 9.35 Definition of the Price List

6. Determine the cost collector (strategy) by selecting the *account assignment object*. The following options are available:

   ▶ The cost center of the applicant, which is determined from the HR-specific user master data.

   ▶ The WBS element of the applicant, which is determined from the HR-specific user master data.

   ▶ You must enter an internal order, a cost center, or a WBS element.

   ▶ A user exit, namely, the BAdI implementation of the QISR2 BAdI. Table 9.4 describes the interface of the ISR_ACCOUNT_ASSIGNMENT_GET method of the QISR2 BAdI. The programming process is similar to that of the QISR1 BAdI.

OBJNR_REAL enables you to provide the object number for the true account assignment in Controlling (CO). OBJNR_STAT enables you to define the statistical account assignment object.

Parameter	Type	Description
FLT_VAL	Importing	Scenario name
GENERAL_DATA	Importing	General ISR data
SPECIAL_DATA	Importing	Form data
OBJNR_REAL	Exporting	True CO account assignment
OBJNR_STAT	Exporting	Statistical CO account assignment

Table 9.4 "ISR_ACCOUNT_ASSIGNMENT_GET" Method

7. After defining your own notification type, check to see if an implementation for the NOTIF_EVENT_POST BAdI with the notification type of your scenario exists. If there is no such implementation, create a new one with your notification type as the filter value. You should use the ISR_CHECK_AT_POST implementation as the template.

9.4.10 Testing the Scenario

The TEST function next to the FORM field in the basic ISR Customizing (see Figure 9.22) enables you to quickly call the form to check any changes made to the form or the Customizing.

1. To do this, you must navigate to the ADDITIONAL DATA FOR SCENARIO Customizing and enter the corresponding server via the SERVER button.

2. If there is no entry for the entry type in the Web (A – ENTRY USING ADOBE PDF), create a new entry.

3. Enter the URL for the server into the SERVER FOR CALL THE ISR FORMS field as follows: *http://<myserver>:<port>/sap/bc/webdynpro/sap/*.

   Replace the *<myserver>* placeholder with your server, and enter the corresponding port for *<port>*.

4. Furthermore, implement the settings from SAP Note 1110677 for activating the testability with the Web Dynpro ABAP component of the ISR in the Customizing.

5. To test the Adobe form, click the TEST button. The system automatically inserts the necessary URL parameters (for example, the scenario). The form for creating a request is started in a browser window.

6. The `ISR_PROCESS_EVENT` function module is another alternative for testing. It enables you to test all backend settings without an Adobe form: the scenario Customizing, the Workflow, and the BAdI implementation. Section 9.7.4 provides a detailed description of the function module.

9.5   Request Forms as Adobe Forms

The interactive Adobe form within the ISR framework must meet specific technical requirements with regard to the interface, the context of the form, and the individual screen elements. Therefore, the basic ISR Customizing provides additional definition and generation aids.

9.5.1   Specific Properties

You define the characteristics in the ISR Customizing as described in Section 9.4.5, Characteristics. The fields in the Adobe form, however, are bound to the context of the form and not to the Customizing of the ISR. So how can you ensure that the form contains the appropriate characteristics?

The interface and the context of the form must meet specific criteria. The options provided by Form Builder for defining the form interface cannot be fully used within the ISR. The reason for this restriction is that the definition of the form context is outsourced to the ISR Customizing. This means that the interface and context must correspond to the characteristics of the Customizing.

The following conditions apply to the usage of interfaces in the ISR:

▶ You can use only DDIC interfaces. It is not possible to use XML interfaces.

▶ The interface must have an ISR-specific data structure.

▶ Only import parameters are used.

▶ It is not possible to link single elements to specific DDIC elements or advanced Form Builder functions. Initializations and form routines are not supported, for example.

▶ You must program data initializations in the appropriate implementation of the QISR1 BAdI (see Section 9.6, Form Flow Logic).

The following conditions apply to the usage of forms in the ISR:

▶ The layout type must be ZERO CLIENT INSTALLATION (ZCI) LAYOUT.

▶ The data context has an ISR-specific data structure and must be copied from the interface on a one-to-one basis.

▶ To use programmed input helps, the script of the screen elements from the ISR library is mandatory. The same holds true for the usage of form events and standardized approval forms.

ZCI in the ISR

Along with the introduction of ZCI technology, all of the provided Adobe forms of the ISR were set from the previous ACF technology to ZCI. The delivery in SAP ERP 6.0 was implemented in SP 5 (see SAP Note 947675). You should use the ZCI Layout type for customer-specific forms within the ISR.

The ZCI technology is described in detail in Section 8.5.2.

9.5.2 Structure of the Interface and Form Context

The ISR framework ensures that the contents of the fields of the Adobe form are transferred to the backend and that field contents that are determined in the backend are correctly mapped in the form. Here, it is critical that the form context meets the ISR criteria. The context only corresponds to the assigned interface. If you use only the functions of the ISR Customizing to generate new and adapt existing forms, this requirement is automatically met.

To ensure correct data binding of the Adobe form at runtime, every characteristic must use the generic table types of the ISR in the context of the Adobe form (see Figure 9.36):

▶ **QISR_TAB_TYPE_DATE**
Characteristics of the date type (DDIC data type: DATS).

▶ **QISR_TAB_TYPE_TEXT**
Characteristics for plain text.

▶ **QISR_TAB_TYPE**
All other characteristics.

Figure 9.36 Interface and Context of an Adobe Form in the ISR

All three table types have the same data structure: `<characteristic>-<DATA>-<FIELD>`. The `<characteristic>` placeholder stands for the name of the characteristic from the ISR Customizing. Due to the generic programming of the ISR Web Dynpro component, this tabular data structure is necessary and must not be changed. The following ISR-specific structures constitute the exception to this rule because they exist in all forms and interfaces of the ISR and thus do not have to be generated in the Web Dynpro component.

▶ **General ISR data** (structure: `GENERAL_DATA`)
The structure provides information on the processors involved and technical information (see Section 9.4.5, Characteristics).

▶ **Form parameters** (structure: `CONTROL_PARAM`)
The structure provides technical information that can be used for script programming. The attributes correspond to those from Section 9.6.2. The `ISR_REVIEW` attribute indicates whether the user is in the second step (CHECK AND SEND) of the request form, and the `ISR_CONFIRMATION` attribute provides the information

that the user is currently in the third and last step (COMPLETED) of the request form.

▶ **UI attributes of a field** (structure: UI_ATTRIBUTES)
This structure contains the layout information from the QISR1 BAdI.

Creating the Context and the Interface

You should only use the GENERATE AND CHANGE ADOBE FORM functions of the ISR Customizing to adapt the context of a form. The interface is automatically modified.

9.5.3 Generating Adobe Forms from Characteristics

During the generation of an Adobe form, the system automatically copies the characteristics of the scenario to the interface and context of the form. For the creation of an Adobe form, a number of configurations are possible:

▶ **You have defined an ISR scenario with characteristics, but the form has not been created yet.**
You generate the form via the GENERATE button (see Figure 9.37). You then have the following options:

  ▶ A blank form

  ▶ A form in the SAP standard (the ISR_FORM_STANDARD form is used as the template)

  ▶ The form with the template of another scenario

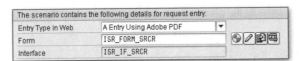

Figure 9.37 Functions for the Generation and Processing of an Adobe Form in the Basic ISR Customizing

In Form Builder, you then design the layout. To define fields with ISR-specific script programming (see Section 9.5.5, ISR Library—Special Screen Elements), use the ISR library—at least at the beginning. Finally, generate the data binding between the layout elements and the context fields. If you use Form Builder to define new fields in the layout for which no characteristics exist, Form Builder asks you when you exit it whether these characteristics should be created (see Section 9.5.4, Generating New Characteristics from the Form).

▶ **You have defined an ISR scenario with characteristics and have a PDF form, but no Form Builder form.**

In this case, you can perform the same steps as described previously. The only difference is that, after the generation, you have to load the PDF into Form Builder and then edit the layout. Then you implement the data binding.

▶ **You have a form defined in Form Builder. This form has the appropriate form fields in the layout but does not have the appropriate context for the ISR.**

There are two "useful" alternatives for customizing the form for the ISR:

▶ If you have defined the corresponding characteristics in the ISR Customizing, enter the name of the form into the ISR Customizing and click on the CHANGE ADOBE FORM button. This brings you to Form Builder, and the system generates the appropriate interface and context. Note that the previous context is overwritten. Now, you need to manually implement the data binding between the layout and context.

▶ If you have not defined the corresponding characteristics in the ISR Customizing yet, enter the name of the form into the ISR Customizing, and click on the IMPORT FORM FIELDS button. Now the system reads the technical names of all layout elements of the form that can be used for data input and generates the characteristics in the ISR Customizing. In addition, it automatically generates the context and the data binding in the form (see Section 9.5.4).

What Happens During Form Generation?

During the generation of a form, the system generates the Workbench object of a form and of an ABAP Dictionary-based interface (DDIC). XML-based interfaces cannot be used within the ISR.

You can specify the technical name of the form and interface in the fields of the ISR Customizing with the same name in advance. You can freely select the name within the framework of the customer namespace of Workbench objects. If you do not specify the names, the system automatically determines these names. To do this, the following logic is used in the customer system; xxxx refers to the four-digit name of the scenario:

▶ Form: ZISR_FORM_xxxx

▶ Interface: ZISR_IF_xxxx

The system automatically copies the characteristics of the scenario that are defined in the ISR Customizing to the DDIC interface and context of the form. The standard fields described in Section 9.5.2 are copied in the same way.

9.5.4 Generating New Characteristics from the Form

If you first define a form without having created an ISR scenario with characteristics in advance, or if you have defined new fields in the layout, you can proceed as follows to make the form usable in the ISR.

1. Call Form Builder via the CHANGE ADOBE FORM button. If you have defined new fields in the layout, these fields are automatically copied as characteristics to the scenario Customizing when you exit Form Builder. During this process, the system automatically defines the data binding of the new fields in the layout. To achieve this, confirm the corresponding dialog box.

2. You can also implement this at a later stage. Click on the corresponding button to carry out the IMPORT FORM FIELDS function in Customizing. The system then uses the technical names of all screen elements that are defined in the form to generate the corresponding characteristics. In addition, it also adapts the corresponding interface and context in the form. Finally, the system generates the data binding between the context elements and the corresponding screen elements of the form; so far, everything has been done automatically. Answer YES in the dialog box to confirm activation of the form.

3. The generated characteristics are declared as UNCATEGORIZED. Therefore, you need to postprocess the Customizing of the characteristics, for example, to create the reference to the Data Dictionary for individual characteristics.

4. If you created the form outside the scenario Customizing, navigate to the Customizing and enter the required form into the FORM field. Then, click on the IMPORT FORM FIELDS button to the right of the input field.

9.5.5 ISR Library—Special Screen Elements

You should use the screen elements from the ISR library for forms with ZCI Layout (see Figure 9.38). In this context, the script is important and not the layout, which you can customize as required.

The library is provided with the SAP GUI. SAP Note 947633 contains current updates for the ISR library, and the entire ISR library is documented in SAP Note 741381.

The advantage—or preferably, the requirement—of the ISR library is that an ISR-specific script (FormCalc or JavaScript) with specific functions is already assigned to the individual elements. For example, if you plan to implement programmed input helps for a form field, you must use this script.

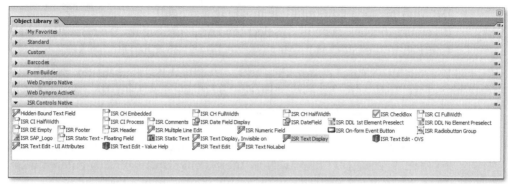

Figure 9.38 ISR Library for Forms with the "ZCI Layout" Type

The critical special screen elements with a specific script include:

- **ISR DDL 1st Element Preselect** (input help)
  The first value pair of the programmed value list is automatically copied for the field value. Section 9.6.3 contains a programming example for a dropdown list box.

- **ISR DDL No Element Preselect** (input help)
  The field can only be populated via a manual selection from the dropdown list box.

- **ISR On-form Event Button** (button)
  Here, the system generates a button with an event. This button can be evaluated in the QISR1 BAdI.

- **ISR Text Edit — Object Value Selector (OVS)** (input help)
  You define the input and output fields of the OVS in Customizing Transaction QISRSCENARIO_OVS. You program this input help in the SET_ADDITIONAL_DATA method of your BAdI implementation, QISR1.

- **ISR Text Edit — Value Help** (input help)
  SAP Note 1035630 provides detailed information on this DDIC-related input help.

- **ISR Text Edit — UI Attributes** (script template)
  SAP Note 925657 contains details on how to control layout properties of individual fields, such as mandatory field, visibility, and ready-for-input status using the QISR1 BAdI.

▶ **ISR Multiple-Line Edit** (multiple-line long text field)
If you use this field, you must select the Long Text flag for the respective characteristic in the ISR Customizing (see Section 9.4.5, Characteristics).

You can also bind the form field to the standard ISR element for comments,
ISR_NEW_LONG_TEXT, from the form context (see Figure 9.39). Here, every newly
entered text is transferred to the subject long text of the notification. It can be
viewed and changed in Transaction IQS22. In this case, you should define a second long text field and bind it to the second standard ISR element for comments
on the ISR_LONG_TEXT display. Now the system displays already-entered texts.
The form in Figure 9.39 shows an example for both long text fields.

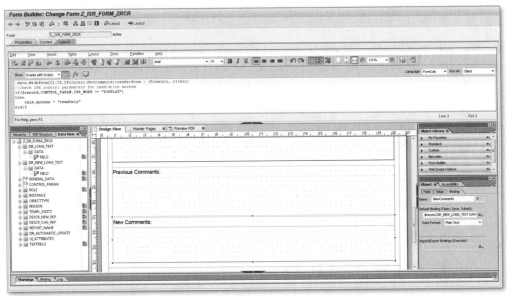

Figure 9.39 Usage of the Standard Long Text Fields "ISR_NEW_LONG_TEXT" and
"ISR_LONG_TEXT" in Form Builder

The following sections introduce simple examples of ISR-specific scripts.

Using the Script to Control the Ready-for-Input Status of Fields

You can easily make the fields editable by adapting the script programming of
individual fields in Form Builder. The standard ISR script for controlling the ready-
for-input status is defined in the ready:form - (formcalc,client) event of a field
(see Listing 9.3).

```
//Check ISR control parameters for read/write access
if($record.CONTROL_PARAM.ISR_MODE == "DISPLAY" |
   $record.CONTROL_PARAM.ISR_FORM_VIEW =="ISR_APPROVE" )
then
        this.access = "readOnly"
endif
```

Listing 9.3 Script for the Ready-for-Input Status

For example, if you remove the query for equality with the ISR_APPROVE event, the corresponding field is ready for input for the approver.

If you have complex requirements for the layout properties, use the dynamic script of the ISR TEXT EDIT – UI ATTRIBUTES script template from the ISR library.

Using the Script to Generate an Event

You can link a button to an event by modifying the script programming of the button. If you click on this button, the BAdI implementation of the QISR1 BAdI is executed, and the system transfers the EVENT of the form to the USER_COMMAND parameter. The standard ISR script for the name of the event is defined in the mouseDown – (FormCalc, client) event of the button (see Listing 9.4).

```
//Set ISR_EVENT for BAdI processing in backend
$record.CONTROL_PARAM.ISR_EVENT = "CUSTOM_EVENT"
```

Listing 9.4 Script for the CUSTOM_EVENT Event

You must also define the mechanism of the event of the Adobe form in the click – (JavaScript, client) event of the field (see Listing 9.5).

```
//Trigger call to backend for
//BAdI user command processing
ContainerFoundation_JS.SendMessageToContainer(event.
  target, "submit", "", "", "", "");
this.access = "readOnly"
```

Listing 9.5 Script for an Event

Enhanced Input Help

SAP ERP 6.0 SP 12 (SAP_APPL) enables you to provide an enhanced input help (Object Value Selector (OVS)) to one or more fields in an Adobe form in the ISR.

SAP Note 906950 provides detailed information on the OVS. You must carry out the following steps to implement an enhanced input help.

1. **Corresponding ISR Customizing**
   You need to define the attributes for the input help in Customizing Transaction QISRSCENARIO_OVS (see Figure 9.40). Select a scenario and navigate to CHARACTERISTICS WITH ENHANCED SEARCH HELP. Define a characteristic as the start field for an input help and check the ACTIVE flag.

Figure 9.40 Customizing of the Enhanced Input Help

Define the input and output fields for the selected start field (you can use all characteristics of the scenario), and specify which type and position the respective field should have:

- B INPUT FIELD AND OUTPUT FIELD
- S INPUT FIELD FOR SEARCH ONLY
- O OUTPUT ONLY

Output fields can be hidden. That means the results list of the input help does not display the field. After the selection of the user in the dialog box of the input help, the value of this field is transferred to the form just like the other selected values.

2. **Screen element in the form**
   Use the ISR TEXT EDIT – OVS or ISR TEXT EDIT – VALUE HELP screen element from the ISR library for enhanced input help.

   Note that you need to enter the corresponding field name in the `Click` action handler in addition to the common data binding and the script of the input help. Find the following line:

```
var fieldName = "FieldNameToBeReplaced";
```

Replace the `FieldNameToBeReplaced` variable with the field name, which you can find in the lower-level Binding tab of the Object tab. Here, the field name is listed as Name.

If the system is supposed to automatically check the value entered in the SAP ERP backend system after the user has made an entry in the input help, insert the following lines in the `Exit` event of the screen element via the script editor of the Adobe form (see Listing 9.6):

```
xfa.record.CONTROL_PARAM.ISR_EVENT.value =
  "<EVENT_NAME>";
xfa.record.GENERAL_DATA.HEADER.EXT_REF_NUMBER.value =
  "VALUE_HELP";
```

Listing 9.6 Additional Script for the Input Help

Replace the `<EVENT_NAME>` placeholder with any event name. You can also use the `CHECK` standard event.

3. **Programming the input help**
   You can program the input help in the scenario-specific implementation of the `QISR1` BAdI in the `SCENARIO_SET_ADDITIONAL_VALUES` or `INT_SERVICE_REQUEST_INIT` method.

   Insert all output values of the output fields in the `ADDITIONAL_DATA` transfer table. This data are then used as the basis of the search. Based on the input, the system delivers the results list to the OVS search fields as a subset of the entries from the `ADDITIONAL_DATA` table at runtime. The table contains the following fields:

   ▶ `FIELDINDEX` field: counter, starting with 1

   ▶ `FIELDNAME` field: characteristic name

   ▶ `FIELDVALUE` field: Value

4. **Tips for the implementation in the QISR1 BAdI**
   The sorting of the rows in the results list is controlled via the FIELDINDEX counter. In the `FIELDNAME` field, you must enter the exact characteristic name, without additional ending, such as `_KEY`, as it is required for the programming of the dropdown list box (see Section 9.6.3, Programming Examples).

Other fields in the form can be programmed as dropdown list boxes. The ISR_CUST_SCENARIO_VALHLP_GET function module provides all of the information from the Customizing of the enhanced input help.

Listing 9.7 illustrates a programming example of the SCENARIO_SET_ ADDITIONAL_VALUES method from the QISR1 BAdI for an enhanced input help. The PERSON characteristic is defined as an OVS, and the maximum results list consists of the FIRSTNAME, LASTNAME, and TITLE output fields. The entries in the ADDITIONAL_DATA table could look as follows; the list contains two data records.

```
METHOD if_ex_qisr1~SCENARIO_SET_ADDITIONAL_VALUES
  DATA: ls_additional_value TYPE qisrsspecial_param.
  ls_additional_value-fieldindex = 1.
  ls_additional_value-fieldname  = ‚FIRSTNAME'.
  ls_additional_value-fieldvalue = ‚Jim'.
  APPEND ls_additional_value TO additional_data.
  ls_additional_value-fieldname  = ‚LASTNAME'.
  ls_additional_value-fieldvalue = ‚Smith' .
  APPEND ls_additional_value TO additional_data.
  ls_additional_value-fieldname  = ‚TITLE'.
  ls_additional_value-fieldvalue = ‚Mr.'.
  APPEND ls_additional_value TO additional_data.
  CLEAR ls_additional_value.

  ls_additional_value-fieldindex = 2.
  ls_additional_value-fieldname  = ‚FIRSTNAME'.
  ls_additional_value-fieldvalue = ‚Linda'.
  APPEND ls_additional_value TO additional_data.
  ls_additional_value-fieldname  = ‚LASTNAME'.
  ls_additional_value-fieldvalue = ‚Green' .
  APPEND ls_additional_value TO additional_data.
  ls_additional_value-fieldname  = ‚TITLE'.
  ls_additional_value-fieldvalue = ‚Mrs.'.
  APPEND ls_additional_value TO additional_data.
  CLEAR ls_additional_value.
```

Listing 9.7 Programming for an Enhanced Input Help (OVS)

Format of Amounts and Quantities

SAP ERP 6.0 Support Package 16 (SP 16, SAP_APPL) enables you to display the format of an amount field value depending on the corresponding currency. Likewise, the format of a value in a quantity field can be displayed depending on the respective quantity unit. For example, a lot of currencies are displayed with two decimal places. The Japanese Yen, however, has no decimal places.

SAP Note 1350278 provides detailed information on amount and quantity fields in ISR.

In the QISR1 BAdI implementation, a reference field needs to be provided via the EXTERNAL_DATA table for this purpose. This reference field provides the data type—currency or quantity unit—and the concrete value for the determination of the correct form of the amount or quantity field. Because the format of the currency or quantity unit can alter in the form after the value has been changed, the formatting needs to be adapted after each form roundtrip.

Listing 9.8 illustrates a programming example of the SCENARIO_ INT_SERVICE_REQUEST_CHECK method from the QISR1 BAdI for an amount field. The value of the REVENUE characteristic is supposed to be displayed correctly in the format according to the JPY (Japanese Yen) reference currency. The entries in the EXTERNAL_DATA table should look as follows: The QISR_FIELDNAME_REF_TYPE field for the reference type needs to receive the value C for an amount field. For a quantity field, it would be the value Q. The programming can be implemented in all methods that provide the EXTERNAL_DATA table as an interface parameter.

> **Tip for Using the SPECIAL_DATA Table**
>
> If the corresponding currency has been entered in the form, you can retrieve the value of the currency from the respective field of the SPECIAL_DATA table. Note that you can only use the appropriate key from SAP Customizing as a reference.
>
> ▶ You can find the currency keys in Transaction OY04 (ISO Codes).
> ▶ You can find the keys for the quantity units in Transaction CUNI.
>
> If the entry in the form does not exactly correspond to this key, you have to implement the appropriate data mapping in your system.
>
> Example: Yen was entered as the permitted value in the form. Prior to the transfer to the EXTERNAL_DATA interface parameter, which is illustrated in Listing 9.8, you have to convert this value into JPY.

```
METHOD if_ex_qisr1~INT_SERVICE_REQUEST_CHECK

* local data
  DATA: ls_external_value TYPE qisrsspecial_param.
```

```
ls_external_value-qisr_fieldname = 'REVENUE'.
ls_external_value-qisr_fieldname_ref = 'JPY'.
ls_external_value-qisr_fieldname_ref_type = 'C'.
APPEND ls_external_value TO external_data.
CLEAR ls_external_value.
```

Listing 9.8 Programming for the Formatting of an Amount Field

9.6 Form Flow Logic

In addition to the definition of the Customizing and the Adobe form, you can now start using programs to control the flow logic of the form with the QISR1 BAdI. An essential aspect of the ISR is its flexibility in manipulating the flow logic of the request form. The ISR framework enables you to control the flow logic of the request form in the backend via the predefined QISR1 BAdI definition. This section uses simple programming examples to show how you can use the BAdI implementation.

To add your own processing logic to a form, select DEFINE BUSINESS-ADD-IN in the basic ISR Customizing. Now you can create, modify, or delete implementations. You can assign a specific BAdI implementation of the QISR1 BAdI definition to each scenario by default. However, if required, you can also use one BAdI implementation for multiple scenarios. You either assign the additional scenario directly to a BAdI implementation as an additional filter value or you enter the scenario into BUSINESS ADD-IN FROM SCENARIO whose BAdI implementation you want to use for the current scenario. This configuration only applies to the QISR1 BAdI.

> **Multiple Assignment of a BAdI Implementation to the Scenario**
>
> You can use the BAdI implementation in multiple scenarios. However, you should link a scenario to the BAdI implementation of another scenario in the basic Customizing if you have many similar scenarios or if you do not want to modify the existing BAdI implementation.

Figure 9.41 shows a diagram of the form flow logic with the times of the calls of individual methods of the QISR1 BAdI. For more information, refer to SAP Note 105505.

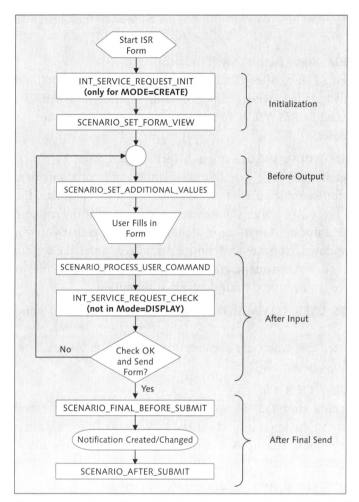

Figure 9.41 Points in Time of the Form Flow Logic with the QISR1 BAdI

In total, nine BAdI methods are available:

▶ **INT_SERVICE_REQUEST_INIT** (initialization)
This method is executed once as the first method when a request form is called for a new request and is used for data initializations in the form. The following parameter values are already defined here:

  ▶ MODE = "CREATE"

  ▶ FORM_VIEW = "ISR_REQUEST"

  ▶ EVENT (empty)

SAP Note 883718 describes how you can also use the method in the Change or Display mode.

▸ **SCENARIO_SET_FORM_VIEW** (setting the form view)
This method is executed once after the INT_SERVICE_REQUEST_INIT method when a request form is called. Section 9.6.2, Default Values for the MODE, USER_COMMAND, and FORM_VIEW Parameters, lists the default values for the FORM_VIEW parameter.

▸ **SCENARIO_SET_ADDITIONAL_VALUES** (input helps)
This method is executed when the request form is started and prior to any new output of the form, for example, after an EVENT. In this method, populate the internal table, ADDITIONAL_DATA, with values that you only need at the runtime of the form and should not be stored in the request. That means that you can set value lists for dropdown list boxes and control parameters here. The system does not automatically delete the internal table, ADDITIONAL_DATA, which means that data that are once set are stored until the form is submitted.

▸ **SCENARIO_PROCESS_USER_COMMAND** (processing your own user commands)
This method is executed first when any event in the request form (CHECK, SUBMIT, USER COMMAND) is triggered.

▸ **INT_SERVICE_REQUEST_CHECK** (check)
This method is executed after the SCENARIO_PROCESS_USER_COMMAND method when a standard event in the request form (CHECK or SUBMIT of a form) is triggered. Therefore, the request data are always checked before the new or modified notification is updated.

▸ **SCENARIO_FINAL_BEFORE_SUBMIT** (check prior to the submit event)
This method is called immediately after the notification has been created.

▸ **SCENARIO_AFTER_SUBMIT** (exit after the submit event)
This method is called after the form data have been posted and the notification has been created.

▸ **POST_NOTIF_POSITION** (determining data for the position of the notification)
This method serves to derive the notification position from the notification data shortly before the notification is posted. It is relevant only if you want to use notification positions.

- **REVERSE_NOTIF_EXTERNAL** (deleting external data separately when a notification is reversed)

  This notification is an exception because it is not processed via the form. Instead, it is used when a service request is reversed in the ISR status overview to allow for request-specific and scenario-specific data changes outside of the actual request.

  This is the case, for example, if you entered additional information on the request in a customer-specific table when creating the request in your scenario to use it for later evaluations. By reversing the request, you can adapt these data.

9.6.1 Data Structures within the ISR Framework

Table 9.5 lists the most important data structures for implementing the BAdI methods. They are provided in most of the methods of the QISR1 BAdI and in the other BAdIs of the ISR (see Section 9.4, Customizing and Programming a Scenario). However, this list is not complete because the other parameters are not relevant for most of the applications. Their relevance is described in the documentation of the QISR1 BAdI.

Parameter	Type	Description
FLT_VAL	QSCENARIO	Current scenario
MODE	QISRDMODE	Describes the edit mode
FORM_VIEW	QISRDFORMVIEW	Current form view
USER_COMMAND	SYUCOMM	Event (standard events and scenario-specific events)
RETURN	BAPIRET1	Return structure for error messages
MESSAGE_LIST	QISRTRETURN	List with messages of various error categories
UI_ATTRIBUTES	QISRTUI_ATTRIBUTES	UI properties of a form field
GENERAL_DATA	QISRSGENERAL_PARAM	General ISR data (applicant, and so on)
SPECIAL_DATA	QISRTSPECIAL_PARAM	Form data
ADDITIONAL_DATA	QISRTSPECIAL_PARAM	Values for input helps

Table 9.5 Interface Parameters of Methods of the QISR1 BAdI

9.6.2 Default Values for the MODE, USER_COMMAND, and FORM_ VIEW Parameters

The following list describes some critical parameters of the BAdIs and the relevance of the corresponding permitted values.

- ▶ **MODE**
  MODE describes the current edit mode. The MODE parameter enables you to design your program logic based on the current mode:
  - ▶ CREATE if the ISR form is called for a new request
  - ▶ CHANGE if the ISR form with the notification number is called to be modified
  - ▶ DISPLAY if the ISR form with the notification number is called to be displayed

- ▶ **FORM_VIEW**
  FORM_VIEW describes the current processor role:
  - ▶ ISR_APPROVE if the approver is processing the form
  - ▶ ISR_REQUEST if the applicant is processing the form
  - ▶ ISR_PROCESS if the processor is processing the form or the notification

- ▶ **USER_COMMAND**
  The standard ISR events in USER_COMMAND are defined as follows:
  - ▶ SEND if the form is sent for a new request/notification
  - ▶ SAVE if the form is saved for an existing request/notification
  - ▶ CHECK if the CHECK button is clicked in the form
  - ▶ ACCEPT if the APPROVED button is clicked in the approval form
  - ▶ REJECT if the REJECT button is clicked in the approval form
  - ▶ BACK if the BACK TO AUTHOR button is clicked in the approval form

In your customer-specific form, you can define any number of events that can be queried in the methods of the QISR1 BAdI via the USER_COMMAND parameter at runtime (see Section 9.6.3, Programming Examples).

9.6.3 Programming Examples

This section provides some simple programming examples. They are designed to introduce you to the programmed form flow logic and illustrate the basic options of the QISR1 BAdI.

Programming Example for a Field Initialization

The NEW_COSTCENTER characteristic is initialized via the INITIATED_BY-MASTER_CCTR standard ISR parameter (see Listing 9.9):

```
METHOD if_ex_qisr1~int_service_request_init
* local data
  DATA: ls_special_data TYPE qisrsspecial_param.

  LOOP AT special_data INTO ls_special_data.
      CASE ls_special_data-fieldname.
    WHEN 'NEW_COSTCENTER'.
      ls_special_data-fieldvalue =
                general_data-initiated_by-master_cctr.
        WHEN OTHERS.
  ENDCASE.
      MODIFY special_data FROM ls_special_data.
      ENDLOOP.
```

Listing 9.9 Field Initialization

Programming Example for a Check

The system returns an error message after a check (see Listing 9.10):

```
METHOD if_ex_qisr1~int_service_request_check
  IF general_data-initiated_by-lastname is initial.
    return-type   = 'E'.
    return-id     = 'QISR'.
    return-number = '046'.
    EXIT.
    ENDIF.
```

Listing 9.10 Programming of an Error Message

Programming Example for a Form Event

The USER_COMMAND or EVENT URLB of the form is processed if it is a new request (see Listing 9.11).

```
METHOD if_ex_qisr1~scenario_process_user_command.
  DATA:      ls_special_data type qisrsspecial_param.
  DATA:      lv_vacation(1)   type c.

* only for new requests
```

```
    CHECK mode = 'CREATE'.
* process user commands
        CASE user_command.
      WHEN 'VACA'.
* read special data VACATION
        LOOP AT special_data INTO ls_special_data.
          IF ls_special_data-fieldname = 'VACATION'.
            lv_vacation = ls_special_data-fieldvalue.
        ENDLOOP.
        READ TABLE special_data INTO ls_special_data
            WITH KEY fieldname = 'ESS_COSTS'.
        IF sy-subrc EQ 0 AND lv_vacation eq 'X'.
*       delete 'ESS_COSTS' if leave is selected
          CLEAR ls_special_data-fieldvalue.
      ENDIF.
        MODIFY special_data FROM ls_special_data
                           INDEX sy-tabix.
    ENDCASE.
```

Listing 9.11 Programming of an Event (User Command)

Programming Example for an Input Help

To implement an input help for a characteristic (for example, SYSTEMNAME) in the QISR1 BAdI, you must populate the internal table, ADDITIONAL_DATA, of the SCENARIO_SET_ADDITIONAL_VALUES method for the key value (for example, SYSTEMNAME_KEY) and the corresponding description (for example, SYSTEMNAME_LABEL). You implement multiple entries in the input help via the sequential numbering in the FIELDINDEX field.

You must define the technical name and the description of the key value in the Customizing of the characteristics (see Figure 9.25). The technical names are used to correctly assign the input values. The ADDITIONAL_DATA table can therefore contain the values of several input helps at the same time.

Either use the ISR_DDL_NoSelected or ISR_DDL_1stSelected layout element from the ISR library (see Section 9.5.5). Figure 9.42 displays the result of the programming example in the Adobe form using the ISR_DDL_NoSelected element. SAP Note 1133359 describes how you can map the dropdown list box as an Extended Value Selector (EVS).

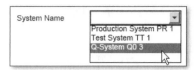

Figure 9.42 Programmed Input Help in the Adobe Form at Runtime

To define an enhanced input help, use the separate Customizing transaction, QISRSCENARIO_OVS, instead of the basic ISR Customizing. The value list is programmed in the SCENARIO_PROCESS_USER_COMMAND method. You can find a programming example in SAP Note 906950. In the Adobe form, use the ISR Text Edit – OVS layout element from the ISR library.

You do not have to implement this method to use the ISR Text Edit – Value Help input help. This input help automatically provides domain-fixed values or an input help that is assigned to a data item. The prerequisite here is that the characteristic in the ISR Customizing is assigned to the respective data item.

An input help with two selection values for the System characteristic is programmed as in Listing 9.12.

```
if_ex_qisr1~scenario_set_additional_values
  DATA: ls_additional_value TYPE qisrsspecial_param.

* first DDLB entry
  ls_additional_value-fieldindex = 1.
  ls_additional_value-fieldname  = 'SYSTEMNAME_KEY'.
  ls_additional_value-fieldvalue = 'PR1'.
  APPEND ls_additional_value TO additional_data.
  ls_additional_value-fieldname  = 'SYSTEMNAME_LABEL'.
  ls_additional_value-fieldvalue = 'Productive System PR 1'.
  APPEND ls_additional_value TO additional_data.

* second DDLB entry
  ls_additional_value-fieldindex = 2.
  ls_additional_value-fieldname  = 'SYSTEMNAME_KEY'.
  ls_additional_value-fieldvalue = 'TT1'.
  APPEND ls_additional_value TO additional_data.
  ls_additional_value-fieldname  = 'SYSTEMNAME_LABEL'.
  ls_additional_value-fieldvalue = 'Test System TT 1'.
  APPEND ls_additional_value TO additional_data.
```

Listing 9.12 Programming of an Input Help for a Dropdown List Box

9.6.4 Reading and Setting the Special Request Fields in BAdI Methods

You can easily access the general request data within the BAdI implementations because it is transferred with the GENERAL_DATA structure to the methods. In contrast, the special request data that are defined as a characteristic in the ISR Customizing are provided as a table, and the table SPECIAL_DATA contains one row for each characteristic.

As you saw in the previous examples, the code can quickly become confusing for more complex programming tasks if you always need to find single field values via the LOOP AT special_data ABAP command. Therefore, SAP provides two function modules to move this tabular data to the corresponding local structures at the beginning of a BAdI method and write it back to the table at the end of the method.

▶ **ISR_SPECIAL_DATA_TO_STRUC**
This function module serves to move the special request data from the SPECIAL_DATA table to a structure. In this process, only the request data are transferred from the table to the structure (see Listing 9.13).

```
  DATA: ls_master_data TYPE bapi2075_7.
* move special request data to structure
  CALL FUNCTION 'ISR_SPECIAL_DATA_TO_STRUC'
      EXPORTING
          it_special_data = special_data
      CHANGING
          cs_data         = ls_master_data.
* addtional processing steps
* ...
* return the special request data
  CALL FUNCTION 'ISR_STRUC_TO_SPECIAL_DATA'
      EXPORTING
          is_data         = ls_master_data
      CHANGING
          ct_special_data = special_data.
```

Listing 9.13 Programming the Data Transfer

▶ **ISR_STRUC_TO_SPECIAL_DATA**
This function module works similar to ISR_SPECIAL_DATA_TO_STRUC, only the other way around.

You can use the same function modules to read and write the ADDITIONAL_DATA transfer table for the input help.

As an alternative to these two function modules, you can use the methods of the CL_ISR_DATA help class. In addition to the already-mentioned options for transferring data to the local structure, this class also provides the option to manipulate the data, for example, by adding, inserting, and deleting data (see Listing 9.14).

```
METHOD if_ex_qisr1~int_service_request_check.

  DATA: BEGIN OF ls_characteristics,
          company_code    TYPE bukrs,
          cost_center     TYPE kostl,
        END OF ls_characteristics.

* copy the form data to class storage
* CL_ISR_DATA
  CALL METHOD cl_isr_data=>set
    EXPORTING
      it_data = special_data.

* read the form data in local structure
  CALL METHOD cl_isr_data=>read
    EXPORTING
      id_index        = 1
    IMPORTING
      es_data_record = ls_characteristics.

* data changes
  IF ls_characteristics-cost_center = '12345678'.
    ls_characteristics-company_code = '1000'.
  ELSE.
    ls_characteristics-company_code = '0001'.
    ENDIF.

* replace the data
  CALL METHOD cl_isr_data=>insert
    EXPORTING
      is_data_record = ls_characteristics
      id_index       = 1
```

```
    RECEIVING
        rt_data         = special_data.

ENDMETHOD.
```
Listing 9.14 Programming with the CL_ISR_DATA Help Class

9.6.5   Error Handling During Checks

You can output error messages within the INT_SERVICE_REQUEST_CHECK and SCENARIO_PROCESS_USER_COMMAND methods to prevent the processing of the service request. To do this, fill the RETURN transfer structure with the respective error message. If you want to output multiple messages, use the MESSAGE_LIST transfer table.

> **Error Handling Controls the Processing of the Request**
>
> If you use Web Dynpro applications in the ISR, you can control the processing of a request by the applicant. If the MESSAGE_LIST transfer table contains one or more messages, an error message from the RETURN structure that was output at the same time is not displayed; however, the messages of MESSAGE_LIST are always displayed. The error message in the RETURN structure prevents the system from sending the request. If the RETURN structure remains empty, the request can be sent despite the messages in the MESSAGE_LIST transfer table, independent of their message category.

9.6.6   Controlling the Field Layout

You can control the layout properties of individual form fields, such as mandatory field, visibility, and ready-for-input status, in the ISR framework. A requirement for this is Support Package 4 of SAP ERP 6.0. SAP Note 925657 provides more information on this topic. You can control the layout properties in the following methods:

▶ INT_SERVICE_REQUEST_CHECK

▶ INT_SERVICE_REQUEST_INIT

▶ SCENARIO_SET_ADDITIONAL_VALUES

▶ SCENARIO_PROCESS_USER_COMMAND

They have the UI_ATTRIBUTES interface parameter. Like the ADDITIONAL_DATA table, this table is usually empty at the ISR runtime and must be filled for the respective characteristics (FIELDNAME). You can assign the following properties to any field of the form using the UI_ATTRIBUTE field:

- ▸ M Mandatory Field and Ready for Input
- ▸ I Ready for Input
- ▸ R Visible and not Ready for Input
- ▸ H Not Visible

You can adapt this property after any standard event or an action in the form for which an event is executed.

9.7   ISR Architecture

This section illustrates the architecture of the ISR framework and provides an overview of the SAP technologies used and their integration with the ISR framework. In addition, it describes the communication between the individual frontend and backend components and the critical interfaces of the ISR, particularly the Web Dynpro applications.

9.7.1   ISR as a Toolset

As described earlier, the ISR uses various applications from SAP NetWeaver and SAP ERP and combines them to form a framework that allows for form-based request scenarios and the involved process for the execution of the required service. To process the process, that is, to forward the request to the processor responsible, it can be integrated with SAP Business Workflow. This is achieved by using the BUS7051 business object of the quality notification — or simply notification — as the runtime object of the service request.

Furthermore, the request scenario is integrated with SAP CO to determine direct and indirect overhead costs of the service request. ISR links these different applications and provides various interfaces so that you can use programs to flexibly control the request form and process.

Figure 9.43 illustrates the communication between the QISR_UI_FORM Web Dynpro component and the backend. The Web Dynpro component communicates with the ISR runtime in the backend via the ISR_PROCESS_EVENT Remote Function Call

(RFC). During ISR runtime, the methods of the QISR1 BAdI (see Section 9.6.1, Data Structures within the ISR Framework) are called at different times.

When the form is sent, the form data are stored separately in the Business Document Service (BDS), that is, the document management of the Knowledge Provider, and the notification is created. Thus, the data are not stored with the form as a PDF. This program design is the main reason why the ISR cannot support the process of entering requests offline. Within the ISR, the Adobe form serves only as the interface layout for entering the request and is always merged with the current data at runtime.

Figure 9.43 Communication between ABAP Design Time and ABAP Runtime

---

Data Storage Separated from the Layout

Only the form data are stored, not the PDF. Technically, the interactive Adobe form serves solely as the input screen. Users can still store a current PDF in Adobe Reader.

When the notification is created, the CREATED event of the business object is triggered and the system generates the corresponding work item in the UWL (in the portal) or in SAP Business Workplace (Transaction SBWP).

9.7.2 Web Dynpro ABAP Component and How to Use It

As described in Section 9.4.4, the UI technology to enter the request is interchangeable. In addition to the interactive Adobe form (available as of SAP ERP 5.0), you can use other form technologies, such as ITS Services, BSP forms, or JSP forms. However, for all request forms as of SAP ERP 5.0, the Adobe form is the standard solution of the ISR and embedded in a Web Dynpro component (see Figure 9.44).

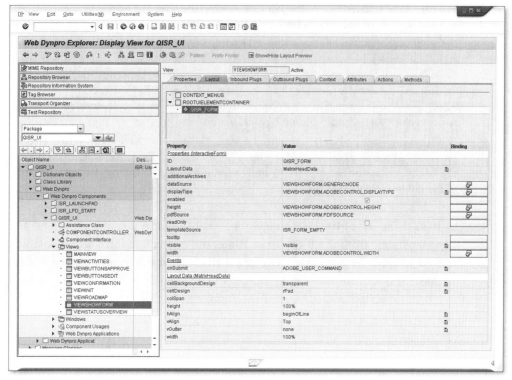

Figure 9.44 Web Dynpro Component "QISR_UI"

Basic Principles of the Web Dynpro Component of the ISR

For integration of the Adobe form, the following Web Dynpro applications, based on Web Dynpro ABAP and Web Dynpro Java, are available:

▶ QISR_UI Web Dynpro ABAP component

▶ PCUI_GP~ISR Web Dynpro ABAP component

Both solutions provide the same functions, particularly for displaying the form—there are no differences.

Both technologies have four Web Dynpro applications, each with identical parameters. The QISR_UI Web Dynpro ABAP component is available as of Support Package 8 of SAP ERP 6.0. However, you should at least use SAP ERP SAP_APPL SP 12. The Web Dynpro Java component has been available as of SAP ERP 5.0 and it is provided in the PCUI_GP software component.

Selection Options for Web Dynpro ABAP or Java

You may have wondered why the ISR Customizing provides the Adobe PDF entry type but no selection options for Web Dynpro ABAP or Java.

Every scenario that deploys the Adobe PDF entry type in the Customizing, and to which an interactive Adobe form is assigned, can be used with both Web Dynpro UI technologies—without having to configure additional settings in the backend. For this reason, no Customizing entry is possible or required for a differentiation between Web Dynpro ABAP and Web Dynpro Java. You decide with your iView or Web Dynpro component which type of Web Dynpro technology you want to use.

The following sections only describe the Web Dynpro ABAP solution—most of the provided ISR scenarios are started via the QISR_UI Web Dynpro ABAP component. Only the Personnel Change Request (PCR) application uses the Web Dynpro Java component of the ISR in SAP ERP 6.0.

The basic principle of the ISR framework is that the form data are processed and stored separately from the form. At runtime, the interactive form serves solely as the input screen. Therefore, the basis for a correct data transfer between the various components of the ISR is the definition of the form fields with identical names in the ISR Customizing and context of the form (see Section 9.5.2, Structure of the Interface and Form Context).

The QISR_UI Web Dynpro component uses InteractiveForm as the screen element. Both the dataSource attribute for the form data and the pdfSource attribute are bound to a context element of the Web Dynpro component, which is not filled until the component is started.

The system generates the context of the Web Dynpro component for the data of the form. The basis for the generation is the list of characteristics from the ISR Customizing. This list is read via an RFC, from which the appropriate context for the form is generated. At the beginning of the form runtime, the name of the form (for example, ISR_FORM_SRCR) is determined via an appropriate Web Dynpro interface and transferred to the InteractiveForm Web Dynpro screen element. Adobe

Document Services (ADS) read the corresponding interactive PDF and display it together with the data of the context.

Web Dynpro Applications of the ISR

The standard interface of the ISR is provided by four Web Dynpro applications, which you can independently integrate with your portal environment. Note that all applications must be started with specific parameters.

▸ **QISR_UI_FORM**

The QISR_UI_FORM Web Dynpro application in the form of a roadmap consisting of three steps and SAP Interactive Forms by Adobe is used for request creation (see Figure 9.3). Required parameters include:

▸ SCENARIO
ISR scenario, must always be specified

▸ NOTIF_NO
Notification number

▸ MODE
Mode

Only specify the notification number if an existing request is changed (MODE = CHANGE parameter) or displayed (MODE = DISPLAY parameter). For new requests (MODE = CREATE parameter), NOTIF_NO remains empty.

▸ **QISR_UI_FORM_APPROVE**

The QISR_UI_FORM_APPROVE application only consists of SAP Interactive Forms by Adobe and is used to approve the request. No roadmap is used here.

However, it makes sense to deploy this application if you use a notification type with approval. The approver is provided with the APPROVE, REJECT, and BACK TO AUTHOR buttons (see Figure 9.10).

The only required parameter is WF_ID (technical number of the workflow item of the approver).

In the standard version of the ISR scenarios, none of the form fields of this application are ready for input. However, by adapting the script programming of individual fields in Form Builder, you can make them ready for input (see Section 9.5.5, ISR Library—Special Screen Elements).

▸ **QISR_UI_FORM_DISPLAY_ONLY**

The QISR_UI_FORM_DISPLAY_ONLY application only serves to display the current status of an ISR form. It contains only the form without input options, roadmaps, or functions in the form of buttons. Required parameters include:

▶ SCENARIO – ISR Scenario

▶ NOTIF_NO – notification number

▶ **QISR_UI_STATUSOVERVIEW**

The QISR_UI_STATUSOVERVIEW application provides the applicant with an overview of all of his requests for the last 365 days and their status (see Figure 9.8). This application can be called without additional parameters.

ISR_SCENARIO_PARAMS for Any Parameters

The ISR_SCENARIO_PARAMS parameter enables you to initialize single or multiple characteristics that are defined in the scenario. This parameter is also used, for example, to define the version of the scenario (see Section 9.4.2).

To initialize multiple fields, use the dollar sign ($) to separate the field and value combinations. Do not leave blanks between these combinations; transfer the values as a continuous string. The prerequisite here is that the parameter must be defined as a characteristic in the ISR Customizing; however, it does not have to be a form field. Depending on the technology, you can use ISR_SCENARIO_PARAMS for all three usage options of the ISR in SAP NetWeaver Portal (see Section 9.7.3) either as a URL parameter (iView) or via the corresponding interface methods of the ISR (Web Dynpro component).

Let's look at an example: The ORDER characteristic should be initialized with the value 000000123456 and the ACCOUNT characteristic with the value 400100. Therefore, the assembled parameter for ISR_SCENARIO_PARAMS is as follows: ISR_SCENARIO_PARAMS=ORDER =000000123456$ACCOUNT=400100.

9.7.3 Usage Options in SAP NetWeaver Portal

The forms of the ISR are available to the user in different ways in SAP NetWeaver Portal:

▶ Direct usage of an ISR Web Dynpro application (for example, QISR_UI_FORM) via a link

▶ ISR Launchpad, embedded in a specific Web Dynpro component

▶ Component use of the QISR_UI Web Dynpro component

ISR Web Dynpro Application in an iView

If you use an ISR Web Dynpro application, you can provide the request as a callable service in the portal. This corresponds to a link to an iView that starts the application in Web Dynpro ABAP (or Web Dynpro Java) of the ISR. The application must be started with the SCENARIO and MODE parameters. Here, SCENARIO corresponds to the four-digit scenario name, for example, SMC1. For a new request, you must specify MODE = CREATE. Section 9.6.2, Default Values for the MODE, USER_COMMAND, and FORM_VIEW Parameters, lists the valid values for the MODE parameter.

A display option in the portal should include one of the corresponding Web Dynpro applications in an iView. Both the Web Dynpro component of the ISR status overview and the UWL access this Web Dynpro application of the ISR (see Figure 9.45).

Figure 9.45 Communication between SAP NetWeaver Portal and Web Dynpro Runtime

You can find generic iViews of the ISR in SAP NetWeaver Portal via the menu path Portal Content • ERP Common Parts.

ISR Launchpad

You can call one or more request forms via buttons within your own component in Web Dynpro ABAP (see Figure 9.46). The advantage of the ISR Launchpad is that, when starting the request form, you can transfer any URL parameters that can be evaluated in the initialization method of the QISR1 BAdI implementation. In addition, a check can be executed in the backend before the form is started, for example, to check whether the user is authorized to start the request form.

Figure 9.46 Start of an ISR Form from the "ISR_LPD_START" Test Application

The SCENARIO_CHECK method of the QISR6 BAdI is called in the ISR_LAUNCHPAD_ SCENARIO_CHECK function module. This function module is executed prior to the start of the request form in the ISR Launchpad. This applies to both the Web Dynpro Java variant and the Web Dynpro ABAP variant of the ISR. This check enables you to prevent the start of the form, for example, due to missing authorizations.

If you use the third variant of the ISR integration (QISR_UI as a component use), you may also integrate this check option with your own Web Dynpro component. To do this, simply integrate the ISR_LAUNCHPAD_SCENARIO_CHECK function module.

Integrating the ISR Launchpad with Programs

This integration type of the ISR application (see Figure 9.47) is programmed in the ISR_LPD_START Web Dynpro component as an example and can be started via the application in Web Dynpro ABAP that has the same name.

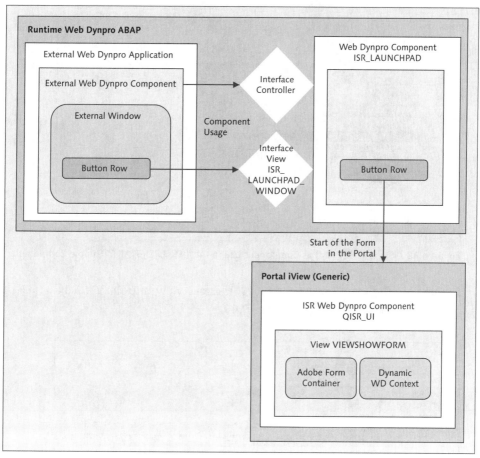

Figure 9.47 Schematic Diagram of the ISR Launchpads in Your Own Web Dynpro Application

The following section describes the steps for integrating the ISR Launchpad:

1. First, specify the ISR_LAUNCHPAD Web Dynpro component as the COMPONENT USE in Transaction SE80 in the surrounding Web Dynpro component (see Figure 9.48).

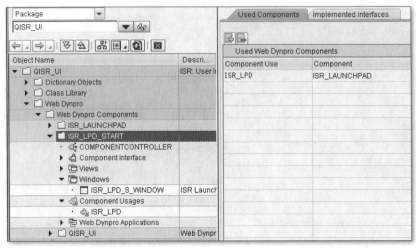

Figure 9.48 ISR_LAUNCHPAD as Component Use in the "ISR_LPD_START" Sample Component

2. Integrate the `ISR_LAUNCHPAD_WINDOW` interface view into the `VIEWCONTAINER` of the appropriate `WINDOW` (see Figure 9.49).

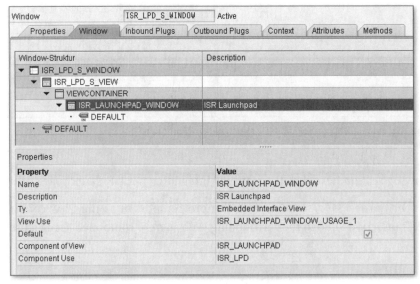

Figure 9.49 "ISR_LAUNCHPAD_WINDOW" Interface View

3. Create a new ABAP class (provider class) that implements the IF_ISR_LPD_PROVIDER interface. You need this class to start the launchpad with the required parameters (see Figure 9.50).

Figure 9.50 Provider Class with Interface

4. Then, generate an instance of the provider class and initialize the ISR Launchpad with the necessary scenario group in the view of the surrounding application. For this reason, the INIT method was created in COMPONENTCONTROLLER in the sample Web Dynpro component, ISR_LPD_START. This method is called in the WDDOMODIFY method of the ISR_LPD_S_VIEW view. You can also define the implementation of the INIT method in your Web Dynpro component in the WDDOINIT method in COMPONENTCONTROLLER if the scenario group is not changed during the execution (see Figure 9.51).

5. Implement the IF_ISR_LPD_PROVIDER~GET_PARAMETERS method to transfer the required call parameters to the ISR request. The method has the EXPORTING parameter, ET_PARAMS, of the QISRTLPD_SCEN_PARAM type, which contains the SCENARIO field. This field, in turn, contains a table with the following fields:

▶ PARAM_INDEX

▶ PARAM_KEY

▶ PARAM_VALUE

Therefore, you can specify a list with parameters you defined yourself for one or more scenarios. PARAM_KEY corresponds to the technical name of the parameter and PARAM_VALUE to the value of the parameter. If you want to transfer one parameter value, enter ‚1' for PARAM_INDEX.

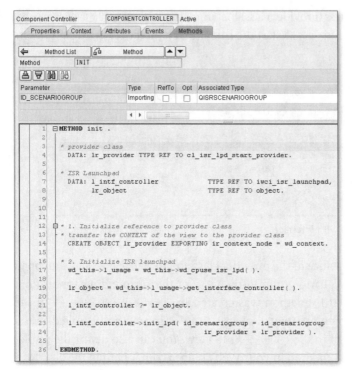

Figure 9.51 Initializing the ISR Launchpad in COMPONENTCONTROLLER

Customizing the ISR Launchpad

Proceed as follows in the Customizing of the ISR Launchpad:

1. First, define an Isr Scenario Group (see Figure 9.52).

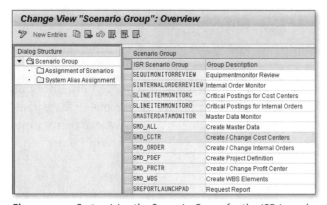

Figure 9.52 Customizing the Scenario Group for the ISR Launchpad

2. Based on this group, define the list of the ISR scenarios that can be started for your ISR Launchpad (see Figure 9.53).

Figure 9.53 Assigned Scenarios of a Scenario Group

3. Finally, specify the order and the text of the buttons. The Customizing for the ISR Launchpad can be found via the menu path CROSS-APPLICATION COMPONENTS • INTERNET/INTRANET SERVICES • INTERNAL SERVICE REQUEST • SCENARIO DEFINITION • DEFINE SCENARIO GROUPS or directly via the VC_ISRGRP view cluster.

QISR_UI Web Dynpro Component as the Component Use

The third option for using the ISR Web Dynpro component is direct integration with your own Web Dynpro component. In this case, the QISR_UI Web Dynpro component is defined as the USED COMPONENT (see Figure 9.54).

Figure 9.54 Schematic Diagram of the "QISR_UI" Web Dynpro Component as a Direct Component Use

The communication with the QISR_UI component takes place via the methods of the InterfaceController. It provides numerous SET/GET methods to determine or modify the data of the form and additional technical control parameters. The central method, `CALL_ISR_PROCESS_EVENT`, is used to call the ISR framework via an `EVENT`. This `EVENT` import parameter processes the standard events of the ISR framework (see Section 9.6.2, Default Values for the MODE, USER_COMMAND, and FORM_VIEW Parameters) or any events you defined yourself that are queried in the corresponding BAdI implementation.

9.7.4 ISR_PROCESS_EVENT RFC

In addition to the mentioned Web Dynpro interfaces, there are other technical interfaces that can also be useful for the implementation of a scenario. In addition, some service modules are available that are useful for the implementation of BAdIs.

RFC `ISR_PROCESS_EVENT` is the central communication interface of the ISR framework between the ISR frontend and the backend. It can be used to simulate the processes of creating, changing, or reading a service request *without* deploying the ISR frontend (Web Dynpro application, Adobe form). In this context, the `QISR1` BAdI is also implemented. Table 9.6 describes the meaning of the individual fields of the interface.

Parameter	Type	Values	Description
`SCENARIO`	Importing		Four-digit scenario name
`MODE`	Importing	`CREATE`, `CHANGE`, `DISPLAY`	Describes the edit mode
`EVENT`	Importing	`SEND`, `SAVE`, `CHECK`, `APPROVE`, etc.	Event (standard events and scenario-specific events)
`NOTIF_NO`	Importing		Notification number if `MODE = CHANGE` or `MODE = DISPLAY`
`NOTIF_NO_OUT`	Exporting		Notification number is output if notification was created
`RETURN`	Exporting		Error message
`DATA`	Tables		Form data and general data
`ADDITIONAL_DATA`	Tables		Values for input helps

Table 9.6 Interface of RFC ISR_PROCESS_EVENT

You do not have to consider the FLAG_INOUT_CONVERSION, FLAG_RESET, ISR_PAGE_IN, ISR_PAGE_OUT, or ISR_FORM_VIEW parameters or additional table parameters for the simulation.

DATA and ADDITIONAL_DATA Table Parameters

The DATA and ADDITIONAL_DATA table parameters have a generic structure and each contain the following fields:

▶ FIELDINDEX

▶ FIELDNAME

▶ FIELDVALUE

DATA contains a list of all characteristics (FIELDNAME) with the corresponding characteristic values (FIELDVALUE). Because a characteristic can include multiple values, each combination of FIELDNAME and FIELDVALUE has a counter in the FIELDINDEX field, which starts with '1.'

ADDITIONAL_DATA contains the values for the input helps. The data formatting is described in Section 9.6.3, Programming Examples.

The following examples describe the possible or necessary parameterization of the ISR_PROCESS_EVENT RFC for various application cases.

Example 1: Starting a Request

To simulate the start of a new service request, start the RFC with the SCENARIO = xxxx (xxxx refers to the scenario name) and MODE = CREATE parameters. The EVENT parameter remains empty. The DATA and ADDITIONAL_DATA tables now contain the initialized characteristics and possible values for the programmed input helps.

Example 2: Submitting a Request

If you want to submit a service request, start the RFC with the SCENARIO = xxxx, MODE = CREATE and EVENT = SEND parameters. In the DATA table, transfer the data that the service request should contain. The NOTIF_NO_OUT return parameter contains the notification number.

If you want to check the data before they are submitted, simply enter EVENT = CHECK for the parameter. If the data are not correct, the system outputs an error message with the RETURN return structure. This also applies to Example 3.

Example 3: Reading an Existing Request

If you want to read a service request, start the RFC with the SCENARIO = xxxx, MODE = DISPLAY, and NOTIF_NO parameters, including the corresponding notification number. The EVENT parameter remains empty. The DATA and ADDITIONAL_DATA tables now contain the list of the characteristic values and possible values for the programmed input helps.

Example 4: Changing an Existing Request

If you want to change a service request, start the RFC with the SCENARIO = xxxx, MODE = CHANGE, EVENT = SAVE, and NOTIF_NO parameters, including the corresponding notification number. In the DATA table, transfer the data that the service request should contain. Note that the transfer of characteristics without characteristic value results in a deletion of an existing characteristic value.

9.7.5　Additional Interfaces and Auxiliary Functions

Table 9.7 lists additional function modules and an ABAP class that are useful for the programming within the BAdI implementation.

Interface	Description
ISR_GENERAL_DATA_GET	Reads general, scenario-specific, and request-specific data of a request from the database or the internal function group storage.
ISR_SPECIAL_DATA_GET	Reads scenario-specific and request-specific characteristic data of a request from the database or the internal function group storage.
Class: CL_ISR_DATA	This help class can be used to facilitate the programming based on the relatively general interface parameters of the BAdI methods for the specific characteristics of a scenario. Section 9.6.4, Reading and Setting Special Request Fields in BAdI Methods, contains a programming example.

Table 9.7　Useful Interfaces for the BAdI Implementation

Interface	Description
ISR_SPECIAL_DATA_TO_STRUC	The function module serves to move the form data from the generically formatted transfer tables of the BAdIs to an appropriate, scenario-specific table or structure. This facilitates the subsequent programming, which is based on the form data. The function module can be used as an alternative to the CL_ISR_DATA class.
ISR_STRUC_TO_SPECIAL_DATA	If you want to change the form data in a BAdI method, this module can be used to move the data from the scenario-specific table or structure to the generic transfer table of the BAdIs.
ISR_NOTIF_REVERSE	This function module is used to reverse ISR requests. This is possible as long as the status of the notification is OPEN. The function module changes the status to COMPLETED. The ISR status overview also displays the REVERSED status. You can carry out your own processings in an implementation of the REVERSE_NOTIF_EXTERNAL method of the QISR1 BAdI. The function module is also used in the ISR status overview.
ISR_REQUEST_GET_RFC	The function module outputs a list of all service requests of any applicant with the current status information. The function module is also used in the ISR status overview.
ISR_ACTOR_FOR_ROLE_GET	This function module can be used, for example, to determine the current processor in a customer-specific workflow template by means of rules. In addition, the CONTAINER_FOR_ACTOR_DET_FILL method of the QISR3 BAdI is implemented to change the data of the workflow container.
Function group: QISR5	The function modules of the QISR5 function group can be used to determine the Customizing settings for a scenario.

Table 9.7 Useful Interfaces for the BAdI Implementation (Cont.)

The BAdI interfaces listed in Table 9.8 can be used within the ISR and were described in detail using programming examples in this chapter. BAdI QISR5 does exist but is usually not used.

BAdl Interface	Purpose	Where Is It Explained?
QISR1	Form programming interface	Section 9.6
QISR2	Account assignment determination	Section 9.4.9
QISR3	Fills the container to determine the processor	Section 9.4.8
QISR4	Executes a function of the activity bar (action box)	Section 9.4.6
QISR6	ISR: Calls in the ISR Launchpad (Web Dynpro)	Section 9.7.3

Table 9.8 BAdl Interfaces of the ISR

9.8 ISR in the Application Basis (ABA)

This section describes the ISR variant in the Application Basis (SAP_ABA software component), which is available with Release SAP NetWeaver EHP2. In the following, this variant is called "ISR (ABA)." The ISR described in the previous sections is to be called "ISR in ECC."

9.8.1 Basic Concept

The concept for the development of ISR (ABA) basically derived from two central considerations:

▶ **ISR only as a form framework**
An application wants to deploy ISR as the form framework but uses its own runtime object. This is due to the fact that there are already applications in the ISR in ECC that deploy the ISR only as a form framework and use their own runtime objects: These are scenarios from the T ("Tax and Revenue Management— TRM") and H ("HCM Processes and Forms") applications. Consequently, these applications also use specific business workflow templates to implement the request process.

▶ **ISR outside of ECC**
Previously, applications outside of ECC were not able to use ISR because the ISR in ECC is provided in the SAP_APPL software component. ISR (ABA), which was

developed in the SAP_ABA software component, can be used in applications such as "SAP Master Data Governance."

Therefore, the ISR (ABA) functions were reduced. The ISR concept, however, was retained and copied from the respective components of the ISR as it is available in ECC 6.0. The consequence and thus the essential difference between the two ISR variants is that the ISR (ABA) does not provide a connection to SAP ERP.

The ISR (ABA) programming is completely new, that is, Customizing tables and views as well as the runtime environment are all new Workbench objects. The technical design is principally analogous to the ISR in ECC 6.0. This section focuses on the differences between ISR (ABA) and ISR in ECC. Figure 9.55 compares the essential technical principles and functions of ISR (ABA) and ISR in ECC.

	ISR in ERP and ECC (Standard Application)	ISR in ECC for Application T (TRM)	ISR in ABA
Software Component	SAP_APPL, since Release 4.6C	IS-PS-CA	SAP_ABA, since Release 7.0 EHP2
Form	Adobe Form (since ECC 5.0) ITS (since 4.6C) JSP and BSP	Adobe Form	Adobe Form
Form Properties	▶ Initialization ▶ Checks ▶ Own Events ▶ Value Help (EVS, OVS)	▶ Initialization ▶ Checks ▶ Own Events ▶ Value Help (EVS, OVS)	▶ Initialization ▶ Checks ▶ Own Events ▶ Value Help (EVS, OVS)
Form Interface	DDIC-Based	DDIC-Based	XML Schema-Based
FPM Application	QISR_UI_FPM_GAF (since ECC 6.0, SP 8)	TRM-Specific Application	APB_ISR_UI_FPM_GAF
Form Data Storage in BDS	ID = Notification Number	ID = Generated OBJECTID	ID = Generated OBJECTID
Runtime BADI/ Runtime API	▶ QISR1 ▶ ISR_PROCESS_EVENT	▶ QISR1 ▶ ISR_PROCESS_EVENT	▶ APB_ISR_PROCESS (Structure Identical to QISR1) ▶ APB_ISR_PROCESS_EVENT
SAP Business Workflow	▶ Yes, Generic Through Notification ▶ Several Approval Steps	Yes, TRM-specific	No
(QM) Message as Runtime Object	Yes	No	No
Status Overview	Yes	No	No
Follow-Up Activities	Yes	No	No
Customizing	▶ QISRSCENARIO (Transaction) ▶ Wizard for New Scenario	Views of VC_SCENARIO (from Transaction QISRSCENARIO) are used.	APB_ISR_CUST (Transaction)
Framework Integration	see Section 9.4.2	TRM (see Section 9.4.2)	SAP Master Data Governance (Optional Via Application)

Figure 9.55 Comparison: ISR in ECC (SAP_APPL), ISR for TRM, and ISR in ABA (SAP_ABA) (Source: SAP)

9.8.2 Defining a Scenario

The basic principle of the Customizing of ISR (ABA) corresponds to that of ISR in ECC. You also have to implement all relevant settings for a scenario.

The DEFINE SCENARIO IMG activity (Transaction APB_ISR_CUST) provides central access to the Customizing of ISR (ABA) scenarios. You can find the Customizing via the menu path CROSS-APPLICATION COMPONENTS • GENERAL APPLICATION FUNCTIONS • GENERIC SAP BUSINESS SUITE FUNCTIONS • BASIC INTERNAL SERVICE REQUEST • DEFINE SCENARIOS.

Here, you can view a list of scenarios. Select a scenario, and go to BASIC DATA and VERSION. This brings you to the basic ISR (ABA) Customizing (see Figure 9.56).

> **ISR (ABA) Scenario**
>
> The formatting (four digits), the customer namespace, and the technical SCENARIO key field, correspond to the ISR scenario in ECC.
>
> ISR (ABA) and ISR in ECC are technically completely independent of each other because new, independent tables and programs were developed for ISR (ABA). So the definitions of the scenarios are also independent of each other. You can even use the same technical names in both ISR variants.

Figure 9.56 Basic ISR (ABA) Customizing

In contrast to ISR in ECC, ISR (ABA) contains only very few settings that are managed in the same way as in the ISR in ECC:

▶ **Application**
You have to assign an application to a scenario. The following applications are available:

▶ Standard Application (no value in the "Application" field)
You use this application if you want to integrate ISR (ABA) with your Web Dynpro application or if you want to use the Web Dynpro application of the ISR (ABA) separately.

▶ SAP Master Data Governance (FM in the "Application" field)
You can use this application only in the identically named framework for managing change requests for master data.

▶ **Version and Validity Period**
The management of version and validity period corresponds to that in the ISR in ECC (see Section 9.4.2). In VERSION AND FORM, enter a unique value for the version number.

▶ **Form Template and Interface**
You can either enter an existing interactive Adobe form or create a new form.

   ▶ If you create a new form, enter a name for the form in the FORM TEMPLATE field, or leave this field blank. In this case, the form name is generated automatically in the following format: APB_ISR_FORM_XXXX (XXXX = technical name of the scenario). Choose GENERATE to generate the new form. Form Builder opens.

   ▶ If you want to change the layout of the form, select CHANGE. Form Builder opens. If you define new fields in the layout, you can automatically transfer these fields as characteristics to the scenario when you exit Form Builder. During this process, the system automatically saves the data binding of the new field in the layout.

The interface of the form is automatically generated when you create the form, and the system enters it in the INTERFACE field. The name of this interface can then no longer be changed manually. If the interface is exchanged in the form, the name of the interface is automatically adapted in the scenario Customizing.

The principle for creating the form as well as the technical basics of the form and the form context fully correspond to the ISR in ECC (see Section 9.5, Request Forms as Adobe Forms). Because ISR (ABA) only supports the Adobe form as an input screen, an ENTRY TYPE is not required—in contrast to ISR in ECC.

ISR (ABA) Form Interface Type

You can only use an XML schema based-interface in ISR (ABA) (see Figure 9.57), while you may only use the DDIC interface in ISR in ECC.

Figure 9.57 ISR (ABA) Interface Type—XML Schema

▶ **Reference scenario**

You use the reference scenario if the form flow logic (see Section 9.8.3, Form Flow Logic) is supposed to be controlled by the scenario defined in this field.

▶ **Characteristics**

Here, you define the fields of the form. The characteristics are defined according to the same roles and restrictions as described in Section 9.4.5, Characteristics. As a result, the options for programmed input helps, control as long text field, as well as the referencing to a data element or a structure from the Data Dictionary are available. In particular, the programmed input help using the OVS is created— as has already been described in Sections 9.6.3, Programming Examples, and 9.5.5, ISR Library—Special Screen Elements (Enhanced Input Help).

For a scenario, you maintain the Customizing for the enhanced input help accordingly via Transaction APB_ISR_CUST_OVS or via the IMG activity, Set Up OVS Input Help. You can find this activity in the IMG under Cross-Application Components • General Application Functions • Generic SAP Business Suite Functions • Basic Internal Service Request • Set Up OVS Input Help. The `APB_ISR_CUST_SCEN_VALHLP_GET` function module provides information on the customizing of an OVS for a scenario.

9.8.3 Form Flow Logic

Like with the ISR in ECC, you can use programs to control the flow logic of the form using the BAdI, `APB_ISR_FORM_PROCESSING`. This BAdI can be implemented via the `APB_ISR_PROCESS` enhancement spot.

To add your one processing logic to a form, choose the IMG activity, BAdI: Form Processing under Cross-Application Components • General Application Functions •

GENERIC SAP BUSINESS SUITE FUNCTIONS • BASIC INTERNAL SERVICE REQUEST • BADI:
FORM PROCESSING.

You can assign a specific BAdI implementation of the APB_ISR_FORM_PROCESSING
BAdI definition to each scenario by default. Enter the relevant scenario as the
filter value. The methods of the APB_ISR_FORM_PROCESSING BAdI definition have a
similar development and usability compared with the equivalent methods of the
QISR1 BAdI. The QISR1 BAdI had more methods, which are insignificant for the
form flow logic in the ISR (ABA). Figure 9.58 provides a schematic comparison of
the methods of the two BAdI interfaces.

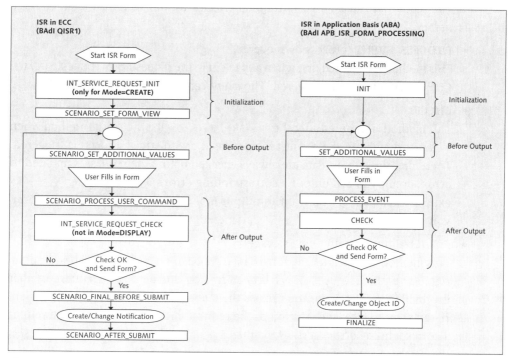

Figure 9.58 Points in Time of the Form Flow Logic—Comparison between ISR in ECC and
ISR (ABA)

Methods

In total, five BAdI methods are available:

▶ **INIT** (initialization)
This method is only called for the initial call of a new request form. In this

context, CT_SPECIAL_DATA is used for the initialization of the provided form fields. The following parameters are defined:

▶ IV_MODE = "CREATE"

▶ IV_EVENT is blank

▶ **SET_ADDITIONAL_ VALUES** (input helps)
In this method, you can fill the internal table, CT_ADDITIONAL_DATA, with value lists for dropdown list boxes and control parameters. These values are not stored in the request. However, they are available during the entire current runtime of the Adobe form.

The value list must be sorted alphabetically by the technical characteristic names.

▶ **PROCESS_EVENT** (process own events)
This method is executed first when any event in the request form (CHECK, SUBMIT, CHECK, IV_EVENT) is triggered. The event can be processed accordingly.

▶ **CHECK**
This method is executed after the SCENARIO_PROCESS_USER_COMMAND method when a standard event in the request form (CHECK or SUBMIT of a form) is triggered. Therefore, the request data are always checked before the request is updated. If errors occur, you can output a corresponding error message via the ES_RETURN export parameter. If you want to output more than one message in the form, you can use the CT_MESSAGE_LIST parameter.

▶ **FINALIZE** (finalize after data storage)
This method is used after the form data have been saved in the database and the request number (IV_OBJECTID) has been created, and before the request number is provided in the screen. You can use the method to execute a follow-up action. If you want to reset the creation of the request in the database, you can output a corresponding error message via the ES_RETURN export parameter. This resets the database entry of the request.

Table 9.9 lists all data structures for the implementation of the methods of the APB_ISR_FORM_PROCESSING BAdI. The meaning and usage of the respective data structure corresponds to the (almost) identically named data structure of the QISR1 BAdI (see Section 9.6.1, Data Structures within the ISR Framework). The programming examples from Section 9.6, Form Flow Logic, can be reused. To do so, simply replace the equivalent data structures.

Parameter	Type	Description
IV_SCENARIO	APB_ISR_SCENARIO	Current ABA scenario—corresponds to FLT_VAL in QISR1
IV_MODE	APB_ISR_MODE	Describes the edit mode
IV_EVENT	APB_ISR_EVENT	Event (standard events and scenario-specific events)—corresponds to USER_COMMAND in QISR1
IV_OBJECTID	APB_ISR_OBJECTID	Object ID
ES_RETURN	BAPIRET1	Return structure for error messages
CT_MESSAGE_LIST	BAPIRET2_T	List with messages of various error categories
CT_UI_ATTRIBUTES	APB_ISR_T_UI_ATTRIBUTE_PARAM	UI properties of a form field
CS_GENERAL_DATA	APB_ISR_S_GENERAL_PARAM	General ISR data
CT_SPECIAL_DATA	APB_ISR_T_SPECIAL_PARAM	Form data
CT_ADDITIONAL_DATA	APB_ISR_T_SPECIAL_PARAM	Values for input helps
CT_EXTERNAL_DATA	APB_ISR_T_SPECIAL_PARAM	Values for control functions

Table 9.9 Interface Parameters of the Methods of the APB_ISR_FORM_PROCESSING BAdI

Default Values for the Parameters MODE and IV_EVENT

The following short list describes the two parameters, Mode and Event, and the relevance of the corresponding permitted values.

▶ **MODE**

MODE describes the current edit mode. The MODE parameter enables you to design your program logic based on the current mode:

- CREATE if the ISR form is called for a new request

- CHANGE if the ISR form with object ID is called to be modified

- DISPLAY if the ISR form with object ID is called to be displayed

- **IV_EVENT**

  IV_EVENT corresponds to the USER_COMMAND parameter in QISR1. The standard ISR events of the IV_EVENT parameter are defined as follows:

  - SEND if the form is sent for a new request

  - SAVE if the form is saved for an existing request

  - CHECK if the CHECK button is clicked in the form

In your customer-specific form, you can define any number of events that can be queried via APB_ISR_FORM_PROCESSING via the IV_EVENT parameter at runtime.

9.8.4 Architecture

The ISR (ABA) supports form-based request scenarios with the options of dynamic programming of input helps, initializations, checks, and own events. These options were described in the previous chapters. Moreover, the ISR (ABA) provides a BAdI interface to flexibly control the request form.

The process that is linked with the request scenario and is used to run the requested service is no longer supported. Consequently, the integration of the business object BUS7051 as the service request's runtime object and the associated Customizing is missing. As a result, integration with Business Workflow is no longer supported automatically. The runtime object of ISR (ABA) must be made available to the application and can be controlled via the BAdI implementation (see Section 9.8.3, Form Flow Logic).

Figure 9.59 illustrates the communication between the APB_ISR_UI_FORM Web Dynpro component and the backend on the one side. The other side shows the integration between ABAP design time and ABAP runtime. This schematic presentation refers to the corresponding Figure 9.43 for the ISR in ECC. Those parts of the architecture that are no longer available in the ISR (ABA) compared with ISR in ECC are indicated in gray. The only technical components left are the components of the ISR (ABA) with the respective, new object names.

Figure 9.59 Communication between ABAP Design Time and ABAP Runtime of the ISR (ABA)

The runtime's Web Dynpro component communicates with the ISR (ABA) runtime in the backend via the APB_ISR_PROCESS_EVENT Remote Function Call (RFC). During ISR (ABA) runtime, the methods of the APB_ISR_FORM_PROCESSING BAdI (see Figure 9.58) are called at different times.

When the form is sent, the form data are stored with a generated, 32-digit OBJECTID in the Business Document Service (BDS) of the Knowledge Provider's document management. The data are not stored with the form as a PDF in ISR (ABA). The Adobe form therefore only serves as the interface layout for entering the request and is always merged with the current data at runtime.

Tip for "Meaningful" Object ID

It is also possible to additionally assign a custom, "meaningful" object ID (maximum length: 20 characters) via the BAdI implementation. This object ID can be transferred in the GENERAL_DATA-HEADER structure in the EXT_REF_NUMBER field. It is updated upon saving.

For integration of the Adobe form, the Web Dynpro applications, APB_ISR_UI and APB_ISR_UI_FPM, which are based on the correspondent Web Dynpro ABAP components, are available:

▶ **Web Dynpro ABAP component APB_ISR_UI**

The APB_ISR_UI Web Dynpro component features the same design and programming as the QISR_UI Web Dynpro component and can thus be integrated as a USED COMPONENT with its own Web Dynpro component (see Section 9.7.3, Usage Options in SAP NetWeaver Portal). Figure 9.60 illustrates the usage of the APB_ISR_UI Web Dynpro ABAP component.

SCENARIO, OBJECTID, and MODE are the parameters required for calling the Web Dynpro application. Table 9.9 provides information on the parameters' meaning.

▶ **Web Dynpro ABAP component APB_ISR_UI_FPM**

The APB_ISR_UI_FPM component is based on Floorplan Manager (FPM) and is only used for demonstration purposes. It is recommended that you use the APB_ISR_UI Web Dynpro component and possibly integrate it with a custom FPM-based application.

Figure 9.60 Schematic Diagram of the APB_ISR_UI Web Dynpro Component as a Direct Component Use

Comparable with ISR in ECC, a APB_ISR_PROCESS_EVENT RFC is available in ISR (ABA). This RFC is the central communication interface of the ISR (ABA) framework between the ISR frontend and the backend. But it can also be used to simulate the processes of creating, changing, or reading a service request *without* deploying the ISR frontend (Web Dynpro application, Adobe form). In this context, the APB_ISR_FORM_PROCESSING BAdI is also implemented. The RFC's interface corresponds to the one of the ISR_PROCESS_EVENT RFC (see Section 9.7.4, ISR_PROCESS_EVENT

RFC). Thanks to Table 9.6, you can understand the meaning easily. The functioning of these two RFCs is completely identical.

9.9   Summary

This chapter introduced you to the concept of the ISR as an application of the interactive Adobe forms within SAP ERP. You now know that the ISR is a framework that you can flexibly configure and that links several SAP components, and you know the prerequisites to use the ISR. A sample scenario was used to illustrate the usage options of the ISR. This chapter also described how you can use the ISR wizard to create a simple ISR scenario together with an Adobe form.

In addition, it introduced the Customizing and BAdI interfaces as the modeling tools of the scenario. Now you can implement complex requirements for the scenario. You learned how you can generate and extend an interactive Adobe form for the ISR framework. This is particularly critical because the ISR framework requires a specific interface and context structure. Furthermore, this chapter illustrated the purpose of the ISR library.

The subsequent sections outlined the basic technical architecture of the ISR. The ABAP interfaces are considerably useful for making the programming of the BAdI implementation of a scenario more efficient.

Finally, you learned about the ISR in the Application Basis (ABA). Chapter 11, ABAP PDF Object, which mainly addresses advanced form developers, provides more information on the ABAP PDF object.

After having discussed online scenarios, we now turn your attention to the implementation of offline scenarios in ABAP. ABAP Offline Infrastructure is used for this purpose, which is basically an extension of the procedure for creating the print output.

10   ABAP Offline Infrastructure

The two previous chapters presented interactive PDF forms as part of an interface technology. Online scenarios were implemented in principle. But Web Dynpro also supports offline scenarios, for instance, by uploading a PDF form. The following now presents interactive PDF forms as the only means for entering data in an offline scenario. This chapter provides step-by-step instructions on how to use ABAP Offline Infrastructure based on a sample scenario. You first learn which scenario is supposed to be implemented. This is followed by a description of how to implement the necessary steps. To do so, you must first configure the email inbound of Business Communication Services and then define an interface. Next, you need to create a form and implement a print program and the offline handler. You can then test the sample scenario.

10.1   Offline Scenarios Using Email Messages

One of the most common procedures for implementing offline scenarios is to send and receive PDF forms via email. The messages are sent and processed automatically in the background. From the technical perspective, this was already possible as of the initial availability of SAP Interactive Forms by Adobe. The sending and processing only had to be programmed manually in ABAP.

In order to drastically reduce the development time required for such scenarios, SAP introduced ABAP Offline Infrastructure with SAP NetWeaver 7.0 Enhancement Package 1 (EHP1) and enhanced it with SAP NetWeaver 7.0 EHP2.

The effort required for development was reduced by combining the programming steps, which repeat in all implementations, and making them available to the developers in ABAP Offline Infrastructure. When you use ABAP Offline Infrastructure, the only task left is to program an offline handler and a print program. Chapter 6 introduced you to the print program. It is just enhanced with an option for sending the generated PDF form.

The offline handler is new and assumes the task of processing the returned PDF forms. It cannot be generalized and automated because different steps, for instance, to start a business process or to validate data, may be necessary depending on the business scenario.

> **Availability of ABAP Offline Infrastructure**
>
> ABAP Offline Infrastructure is available as of SAP NetWeaver 7.0 EHP1 and only in ABAP. There is no comparable infrastructure in Java. Naturally, you still require the SAP NetWeaver Java stack on which an ADS instance runs.
>
> As of SAP NetWeaver 7.0 EHP2, another function module is provided that converts form data (XML format) into the Dictionary-based interface. This functionality is used in this chapter.

10.2 Address Updating in the Flight-Booking Model as a Sample Scenario

In this sample scenario, customers are to be provided with the option to update their address using an interactive PDF form. An update of the address data record may be desirable for different reasons, for instance, to update the address list at regular intervals or to offer customers an easy option to update the address. In this case, the customer—if he received the PDF from in advance—can send the form whenever his address has changed without registering in a portal, logging on, or having to find out the appropriate procedure.

The flight-booking model can be reused for the implementation of the sample scenario. It provides a corresponding structure of the SCUSTOM type and an associated, populated table for the address data records. This data structure also includes the customer's email address. All information required is therefore available.

> **Business Scenarios with Same Structure as the Sample Scenario**
>
> The following business scenarios have a similar structure as our example; their implementation, however, would go beyond the scope of this book:

- Updating vendor master data, for instance, every two years
- Automated time recording by a group lead, who receives a time recording form for his team every Monday and must return it at the end of the week
- Reading the (power) meter readings by customers of a (power) supplier

The call of an ABAP program and the selection of a customer number will be the trigger for sending a PDF form for the address update. An interactive PDF form is generated that contains the currently saved address of the customer. This form is then sent to the customer via email.

After the customer has received the email, he can open the PDF from and update the address. The customer then signs the PDF form digitally and saves the PDF form for reference on his computer. As the last step, he clicks on the SEND UPDATE button in the form. This starts the customer's email program, and a new email message is opened in which the address field is already populated. The filled-out PDF form is already included as an attachment. The customer then confirms the actual sending of the email in the email program.

The email address to which the form was sent is a system email address; that is, it is not assigned to a user. After receipt, the PDF form included in the attachment is processed. The new address data are extracted and the digital signature is validated for security reasons.

- The address data record is to be updated only if the signature is valid.

- If the digital signature is invalid, the address data are rejected.

The address update process is completed in both cases.

Complex Business Scenarios

The example described here is a simple scenario. In particular, it did not consider how to prevent multiple sending of the email message by the customer and the resulting multiple processing of a PDF form. Also not considered was how individual forms can be assigned to business processes.

Both can be implemented via an automatically assigned ID label that is part of the data defined in the PDF form. The definition and processing of this ID label depends on the scenario. For this reason, it cannot be provided as part of ABAP Offline Infrastructure.

The first step in implementing the sample scenario is to configure Business Communication Services for sending and receiving email messages.

10.3 Configuring the Email Inbound

The email inbound is configured using Transaction SO50 (Exit Rules for Inbound Processing). You obtain detailed information if you call HELP • HELP ON APPLICATION in Transaction SO50. The following describes only the steps required for configuring the email inbound.

1. Start Transaction SO50.

2. Select the CREATE button.

3. Choose the INTERNET MAIL entry as the communication type (see Figure 10.1).

Figure 10.1 Configuring the Email Inbound

4. As the RECIPIENT ADDRESS, enter an address for the domain under which your SAP system can be addressed by email from the Internet. Select "pdf" as the NAME, for example. The address may then look as follows: *pdf@nameofyourcompany.com*.

5. Set the document type (DOCUME... column) to "*."

6. Enter the generic exit handler that is provided by ABAP Offline Infrastructure as the EXIT NAME. Its name is `CL_FP_INBOUND_HANDLER`.

7. Change the CALL SEQUENCE (see last column) so that this exit handler is called first. To define the sequence, simply enter the number in the last column.

8. Save your settings.

Inbound mails that are sent to this address are now automatically transferred to ABAP Offline Infrastructure, where they are processed and then forwarded to your own handler later on.

The next steps involve the sending of documents.

10.4   Using ABAP Offline Infrastructure

After you have successfully configured Business Communication Services, you now gradually implement the sample scenario. In the first step, you create an ABAP Dictionary-based interface with the corresponding context.

> **ABAP Offline Infrastructure Does Not Support Version Management**
>
> For offline scenarios, you must bear in mind that PDF forms may be circulating for a longer period of time. If you want to change an existing scenario, you must take special measures because ABAP Offline Infrastructure in its current version does not support the versioning of forms. If changes go beyond purely visual modifications (that is, changes to the data structure), you must work with copies of the interface, the form, and the programs.

10.4.1   Creating the Offline Handler

Before you create the interface and the form, you must first create an empty offline handler because this is the location where you must store the form. A form for offline scenarios can be activated only if you specify a handler, which then receives the data at runtime later on. An offline handler is an ABAP class which implements the IF_FP_OFFLINE interface.

The actual implementation of the handler is done in Section 10.4.5, Processing Forms Received.

Figure 10.2   Creating the Offline Handler

1. Start Transaction SE24, and create a new class, ZCL_IFBA_BOOK_OFFLINE.

2. In the subsequent dialog (see Figure 10.2), enter a DESCRIPTION of the class and SAVE.

3. Select $TMP as the package or click on the LOCAL OBJECT button.

4. Select the INTERFACES tab in the CLASS BUILDER.

5. Enter IF_FP_OFFLINE under INTERFACE, and activate the object (see Figure 10.3).

Figure 10.3 Offline Handler

In Section 10.4.5, Processing Forms Received, you will implement the two predefined methods, GET_INSTANCE and HANDLE_PDF. But first, let's create the form for the PDF generation.

10.4.2 Interface and Context

To create an interface, proceed as described in Section 4.2, Interface of a Form.

1. Create a Dictionary-based interface with the name Z_IFBA_BOOK_OFFLINE_INTERFACE.

2. Create an import parameter CUSTOMER of the SCUSTOM type.

3. Create another EMAIL parameter of the AD_SMTPADR type.

4. Activate the interface. Figure 10.4 shows the completed interface.

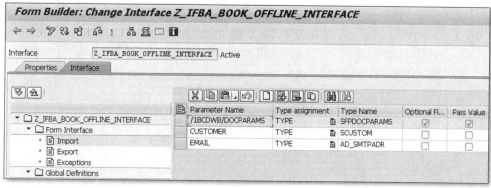

Figure 10.4 Form Interface for the Offline Example

Create the form context as described in Section 4.3, Context of a Form.

1. Create a Z_IFBA_BOOK_OFFLINE_FORM form and select Z_IFBA_BOOK_OFFLINE_
   INTERFACE as the interface.

2. Drag and drop the CUSTOMER structure and the EMAIL field from the interface to
   the context. The result is shown in Figure 10.5.

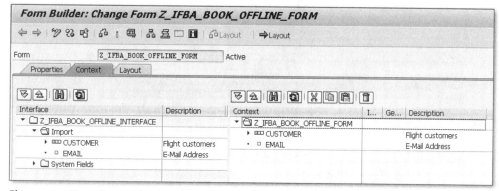

Figure 10.5 Form Context for the Offline Example

You now need to publish the offline handler created in Section 10.4.1 in the
form.

1. Select the PROPERTIES tab in Form Builder.

2. Enter the `ZCL_IFBA_BOOK_OFFLINE` class in the INBOUND HANDLER field. You can use the input help here. The result set is already restricted to valid implementations (see Figure 10.6).

Figure 10.6 Offline Handler Has Been Created

3. Save the form. Note, however, that you cannot activate the form yet because you have not defined any layout yet.

After you have defined the interface and the corresponding context, you can start to create the address update form.

10.4.3 Creating the Form Template

The following description assumes that you are already familiar with form creation. For this reason, the description is kept very short. Should you require a more comprehensive description, you can refer to Chapters 5, Creating Form Templates, and 7, Advanced Form Template Creation. Figure 10.12 shows the complete form template for orientation.

1. If you are no longer in Transaction SPF, start this transaction. Then open the Z_IFBA_BOOK_OFFLINE_FORM form in change mode, and navigate to the LAYOUT tab.

2. Drag and drop a TEXT form field from the STANDARD library to the form template.

3. Enter the following text in this form field: "Address Change Order." You can format it by setting the FONT SIZE to 14 and the STYLE to BOLD (FONT palette).

4. Then insert a blank line and the following text: "You can modify your address directly on this form. To send it for processing follow the instructions below."

5. Below, add a subform to the form template. Increase this form template so that the space allows for five text fields.

6. Then drag and drop the following nodes from the DATA VIEW to the subform in the sequence indicated (Figure 10.12 shows the arrangement in the form): ID, NAME, STREET, POSTCODE, CITY, and TELEPHONE.

7. Besides the arrangement, you can also adapt the size of the individual text fields. Remember to allow for space for the caption if required.

8. In the next step, you edit the ID form field (see hierarchy). First, navigate to the VALUE tab of the OBJECT palette, where you select the READ ONLY entry for the TYPE.

9. Then go to the FIELD tab, and select the entry, NONE, for the APPEARANCE.

10. Subsequently, add another TEXT form field to the form template. Position it below the subform.

11. Enter the following text in this form field: "After finishing your updates please sign the form with a digital signature. Then click on the 'Send update' button to submit the form for processing to us." Enter the following in a new line: "Thank You!"

Alternative Scenario without Signature Field

At this point, you must decide whether you want to implement the scenario with a digital signature. If you do not have a certificate or a secure ADS connection, you can also reproduce this scenario without the digital signature. Simply leave out the signature form field and the program lines for validating the signature in Listing 10.2. In this case, you can skip the next section.

Adding the Logic for the Signature Field

To add the signature field and configure the locking of form fields, proceed as follows:

1. Add a SIGNATURE FIELD below the text and increase this field.

2. Change the caption to "Sign to confirm." Leave sufficient space for the caption.

3. Navigate to the SIGNATURE tab of the OBJECT palette.

4. Check whether the LOCK FIELDS AFTER SIGNING option is selected. Select it if it is still disabled.

5. Choose NEW/MANAGE COLLECTION (see Figure 10.7).

Figure 10.7 Menu Item for Creating a New Collection

6. The COLLECTION LIST dialog is displayed. Click on the NEW button.

7. The system displays a new collection list. Enter the name "ListOfFields" for the collection (see Figure 10.8).

Figure 10.8 Dialog for Editing Collection Lists

8. Then click on MODIFY...

9. The system opens the dialog, COLLECTION EDITOR [LISTOFFIELD], where you select all fields except for BUTTON1 (see Figure 10.9). This button is to remain active (in other words, not locked) after signature so that the PDF form can be returned.

10. To perform the selection in the dialog with only a few steps, you can select the checkbox directly next to the DATA root node and then deselect the checkbox for BUTTON1.

11. Click on OK to close the dialog.

12. Close the COLLECTION LIST dialog by clicking on CLOSE.

Figure 10.9 Selected Form Fields in the Collection Editor

13. Subsequently check whether the ALL FIELDS IN DOCUMENT option is selected in the SIGNATURE TAB.

Adding a Button to Send the PDF Form Via Email

You now want to send the filled-out and signed form via email. To enable easy handling for the user, you provide a button in the form. If the user clicks on this button, the sending of an email message is triggered.

The recipient address is defined during configuration and is therefore a dynamic parameter. So that the recipient address does not have to be defined in the form and thus need to be changed in the form template with every modification of the configuration, it is transferred by the print program in this example. The recipient address is defined for the SEND UPDATE button using a script program.

To create the button for returning the form with the previously described properties, perform the following steps:

1. First add a regular button to the form template. Position it to the right of the signature field.

2. Adjust the size of the button so that the following text is visible as the caption: "Send update."

3. Select the button, and navigate to the FIELD tab of the OBJECT palette, where you change the CONTROL TYPE from NORMAL to SUBMIT. Another tab with the name SUBMIT becomes visible (Figure 10.10).

4. Navigate to the SUBMIT tab of the OBJECT palette. For SUBMIT AS, select the PDF entry.

5. Enter the following in the SUBMIT TO URL: field: "mailto:a@b.com." This is required because the field must not remain empty. If you do not make this selection, you receive a yellow warning and an error message during testing when you open the PDF form. Figure 10.11 shows what the SUBMIT tab is supposed to look like after the last two steps.

6. Then go to the script editor, and select the `layout:ready` event in the SHOW dropdown list. Remember that for these steps you must select the button which you have added in this section.

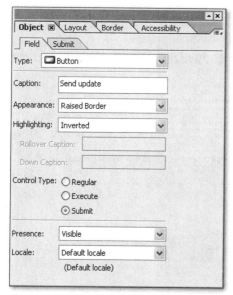

Figure 10.10 Field Tab for the Submit Button

Figure 10.11 Submit Tab for the Email Message Button

7. Enter Listing 10.1 in the script editor. Section 7.3.6, Determining the Recipient Address for an Email Message at Runtime provides a description of this procedure (changing an attribute value of a form field at runtime).

```
this.resolveNode("#event.#submit").target =
                    "mailto:"+$record.EMAIL.value;
```

Listing 10.1 Script Program For Defining the Recipient Address

The creation of the SUBMIT button and the form template is now complete. You can now save the form template.

Figure 10.12 shows the complete form template as a reference for the arrangement and captions of the individual form fields.

Figure 10.12 Form Template for the Address Update as a Reference

You have just created the form template and can now activate the form object as the last step.

As the next step, you will create the print program for generating and sending the PDF form.

10.4.4 Generating and Sending the Form

The program for sending has a structure similar to the one that was discussed in Section 6.1, Print Program. Its task is to determine all address information dependent on the customer number and send the information to the defined email address.

But because email addresses are not valid in the sample database or because the PDF documents would not reach the recipient, the first email address is overwritten with a value that you specify in the selection screen.

This enables you to enter your own email address as the recipient and simulate the scenario. The second email address is the address for inbound processing, which you have defined in Section 10.3, Configuring the Email Inbound.

Listing 10.2 shows the complete program for generating and sending a form.

The gs_docpar-fillable = 'F' assignment is the essential statement for the offline infrastructure. As a result, additional information required for subsequent inbound processing is added to the PDF document at runtime.

Normally you would define the email address of the user via the gv_mail = gs_customer-email. statement. As mentioned previously, you could not receive the PDF then. You therefore define your own address using the gv_mail = p_mail. assignment.

The PDF is sent via email at the end of the program.

The submit process from the SAP system typically occurs after a configurable period of time. You can start the submit process via Transaction SCOT. The online help for this transaction provides further information on the email dispatch, which is not part of this book.

```
PROGRAM z_ifba_book_offline.
INCLUDE fp_utilities.

PARAMETER: p_mail    TYPE ad_smtpadr DEFAULT
                          'yourname@nameofyourcompany.com'
                          LOWER CASE OBLIGATORY,
           p_rmail   TYPE ad_smtpadr DEFAULT
                          'pdf@nameofyourcompany.com'
                          LOWER CASE OBLIGATORY,
           p_custid TYPE scustom-id DEFAULT 12 OBLIGATORY,
           p_conn    TYPE rfcdest OBLIGATORY.
DATA: gs_customer TYPE scustom,
      gv_fmname    TYPE rs38l_fnam,
      gs_outpar    TYPE sfpoutputparams,
      gs_docpar    TYPE sfpdocparams,
      gs_output    TYPE fpformoutput,
      gv_error     TYPE string,
```

```
     gv_mail      TYPE ad_smtpadr.

INITIALIZATION.
  MOVE cl_fp=>get_ads_connection( ) TO p_conn.

AT SELECTION-SCREEN ON VALUE-REQUEST FOR p_conn.
  PERFORM value_help_for_destination USING 'P_CONN'.

START-OF-SELECTION.
  SELECT SINGLE * FROM scustom INTO gs_customer
                  WHERE id = p_custid.
  IF gs_customer IS INITIAL.
    MESSAGE ID 'AD' TYPE 'E' NUMBER '718' WITH 'SCUSTOM'.
  ENDIF.

  TRY.
      CALL FUNCTION 'FP_FUNCTION_MODULE_NAME'
        EXPORTING
          i_name     = 'Z_IFBA_BOOK_OFFLINE_FORM'
        IMPORTING
          e_funcname = gv_fmname.
    CATCH cx_fp_api.
      MESSAGE ID 'FPAPIGENERIC' TYPE 'E' NUMBER '000'
              WITH 'Z_IFBA_BOOK_OFFLINE_FORM'.
  ENDTRY.

  gs_outpar-getpdf     = abap_true.
  gs_outpar-nodialog   = abap_true.
  gs_outpar-connection = p_conn.
  CALL FUNCTION 'FP_JOB_OPEN'
    CHANGING
      ie_outputparams = gs_outpar
    EXCEPTIONS
      cancel          = 1
      usage_error     = 2
      system_error    = 3
      internal_error  = 4
      OTHERS          = 5.
  IF sy-subrc IS NOT INITIAL.
    MESSAGE ID sy-msgid TYPE sy-msgty NUMBER sy-msgno
            WITH sy-msgv1 sy-msgv2 sy-msgv3 sy-msgv4.
  ENDIF.
```

```abap
* Offline handling!
  gs_docpar-fillable = 'F'.
  CALL FUNCTION gv_fmname
    EXPORTING
      /1bcdwb/docparams  = gs_docpar
      customer           = gs_customer
      email              = p_rmail
    IMPORTING
      /1bcdwb/formoutput = gs_output
    EXCEPTIONS
      usage_error        = 1
      system_error       = 2
      internal_error     = 3
      OTHERS             = 4.
  IF sy-subrc IS NOT INITIAL.
    CALL FUNCTION 'FP_GET_LAST_ADS_ERRSTR'
      IMPORTING
        e_adserrstr = gv_error.
    IF NOT gv_error IS INITIAL.
      MESSAGE gv_error TYPE 'E'.
    ELSE.
      MESSAGE ID sy-msgid TYPE sy-msgty NUMBER sy-msgno
              WITH sy-msgv1 sy-msgv2 sy-msgv3 sy-msgv4.
    ENDIF.
  ENDIF.

  CALL FUNCTION 'FP_JOB_CLOSE'
    EXCEPTIONS
      usage_error    = 1
      system_error   = 2
      internal_error = 3
      OTHERS         = 4.
  IF sy-subrc IS NOT INITIAL.
    MESSAGE ID sy-msgid TYPE sy-msgty NUMBER sy-msgno
        WITH sy-msgv1 sy-msgv2 sy-msgv3 sy-msgv4.
  ENDIF.

* Usually, email should be sent to gs_customer-email,
* but for test purposes we use the email address
* from the selection screen.
* gv_mail = gs_customer-email.
  gv_mail = p_mail.
  PERFORM send_mail USING gs_output-pdf gv_mail.
```

```
FORM send_mail USING pv_pdf TYPE xstring
                    pv_mail TYPE ad_smtpadr.
  DATA: lt_content        TYPE solix_tab,
        lv_length         TYPE so_obj_len,
        lv_subject        TYPE so_obj_des,
        lo_document       TYPE REF TO cl_document_bcs,
        lv_message_subject TYPE string,
        lv_error          TYPE string,
        lo_send_request   TYPE REF TO cl_bcs,
        lo_recipient      TYPE REF TO cl_cam_address_bcs,
        lx_exception      TYPE REF TO cx_bcs.

  lt_content = cl_document_bcs=>xstring_to_solix( pv_pdf ).
  lv_length  = xstrlen( pv_pdf ).
  lv_subject = 'IFbA Offline Demo'.
  TRY.
      lo_document = cl_document_bcs=>create_document(
          i_type    = 'PDF'
          i_subject = lv_subject
          i_length  = lv_length
          i_hex     = lt_content ).
      lo_send_request = cl_bcs=>create_persistent( ).
      lo_send_request->set_document( lo_document ).
      lv_message_subject =
              'Please check your data'(001).
      lo_send_request->set_message_subject(
                          lv_message_subject ).
      lo_recipient =
        cl_cam_address_bcs=>create_internet_address(
                      i_address_string = pv_mail ).
      lo_send_request->add_recipient( i_recipient =
                                  lo_recipient ).
      lo_send_request->send( i_with_error_screen =
                                  abap_true ).
    COMMIT WORK.
    MESSAGE ID 'SO' TYPE 'S' NUMBER '024'.
  CATCH cx_bcs INTO lx_exception.
    lv_error = lx_exception->get_text( ).
    MESSAGE lv_error TYPE 'E'.
  ENDTRY.
ENDFORM.
```

Listing 10.2 Generating and Sending the PDF Document

With this program, you can generate and send a form as it is required for ABAP Offline Infrastructure.

Start the program in Transaction SE38. You can enter the customer number and email addresses in the selection screen (see Figure 10.13). After execution, you should have a PDF in your email inbound that can be filled out.

Figure 10.13 Sending the PDF Document

The last step before you can test the scenario is to program the offline handler.

10.4.5 Processing Forms Received

To be able to process the incoming forms, you have already created an offline handler in Section 10.4.1. Next, you will define the logic for the actual processing in the ZCL_IFBA_BOOK_OFFLINE class. This class has two predefined interface methods (see Figure 10.14):

▶ IF_FP_OFFLINE~GET_INSTANCE

▶ IF_FP_OFFLINE~HANDLE_PDF

Figure 10.14 Offline Handler Methods

Initially, implement the IF_FP_OFFLINE~GET_INSTANCE method, which is required for instantiation at runtime. The inbound processing initially calls the general handler, CL_FP_INBOUND_HANDLER, which determines the name of the assigned form in the form data. Based on this name, you then define the name of the offline handler, which you will implement in the following.

1. Double-click on the IF_FP_OFFLINE~GET_INSTANCE method to navigate to the source code editor.

2. Enter CREATE OBJECT ro_instance TYPE zcl_ifba_book_offline. as the program code (see Figure 10.15).

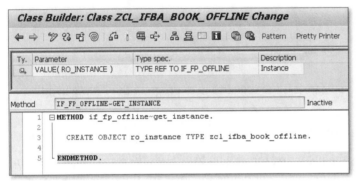

Figure 10.15 Returning the Reference to the Offline Handler

3. Save the class.

Next, implement the actual processing in the IF_FP_OFFLINE~HANDLE_PDF method. Listing 10.3 shows the complete coding.

At this point, the call of the FP_FUNCTION_MODULE_NAME function module may be new to you. So far, its only purpose was to determine the generated function module of a form. Since SAP NetWeaver 7.0 EHP2, it has been enhanced with an additional return parameter EV_FUNCNAME_INBOUND. Put simply, this function module is the opposite to a "normal" function module. It can fill the Dictionary structures from the XML data that is contained in a PDF. Without this module, you had to parse the XML data itself.

After you have called the generated inbound function module, the two parameters, CUSTOMER and EMAIL, are available, which you have created in Section 10.4.2, Interface and Context.

► You do not need the value of EMAIL; this only involves the address to which the PDF document was returned.

► The CUSTOMER parameter, however, contains all data from the form, including the updated address.

Before you write the update data to the database, the digital signature must be checked. Only if the PDF document is signed and the signature is valid will the data be accepted. This is done using the ABAP PDF object. For details on checking digital signatures, refer to Section 11.4.3, Validation of a Digital Signature.

If the signature is valid, the data are updated in the database using the MODIFY statement.

In a real-life scenario, you would certainly write an application log, forward the mail to an agent in case of an error, or start a workflow. In this example, further processing is simply aborted. Moreover, the method checks all signatures and whether these are valid for the highest version number; in this example, only one signature is generated if you do not generate and sign various versions when filling out the form.

Despite these simplifications, you are now familiar with the basic steps for automatic email inbound processing with interactive PDF documents. The extension of the example (see Listing 10.3) in a real-life scenario strongly depends on the respective requirements.

```
METHOD if_fp_offline~handle_pdf.
  DATA: lv_fm_name     TYPE rs38l_fnam,
        ls_customer    TYPE scustom,
        lv_email       TYPE ad_smtpadr,
        lo_pdfobj      TYPE REF TO if_fp_pdf_object,
        lv_maxversion  TYPE i,
        lt_signatures  TYPE tfpsignature,
        ls_signature   TYPE sfpsignature.

* Check parameters.
  IF iv_form_name IS INITIAL OR iv_pdf IS INITIAL OR
     iv_xml IS INITIAL.
    RAISE EXCEPTION TYPE cx_fp_offline
      EXPORTING textid = cx_fp_offline=>cx_fp_offline.
  ENDIF.

* Get name of inbound handler for XML->DDIC conversion.
```

```abap
    TRY.
        CALL FUNCTION 'FP_FUNCTION_MODULE_NAME'
            EXPORTING
              i_name                = iv_form_name
            IMPORTING
              ev_funcname_inbound = lv_fm_name.
      CATCH cx_fp_api.
        RAISE EXCEPTION TYPE cx_fp_offline
            EXPORTING textid = cx_fp_offline=>cx_fp_offline.
    ENDTRY.

* Convert XML: Get customer record.
* Note: lv_email only contains the receiving address.
    CALL FUNCTION lv_fm_name
      EXPORTING
        iv_xml_data     = iv_xml
      IMPORTING
        customer        = ls_customer
        email           = lv_email
      EXCEPTIONS
        usage_error     = 1
        system_error    = 2
        internal_error  = 3
        OTHERS          = 4.
    IF sy-subrc IS NOT INITIAL.
      RAISE EXCEPTION TYPE cx_fp_offline
          EXPORTING textid = cx_fp_offline=>cx_fp_offline.
    ENDIF.

* Verify signature.
    TRY.
        lo_pdfobj =
          cl_fp=>get_reference( )->create_pdf_object( ).
        lo_pdfobj->set_document( pdfdata = iv_pdf ).
        lo_pdfobj->set_task_getsignatures( ).
        lo_pdfobj->execute( ).
        lo_pdfobj->get_signatures(
          IMPORTING
            numversions = lv_maxversion
            signatures  = lt_signatures ).
      CATCH cx_fp_runtime.
        RAISE EXCEPTION TYPE cx_fp_offline
            EXPORTING textid = cx_fp_offline=>cx_fp_offline.
    ENDTRY.
```

```
IF lt_signatures IS INITIAL.
  RAISE EXCEPTION TYPE cx_fp_offline
    EXPORTING textid = cx_fp_offline=>cx_fp_offline.
ENDIF.
LOOP AT lt_signatures INTO ls_signature.
  IF NOT (
      ls_signature-status = if_fp_pdf_security_status=>ok
    AND
      ls_signature-maxversion = lv_maxversion ).
    RAISE EXCEPTION TYPE cx_fp_offline
      EXPORTING textid = cx_fp_offline=>cx_fp_offline.
  ENDIF.
ENDLOOP.

* Update customer record on DB.
  MODIFY scustom FROM ls_customer.

ENDMETHOD.
```

Listing 10.3 Evaluating the Inbound Data

Save and activate the class. You have now created all components required (interface, form, email dispatch, inbound processing, and offline handler) and can start the scenario.

Security for Offline Scenarios

The validation of the digital signature is a first step in ensuring the security of offline scenarios. In this example, however, you have checked the validity of only the signature (see Section 11.4.3, Validation of a Digital Signature, to obtain further details on the validation of digital signatures).

Another step is the assignment of certificates to users. This cannot be implemented by ADS because ADS does not include any user administration and because this should be part of the existing user administration to not double the effort required for configuration and maintenance. ADS supports an assignment only if a high volume of information on the digital signature is returned (see the example in Section 11.4.3).

Another step is the *certification of forms* before they are sent. This enables the customer to trace the creator of a form. Moreover, prior to processing, you can check whether the certification is still intact. If not, the form was changed and the processing must be terminated for security reasons.

You must also consider the security of the communication channel itself. If this is not possible or would be too expensive, you can utilize Adobe LiveCycle Rights Management to implement a targeted control of the access rights.

10.5 Testing the Offline Scenario

To go through the entire scenario and check its proper functioning, proceed as follows:

1. Start the z_ifba_book_offline program in Transaction SE38.

2. In the selection screen, enter the parameters in accordance with your configuration (see Figure 10.13).

3. Execute the program.

   This is the point where the work with the scenario starts from the perspective of the customer who is supposed to update an address.

4. You should have an email in your inbox after a short period of time. This email should be similar to the one illustrated in Figure 10.16.

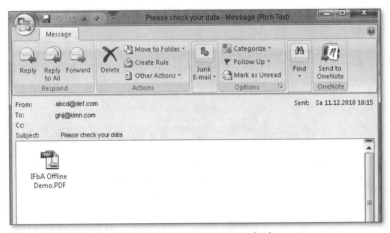

Figure 10.16 Received Email with a PDF Form Attached

5. Save the PDF file from the attachment, and then open it using Adobe Reader.

6. Fill out the PDF form. The customer number cannot be changed. All other fields from the form are ready for input.

7. After you have filled out the form, you need to sign it by clicking on the signature form field and selecting an available certificate. This step is necessary if you have decided on a scenario that is implemented with a digital signature.

8. Figure 10.17 shows what the PDF form looks like after it has been signed.

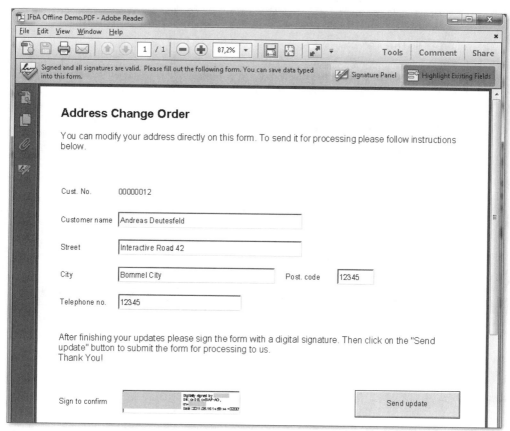

Figure 10.17 Filling Out the PDF Form in Adobe Reader

9. Now click on the SEND UPDATE button. The dialog shown in Figure 10.18 opens where you can select the desktop email application.

10. Select the applicable option.

11. If you have a desktop email application on your computer and select the corresponding option, a window is opened to create an email message (see Figure 10.19).

Figure 10.18 Selection Dialog of the Email Program

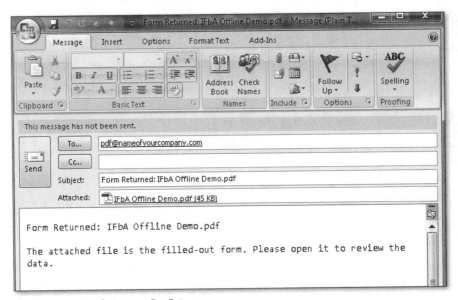

Figure 10.19 Email Message For Return

12. The recipient address is already entered for the email message. If the scenario was implemented correctly, this is the address you have configured and entered in the selection screen of the program for sending the PDF form.

13. Click on the SEND button to confirm dispatch. The email message is returned for further processing.

The scenario can be further enhanced to increase user-friendliness. In this case, a confirmation email is sent to the customer to inform him about the successful receipt and processing of the PDF form. This email message, in turn, can contain a print form. This book already imparted the knowledge that is required to implement this.

The perspective of the customer who received the form for the address update and returned it in the previous step ends here.

The next step involves the processing of the PDF form received by the customer. This is done without any manual steps. You can check the proper functioning by performing the following steps:

1. Start Transaction SE16 (Data Browser) and enter the "SCUSTOM" in the TABLE NAME field (see Figure 10.20).

Figure 10.20 Selecting the SCUSTOM Table

2. A selection screen for the SCUSTOM table opens. In the ID field, enter the customer number that you have entered as the parameter for the z_ifba_book_offline program in the second step of this section (see page 628). In this example, the value is "12" (see Figure 10.21).

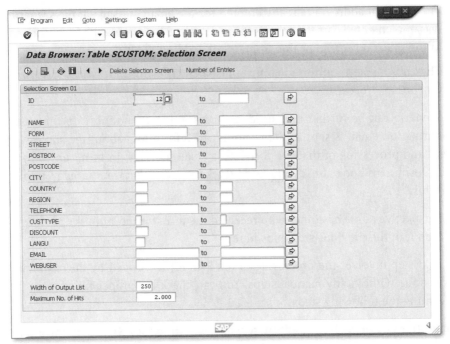

Figure 10.21 Selecting the Customer Number Used (12)

3. Choose EXECUTE.

4. The entry is output in the table for the customer as shown in Figure 10.22.

Figure 10.22 Updated Data Record in the SCUSTOM Table

If the offline handler was implemented correctly, the table entry shows the values entered in the PDF form (in the fields that were available in the form, for instance, NAME). The correct functioning of the scenario implementation was thus checked.

10.6　Summary

This chapter introduced you to ABAP Offline Infrastructure. You first got to know an introductory sample scenario, whose implementation was then described step by step. The implementation of the scenario was then tested to illustrate its functioning.

In the course of this book, you have been introduced to several runtime environments and their usage. If you require more flexibility for creating and processing both print forms and interactive PDF forms, refer to Chapter 11, ABAP PDF Object, where you can obtain information on how to access the ADS functionality via the ABAP PDF object.

The ABAP PDF object is the interface to Adobe Document Services (ADS). It provides access to various functions that can be used in ABAP programs and provides a high level of flexibility, particularly in offline scenarios.

11 ABAP PDF Object

So far, you have used ADS only in conjunction with form output and interactive online scenarios. You have used a function module interface that automatically calls the required functions of ADS and processes the result in the system. However, you have not communicated with ADS directly—this task is assumed by the form runtime environment.

In addition, you were introduced to different frameworks, such as Web Dynpro ABAP and Internet Service Request (ISR). All of these frameworks have been specially designed for their respective application and provide functions that are relevant for the appropriate scenarios. However, individual frameworks do not provide all of the functions of ADS. For example, Web Dynpro ABAP does not offer a connection to the SAP spool system, and the form runtime environment has no interface for digital signatures.

11.1 Overview

This chapter discusses the ABAP Portable Document Format (PDF) object that provides you with comprehensive functions for processing PDF documents. It is an interface that uses the methods of ADS, which enables you to implement your requirements very flexibly.

In some cases, however, you must handle details that are otherwise assumed by the frameworks. This, in turn, increases the programming effort. For example, if you want to create a PDF, you must provide an XML data stream and the form in binary format or via a URL. Otherwise, this is done by the form runtime environment. However, there are several options for retrieving this information.

You can also use the PDF object to create a print output. Because you then must assume the administration of spool requests and the communication with the spool system yourself, it is recommended that you use the function module interface as described in Chapter 6, Form Output. Therefore, this chapter focuses on the options for calling ADS in offline scenarios.

Section 11.2, Instantiating the PDF Object, provides a general overview of the PDF object and describes its basic functioning. This is followed by the steps required to develop an offline scenario with interactive PDF forms. Here, the focus is on the processing steps that require a functionality of ADS and how you can use them via the PDF object.

The creation of interactive PDF documents as the first step is detailed in Section 11.3, Creating a PDF Document. Section 11.4, Processing an Interactive PDF Document, describes how you can process a filled-out PDF document after it has been received in the SAP system. This section also discusses the extraction of data (see Section 11.4.2, Data Extraction) and the validation of digital signatures (see Section 11.4.3, Validation of a Digital Signature). Section 11.5, Certifying PDF Documents, describes how to certify PDF documents and check the validity of the certification during processing. Chapter 10, ABAP Offline Infrastructure, already addressed this topic. Section 11.6, Job Profile, briefly describes the option of transferring job profiles when calling Adobe Document Services. Finally, the chapter is rounded off with an overview of additional methods for the PDF object (see Section 11.7, Additional Methods of the PDF Object).

Note of the Following Presentation

For the sake of simplicity, local files are used in this chapter to focus the examples on the essential aspects.

11.2   Instantiating the PDF Object

The IF_FP_PDF_OBJECT interface for the PDF object provides all of the methods that you need for accessing ADS. The implementing class of this interface is CL_FP_PDF_OBJECT.

You can create an instance of this class via the factory class, `CL_FP` (see Listing 11.1). You need this coding in all of the programs that work with the PDF object. After that, you can access all methods of the PDF object via the `l_pdfobj` reference.

```
DATA: l_fp      TYPE REF TO if_fp,
      l_pdfobj  TYPE REF TO if_fp_pdf_object,
      l_fpex    TYPE REF TO cx_fp_runtime,
      l_err     TYPE string.
* Get FP reference.
l_fp = cl_fp=>get_reference( ).
TRY.
*    Create PDF Object.
     l_pdfobj = l_fp->create_pdf_object( ).
   CATCH cx_fp_runtime_internal
         cx_fp_runtime_system
         cx_fp_runtime_usage INTO l_fpex.
     l_err = l_fpex->get_errmsg( ).
     MESSAGE l_err TYPE 'E'.
ENDTRY.
```

Listing 11.1 Instantiating the PDF Object

If you do not specify a connection to ADS, the system uses the standard connection with the name ADS. If you have created additional connections in your system, you can transfer them when creating the reference. The CREATE_PDF_OBJECT method has an optional parameter, CONNECTION, via which you can transfer the connection.

Because errors can occur during the method calls, you must catch multiple exceptions. The three following exception classes derive from CX_FP_RUNTIME. In Listing 11.1, all exceptions are processed collectively:

▶ **CX_FP_RUNTIME_INTERNAL**
The exception class, CX_FP_RUNTIME_INTERNAL, is intended for internal errors of the PDF object and you will hardly ever come across it.

▶ **CX_FP_RUNTIME_SYSTEM**
The exception class, CX_FP_RUNTIME_SYSTEM, is primarily used if a serious error occurs in the processing done by ADS.

▶ **CX_FP_RUNTIME_USAGE**
The CX_FP_RUNTIME_USAGE exception is triggered if you call the PDF object incorrectly or provide insufficient information for a scenario.

The PDF object contains a lot of methods. Therefore, you are first provided with a brief overview of the different types of methods.

► The methods of the PDF object are subdivided into different groups. For example, you can use the SET methods to set different data—an example is the SET_DATA method to specify XML data.

► Another group is formed by the SET_TASK methods that communicate the tasks to the PDF object. Here, you can specify, for example, whether you want to create a PDF document (SET_TASK_RENDERPDF) or extract the data from a PDF (SET_TASK_EXTRACTDATA).

► The EXECUTE method is the method that calls ADS. You must set all data and specify the task of the PDF object prior to this call.

► GET methods deliver results that are provided depending on the task, for example, a PDF document or an XML data stream.

► You need the RESET method to reuse the instance of the PDF object after a call to ADS. This method resets the internal data.

When you call the EXECUTE method, the system checks the input data for completeness and creates the work instructions for ADS. Then the actual call is implemented via the Web service interface. If the call was successful, that is, no exception was triggered, you can call the result via different GET methods. For example, if you requested a PDF document, you can receive it via the GET_PDF method. If you schedule another call to ADS and want to reuse the instance of the PDF object, you must reset the PDF object via the RESET method.

The following sections of this chapter describe the different application scenarios of the PDF object, including sample programs that are provided as test programs by SAP (a test program exists for each method). You can use these programs to familiarize yourself with and test the options of the PDF objects. After that, you can copy the method calls into your own programs. The basic structure is always identical:

1. Creating the instance
2. Setting the data
3. Specifying the task
4. Calling ADS
5. Retrieving results

11.3 Creating a PDF Document

The creation of a PDF document is the primary function of Adobe Document Services. Chapter 6 described how you can create a PDF document via the function module interface and return it to the application. In this process, you can define various properties, for example, whether the PDF is interactive, whether additional usage rights are assigned, or whether it is a dynamic interactive PDF document. The data for the form were provided either as Dictionary objects or as XML data stream.

To create a PDF document, you need a form and a data stream. However, you can also create a PDF document without transferring a data stream. This is particularly useful for interactive scenarios; however, values are frequently predefined here.

The PDF object includes methods in its interface that you can use to control the PDF creation. This can be important, for example, if the functions are not provided via the superordinate interfaces.

Let's first look at the form: Where can you obtain a form for document creation? The PDF object cannot access the form repository that was described in Chapter 4, Interface and Form Context. You can use Transaction SFP to maintain forms that are evaluated by the form runtime environment and provided to the PDF object. If you use the PDF object directly, you must retrieve the form yourself. Proceed as follows:

1. For simplicity, let's assume that the form is saved locally on your computer. You can find a sample form and a corresponding data record relative to the installation directory of Adobe LiveCycle Designer *\EN\Samples\Purchase Order\ Schema*. There you will find two folders called FORMS and DATA. The FORMS folder includes the form *Purchase Order.xdp;* the DATA folder contains the XML data record *Purchase Order.xml*.

2. To create a PDF from these two files, use the test program, `FP_PDF_TEST_01`. Enter the complete path of the *Purchase Order.xml* file as the XFD FILENAME via the input help. Select the *Purchase Order.xdp* file under XFT FILENAME. You can leave the other fields as they are.

3. Select EXECUTE to display the finished PDF.

Now, take a closer look at the test program to better understand the methods of the PDF object. Listing 11.2 shows the relevant part. The other parts of the program deal with importing files, error handling, and PDF display.

```
l_pdfobj = l_fp->create_pdf_object( ).
l_pdfobj->set_template( xftdata = l_xft locale = l_locale ).
l_pdfobj->set_data( formdata = l_xfd ).
l_pdfobj->set_task_renderpdf( ).
l_pdfobj->execute( ).
l_pdfobj->get_pdf( IMPORTING pdfdata = pdfresult ).
```

Listing 11.2 Creating a PDF Document

Listing 11.2 illustrates the following case:

► After the instantiation of the PDF object, the system calls the SET_TEMPLATE method to transfer the content of a form. You will learn how you can transfer a form via a reference later on. In this process, the system also sets the locale—a combination of language and country, for example, de_DE or en_US.

► The XML data is specified via the SET_DATA method.

► A PDF creation is requested by calling the SET_TAST_RENDERPDF method to communicate the task to be sent to the PDF object.

► Now, all information for creating a document is available; this is done via the call of the EXECUTE method. Only now is ADS called and contents transferred.

► Retrieve the result—the finished PDF document—via the GET_PDF method. This method also returns the number of pages created; the parameter is called RENDERPAGECOUNT and is an integer type.

11.3.1 Retrieving a Form

In a real-life scenario, the form and the data stream are not available on your local PC and you must retrieve the form from the respective storage. If the form was created using Transaction SFP, you can use an Application Program Interface (API) to read the form. This chapter does not detail the complex API of the SAFPAPI package, which provides comprehensive functions for form processing. You need this package if you want to generate forms via API. But because you want to determine the form content only at runtime, you can also use a help class for access.

This help class is called `CL_FP_WB_HELPER` and offers interesting methods for accessing interfaces and forms. The method used to read a form at runtime is called `FORM_LOAD_FOR_RUNTIME`. However, this method does not provide the content of the form, only a reference to a form workbench object. The code fragment from Listing 11.3 shows how you can retrieve the form content.

```
DATA: l_wb_form TYPE REF TO if_fp_wb_form,
      l_form    TYPE REF TO if_fp_form,
      l_layout  TYPE REF TO if_fp_layout,
      l_content TYPE FPCONTENT.
l_wb_form = cl_fp_wb_helper=>form_load_for_runtime(
              i_name = l_name i_language = l_language ).
l_form ?= l_wb_form->get_object( ).
l_layout = l_form->get_layout( ).
l_content = l_layout->get_layout_data( ).
```

Listing 11.3 Reading the Form Content

The `FORM_LOAD_FOR_RUNTIME` method expects the name (`FPNAME` data type) and language (`LANGU` data type) as parameters. The result—a reference to `IF_FP_WB_FORM`—is used to determine the reference to a form object (`IF_FP_FORM`). This object, in turn, provides the `GET_LAYOUT` method to access the layout object (`IF_FP_LAYOUT`); the actual form content is now available in binary form via the `GET_LAYOUT_DATA` method (the `FPCONTENT` data type corresponds to the `XSTRING` ABAP data type).

Note on Error Handling in the Examples

This example does not contain any error handling. Therefore, note that you must catch the corresponding exceptions of the method, for example, if the required form does not exist.

You can transfer the form that you read as shown in Listing 11.3 to the PDF object via the `SET_TEMPLATE` method (see Listing 11.2).

11.3.2 Transferring a Form via a Reference

If you provide the forms separately and enable HTTP access, you can transfer a link to the form instead of the form itself. To do this, select the `XFTFILE` parameter instead of `XFTDATA` when calling the `SET_TEMPLATE` method. You can transfer HTTP or FILE references, which may refer to a file in a directory.

Note, however, that ADS must have access via the specified URL. This is the task of the form runtime environment because only a logical connection can be transferred. ADS retrieves the logon data via a Destination service (the configuration is described in Chapter 3, Installation and Configuration).

Therefore, the simplest way is to read the form separately and transfer it to the PDF object as content; however, no caching options are available this way. Therefore, the creation of the PDF document via the function module interface is preferred.

11.3.3 Creating an Interactive PDF Document

To ensure that the PDF is created as an interactive document, only a minor modification for calling the SET_TEMPLATE method is necessary. To do this, set the FILLABLE parameter to 'X'. If you want to create a dynamic interactive PDF, also set the DYNAMIC parameter to 'X' when calling the SET_TASK_RENDERPDF method.

You can use the PRINTABLE and CHANGESRESTRICTED parameters to restrict the change options. By default, you always create a PDF document that you can print from Adobe Reader. But if you set the PRINTABLE parameter to its initial value, you can no longer print the PDF. The CHANGESRESTRICTED parameter controls whether you may fill or sign a PDF document; you can also restrict the sticky note function with this parameter.

These functions are activated by default. Table 11.1 contains a list of the possible values.

Value	Allowed Functions
space	All changes
A	Only additional contents
F	Filling and signing
N	Filling, signing, and annotations
X	No changes allowed

Table 11.1 Values for the Change Options of a PDF Document

Now let's create a small program with which you can create different types of PDF documents for testing purposes and that enables you to create an interactive PDF document that is optionally dynamic. An XML file with data is supposed to be optional so that you can receive an empty interactive PDF document. This is needed in Section 11.4 for simulating an offline scenario.

Listing 11.4 shows the program's code.

```
PROGRAM z_ifba_book_pdf.
TYPE-POOLS abap.
INCLUDE fp_utilities.
PARAMETERS:
    p_xfd  TYPE localfile VISIBLE LENGTH 64,
    p_xft  TYPE localfile VISIBLE LENGTH 64 OBLIGATORY,
    p_pdf  TYPE localfile VISIBLE LENGTH 64 OBLIGATORY,
    p_int  TYPE abap_bool DEFAULT abap_true AS CHECKBOX,
    p_dyn  TYPE abap_bool AS CHECKBOX.
DATA: l_fp        TYPE REF TO if_fp,
      l_pdfobj    TYPE REF TO if_fp_pdf_object,
      l_xft       TYPE xstring,
      l_xfd       TYPE xstring,
      l_pdfresult TYPE xstring,
      l_fpex      TYPE REF TO cx_fp_runtime,
      l_error     TYPE string.
AT SELECTION-SCREEN ON VALUE-REQUEST FOR p_xfd.
  PERFORM value_help_for_file USING 'XML' CHANGING p_xfd.
AT SELECTION-SCREEN ON VALUE-REQUEST FOR p_xft.
  PERFORM value_help_for_file USING 'XDP' CHANGING p_xft.
AT SELECTION-SCREEN ON VALUE-REQUEST FOR p_pdf.
  PERFORM value_help_for_output_file USING 'PDF'
                                     CHANGING p_pdf.
START-OF-SELECTION.
  IF p_xfd IS NOT INITIAL.
    PERFORM load_file USING p_xfd CHANGING l_xfd.
  ENDIF.
  PERFORM load_file USING p_xft CHANGING l_xft.
* Get FP reference.
  l_fp = cl_fp=>get_reference( ).
  TRY.
*    Create PDF Object.
    l_pdfobj = l_fp->create_pdf_object( ).
*    Set template.
    l_pdfobj->set_template( xftdata = l_xft
                            fillable = p_int ).
*    Set data.
    IF l_xfd IS NOT INITIAL.
```

```
        l_pdfobj->set_data( formdata = l_xfd ).
      ENDIF.
*     Tell PDF object to create PDF.
      l_pdfobj->set_task_renderpdf( dynamic = p_dyn ).
*     Execute, call ADS.
      l_pdfobj->execute( ).
*     Get result.
      l_pdfobj->get_pdf( IMPORTING pdfdata = l_pdfresult ).
    CATCH cx_fp_runtime_internal
          cx_fp_runtime_system
          cx_fp_runtime_usage INTO l_fpex.
      l_error = l_fpex->get_errmsg( ).
      MESSAGE l_error TYPE 'E'.
  ENDTRY.
  PERFORM download_file USING l_pdfresult p_pdf.
```

Listing 11.4 Flexibly Creating Interactive PDF Documents

For testing purposes, you can create any forms that you created using Adobe Live-
Cycle Designer. If you define an XML file, the XML structure must suffice for the
schema of the form design.

Interactive Forms Can Be Created via the Form Interface

You can also create an interactive or dynamic form with restricted change options via
the function module interface.

Listing 11.5 shows an example of how you must change Listing 11.6 from Section
6.4.2, Returning Documents, to receive a dynamic interactive PDF document that
you may only fill out and sign.

```
  ...
* Request PDF document.
  gs_outputpar-nodialog = abap_true.
  gs_outputpar-getpdf   = abap_true.
..gs_outputpar-pdfchangesrestricted = 'F'.
  CALL FUNCTION 'FP_JOB_OPEN'
    CHANGING
      ie_outputparams = gs_outputpar
    EXCEPTIONS
  ...
* Set language and country.
  gs_docparams-langu        = p_langu.
```

```
    gs_docparams-country      = p_ctry.
    gs_docparams-fillable     = abap_true.
    gs_docparams-interactive  = abap_true.
* Call generated function module (form).
    CALL FUNCTION gv_fmname
      EXPORTING
...
```

Listing 11.5 Example for Restricted Change Options

11.3.4 Usage Rights

When an interactive PDF document is created via ADS, usage rights are added to the document by default. This enables the user not only to change values in an interactive PDF document but also to save them or send them via email. In addition, the user can also add a digital signature or annotations to the document.

There are many different usage rights that are summarized in categories and are available as attributes in the IF_FP_PDF_USAGE_RIGHTS interface. Most of the following usage rights are added to the interactive PDF document by default; if not, this is indicated in the text.

▶ **DOCRIGHTS**

The FULLSAVE usage right enables you to save the document with all changes. This usage right is not set by default and is the only usage right from the DOCRIGHTS category.

▶ **FORMRIGHTS**

The usage rights FILLIN, ADD, and DELETE enable you to fill out, add, and delete fields. IMPORT or EXPORT enable the import or export of form data. SUBMITSTANDALONE enables the offline transfer, while SPAWNTEMPLATE enables the creation of new pages. ONLINE is required for calling Web services from the form, and BARCODE activates a 2D bar code functionality. The usage rights IMPORT and BARCODE are not set by default.

▶ **SIGNRIGHTS**

For working with digital signatures, you must set the usage right MODIFY.

▶ **ANNOTRIGHTS**

The usage rights CREATE, DELETE, MODIFY, COPY, IMPORT, and EXPORT are available for working with annotations. The usage right ONLINE, for uploading and downloading annotations, is not set by default.

▶ **EMBEDFILERIGHTS**

To work with file attachments, you must set the usage rights `CREATE`, `DELETE`, `MODIFY`, and `IMPORT`.

▶ **No usage rights**

If you do not want to set usage rights during the creation of interactive PDF documents, you must call the `SET_USAGERIGHTS` method prior to the call to ADS.

Here, you can use the `DEFAULT_RIGHTS` parameter to control whether or not you want to use the standard rights. If you set the parameter to `ABAP_FALSE`, no rights are set.

▶ **Individual usage rights**

If you want to use only some rights, set the parameter to `ABAP_FALSE` and transfer the desired rights together with the `RIGHTS` table parameter.

The structure of the table consists of two fields, `RIGHT` and `VALUE`. In the `RIGHT` field, you can transfer the `IF_FP_PDF_USAGE_RIGHTS=>ANNOTRIGHTS` value, and in the `VALUE` field the `IF_FP_PDF_USAGE_RIGHTS=>ANNOTRIGHT_CREATE` value, for example. Note that the usage rights,, `BARCODE` and `ONLINE` are not part of the credential and can therefore not be used presently.

Listing 11.6 shows how you can extend Listing 11.4 so that the user can only add and change annotations to an interactive PDF document. Insert the lines directly before calling the `EXECUTE` method.

```
* No default usage rights
* Only allow create/modify annotations
DATA: l_right   TYPE sfpuright,
      lt_rights TYPE tfpuright.
l_right-right = if_fp_pdf_usage_rights=>annotrights.
l_right-value = if_fp_pdf_usage_rights=>annotright_create.
APPEND l_right TO lt_rights.
l_right-right = if_fp_pdf_usage_rights=>annotrights.
l_right-value = if_fp_pdf_usage_rights=>annotright_modify.
APPEND l_right TO lt_rights.
CALL METHOD l_pdfobj->set_usagerights
  EXPORTING
    default_rights = abap_false
    rights         = lt_rights.
```

Listing 11.6 Defining Usage Rights

When you execute the changed program, you can only add or change annotations in the PDF; you cannot change the values in the form.

Default usage rights are also assigned to interactive PDF documents that are created via the function module interface. This is done automatically when you set the `FILLABLE` parameter to `ABAP_TRUE` during the creation of the documents (see Section 6.4.2). If you want to create a document without usage rights via the function module interface, set the `FILLABLE` parameter to `'N'`.

When you have created an interactive PDF document, you can add usage rights later on. To do this, refer to the `FP_PDF_TEST_27` test program that can read an existing PDF file, add a usage right, and save the new PDF.

11.4 Processing an Interactive PDF Document

The Web Dynpro ABAP and ISR frameworks presented in this book are specialized for processing online scenarios. However, interactive PDF documents also support numerous functions that are required in offline scenarios. The complete implementation of an interactive offline scenario would go beyond the scope of this book because many different options for interactive PDF documents can be received in the system. Furthermore, the requirements of how to handle data are characterized by different aspects. Therefore, this chapter focuses on the essential points and presents the functions of the PDF object that support you in the processing of interactive PDF documents.

The core functions for processing are always identical regardless of how documents were received in the system. Therefore, for better understanding, it is sufficient to simulate an offline scenario based on examples. The concepts presented can be found in every implementation.

An offline scenario consists of three steps:

1. An interactive PDF document is provided. It can contain prepopulated data and be sent to a user via email or be provided for download on an Internet page.
2. The user fills in the form with data and adds a digital signature, if necessary.
3. The completed and possibly signed form is sent via email or uploaded in a portal to the system for processing.

We have already discussed the necessary functions of ADS for the first step, that is, providing an interactive PDF document. You can create such a document either via the generated function module interface or directly via the PDF object (see Section 11.3.3, Creating an Interactive PDF Document). Here, you can also influence the usage rights (see Section 11.3.4, Usage Rights).

During the creation, you can partially predefine data. The finished PDF document is then sent via email or provided for download. If your scenario requires unique identification when it is received, you can generate hidden data in the PDF document. Here, it is sufficient to transfer the data in the form context (or simply in the XML data stream if you work with the PDF object directly) during document creation; the fields do not have to be bound to the form. The hidden data can be read later on, which enables an identification of the scenario and a unique assignment of the document. However, the exact implementation depends on the specific requirements.

11.4.1 Filling Out an Interactive PDF Document

Now we will create an interactive PDF document as described in Section 11.3, using the purchase order example. You can find all of the required data in the installation directory of Adobe LiveCycle Designer.

1. Start the Z_IFBA_BOOK_PDF program and specify the sample form and the data record.

2. As PDF FILENAME, specify the target file in which the finished PDF document is to be saved. The checkboxes for an interactive or dynamic document are set so that an interactive, not dynamic, document is created.

3. If you open the created PDF document with Adobe Reader, you can change the field values. For example, change the quantities in the purchase order. You can see that the total is adapted automatically.

4. At the bottom left, there is a signature field. Simply click on it to sign the document digitally. Select a DIGITAL ID and click on SIGN (see Figure 11.1). In the figure, some fields are grayed out for security reasons.

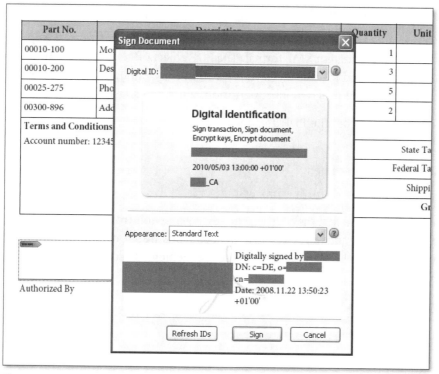

Part No.			Quantity	Unit
00010-100	Mo		1	
00010-200	Des		3	
00025-275	Pho		5	
00300-896	Add		2	
Terms and Conditions				
Account number: 1234				

Figure 11.1   Signing a PDF Document

5. Adobe Reader now prompts you to save the document. Enter a file name and save the document. The document is now digitally signed and displayed accordingly by Adobe Reader (see Figure 11.2).

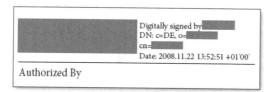

Figure 11.2   Signature in a PDF Document

6. The completed and signed PDF document can now be sent via email.

The following descriptions focus on the processing of the document after it has been received by the system. The following sections detail how to extract data from a PDF document and check the digital signature.

11.4.2 Data Extraction

An important functionality for processing interactive PDF documents is the option to extract data provided in XML format. The PDF object offers methods to transfer a PDF document and to read the XML data from it by calling ADS. To do this, a complete application program must perform the following tasks:

1. Extracting data from the PDF document

2. XML processing

3. Identifying the document

4. Starting a process for further processing

This book details the first task, that is, the data extraction from a PDF document. The XML processing and the assignment of documents are strongly characterized by the application and the scenario and must be implemented accordingly depending on the respective requirement.

Listing 11.7 shows the basic steps of data extraction:

```
l_pdfobj = l_fp->create_pdf_object( ).
l_pdfobj->set_document( pdfdata = l_pdf ).
l_pdfobj->set_task_extractdata( ).
l_pdfobj->execute( ).
l_pdfobj->get_data ( formdata = l_data ).
```

Listing 11.7 Calling the PDF Object for Data Extraction

1. Transfer an existing document to the PDF object via the SET_DOCUMENT method.

2. Select the data extraction by calling the SET_TASK_EXTRACTDATA method.

3. ADS is called via the EXECUTE method.

4. The data of the document are available and can be retrieved using the GET_DATA method.

The complete program (FP_PDF_TEST_03) is available in your system. In the selection screen, select a PDF file and specify a target file to save the XML data. If you create an interactive PDF document via the program from Listing 11.4, you can extract the data with the FP_PDF_TEST_03 program.

1. Specify the file as the PDF document that contains the changed values and the signature from Section 11.4.1, Filling Out an Interactive PDF Document.

2. Open the created XML file and check to see whether it contains the changed values. Now these data can be processed by an application. The values are not saved in the local files.

3. The PDF object returns the data directly to the calling application. The test program saves the files locally to make working with the PDF object as easily as possible.

4. A real application would now receive the data and start a workflow for further processing, if necessary.

5. For processing the XML data, use the XML processor in ABAP to map the values from the XML data stream to the Dictionary fields.

Data Extraction from Interactive PDF Documents Only

If you try to extract data from a noninteractive PDF document, ADS triggers an error message that is forwarded as an exception to the calling program via the PDF object.

You can extract data only from interactive PDF documents based on the XML Forms Architecture (XFA) technology by Adobe.

11.4.3 Validation of a Digital Signature

To exclude or recognize data manipulations, the document was digitally signed in Section 11.4.1. If the data is changed later on, the signature becomes invalid. The PDF object provides a method to check all signatures of a PDF document.

A unique identification of the sender is also necessary to ensure that the signature was done by the person responsible. This task is not covered by ADS; instead, ADS validates the signatures and then detects manipulations. The assignment between the signature and the user must be carried out separately.

Listing 11.8 provides the methods required for determining the signature:

```
l_pdfobj = l_fp->create_pdf_object( ).
l_pdfobj->set_document( pdfdata = l_pdf ).
l_pdfobj->set_task_getsignatures( ).
l_pdfobj->execute( ).
l_pdfobj->get_signatures( IMPORTING signatures = l_sigs ).
```

Listing 11.8 Calling the PDF Object for Determining the Digital Signatures

- Transfer the signed PDF document to the PDF object, as described in Section 11.4.2, during data extraction by calling the SET_DOCUMENT method.

- Use SET_TASK_GETSIGNATURES to activate the signature determination.

- After you call ADS via EXECUTE, you are provided with the signature information via the GET_SIGNATURES method.

SAP provides a test program for determining signatures. This is the FP_PDF_TEST_12 program that only tests PDF files and outputs information about the contained signatures on the screen.

Digital Signatures Require a Secure Connection!

Up to now, you have not had to consider the connection to ADS for the instantiation of the PDF object. If you do not specify any connection, the system automatically selects the connection with the name ADS.

If you implement security-relevant operations, for example, signature determination, the system checks whether a Secure Socket Layer (SSL) connection is used. If the connection is secured only with a standard authentication (user name and password), an error message is created when the SET_TASK_GETSIGNATURES method is called.

To work with digital signatures, you must either secure the ADS connection or set up a second secure connection, for instance, ADS_SSL, which you configure accordingly. You must explicitly notify the connection name to the PDF object. This is done using the following call:

```
l_pdfobj = l_fp->create_pdf_object( connection = 'ADS_SSL' ).
```

Now, run the FP_PDF_TEST_12 program and enter the document from Section 11.4.1, Filling Out an Interactive PDF Document, as the PDF file that you digitally signed (see Figure 11.1). The result is shown in Figure 11.3.

Short text	Value
Field Name	SignatureField1
Status	All Checks OK
Signatory	
Date and Time	Sat Nov 22 2008 13:52:51 GMT+0100
Location	
Information About Contact	
Legal Attestations	
Rights (See Interface IF_FP_PDF_SECURITY_PERMISSIONS)	All
Reason	null
Version	1
Highest Version Still Valid for This Version	1

Figure 11.3 Result of the Signature Check

- The Status field indicates whether the signature is valid. If the message "Cannot check signature" is displayed in the status field, you must check the configuration of the Trusted Anchors as described in Section 3.5.2, Credentials, Trusted Anchors, Certificate Revocation Lists.

- If you change and save the PDF with Adobe Reader after signing it, a new version is created internally that is also displayed in Adobe Reader. As a result, the signature is no longer valid in Version 2. If you rerun the FP_PDF_TEST_12 test program, the result remains as shown in Figure 11.3. Version 1 is still specified as the highest version.

- The test program does not show that there is a second version. The GET_SIGNATURES method of the PDF object returns the table with the signatures and a numeric value, NUMVERSIONS, which specifies the number of versions contained in the PDF document. To determine whether no changes have been made to the document after signing it, you must check that the signature itself is valid and that it is valid for the highest version.

- If there are multiple signature fields on a form, you receive information for each signature about the validity and the versions of the document.

11.5   Certifying PDF Documents

So far, this chapter has focused on the signature of a PDF document that was made by a user. The focus has been on whether the data of a document had been modified after the signature and which version the user had signed.

However, there is an essential aspect in offline scenarios that should be considered: the integrity of the document itself.

A user who fills out and signs an interactive PDF document certainly wants to be able to rely on the trustworthiness of the document. For this purpose, the enterprise that sends a PDF document can certify the document. The certificate can then be checked in Adobe Reader.

After filling out, signing, and returning the PDF document, however, the recipient should also check that no modifications were made to the document itself. For example, the recipient could change the document structure before signing the document. If he signs it afterward, the modification will not be displayed with the signature. The solution of this, again, is to certify the PDF document itself because this can be checked on the server side. Filling out and signing the document in the usual way does not infringe on the certificate — but modifications to the document itself would be noticed.

Listing 11.9 shows the basic steps of the certification of a PDF document.

```
l_pdfobj = l_fp->create_pdf_object( ).
l_pdfobj->set_document( pdfdata = l_pdf ).
l_pdfobj->set_certification(
          keyname   = 'cert_valid'
          fieldname = 'data[0].#subform[0].SigField1[0]'
          reason             = 'reason'
          location           = 'location'
          contactinfo        = 'contact info'
          legalattestations = 'legal attestations'
          permissions        = 'permissions' ).
l_pdfobj->execute( ).
l_pdfobj->get_pdf( IMPORTING pdfdata = l_pdfresult ).
```
Listing 11.9 Certifying a PDF Document

1. Transfer an existing document to the PDF object via the SET_DOCUMENT method.

2. Select the data required for the certification and the certificate itself by calling the SET_CERTIFICATION method.

3. ADS is called via the EXECUTE method.

4. You can then access the certified document using the GET_DOCUMENT method.

The entire program is available in your system: It is the FP_PDF_TEST_09 program. After having started the program (F8 key), you can specify a PDF file for certification in the selection screen. A second file is supposed to be used for the output. The ADS connection needs to be secured via SSL (Secure Sockets Layer). You also have to specify the name of the certificate (see Section 3.5.2, Credentials, Trusted Anchors, Certificate Revocation Lists).

An interactive PDF document may contain several signature fields. There needs to be a field for each signature. The certification also requires such a specific field. You have to use a special syntax to define the SIGNATURE FIELD for adding the certificate. A signature field at the highest level always begins with 'data[0].#subform[0]'. This is followed by the field name (here: SigField1[0]) as it is defined in the hierarchy view in Adobe LiveCycle Designer.

If the certified PDF document is sent and opened in Adobe Reader, the recipient is informed if the document has been modified since the certification (see Figure 11.4).

This certificate is still valid when the document has been filled out and signed. After the document has been returned, the receiving system can check this certificate. For this purpose, the PDF object provides an additional function—server-side checks of certifications. In the previous section, the certification was implemented via the server; the check was performed by the recipient in Adobe Reader. The following describes the steps for checking certifications via the ABAP system. Listing 11.10 shows the basic steps for this.

```
l_pdfobj = l_fp->create_pdf_object( ).
l_pdfobj->set_document( pdfdata = l_pdf ).
l_pdfobj->set_task_getcertification( ).
l_pdfobj->execute( ).
l_pdfobj->get_certification( IMPORTING
            status      = l_status
            certificate = l_certificate ).
```

Listing 11.10 Determining the Certificate of a PDF Document

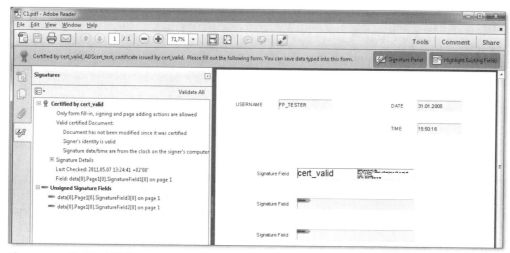

Figure 11.4 Certified PDF Document

1. Transfer an existing document to the PDF object via the SET_DOCUMENT method.

2. Activate the check of the certification by calling the `SET_TASK_GETCERTIFICATION` method.

3. ADS is called via the `EXECUTE` method.

4. You can then access the result of the check using the `GET_CERTIFICATION` method.

This program is also available in your system: It is the `FP_PDF_TEST_10` program. You can specify a PDF file that is supposed to be checked in the selection screen. The ADS connection also needs to be secured via SSL in this case. The calling program displays the result of the check (see Figure 11.5).

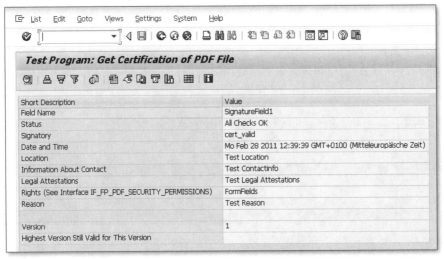

Figure 11.5 Certificate Is Valid

ADS determines whether the document has been changed after the certification. Figure 11.6 shows the result.

As already mentioned, filling out and digitally signing a PDF document does *not* make the certification of this document invalid. This way, you can check whether a PDF document was sent by yourself and was not modified during the transfer or by the user.

These are the essential ADS functions for processing interactive PDF documents in offline scenarios. Sections 11.6, Job Profiles, and 11.7, Additional Methods of the PDF Object, describe further functions for PDF documents.

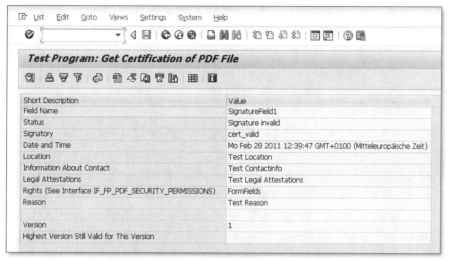

Figure 11.6 Validity of the Certification Was Destroyed

11.6 Job Profiles

PDF objects also enable you to determine the job profiles that are installed on ADS. You can then use them in a print program, for example.

The method is GET_JOB_PROFILES and it returns a table of the TFPJOBPROFILE type as the result. The structure of the table type is SFPJOBPROFILE, a combination of the job profile name and a description.

The name has the form that is expected for the call of the FP_JOB_OPEN function module in the IE_OUTPUTPARAMS-JOB_PROFILE parameter, for example.

If you use the PDF object directly, you can also use a job profile—you can transfer it using the SET_JOB_PROFILE method.

11.7 Additional Methods of the PDF Object

The PDF object provides many more functions that are described in the online help. Just start Transaction SFP and follow the menu path HELP • APPLICATION HELP.

► Under REFERENCE, you can find the entry, RUNTIME API OF THE PDF DOCUMENT OBJECT. There, all methods, including their parameters, are displayed.

▸ Look at the section called "Example and Test Programs." Here, you can find more than 20 test programs that you can use to test the individual methods of the PDF object. Some of the test programs, for example, PDF creation, data extraction, or check of digital signatures, have already been presented in this chapter.

▸ FP_PDF_TEST_15 is another interesting program that you can use to determine file attachments of a PDF document.

▸ You can add files to a PDF document using the methods in the FP_PDF_TEST_16 program.

▸ The FP_PDF_TEST_20 program details how you can influence the initial display of a PDF document when it is opened in Adobe Reader.

▸ If a user added annotations to a PDF document, you can display them using the FP_PDF_TEST_14 program.

▸ Check your system to find out which test programs exist according to the FP_PDF_TEST_* pattern. Some of the functions may be useful in your application scenarios.

11.8 Summary

This chapter presented the ABAP PDF object that provides you with all of the functions of ADS in an ABAP environment. You learned the basic functioning of the PDF object and can now create PDF documents interactively. You also learned how to access forms from the form storage.

You were introduced to the most important steps for an offline scenario. A completed PDF document that is possibly prepopulated with values is signed digitally and sent to ADS for processing. In addition, this chapter described how you can determine the XML data that have been entered or changed by a user. This chapter also detailed checking digital signatures. For interactive offline scenarios, certified PDF documents are essential. They were also discussed in Chapter 10, ABAP Offline Infrastructure.

There are additional functions of the PDF object that you can view based on test programs delivered by SAP.

Chapter 12, Offline Scenarios via Web Services, presents an example of how you can implement an offline scenario using a Web service.

This chapter describes how you can implement offline scenarios using Web services and details two variants—the use of Web service-based data connections and the Simple Object Access Protocol (SOAP) object in JavaScript—based on examples.

12 Offline Scenarios via Web Services

The query and transmission of data via a Web service is an alternative to processing interactive Portable Document Format (PDF) forms in the backend, which was described in Chapter 11, ABAP PDF Object. The Web service reads and updates business data in the SAP system. This chapter provides the basics and usage options for integrating interactive PDF forms with Web services.

12.1 Overview

An interesting alternative for processing a PDF document in SAP systems is by direct link via Web services. In PDF forms, you have the option to call a Web service and to transfer data at the same time. You can also use the return values of Web services to update form fields and tables, for example.

There are two variants for using Web services:

▶ **WSDL-based data connection**
In this procedure, you define a data connection for a Web service. Request and response parameters are then available via the data view. The parameters can be used for form generation via the known graphical-visual methods.

▶ **Usage of the SOAP object in JavaScript**
Using the SOAP object in JavaScript enables you to write script programs that call Web services. These programs must read and update form fields themselves, which is a disadvantage compared to the WSDL-based data connection.

This chapter is not aimed at developing complex scenarios, but rather at introducing you to the procedure for the two implementation approaches. This information will enable you to decide for yourself whether Web services are an option for implementing a connection to an SAP system.

> **Enhanced Function for WSDL Data Connections in Adobe LiveCycle Designer 8.2 and Adobe Reader 9**
>
> Adobe LiveCycle Designer 8.2 provides enhanced functions for WSDL data connections for the support of authentication at the transport and notification level. To use these functions, you need to have Adobe Reader Version 9 or higher.

12.2   Using WSDL Data Connections

This section considers the first example of WSDL data connection. To do this, first generate a Web service from a Business Application Programming Interface (BAPI). Then create a form template that uses this Web service via a WSDL data connection. After you have generated an interactive PDF form from the form template, you can test it in Adobe Reader.

12.2.1   Creating a Web Service Based on a BAPI

For this first example, we will generate a Web service for a BAPI of the flight customer database; here, only one function for querying all customers through the Web service is provided.

> **Generating Web Services in this Book**
>
> The procedure presented in this chapter is not a general introduction to the generation and usage of Web services for SAP systems. Rather, it is a simple and quickly reproducible instruction to obtain a Web service that can be called to illustrate the PDF form techniques presented here.
>
> The Web services were generated on an SAP system based on SAP NetWeaver 7.0 SP 12. The dialogs may appear different in other release versions. The Web services do not have to be developed with the same SAP NetWeaver release or provided on the same system as ADS.

Creating a Web Service for BAPI

To create a Web service for a BAPI, proceed as follows:

1. Log on to your SAP system and start the ABAP Development Workbench using Transaction SE80.

2. Have the system display all local objects for your user. Select LOCAL OBJECTS from the dropdown list and click on the button for updating the display (the glasses icon). The screen should now look as illustrated in Figure 12.1.

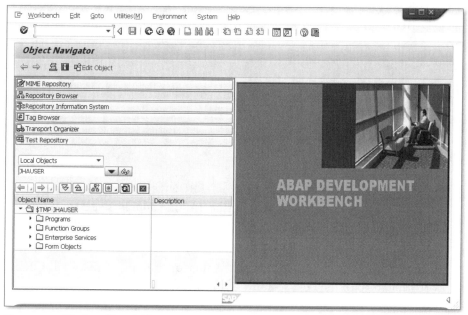

Figure 12.1 Display of Local Objects

3. To start the creation of a Web service, right-click on the $TMP node in the object hierarchy to open the context menu. Follow the menu path CREATE • ENTERPRISE SERVICE/WEB SERVICE • WEB SERVICE.

   Then, a wizard opens that helps you create a service definition. To set up the service, proceed as follows:

4. Read the first screen of the wizard and then click on the CONTINUE button.

5. Fill out the second screen (CREATE SERVICE) as follows (see Figure 12.2): Enter Z_IFBA_BOOK_CUSTOMERS as the name of the service definition and "Returns customer list." as the short text. Choose BAPI as the ENDPOINT TYPE and confirm this step by clicking on the CONTINUE button.

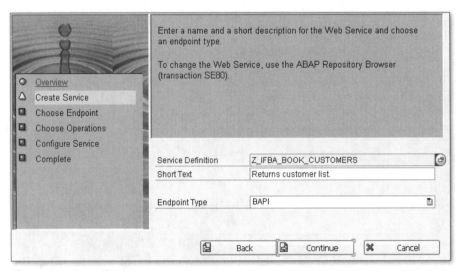

Figure 12.2 Create Service

6. In the third screen (CHOOSE ENDPOINT) enter BC-DWB as the application (see Figure 12.3). Choose FLIGHTCUSTOMER for the BAPI; to do this, select SCUSTOMER in the input help. Click on CONTINUE.

7. In the following screen (CHOOSE OPERATIONS), select the GETLIST operation as illustrated in Figure 12.4. Deselect the other operations, if required. Choose CONTINUE to go to the next screen.

Figure 12.3 Choose Endpoint

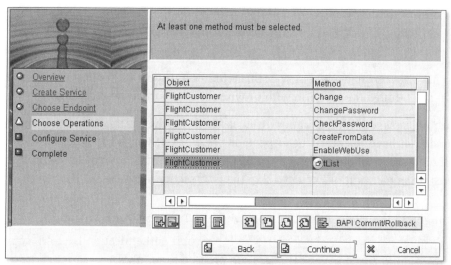

Figure 12.4 Choose Operations

8. In the CONFIGURE SERVICE screen (see Figure 12.5), select the RELEASE SERVICE FOR RUNTIME. Note that the Web service requires the user name and password for transport authentication (due to the selected profile). Click on CONTINUE to confirm.

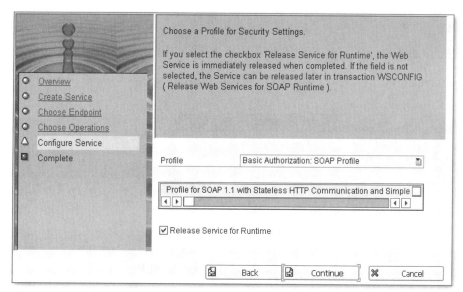

Figure 12.5 Configure Service

9. Confirm the last step, Complete, by clicking on the CONTINUE button. In the next dialog, CREATE OBJECT DIRECTORY ENTRY, select LOCAL OBJECT for the $TMP package.

You have now created a Web service that requires transport authentication. You can then run through the scenario with or without transport authentication.

Without transport authentication, it is easier to reproduce the example because you do not have to enter a user name or password. If you want to start without authentication, follow the steps in the next section. If you want to work with transport authentication, you can skip the next section.

Configuring the Web Service for Removing the Transport Authentication

To be able to reproduce the scenario with transport authentication later on, copy the previously created Web service. Then proceed as follows:

1. Start Transaction SE80.

2. Navigate to the local objects, and open the SERVICE DEFINITIONS subfolder of the ENTERPRISE SERVICES folder.

3. Right-click on the Z_IFBA_CUSTOMERS entry to open the context menu.

4. Here, select the COPY... MENU ITEM. This opens the dialog shown in Figure 12.6.

5. Enter Z_IFBA_BOOK_CUSTOMERS_AUTH into the TO SERVICE DEFINITION field. This is the name under which you can find the Web service that requires authentication.

You have now created the copy of the Web service.

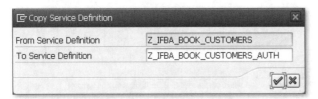

Figure 12.6 Copying the Web Service Definition

The following section describes how you configure the Web service called Z_IFBA_BOOK_CUSTOMERS so that no transport authentication is required.

Start Transaction WSCONFIG to configure the Z_IFBA_BOOK_CUSTOMERS Web service. Proceed as follows:

1. Select the previously created Web service (Z_IFBA_BOOK_CUSTOMERS) as the Service Definition and Variant; it is recommended that you use the input help here.

2. Then REFRESH the screen.

3. Double-click on the Web service that appears below RELEASED WEB SERVICES. This opens a new screen.

4. In this screen, you can find the ICF DETAILS BUTTON. Click on this button to go to the next screen.

5. There, double-click on the (Web) service. You must expand the hierarchy tree under VIRTUAL HOSTS/SERVICES.

> **Communication User**
>
> If you want to, and have the appropriate rights, you can create a communication user and use it instead of your own user data throughout this chapter. Communication users cannot log on to an SAP system and therefore should be used for security reasons.

The screen shown in Figure 12.7 should now appear. In the figure, the LOGON DATA tab is already displayed and the changes described in the following have been implemented for defining a user for the Web service.

1. Switch to change mode.

2. Enter a client, user, and password (for example, your login data or a communication user).

3. Save the changes. Because no productive scenario is developed here, you can ignore the message about not using a dialog user.

Accessing the WSDL File of the Web Service

To create a WSDL-based data connection, you need the URL for the Web service. This can be called using Transaction WSADMIN.

1. At this point, start Transaction WSADMIN.

2. In the screen that opens, expand the hierarchy tree for SOAP APPLICATION FOR BAPIS until you reach the Web service you just created (see Figure 12.8).

Figure 12.7 Processing the Internet Communication Framework (ICF) Details

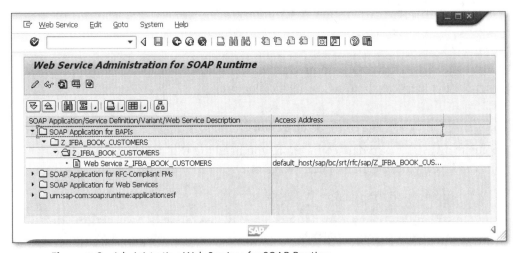

Figure 12.8 Administration Web Services for SOAP Runtime

3. Select your Web service, go to the WEB SERVICE menu, and choose the WSDL menu item.

4. In the following dialog, select Document Style so that the parameters are transferred in document format; confirm your selection. Displaying the content of the WSDL file is started externally in the default browser.

If you did not deactivate transport authentication, you first have to authenticate yourself in a dialog as shown in Figure 12.9 (for example, with a communication user).

Figure 12.9 Authentication When Calling the WSDL File

You should continue with the creation of a form template (see Section 11.2.2, Creating the Form Template) when the WSDL file is displayed as illustrated in Figure 12.10.

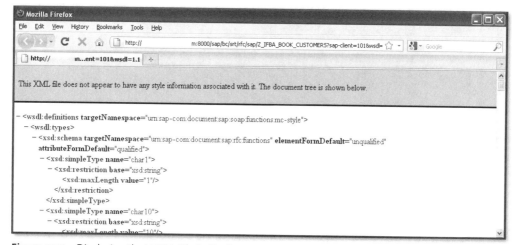

Figure 12.10 Displaying the WSDL File in the Browser

12.2.2 Creating a Form Template

After you have created the Web service, you can continue with the creation of the form template that uses the Web service. To do so, use Transaction SFP to start Form Builder.

Creating a Form Interface

First, you need an interface for the form template. Proceed as follows:

1. Create a new interface called Z_IFBA_BOOK_WS_INTERFACE1.

2. Add a parameter to the interface and call it CUSTOMERS. The type assignment is TYPE and the type name is TY_CUSTOMERS.

3. Save the interface and activate it in the last step.

The interface should now appear as illustrated in Figure 12.11.

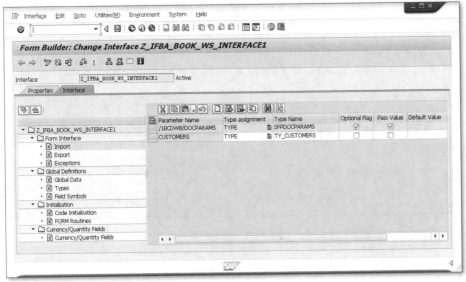

Figure 12.11 Z_IFBA_BOOK_WS_INTERFACE1 Interface

Creating the Form Design

After you have created the interface, you can create the form. Proceed as follows:

1. Create a new form called Z_IFBA_BOOK_WS_FORM_01. You can enter "test form for Web service" as the description.

2. Select the previously selected interface, `Z_IFBA_BOOK_WS_INTERFACE1`, and save the form as a local object.

3. Add the `CUSTOMERS` parameter to the context of the form. The context should now appear as illustrated in Figure 12.12.

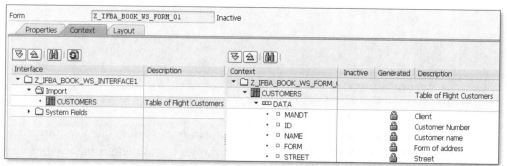

Figure 12.12 Context for the Form

4. When this is done, switch to the LAYOUT view and look at the data view. Below the `Z_IFBA_BOOK_WS_FORM_01` node, you can find the `CUSTOMERS` table structure for storing customer information.

Next, proceed as follows to create the WSDL-based data connection:

1. Right-click on the data view to open the context menu and follow the NEW DATA CONNECTION... menu path.

2. In the following dialog, enter "IFBA_BOOK_WebService" as the name of the data connection and select WSDL FILE as the option for the data description. This is shown in Figure 12.13. Click on NEXT.

3. In the next step, enter the URL for the WSDL file of the Web service. You can copy it from the browser window that you opened for displaying the WSDL file. Then click on NEXT.

4. This opens the dialog for authentication shown in Figure 12.14. Enter the user name and password of a user (for example, of a communication user).

5. In the following step, you must select one operation—namely the operation that you have provided via the Web service in Creating a Form Interface in Section 12.2.2. Select the operation and click on NEXT.

Figure 12.13 Creating a New Data Connection

6. This opens a dialog (see Figure 12.15) in which you can define the authentication parameters for the Web service (for transport and notification level). Select the REQUIRES HTTP/HTTPS AUTHENTICATION and ACCEPTS USER NAME AND PASSWORD options.

7. Complete the creation of the new data connection by clicking on the FINISH button.

Figure 12.14 Authentication for the Data Connection

The Web service now appears in the data view. It has its own icon to differentiate itself from the other data connections. Below the new data connection, you can find the structure for the request and the response of the Web service. In addition, there is a button for calling the Web service. Adobe LiveCycle Designer has automatically generated a button that you can add to a form template via the data view.

Next, customize the data view so that it appears as illustrated in Figure 12.16. To do this, expand or collapse the corresponding node in the data view using the plus (+) and minus icons (–).

Figure 12.15 Authentication Options for WSDL Data Connections

Figure 12.16 Data View

> **WSDL-Based Data Connection**
>
> WSDL-based data connections are active only at runtime. They are not part of the data's structure description that is based on the form.

After you have set up the data connection for the Web service, you can supplement the form template for the use of the Web service. Proceed as follows:

1. First, insert the button for calling the Web service (FLIGHTCUSTOMERGETLISTBTN) from the DATA VIEW in the top-left corner of the first page.

2. Then, drag and drop the MAXROWS field, which you can find under FLIGHTCUS-TOMERGETLIST REQUEST. Position it on the right-hand side of the button and set the default binding to NONE because the value of this field is not supposed to be saved.

3. Click on the button for the Web service call and navigate to the OBJECT palette. There, on the EXECUTE tab, you can find information about the Web service and operation saved for the button.

   In addition, the RE-MERGE FORM DATA option is available. Select this option. This results in the re-merge of the form after the call of the Web service and is required because a table structure is expected as the return of the Web service and also because the table in the form is to be organized according to the received structure.

4. Next, drag and drop the table from the data view. To do this, select the table structure, which you can find under the node for FLIGHTCUSTOMERGETLIST RESPONSE. The name of the table node is CUSTOMERLIST and the individual table rows are ITEM nodes.

5. Position the table below the button and as close to the left border as possible.

6. Then delete the columns COUNTRYISO, REGION, POBOX, and EMAIL from the table. To do so, highlight the respective column and remove it via the menu path TABLE • DELETE • COLUMN. You must do this because you require more space for the columns CUSTOMERID, CUSTNAME, STREET, and CITY to fit the corresponding text later on.

7. Finally, enlarge the four columns just mentioned.

Figure 12.17 shows what the form template is supposed to look like at this point. If the screen also shows warnings (the yellow exclamation marks), you can ignore them because they will be fixed in the next steps, because the data binding of the table has not been specified yet.

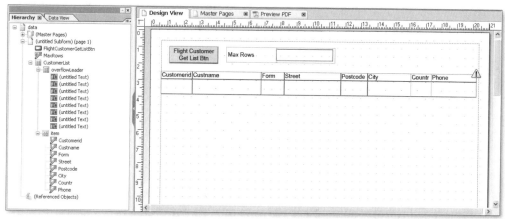

Figure 12.17 Structure of the Form Template

Now select any cell of the table's data row and navigate to the BINDING tab of the OBJECT palette. In this tab, you can find an area for the IMPORT/EXPORT BINDINGS. Enter some text in the first text field, for example, "Street" if you selected the cell of the STREET column. According to this, the import/export binding is used instead of the default binding for the binding to Web services.

Import/Export Binding of Form Fields

The import/export binding is a runtime property. At runtime, a form field can be bound to multiple Web services at the same time and have both import and export bindings (for example, a response parameter of a Web service can be used as a request parameter of another Web service).

Do not confuse import/export binding with the default binding to the form's data structure.

Because the import/export binding is a runtime property, you must implement the binding to the data structure in the next step. To do this, you specified a structure in the interface and in the context at the beginning of this example. Navigate to the hierarchy and carry out the following steps:

1. Select the CUSTOMERLIST table and set the default binding to NONE.

2. Select the ITEM row under CUSTOMERLIST. Then set the default binding to `$record.CUSTOMERS.DATA[*]`.

3. Navigate to the data view and expand it so that you can view all nodes under the menu path Z_IFBA_BOOK_WS_FORM_01 • CUSTOMERS • DATA.

4. Specify the data binding for all cells of the table. To do so, drag and drop the respective data node from the data view to the respective cell.

5. All warnings with regard to the data binding have disappeared and the form template is now complete.

Finally, you must save and activate the form so that you can test it in the next step.

12.2.3 Testing the Form Template

To test the form template, you must create a PDF file for the form in the next step. The PDF preview of Adobe LiveCycle Designer cannot be used because you first must add corresponding usage rights to the PDF for calling the Web services.

Creating a Program for Generating a PDF

Section 11.3.1, Retrieving a Form, already described the basics for creating the program. Here, Listing 12.1 references a program that outputs a form as an interactive PDF form that was created using Transaction SFP.

Use Transaction SE38 (ABAP Editor) to create a new test program called Z_IFBA_BOOK_SFP_PDF and utilize Listing 12.1 as the program code. The program has been developed especially for the test in this chapter, whereas the form is referenced via a name from the form storage of the SAP system. It does not use data for generating the PDF form. Run the program, select Z_IFBA_BOOK_WS_FORM_01 as the form template, and enter "Z_IFBA_BOOK_WS_FORM_01.PDF" as the name of the PDF to be created.

```
PROGRAM z_ifba_book_sfp_pdf.
TYPE-POOLS abap.
INCLUDE fp_utilities.
PARAMETERS:
    p_frm TYPE fpwbformname OBLIGATORY,
    p_pdf TYPE localfile VISIBLE LENGTH 64 OBLIGATORY,
    p_int TYPE abap_bool DEFAULT abap_true AS CHECKBOX,
    p_dyn TYPE abap_bool AS CHECKBOX.
```

```
DATA:
    l_fp        TYPE REF TO if_fp,
    l_pdfobj    TYPE REF TO if_fp_pdf_object,
    l_xftref    TYPE string,
    l_pdfresult TYPE xstring,
    l_fpex      TYPE REF TO cx_fp_runtime,
    l_fpex_api  TYPE REF TO cx_fp_api,
    l_error     TYPE string.

AT SELECTION-SCREEN ON VALUE-REQUEST FOR p_pdf.
  PERFORM value_help_for_output_file USING 'PDF'
                                     CHANGING p_pdf.
START-OF-SELECTION.

* Determine the URL for the form.
  TRY.
      cl_fp_wb_helper=>form_layout_exists( i_name = p_frm ).
    CATCH cx_fp_api_usage. "#EC NO_HANDLER
    CATCH cx_fp_api_repository INTO l_fpex_api.
      IF l_fpex_api->textid =
        cx_fp_api_repository=>object_already_exists.
        l_xftref = cl_fp_wb_helper=>form_layout_url(
                                   i_name = p_frm
                                   i_dest_path = 'X' ).
      ELSE.
        MESSAGE ID 'FPRUNX' TYPE 'E' NUMBER '050'
                WITH sy-langu.
      ENDIF.
  ENDTRY.

* Get FP reference.
  l_fp = cl_fp=>get_reference( ).
  TRY.

*   Create PDF Object.
    l_pdfobj = l_fp->create_pdf_object( ).

*   Set template.
    l_pdfobj->set_template( xftfile = l_xftref
                            fillable = p_int ).
```

675

```
*   Tell PDF object to create PDF.
    l_pdfobj->set_task_renderpdf( dynamic = p_dyn ).

*   Execute, call ADS.
    l_pdfobj->execute( ).

*   Get result.
    l_pdfobj->get_pdf( IMPORTING pdfdata = l_pdfresult ).
    CATCH cx_fp_runtime_internal
          cx_fp_runtime_system
          cx_fp_runtime_usage INTO l_fpex.
      l_error = l_fpex->get_errmsg( ).
      MESSAGE l_error TYPE 'E'.
  ENDTRY.

    PERFORM download_file USING l_pdfresult p_pdf.
```
Listing 12.1 Test Program for Generating Interactive PDF Forms

Offline Test of the Generated PDF

In the previous section, you generated a PDF file that you can now test offline. Proceed as follows:

1. Double-click on the PDF file, *Z_IFBA_BOOK_WS_FORM_01.PDF*, to open it in Adobe Reader. The table for the customer information does not show rows.

2. In the MAXROWS field, enter the number of table rows to be returned. Select a small number (for example, ten) because pagination has not been specified in the form template. As an exercise, you can first implement the pagination and then test the form with larger tables.

3. Click on the button for calling the Web service.

4. A security warning appears because the PDF wants to call a Web service. At this point, you can decide whether you want to allow or block this for the PDF.

   Because the created Web service is to be called, you can allow it. You can also specify that Adobe Reader remembers this for the Web service. Then, the warning is not displayed if you want to test different values for the number of rows returned.

5. Next, the dialog for authentication opens, which is shown in Figure 12.18. Enter the user name and password of a user that is allowed to call the Web service.

Figure 12.18 Authentication Dialog for the Web Service Call

Figure 12.19 illustrates what the result of a test run can look like. Note that the MAXROWS text field has no data binding and therefore does not contain any value after the re-merge.

Figure 12.19 Test of the Form Template in Adobe Reader

You should implement another test to check whether the data received from the Web service has been merged with the PDF form. To do this, carry out the following steps:

1. Open the PDF form and fill the table for the customer information by calling the Web service.

2. Save the PDF form and exit Adobe Reader.

3. Reopen the PDF form and check to see whether the table for the customer information is empty.

To work properly, you specify the default binding for the table during the creation of the form template.

Security Settings in Adobe Reader

Adobe has integrated numerous new security settings and confirmation dialogs with Adobe Reader 9. They are particularly relevant if you access the Internet from a PDF. So read these kinds of dialogs carefully before confirming them. This chapter solely discusses the dialogs that are relevant for this scenario.

12.3 Using the SOAP Object in JavaScript

This section describes the use of the SOAP object based on a second example. To obtain Web services with very simple interfaces, you must first create function modules and then generate the corresponding Web services for these function modules. Then you create a form template and program script programs that call the previously created Web services via the SOAP object.

12.3.1 Creating a Web Service on the Basis of a Function Module

In this section, we will create the Web services that are used in a PDF form later on. First, let's look at two of the Web services that can be called without a transport authentication and one that can be called with a transport authentication. To do this, you must carry out the following three steps sequentially:

1. Create a function group.

2. Create two function modules.

3. Create three Web services for the function modules.

Creating a Function Group

Proceed as follows to create a function group:

1. Start Transaction SE80 to open the Object Navigator.

2. Have the system display the local objects from the $TMP package.

3. Right-click on it to open the context menu of the $TMP package in the object hierarchy. Follow the menu path CREATE • FUNCTION GROUP.

4. In the following dialog, enter Z_IFBA_BOOK_FCT_GROUP as the name of the function group and "A function group for the IFBA book" as the short text.

5. Save the function group and specify it as a local object.

You have now created a function group. In the next step, we will add two function modules to this group.

Creating Two Function Modules

To create the Z_IFBA_BOOK_SUQARE function module, proceed as follows:

1. Open the context menu for the Z_IFBA_BOOK_FCT_GROUP function group and follow the CREATE • FUNCTION MODULE menu path.

2. In the following dialog, enter Z_IFBA_BOOK_SQUARE as the name and "Returns the square of the input parameter." as the short text. Then save the function module.

3. In the screen of the function module, first go to the ATTRIBUTES tab and select the REMOTE-ENABLED MODULE option for the processing type so that you can create a Web service from this module (see Figure 12.20).

4. Go to the IMPORT tab to determine an input parameter. Create a parameter called INPUT, specify TYPE as the typing and I as the associated type, and select the PASS VALUE option.

Figure 12.20 Properties of a Function Module

5. Go to the EXPORT tab to determine a return parameter. Create a parameter called OUTPUT, with TYPE as the typing and I as the associated type. Then, select the PASS VALUE option (see Figure 12.21).

Figure 12.21 Determining the Import Parameter

6. Go to the SOURCE CODE tab and supplement the source code analog with Listing 12.2. The function from Listing 12.2 calculates the square of an input parameter and returns it.

```
FUNCTION Z_IFBA_BOOK_SQUARE.
*"----------------------------------------------------------
*"*"Local interface:
*"  IMPORTING
*"      VALUE(INPUT) TYPE  I
*"  EXPORTING
*"      VALUE(OUTPUT) TYPE  I
*"----------------------------------------------------------
OUTPUT = INPUT * INPUT.
ENDFUNCTION.
```

Listing 12.2 Source Code of the Z_IFBA_BOOK_SQUARE Function Module

7. Save the function module, check it, and then activate it.

8. It is recommended that you test the function module in the last step. To do this, expand the object hierarchy until you can view the Z_IFBA_BOOK_SQUARE node.

9. Open the context menu, follow the TEST • TEST menu path, and test the function module. If everything runs smoothly, that is, if a square is returned for an input (see Figure 12.22), you have created the first function module successfully. We will set up a Web service for the function module later on.

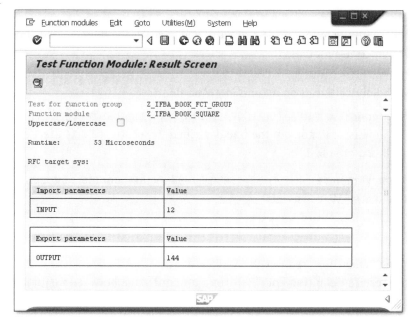

Figure 12.22 Test the Function Module

681

Repeat the procedure to create a second function module. In doing so, note the following:

1. The name of the second function module is Z_IFBA_BOOK_TIME and the short text is "Returns a random value between 0 and 9."

2. The function module has no import parameters.

3. The name of the export parameter is L_INT.

4. The listing of the source code is shown in Listing 12.3. Remember that it must be a remote-enabled module.

```
FUNCTION Z_IFBA_BOOK_TIME.
*"----------------------------------------------------------
*"*"Local interface:
*"  EXPORTING
*"     VALUE(L_INT) TYPE  I
*"----------------------------------------------------------
DATA: l_time TYPE syuzeit.
GET TIME FIELD l_time.
l_int = l_time+5(1).
ENDFUNCTION.
```

Listing 12.3 Source Code of the Z_IFBA_BOOK_TIME Function Module

Do not continue with the following section until you have successfully created and tested the two function modules.

Creating a Web Service Based on a Function Module

To create a Web service for the Z_IFBA_BOOK_TIME function module, proceed as follows (the procedure is analogous to the one described in Section 12.2.1, Creating a Web Service-Based on a BAPI):

1. Open the context menu for the Z_IFBA_BOOK_TIME function module. Follow the menu path CREATE • WEB SERVICE.

2. Click on CONTINUE to confirm the first screen of the wizard, CREATE SERVICE DEFINITION.

3. In the second screen for creating the service, enter Z_IFBA_BOOK_TIME as the name of the service definition and "Returns a random value between 0 and 9." as the short text. The ENDPOINT TYPE has already been selected correctly; confirm your entries with CONTINUE.

4. In the CHOOSE ENDPOINT screen, the correct function module has already been selected. You only need to select the NAME MAPPING option and click on CONTINUE to confirm.

5. In the CONFIGURE SERVICE screen, select RELEASE SERVICE FOR RUNTIME and click on CONTINUE to confirm.

6. Click on the COMPLETE button of the wizard and create the Web service as a local object.

7. Configure the Web service as described in Configuring the Web Service in Section 12.2.1.

8. Repeat this procedure for the Z_IFBA_BOOK_SQUARE function module. Enter "Returns the square of the input parameter." as the short description.

9. Ultimately, you need another Web service that requires a transport authentication. To do this, use the Z_IFBA_BOOK_SQUARE function module again. You must take the following aspects into account during the creation of this Web service:

   ▸ The name of the service definition is Z_IFBA_BOOK_SQUARE_SEC.

   ▸ The last step — the configuration of the Web service — is not implemented.

As a reference, Figure 12.23 illustrates the object hierarchy in the ABAP Development Workbench. Compare it with your hierarchy:

▸ Below FUNCTION MODULES, there is a function group called Z_IFBA_BOOK_FCT_GROUP.

▸ Below this function group, the two function modules, Z_IFBA_BOOK_SQUARE and Z_IFBA_BOOK_TIME, should be available.

▸ In the ENTERPRISE SERVICES category, you should find the four created Web services under SERVICE DEFINITIONS (three for the function modules and one for the BAPI).

Call the WSDL file in the Web browser for all three Web services using Transaction WSADMIN so that you can copy the URL of the individual Web services later on. The procedure is described in Accessing the WSDL File of the Web Service in Section 12.2.1. You can find the Web services for the function module under SOAP APPLICATION FOR RFC-COMPLIANT FMs in Figure 12.8, Section 12.2.1. If you call the WSDL file for the Z_IFBA_BOOK_SQUARE_SEC Web service, the system will prompt you for a user name and password. Enter a user that is valid for the client used.

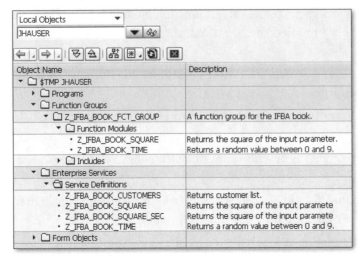

Figure 12.23 Object Navigator of the ABAP Development Workbench

12.3.2 Creating a Form Template

To create a form template that uses the previously created Web services, start Transaction SFP in the next step.

Creating a Form Interface

This section describes a simple example for testing the Web services. For this reason, the interface remains empty. Proceed as follows:

1. First, create a new interface called Z_IFBA_BOOK_WS_INTERFACE2. Enter "Interface for the function module test." as the short description. Leave the interface type as ABAP Dictionary-based Interface.

2. Save the interface as a local object.

3. Finally, activate the interface.

Creating the Form Design

Proceed as follows to create the form design.

1. Create a new form called Z_IFBA_BOOK_WS_FORM_02; the short description is "Form for a function module test."

2. Use the newly created interface, Z_IFBA_BOOK_WS_INTERFACE2.

3. Save the form as a local object.

4. Because the interface is empty, you cannot create a context. This is not a problem because the context is not required in this example. Go to the LAYOUT tab.

12.3.3 Implementing the Web Service Calls

The following examples describe the call to a Web service by means of the SOAP object in JavaScript.

- ▶ The first example processes a return parameter.
- ▶ The second example uses a parameter for the call.
- ▶ The third example calls a Web service that requires transport authentication.
- ▶ The last example transfers a user name and password in an authentication object so that the user is not asked for it.

You can find a figure of the finished form template as a reference at the end of this section. You can test each example individually or summarize all examples in one form template and then test them. The test of the form is described in Section 12.3.4, Testing the Form Template.

Calling the Z_IFBA_BOOK_TIME Web Service

This first example introduces you to using the SOAP object and calling the Z_IFBA_BOOK_TIME Web service. The return result is copied to a text field. Carry out the following steps to create the form templates:

1. The first page of the form is untitled. Rename the page "Page1."

2. Add a button to the form. Position this button in the top-left corner of the first page and change the label to "Call TIME."

3. Then add a text field to right of the button. Change the label to "Result."

4. Click on the button and have the system display the script for the click event; it should be empty. Change the language to JAVASCRIPT.

5. Enter Listing 12.4 as the script for the click event.

```
// URL pointing to the WSDL
var cURL =
"http://XXX.com:YYY/sap/bc/srt/rfc/sap/
  Z_IFBA_BOOK_TIME?sap-client=101&wsdl=1.1";
```

```
// Connect to web service
var service = SOAP.connect(cURL);
// Call operation "ZIfbaBookTime" and keep the result in
// a variable
var result = service.ZIfbaBookTime();
// Update textfield on form with the result returned from
// the web service
xfa.resolveNode
   ("data.Page1.TextField2").rawValue = result;
```

Listing 12.4 Calling the Z_IFBA_BOOK_TIME Web Service

Line Breaks in Listings

These listings contain line breaks within the strings for formatting reasons. Leave these line breaks out when entering the listings.

6. Replace the URL for the Web service (cURL variable) by copying the URL from the browser that displays the WSDL file for the Z_IFBA_BOOK_TIME function module and inserting it into the script.

7. You can add another line in the area below the button and the text field to separate this area.

The script in Listing 12.4 establishes a connection to the Web service. To do this, the connect method of the SOAP object is used. This method requires a URL that points to the WSDL of the Web service as a parameter. The return value is a proxy object for the Web service that provides a method for each operation of the Web service. In this example, you can call the ZIfbaBookTime method because this is the operation provided by the Web service. In this first and rather simple example, the return value of the Web service call can be directly assigned to the text field.

Calling the Z_IFBA_SQUARE Web Service

The second example transfers a request parameter for the call of the Z_IFBA_BOOK_SQUARE Web service. In comparison to the previous example, this example considers the creation and processing of the request and response structures.

1. Add another button to the form template and change the label to "Call SQUARE."

2. Then insert two more text fields to the right of the button you just inserted. Change the label of the first text field to "Input" and the label of the second text field to "Output."

3. Click on the button and have the system display the script for the `click` event. Change the language to JavaScript.

4. Copy the script from Listing 12.5 and adapt the URL for the Web service just as in the previous example. However, this example uses the Z_IFBA_BOOK_SQUARE Web service.

```
// URL pointing to the WSDL
var url = "http://XXX.com:YYY/sap/bc/srt/rfc/sap/
  Z_IFBA_BOOK_SQUARE?sap-client=101&wsdl=1.1";
// Create request structure, read Input out of text field
var request = {
        "urn:sap-com:document:sap:soap:functions:
         mc-style:ZIfbaBookSquare" :
        {Input:
          xfa.resolveNode("data.Page1.TextField2").
          rawValue}
};
// Call web service using SOAP object
var response = SOAP.request ({
        cURL: url,
        oRequest: request,
        cAction:
          "urn:sap-com:document:sap:soap:functions:
          mc-style"
});
// Now update the text field with the response
// access response array
// see WSDL/web service definition for identifiers
var result =
response["urn:sap-com:document:sap:soap:functions:
  mc-style:ZIfbaBookSquareResponse"]["Output"];

// Set rawValue of corresponding text field
xfa.resolveNode("data.Page1.TextField3").rawValue
                                        = result;
```

Listing 12.5 Calling the Z_IFBA_BOOK_SQUARE Web service

5. You can also add another line to separate the area.

The second example (see Listing 12.5) does not use the `connect` method for the SOAP object but instead calls the `request` method. For this reason, a `request` object was created; it is important to know the structure and the names of the request's fields. You need to look at the WSDL file to determine the namespaces. There you can then find the namespace, `urn:sap-com:document:sap:soap:functions:mc-st yle`, which is used in the example. Other parameters are the URL of the WSDL for the Web service and the `cAction` string that is written in the SOAP header and is an optional parameter. Because it is in the SOAP header, it can be read by a firewall, for example.

Finally, the return value (`result`) is read from the returned structure (`response`). Here, it is important again to know the structure and the name of the fields. In the present example, `Output` is a field below the `ZIfbaBookSquareResponse` response structure. The namespace is the same as for the request structure.

Calling the Z_IFBA_BOOK_SQUARE_SEC Web Service

This example is a variant of the previous example: A Web service is called that requires authentication at transport level. The difference does not become apparent until runtime when you test the form.

To create the appropriate form template, repeat the example from Calling the Z_IFBA_SQUARE Web Service in Section 12.3.3. However, note the following:

▶ Enlarge the button and change the label to "Call SQUARE_SEC."

▶ Use the `Z_IFBA_BOOK_SQUARE_SEC` Web service instead of the `Z_IFBA_BOOK_SQUARE` Web service when you determine the URL (see Listing 12.5).

Automatic Authentication for Calling a Web Service

In contrast to the previous example, the fourth example does not prompt for the authentication in a dialog, but transfers the required information, that is, the user name and the password, already in the script program for the call to the SOAP object. Repeat the second example and note the following:

1. Enlarge the button and change the label to "Call SQUARE_SEC Auth Obj."

2. Use the `Z_IFBA_BOOK_SQUARE_SEC` Web service instead of the `Z_IFBA_BOOK_SQUARE` Web service when you determine the URL.

3. Replace the Web service call in the script (SOAP.request) by the script shown in Listing 12.6.

4. In the script program, rename both text fields to TextField6 and TextField7. For the oAuthenticator object, adapt the values for <user-id> and <password> according to your system. Utilize a valid user name and password for the client you use.

```
// Create object for authentication
var oAuthenticator =
{
Username: "<user-id>",
Password: "<password>"
};
// Call web service using SOAP object
var response = SOAP.request ({
        cURL: url,
        oRequest: request,
        cAction: "urn:sap-com:document:sap:soap:
          functions:mc-style",
        oAuthenticate: oAuthenticator
});
```

Listing 12.6 Extension to the Use of an Authentication Object

The script program for the fourth example (Listing 12.6) combines an object for authentication (oAuthenticator) and contains a user name and a password. The object is transferred as an additional parameter for the call of the request method.

Note that the password and the user name do not have to be contained in the script program. They can also originate from fields of the form (for example, you can use the PASSWORD field).

Finished Form Template

If you have completed and followed all of the examples sequentially, the form template should appear as illustrated in Figure 12.24. The figure shows the positioning of the individual form fields and the script for the click event of the first example.

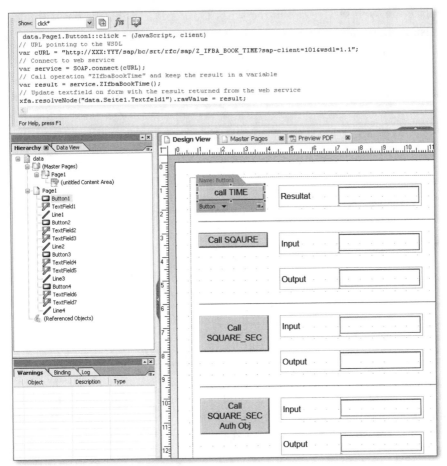

```
Show: click*                    fn
   data.Page1.Button1::click - (JavaScript, client)
// URL pointing to the WSDL
var cURL = "http://XXX:YYY/sap/bc/srt/rfc/sap/Z_IFBA_BOOK_TIME?sap-client=101&wsdl=1.1";
// Connect to web service
var service = SOAP.connect(cURL);
// Call operation "ZIfbaBookTime" and keep the result in a variable
var result = service.ZIfbaBookTime();
// Update textfield on form with the result returned from the web service
xfa.resolveNode("data.Seite1.Textfeld1").rawValue = result;

For Help, press F1
```

Figure 12.24 Structure of the Form Template

12.3.4 Testing the Form Template

To test a form template, you must first create a PDF and save it as described in Section 12.2.3, Testing the Form Template. You can then open the PDF file in Adobe Reader and test the Web service calls.

The following describes the test results you can expect for the four examples:

▶ **Calling the Z_IFBA_BOOK_TIME Web service**
 After you click on the CALL TIME button, a security warning is displayed because you called an external Web service. You must allow it for the test. After a short

period of time, a number between 0 and 9 is displayed in the RESULT text field.

This example deliberately uses a Web service that returns different results — so if you click on the button repeatedly, you can see that the Web service has really been called multiple times.

▶ **Calling the Z_IFBA_BOOK_SQUARE Web service**
To test the second example, enter a figure in the INPUT field. Then click on the CALL SQUARE button. Then permit access to the Web service. After a short period of time, the OUTPUT field shows the square of the figure entered in the INPUT field.

Note that no error handling has been implemented for the examples. You can repeat the call with different values in this example as well.

▶ **Calling the Z_IFBA_BOOK_SQUARE_SEC Web service**
This example behaves like the previous one. The only difference is that the dialog for the transport authentication is displayed (see Figure 12.25). To continue, you must enter a valid user and the corresponding password for the selected client. If required, uncheck the SAVE THIS INFORMATION option.

Figure 12.25 Dialog for the Authentication

▶ **Automatic authentication for calling a Web service**
This example behaves exactly like the second example. By using an authentication object, the authentication is implemented automatically. Although you use the Web service that requires authentication, you cannot distinguish between this example and the second example.

Now you know the most important procedures for using Web services. The next section provides some remarks for frequently asked questions.

12.4 Tips for Using Web Services

This section summarizes tips and procedures for the use of Web services.

12.4.1 Calling the Web Service in the Click Event

You do not have to use the button generated by Adobe LiveCycle Designer to call a Web service. You can implement this yourself in a script. Listing 12.7 shows what the script line needs to look like in JavaScript to call the Web service that you created in Section 12.2, Using WSDL Data Connections, and used in the form template. Note that the name of the data connection is used for the Web service. In this example, the name is IFBA_BOOK_WebService.

```
xfa.connectionSet.IFBA_BOOK_WebService.execute(1);
```
Listing 12.7 Calling the Web Service of a Data Connection

The parameter specifies whether the form is re-merged (value 1) or not (value 0) after the call to the Web service. If the form is re-merged, the execution of the script program aborts at this point.

12.4.2 Calling the Web Service Automatically When Opening the Form

A Web service does not always have to be called as a reaction to a user interaction; it can also, for example, be implemented automatically by a script in the form:ready or Layout:ready event. This way, the form can request data before it is displayed to the user or it can be checked to see whether the required SAP system can be accessed, for example.

12.4.3 Calling Multiple Web Services Using a Button

There are cases in which multiple Web services are called consecutively (for example, to read details for a business partner that is not determined until the call of the first Web service). Here, you can use the procedure described in Section 12.4.1, Calling a Web Service in the Click Event.

You can also implement multiple calls of different Web services consecutively in a single script. Note that as soon as the form must be re-merged by setting the parameter to 1, the execution of the script program is aborted accordingly.

12.5 Summary

Web services are a simple and elegant method of connecting interactive PDF forms with an SAP system; for this reason, two different approaches are available:

- ▶ You can use the WSDL-based data connection. In this approach, the request and response parameters are provided via the data view together with a ready-to-use button. As of Adobe LiveCycle Designer 8.2 and Adobe Reader 9, authentication at transport and notification level is supported. They can also be used for the graphical interactive procedure of creating form templates.
- ▶ The second approach, using the SOAP object in JavaScript, provides more flexibility but also involves more programming effort. The request and the processing of the responses must be programmed in JavaScript. The SOAP object enables an authentication at transport level by means of user name and password.

You got to know both approaches, based on examples, in this chapter.

The last chapter of this book is dedicated to the advanced administration and configuration of ADS. It describes the configuration of a secure connection to ADS and then presents the job profile management. The chapter concludes with a description of how to obtain and install the XDC Editor.

13 Advanced Installation and Configuration

A secure connection to ADS is required for scenarios in which security is of relevance, for instance, when electronic signatures are verified or PDF documents certified. The configuration of a secure connection requires knowledge of the administration of ABAP and Java systems.

This chapter first describes the configuration of a secure connection and then presents job profiles and their management. This functionality is made available by SAP NetWeaver Administrator. Using job profiles, you can modify requests to the ADS prior to their execution without changing the print programs. This way, you can activate duplex print retroactively or modify usage rights.

Finally, you learn how to obtain and install the XDC Editor, which is required if you need to adapt XDC files for a specific printer. For this purpose, the control commands for this printer are presented.

13.1 Configuring a Secure Connection to ADS

In Chapter 3, Installation and Configuration, you learned how to create a default ADS connection. This connection was named ADS. In this section, you now will learn how to create a secure ADS connection. The name of this connection will be ADS_SSL, and it can be used in all previous examples instead of the connection ADS. Furthermore, this secure connection also supports scenarios in which an electronic signature needs to be validated.

The basis for creating a secure connection is that you have the option to sign certificates or have them signed. This is usually done by an official certification authority.

If you have your own (sub)certification authority, or if certificates can be sent to an official certification authority (CA for short), you can skip the next section. Here is described how you can set up an unofficial certification authority to later on sign certificates for the secure connection yourself.

> **Required Knowledge**
>
> This chapter requires knowledge of digital certificates and cryptographic procedures.

13.1.1 Setting Up Your Own Certification Authority

To create your own certification authority, you must first download and install the OpenSSL software. Proceed as follows:

1. Download OpenSSL. Use Version 0.9.8 because Version 1.0 caused problems in the past. For Windows, you can download the relevant version at *http://slproweb.com/*.

2. After download, install OpenSSL in the OPENSSL directory. Choose the THE OPENSSL BINARIES (/BIN) DIRECTORY setting for COPY OPENSSL DLLS TO.

Next, you must modify the *openssl.cfg* file in the *OpenSSL/bin* directory.

1. To do so, open the *openssl.cfg* file with a text editor, which also supports Unix files.

2. Then go to the [CA_default] section. You can search for this section in the text editor. Multiple default parameters are defined in every section.

3. Set the following default value, dir = ../IFbABook.

4. Then set the default value, default_days   = 1460 (or more days as required).

5. Go to the [policy_match] section.

6. Set the default value, stateOrProvinceName = optional.

7. Go to the [req_distinguished_name] section.

8. In this area, set `countryName_default = DE` and further default values as required.

9. Go to the `[ req_attributes ]` section.

10. Comment out the two entries, `challengePassword` and `unstructuredName`, via `#`.

11. Save the files, and close the text editor.

12. Create a new directory with the name, *IFbABook*, in the *OpenSSL* directory.

13. Then create the following five subfolders: certs, crls, newcerts, private, and requests.

14. Now create two new files in the *IFbABook* directory.

15. The first file has the name *serial* (without file extension) and its content is the character string "01". This is the sequential serial number for certificates issued.

16. Then create an empty file with the name *index.txt*.

This concludes the preparations for creating a certification authority.

Next, you can create a certification authority. If the system queries a password (pass phrase), you can enter "ifbabook" in this example.

Proceed as follows to create a certification authority:

1. Go to the *\OpenSSL\IFbABook* directory in the command field. Execute the following three commands in the given sequence.

2. To generate an RSA private key with a length of 2048 bits for the certification authority, run the following command: `..\bin\openssl.exe genrsa -des3 -out private\cakey.pem 2048`

3. To create a root certificate for the certification authority with a validity of 12 years (4,380 days), execute the following command (see Figure 13.1):

   `..\bin\openssl.exe req -new -x509 -days 4380 -key private\cakey.pem -out cacert.pem`

4. When you execute the command, you must enter parameters. Use "DE" for the COUNTRY NAME, "Walldorf" for the LOCALITY NAME, "IFbABook" for the

ORGANIZATION NAME, and "IFbABookCA" for the COMMON NAME. You can leave all other parameters empty.

Figure 13.1 Creating a Root Certificate for the Certification Authority

5. In the last step, you must export the public key of the certification authority as an X.509 certificate using the following command:

```
..\bin\openssl.exe x509 -in cacert.pem -outform der -out
CA_public.der
```

In the last step, you exported the public key of the certification authority (in the *CA_public.der* file) and thus completed the creation of a certification authority. You will need the public key later on to configure trusted certification authorities.

By means of the certification authority, you can sign certificates for the SSL connection. This task is usually assumed by an official certification authority. For the description in this book, however, it is sufficient to use your own unofficial certification authority.

13.1.2 Creating an SSL Client Identity in the ABAP System

To create a secure connection, you must first create an SSL client identity with the associated certificates. To do so, proceed as follows:

1. Start Transaction STRUSTSSO2.

2. Then select the ENVIRONMENT • SSL CLIENT IDENTITIES menu path (see Figure 13.2).

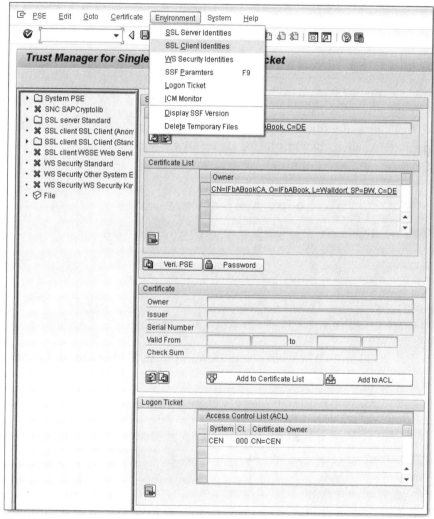

Figure 13.2 Transaction STRUSTSSO2

3. The CHANGE VIEW "SSL CLIENT IDENTITIES OF SYSTEM" opens. To enter a new identity, click on NEW ENTRIES (see Figure 13.3).

Figure 13.3 Overview of Existing SSL Client Identities

4. Now, create new identities. The name of the IDENTITY is "ADSSSL." Enter "ADS SSL Identity" as the DESCRIPTION (see Figure 13.4).

Figure 13.4 Creating a New SSL Client Identity

5. Save the new identity by clicking on the SAVE icon. You can create the identity as a local object.

Figure 13.5 SSL Client Identities after Creating the ADSSSL Identity

When you return to the overview, you can view the newly added identity (see Figure 13.5).

Creating a Client Certificate

Next, you must create a client certificate for the new client identity. Note that the company and country in this example must match with the information of the certification authority. Proceed as follows:

1. Right-click on the new client identity (ADSSSL) to open the corresponding context menu.

2. Choose CREATE from the context menu.

3. Fill out the dialog and create the certificate by clicking on the green checkmark (see Figure 13.6).

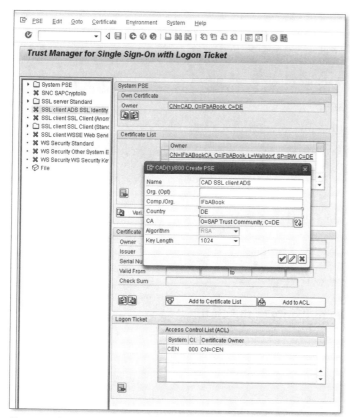

Figure 13.6 Creating a Client Certificate

Figure 13.7 shows the created client certificate.

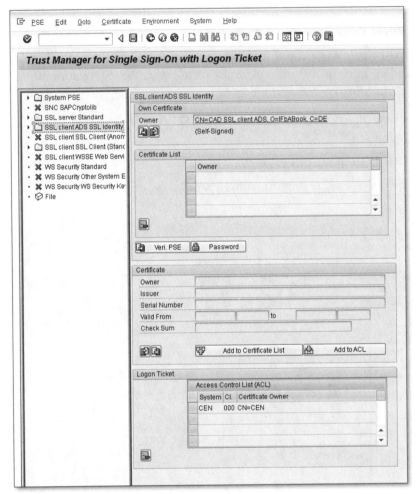

Figure 13.7 Created Client Certificate

Adding the Certification Authority to the Certificate List

To add the certification authority to the certificate list, proceed as follows:

1. Select IMPORT from the CERTIFICATE menu.

2. Choose the public key of the certification authority as the certificate to be imported. This public key has been created previously and saved under the file name *CA_public.der* (see Figure 13.8).

3. The details of the certification authority are shown in the CERTIFICATE area (see Figure 13.9).

4. Click on the ADD TO CERTIFICATE LIST button (see Figure 13.9).

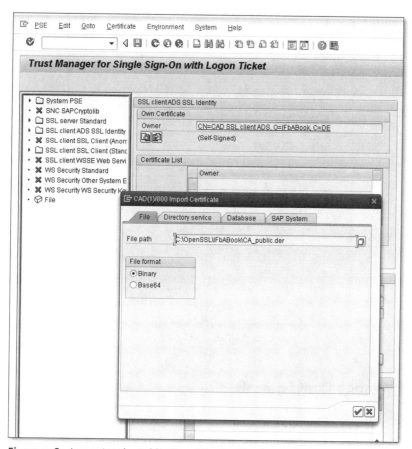

Figure 13.8 Importing the Public Key of the Certification Authority

You have thus published the certification authority in the ABAP system.

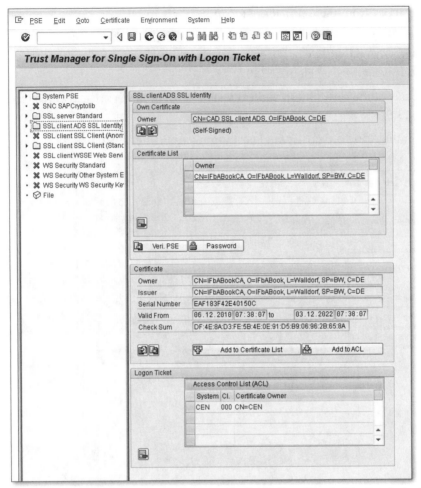

Figure 13.9 Client Certificate After Importing the Public Key of the Certification Authority

Creating and Signing a Client Certificate

Next, you must create a client certification and then sign it (with your own certification authority). Proceed as follows:

1. First, double-click on your own certificate to select it.

2. The certificate information is shown in the CERTIFICATE area.

3. Choose the EDIT • CREATE CERTIFICATE REQUEST menu item (see Figure 13.10).

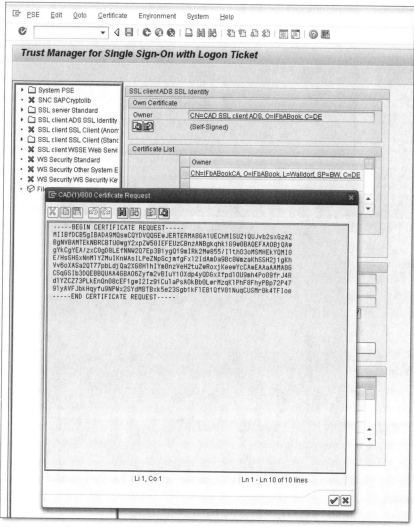

Figure 13.10 Certificate Request

4. A dialog opens where you click on the SAVE AS LOCAL FILE button to open the dialog shown in Figure 13.11.

Figure 13.11 Saving the Certificate Request

5. Use "ADS_SSL_Client.pem" as the file name and save the files in the *requests* directory.

6. Navigate to the command field input.

7. To sign, execute the following command (see Figure 13.12):
```
..\bin\openssl ca -in requests\ADS_SSL_Client.pem
  -out certs\ADS_SSL_Client.pem -notext
```

Figure 13.12 Signing the Certificate Request

8. The request is located in the `requests` folder and the output is made in the `certs` folder.

9. Next, open the signed certificate (the *ADS_SSL_Client.pem* file from the `certs` folder), as well as the certificate of the certification authority (*cacert.pem*) with the text editor.

10. Copy the entire content of the signed certificate to the clipboard.

11. Then go to the certificate of the certification authority and supplement it by inserting the content of the clipboard.

12. Save the changed certificate under a new file name to be able to read it in the next step.

13. Go back to the SAP GUI user interface.

14. Import the previously saved file via the EDIT • IMPORT CERTIFICATE RESPONSE menu item. The result should appear as illustrated in Figure 13.13.

Figure 13.13 Imported Certificate Response

15. Then choose EXPORT in the CERTIFICATE menu.

16. Use the *ADS_SSL_Client.crt* file name and click on SAVE.

You have just created a client certificate and signed and exported it for usage in the Java system.

Restarting the Internet Communication Manager (ICM) in the ABAP System

For changes to become effective and to complete the configuration in the ABAP system, you must restart the Internet Communication Manager as the last step. Proceed as follows:

1. Call Transaction SMICM.

2. Select all threads displayed.

3. Choose the ADMINISTRATION • ICM • EXIT SOFT • GLOBAL menu item to stop the threads. Stopping the threads causes a restarting of the ICM.

13.1.3 Configuring the Java System and ADS

After the preparations in the ABAP system, you must now configure the Java system on which ADS runs.

Configuring Trusted Certificates

First, you must add the private key of the certification authority to the list of trusted certificates. When you use the private key of your own certification authority, you can also sign certificates directly upon creation. If the private key does not exist, you must first export new certificates and then sign and import them.

You can add the private key of the certification authority to the list of trusted certificates as follows:

1. Navigate to the command field input.

2. Export the private key of the certification authority as PKCS#12 Key Pair (in a file called *CA_private.p12*) using the following command:
   ```
   ..\bin\openssl pkcs12 -export -in cacert.pem -inkey
     private\cakey.pem -certfile cacert.pem -out CA_private.p12
   ```

3. Then start SAP NetWeaver Administrator by entering the following URL in a Web browser: *http://<server>:5<InstanceNumber>00/nwa*.

4. Choose CONFIGURATION MANAGEMENT • SECURITY • CERTIFICATES AND KEYS.

5. Select the TRUSTEDCAS entry in the KEY STORAGE VIEWS area.

6. To import the private key of the certification authority to the key storage for TrustedCAs, click on IMPORT ENTRY.

7. A dialog opens in which you select "PKCS#12 Key Pair" as the ENTRY TYPE (see Figure 13.14).

8. Then select the *CA_p6rivate.p12* file and enter the previously used password.

9. Click on IMPORT to start the import.

Figure 13.14 Importing the Private Key into the Key Storage

10. Now use the same procedure to import the public key of the certification authority. "X.509 Certificate" is the ENTRY TYPE. Choose the *CA_public.der* file and click on IMPORT (see Figure 13.15).

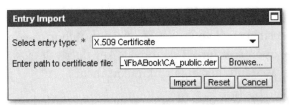

Figure 13.15 Importing the Public Key of the CA into the Key Storage

You have thus published the certification authority in the Java system.

Configuring the Service_SSL Key Store

In the next step, you must configure the already existing key store, "Service_SSL." Proceed as follows:

1. Select the key storage view with the name SERVICE_SSL in the KEY STORAGE VIEWS area.

2. Then delete the template certificates by selecting them and removing them with the DELETE button. You can use the certificate details to check whether these are your own or template certificates.

3. Create a new certificate entry by clicking on the CREATE button.

4. Use the following parameters in the ENTRY SETTINGS step (see Figure 13.16):

   ▶ NAME: ssl-credentials (use the name with this exact spelling)

   ▶ ALGORITHM: RSA

   ▶ KEY LENGTH: 2048

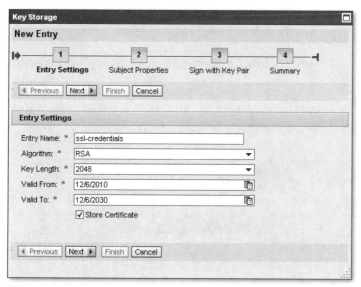

Figure 13.16 Entry Settings Step for the Certificate Entry

5. Use the following values in the SUBJECT PROPERTIES step (see Figure 13.17):

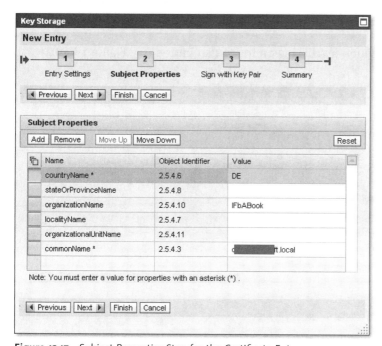

Figure 13.17 Subject Properties Step for the Certificate Entry

> ▶ COUNTRYNAME: DE

> ▶ ORGANIZATION: IFbABook

> ▶ COMMONNAME: Complete domain name of the server (for instance, "a.b.com")

6. In the SIGN WITH KEY PAIR step, select the imported certification authority "CA_private" for the SIGNING KEY PAIR (see Figure 13.18).

Figure 13.18 Selecting the Key Pair

7. Confirm the creation by clicking on the FINISH button (see Figure 13.19).

Figure 13.19 Details on the Signing Key Pair

You have just configured the "Service_SSL" key store.

Creating a New Key Store View

To create a new key storage view for storing the ADS certificates, proceed as follows:

1. Click on ADDVIEW IN THE KEY STORAGE VIEWS area.

2. The name of the IDENTITY is "ADSCerts." Enter "View for ADS Certificates" as the DESCRIPTION (see Figure 13.20).

3. Click on CREATE to create the view.

Figure 13.20   Creating a View for the ADS Certificates

Generating and Exporting Certificates for the ADSUser

Next, you must create a certificate entry for the ADSUser and export the associated public key. Proceed as follows:

1. Click on CREATE under the ADSCERTS view. Figures 13.21 through 13.23 shows the individual steps.

2. Choose the following parameters in the ENTRY SETTINGS step (see Figure 13.21):

   ▶ ENTRY NAME: ADSUser

   ▶ ALGORITHM: RSA

   ▶ KEY LENGTH: 2048

   ▶ VALID FROM/VALID TO: The period of time in which the certificates are to be valid

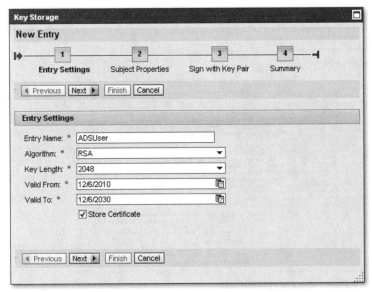

Figure 13.21   Entry Settings Step for the Certificates of the ADSUser

3. Use the following parameters in the SUBJECT PROPERTIES step (see Figure 13.22):

   ▶ NAME: ADSUser

   ▶ ORGANIZATION: IFbABook

   ▶ COMMONNAME: ADSUser

4. Now, in the SIGN WITH KEY PAIR step, use the imported certification authority "CA-Private" for the SIGNING KEY PAIR (see Figure 13.23):

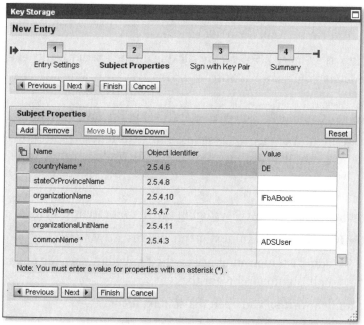

Figure 13.22 Subject Properties Step for the Certificates of the ADSUser

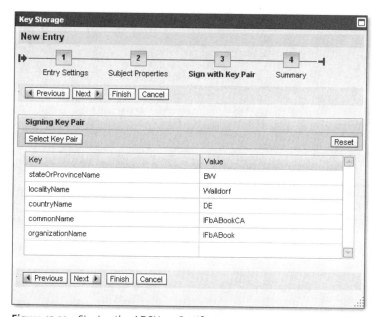

Figure 13.23 Signing the ADSUser Certificate

5. Click on the FINISH button to complete the creation of the ADS certificate.

6. Select the ADSUSER-CERT entry in the ADSCERTS area.

7. Save the public key as a Binary X.509 file by clicking on the EXPORT ENTRY button. Use the predefined file name, *ADSUser-cert.crt*.

Restarting the Internet Communication Manager (ICM) in the Java System

You must now restart the ICM of the Java system. Proceed as follows:

1. Open the page *http:<Server>:<Port>/startPage*.

2. Choose SAP MANAGEMENT CONSOLE.

3. Open the current instance of the ADS system in the MANAGEMENT CONSOLE.

4. Right-click on the ICM to open its context menu and choose MANAGE.

5. Log on to the Web administration interface as the "webadm" user (or under another user with administration rights for the ICM).

6. Select RUNNING (under STATUS:) and open the context menu.

7. Choose RELOAD CONFIGURATION to restart the ICM (see Figure 13.24).

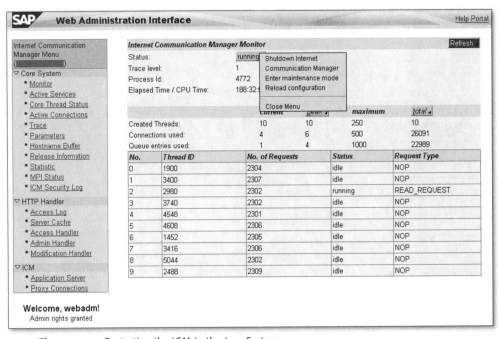

Figure 13.24 Restarting the ICM in the Java System

Configuring SSL in the Java System

Next, you must configure SSL in the Java system. Proceed as follows:

1. Go back to SAP NetWeaver Administrator. Select CONFIGURATION MANAGE-MENT • SECURITY • SSL to go to the SSL configuration.

2. If SSL is not enabled, activate it with the following settings (see Figure 13.25).

   ▸ In the AS JAVA INSTANCES area, click on EDIT.

   ▸ Use 50001 for the SSL PORT if your instance number is 00 (the default port is 5<InstanceNumber>01).

   ▸ Choose REQUEST for the CLIENT AUTHENTICATION MODE.

   ▸ Utilize INSTANCE DEFAULT as the KEYSTORE VIEW NAME.

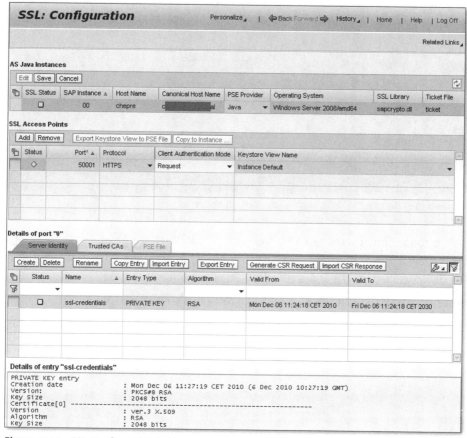

Figure 13.25 SSL Configuration in the Java System

3. Call the management of the Java system properties by selecting the CONFIGURA-TION MANAGEMENT • INFRASTRUCTURE • JAVA SYSTEM PROPERTIES menu item.

4. Go to the SERVICES tab and select the USER MANAGEMENT ENGINE entry.

5. Select the UME.LOGON.ALLOW_CERT line in the PROPERTIES tab.

6. Click on the MODIFY button to open another dialog window. Choose `true` as the value (Figure 13.26). Click on SAVE to save your changes.

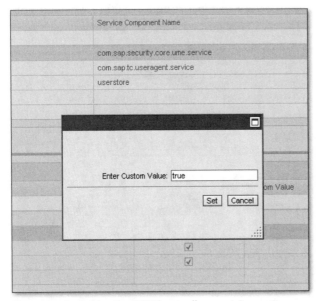

Figure 13.26 Setting the UME.logon.allow_cert Properties

7. Go to the initial screen of SAP NetWeaver Administrator, and call the identity management configuration by selecting the following menu item: CONFIGURA-TION MANAGEMENT • SECURITY • IDENTITY MANAGEMENT.

8. Choose ADSUSER in the SEARCH area. You can also browse for "*ads*."

9. In the CERTIFICATES tab, upload the public key of the ADSUser certificate. Click on MODIFY to accept the changes.

10. Select the *ADSUser-cert.crt* file in the CERTIFICATE UPLOAD area and start the upload by clicking on the UPLOAD CERTIFICATE button.

11. Upload the public key of the SSL client identity of the ABAP system. To do so, choose the previously exported ABAP certificate (the *ADS_SSL_Client.crt* file) and click on the UPLOAD CERTIFICATE button.

The screen for identity management should look like the one shown in Figure 13.27. You can view the two uploaded certificates under DETAILS OF USER ADSUSER.

For the changes to become effective, you must now restart the ICM once again.

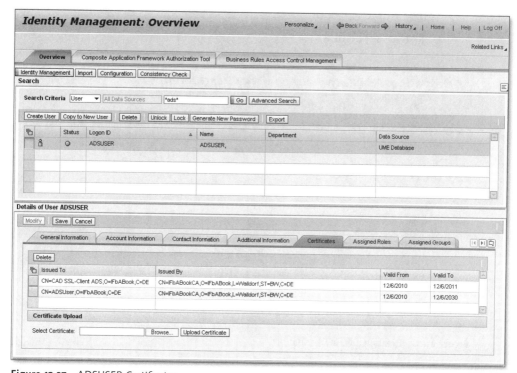

Figure 13.27 ADSUSER Certificates

Creating a New Destination

As the next step, you must create a new destination. To do this, carry out the following steps:

1. Go to the destination management by calling the following menu item: SOA MANAGEMENT • TECHNICAL CONFIGURATION • DESTINATION TEMPLATE MANAGEMENT.

2. Click on NEW to create a new destination.

3. Use the following values in the GENERAL step (Figure 13.28):

   ▸ DESTINATION TYPE: WSIL

   ▸ DESTINATION NAME: SecureConfigPort_Document

   ▸ URL: *https://<Java system of ADS>:<SSL Port>/inspection.wsil/*

   ▸ SYSTEM: Java

   ▸ SYSTEM NAME: <blank>

   ▸ HOST NAME: <blank>

Figure 13.28 Creating a New Destination

4. Use the following parameters in the SECURITY step (see Figure 13.29):

   ▸ AUTHENTICATION: User ID/Password

   ▸ USER ID: ADSUser

   ▸ PASSWORD: password of the ADSUser

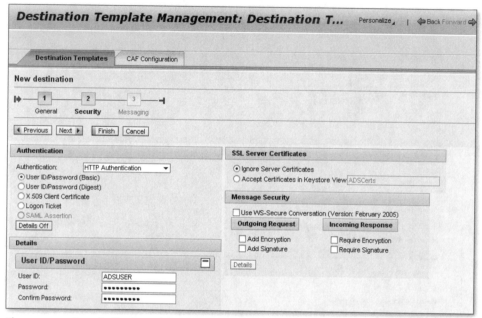

Figure 13.29 Security Settings of the New Destination

You have now created a new destination with the name, SECURECONFIGPORT_ DOCUMENT.

Adapting the FP_ICF_DATA_XXX Destination

In the default configuration, the FP_ICF_DATA_XXX destination is configured for an unsecured connection. It must be reconfigured if a secure connection is used:

1. In the initial screen of SAP NetWeaver Administrator, choose SOA MANAGEMENT • TECHNICAL CONFIGURATION • DESTINATIONS.

2. First, adapt the destination with the name FP_ICF_DATA_<ABAP SYSTEM ID>. To do so, select it.

3. Go to the CONNECTION AND TRANSPORT tab and use the following values (see Figure 13.30):

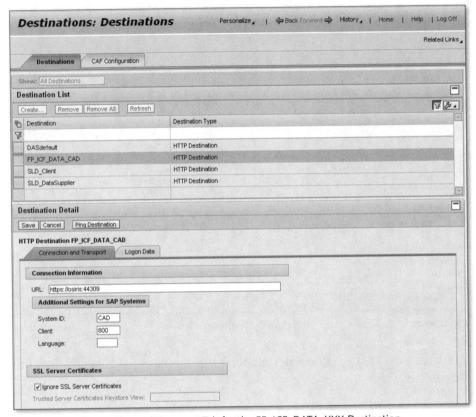

Figure 13.30 Connection and Transport Tab for the FP_ICF_DATA_XXX Destination

- ▸ HOSTING SYSTEM: Local J2EE System CET
- ▸ DESTINATION NAME: FP_ICF_DATA_<ABAP system ID>
- ▸ DESTINATION TYPE: HTTP
- ▸ URL: *https://<ABAP server>:<SSL port of the ABAP server>*
- ▸ SYSTEM ID: <ABAP system ID>
- ▸ CLIENT: <client in which ADSUSER is located>

4. Then switch to the LOGON DATA tab (Figure 13.31). Use the following parameters for the configuration:

- ▸ AUTHENTICATION: Basic
- ▸ USER NAME: ADS_AGENT
- ▸ PASSWORD: <password of ADS_AGENT>

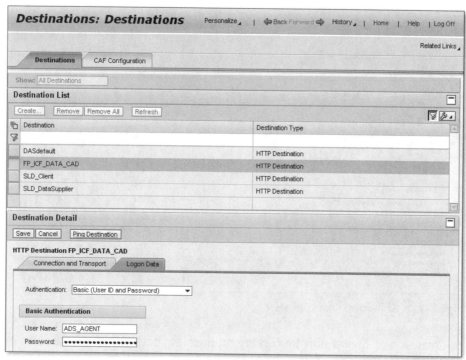

Figure 13.31 Logon Data Tab for the FP_ICF_DATA_XXX Destination

The FP_ICF_DATA_XXX destination has been created.

Creating a Logical Port

A new logical port is required for the secure call of ADS. It is the secured counterpart for the unsecured logical port named "ConfigPort_Document." To create a new logical port, proceed as follows:

1. Switch to the Single Service Administration area, where you must call the SOA Management • Application and Scenario Communication • Single Service Administration menu item in the initial screen.

2. Go to the Consumer Proxies tab.

3. Search for the consumer proxy "DestinationSi" using the filter function.

4. Select DestinationSI, and switch to the Configuration tab (see Figure 13.32).

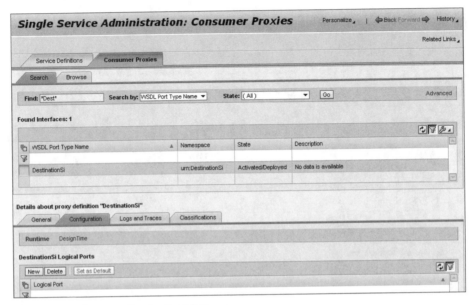

Figure 13.32 Consumer Proxies Overview

5. Create a new logical port by clicking on the New button in the lower area of the screen.

6. Go through the individual steps and use the following parameters.

> ▶ In the Source step, select the Enter Manually option (see Figure 13.33).

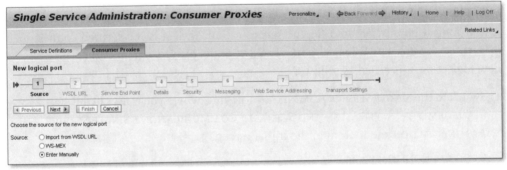

Figure 13.33 Creating a New Logical Port

▸ In the DETAILS step (see Figure 13.34), use "SecureConfigPort_Document" for the LOGICAL PORT NAME and *https://<FQDN des ADS>:<SSL Port>/inspection. wsil for* WEB SERVICES END POINT URL.

▸ In the AUTHENTICATION step, choose AUTHENTICATION: HTTP with user ID and password and ADSUSER for the USER ID.

Figure 13.34 Details of the Logical Port

Configuring a Trusted Anchor for ADS

Next, you create a trusted anchor for ADS. The certification authority is added to this trusted anchor to classify it as trusted. So if a digital signature is available in a PDF form and the certificate for the signature originates from this certification authority, the signature is accepted as valid. You can also add further certification authorities in parallel.

Create the trusted anchor as follows:

1. Go to the ADS configuration by selecting CONFIGURATION MANAGEMENT • INFRA-STRUCTURE • ADOBE DOCUMENT SERVICES.

2. Choose TRUSTED ANCHORS from the SHOW dropdown list. Then click on the MANAGE CER FILES... button.

3. To insert the public key of the certification authority, click on the ADD NEW FILE... button.

4. A dialog opens in which you click on BROWSE... to select the *CA_public.der* file (see Figure 13.35).

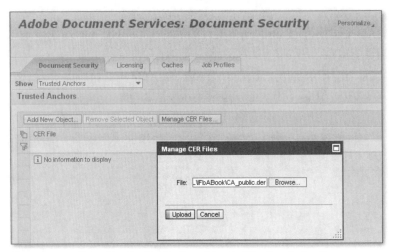

Figure 13.35 Uploading the Public Key of the Certification Authority

5. Then choose UPLOAD to start the upload.

As the last step, you create the actual trusted anchor.

1. For this purpose, click on the ADD NEW OBJECT... button.

2. Choose *CA_public.der* from the dropdown list and select all three options (see Figure 13.36).

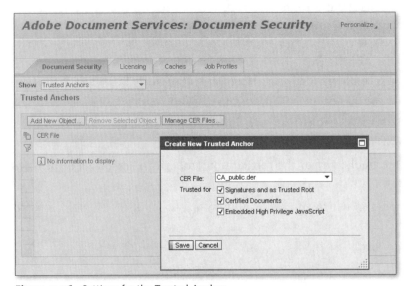

Figure 13.36 Settings for the Trusted Anchor

3. Choose SAVE to save and thus create the trusted anchor.

Figure 13.37 shows the newly created trusted anchor.

Figure 13.37 Created Trusted Anchor

This concludes the preparations for creating a secure connection. The only task left is to create the actual secure connection.

13.1.4 Creating a Secure Connection in the ABAP System

Finally, you must create the actual ADS connection. Proceed as follows:

1. Start Transaction SM59.

2. Double-click on the ADS destination under HTTP CONNECTIONS.

3. Follow the menu path, CONNECTION • COPY.

4. Enter ADS_SSL as the name of the new destination. This is the secure ADS connection.

5. Switch to change mode.

6. Enter the following information in the TECHNICAL SETTINGS tab (see Figure 13.38):

   ▸ TARGET HOST: the fully qualified domain name of the target host

   ▸ SERVICE NO.: 50001 (or the SSL port through which ADS can be reached)

   ▸ PATH PREFIX: */AdobeDocumentServicesSec/Config?style=rpc*

Figure 13.38 Technical Settings for the RFC Destination

7. Enter the following information in the Logon & Security tab (see Figure 13.39):

- ▸ Logon Procedure: Basic Authentication
- ▸ SSL: Active
- ▸ SSL Client Certificate: ADSSSL (the created client identity)
- ▸ User: ADSUSER

A secure ADS connection with the name ADS_SSL is now available.

Figure 13.39 Logon and Security for the RFC Destination

Testing the Secure Configuration

You can use the same programs as for a connection without SSL for testing (that is, all examples provided in this book). The tests fail if the configuration is incorrect or if errors occur in the certificate creation.

Because you require the secure connection for the tests, you cannot start testing until you have completed the configuration.

13.2 Managing and Creating Job Profiles

The use of job profiles enables you to modify parameters for creating an output by ADS. This is done before the output is generated and without changing the print program or the Web Dynpro application.

This can be used, for example, to enable duplex printing retroactively or add usage rights for the paper form barcode (which is not done by default). Job profiles are provided together with ADS for these cases.

Other job profiles to be defined by the user can modify the usage rights, for instance, to disable file attachments, switch of commenting, or specify the initial appearance in Adobe Reader (for example, you can always display the complete first page). Section 13.2.3, Creating a New Job Profile, presents the various areas in which you can make settings.

13.2.1 Calling the Job Profile Management

The user interface for managing and creating job profiles is provided as part of SAP NetWeaver Administrator. Follow the steps below to navigate to the job profile management:

1. Enter the URL for SAP NetWeaver Administrator in a Web browser (usually, *http:<server>:<port>/nwa*).

2. A logon screen appears. Log on as a user that has ADS administration rights.

3. Go to the Configuration area and then to the Infrastructure area below.

4. Select Adobe Document Services there.

5. To navigate to the management of job profiles, choose the Job Profiles tab. The screen shown in Figure 13.40 should now appear.

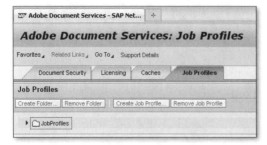

Figure 13.40 Job Profile Management

13.2.2 Managing Job Profiles

In ADS, job profiles are managed in two categories (presented as directories):

▶ The *first* category has the name ADOBE and contains the provided job profiles. These cannot be changed.

▶ The *second* category involves the *Custom* directory. In this directory, the administrator can create new job profiles or change the ones contained therein.

Figure 13.41 shows an overview of the categories and the provided job profiles.

Figure 13.41 Categorization of Job Profiles

Before you create a new job profile in the next section, you first need to create a new directory. Proceed as follows:

1. Select the *Custom* directory.

2. Click on the CREATE FOLDER... button to create a new directory.

3. Enter "IFbABOOK" in the dialog that now appears. Click on SAVE.

13.2.3 Creating a New Job Profile

The next step is to create a new job profile. Proceed as follows:

1. Click on the CREATE JOB PROFILE button.

2. Enter "IFbABookSampleJobProfile" for the JOB PROFILE NAME in the dialog that now appears. Enter "A sample Job Profile for the IFbA Book." under DESCRIPTION.

3. The job profile is created when you click on the SAVE button.

This takes you to the screen shown in Figure 13.42, in which the SUBPROFILES tab is selected. Subprofiles allow you to reuse existing (sub)profiles. This is useful if you want to reuse settings for one or more tabs in various job profiles.

Figure 13.42 Newly Created Job Profile

You can make settings for job profiles in five areas (PRINT, DOCUMENT, INITIAL VIEW, USAGE RIGHTS, and CERTIFICATION). Each tab includes a checkbox with which you can specify whether the job profile determines options for this area anew. If this checkbox is selected, the fields in the tab become active. At runtime, the options sent to ADS are then replaced by those in the job profile. Every tab directly provides information on the individual options in the HELP area.

You can now modify the job profile in such a way that the Initial View settings are specified, which are relevant when you open the PDF form in Adobe Reader. Proceed as follows (see Figure 13.43):

1. Choose the INITIAL VIEW tab.

2. To specify that the job profile overwrites the Initial View settings, activate the SET INITIAL VIEW checkbox.

Figure 13.43 Modifying a Job Profile

3. Another example would be the following: You can specify for the job profile that Adobe Reader always displays the complete first page when you select the FIT PAGE option for MAGNIFICATION MODE.

4. Click on the SAVE button under the name of the job profile.

You have just created a job profile that you can use in the examples of Chapters 6 and 8. You can view the options in the tabs. As was already mentioned, the description of the options is directly provided in the HELP area (see Figure 13.42, for example).

13.3 Installing and Using the XDC Editor

You can use the XDC Editor to edit XDC files (see Figure 13.44). It is provided as a plug-in for the Eclipse development environment. You can download the XDC Editor via the SDN.

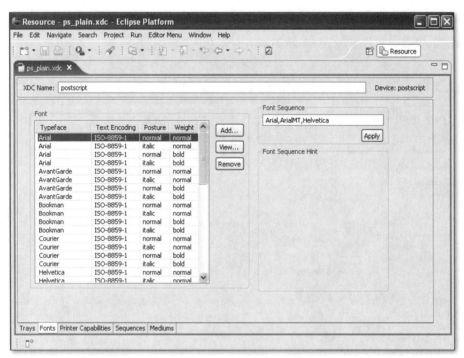

Figure 13.44 XDC Editor

1. To do this, go to *http://sdn.sap.com* and log on or register.

2. In the main navigation, select DOWNLOADS and then APPLICATION SERVER TOOLS. From the available downloads, select XDC EDITOR FOR SAP INTERACTIVE FORMS BY ADOBE.

3. After you have downloaded the ZIP archive, unpack it to a directory of your choice and follow the installation instructions in the *XDCEditor_Readme.htm* file.

After successful installation, you can either open and change existing XDC files or create a new XDC file. If you create a new XDC file (FILE • NEW • OTHER...), you must select the ADOBE XFA DEVICE CONFIGURATION FILE (XDC) under ADOBE XDC EDITOR. Additionally, you must specify which XDC file you want to use as the basis. For example, select "ps_plain.xdc" if you want to create an XDC file for a specific PostScript printer. Finally, save the XDC file with a new name.

SAP Note 1122142 describes in detail how you can edit XDCs using this tool. Further information is available in the application help (HELP • HELP CONTENTS) of Eclipse after plug-in installation.

13.4 Summary

In the final chapter of this book, you were introduced to advanced configuration and administration topics. You require this knowledge if you want to move beyond the simple application scenarios of SAP Interactive Forms by Adobe and implement more complex scenarios.

The Authors

Dr. Jürgen Hauser has worked for Adobe Systems since 2005. His responsibilities include representing Adobe at SAP AG in Walldorf, Germany; product management for SAP Interactive Forms by Adobe; and additional duties, such as serving as a local contact for Adobe Flex and Adobe AIR. He has presented SAP Interactive Forms by Adobe at numerous conferences and events worldwide. As a product manager, he has also been responsible for Adobe LiveCycle Mosaic, a product for the creation of composite rich Internet applications, since 2010. In autumn 2010, he moved to the US in order to work at Adobe Systems, Inc.

He previously worked as a project manager and system architect for a large German consulting firm. After finishing his studies in computer science, with a minor in mathematics, he participated in the Distributed Systems research group. He earned his doctorate in multimedia systems from the University of Stuttgart, Germany.

Andreas Deutesfeld studied physics and computer science at the Johannes Gutenberg University in Mainz, Germany. After finishing his studies, he joined SAP AG in Walldorf, Germany, in 1996. His work focused on form technologies in the development of SAP NetWeaver. He has conducted numerous workshops and classes and consulted for many projects on this topic. Since 2003, he has been heavily involved as a development architect in the design and implementation process of the form solution, SAP Interactive Forms by Adobe. He lives in a small town on the Rhine with his wife and son.

Dr. Stephan Rehmann holds a PhD in low-temperature physics from the University of Bayreuth, Germany. He joined SAP AG in 1998 and worked in the development division of the overhead cost-controlling product team. Later, he was responsible for the ISR framework for SAP ERP, among other things. At present, he works as a development architect in the development department of SAP ERP Financials in the cost accounting area.

Thomas Szücs was a senior software developer at SAP AG for the Web Dynpro ABAP division, where he was in charge of Adobe integration, among other projects. After almost nine years at SAP working on SD, CRM, and SAP NetWeaver, he now works as a senior solution architect at Corporate Business Solutions GmbH in Heidelberg, Germany. He is married and lives near Bruchsal, Germany, with his family.

Index

T